Apple Pro Training Series

OS X Support
Essentials 10.10

Kevin M. White and Gordon Davisson

Apple
Certified

Apple Pro Training Series: OS X Support Essentials 10.10
Kevin M. White and Gordon Davisson
Copyright © 2015 by Peachpit Press

Peachpit Press
www.peachpit.com

To report errors, please send a note to *errata@peachpit.com*.
Peachpit Press is a division of Pearson Education.

Apple Series Editor: Lisa McClain
Production Editor: Tracey Croom
Technical Editor: Adam Karneboge
Apple Reviewer: Yulia Stolerman
Apple Project Managers: Yulia Stolerman, Debra Otterstetter
Copy Editors: Leslie Tilley, Kim Wimpsett

Proofreader: Darren Meiss
Production Services: Happenstance Type-O-Rama
Indexer: Jack Lewis
Cover Illustration: Paul Mavrides
Cover Production: Cody Gates, Happenstance Type-O-Rama

ISBN 13: 978-0-13-401471-5
ISBN 10: 0-13-401471-5
9 8 7 6 5 4 3 2 1 Printed and bound in the United States of America
Alternate Binding:
ISBN 13: 978-0-13-403768-4
ISBN 10: 0-13-403768-5
9 8 7 6 5 4 3 2 1 Printed and bound in the United States of America

I could not have made this journey without the support of my family and loving wife, Michelle.

This book is dedicated to my greatest works: Logan, Sawyer, and Emily.

— *Kevin White*

Much appreciation to my amazing wife, Berit Benson, and her uncanny ability to sense when I needed coffee the most.

— *Gordon Davisson*

Acknowledgments In addition to the amazing Peachpit staff members who were instrumental in completing this work, we would like to thank the development team for their hard work: Adam Karneboge, Yulia Stolerman, and Craig Cohen. Additional thanks go out to Debbie Otterstetter, John Signa, Shane Ross, Eugene Evon, Cindy Waller, Arek Dreyer, Ben Greisler, Schoun Regan, Patrick Gallagher, and Timothy Perfitt. Also, the accuracy of this guide has been greatly enhanced by feedback from those who reviewed early versions of the guide, including attendees of the Yosemite Support Essentials beta class.

Contents at a Glance

Table of Contents

Data Management

System Management

About This Guide

This guide serves as a tour of the breadth of functionality of OS X Yosemite and the best methods for effectively supporting users of OS X systems. It is intended for both self-paced learners and those participating in an instructor-led course. This guide is the curriculum for the official Apple training course Yosemite 101: OS X Support Essentials 10.10, a three-day, hands-on course that provides an in-depth exploration of how to troubleshoot on OS X Yosemite. This course is facilitated by an Apple Certified Trainer and is organized into multiple lessons, each containing instructor presentations followed by related student exercises.

The primary goal of this guide is to prepare help desk specialists, technical coordinators, service technicians, system administrators, and others who support Mac users to knowledgeably address customer concerns and questions. This goal includes providing learners with the ability to return a Mac computer running OS X back to normal operation using the proper utilities, resources, and troubleshooting techniques.

Whether you are an experienced system administrator or just want to dig deeper into OS X, you'll learn in-depth technical information and procedures used by Apple-certified IT professionals to install, configure, maintain, and diagnose Mac computers running OS X.

> **NOTE** ▶ Unless otherwise specified, all references in this guide to OS X or OS X Yosemite refer to version 10.10, which was the most current version available at the time of writing. Due to subsequent updates, some screens, features, and procedures may be slightly different from those presented in these pages. When available, you can access updates to this guide on the Update tab for the book at www.peachpit.com/apts.osxyosemite#updates.

GOALS

▶ Explain how this guide is organized to facilitate learning

▶ Set up an environment for self-paced exercises

▶ Introduce Apple Training and Certification courses and exams

Learning Methodology

Each lesson in this guide is designed to help experienced users become experts who are able to support other OS X users by:

▶ Providing knowledge of how OS X works

▶ Showing how to use diagnostic and repair tools

▶ Explaining troubleshooting and repair procedures

For example, in Lesson 20 "Network Essentials", you'll learn basic networking concepts (knowledge). You'll experience using network configuration and troubleshooting applications like Network preferences and Network Utility (tools). And you'll explore methods for resolving network issues (procedures). In addition, each lesson includes troubleshooting techniques for dealing with common issues related to the topic at hand.

This guide assumes a basic level of familiarity with OS X at the user level. This guide does not cover basic usage of the system, but a good place to start is the Apple Mac Basics support site, www.apple.com/support/macbasics/. Again, it's strongly suggested that you be comfortable using a Mac before you begin the exercises in this guide.

Lesson Structure

Each lesson in this guide contains a reference section followed by an exercise section.

> **NOTE** ▶ "Note" resources, like this one, offer important information or help clarify a subject. For example, some of the exercises in this guide may be disruptive. Consequently, it's recommended that you perform these exercises on an OS X computer that is not critical to your daily productivity.

The reference sections contain initial explanatory material teaching essential concepts. The exercise sections augment your understanding of concepts and develop your skills through step-by-step instruction for both self-paced learners and the hands-on portions of an instructor-led course.

> **TIP** ▶ "Tip" resources, like this one, provide helpful hints, tricks, or shortcuts. For example, when discussing the process of downloading from the Mac App Store, you could be told how to check the progress of the download.

Throughout this guide you'll find references to Apple Support articles. These articles can be found at the Apple Support website (www.apple.com/support/), a free online resource containing the very latest technical information for Apple products. We strongly encourage you to read the suggested documents and search the Apple Support website for answers to any problems you encounter.

> **MORE INFO** ▸ The "More Info" resources, like this one, provide ancillary information. These resources are merely for your edification, and are not considered essential for the coursework.

Lesson files and bonus materials are available online when you redeem the access code supplied with your guide at www.peachpit.com/redeem. The "Lesson Review Questions & Answers" appendix recaps each lesson through a series of questions that reinforce the material you learned in the guide. You can refer to the lessons and various Apple resources, such as the Apple Support website and documentation, mentioned in the guide. Answers are also provided to confirm your understanding of the concepts. The "Additional Resources" appendix contains a list of relevant Apple Support articles and recommended documents related to the topic of each lesson. The "Updates & Errata" document contains updates and corrections to the guide.

Exercise Requirements

This guide is written so that both the self-paced learner and those attending an Apple Authorized Training Center or Apple Authorized Training Center for Education (AATC or AATCE) can complete most of the exercises using the same techniques. Those attending the Yosemite 101 course at an AATC or AATCE will have the appropriate exercise setup provided as part of the training experience. On the other hand, self-paced learners attempting these exercises will have to set up an appropriate environment using their own equipment.

> **NOTE** ▸ Some of these exercises can be disruptive—for example, they may turn off network services temporarily—and some, if performed incorrectly, could result in data loss or damage to system files. Consequently, it's recommended that you perform these exercises on an OS X computer that is not critical to your daily productivity. Apple Inc. and Peachpit Press are not responsible for any data loss or any damage to any equipment that occurs as a direct or indirect result of following the procedures described in this guide.

Mandatory Requirements

To perform the exercises in this guide, you must have some basic necessities:

▶ Mac computer meeting the requirements to run OS X Yosemite

▶ OS X Yosemite ("Exercise 1.2 Upgrade to OS X Yosemite" on page 30 includes instructions for downloading Yosemite if you do not already own it)

▶ A high-speed Internet connection

▶ Student Materials demonstration files, which can be obtained by redeeming the code provided with your guide (instructions to redeem the code and download are included in "Exercise 2.5 Download the Student Materials Independently" on page 76)

Optional Add-Ons

Most of these exercises assume access to one or more of the following additional resources (specific resources needed for each exercise are listed at the beginning of the exercise):

▶ An iCloud account. You can use an existing iCloud account or set up a new free account during the exercises.

▶ An Apple ID that can make purchases from the Mac App Store. You can use an existing account or set up a new account during the exercises. You do not have to enter a credit card or payment information to download free items.

▶ An erasable external USB, FireWire, or Thunderbolt disk with a capacity of at least 1 GB (or 8 GB for "Exercise 3.2 Create an OS X Install Disk" on page 99).

▶ An isolated network or subnet with an exercise-specific configuration. This can be facilitated with something as simple as a small network Wi-Fi router with multiple Ethernet ports. For example, the Apple AirPort Extreme (www.apple.com/airportextreme/) would be a good choice. Instructions for the general setup of an exercise network and specific instructions for the configuration of AirPort Extreme are available with the lesson files and bonus material when you redeem the access code provided with this guide at www.peachpit.com/redeem.

▶ A Wi-Fi interface in your computer and access to at least two Wi-Fi networks (at least one of which is visible).

▶ An additional Mac system running OS X Yosemite.

▶ A FireWire or Thunderbolt cable (as appropriate) to connect the two computers.

▶ Optionally, the additional Mac system can have OS X Server installed and set up with an exercise-specific configuration. Any Mac that can run OS X Yosemite can run OS X Server after purchasing it from the Mac App Store for $19.99. Specific instructions for configuring an OS X Server for exercise use are available with the lesson files and bonus material when you redeem the access code provided with this guide at www.peachpit.com/redeem.

▶ If your computer has a Retina display, a magnifying glass may be helpful for "Exercise 27.2 Use Single-User Mode" on page 925.

If you lack the equipment necessary to complete a given exercise, you are still encouraged to read the step-by-step instructions and examine the screenshots to understand the procedures demonstrated.

Exercise Order

The exercises in this guide are designed to be relatively independent of each other, so that you can complete them out of order or skip exercises. However, there are some exercises you must perform in the correct order:

▶ If your computer is not running OS X Yosemite yet, you must perform the appropriate exercises in Lesson 1 "Install OS X Yosemite" to upgrade or reinstall it.

▶ You must perform the appropriate exercises in Lesson 2 "Setup and Configuration" to set up your computer for any of the later exercises.

▶ "Exercise 5.1 Manage User Accounts" on page 145 and "Exercise 6.1 Restore a Deleted User Account" on page 166 create user accounts that many later exercises depend on.

Some exercises also have specific dependencies on other exercises; these will be listed as prerequisites at the beginning of the exercise.

Apple Training and Certification

The Apple Training and Certification program is designed to keep you at the forefront of Apple technology. Certification creates a benchmark to demonstrate your proficiency in specific Apple technologies and gives you a competitive edge in today's evolving job market.

Certification exams are delivered at Apple Authorized Training Centers around the world.

Reading this guide or attending the Yosemite 101 course will help prepare you to pass the OS X Support Essentials 10.10 Exam and become an Apple Certified Support Professional (ACSP) and/or Apple Certified Technical Coordinator (ACTC).

▶ ACSP certification verifies an understanding of OS X core functionality and an ability to configure key services, perform basic troubleshooting, and support multiple users with essential OS X capabilities.

▶ ACSP certification is designed for the help desk professional, technical coordinator, or power user who supports OS X users, manages networks, or provides technical support for the Mac.

▶ Students earn ACSP certification by passing the OS X Support Essentials 10.10 Exam. Visit training.apple.com/certification/osxyosemite to review the OS X Support Essentials Exam Prep Guide.

▶ ACTC certification verifies a foundation in OS X and OS X Server core functionality and an ability to configure key services and perform basic troubleshooting. ACTC certification is intended for OS X technical coordinators and entry-level system administrators who maintain small-to-medium networks of computers using OS X Server.

▶ Students earn ACTC certification by passing both the OS X Support Essentials 10.10 Exam and OS X Server Essentials 10.10 Exam. (To prepare for the latter exam, attend the Yosemite 201 course or read *Apple Pro Training Series: OS X Server Essentials 10.10*.)

MORE INFO ▶ To read OS X Technical White Papers and learn more about all Apple certifications, visit http://training.apple.com.

NOTE ▶ Although all the questions in the OS X Support Essentials 10.10 Exam are based on material in this guide, nothing can substitute for time spent learning the technology. After you read the book and/or take the class, spend time increasing your familiarity with OS X on your own to ensure your success on the certification exam.

Installation and Configuration

Lesson 1
Install OS X Yosemite

Every Mac computer has some version of OS X preinstalled when it's built, usually the latest available at the time. Thus, every Mac will at some point need a later version of the operating system to provide the latest features and updates, and because OS X Yosemite is free, anyone can upgrade at no cost. This lesson guides you through both upgrading an existing system and performing a new installation. It also includes troubleshooting issues that may arise during these processes.

> **NOTE ▶** Several of the operations covered in this lesson involve significant changes to your Mac computer's setup. Many of them are difficult to reverse, if not irreversible. If you plan to follow the exercises in this lesson, you should do so on a spare computer or an external disk that does not contain critical data.

GOALS

▶ Prepare a computer for an upgrade to OS X Yosemite

▶ Prepare a computer for a new installation of OS X Yosemite

▶ Successfully upgrade or install OS X Yosemite

▶ Troubleshoot potential installation problems

Reference 1.1
About OS X Yosemite

OS X Yosemite is the latest version of the Apple desktop and portable computer operating system. Since its introduction in 2001, OS X has become an increasingly attractive alternative to other operating systems because of its combination of innovative technologies. OS X is the only operating system that combines a powerful open source UNIX foundation with a state-of-the-art user interface, offering all the ease of use Apple is known for. Furthermore, Apple provides an exceptional development platform, as evidenced by the large selection of high-quality third-party software titles available for OS X.

What's New in OS X Yosemite

In addition to the features found in previous versions, OS X Yosemite includes dozens of new features. The central theme of recent OS X upgrades is the marriage of the best features in iOS with the flexibility of the Mac operating system. OS X Yosemite pushes this connection further than previous OS X upgrades by introducing a complete OS X interface redesign that closely matches the style of iOS 8. This visual update also includes enhancements to often-used system features, like Spotlight search and Notification Center, that make them even more powerful and easy to use.

Further, OS X Yosemite and iOS 8 also now share a deeper connection with new continuity technologies that allow users to instantly transfer phone calls, messages, and documents between nearby devices. For example, you can answer a call on an iPhone with iOS 8 and instantly transfer that call to a Mac with OS X Yosemite.

OS X Yosemite also features increased integration with iCloud, allowing users' local account passwords to be tied to their iCloud accounts. Finally, in OS X iCloud Drive is fully integrated with the Finder, allowing users to access documents in iCloud just as they would a local document.

> **MORE INFO** ▶ A full list of the new OS X Yosemite features can be found at www.apple.com/osx/all-features/.

Integration Through Standards

Much of the success of OS X can be attributed to Apple embracing industry-standard formats and open-source software. Nearly every technology in OS X is based on well-known standards. Adoption of common standards saves engineering time and allows for much smoother integration with other platforms. When Apple developers must engineer a technology for a new feature, Apple often releases the specs to the developer community, fostering a new standard. An example of this is Bonjour network discovery, which Apple pioneered and has maintained as an industry-standard protocol commonly known as Multicast DNS (mDNS), for others to develop and use.

Some examples of common standards supported by OS X are:

► Connectivity standards—Universal Serial Bus (USB), IEEE 1394 (FireWire), Thunderbolt, Bluetooth wireless, and the IEEE 802 family of Ethernet standards

► File system standards—File Allocation Table (FAT), New Technology File System (NTFS), ISO 9660 optical disc standard, Universal Disk Format (UDF), and the Xsan file system based on the StorNext file system

► Network standards—Dynamic Host Configuration Protocol (DHCP), Domain Name System (DNS), Hypertext Transfer Protocol (HTTP), Internet Message Access Protocol (IMAP), Simple Mail Transfer Protocol (SMTP), File Transfer Protocol (FTP), Web Distributed Access and Versioning (WebDAV), and Server Message Block/Common Internet File System (SMB/CIFS) including SMB3

► Application and development standards—Single UNIX Specification v3 (SUSv3), Portable Operating System Interface (POSIX), C and C++, Objective C, Ruby, Python, and Perl

► Document standards—ZIP file archives, Rich Text Format (RTF), Portable Document Format (PDF), Tagged Image File Format (TIFF), Joint Photographic Expert Group (JPEG), Portable Network Graphics (PNG), Advanced Audio Coding (AAC), and the Moving Picture Experts Group (MPEG) family of media standards

Reference 1.2
Installation Choices

How much of this lesson you'll want to complete depends on the state of your Mac. You can read through the entire lesson, but you probably won't want to attempt all the techniques described here on your working Mac.

TIP ► If you don't know what version of OS X your Mac is running, simply choose About This Mac from the Apple menu.

Odds are, your Mac falls into one of the following general categories:

Running OS X Yosemite with No Significant Problems

If this is the case, upgrading isn't necessary, and you probably don't want to reinstall the operating system. You may still wish to read through this lesson, but don't perform any of the exercises.

Running OS X Yosemite but Has Significant Problems

If this is the case, back up important data, erase the system disk, and perform a "clean" installation. You should have access to Time Machine and OS X Recovery. However, keep in mind that restoring a full system backup may also restore the problematic items, so you may need to manually restore individual items to result in a stable system.

You will be best served by first familiarizing yourself with Lesson 16 "Time Machine", and Lesson 3 "OS X Recovery" and then returning to this lesson to learn about reinstallation options. When you're ready for reinstallation, read "Reference 1.4 Preparing the System Disk" on page 14 and "Reference 1.5 Upgrading and Installing" on page 17. Then perform the steps outlined in "Exercise 1.3 Erase a Mac System and Install OS X Yosemite" on page 33.

Running OS X v10.6, OS X Lion, OS X Mountain Lion, or OS X Mavericks with No Significant Problems

If this is the case, you can perform a standard upgrade-in-place installation of OS X Yosemite.

To perform a standard upgrade installation, read "Reference 1.3 Before Upgrading a Previous System" on page 7 and "Reference 1.5 Upgrading and Installing" on page 17. Then perform the steps outlined in "Exercise 1.1 Prepare a Mac for Upgrade" on page 23 and "Exercise 1.2 Upgrade to OS X Yosemite" on page 30.

Running OS X v10.6, OS X Lion, OS X Mountain Lion, or OS X Mavericks but Has Significant Problems

If this is the case, back up important data, and then create an external OS X Recovery disk. After starting up the Mac from the OS X Recovery system, you can erase the built-in system disk and perform a "clean" installation. You have access to Time Machine but not the Yosemite version of OS X Recovery, so you will be best served by first familiarizing yourself with Lesson 16 "Time Machine". You also need to create an external OS X Recovery disk, as covered in "Exercise 3.2 Create an OS X Install Disk" on page 99. Once you have access to the Yosemite version of OS X Recovery, you can return to this lesson to learn about reinstallation options.

When you're ready to reinstall, read "Reference 1.4 Preparing the System Disk" on page 14 and "Reference 1.5 Upgrading and Installing" on page 17. Then perform the steps outlined in "Exercise 1.3 Erase a Mac System and Install OS X Yosemite" on page 33.

Running a Version of OS X Prior to v10.6 and You Want to Upgrade

Apple doesn't officially support upgrading to OS X Yosemite from any version of OS X prior to v10.6.8. If you don't have access to the OS X v10.6 installer, you can purchase it on DVD from the Apple Online Store (Apple part number: MC573Z/A).

Once you have access to the OS X v10.6 installation media, perform the necessary updates to get the Mac to OS X v10.6.8, and then follow the standard recommendations for upgrading to OS X Yosemite, as covered in this lesson.

Reference 1.3
Before Upgrading a Previous System

Every Mac ships with OS X installed, so the majority of OS X Yosemite installations are upgrades. In addition to the existing operating system that the installer will upgrade, the system will probably also contain important user data.

The OS X installation process is designed to retain nonsystem data, like user accounts and additional applications, during an upgrade installation. With every new release of OS X, millions of Mac systems are successfully upgraded without issues.

However, upgrading an operating system is a complicated process and not entirely risk free. Apple engineers work hard to ensure the OS X upgrade process is reliable, but other variables involved could still lead to issues. For instance, hardware failure could prevent a successful upgrade installation. For these reasons, you should take some preparatory steps to prevent installer issues and data loss.

Verifying Installation Requirements

It's important to understand the installation requirements for the copy of OS X you plan to use, and also the requirements of the particular Mac you intend to install it on. If you're not sure of the computer's specifications, use the System Profiler or System Information application to view its status.

> **TIP** In OS X v10.6, the application that gathers system information is named System Profiler. In OS X Lion, Mountain Lion, Mavericks, and Yosemite systems, it's called System Information.

You can find System Profiler or System Information in the /Applications/Utilities folder. In either application, verify the computer's specifications by selecting and viewing the various content areas in the Hardware section.

Specifically, before installing OS X Yosemite, you should note the computer's memory capacity and serial number. You should also check the Serial-ATA section for the amount of free space on the system disk, often named Macintosh HD.

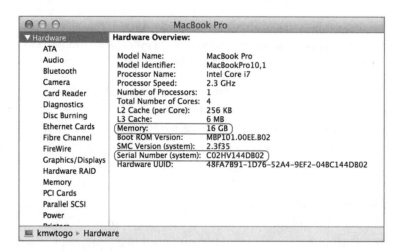

Upgrading to OS X Yosemite has the following general requirements:

▶ OS X v10.6.8 or later

▶ 2 GB of memory

▶ 8 GB of available space

► Apple ID (for some features)

► Compatible Internet service provider (for some features)

Beyond this, you need to find out if your specific Mac model is supported. Once you have the Mac computer's serial number, you can check it against the Apple Support Tech Specs website (http://support.apple.com/specs/). Once you have navigated to this website, click the Browse by Product button at the top-right corner, and then enter the serial number in the search field.

The search should return the specific model name for the Mac. For example, the preceding screenshot shows a Mac identified as a MacBookPro10,1. Although that is a specific identifier, it's not the name that Apple has defined for technical specifications. Entering this Mac computer's serial number in the Apple Support Tech Specs website returns the official name of "MacBook Pro (Retina, 15-inch, Mid 2012)."

Knowing the full model name of your Mac is important, as OS X Yosemite supports only the following Mac models:

► iMac (Mid 2007 or newer)

► MacBook (Late 2008 Aluminum, or Early 2009 or newer)

► MacBook Air (Late 2008 or newer)

► MacBook Pro (Mid/Late 2007 or newer)

► Mac mini (Early 2009 or newer)

► Mac Pro (Early 2008 or newer)

► Xserve (Early 2009)

> **MORE INFO** ► This seemingly arbitrary selection of Mac models actually share a specific new feature for their respective model lines. Each model is the first in its line to support 64-bit EFI firmware.

> **MORE INFO** ► Some OS X Yosemite features have additional requirements beyond these minimum system requirements. You can learn more about feature-specific requirements at the OS X technical specifications website, www.apple.com/osx/specs/.

Preparing for an Upgrade Installation

Although you could jump right into the OS X upgrade installation without any preparation, completing some preliminary steps reduces the chances of upgrade problems or losing important data. You should take four crucial steps before any system upgrade installation:

▶ Verify application compatibility.

▶ Back up important files and folders.

▶ Back up critical settings.

▶ Check for Apple software and firmware updates.

> **NOTE** ▶ This may seem like a no-brainer, but obviously you don't want to lose power halfway through an upgrade installation. Plug any portable Mac into AC power for the duration of the installation process to ensure it can complete.

Verify Application Compatibility

When moving to a new operating system, third-party applications may require updates to function properly. Once again, you can use System Profiler or System Information to easily collect a list of installed applications.

If you're using the earlier System Profiler application, verify that View > Full Profile is selected, to reveal the Applications section in the Contents list. Selecting Applications from the Contents list prompts the system to scan common locations on the local disk for available applications.

You don't have to worry about the applications installed as part of the operating system; those are replaced when you install the new system. However, you may have to do your own research by visiting vendors' websites to determine if third-party applications require updates.

OS X also includes a list of known incompatible software. If the OS X Installer application detects incompatible software during an upgrade, it usually moves that software to an Incompatible Software folder. In some cases, however, the incompatible software isn't moved, but the operating system prevents you from opening it and displays a warning dialog stating that the software is known to be incompatible. You can find out more about this feature in Apple Support article HT201861, "OS X: About the incompatible software folder."

Back Up Important Files and Folders

Experienced computer users know to keep backups of their important files and folders. Having a current backup is even more important when making significant changes to the computer, such as installing a new operating system. If it's done improperly, it could result in complete data loss.

If the Mac system is already running OS X v10.5 or later, you can use the built-in Time Machine software to easily create a backup before you start your installation. Using Time Machine is covered in Lesson 16 "Time Machine".

Document Critical Settings

Apple has designed the OS X Installer to help ensure that previous settings are not lost when you upgrade OS X. Nonetheless, some settings are so critical to your computer's function that you need to document them in case something goes wrong.

Specifically, network settings are critical, and they should be documented before a system upgrade is attempted. Network settings for all previous versions of OS X are located in the Network pane of System Preferences, accessed from the Apple menu. Avoid missing settings by navigating through all the available network interface and configuration tabs.

> **TIP** You can quickly document your settings by using the screen capture keyboard shortcut, Command-Shift-3, to create screenshots of the dialogs one by one.

Apple Software Update

As mentioned previously, to upgrade to OS X Yosemite, you must have OS X v10.6.8 or later. In addition, other Apple software has also been updated in preparation for this release. For example, both the iLife and iWork suites have undergone numerous between-

OS X releases. You should ensure that the Mac you're going to upgrade has all available Apple software updates.

Assuming the Mac is connected to the Internet, choose Software Update from the Apple menu. Then install all available updates. If no updates are found, your Mac is running the latest software, which ensures a smooth OS X upgrade.

More recent versions of OS X use the Mac App Store for accessing software updates. In this case, selecting Software Update will automatically open the Mac App Store, and OS X Yosemite will be listed as the first upgrade item. You can certainly start the upgrade process from here, but be sure you have completed all the suggested upgrade preparation steps before selecting the option to perform the free upgrade. Details on the upgrade process are covered in "Reference 1.5 Upgrading and Installing" on page 17, later in this lesson.

Firmware Updates

Some Mac computers may require a firmware update to properly access all the OS X Yosemite features. Firmware is low-level software that facilitates the startup and management of system hardware. Apple may release firmware updates for some Mac models so they operate properly with new system software, although these updates occur less frequently than normal software updates. Often these updates are caught by the software update mechanism or are installed automatically via the OS X installation process. How-ever, in some cases a Mac may require manual firmware updates. It's always best to check for firmware updates before installing a later version of OS X.

The default view for System Profiler or System Information (again, found in the /Applica-tions/Utilities folder) identifies the versions of the two types of firmware on Intel-based Mac computers. The first, listed as Boot ROM Version, is for the Extensible Firmware Interface (EFI), which is responsible for general hardware management and system startup.

The second, listed as SMC Version, is the System Management Controller (SMC) firm-ware, which is responsible for managing hardware power and cooling. Once you have located your computer's firmware versions, you can determine if you have the latest updates by accessing Apple Support article HT201518, "EFI and SMC firmware updates for Intel-based Macs." In this article, Mac models are listed by their model identifier, which can also be located in the same System Information view as the firmware version.

NOTE ▶ The OS X installation process will automatically upgrade the firmware on many late-model Mac computers with a version later than what is listed on the Apple Support website. In other words, you only need to be concerned if your Mac comput-er's firmware version is older than what's listed on the Apple Support website.

If you determine that your Mac requires a firmware update (if it was not updated by the automatic software updates), you need to find the correct update at the Apple Support Download website, http://support.apple.com/downloads. Like other system software updates, a firmware update requires administrative user authorization and a restart.

However, some older Mac computers have an extra requirement for firmware updates: After the initial installation process, you must shut down and then restart the computer by holding down the power button until you hear a long tone. This initiates the remainder of the firmware update process. Be sure to read any instructions that come with a firmware updater carefully! Failing to properly update a Mac computer's firmware could lead to hardware failure.

> **NOTE ▶** If you experience an unsuccessful update on an older Mac, you can restore your Mac computer's firmware with a Firmware Restoration CD. You can find out more about acquiring and using this CD from Apple Support article HT201692, "About the Firmware Restoration CD (Intel-based Macs)."

Keeping Up to Date

For the most recent information on the installation process, your best source is the Apple Support website. A good place to start is the OS X Yosemite support page at www.apple.com/support/osx/. Any time you intend to install OS X, visit these resources to catch any recently discovered issues. The Apple Support articles are sprinkled throughout this guide for a reason: They are the best source for official, up-to-date support information.

Reference 1.4
Preparing the System Disk

Whether you need to perform an erase and install for a "clean" system or you are planning on changing the disk structure by repartitioning the existing disk or adding a new disk, you have to prepare the system disk before installing OS X. Specifically, OS X installs only on disks that are partitioned via the GUID partition table (GPT) scheme and contain at least one Mac OS Extended (Journaled) formatted volume.

> **NOTE ▶** Any disk containing OS X v10.6 or later is already properly formatted for OS X Yosemite. In other words, if you only need to upgrade a working OS X system, you don't need to make any system disk changes, and you can simply follow the steps in "Exercise 1.2 Upgrade to OS X Yosemite" on page 30.

New OS X Installation (aka Clean Install)

Erasing the system disk before a system installation may be necessary for various reasons. Obviously, doing this erases any existing data, but sometimes this may be required. As one example, if you are upgrading the computer's internal disk to a bigger or faster disk, it must be properly formatted for OS X. Or, if an operating system has serious issues, erasing and installing a "clean" copy of OS X may resolve the situation.

Reasons for repartitioning your system disk are a bit more complex, so they are covered in the next section. Nevertheless, the process of repartitioning may require erasing data on the disk, which is thus often done prior to installing OS X. You use Disk Utility for both erasing and repartitioning the disk. Disk Utility can be found on any Mac in the /Applications/Utilities folder or, as covered later in Lesson 3 "OS X Recovery", from OS X Recovery. If you're going to make changes to the system disk before you install OS X, be sure to start up from a system on another, physically different, disk.

> **MORE INFO** ▶ This lesson does not include details about erasing or repartitioning disk; these procedures are covered extensively in Lesson 9 "File Systems and Storage". Specific steps can be found in Apple Support article, HT202796, "OS X: Installing OS X on an external volume."

Understanding Partitioning Options

Before selecting a destination disk, you may want to pause and consider the various disk partition methodologies that are available as installable OS X destinations. Most Mac computers have a single disk, formatted with a single large system volume that defines nearly the entire space on that disk. This is the OS X default partition setup. However, by repartitioning the disk, you can choose to break up that single large volume into separate smaller volumes. This allows you to treat a single physical storage device as multiple separate storage destinations.

Just as installing a new operating system has long-lasting ramifications for how you use your computer so does your choice of partitioning. Thus, before you install a new operating system, you should consider your partition philosophy. The following lists present the pros and cons of various partition options. Again, many of these concepts are further discussed in Lesson 9 "File Systems and Storage".

Single Partition for System Volume

▶ Pros—Most OS X systems are formatted with a single large system volume by default, so no disk partitioning changes are necessary. Also, a single system volume is often the most efficient use of space on your disk, as having separate partitions can potentially lead to wasted space if not sized correctly.

▶ Cons—Having only a single system volume limits administrative flexibility. For example, some testing and recovery tasks require the use of another storage volume. With only a single local volume, you will have to use an additional physical storage device to accommodate those needs.

Multiple Partitions

▶ Pros—Multiple partitions allow you to have multiple operating systems and multiple storage volumes on a single device. Having multiple operating systems allows you to run different versions of OS X or even other third-party operating systems and software from one disk. Or you can create utility systems that can be used to repair the primary system or test new software. Also, with multiple storage volumes, replacing a damaged operating system can be much easier if all the user's data resides on another nonsystem volume.

▶ Cons—Most disks need to be repartitioned to accommodate multiple volumes. While OS X Yosemite supports dynamic partitioning without losing data, it can do so only when working within the free space of a disk. Therefore, certain partition configurations may require you to completely erase the disk. Any future partition changes may require you to sacrifice data on the disk as well. Additionally, several technologies in OS X become more complicated to manage when using multiple volumes on single disk. Finally, multiple volumes can be very space-inefficient if you don't plan carefully, as you may end up with some volumes underused or others that run out of space too soon.

NOTE ▸ A multiple-partition system can cause the following complications: Boot Camp Assistant cannot add more partitions to a multiple-partition disk; enabling FileVault encrypts only the system volume, leaving other volumes unencrypted; and additional partitions on Fusion Drive volumes cannot take advantage of fast flash storage.

Reference 1.5
Upgrading and Installing

Apple is known for designing every operation to be as easy as possible, and the OS X installation process is an example of this ease. Most users can easily complete the installation with no training. However, anyone tasked with supporting OS X computers should be fully familiar with all the procedures needed to ensure a smooth installation.

Acquiring the OS X Installer

OS X Yosemite is a free upgrade that is available for download only from the Mac App Store. However, once you have downloaded the OS X installer, you can also create your own external OS X Install disk by following the instructions in "Exercise 3.2 Create an OS X Install Disk" on page 99.

If you are acquiring OS X Yosemite for the first time, the process is as simple as purchasing a new application from the Mac App Store. Also, as covered previously, more recent versions of OS X will automatically prompt you to upgrade to OS X Yosemite when performing a routine software update.

Using the Mac App Store does have a few prerequisites, though:

▸ You must be running OS X v10.6.8 or later.

▸ You must be connected to the Internet, ideally at broadband speeds. The OS X Installer is just over 5 GB, so it can take awhile to download even on "fast" connections.

▸ In order to download an item from the Mac App Store, you must sign in with an Apple ID. This is because even items that are free in the Mac App Store, like the OS X Yosemite Installer, must be purchased using an Apple ID with verified billing information. If you have previously purchased items from an online Apple store, like iTunes or the Mac App Store, your billing information is likely already configured. However, if you have yet to purchase items from an Apple online store, you can set up your billing information within the Mac App Store.

MORE INFO ▶ Details on the Mac App Store are covered in Lesson 17 "Application Installation".

Assuming you meet these criteria, simply open the Mac App Store from the Apple menu. OS X Yosemite will likely remain as one of the featured items on the store, so it should be easy to find. The Yosemite installer may also appear in the software updates list, which appears when you click the Updates button in the Mac App Store toolbar. To download the Install OS X Yosemite application to your Mac, just click the Free Upgrade or Download button. The installer automatically opens once the download is complete, but you can also find it in the Applications folder if necessary.

NOTE ▶ If you already have OS X Yosemite installed on your Mac, the Mac App Store may show that it's already installed or downloaded. In this case, the OS X Yosemite installer may still be in the Applications folder. If not, you also have access to the installer via the steps covered in Lesson 3 "OS X Recovery".

Newer Mac Systems

New Mac computers usually ship with a release of OS X engineered specifically for that model. Additional bundled software may also be included. This guide assumes that you are using a standard copy of OS X Yosemite, so you may find that some details vary if you are using a computer-specific install.

While OS X Yosemite is compatible with hardware from several years preceding its release, a specific version of OS X does not support hardware that is newer than the operating system release. In other words, you could come across a Mac that's newer than the OS X Yosemite installer you're trying to use. In this case, the installation may fail to start up the Mac or simply refuse to install in the first place. If that happens, use the original OS X Recovery system that came with the Mac.

MORE INFO ▶ See Apple Support article HT1159, "Mac OS X versions (builds) for computers," and article HT201686, "Don't install a version of Mac OS X earlier than what came with your Mac."

Install OS X Yosemite

The installation process itself involves just a few simple choices up front, followed by the actual installation. This means you need to spend only a few moments choosing the installation destination, and then you can leave the computer unattended while the installation completes.

TIP ▶ If a power loss or disk disconnection occurs, simply restart the installation.

Upgrade Versus Install

The installer automatically chooses the appropriate installation type for your selected destination: upgrade or new. Upgrade installations take an existing OS X system and upgrade it to a later version. New installations place a new copy of OS X on a disk without an existing system.

In either case, the installer never deletes nonsystem data on the selected destination. Specifically, the OS X installer is designed to ensure that third-party applications and user data remain functional after an installation. As far as installation destinations go, the OS X installer can upgrade the system your Mac is currently running from, or you can install to another disk attached to your Mac.

NOTE ▶ You cannot upgrade OS X if any other users are currently logged in to the Mac via fast user switching. You need to either have those users log out of their sessions or restart the computer to forcibly end the other user sessions.

Performing a Clean or New Installation

As covered previously, if you want to perform an erase and install, also known as a clean installation, you must manually erase the destination system disk using Disk Utility before running the OS X installer. If the destination is another system disk, like an external disk, you can erase and install from your currently running Mac. However, if you want to erase the system disk your Mac is currently running from, you need to start up from another system, as covered in Lesson 3 "OS X Recovery".

The Installation Destination

During installation of OS X Yosemite, the only choice you need to make is the installation destination—you are simply selecting the disk volume where OS X will be installed. This can be an internal or an external disk, as long as it's properly formatted. The default selection is the current startup disk; you have to click the Show All Disks button to choose an alternate destination.

You may notice that the installer does not let you select certain disks or partitions. This is because the installer has determined that your Mac cannot start from that location. Possible reasons include:

▶ The disk does not use the proper partition scheme for your Mac. Intel Mac computers use the GUID partition table (GPT) scheme. You can resolve this issue by repartitioning the disk using Disk Utility.

▶ The specific partition is not formatted properly. OS X requires a partition formatted as a Mac OS Extended (Journaled) volume. You can resolve this issue by erasing the partition using Disk Utility.

▶ The OS X Installer does not support installing to a disk containing Time Machine backups. For more information, see Apple Support article HT203322, "OS X: Cannot install on a volume used by Time Machine for backups."

Again, the system automatically determines if the selected destination already has a version of OS X installed. If there is an existing system, the installer upgrades the system to the new version.

Reference 1.6
Installer Troubleshooting

For most systems the OS X installation is painless and reliable. Yet, as with any complicated technology, problems may arise. The good news is that the OS X installer has the ability to "back out" of an installation and restore the previous system. If this happens, obviously the installation was not successfully completed, but at least you still have a functioning Mac.

Thoroughly verifying that your computer meets the requirements for OS X Yosemite and completing the installation preparation steps as outlined in this lesson will go a long way toward preventing or resolving any serious problems.

General OS X Installer Troubleshooting

Beyond the preparation steps covered earlier in this lesson, the most common installation failures arise from problems with the destination disk. For example:

► The installer may be unable to verify the selected disk or partition. This indicates serious disk problems. Refer to the troubleshooting steps in Lesson 9 "File Systems and Storage", to resolve this issue.

► An error message may appear saying that some features of OS X are not supported on the selected disk. This happens if your system disk is a software RAID (Redundant Array of Independent Disks) set or uses nonstandard Boot Camp partitioning. In this case, the installer cannot create an OS X Recovery HD, but you can still install OS X Yosemite.

   MORE INFO ► See Apple Support article HT201316, "OS X: 'Some features of Mac OS X are not supported for the disk (volume name)' appears during installation."

► In some cases, even when a disk is partitioned and formatted properly, the installer does not let you select that disk. This error most often occurs when there is also a Boot Camp partition on the disk. The resolution in this case involves slightly decreasing the size of the Mac partition to make room for the OS X Recovery HD.

MORE INFO ▶ See Apple Support article HT203482, "Installer reports 'OS X could not be installed on your computer' or 'This disk cannot be used to start up your computer'"

The OS X Installer Log

The granddaddy of all troubleshooting resources for OS X is the log file. Nearly every process writes entries in a log file, and the installer is no exception. The Installer log contains progress and error entries for nearly every step of the installation process, including steps not shown by the standard interface.

During the installation process, you can access the Installer log by simply choosing Installer Log from the Window menu. Information in the Installer log helps you to more precisely pinpoint problems or verify installation.

TIP ▶ You can also use this technique to check on the progress of any general software installation via the Installer application.

TIP ▶ After installation, you can access the Installer log on a normally running Mac from the /Applications/Utilities/Console application. Once Console is open, expand the /var/log folder, and then select install.log.

You can leave the Installer log window open during the entire installation process to monitor its progress. You may find that, even during a successful installation, the installer reports many warnings and errors. Many of these reported issues are benign, and you should only concern yourself with them if you are trying to isolate a show-stopping problem. When the installation is successfully completed, the summary entries in the Installer log look similar to those in the preceding screenshot.

Exercise 1.1
Prepare a Mac for Upgrade

▶ **Prerequisite**

▶ This exercise is necessary only if you are upgrading your computer from an
earlier version of OS X to Yosemite.

In this exercise, you will verify that your computer's hardware and firmware support OS X
Yosemite, as well as check for old software and record important settings.

Use System Information (or System Profiler) to Check Hardware, Firmware, and Application Compatibility

1   If necessary, log in to your existing administrator account on your computer.

2   In the Finder, navigate to the /Applications/Utilities folder (you can use the Finder
keyboard shortcut Command-Shift-U).

3   Open the System Information or System Profiler utility (its name depends on which
version of OS X you are using).

System Information

4   If necessary, select the Hardware entry in the sidebar.

5   Verify that the Memory entry is at least 2 GB. If it is less than that, you cannot use
Yosemite on this computer.

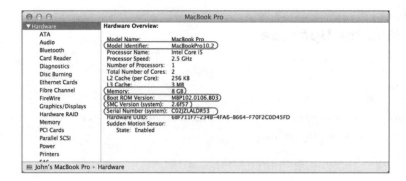

6   Make notes of the Model Identifier, Boot ROM Version, SMC Version, and Serial Number entries:

Model Identifier: _____

Boot ROM Version: _____

SMC Version: _____

Serial Number: _____

7   Select the sidebar entry for the bus your computer's startup disk is attached to (for most models, this is the Serial-ATA or SATA/SATA Express bus).

8   If necessary, select your startup disk in the listing at the top right.

9   Find your startup volume in the listing at the bottom right, and verify that it has at least 8 GB of available space. Ideally, there should be a lot more than 8 GB available, but 8 GB is the minimum requirement for installing OS X Yosemite.

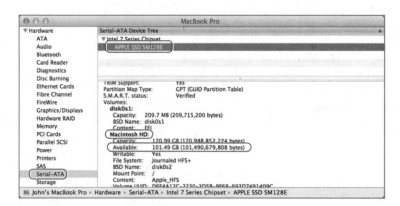

10 In the sidebar, under Software, select Applications, and wait for it to gather information on the applications installed on your computer.

11 Click the heading for the Last Modified column on the right. If the column's triangle is pointing down, click again so that it points up.

Your applications are listed with the oldest ones at the top. In general, your oldest applications are the most likely to be incompatible with newer versions of OS X. You may want to research the older applications to see whether they are compatible with OS X Yosemite or whether updates are available for them. Often, the developer's website has information about compatibility and updates.

12 Click the heading for the Kind column.

13 Scroll through the list to see if you have any PowerPC or Classic applications. These kinds of applications are not supported by OS X Yosemite. Some applications may have a blank in this column; this does not indicate a problem.

14 Quit System Information/System Profiler.

15 Open Safari, and navigate to the OS X support page (www.apple.com/support/osx/).

This page has links to support information on OS X Yosemite.

16 Click the "Upgrade to Yosemite" link.

This page has information and links about upgrading to OS X Yosemite, including requirements for installing Yosemite.

17 Navigate to the Apple Tech Specs website (http://support.apple.com/specs/).

18 Click the Browse by Product button.

19 Enter your computer's serial number (recorded in step 6) in the Search Tech Specs field, and press Return.

A link to your computer's technical specs, listed by its model name, appears. Verify that the model name is on the list of supported models in "Reference 1.3 Before Upgrading a Previous System" on page 7.

20 If you want, click the link to view your computer's detailed specifications.

21 In the search field near the upper-right corner of the Apple webpage (*not* the field in the Safari toolbar), enter HT1237, and press Return.

This takes you to the Apple Support article HT1237, "EFI and SMC firmware updates for Intel-based Macs."

22 Find your model in the list. Note that you can find it by either model name (which you found in step 19) or its model identifier (which you found in step 6).

23 Verify that the Boot ROM and SMC versions listed match what you found in step 6. If they do not, update your computer's firmware before upgrading OS X. The easiest way to do this is with automatic software updates (note that it checks other things, so you should run it even if your firmware is up to date).

NOTE ▶ You can find more information about automatic software updates in Lesson 4 "OS X Software Updates".

24 From the Apple menu, choose Software Update, and wait while your software and firmware are checked for updates.

25 If a message appears informing you that "Your computer is up to date" or there are "No Updates Available," proceed to the "Document Network Settings" section of this exercise.

26 If you are using Mac OS X v10.6 or OS X v10.7 and a dialog appears informing you that updates are available for your computer, click Show Details to view the updates it found.

Look through the available updates, and deselect any that you do not want to perform at this time. Then click Install *x* Items, where *x* is the number of items you have chosen to install, and follow any prompts and instructions to complete the updates. Note that the process for updating firmware can vary from model to model.

27 If you are using OS X v10.8 or OS X v10.9 and the App Store lists available updates, click the Update buttons for any updates you want to install. Note that you may have a "More" option available to show a more detailed list of system updates and an Update All button to install all available updates. Follow any prompts and instructions to complete the updates. Note that the process for updating firmware can vary from model to model.

OS X v10.8 and OS X v10.9 use an update process similar to that of OS X Yosemite, so you can refer to Lesson 4 "OS X Software Updates" for more information about the update process.

28 After the updates have finished, repeat starting at step 24 to verify that all updates installed successfully and that no more updates have become available.

Document Network Settings

1 From the Apple menu, choose System Preferences.

2 In System Preferences, click Network.

3 Select each of the network services (listed on the left of the preference pane), and record any special settings assigned to them. You need to click the Advanced button for each service to see the full settings. Generally, the easiest way to do this is to take screenshots with the shortcut Command-Shift-3 to give you a "permanent" record to work from.

4 If your computer has more than one location defined, repeat this process for each location.

Back Up Your Data

In case anything goes wrong during the system upgrade or any of the exercises in this guide, back up any important data on the computer (including the settings recorded earlier in this exercise). OS X includes a backup utility, Time Machine, which is documented in Lesson 16 "Time Machine". There are also many third-party options for backing up OS X computers.

Whichever backup option you choose, make sure your backup is up to date and includes all important data before proceeding. The process depends on your chosen backup solution, but usually the best test is to try restoring critical data from the backup.

Exercise 1.2
Upgrade to OS X Yosemite

▶ **Prerequisites**

▶ This exercise is necessary only if you are upgrading your computer from an earlier version of OS X to Yosemite.

▶ Your computer must be running OS X version 10.6.8 or later to perform this exercise.

▶ Perform "Exercise 1.1 Prepare a Mac for Upgrade" on page 23 before beginning this exercise.

In this exercise, you will download OS X Yosemite from the Mac App Store and install it as an upgrade on your computer.

Use the App Store to Download the Installer

1   Log in to your existing administrator account on your computer.

2   From the Apple menu, choose App Store. If App Store is not one of the choices in the Apple menu, you may be running a version of OS X earlier than OS X v10.6.8, in which case you cannot use this method to upgrade to OS X Yosemite.

3   In the search field of the App Store window, enter Yosemite, and press Return.

4   Find OS X Yosemite in the search results, and click the button under its name (it is labeled either "DOWNLOAD" or "GET").

5   If a dialog appears asking you to sign in, you will need to either sign in to an Apple ID account or create a new Apple ID to download Yosemite. See Lesson 17 "Application Installation" ("Reference 17.1 The Mac App Store" on page 475 and "Exercise 17.1 Use the Mac App Store" on page 505) for more information about using Apple IDs with the App Store.

6   If the App Store requests any additional information, supply it as requested.

7   Wait for the Install OS X Yosemite app to download.

    When the download is complete, the app opens automatically.

    NOTE ▶ The installation process deletes the installer application. If you want to upgrade several computers or create an OS X Yosemite install disk, quit the installer, and make a copy of it before proceeding. You can find the process for creating an install disk in "Exercise 3.2 Create an OS X Install Disk" on page 99.

Upgrade Your Computer to OS X Yosemite

1   If necessary, open the Install OS X Yosemite application.

2   At the Welcome screen, click Continue.

3   Read the license agreement, and if its terms are acceptable to you, click Agree.

4   In the confirmation dialog that appears, click Agree.

At this point, you can select the install destination.

5   The default selection is the current startup volume; if other volumes are available, click the Show All Disks button to select a different destination.

6   Click Install to start the installation. If you are warned about not being connected to a power source, connect your power adapter before continuing.

7   Enter the password of your administrator account to authorize the installation.

To see the details of the installation process, follow the instructions in "Exercise 1.4 Verify System Installation" on page 40 as soon as the installation has started.

The installation normally completes automatically without further interaction, although it will restart several times during the process.

The first time you log in to your account after upgrading, you may be prompted to sign in with your Apple ID. You can skip this step by selecting "Don't sign in" because you will explore the Apple ID and iCloud features of OS X Yosemite in later exercises.

Now that your computer is running OS X Yosemite, follow the instructions in "Exercise 2.2 Configure an Existing OS X System for Exercises" on page 63 to set up your computer for the rest of the exercises in this guide.

Exercise 1.3
Erase a Mac System and Install OS X Yosemite

▶ **Prerequisites**

▶   This exercise is necessary only if your computer needs to be erased before installing OS X Yosemite, as covered in "Reference 1.2 Installation Choices" on page 5.

▶   You need an OS X Yosemite recovery partition or a Yosemite install disk (see Lesson 3 "OS X Recovery" for details).

WARNING ▶ This exercise erases all existing data on your computer. If you want to keep any of this data, you must ensure that it is safely backed up to another computer or disk.

If your computer is having trouble, it may be best to erase the existing data and start over with a clean installation of OS X Yosemite. To do this, you must start up from another disk, erase your computer's internal disk, and then install a new operating system.

Start Up from Recovery or an Install Disk

1   Before proceeding with this exercise, make sure all the files you want to preserve from this computer are safely backed up elsewhere.

2   If your computer is running, shut it down.

3   If you are replacing an existing installation of OS X Yosemite (and want to perform the installation from the computer's existing Yosemite recovery partition), press the power button on your computer to turn it on, and then immediately press and hold the Command and R keys until you see the Apple icon appear in the middle of the screen. Once you see the Apple icon, release the keys and skip ahead to the next section, "Erase Your Computer's Disk Drive" on page 35.

4   If you are using an external Yosemite install disk, connect the disk to your computer.

5   Press the power button on your computer to turn it on, and then immediately press and hold the Option key until you see a row of icons appear on the screen.

Macintosh HD   Install OS X Yosemite

6   Click the recovery disk or partition's icon. Depending on the type and version of disk you are using, it may be labeled Recovery HD (if it is an OS X v10.7 recovery partition), Recovery-10.x (if it is a recovery partition), or Install OS X Yosemite (if it is an install disk).

7   Click the arrow that appears under the icon.

The computer starts up into the installer/recovery environment. Lesson 3 "OS X Recovery" has more information about using these modes.

Erase Your Computer's Disk Drive

1   If a language selection screen appears, select your preferred language, and click the right-arrow button to continue.

2   Open Disk Utility.

▶   If an OS X Utilities window appears, select Disk Utility, and click Continue.

▶   If an installer screen appears instead, choose Utilities > Disk Utility.

Disk Utility opens. Lesson 9 "File Systems and Storage" has more information about using Disk Utility.

3   From the sidebar, select the disk or volume you want to install Yosemite on.

NOTE ▶ Selecting a disk (the top entry) will erase the entire disk and all data on it. If you would prefer to erase only a single partition, you can select the partition's entry under the disk drive in the sidebar. If you choose this option, you must also verify that the disk is formatted with a GUID partition table (GPT). See Lesson 9 "File Systems and Storage" for more details on disk formatting and erasure options.

4   Click the Erase tab near the top of the Disk Utility window.

5   From the Format pop-up menu, choose Mac OS Extended (Journaled).

6   Enter a new name for your computer's disk. The rest of this guide assumes that it is named Macintosh HD.

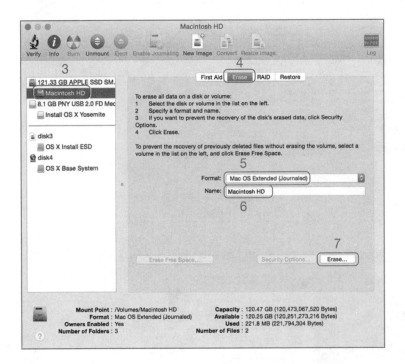

7   Click the Erase button near the bottom right of the Disk Utility window.

8   In the confirmation dialog that appears, click Erase.

9   From the menu bar, choose Disk Utility > Quit Disk Utility.

Install OS X Yosemite

1   If an OS X Utilities window appears, select Install OS X or Reinstall OS X, and click Continue.

2   In the Install OS X window, click Continue.

3   If you are notified that your computer's eligibility will be verified with Apple, click Continue.

4   Read the license agreement, and if its terms are acceptable to you, click Continue.

5   In the confirmation dialog that appears, click Agree.

6   Select your computer's disk drive from the list of available volumes, and click Install.

7   If you are prompted to, enter your Apple ID to sign in to the App Store. See Lesson 17 "Application Installation" ("Reference 17.1 The Mac App Store" on page 475 and "Exercise 17.1 Use the Mac App Store" on page 505) for more information about using Apple IDs with the App Store.

To see the details of the installation process, follow the instructions in "Exercise 1.4 Verify System Installation" on page 40 as soon as the installation begins.

The installation completes automatically without further interaction, although it will restart several times during the process.

Upon restart, you are greeted by the full Setup Assistant experience, as covered in Lesson 2 "Setup and Configuration". Follow the instructions in "Exercise 2.1 Configure a New OS X System for Exercises" on page 60 to set up your computer for the rest of the exercises in this guide.

Exercise 1.4
Verify System Installation

▶ **Prerequisite**

▶ You must have started installing OS X Yosemite using the instructions in
"Exercise 1.2 Upgrade to OS X Yosemite" on page 30 or "Exercise 1.3 Erase a
Mac System and Install OS X Yosemite" on page 33 to perform this exercise.

In this exercise, you use the Installer log to examine the installation process as it happens.

Examine the Installer Log

Any time during the installation process, you can bring up the Installer log by following
these steps:

1   If the installer is running in full-screen mode, you can't see the menu bar. Move your
mouse to the top of the screen to reveal the menu bar.

2   Choose Window > Installer Log (or press Command-L).

3   Choose Show All Logs from the Detail Level pop-up menu to view the entire contents
of the Installer log.

4   Use the Spotlight search field in the toolbar to isolate specific entries in the Installer
log.

5   To save the Installer log, click the Save button in the toolbar.

NOTE ▶ The installer restarts the computer partway through the installation process. When the computer restarts for the second phase, the log window does not automatically reopen.

TIP ▶ The Mac does not automatically restart after the second phase as long as the Installer Log window is the foremost window.

Lesson 2
Setup and Configuration

Providing competent system configuration is a primary concern of technical support personnel. This lesson focuses on both initial setup and ongoing system configuration. Preliminary OS X configuration is handled via Setup Assistant, while subsequent configuration is almost entirely handled via System Preferences and configuration profiles. Finally, this lesson introduces the tools used to gather and verify system information.

GOALS

▸ Complete the initial configuration of an OS X system

▸ Adjust common system settings

▸ Identify and install a configuration profile

▸ Examine and verify system information

Reference 2.1
Setup Assistant

If you are using a new system for the first time or you have just completed an upgrade installation of OS X, you will be presented with Setup Assistant. For new systems or clean installations of OS X, this application will guide you through the preliminary configuration required for a new system.

If you have just upgraded an existing system from a previous version of OS X, Setup Assistant will also open, but you will be presented with fewer configuration steps compared to a new system. Most importantly, in this case you will be prompted to enter your Apple ID information to complete the iCloud setup. Even if you previously set up iCloud on an existing system, when Setup Assistant is running you will need to reenter your authentication information to complete the upgrade to OS X Yosemite.

Keep in mind that setting up iCloud is optional. However, it is free of charge, and as you'll see throughout this guide, many powerful OS X features require an iCloud account.

Several of the steps in Setup Assistant can be skipped, but the required steps are necessary for good reason. Any of the configurations made using Setup Assistant can be easily changed later by accessing the corresponding settings, as covered in "Reference 2.2 System Preferences" on page 52.

NOTE ▶ Attempting to use the Command-Q keyboard shortcut in Setup Assistant will not allow you to quit the process or skip any screens. Instead, you must choose to either shut down or continue.

NOTE ▶ OS X systems managed by a school or business may present different Setup Assistant options than the defaults shown here. In certain managed situations, some of the default screens may be skipped and you may encounter additional organizational configuration screens. These differences are controlled by an administrator via mechanisms outside the Mac. Thus, you may have to contact the organization's primary administrator to properly complete the Setup Assistant process.

Setup Assistant: Country and Keyboard

The first Setup Assistant screen allows you to select your country; this ensures that the applications on your system use appropriate language and dialect. This information is also used to complete the registration process. At this point, you also select the primary keyboard layout. Both language and keyboard layout settings can be changed later from Language & Region preferences.

Setup Assistant: Network Settings (Optional)

Setup Assistant will attempt to establish a connection to the Internet by automatically configuring the Mac computer's network settings. It will first attempt to automatically configure via DHCP on an Ethernet network or open Wi-Fi network. If a connection is made this way, you won't be prompted to set up networking.

Otherwise, the assistant will try to figure out which type of network connection you need to set up and present you with the appropriate configuration screen. On most Mac computers, this will be the Wi-Fi network setup screen, where you can select a wireless network and authenticate to it. Alternatively, you can postpone setting up networking at this point, and do it later from Network preferences. Lesson 20 "Network Essentials" covers this topic in greater detail.

Setup Assistant: Transfer Information (Optional)

Using this optional utility, also known as Migration Assistant, you can transfer computer and user information from another computer or a backup to the new system. Completing the transfer from another system enables you to skip most of the remaining steps of Setup Assistant, as the configuration is gathered from the previous system. Lesson 6 "User Home Folders" covers transferring information via Migration Assistant in greater detail.

If you do not have a previous system to migrate settings and data from, simply leave the default choice, and click Continue to proceed with the Setup Assistant process.

Setup Assistant: Apple ID and iCloud (Optional)

Again, both new systems and systems upgraded to OS X Yosemite may prompt you to enter your Apple ID authentication. New systems will present this screen only if the Mac is connected to the Internet.

At this screen you can enter an existing Apple ID, recover a lost Apple ID, or create a new Apple ID. An Apple ID is free to set up and provides login access for all Apple online and store services. If you have ever purchased anything online from Apple, such as from the iTunes Store, you already have an Apple ID.

Once it's entered, your Apple ID is automatically configured for several services, including the Mac App Store, the iTunes Store, Messages, FaceTime, Game Center, and iCloud. Also, in subsequent Setup Assistant steps, this Apple ID will be pre-entered for optional configuration of computer account setup and system registration. If you use separate Apple IDs for iCloud and iTunes purchases, you also have the option to enter both Apple IDs during the Setup Assistant process.

> **NOTE ▶** If you're entering an Apple ID that hasn't been used in a while, you may be prompted to change the security settings for the account. Be sure to take these important steps; they protect your account if you lose the password.

NOTE ▶ If you're entering an Apple ID that is configured for two-step identity verification, you will be required to enter your password along with a four-digit verification code that will be sent to a trusted device.

iCloud is a free cloud-storage and communication service that you can set up on any Apple device. Though not required for completing Setup Assistant, iCloud is the easiest way to share information between OS X, iOS, and even Windows devices. As you will see throughout this guide, OS X Yosemite features deep integration with iCloud services.

Only Apple IDs that have signed into iCloud on a Mac or iOS device have access to iCloud services. If an existing Apple ID has never been used for iCloud, entering this account during Setup Assistant will upgrade the Apple ID to include iCloud services. Further, Setup Assistant will automatically configure your Mac to use iCloud for most services.

The following iCloud services will be enabled by default in most cases: iCloud Drive, Photos (if iPhoto or Aperture is installed), Contacts, Calendars, Reminders, and Safari. If the Apple ID you enter belongs to the @mac.com, @me.com, or @icloud.com domain, then Mail and Notes are also automatically configured.

NOTE ▶ If you're entering an Apple ID that belongs to someone under the age of 13 (made possible via Apple ID for Students or iCloud Family Sharing), no iCloud services will be enabled by default.

Later steps in Setup Assistant will prompt you to enable the iCloud Keychain and Find My Mac services. After setup, you can verify and modify iCloud service settings from iCloud preferences. iCloud is covered in this guide where appropriate, specifically Lesson 7 "System Security", Lesson 18 "Document Management", and Lesson 23 "Network Services".

MORE INFO ▶ For more information about Apple ID, see Apple Support article HT5622, "Frequently asked questions about Apple ID." For more information about two-step verification, see Apple Support article HT5570, "Frequently asked questions about two-step verification for Apple ID." For more information about creating an iCloud account, see Apple Support article HT201309, "Creating an iCloud account: Frequently Asked Questions."

Setup Assistant: Enable Find My Mac (Optional)

If you previously entered an Apple ID, you will be prompted to enable the Find My Mac feature. Find My Mac, as the name implies, is an iCloud service that helps you locate your computer should it be lost or stolen. After setup, you can verify and modify Find My Mac service settings from iCloud preferences.

Find My Mac relies on Location Services, which allows applications to locate your Mac using a Wi-Fi-based geolocation technology. Location Services is enabled by default with OS X Yosemite. You can further adjust Location Services in Security & Privacy preferences. Lesson 7 "System Security" covers Find My Mac and Location Services in greater detail.

Setup Assistant: Terms and Conditions

Accepting the Apple terms and conditions is the only registration requirement you must complete to use OS X. The content of the Terms and Conditions page will vary depending on whether you entered an Apple ID in the previous step. Accepting the terms and conditions does not send any personal or technical information to Apple. In fact, you can accept them even if your Mac is offline and never accesses the Internet.

> **MORE INFO** ▶ For more information about Apple terms and conditions, visit the Apple Legal website at www.apple.com/legal/.

Setup Assistant: Create Your Computer Account

After the Terms and Conditions step, you arrive at one of the most important steps of the setup process, the "Create a Computer Account" screen. Here you create the initial administrative user account for the system. At first, this account will be the only administrative user account allowed to modify system settings, including the creation of additional user accounts. Therefore, until you create additional administrative user accounts, you *must* remember the authentication information for this account.

If you previously entered an Apple ID, that information will be used to populate the fields. As a default in OS X Yosemite, you can now use your Apple ID (or iCloud account) name and password to create the new computer user account.

NOTE ▸ The OS X interface sometimes uses "iCloud account" instead of "Apple ID." However, because all Apple services, including iCloud, are accessed via Apple ID authentication, this guide uses the term "Apple ID" when discussing Apple service authentication.

When you use an Apple ID to create a computer account, the full name and password are based on that Apple ID. The account name, used to create the user's home folder, is pre-populated, but you can enter a different name if you like. After user creation, the full name and password will be the same as the Apple ID linked with this computer account.

However, you don't have to link a local account with an Apple ID. Simply deselect the option "Use my iCloud account to log in." Then you can define any local account name and password you like. Note that even when you choose to create a user account that is not linked with an Apple ID, the option to allow your Apple ID to reset the password is still enabled by default. This option can be deselected as well.

Deselecting these options will not disable normal iCloud services for the account you are creating. Because Apple ID authentication was entered earlier in the Setup Assistant process, iCloud services will still be enabled for this local account once setup is complete. After setup, you can modify local user accounts from the Users & Groups preferences, and adjust iCloud service settings from the iCloud preferences. Additional user account creation and management are detailed in Lesson 5 "User Accounts".

Finally, below the user information, you'll note OS X is configured to automatically set the time zone based on the computer's location. The system is also configured to automatically set the date and time using the Apple time servers. Both of these settings require an Internet connection. If no connection is available, the system will pick Cupertino, California for the time zone and use the system's built-in hardware clock setting for the date and time. After setup, you can verify and modify these settings from the Date & Time preferences.

Setup: iCloud Keychain (Optional)

After creating the local administrator account, if you previously entered an Apple ID, you will be prompted to optionally enable iCloud Keychain. This feature securely saves your private information, like service usernames and passwords, to your iCloud account. This allows for easy access from multiple devices. Enabling iCloud Keychain will prompt you to set up two-step verification for any Apple IDs that don't have this feature enabled.

If you choose to not set up iCloud Keychain at this point, you can do so later from the iCloud Preferences. Lesson 8 "Keychain Management" covers this topic in greater detail.

Setup: iCloud Drive (Optional)

If you previously entered an Apple ID that has not been upgraded to the new iCloud Drive service, you will be prompted to upgrade your previously stored iCloud documents. This one-time process is required if you intend to access documents stored in iCloud on OS X Yosemite and iOS 8 devices.

If you choose not to upgrade to iCloud Drive at this point, you can do so later from the iCloud preferences. Lesson 18 "Document Management" covers this topic in greater detail.

Setup: FileVault Disk Encryption (Optional)

OS X Yosemite includes FileVault, which can be used to protect the system volume by encrypting its contents. If you are working through Setup Assistant on a late-model portable Mac that doesn't have FileVault enabled, you may be prompted to enable this feature. This screen will appear on both new systems and systems upgraded to OS X Yosemite, but only if the system has a single local user account and that account has signed into iCloud.

If you select the option to turn on FileVault, after Setup Assistant is complete, the system will begin to encrypt the contents of the system volume. The computer will not have to restart, and the encryption will complete silently in the background. Because this option appears only on systems with a single local user account, only that local account will be allowed to unlock the encrypted system during startup. If the account password is lost, the disk will remain locked unless it is reset using a FileVault recovery key.

The second option on this screen allows you to save the FileVault recovery key to the iCloud account. If you don't choose the option to allow iCloud to unlock the disk, then you will be presented with another screen showing the FileVault recovery key. In this case, you are responsible for manually saving the recovery key to a safe location.

If you choose not to enable FileVault at this point, you can do so later from the Security & Privacy preferences. Lesson 10 "FileVault" covers this topic in greater detail.

Setup: Diagnostics & Usage (Optional)

By default, OS X is configured to automatically send diagnostic and usage information to Apple and third-party developers. Both of these feedback mechanisms allow developers to improve system and application performance. Providing this type of feedback may be a privacy concern for some, so it can be disabled as well. After setup, you can verify and modify these settings from the Security & Privacy preferences, as covered in Lesson 7 "System Security".

Setup: Register Your Mac (Optional)

Finally, the registration process allows you to optionally send system registration information to Apple. This information is used to associate your contact information with the Mac hardware. This information is primarily used to facilitate AppleCare support.

Again, if you previously entered an Apple ID, Setup Assistant optionally submits the registration based on your Apple ID account. If you didn't enter an Apple ID, you can manually enter your contact information here. Or, to postpone registration, click the Skip button.

Reference 2.2
System Preferences

Once Setup Assistant has completed the initial configuration, you have various system tools to use for administration and troubleshooting. The System Preferences application is the primary interface for adjusting user and system settings.

You will use System Preferences throughout this guide and any time you are setting up or reconfiguring a Mac system. The quickest access to System Preferences is from the Apple menu, because it's available from any application that shows the menu bar.

TIP ▶ The System Preferences application can also be found in the /Applications folder. You can use any shortcut method you like to access the System Preferences application, including clicking its icon in the Dock. With a default installation of OS X, System Preferences appears in the Dock, but it can also be removed like any other icon in the Dock.

When you open System Preferences, you'll notice it is divided into four or five separate rows of icons. These rows represent different categories of System Preferences. (Unlike previous OS X versions, Yosemite does not label categories.)

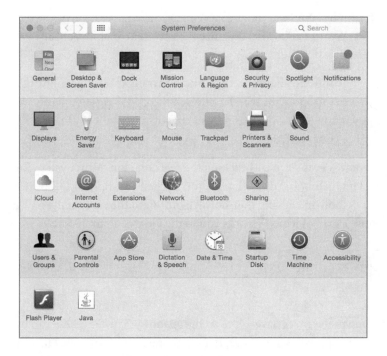

The individual System Preferences are organized as follows:

▶ First row, personal—These preferences generally affect only settings for the active user account. In other words, for most of the System Preferences in this category, each user has his or her own discrete settings.

▶ Second row, hardware—These preferences are specific to hardware settings. For example, the Energy Saver and Printers & Scanners preferences in this category affect every user on the Mac, and thus they require administrator user access to be changed.

▶ Third row, Internet and wireless

▶ Fourth row, system—These preferences have a systemwide effect when changed. Consequently, most of the preferences in this category require administrative access. An additional preference you may find in this row is Profiles preferences, which appears only when profiles are installed. Profiles are covered in "Reference 2.3 Profiles" on page 55.

▶ Fifth row, other—These preferences are not part of the standard OS X installation. The developers of third-party preferences decide whether their preferences require administrative access, so you may not see icons in this row.

TIP ▶ While you're in System Preferences, the View menu can give you quick access to all the preferences. You can choose to organize the preferences alphabetically or hide individual preferences.

TIP ▶ If you are ever confused about where to find a particular setting among the various preferences, use the Spotlight search option in the upper-right corner of the System Preferences window. Entering text in this field will automatically highlight preferences containing your search criteria.

Accessing a set of preferences is as simple as clicking the relevant icon. Most System Preferences changes are instantaneous and don't require you to click an Apply or OK button. In the System Preferences toolbar, clicking the Show All button to the right of the navigation arrows (representing a grid of icons) returns you to the view of all preferences.

You may notice that some preferences have a lock in the lower-left corner. These can be accessed only by an administrative user account. If a set of preferences you need to access is locked from editing, simply click the lock icon, and then authenticate as an administrative user to unlock it.

If you are logged in as a nonadministrative user in OS X, more preferences will be locked than if you are logged in as an administrative user. For example, if you are logged in as an administrative user, App Store preferences will not show the lock icon, whereas if you are logged in as a nonadministrative user, App Store preferences will be locked by default.

The lock icon appears in a variety of places, not just in System Preferences. The lock icon is a general indication that access to the item requires administrative authentication. This is often the case when an item represents a change that affects all users.

Reference 2.3
Profiles

An alternative method for system setup is to install profiles. Profiles were originally created to provide easy configuration and management for iOS devices, but they are now also used in OS X.

A profile is a document that includes instructions for specific settings. For example, profiles can contain settings for Internet accounts or network preferences. Profile documents can be identified by their icon and the filename extension of .mobileconfig.

Trust_Profile_for_Pretend
co.mobileconfig

When a profile is installed, user and system settings are automatically configured based on the profile's content. Thus, an administrator can create a profile that contains a complex variety of settings and then share this profile document with multiple users. The users can then easily install the profile themselves instead of having to manually configure settings. In other words, profiles can save both administrators and users a lot of time.

Both Apple and third-party developers provide software for creating profiles. Apple alone is responsible for several tools that can create profiles, including Xcode, the Apple Configurator application, and the Profile Manager service of OS X Server.

Different general types of profiles are tailored to specific purposes. For example, configuration profiles contain settings that automatically configure certain functions. Trust profiles contain digital certificates, which are used to validate and secure service connections. Enrollment profiles are used to establish a connection to a profile management service, more commonly known as a Mobile Device Management (MDM) service.

Administrators can provide profiles through any means that one would use to share any other document. For example, an administrator could send a profile via email or make it available as a download from a link on a website. Alternatively, administrators can automatically push profiles to an OS X system that is enrolled in an MDM service like that provided by the Profile Manager service of OS X Server. Details on the creation of profiles is beyond the scope of this guide, but every Mac administrator should be familiar with how to identify and verify these profiles.

MORE INFO ▸ You can find more information about managing OS X and iOS using profiles in *Managing Apple Devices* (Peachpit Press).

If you are presented with a profile that needs to be installed, simply double-click the file to install it. This automatically opens the profile document in the Profiles pane of System Preferences. Profiles preferences appear only when profiles are installed.

From Profiles preferences, any user with administrative privileges can install, verify, or delete a profile. The screenshot above shows an installed trust profile that contains a digital certificate. Delivering this type of information via a profile is ideal, because it simplifies a process that would take several more complicated steps using a traditional method.

NOTE ▸ The installation of some profiles may require entering additional authentication information. For example, a profile that configures VPN settings will likely require that the user enter a password to authenticate a VPN session.

Verifying the results of an installed profile is a bit more difficult, as the profile could contain multiple settings that affect a variety of different services and applications. However, inspecting the details section of an installed profile in Profiles preferences is a good starting point. Again, in the previous example, the Details section shows that this a trust profile containing a digital certificate. As covered in Lesson 8 "Keychain Management", you can open the Keychain Access application to verify the installation of this certificate.

Reference 2.4
System Information

Knowledge of your Mac computer's specifications is always important when installing new software, updating installed software, performing maintenance, or troubleshooting a problem. In this section you will learn how to gather essential system information with the About This Mac window and the System Information application.

About This Mac Window

Your first stop in discovering a Mac computer's specifications is the About This Mac window. You can open it from any application by choosing About This Mac from the Apple menu.

For OS X Yosemite, the traditional simple About This Mac window has been replaced by a much more comprehensive system overview interface. Now the initial view of the About This Mac window shows you the system software version, Mac model name, processor type and speed, total system memory, graphics card information, and Mac serial number. Clicking the system version number reveals the system build number.

NOTE ▶ Mac computers that have had their logic boards improperly replaced may not display the serial number in the About This Mac window.

Of the information in the About This Mac window, a few items are key to the identification of the OS X system and Mac hardware:

▶ System version number—This number represents the specific system software version currently installed on the computer. The first part, 10, obviously represents the tenth generation of the Mac operating system. The second section, 10, represents the tenth major release of OS X. The final portion, if any, represents an incremental update to the operating system. Incremental updates generally offer very few feature changes but often include a number of security and bug fixes.

▶ System build number—This appears when you click the system version number and is an even more granular representation of the specific system software version installed on the computer. Apple engineers create hundreds of versions of each system software release as they refine the product. The build number is used to track this process. Also, you may find that the computer-specific builds of OS X that come preinstalled on new Mac hardware differ from the standard installation builds. This is an important detail to note if you are creating system images for mass distribution, as computer-specific builds of OS X may not work on other types of Mac hardware.

▶ Mac model name—The Mac computer's model name is most often derived from the product marketing name for the Mac, followed by a relative release date. For example, the screenshot above was taken on a "MacBook Pro Retina, Mid 2012." Because Apple releases very few Mac models each year, this naming convention is specific enough for hardware support identification.

▶ Mac serial number—The hardware serial number is also located somewhere on the Mac case, but sometimes it can be quite difficult to find. As it is on many other mass-produced products, the serial number is a unique number used to identify that particular Mac for maintenance and service issues.

Clicking the buttons across the About This Mac window's toolbar reveals more details about the computer's hardware and support options. Quite possibly the best feature of this window is the Support and Service buttons, which link directly to specifically useful areas of the Apple Support website. The contents of the links are generated dynamically to show the most up-to-date support information about OS X and your Mac. For example, the Specifications link opens a webpage with the full specifications for your specific Mac.

System Information Application

The information in the About This Mac window is only the tip of the iceberg compared with what you can find via the System Information (formerly System Profiler) application. From the About This Mac window, click the System Report button to open System Information. This opens a new System Information window revealing all available reporting options.

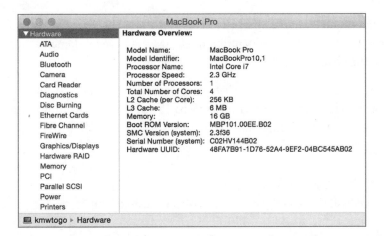

You will use System Information to locate critical system details in nearly every lesson of this guide. Additionally, one of the most important uses of System Information is as a documentation tool. Any time you need to document the current state of a Mac, you can use System Information to create a detailed system report by choosing File > Save from the menu. This creates a System Information-specific file (.spx filename extension) that can be opened from other OS X systems.

> **TIP** ▶ For quick access to the System Information application, select the Apple menu, and then hold down the Option key. The About this Mac menu option changes to System Information while the Option key is depressed.

Exercise 2.1
Configure a New OS X System for Exercises

▶ **Prerequisites**

  ▶ This exercise is necessary only if you have not already set up your computer. If you are using a Mac computer with existing accounts, perform "Exercise 2.2 Configure an Existing OS X System for Exercises" on page 63 instead.

  ▶ Your computer must have a new installation of OS X Yosemite and not have been set up yet.

The initial OS X configuration is simple, thanks to Setup Assistant. However, in this lesson you will learn how a few of these initial configuration settings can have fundamental and widespread effects on the system.

In this exercise, you will configure a clean installation of OS X on your class computer. Configuring OS X for this class entails answering a few basic questions and setting up the initial administrator user account. Completing these tasks will acquaint you with the Setup Assistant application.

Configure OS X with Setup Assistant

The following steps walk you through the basic setup of OS X using Setup Assistant:

1   At the Welcome screen, select the appropriate region, and click Continue.

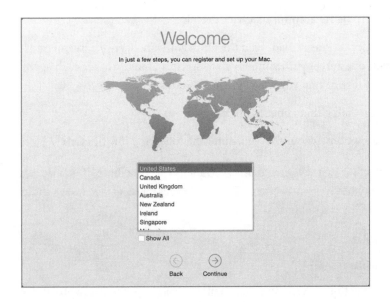

NOTE ▶ If you pause for a few moments at the Setup Assistant Welcome screen, the VoiceOver tutorial begins. This is an optional tutorial that explains how to use the VoiceOver assistance technology designed for visually impaired people.

2   At the Select Your Keyboard screen, select the appropriate keyboard layout, and click Continue.

Setup Assistant evaluates your network environment and tries to determine whether you are connected to the Internet. This can take a few moments.

3   If you are asked to select your Wi-Fi network or how you connect to the Internet, configure it appropriately for your Internet connection. If you are performing this exercise in a class, please ask your instructor how you should configure your computer.

If you are not asked about your Internet connection, your computer's network settings have already been configured via DHCP, and you may move on to step 4.

4   At the "Transfer Information to This Mac" screen, select "Don't transfer any information now," and click Continue.

If you were replacing a computer, the other options would assist you in migrating user data and system information from the old computer to the new one.

5   If the "Sign in with Your Apple ID" screen appears, select "Don't sign in," click Continue, and then click Skip in the confirmation dialog that appears.

You will set up an Apple ID account in a later exercise.

6   At the Terms and Conditions screen, read the OS X software license agreement. If there is more than one agreement, you may need to click "more" under each agreement to get the full text. When you have finished reading, click Agree.

7   In the confirmation dialog that appears, click Agree.

8   At the Create a Computer Account screen, enter the following information:

> **NOTE** ▶ It is important that you create this account as specified here. If you do not, future exercises may not work as written. This guide uses **this bold blue text** to indicate text that you should enter exactly as shown.

Full name: **Local Admin**

Account name: ladmin

If you are performing this exercise in a class, enter ladminpw in the Password and Verify fields. If you are performing this exercise on your own, select a more secure password for the Local Admin account. Be sure to remember the password you have chosen since you will need to reenter it periodically as you use this computer.

You may provide a password hint and change the other options if you want.

Deselect the option "Set time zone based on current location."

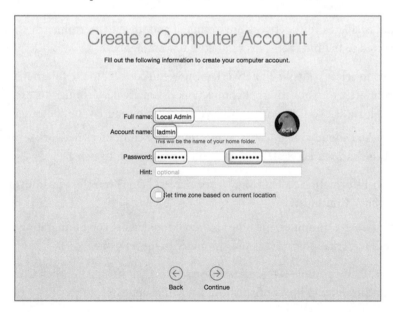

9   Click Continue.

10 If you are prompted to, select your location to set the computer's time zone; then click Continue.

11 If you are prompted to share diagnostics and usage, choose whether you want to share diagnostic information with Apple and app developers, and then click Continue.

12 If you are presented with a Register screen, select "Don't register," and click Continue.

13 When asked whether you are sure you don't want to register, click Skip.

Skip "Exercise 2.2 Configure an Existing OS X System for Exercises" on page 63 and proceed to "Exercise 2.3 Examine System Preferences" on page 66 to configure your preference settings.

Exercise 2.2
Configure an Existing OS X System for Exercises

▶ **Prerequisites**

▶   Your computer must be running OS X Yosemite.

▶   Your computer must already have been set up, and you must have an existing administrator account on it. If your computer has not been set up (that is, if the initial administrator account has not been created), perform "Exercise 2.1 Configure a New OS X System for Exercises" on page 60 instead.

To provide a consistent environment for the rest of the exercises in this guide, you will use System Preferences to create a new administrator account.

Create a New Administrator Account in System Preferences

1   If necessary, log in to your existing administrator account.

2   From the Apple menu, choose System Preferences.

3   In System Preferences, click Users & Groups.

4   In the lower-left corner, click the lock icon.

5   In the dialog that appears, enter the password for your existing administrator account, and click Unlock.

6   Click the Add (+) button below the user list.

7   In the dialog that appears, enter the following information:

NOTE ▶ It is important that you create this account as specified here. If you do not, future exercises may not work as written. If you already have an account named "Local Admin" or "ladmin," you will have to use a different name here, and then remember to use your substitute name throughout the rest of the exercises. This guide uses **this bold blue text** to indicate text that you should enter exactly as shown.

New Account: choose Administrator

Full Name: **Local Admin**

Account Name: **ladmin**

Password: select "Use separate password"

If you are performing this exercise in a class, enter **ladminpw** in the Password and Verify fields. If you are performing this exercise on your own, select a more secure password for the Local Admin account. Be sure to remember the password you have chosen, since you will need to reenter it periodically as you use this computer.

You may provide a password hint if you want.

8   Click Create User.

9   If you are prompted to turn off automatic login, click "Turn Off Automatic Login."

10 Quit System Preferences, and log out.

11 At the login screen, select the Local Admin account, and enter its password (ladminpw, or whatever you chose earlier).

12 Press Return.

13 When you are prompted to sign in with your Apple ID, select "Don't sign in," and click Continue.

You will set up an Apple ID account in a later exercise.

14 When a dialog appears asking if you are sure you want to skip signing in, click Skip.

15 If you are prompted to share diagnostic data with app developers, choose whether you want to do so, and click Continue.

Proceed to "Exercise 2.3 Examine System Preferences" on page 66 to configure your preference settings.

Exercise 2.3
Examine System Preferences

▶ **Prerequisite**

- ▶ You must have created the Local Admin account in either "Exercise 2.1 Con-figure a New OS X System for Exercises" on page 60 or "Exercise 2.2 Config-ure an Existing OS X System for Exercises" on page 63.

In this exercise, you will configure some preference settings to make the rest of the exercises easier. This will also give you an introduction to configuring application and system preferences in OS X.

Adjust Finder Preferences

The OS X default Finder settings make it easy for users to find and work with their own files but are not optimal for system administrators who frequently access files outside their home folder. Since you will be exploring the OS X system more than working with your own files, some customization is in order.

1   If a notification informs you that software updates are available for your computer, click Later, and select Remind Me Tomorrow from the pop-up menu that appears.

You will install updates during the Lesson 4 "OS X Software Updates" exercises.

2   If a notification suggests turning on auto updates, click Not Now.

3   If any dialogs open with a "Do you want to use *<some volume>* to back up with Time Machine?" prompt, click Don't Use in each dialog.

4   From the menu bar, choose Finder > Preferences. If you prefer, you can use the keyboard shortcut Command-Comma instead.

The Finder is actually an application, and its preferences can be configured in much the same way as any other OS X application.

5   Select the options to show hard disks and connected servers on the desktop.

6   From the "New Finder windows show" pop-up menu, choose your startup volume (typically named Macintosh HD).

7   At the top of the Finder Preferences window, click the Sidebar button.

8   Select "ladmin" in the Favorites section of the sidebar and "Hard disks" in the Devices section. Note that "Hard disks" should be fully selected (a checkmark in the check-box), not just partially enabled (a dash in the checkbox).

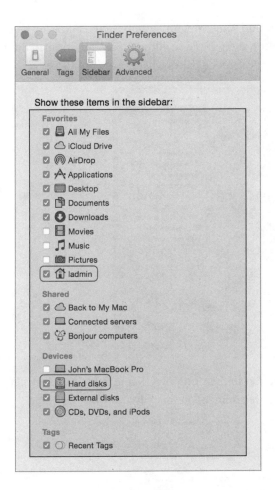

9   Close the Finder Preferences window

Set the Computer Name

If you are performing these exercises as part of a class, your computer will have the same name as all the other students' computers. To avoid confusion, give your computer a unique name.

1   From the Apple menu, choose System Preferences.

2   In System Preferences, click Sharing.

Note that if you aren't sure where to find something in System Preferences, you can use the Spotlight search field in the top right of the window. It searches for matching or related settings and highlights the preference panes where they are located.

3   Enter a unique name for your computer in the Computer Name field. If you are performing these exercises in a class, it's recommended that you use your full name.

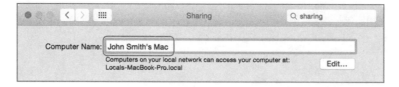

4   Press Return.

Notice that your local host name (.local name) that is displayed under your computer name updates to match your new computer name.

5   If you are performing these exercises on your own, click the Show All (grid icon) button in the toolbar, and then skip ahead to "Adjust Your Trackpad/Mouse Preferences" on page 71.

6   If you are performing these exercises in a class, select the Remote Management check-box.

NOTE ▶ In a classroom situation, remote management will allow your instructor to control the keyboard and mouse, gather information, and update your Mac throughout this course, enabling him or her to assist you with steps and exercises if necessary.

A dialog asks what you want users to be able to do using remote management.

7   Hold down the Option key while clicking one of the checkboxes to select all the options in the dialog.

8   Click OK.

9   Click the Show All (grid icon) button to show all the preference panes.

Adjust Your Trackpad/Mouse Preferences

In OS X you can customize the user interface to fit your personal preferences. For example, depending on what you are used to, you may want to change the default scrolling behavior. Also, you can control how the system recognizes primary and secondary mouse clicks (analogous to left- and right-clicks in other operating systems).

Note that since Control-click always works as a secondary click, these instructions describe it as Control-click.

1   If you are using a trackpad, select the Trackpad pane.

▶   Adjust the "Tap to Click" and "Secondary click" options to your liking. (These functions are used for opening shortcut menus, normally the right mouse button or Control-click.)

▶   Click "Scroll & Zoom," and use the "Scroll direction: natural" option to adjust which direction it works. The default is that moving two fingers up moves the window's contents up.

▶   Check the other options under "Scroll & Zoom" and "More Gestures" and make any appropriate changes.

2   If you are using a mouse, select the Mouse pane.

▶   If your mouse has a scroll wheel (or equivalent), use the "Scroll direction: natural" option to adjust in which direction it works. The default is that pushing the wheel up moves the window's contents up.

▶   If your mouse has multiple buttons, use the "Primary mouse button" option to control which button is the primary (used for selecting, usually the left button) and which button is the secondary (used for opening shortcut menus, usually the right button or Control-click).

3   Quit System Preferences.

Proceed to either "Exercise 2.4 Download the Student Materials in a Classroom" on page 73 or "Exercise 2.5 Download the Student Materials Independently" on page 76, depending on whether you are performing these exercises in a classroom or independently.

Exercise 2.4
Download the Student Materials in a Classroom

► **Prerequisites**

► You must have performed "Exercise 2.3 Examine System Preferences" on page 66.

► You must be performing these exercises in a class or have set up your own server configured as in the Mainserver Setup Instructions. If you are following these exercises on your own and have not set up a server to support the exercises, perform "Exercise 2.5 Download the Student Materials Independently" on page 76 instead.

NOTE ► This exercise is written for students performing these exercises in a classroom environment. You can also use this exercise if you have set up another Mac computer as a server to support these exercises. If you want to do this, navigate to www.peachpit.com/redeem, enter your guide's access code (provided on a card in the back of the printed version of this guide and on the "Where Are the Lesson Files?" page of the electronic version of this guide), and follow the instructions provided with the code. Then download the Mainserver Setup Instructions file onto the computer you will use as a server, and follow the enclosed instructions.

If you are following these exercises on your own and have not set up a server to support the exercises, perform "Exercise 2.5 Download the Student Materials Independently" on page 76 instead.

In this exercise, you will download the student materials required for the rest of the exercises in the guide.

Connect to Mainserver

You will now connect to the file server (called Mainserver) to download the student materials. The details of networking, connecting to, and providing network services will be covered in later lessons.

1   If necessary, open a new Finder window by choosing File > New Finder Window or using the shortcut Command-N.

Look for the server named Mainserver in the Shared section of the sidebar. If Main-server is not shown, click All to view all the shared items.

2   Select Mainserver. If you had to click All in the previous step, you will have to double-click the Mainserver icon.

3   opy the folder by choosing Edit .

Copy the StudentMaterials Folder to Your Computer

1   Inside the Public folder, select (single-click) the StudentMaterials folder.

2   Copy the folder by choosing Edit > Copy "StudentMaterials", by pressing Command-C, or by Control-clicking the folder and choosing Copy "StudentMaterials" from the shortcut menu.

3   Open the Macintosh HD (either from your desktop or the Finder window's sidebar).

4   Open the Users folder.

5   Open the Shared folder.

6   Paste the StudentMaterials folder into the Shared folder by choosing Edit > Paste Item, by pressing Command-V, or by Control-clicking in the Shared folder and choosing Paste Item from the shortcut menu.

This creates a copy of the student materials on your computer. If your instructor has included software updates in the student materials, it may take several minutes to download them. You do not need to wait for it to finish.

7   Drag your copy of the StudentMaterials folder to the right side of the dividing line in the Dock. (The Dock is divided into two sections; the left side holds applications, and the right side holds folders and documents.) Be sure to place it between other entries (so it is added to the Dock) rather than over another entry (which would move it into that folder).

You will be opening the StudentMaterials folder frequently, and this gives you an easy shortcut to it.

8   Optionally, you can also drag the StudentMaterials folder to the Finder's sidebar in the Favorites section to give yourself another shortcut to access it. As in the Dock, be sure to place it between other entries.

9   Choose Go > Applications (or use the shortcut Command-Shift-A).

10   Drag the TextEdit application into the left side of your Dock so that you will always have an easy way to launch it.

11   If necessary, wait for the StudentMaterials folder to finish downloading to your computer.

12   Unmount Mainserver by clicking the eject icon next to it in the Finder sidebar.

You should now skip "Exercise 2.5 Download the Student Materials Independently" on page 76 and proceed to "Exercise 2.6 Install a Configuration Profile" on page 79.

Exercise 2.5
Download the Student Materials Independently

▶ **Prerequisites**

- ▶ You must have performed "Exercise 2.3 Examine System Preferences" on page 66.

- ▶ You must have your guide's access code (provided on a card in the back of the printed version of this guide and on the "Where Are the Lesson Files?" page of the electronic version of this guide).

- ▶ Do not perform this exercise if you are in a class or have set up your own server configured as in the Mainserver Setup Instructions file. If you have access to a server configured to support these exercises, perform "Exercise 2.4 Download the Student Materials in a Classroom" on page 73 instead.

In this exercise, you will download the student materials required for the rest of the exercises in the course.

Download the StudentMaterials Folder from the Web

You will now connect to the Pearson Education web server to download the student materials.

1   Open Safari.

2   Navigate to www.peachpit.com/redeem.

3   Enter the access code (provided on a card in the back of the printed version of this guide and on the "Where Are the Lesson Files?" page of the electronic version of this guide).

4   If you already have a Peachpit account, sign in to it. If you do not, follow the prompts to create one.

5   Click the Lesson & Update Files tab.

> **NOTE ▶** If you purchase or redeem a code for the electronic version of this guide directly from Peachpit, the student materials will automatically appear on the Lesson & Update Files tab without the need to redeem an additional code.

> **NOTE ▶** If you have access to another computer running OS X Yosemite and want to configure it as a server to support these exercises, do not download the student materials here. Instead, download the Mainserver Setup file onto the computer you will use as a server, and follow the enclosed Mainserver Setup Instructions.

6   Click the link to download the student materials.

The student materials for these exercises will be downloaded as a ZIP archive and automatically expanded into the StudentMaterials folder.

7   Click the Downloads (down-arrow icon) button near the top right of the window.

8   Click the view (magnifying-glass icon) button next to StudentMaterials.

Your Downloads folder opens in the Finder, showing the StudentMaterials folder inside it.

9   On your desktop, find the icon for your startup disk (generally Macintosh HD), and double-click it.

This opens a new Finder window showing the contents of the startup disk.

10 Open the Users folder.

11 Open the Shared folder.

12 Drag the StudentMaterials icon from the Downloads folder into the Shared folder.

13 Close the Downloads folder.

14 Drag the StudentMaterials icon from the Shared folder to the right side of the dividing line in the Dock. (The Dock is divided into two sections; the left side holds applications, and the right side holds folders and documents.) Be sure to place it between other entries (so it is added to the Dock) rather than over another entry (which would move it into that folder).

You will be opening the StudentMaterials folder frequently, and this gives you an easy shortcut to it.

15 Optionally, you can also drag the StudentMaterials folder to the Finder sidebar in the Favorites section to give yourself another shortcut to it. As in the Dock, be sure to place it between other entries.

16 Choose Go > Applications (or use the shortcut Command-Shift-A).

17 Drag the TextEdit application into the left side of your Dock so that you will always have an easy way to launch it.

Exercise 2.6
Install a Configuration Profile

▶ **Prerequisite**

▶ You must have downloaded the StudentMaterials folder, using the instructions in either "Exercise 2.4 Download the Student Materials in a Classroom" on page 73 or "Exercise 2.5 Download the Student Materials Independently" on page 76.

In addition to manually configuring settings on OS X computers, you can control a computer's settings by installing profiles. This capability allows you to easily standardize the configuration across multiple computers.

In this exercise, you will demonstrate this by setting your Energy Saver settings with a configuration profile.

Change Your Energy Saver Settings with a Configuration Profile

1 If necessary, open System Preferences by choosing it from the Apple menu.

2 Select the Energy Saver pane.

3 Note your computer's sleep settings. Depending on the model you are using, they may differ from those shown here.

4 Quit System Preferences.

5 Open the StudentMaterials folder. Remember that you put a shortcut to it in your Dock.

6 Open the Lesson2 folder.

7 Open Energy_Saver.mobileconfig.

The profile automatically opens in the Profiles pane of System Preferences.

8 Click Show Profile to display the details of the profile and its payload (the settings it contains). You will need to scroll down to see its full contents.

9 Click Continue.

10 Click Install.

11 Enter the Local Admin account's password (**ladminpw**, or whatever you chose earlier) when prompted.

The Profile pane now lists the configuration profile as installed.

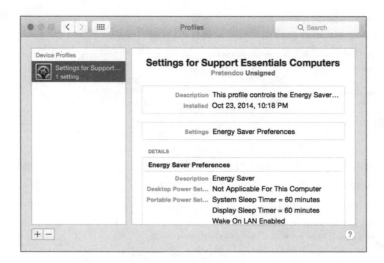

12 Click the left-arrow button in the toolbar, and then select the Energy Saver pane.

The Energy Saver settings have changed to match those in the profile.

NOTE ▶ Although the new Energy Saver settings take effect immediately, the display in System Preferences does not always update. If you still see the old settings, try logging out and back in to the Local Admin account, and then recheck System Preferences.

13 Quit System Preferences

Exercise 2.7
Examine System Information

System Information is the primary tool for gathering configuration information in OS X.
In this exercise, you will explore its features.

Use About This Mac and System Information

System Information displays information and options for repair and warranty coverage of
your computer.

1 From the Apple menu, choose About This Mac.

A dialog appears showing basic information about your computer.

2 Click the OS X version number (below the large "OS X Yosemite"). The build number
(a more specific identifier for the version of OS X you are using) is displayed.

3 Click through the Displays and Storage tabs in the About window's toolbar to view
more information about your computer's hardware configuration.

4 Click the Service tab.

5 Click "Check my service and support coverage status."

6 In the confirmation dialog that appears, click Allow.

Safari opens and shows your computer's model name and warranty status.

7 Quit Safari.

8 In the About window, click Overview.

9 Click the System Report button.

System Information displays a more detailed report of the hardware, network, and software configuration of your computer.

10 Explore the system report by clicking various categories of information in the report's sidebar. Note that some categories may take a while to load.

11 From the menu bar, choose File > Save, enter a name for your system's report, and then click Save.

When saving reports like this, it is usually best to choose a naming convention that includes the computer name (or other identifier) and the date.

This finishes gathering information on your computer and saves it in a report that documents your computer's current status.

12 Quit System Information.

TIP You can also find the System Information application in the /Applications/ Utilities folder or in the Other section of Launchpad. You can use any shortcut method you like to access the System Information application, including placing it in the Dock.

TIP You can also directly access System Information from the Apple menu by holding the Option key. This changes the About This Mac menu choice to System Information. When opening System Information directly, you will skip the summary About This Mac window and instead be presented with the full system report.

Lesson 3

OS X Recovery

From a troubleshooting viewpoint, one of the most useful OS X features is the OS X Recovery system. Via OS X Recovery, you can not only reinstall OS X but also access a variety of administration and troubleshooting utilities. OS X Recovery replaces functionality previously accessed from an OS X installation DVD. The primary difference is that the OS X Recovery system is, by default, located on the primary system disk. This allows easy access to recovery utilities without the need for additional media.

In this lesson, you will learn how to access OS X Recovery on both new Mac computers that came with OS X preinstalled and on systems that have been upgraded to OS X Yosemite. You will also briefly explore the utilities available from OS X Recovery. As long as you don't make any permanent changes using the utilities in OS X Recovery, you can safely explore without damaging your primary OS X system. Finally, you will learn how to create an external OS X install disk that can be used in cases where the local OS X Recovery system isn't available.

GOALS

▶ Access the utilities available in OS X Recovery

▶ Reinstall OS X from OS X Recovery

▶ Create an external OS X recovery disk

Reference 3.1
Startup from OS X Recovery

Mac systems running OS X Yosemite, including both systems that shipped with OS X Yosemite and upgraded systems, include a hidden OS X Recovery system on the local system disk. To access this copy of OS X Recovery, simply restart the computer while holding down Command-R. In most cases, once the OS X Recovery system fully starts, the OS X Utilities window appears. From there you can install (or reinstall) OS X and choose from a variety of maintenance applications. If, however, the OS X Installer appears, you can continue with the installation if you need to, or quit the installer (using the Command-Q keyboard shortcut) to return to the OS X Utilities window.

NOTE ▶ The OS X Recovery system partition, dubbed Recovery HD, is a hidden partition that, by default, does not appear when a Mac is running OS X. The Recovery HD partition is automatically created during OS X installation from the last 650 MB or so of the system volume. You can verify the existence of the Recovery HD partition by examining the internal disk using the System Information application.

If for some reason OS X Recovery doesn't start or isn't installed on the local system disk, you have three alternatives for accessing it:

▶ If you have a Mac model released in mid-2010 or later—If your Mac has the latest firmware updates, it can access OS X Internet Recovery. If the local OS X Recovery system is missing, late-model Mac computers should automatically attempt to access OS X Internet Recovery. You can also force a system to start up to OS X Internet Recovery by holding down Command-Option-R. When you do this, your Mac tries to redownload the OS X Recovery system from Apple servers. If successful, this process re-creates the local Recovery HD partition.

MORE INFO ▶ For more about using OS X Internet Recovery, see Apple Support article HT4718, "OS X: About OS X Recovery," and article HT202313, "Computers that can be upgraded to use OS X Internet Recovery."

▶ If you have an external OS X recovery disk—Connect the recovery disk to your Mac, and restart while holding down the Option key. This opens Startup Manager, where you can use the arrow and Return keys or the mouse or trackpad to select the external OS X recovery disk. The default name for an external OS X recovery disk created using the methods outlined in this lesson is "Install OS X Yosemite." "Reference 3.3 External OS X Recovery Disk" on page 92 and "Exercise 3.2 Create an OS X Install Disk" on page 99 cover creating this disk in greater detail.

▶ If you have a local Time Machine backup disk—The Time Machine backup service automatically creates a hidden OS X Recovery system on local backup disks. To access this system, connect the Time Machine backup disk to your Mac, and restart while holding down the Option key. This opens the Mac computer's Startup Manager, where (as above) you can use the arrow and Return keys or the mouse or trackpad to select the Time Machine backup disk. Lesson 16 "Time Machine" covers this topic in greater detail.

NOTE ► If the Time Machine backup disk is encrypted, you have to enter the disk encryption password to successfully start up the OS X Recovery system. This password is unique to the encrypted backup disk and is not associated with or synchronized to any user account passwords. Again, Lesson 16 "Time Machine" covers this topic in greater detail.

Reference 3.2
OS X Recovery Utilities

OS X Recovery is a useful administrative and troubleshooting resource. When you start up from this system, you have access to several system-administration and maintenance tools.

This system even has a few utilities you cannot find anywhere else in OS X. Again, in most cases, when you first start the OS X Recovery system, you see the OS X Utilities window.

NOTE ► When a Mac is started up from OS X Recovery, Ethernet and Wi-Fi networking are available if the network provides DHCP services. Ethernet is automatically enabled if the Mac physically connected to the network. If a Wi-Fi network isn't automatically connected, you can select one from the Wi-Fi menu item.

NOTE ► If manual network setup is required during use of OS X Recovery, refer to instructions in Apple Support article HT200168, "Using Lion Recovery when no DHCP service is available."

NOTE ▶ While running from OS X Recovery, if the Mac computer's system disk is protected by FileVault, any access to this disk first requires that you unlock the disk. In most cases, any local user's password on the system will unlock the system FileVault disk. Lesson 10 "FileVault" covers this topic in greater detail.

From the OS X Utilities window in OS X Recovery, you can access the following functions:

▶   Restore From Time Machine Backup—Use this to restore a full-system Time Machine backup from either a network or a locally connected disk. Lesson 16 "Time Machine" covers this topic in greater detail.

▶   Install OS X or Reinstall OS X—As the name implies, this option opens the OS X Installer. If you are running from an OS X Install disk, the disk contains all the OS X installation assets. However, the local hidden Recovery HD and disks created with OS X Recovery Disk Assistant do not contain the installation assets and thus require Internet access to reinstall OS X. Further, the OS X Installer must verify that the user is allowed access to the OS X Yosemite assets. On older Mac computers that have been upgraded to OS X Yosemite, you must verify the installation by providing the Apple ID used to purchase OS X. For Mac computers that shipped with OS X Yosemite, this verification is automatic. Lesson 1 "Install OS X Yosemite" covers this topic in greater detail.

▶   Get Help Online—This option opens Safari, taking you directly to the Apple Support website.

▶   Disk Utility—This application handles storage-related administration and maintenance. It is especially useful when the Mac has started up from OS X Recovery, because Disk Utility can be used to manage a system disk that otherwise can't be managed when in use as the startup disk. Specifically, Disk Utility can be used to prepare a disk for a new installation of OS X or to attempt repairs on a disk that fails installation. Lesson 9 "File Systems and Storage" covers this topic in greater detail.

▶   Startup Disk (by clicking the close button or quitting)—If you attempt to quit the OS X Utilities window, you will see a prompt to start the Startup Disk utility. From this utility you can select the default system startup disk. The default startup disk can be overridden using any of the alternate startup modes discussed in Lesson 27 "System Troubleshooting".

Wait, there's more. OS X Recovery has a few extra utilities tucked away in the Utilities menu at the top of the screen:

► Firmware Password Utility—This utility allows you to secure the Mac computer's startup process by disabling all alternate startup modes without a password. You can disable or enable this feature and define the required password. Learn more about firmware passwords in Lesson 7 "System Security".

► Network Utility—This is the primary network and Internet troubleshooting utility in OS X. Its primary use in OS X Recovery is to troubleshoot any network issues that could prevent the download of OS X installation assets. The Network Utility is further discussed in Lesson 22 "Network Troubleshooting".

► Terminal—This is your primary interface to the UNIX command-line environment of OS X. The most useful command you can enter from here is resetpassword followed by pressing the Return key.

► Reset Password opened via Terminal—This utility lets you reset the password of any local user account, including the root user's, on the selected system disk. Obviously, this utility can pose a serious security threat, and consequently it can only be run from OS X Recovery. Further, it's hidden from plain view, as you can only open it by entering the resetpassword command in the Terminal. You can find out more about Reset Password in Lesson 7 "System Security".

NOTE ▶ The utilities available from OS X Recovery can certainly be used to compromise system security. Then again, any system whose default startup disk can be overridden during startup is wide open to compromise. Therefore, in secured environments, it's often necessary to use the Firmware Password Utility to help protect your systems.

Reference 3.3
External OS X Recovery Disk

In some cases, a Mac with OS X installed does not have a local Recovery HD. For example, if you just replaced the internal disk with a new disk, nothing will be on the new disk. Also, OS X systems on RAID (Redundant Array of Independent Disks) sets and disks with nonstandard Boot Camp partitioning will not have a local Recovery HD. In these cases, you would need to start up from an external OS X recovery disk. Also, having an external OS X recovery disk handy can be a real lifesaver should you come across a Mac with a dysfunctional system disk.

NOTE ▶ When creating your own OS X recovery disks, be sure to keep track of the specific version of OS X you are using. As covered in Lesson 1 "Install OS X Yosemite", newer Mac systems do not support older versions of OS X and may require computer-specific builds of OS X. Thus, you should always keep your OS X recovery disks updated to the latest version of OS X available from the Mac App Store.

OS X Yosemite supports a do-it-yourself solution to convert a standard disk into an OS X recovery disk. This method involves using a special command-line tool, named createinstallmedia, found in the Install OS X Yosemite application. This tool copies both an OS X Recovery system and the full OS X installation assets to an external disk. Consequently, this method requires a disk of at least 8 GB, which is a very common size for a small USB flash drive. "Exercise 3.2 Create an OS X Install Disk" on page 99 outlines the steps necessary to create this type of disk.

NOTE ▶ It's not recommended to use the legacy Recovery Disk Assistant method to create external OS X recovery disks for OS X Yosemite.

Exercise 3.1
Use OS X Recovery

▶ **Prerequisite**

▶ Your computer must have a local hidden Recovery HD partition. This partition is normally created by the OS X Yosemite installation process.

In this exercise, you will start up your computer in OS X Recovery. OS X Recovery is stored on a hidden partition named Recovery HD that is created automatically when OS X is installed on the hard disk. You will review the included utilities as well as how OS X Recovery can reinstall the system.

NOTE ▶ You will not perform an installation, but you will get an opportunity to look at the steps leading up to the installation.

Start Up Using OS X Recovery

To access the Installer and other utilities in OS X Recovery, you need to start up from the hidden Recovery HD partition.

1   If your computer is on, shut it down by choosing Shut Down from the Apple menu.

2   Press the power button on your computer, and then hold down Command-R until the gray Apple logo appears on the screen.

     When you hold down Command-R during startup, the computer attempts to start up using a recovery partition on the hard disk.

     If no recovery partition is available, Mac computers with newer firmware can start up from an Apple server over the Internet and get access to the OS X Recovery features.

     If your computer starts up to the login screen instead of OS X Recovery, you may not have held Command-R long enough. If this happens, click the Shut Down button and try again.

3   If a language selection screen appears, select your preferred language, and click the right-arrow button.

4   After OS X Recovery starts up, you see an OS X Utilities window. This window is the primary interface for OS X Recovery.

If you see a Welcome screen instead, you probably pressed Command-R too late or did not hold it down long enough. You can start over by pressing Command-Q and then clicking the Shut Down button.

Examine the Utilities Available in OS X Recovery

While using OS X Recovery, you have access to some utilities for recovering, repairing, and reinstalling OS X. In this part of the exercise, you will familiarize yourself with some of these utilities.

NOTE ▶ In OS X Recovery, if the Mac computer's system disk is protected by File-Vault, any access to this disk will require the disk to be unlocked first. In most cases, any local user's password on the system should be allowed to unlock the system File-Vault drive. Lesson 10 "FileVault" covers this topic in greater detail.

View Help for OS X Recovery

You will use Safari to view the built-in instructions of OS X Recovery and to browse the web.

1   Select Get Help Online, and then click Continue.

Safari opens and displays a document with information about how to use OS X Recovery. Take a moment to skim the document.

This document is stored on the Recovery HD partition, but as long as you have an Internet connection available, you can also use Safari to view online documentation such as the Apple Support articles.

2   If a dialog indicates that Safari wants to use the "login" keychain, leave the Password field blank, and click OK.

3   Click in the "Search or enter website name" field, and then click the Apple icon that appears below it.

Safari now displays the Apple website.

4   If Safari displays a message that says "You are not connected to the Internet," you can join a wireless network using the Wi-Fi icon near the right side of the menu bar.

5   Click the Support link near the top right of the page.

6   You are taken to the Apple Support site. If you were experiencing a problem with your computer, this would be a good place to look for solutions and information. You will use some of the Apple Support resources later in this guide.

7   From the menu bar, choose Safari > Quit Safari (or press Command-Q) to return to the main utilities screen.

Note that closing the Safari window does not quit Safari. This is common among Mac applications, but if you are accustomed to using Microsoft Windows, it may be contrary to your expectations. Generally, the best way to quit a Mac application is to choose Quit <Application Name> from the application menu (the menu next to the Apple menu, named for the current application); or you can use the keyboard shortcut Command-Q.

Examine Disk Utility

Disk Utility is provided in OS X Recovery to allow you to repair, image, reformat, or repartition your computer's disk.

1 Select Disk Utility, and then click Continue.

In the device list on the left, you will see your startup disk and an OS X Base System disk image. Note the primary entry for each disk device and an indented list of volumes on each device (discussed in more detail in Lesson 9 "File Systems and Storage").

2 Select the lower entry for your startup volume. Depending on whether the volume is being managed by Core Storage, it may be labeled "Macintosh HD" or with a description of the physical disk. See "Core Storage" on page 250 for more information on Core Storage.

Notice the options available to perform on the volume. If the volume is being managed by Core Storage, you'll see just First Aid, Erase, and Restore tabs; if not, you'll also see a RAID tab.

Among the reasons Disk Utility is provided in OS X Recovery is to allow you to verify or repair the startup volume's file structure or, if necessary, to erase the volume before reinstalling OS X.

3   Select the upper entry that represents your startup volume, and note how the available options change.

4   Quit Disk Utility by choosing Disk Utility > Quit Disk Utility or by pressing Command-Q.

You are returned to the main utilities screen.

Examine Time Machine Restoration

If you backed up your computer with Time Machine, OS X Recovery has the capability to do a full system restoration from that backup. Setting up Time Machine is covered in "Reference 13.4 File Archives" on page 388.

1   Select Restore From Time Machine Backup, and then click Continue.

A page of notes on the restoration process appears. It is important to note that this restoration interface will erase all current data and replace it from the backup; other restoration interfaces that let you control which files or folders are restored are examined in "Reference 16.3 Restoring from Time Machine " on page 452.

2   Click Continue.

The "Select a Backup Source" screen appears. If you had configured a Time Machine backup target, it would be available here as a source for restoring your system. For more information about Time Machine, see Lesson 16 "Time Machine".

3   Click Go Back to return to the Restore Your System screen.

4   Click Go Back again to return to the main utilities screen.

Examine the OS X Installer

Now you will examine the reinstallation process, but you will not perform the installation. By going through the following steps, you can experience the configuration of an installation without actually waiting for the OS X software to be copied to your system.

1   Select Reinstall OS X, and then click Continue.

The OS X Yosemite Installer opens.

2   Click Continue.

A dialog appears indicating that this computer's eligibility will be verified with Apple.

3 Click Continue.

4 At the license agreement, click Agree.

5 In the license confirmation dialog, click Agree again.

The OS X Yosemite Installer displays a list of partitions where you could install or reinstall OS X.

NOTE ▶ Do not click the Install button; otherwise, the Installer reinstalls OS X, which you do not want to do at this time.

6 Quit the Installer.

Verify Your Startup Disk and Restart

The Startup Disk utility allows you to select the volume from which to start up. If you are having problems during system startup from your computer's internal disk, you could connect a second disk with OS X installed and use Startup Disk to configure the computer to start up from the new disk.

1 From the Apple menu, choose Startup Disk. Notice that Startup Disk shows you a list of all startup volumes. Available options may include Network Startup or one or more NetBoot images, depending on what Startup Disk finds on your network.

2 Verify that your computer's normal startup volume (typically named Macintosh HD) is selected; if necessary, select it.

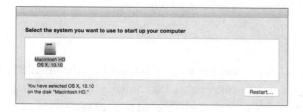

3 Click Restart.

4 In the confirmation dialog, click Restart.

You could also restart without using the Startup Disk utility by choosing Apple menu > Restart.

Exercise 3.2
Create an OS X Install Disk

▶ **Prerequisites**

- ▶ You need an erasable external disk with a capacity of at least 8 GB.
- ▶ You must have created the Local Admin account ("Exercise 2.1 Configure a New OS X System for Exercises" on page 60 or "Exercise 2.2 Configure an Existing OS X System for Exercises" on page 63).

In this exercise, you will create an OS X install disk, which includes not only the OS X Recovery environment and tools but also a full set of installation assets. With a disk created by this method, you can reinstall OS X Yosemite without needing to redownload the Installer application from the Internet.

NOTE ▶ When creating your own OS X install disk, make sure to keep track of the specific version of OS X you are using. As covered in "Exercise 1.3 Erase a Mac System and Install OS X Yosemite" on page 33, newer Mac systems do not support older versions of OS X and may require computer-specific builds of OS X. As such, you should always keep your OS X install disks updated to the latest versions of OS X available from the Mac App Store.

Acquire a Copy of the Install OS X Yosemite Application

If you upgraded to OS X Yosemite following the instructions in "Exercise 1.2 Upgrade to OS X Yosemite" on page 30 and saved a copy of the Installer application, you may use it and skip this section. If you are performing these exercises as part of a class, the instructor may have provided a copy in the StudentMaterials/Lesson3 folder. Otherwise, you can redownload the Installer with the following procedure:

1   From the Apple menu, choose App Store. For more about the Mac App Store, see Lesson 17 "Application Installation".

2   In the search field of the App Store window, enter Yosemite, and press Return.

3   Find OS X Yosemite in the search results, and click the DOWNLOAD or GET button under its name.

4   Click Continue in the confirmation dialog that appears, and then wait while the installer application downloads.

When it finishes downloading, the installer application will open automatically.

5   Quit both Install OS X Yosemite and the App Store.

Reformat the External Disk

Most external disks come preformatted with the MBR partition scheme; to allow an Intel Mac computer to start up from it, you must reformat this disk with the GUID partition table (GPT) scheme. For more information about disk formats, see Lesson 9 "File Systems and Storage".

> **WARNING ▶** This operation will erase all information on the external disk. *Do not* perform this exercise with a disk that contains any files you want to keep.

1   Open Disk Utility. It is located in the Utilities folder, which is inside the Applications folder. You can navigate to this folder in the Finder by using the Finder shortcut Command-Shift-U, or you can open Launchpad in the Dock, and then select the Other icon in Launchpad.

2   Plug the external disk into your computer.

3   If you are prompted for a password to unlock the disk, the disk is encrypted and cannot be used for this exercise. If this happens, eject the disk, and use a different disk for the exercise.

4   Select the external disk device entry in the Disk Utility sidebar. Be sure to select the device entry, not the volume entry indented beneath it.

5   Check the partition map scheme listed at the bottom of the window.

Depending on what this disk was used for most recently, the partition scheme could be anything. To convert it to the GPT scheme, you will erase the disk. If it is already using the GPT scheme, this is not strictly necessary, but you should erase it just to be sure.

It is also possible to partition the disk and use only part of it for the installer volume. See "Repartitioning a Disk" on page 254 for more information about the partitioning procedure.

6   Click the Erase tab.

7   Choose Mac OS Extended (Journaled) from the Format pop-up menu, and give the disk a descriptive name.

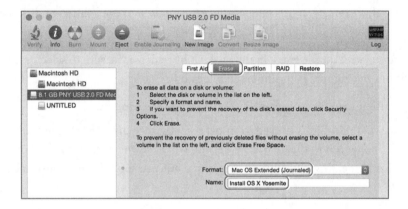

8   Click the Erase button near the bottom right of the window.

9   In the confirmation dialog, click Erase.

10   Verify that the Partition Map Scheme entry is now GUID Partition Table.

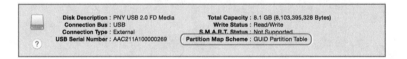

Since you erased the entire disk, rather than a single volume within the disk, Disk Utility has rebuilt the partition map as well. Although a Mac OS Extended volume can be created under any supported partition scheme, Disk Utility created a GUID partition table because it is the best fit.

11   Quit Disk Utility.

Create an OS X Install Disk

1   Open Terminal from the Utilities folder.

2   Switch to the Finder, and open the Applications folder. You can do this by choosing Go > Applications or using the keyboard shortcut Command-Shift-A.

3   Control-click the Install OS X Yosemite application, and choose Show Package Contents from the shortcut menu that appears.

    For more about packages, see "Reference 13.2 Bundles and Packages" on page 381.

4   Inside the installer package, open the Contents folder, and then open the Resources folder inside that.

5   Drag the file named "createinstallmedia" from the Finder window into the Terminal window.

    This inserts the full path to "createinstallmedia" into Terminal.

6   Switch back to Terminal, and press Return.

    This executes "createinstallmedia" as a command-line program. It prints a usage summary, explaining how to use the program.

7   Begin another command by typing "sudo " (note that there must be a space at the end), but do not press Return until step 13.

8   Drag "createinstallmedia" from the Finder window into the Terminal window again.

9   In Terminal, enter the text "--volume " (note that there are two dashes at the beginning, and a space at the end).

10 Drag the Install Yosemite (or whatever you named it) volume icon from the desktop to the Terminal window.

11 In Terminal, enter the text "--applicationpath " (again, there are two dashes at the beginning, and a space at the end).

12 In the Finder, navigate back to the Applications folder, and drag the Install OS X Yosemite application to the Terminal window.

At this point, the Terminal command should look something like this (although the lines may wrap at a different point):

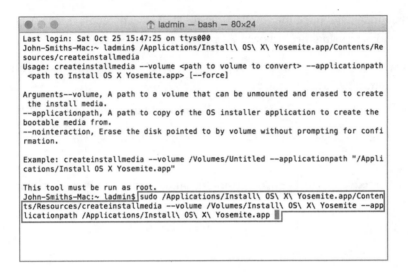

13 Switch to Terminal, and press Return.

This operation requires admin access, so it prompts for your password.

14 Enter the Local Admin account's password (**ladminpw**, or whatever you chose when you created the account), and then press Return. Note that nothing displays as you type.

15 Since this operation will erase the disk, you are prompted to confirm the operation. Verify that the volume name (listed after "/Volumes/") is the one you intend to use, and then enter "**Y**", and press Return.

16 Wait as the install disk is prepared. This may take several minutes.

When the process is complete, it prints "Copy complete." followed by "Done."

17 Quit Terminal.

Test the OS X Install Disk

If you want, you can now test the installer disk, although you should not actually reinstall OS X Yosemite.

1   Restart your computer by choosing Apple menu > Restart and then clicking Restart in the confirmation dialog.

2   Press and hold the Option key until you see a row of icons appear on the screen.

3   Click the install disk's icon.

4   Click the arrow that appears under the icon.

The computer starts up into the installer environment, which is similar to the recovery environment. You can explore it as much as you want, but do not reinstall OS X Yosemite at this time.

5   When you have finished, choose Apple menu > Restart to restart your computer normally.

Lesson 4
OS X Software Updates

Adding new capabilities is the very reason "software" exists. It's expected that you will add new applications to increase the capabilities of your Mac and, as products are refined, new software updates as well. In this lesson, you will configure and use the OS X software update technology, which is an automatic method to keep all your Apple-sourced software up to date. You will also explore an alternative to automatic software updates: manually downloading and installing software update packages.

GOALS

▸ Configure automatic software update settings

▸ Automatically update Apple-sourced software

▸ Manually update Apple software

Reference 4.1
Automatic Software Updates

Keeping current with software updates is an important part of maintaining a healthy computer. For that reason, OS X includes an easy-to-use software update mechanism that automatically checks the Apple servers via the Internet to make sure you're running the latest Apple-sourced software. Automatic software update checking is enabled by default as soon as you start using your Mac.

Both automatic and manual software updates require an Internet connection to download update installers. The automatic software update mechanism checks only for updates of currently installed Apple-sourced software, including software included with OS X and any software purchased from the Mac App Store.

Installing Mac App Store software updates requires appropriate Apple ID authentication. If you have not previously signed in to the Mac App Store from the computer you're working on, you will be required to authenticate with an Apple ID. If a Mac App Store item was installed with a different Apple ID, and you wish to update the item, you must authenticate with the Apple ID used to purchase the original item.

> **NOTE** ▸ Some software updates require that you also agree to a new Apple Software License Agreement.

> **NOTE** ▶ In OS X Yosemite, both administrative and standard users are allowed to install system software updates via the Mac App Store. If your organization restricts this type of activity for nonadministrative users, you can disable automatic software updates, as covered in "Automatic Software Update Preferences" on page 112 later in this lesson.

Automatic Software Update Behavior

OS X Yosemite features unified software updates via integration with the Mac App Store, meaning that all software you have installed from the Mac App Store, including OS X itself and applications created by either Apple or third parties, are updated from a single location. Further, software update is integrated with the Notification Center to let you know as soon as new updates are available for installation.

> **MORE INFO** ▶ Although it's covered here in terms of its update abilities, using the Mac App Store to install new applications is discussed further in Lesson 17 "Application Installation".

Assuming the default settings, updates for important system files and security software are always automatically downloaded and installed. On the other hand, by default, most OS X system and Mac App Store updates are automatically downloaded in the background but not installed. In this case, when updates are ready to be installed, a Mac App Store notification displays, stating "Updates Available."

From this notification you can click Restart, which will immediately install the updates, or click Later to display a menu enabling you to defer the update until a more convenient time. This is especially useful because some system updates prevent you from using the computer while the installation completes, in addition to requiring a restart.

The last item in this menu allows you to enable automatic updates for Mac App Store items. This option is not enabled by default on new OS X systems.

TIP ▶ When software updates are available, a number badge (indicating the number of available updates) will appear next to the Mac App Store icon, the Mac App Store toolbar Updates button, and the App Store selection in the Apple menu. Also, when you try to restart or shut down the computer, you may be reminded to install available updates.

Again, by default on OS X, Mac App Store updates will not automatically install. You may, however, receive an additional notification to "Turn on Auto Updates."

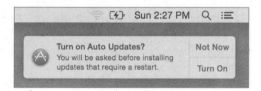

Clicking the Turn On button from this notification enables automatic installation for Mac App Store items. As stated previously, important system and security software are always updated.

After deferring updates, when you are ready to install updates or want to manually check for new updates, you can do so at any time using the following methods:

▶ In the About This Mac window, click the Software Update button.

▶ In the App Store preferences, found in the System Preferences application, click the Check Now button.

▶ In the toolbar of the Mac App Store, click the Updates button.

App Store Update Details

When the Mac App Store opens to show you new updates, each update is listed with information about the software update contents. The information provided includes the update name, version, and a description. Updates that require a system restart include a notice below the update's name.

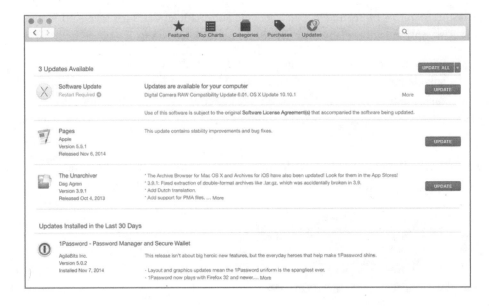

As in the screenshot above, the Updates list is split into three sections:

▸ At the very top are OS X software updates—This section contains only updates for OS X itself or updates for Apple software installed outside of the Mac App Store. (This is similar to the software update mechanism available in earlier versions of OS X.) To simplify the view, multiple software updates in this top section are hidden. You can see all the updates and their descriptions by clicking the More link next to the Update button in the top section.

▸ In the middle are individual Mac App Store updates—Items purchased from the Mac App Store, aside from OS X itself, always appear as separate update items. In this screenshot, both Pages and The Unarchiver require updates. Again, you can see more information about any individual software update by clicking the More link in the description.

▸ At the very bottom are previously installed updates—This section lists only updates installed by this user from the Mac App Store within the last 30 days. It does not list updates installed outside of the Mac App Store or by other users. A complete list of installations can be viewed using System Information, as covered in "Reference 4.3 Installation History" on page 117.

NOTE ▶ If you don't believe the items listed in the Updates view to be accurate, you can refresh available updates by choosing Store > Reload Page from the menu bar or by pressing Command-R.

NOTE ▶ Administrators can configure a custom Software Update service to help them manage updates. If this service is configured, the Software Update area shows the name of the server and lists the available updates. Although this process is not covered in this guide, you can find out more about it in the companion guide, *OS X Server Essentials 10.10: Using and Supporting OS X Server on Yosemite.*

To install a single update, simply click the corresponding Update button, or click the Update All button to install all available updates. If none of the updates requires a restart for installation, the software automatically installs without any further interaction.

However, if any of the updates requires a restart after the install process, you are given the option to restart or again defer the installation. If the update items have already been downloaded, a notification displays.

If any of the update items hasn't been downloaded, a different dialog appears so that you can confirm you want to download the items and then restart.

In either case, when you select a restart option, the system verifies the downloaded updates, logs out the current user, installs the updates, restarts the system, and then automatically logs back in to the user account that initiated the updates.

You can, of course, choose the Not Now button, but you will eventually have to restart to take advantage of the new software. Alternatively, if updates requiring a restart are already downloaded, you can choose an automatic installation option from the Later pop-up menu in the restart notification (shown previously) or from the pop-up menu to the right of the Update All button in the Mac App Store. This allows you to automatically defer the software installation and system restart to a time when it's more convenient.

iLife and iWork Updates

Although most new Mac systems come with the iLife and iWork apps installed, these apps will probably need to be updated. This requires that a user "adopt" or "accept" the free iLife and iWork software licenses that came bundled with the Mac by first signing in to the Mac App Store with his or her Apple ID. For more information about accepting these applications, see Apple Support article HT203658, "Alerts may occur when accepting bundled applications from the Mac App Store."

Older Mac systems upgraded to OS X Yosemite that also have a previous version of the iLife and iWork apps can upgrade, for free, to the latest Mac App Store versions. The software update process automatically detects these updates, but you have to authenticate with an Apple ID to accept the licenses for the new versions. For more information about updating these applications, see Apple Support article HT201064, "Update to newer versions of Apple apps on your Mac using the Mac App Store."

> **TIP** ▶ Once a user's Apple ID has been used to accept the license for an application, that user can install the application on any other Mac by signing in to the Mac App Store. In other words, a user can accept the iLife and iWork applications from a new Mac and then sign in on an older Mac to install the latest versions of the applications.

Automatic Software Update Preferences

App Store preferences, accessed via the System Preferences application, enable you to control the software update automation. Changes made in App Store preferences apply systemwide, to all users.

From the App Store preferences, you can enable or disable the following options:

▶ Automatically check for updates—When this option is enabled, the system checks for updates once a day. Note that "check" means that only a small amount of Internet bandwidth is needed to determine if updates are needed.

▶ Download newly available updates in the background—In this case, the update system may need to use a large amount of bandwidth to download updates. It's not uncommon for OS X system updates to weigh in at over 1 GB. Also, because this option will automatically download updates for applications purchased from the Mac App Store, systems with more applications will likely use more bandwidth.

▶ Install app updates—This option is not enabled by default, but, as covered previously, the system prompts you to enable this option via a notification. Once it's enabled, you are notified after new Mac App Store items are automatically updated or if you need to quit the application to apply the update. Importantly, automatic Mac App Store updates do not require a system restart.

▶ Install OS X updates—This option is not enabled by default, but, as covered previously, you can also enable this option via a notification. Once it is enabled, you will be notified after new OS X system items are automatically updated, as long as they don't require a restart. Again, any OS X updates that require a system restart allow you restart immediately or wait until later.

▶ Install system data files and security updates—If Apple deems these updates important enough that they should be always installed, it's a best practice to leave this option enabled. Keep in mind, though, that some system and security updates require that the system be restarted.

▶ Automatically download apps purchased on other Macs—This feature is disabled by default. If this feature is enabled, when you are signed in to the Mac App Store with an Apple ID, new installations made from another Mac using the same Apple ID will automatically install on this Mac as well. This is handy for those who use multiple Mac systems.

In App Store preferences, you can also click the Check Now button to manually open the Updates section of the Mac App Store.

MORE INFO ▶ Standard users can be individually restricted using parental controls, which include the ability to block access to the Mac App Store. You can find out more about parental controls in Lesson 5 "User Accounts" and more about the Mac App Store in Lesson 17 "Application Installation".

Reference 4.2
Manual Software Updates

Before the Mac App Store or automatic software updates, all Mac software was acquired and installed manually. Fortunately, OS X has always featured relatively simple software installation. In fact, many applications require only that the user copy a single application file to the local Applications folder. On the other hand, more complex software may require multiple resources to be placed in a variety of specific locations on your Mac.

A prime example of a complicated software installation is any system software update. In some cases it may be more convenient to manually install an update, as opposed to using automatic software update via the Mac App Store. For example, perhaps you need to install a particularly large software update for a system with limited Internet bandwidth. It may be better to manually download the update to a portable flash disk at a location with more bandwidth, and then use the flash disk to apply the update to the Mac that needs it. An experienced OS X support specialist will always have an external disk with the most common large updates handy for just such an occasion.

TIP ▶ You have the option of manually downloading and installing Apple software updates. You can find all Apple updates at http://support.apple.com/downloads/. After you download the updates, use the Installer application to apply them.

Installer Application

The Installer application makes complicated application installations simple. Often, software developers will create an "installer package" with all the instructions and resources necessary for the Installer application to set up the new software on your system.

MORE INFO ▶ Though it's covered briefly here, installing new applications is discussed further in Lesson 17 "Application Installation".

BrotherPrinterDrivers.pkg

Double-clicking one of these software installer packages opens the Installer application and begins the installation process. Much like the OS X installation process, the Installer application guides you through the steps necessary to install or update software. This may include agreeing to software licenses, selecting a destination, selecting package options, and authenticating as an administrative user.

Unlike the Mac App Store, the Installer application requires administrative access to install many items. This security mechanism is in place because anyone is allowed to make and distribute traditional OS X installer packages, including those who may have nefarious goals. Another mechanism in OS X, known as Gatekeeper, also provides an additional level of protection against unknown installation packages and software. You can find out more about Gatekeeper in "Gatekeeper" on page 498.

NOTE ▶ Third-party software developers may choose to use a proprietary, non-Apple installer for their product. These installers behave differently from the Apple Installer.

Advanced Installer Features

If you're curious about what an installation package is actually doing to your Mac, you have two ways to find out. First, you can view the Installer log at any time while using the Installer application by choosing Window > Installer Log or pressing Command-L. The Installer log is a live view of any progress or errors reported during the installation process.

TIP After installation, you can access the Installer log from the /Applications/Utilities/Console application. Once Console is open, select /var/log/install.log.

The second method allows you to inspect the content of an installer package before installation. After opening an installer package in the Installer application and passing the initial welcome and license screens, you can preview the list of files to be installed by choosing File > Show Files or pressing Command-I.

TIP Save time looking for what you need by using the search field in the toolbar when examining the Installer log or file list.

Apple has endeavored to increase the security and reliability of software installation packages by supporting signed packages. These packages contain special code used to validate the authenticity and completeness of the software during installation. This makes it nearly impossible for malicious parties to insert illegitimate files in trusted installation packages.

You can recognize a signed installer package by the small lock icon in the far right of the installer window title bar. Clicking this icon displays details about the signed package, including its certificate status.

Reference 4.3
Installation History

The automatic software update mechanism in OS X makes it incredibly easy for the average user to maintain an up-to-date system—so much so that the user often isn't even aware of how many updates or installations have been applied. Yet from a support perspective, it's important to know exactly which installations have taken place.

As you may have seen, the update screen in the Mac App Store shows recently installed updates. However, this list of updates doesn't show the complete history of all installations, but only recent installations from the Mac App Store, and only for the currently logged-in user account.

Fortunately, the System Information application features a complete installation history report. To view this history, open /Applications/Utilities/System Information, and then select the Installations item in the left column. This interface shows all software installed via the Mac App Store or the Installer application, including both new and update installations from either Apple or third parties. You can see the name, version, acquisition source, and date installed.

Exercise 4.1
Manually Install Software Updates in a Classroom

▶ **Prerequisites**

- ▶ This exercise is for students performing these exercises in a classroom environment. If you are following these exercises independently, perform "Exercise 4.2 Manually Install Software Updates Independently" on page 119 instead.

- ▶ You must have created the Local Admin account ("Exercise 2.1 Configure a New OS X System for Exercises" on page 60 or "Exercise 2.2 Configure an Existing OS X System for Exercises" on page 63).

If your instructor has chosen to download any software updates and distribute them as part of the student materials, you can follow these steps to install them. Your instructor will tell you whether you need to do this.

Install Updates from StudentMaterials

1   In the Finder, open the Lesson4 folder inside the StudentMaterials folder. Remember that you created a shortcut to the StudentMaterials folder in your Dock.

2   For each software update in this folder (note: your instructor may additionally specify an order in which they should be installed), do the following:

▶   Open the disk image file. After a short time, a new volume mounts. It contains the update package.

▶   Open the update package. The installer opens and walks you through the installation process.

▶   Continue through the installer prompts, and agree to the license agreement if required.

▶   When prompted, authenticate as Local Admin again (password: ladminpw, or whatever you chose when you created the account). Installing software updates manually requires administrative privileges.

▶   When each update has installed, click Close or Restart as appropriate.

3   Repeat these steps until all the updates have been installed.

4   If you did not restart, eject the disk image or disk images before proceeding. You can do this by Control-clicking in the background of the image's window and choosing Eject from the shortcut menu.

Exercise 4.2
Manually Install Software Updates Independently

▶   **Prerequisites**

▶   This exercise is for students performing these exercises independently. If you are performing these exercises in a classroom environment, perform "Exercise 4.1 Manually Install Software Updates in a Classroom " on page 118 instead.

▶   You must have created the Local Admin account ("Exercise 2.1 Configure a New OS X System for Exercises" on page 60 or "Exercise 2.2 Configure an Existing OS X System for Exercises" on page 63).

If you want to keep a copy of an update or want to install additional software (such as printer drivers) available for download from the Apple Support site, this exercise shows you how to download and install updates manually.

Download an Update from the Internet

1   Open Safari.

2   Navigate to http://support.apple.com/downloads/.

   This page shows the featured updates Apple has made available for download. If you do not see the update you want, click "Browse by Product," and then either browse for it by product category or enter its name in the Search Downloads field.

   The following screenshots use the Savin Printer Drivers package as an example, but you can choose any update for which your computer is eligible.

3   When you find the update you want to install, click its Download button.

4   Wait for the download to complete. Note that a progress indicator in the Safari Downloads button, near the top right of the window, shows the status of the download.

5   Click the Downloads (down-arrow icon) button near the top right of the window.

6   Click the View (magnifying-glass icon) button next to the update you downloaded.

   Your Downloads folder opens in the Finder, and the disk image containing the update is selected.

Install the Update

1   Open the disk image file.

   The disk image mounts, and you will see the installer package it contains.

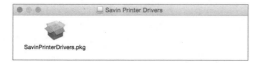

2   Open the installer package.

The installer opens and walks you through the installation process.

3   Continue through the installer prompts, and agree to the license agreement if required.

4   When prompted, authenticate as Local Admin (password: ladminpw, or whatever you chose when you created the account).

Manual software updates usually require administrative privileges to install.

5   After the update installs, click Close or Restart as appropriate.

6   If you did not restart, eject the disk image before proceeding. You can do this by Control-clicking in the background of the image's window and choosing Eject from the shortcut menu or by using the Eject button next to the disk image's name in the Finder sidebar.

Exercise 4.3
Use Automatic Software Update

▶ **Prerequisite**

▶   You must have created the Local Admin account ("Exercise 2.1 Configure a New OS X System for Exercises" on page 60 or "Exercise 2.2 Configure an Existing OS X System for Exercises" on page 63).

In this exercise, you will use the automatic update feature of the Mac App Store to check for, download, and install updates for OS X. You will also see how to view installed software and updates.

Check Your App Store Preferences

1   From the Apple menu, choose System Preferences.

2   Select the App Store pane.

Notice that by default the system will automatically download new updates in the background and then notify you when they are ready.

3   Quit System Preferences.

Update Your Software

1   From the Apple menu, choose App Store.

2   In the App Store toolbar, click Updates.

The App Store checks for new software.

3   If you see a message that says "No Updates Available," your computer is up to date. Skip the rest of this section and proceed to ""Check Installed Updates" on page 124".

4   Click the small triangle next to the Update All button. A pop-up menu appears, with options to install updates later.

5   Click elsewhere to dismiss the pop-up menu.

6   Decide which updates you want to install on your computer.

7   If there is more than one update, you can click More to see a detailed list. Click the Update buttons for the updates you want to install, or click Update All if you want all available updates.

8   If any of the updates are subject to license agreements, you are prompted to agree to them. Read the agreements, and if they are acceptable, click Agree.

9   If you are prompted to restart your computer, click Restart or Download & Restart. Then, log back in to the Local Admin account, and check for more updates by repeating this exercise.

10 If a dialog appears asking if you want to automatically update OS X, click Not Now to keep your current update preference.

11 When all updates have been installed, quit the App Store.

Check Installed Updates

1 Hold down the Option key while you choose System Information from the Apple menu.

System Information opens and displays its report.

2 In the Software section of the sidebar, select Installations.

A list of installed software and updates appears, including the updates you just installed. You can select specific updates from the list to get more information about them.

3 Quit System Information.

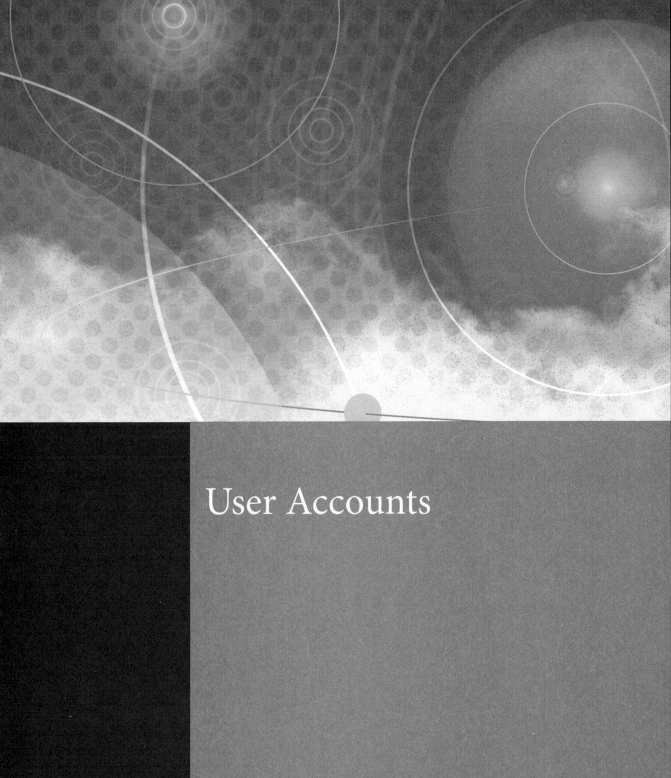

User Accounts

Lesson 5
User Accounts

One of the hallmarks of a modern operating system is support for multiple user accounts. OS X delivers this in spades, with a robust, secure, sophisticated multiuser environment. The UNIX foundation of OS X is the foundation of this environment. UNIX operating systems have a long history of providing such services. And Apple has made many improvements to the UNIX functionality such as advanced user-management features and streamlined administration tools, all with traditional Apple ease of use.

In this lesson, you will explore the technologies that allow individuals to log in and use a Mac. You will also learn how to create and manage multiple user accounts in OS X.

GOALS

▶ Recognize various user account types and user attributes

▶ Create and manage user accounts

▶ Adjust login and fast user switching settings

Reference 5.1
User Account Essentials

With the exception of the rarely used OS X Recovery system or single-user modes, you must log in with a user account to perform any task on a Mac. Even when the computer has just been started up and is showing the login window, and you haven't yet authenticated, the system is still using a handful of system user accounts to maintain background services. Every single file and folder on a Mac computer's hard disk, every item and process, belongs to some type of user account. Consequently, you need a thorough understanding of user accounts to effectively administer and troubleshoot OS X.

> **NOTE** ▶ OS X defaults to requiring a user login even if only a single user account is created for the system. This setting enhances security, and it is necessary if the user is to enable FileVault.

NOTE ▶ This lesson focuses on user accounts that are available only to a single local Mac. Network user accounts, on the other hand, are available to multiple Mac computers and are hosted from shared directory servers. You can find out more about network user accounts in *OS X Server Essentials 10.10: Using and Supporting OS X Server on Yosemite.*

User Account Types

The majority of home Mac users are only aware of, and therefore only use, the account created when their computer was initially set up with Setup Assistant. OS X is engineered to mimic a single-user operating system by default. However, OS X supports multiple simultaneous user accounts. The system also supports several types of user accounts to facilitate different levels of access. Essentially, you choose a specific account type to grant the defined level of access that best meets the user's requirements.

User accounts are categorized into five types: standard accounts, administrative accounts, the guest account, sharing-only accounts, and the root account. Apple has made these different account types available to provide greater flexibility for managing user access. Because each account type is designed to allow different levels of access, you should also be aware of each account type's potential security risk.

Standard Accounts

Standard accounts strike the best balance between usability and security; they are also commonly used when multiple people share a computer. This account type is very secure, assuming an appropriate password is set. Standard accounts have read access to most items, preferences, and applications.

Standard user accounts are allowed to use nearly all the resources and features of the Mac, but they generally can't change anything that might affect other users on the system. The lone exception to this rule is that standard account users can install application and system updates from the Mac App Store. This ability includes applying system updates, which obviously have systemwide effects. If your organization restricts this type of activity for standard account users, then an administrator can disable automatic software updates from App Store preferences in the System Preferences application.

NOTE ▶ Standard accounts can be further restricted using parental controls, including the ability to block access to the Mac App Store. The "managed" account type is a standard account with parental controls enabled, as covered in "Reference 5.3 Parental Controls" on page 138

Even though standard accounts are allowed full access to the Mac App Store, they are not allowed to manually modify the /Applications folder or use other traditional installation methods. This means that standard account users are not allowed to install most software distributed outside the Mac App Store. This may seem unfair for developers that don't distribute via the Mac App Store. However, Apple has instituted tight controls over Mac App Store distribution that provide assurance that the content remains safe for standard account users to install.

Administrative Accounts

Administrative accounts aren't much different from standard accounts, with one important distinction: Administrative accounts are part of the admin group and are allowed full access to almost all applications and preferences, and most system files. By default, administrative account users do not have access to protected system files or other users' items outside of shared items like the Public folders. Despite this, administrative account users can bypass these restrictions both in the graphical environment and using Terminal, if needed. For example, administrative account users are allowed to install and run any software as long as they successfully authenticate when the installer application asks for authorization.

Because an administrative account is the initial account type created when the Mac is configured for the first time using Setup Assistant, many use this as their primary account type. This is advantageous because it lets the user change literally anything on the computer, as is required for system management. The downside is that this user is allowed to make changes or install software that can render the system insecure or unstable.

Additional administrative accounts can be used for daily tasks, but this isn't always the best idea, because, again, all administrative accounts are created equal. In other words, all administrative accounts have the ability to make changes to anything on the system, including deleting or changing the passwords to other administrative user accounts. Administrative users can also change the administrative rights for any other user account, either disabling current administrators or changing standard users into administrators. Further, opening poorly written or intentionally malicious software as an administrative user could seriously harm the system software.

Most significantly, though, any administrative user can enable the root account or change an existing root account password using the Directory Utility application located in the /System/Library/CoreServices/Applications folder. For these reasons, you should seriously consider limiting the number of administrative user accounts on your Mac systems. Additional standard accounts can be created for more secure daily use, but managing OS X requires access to at least one administrative account.

Guest Account

Because enabling the guest account may be considered a security risk, it is disabled by default on OS X. Once enabled, the default guest account is similar to a nonadministrative user, but without a password. Anyone with physical access to the computer can use it to log in.

However, when the guest user logs out, the guest account's home folder is deleted, including any home folder items that would be normally saved, like preference files or web browser history. The next time someone logs in as a guest, a brand-new home folder is created for that user.

Even though the guest home folder is deleted every time a guest logs out, the obvious security risk here is that literally anyone has access equivalent to that of a standard user account, including access to the /Users/Shared folder and users' Public folders. Unlike the guest user's home folder, the contents of these other folders remain after the guest logs out. This means a guest user could execute some potentially nasty applications or fill your disk with unwanted files. Guest users can also restart or shut down your Mac, potentially allowing them to compromise the system during startup.

Fortunately, parental controls enable you to restrict the guest account from running unapproved applications or restarting the Mac. Giving the guest account only limited access, as covered in "Reference 5.3 Parental Controls" on page 138, can provide a safe mechanism for temporary user access. Additionally, you can change the access permissions on shared folders so the guest account is not allowed to copy any items to your disk. Changing file and folder permissions is covered in Lesson 11 "Permissions and Sharing".

> **NOTE ▶** Enabling Find My Mac on a system will also enable the guest account for local login. It's a trap—for the thief! The intent is that a stolen Mac will be locked when found; however, the culprit can choose Guest as a login option upon system startup or wakeup, which allows limited access to the system. Assuming the default settings, the thief would be allowed only to select a Wi-Fi network and use Safari. When the stolen Mac is back online, the owner can use Find My Mac to locate it. You can find out more about this in "Find My Mac" on page 197.

Sharing-Only Accounts

OS X allows special user accounts to be created that have access only to shared files and folders. Sharing-only accounts have no home folder and cannot log in to the Mac computer's user interface or Terminal. Sharing-only user accounts are, by default, allowed file sharing access to users' Public and Drop Box folders, so, like the guest user, these users could potentially fill the disk with unwanted files.

On the other hand, sharing-only user accounts cannot log in to the Mac otherwise, and can be required to use a password, so designating sharing accounts is generally much safer than using the guest account for file sharing. You can further control sharing-only account users' access to your files by adjusting file and folder permissions

Root Account

The root account, also known as the System Administrator, is turned off by default on OS X clients, and for good reason: The root account has unlimited access to everything on the Mac, and a user logged in as root could do anything at all with the system. The root account can read, write, and delete any file; modify any setting; and install any software. Since many system processes run as the root account, it needs to exist on the system; otherwise, OS X wouldn't be able to start up.

The potential for nefarious activity is literally unlimited with root account access. To help prevent abuse of this account, the default OS X configuration does not have a password set for the root account, therefore you cannot log in with the account.

However, as covered previously, any administrative user can choose to enable the root account or change an existing root account password using the Directory Utility application. Again, because it only takes an administrative account to initially access the root account, strictly limiting administrative usage is the key to safeguarding the root account.

> **NOTE ▶** Anyone with access to OS X Recovery can reset the password for any local account, including the root account. If security is a concern in your environment, it's highly recommended that you enable FileVault and/or set a firmware password to restrict OS X Recovery access. Enabling FileVault is covered in Lesson 10 "FileVault". Setting a firmware password is covered in "Reference 7.5 Firmware Password" on page 200.

Local Group Accounts

Essentially, a group account is nothing more than a list of user accounts. Groups are primarily used to allow greater control over file and folder access. OS X uses several dozen built-in groups to facilitate secure system processes and sharing. For instance, all user accounts are members of the staff group; administrative user accounts are also members of the admin group; and the root account has its own group, known as wheel. Using groups to manage sharing is discussed in Lesson 11 "Permissions and Sharing".

NOTE ▶ Standard accounts are always members of the staff group, and administrative accounts are always members of both the staff and admin groups.

Reference 5.2
User Account Management

Once you have a fundamental understanding of OS X user accounts, you're ready to create new users and manage existing users. In this section, you'll examine both simple methods and more complex, yet more flexible, methods for managing local user accounts.

Users & Groups Preferences

In OS X, the Users & Groups preferences window in System Preferences is the primary interface for managing local user accounts, local group accounts, and login settings. From this preference pane, local users can manage basic settings for their own accounts, and any user with administrative privileges can unlock this pane and manage attributes for all local accounts.

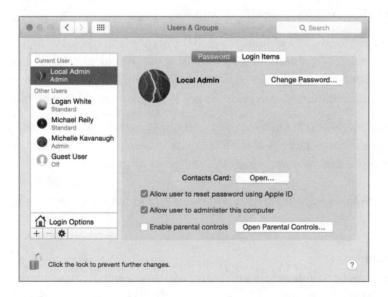

Creating New User Accounts

From Users & Groups preferences, after authenticating as an administrator, you can manage any account by simply selecting it from the list and then modifying items to the right. Start a new account by clicking the small plus button at the bottom of the Users & Groups list. A dialog appears where you can define the basic attributes for the new user account.

A new feature in OS X Yosemite allows local standard and administrator user accounts to use their Apple ID (iCloud) password as their computer login. In this case, when creating a new local user account, an administrator only needs to enter a full name, account name, and the user's Apple ID. The first time the user logs in, he or she enters that same password, and that links the Apple ID with the local account. The iCloud service is then automatically enabled for this user's local account without any additional configuration, which is not the case for normal local user accounts.

When an Apple ID is used for authenticating a local account, password changes are automatically synchronized between the Apple ID and the local computer account. In other words, when users change their Apple ID password, the local computer login password changes as well. However, if users want to separate their Apple ID password from their local computer account, they can do so from either the User & Groups or iCloud preferences. You can find out more about password changes in Lesson 7 "System Security".

> **NOTE** ▶ Internet access is required the first time an Apple ID authenticated user logs in. Internet access is also required to synchronize any Apple ID password changes with the local account.

If you require the traditional local account password, this option is still available by setting a separate password. In this case, the administrator defines the initial password to be used by the user.

When users first log in, they are still prompted to sign in with their Apple ID to enable iCloud services, but the Apple ID password is not linked with their local account password. Users who want to associate their Apple ID with their local computer account can do so from the Users & Groups preference. Again, you can find out more about password changes in Lesson 7 "System Security".

New User Setup Assistant

The first time new users log in to an OS X system, they are presented with a new user Setup Assistant. This is the same process described in Lesson 2 "Setup and Configuration", only in this case it is abbreviated to the point where the user is asked to either enter an Apple ID or verify the currently configured Apple ID. Users can choose not to sign in, but if they do enter their Apple ID information, then the system automatically sets up nearly all OS X features that require an Apple ID. This includes iCloud services and the various Apple stores.

> **NOTE** ▶ If you're entering an Apple ID that belongs to someone under the age of 13 (made possible via Apple ID for Students or iCloud Family Sharing), no iCloud services are enabled by default.

This per-user Apple ID setup will not set up Back to My Mac or Find My Mac services, as allowing other users to change these settings may be considered a security risk. Further, these services can be set up only once for each Mac, as they are systemwide settings.

If two-step verification is enabled for the user's Apple ID, the user will also have to provide a verification code. The user may also be asked to update his or her iCloud documents to the new iCloud Drive service, as detailed in Lesson 18 "Document Management". Finally, the user will be prompted to accept a new Terms and Conditions agreement before the new user Setup Assistant completes.

User Account Attributes

Although the login window lets you log in to the Mac environment, it's the Open Directory system that's responsible for maintaining the account information. Open Directory stores local user account information in a series of XML-encoded text files located in the /var/db/dslocal/nodes/Default/users folder. This folder is readable only by the System Administrator (root) account, but if you were to inspect these files, you would discover they are organized into lists of user attributes and their associated values.

Fortunately, most of these attributes can also be easily accessed from Users & Groups preferences. An administrator can access these normally hidden user account attributes by using a secondary (or Control-) click on a user account to display the Advanced Options dialog.

Each user has a variety of attributes that define the account details. And although you can easily edit these attributes to make a desired change or fix a problem, you can just as easily break the account by entering improper information. For example, you can restore access to a user's home folder by correcting the Home Directory information, or you can accidentally prevent a user from accessing his or her home folder by mistyping this information.

User account attributes include:

▶ User ID—A numeric attribute used to identify the account with file and folder ownership. This number is almost always unique to each account on a single system, though overlaps are possible. User accounts start at 501, whereas most system accounts are below 100. It's important to note that the user ID is only "unique" from those of other users on the local system. Every other Mac system uses similar ID numbers, so between computers, this uniqueness is lost. For example, every first user created on a Mac computer will have the ID number 501. Further, if you delete a user, that user's ID is now up for grabs, and the system will reuse it for a new user.

▶ Group—The user's primary group. As covered previously, the default primary group for all local users is the staff group. This means that when you create a new file, it belongs to your user account and to the staff group.

▶ Account name—Sometimes also referred to as "short name," this is the name used to uniquely identify the account and by default also to name the user's home folder. A user can use either the full name or the account name, interchangeably, to authenticate. However, no other account on the system can have the same account name, and it cannot contain any special characters or spaces. Special characters not allowed include commas, slashes, colons, semicolons, brackets, quotes, and symbols. Allowed characters include dashes, underscores, and periods.

▶ Full name—The full name of the user. It can be quite long and contain nearly any character. However, no other account on the system can have the same full name. You can easily change the full name later, at any point.

▶ Login shell—This file path defines the default command-line shell used in Terminal by the account. Any user who is allowed to use the command line in Terminal has this set to /bin/bash by default. Both administrative and standard users are given this access by default.

▶ Home directory—This file path defines the location of the user's home folder. All users except for sharing users, who do not have home folders, have this set to /Users/ <name>, where <name> is the account name.

▶ Universally Unique ID (UUID)—Sometimes also referred to as Generated UID, or GUID, this alphanumeric attribute is generated by the computer during account creation and is unique across both space and time: Once the attribute is created, no system anywhere will ever create an account with the same UUID. It is used to refer to the user's password and for group membership and file permissions. It's important to note that while UUIDs may be truly unique, one Mac won't be able to identify another's UUIDs. In other words, UUIDs created on one Mac are not known by another. Thus, locally created UUIDs cannot be used between Mac computers for mutual identification.

▶ Alias names—Used to associate the local Mac user account with other service accounts. For example, a user's Apple ID can be associated with a local account. This attribute is optional for OS X, but is required for integration with Apple Internet services like iCloud and its Back to My Mac feature.

NOTE ▶ Local user account passwords are stored as an encrypted attribute to enhance security. Password management is covered in detail in Lesson 7 "System Security".

Reference 5.3
Parental Controls

OS X includes an extensive collection of managed preferences that let you further restrict what users can and cannot do. Apple labels these managed preferences "parental controls," but they are also applicable in business and institutional settings. Because parental controls are designed to further limit standard user accounts, they cannot be applied to an administrative user.

> **MORE INFO** ▶ Parental controls make up a limited subset of a much more extensive profile management system known as Mobile Device Management, or MDM. OS X Server includes an MDM service called Profile Manager. You can find out more about this from *OS X Server Essentials 10.10: Using and Supporting OS X Server on Yosemite.*

> **TIP** ▶ You can use the Action pop-up menu (gear icon) at the bottom of the Parental Controls user list to copy and paste complex settings from one user to another.

Management options available via parental controls include the following:

▶ Use Simple Finder to show only the items most important to your managed user.

▶ Create a list that defines which applications or widgets a user is allowed to open. Users cannot open any application or widget not specified in the list. You can also limit

applications available from the Mac App Store based on the minimum age recommen-
dation.

MORE INFO ► Find out more about restricting access to the Mac App Store in Lesson
17 "Application Installation".

► Enable automatic Safari website content filtering, or manually manage a list of permitted websites or a combination of both automatically and manually permitted websites.

► Limit Game Center, Mail, and Messages to allow exchanges only with approved
addresses.

► Set weekday and weekend time-usage limits.

► Hide profanity in the built-in dictionary.

► Restrict access to the built-in camera, dictation services, printers, password changes,
optical media, and the Dock.

► Maintain Safari, Messages, and application usage logs. The logs show both allowed
and attempted-but-denied access.

NOTE ► The iBooks application also features settings that allow you to restrict access
to the online iBookstore and books with explicit content. However, these settings are
not found in Parental Controls preferences but are instead located in the iBooks application preferences.

NOTE ► Most third-party applications don't honor the parental controls content filters or account limit settings. Examples include the Firefox browser and Outlook
email client. You can, however, easily remedy this by using parental controls to restrict
access to those applications, as described above.

Reference 5.4
Login and Fast User Switching

The login window may look simple, but because it's the front door to your Mac, as an
administrator, you should become familiar with the security options for managing login
behavior. Primarily, these options provide either higher security or greater accessibility.
Additionally, OS X allows multiple users to be logged in at the same time via fast user
switching. However, this feature is not without issues inherent to having multiple users
attempting to access resources simultaneously.

Login Window Options

You can adjust the behavior of the login window from the Users & Groups pane by authenticating as an administrative user and then clicking Login Options at the bottom of the user accounts list.

Login window options include the ability to:

► Enable or disable automatic login as the Mac starts up. This option is off in OS X by default, unless during the OS X Setup Assistant process the user deselected the option to require a password for login. Obviously, you can define only one account for automatic login.

► Choose whether the login window shows a list of available users, the default setting, or blank name and password fields. Choosing to have name and password fields is more secure.

► Select the availability of Restart, Sleep, and Shut Down buttons at the login window. Mac computers in environments that require more stringent security should not have these buttons available at the login window.

► Specify whether users can use the input menu. This allows users easy access to non-Roman characters, like Cyrillic or Kanji, at the login window.

▶ Determine whether the login window will show password hints after three failed password attempts. This may seem like an insecure selection, but remember that password hints are optional for each user account.

▶ Disable the fast user switching menu and adjust the look of the menu item. In other words, the fast user switching menu can appear as the user's full name, account name, or the generic user icon.

▶ Enable users to take advantage of VoiceOver audible assistant technology at the login window.

▶ Configure the Mac to use accounts hosted from a shared network directory. You can find out more about this from *OS X Server Essentials 10.10: Using and Supporting OS X Server on Yosemite.*

TIP ▶ You can configure a short three-line message for the login window from Security & Privacy preferences, as covered in Lesson 7 "System Security". If your organization requires a full login banner, you can configure it via the instructions in Apple Support article HT202277, "How to create a Login window banner in OS X Lion."

Fast User Switching

It's easy to imagine a situation where two users want to use a Mac computer at the same time. Although it's not possible for two users to use the Mac computer's local graphical interface simultaneously, it is possible for multiple users to remain logged into the Mac at the same time.

Fast user switching lets a Mac move between user accounts without users having to log out or quit open applications. This allows a user to keep work open in the background while one or more other users are also logged in to the computer. Returning users can later resume tasks instantly, right where they left off.

NOTE ▶ Fast user switching is not recommended for or compatible with network user accounts.

Fast user switching is enabled by default in OS X, but the fast user switching menu doesn't appear until additional local user accounts are created. This menu item appears on the far right, next to the Spotlight search menu. By default, the fast user switching menu appears as your user account full name. If you don't see this menu item, you can turn it on from the Login options pane of Users & Groups preferences. When another user is logged in, you can initiate the switch to another user by simply selecting that user's name from the fast user switching menu and then entering the appropriate password.

TIP ▶ You can move the fast user switching menu item, or any other menu item on the right side of the menu bar, by dragging the item while holding down the Command key.

Fast User Switching Contention Issues

Apple has endeavored to make fast user switching a reliable feature. Many of the built-in OS X applications are fast user switching savvy. For instance, when you switch between accounts, iTunes automatically mutes or unmutes your music, Messages toggles between available and away chat status, and Mail continues to check for new messages in the background. However, in some circumstances, resource contention may occur when more than one user attempts to access an item.

Examples of fast user switching resource contention include:

▶ Application contention—Some applications are designed such that only one user at a time can use them. If other users attempt to open these applications, they encounter an error dialog, or the application simply doesn't open. Most of the applications that fall into this category are professional applications, which tend to be resource intensive, so it's better to keep only one instance running at a time.

▶ Document contention—Sometimes one user has a document open and remains logged in with fast user switching, often preventing other users from fully accessing the document. As an example, Microsoft Office applications such as Word and Excel allow other users to open a document as read-only, and display an error dialog if the user tries to save changes. Other applications do not allow other users to open the document at all. In the worst-case scenario, an application allows two people to edit the file simultaneously, but will save only changes made by the user who saved last. In this case, the application's developers simply didn't account for the possibility that two users might edit the same document at the same time, so you often won't even see an error message.

▶ Peripheral contention—Many peripherals can be accessed by only one user at a time. This becomes a fast user switching issue if a user leaves an application running that has attached itself to a peripheral. The peripheral will not become available to other applications until the original application is quit. Examples of this include video cameras, scanners, and audio equipment.

Fast User Switching Storage Issues

Fast user switching also has interesting ramifications for nonsystem disks. For example, if one user attaches an external storage device, the disk is available to all other users on the system, even if they weren't logged in when the storage was attached. Mounted disk images are handled a bit more securely. Only the user who mounted the disk image has full read/write access to it. However, other users may still have read access to the mounted disk image.

Shared network volumes remain secure in a fast user switching environment. By default, only the user who originally connected to the share can access it. Even if multiple users attempt to access the same network share, the system automatically generates multiple mounts with different access for each user. The exception to this rule is network home folder shares used by network accounts. While one network user can successfully log in, additional network users from the same server will not be able to access their network home folders. For this reason, fast user switching does not support network accounts.

Resolving Fast User Switching Issues

Unfortunately, because each resource and application can act differently, fast user switching issues are not always consistently reported or readily apparent. OS X doesn't have a "fast user switching is causing a problem" dialog. Still, if you are experiencing access errors for files, applications, or peripherals, your first step should be to check if any other users are still logged in. If so, have them log out and then reattempt access to the previously inaccessible items.

If you cannot log out the other users—perhaps because they are currently unavailable and you don't know their passwords—your options are to force the other users' suspect applications to quit or to force the other users to log out by restarting the Mac. Changing a logged-in user's password isn't an option at this point, because administrators cannot manage user accounts that are currently logged in. These accounts will be dimmed and not available in Users & Groups preferences, as shown by the Michelle account in the following screenshot.

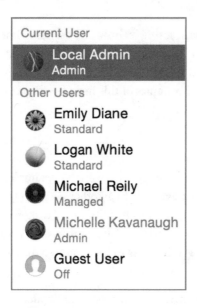

Thus, an administrator will have to either force the other users' applications to quit or restart the Mac to free up any contested items or make any changes to the logged-in users. Neither option is ideal, because forcing an application to quit with open files can result in data loss. If you have no other choice, though, you can force an open application to quit, using techniques covered in Lesson 19 "Application Management and Troubleshooting".

> **TIP** ▸ If you have already set the master password, you can reset a currently logged-in user's password from the login window using the master password. Setting the master password and resetting a user's password is covered in Lesson 7 "System Security".

However, attempting to restart reveals another fast user switching issue: If any other users are still logged in, an administrator will have to force those users' open applications to quit in order to restart. The system makes it easy for an administrator to force these applications to quit via an authenticated restart dialog, but once again, this may cause data loss to any open files.

Exercise 5.1
Manage User Accounts

> **Prerequisites**
>
> ▶ You must have created the Local Admin account ("Exercise 2.1 Configure a New OS X System for Exercises" on page 60 or "Exercise 2.2 Configure an Existing OS X System for Exercises" on page 63).
>
> ▶ This exercise is required for most of the remaining exercises, so do not skip this exercise.

You already created an administrator account during the initial configuration of your computer. You will now create additional accounts to gain a better understanding of the user experience. The next user account will be a standard user. It is a best practice to use a standard user account for your day-to-day use. You should use the Local Admin account only for system administration tasks such as software installation and system configuration, and you can perform most of these tasks while logged in as a standard user, simply by providing the administrator account's name and password.

You will also have the option to link the new account to an iCloud account to allow access to Apple-provided cloud services. This is not required but is recommended and will enable you to do other exercises later in this guide that take advantage of iCloud.

Create a Standard User Account

These steps guide you through account creation:

1   If necessary, log in as Local Admin (password: ladminpw, or whatever you chose when you created the account).

2   Open System Preferences, and click Users & Groups.

3   Unlock the Users & Groups preferences by clicking the Lock button and authenticating as the Local Admin user.

4   Click the New User (+) button beneath the account list, and enter the following information:

New Account: Standard

Full Name: Chris Johnson

Account Name: chris

You now have the option of linking the Chris Johnson account to an Apple ID/iCloud account and using the iCloud account's password to log into the Chris Johnson account.

▶   If you are performing these exercises in a classroom environment, the instructor will provide you with an Apple ID to use. In this case, select "Use iCloud password," and enter the instructor-provided Apple ID.

▶ If you are performing these exercises on your own, have an existing Apple ID that you want to use, and are connected to the Internet, select "Use iCloud password," and enter your Apple ID.

▶ If you are performing these exercises on your own, do not have an existing Apple ID, do not want to use your ID for these exercises, or are not currently connected to the Internet, select "Use separate password," and enter a password for the Chris Johnson account. Be sure to remember the password you have chosen because you will need to reenter it periodically as you use this computer. If you want, you can provide a hint to help you remember the password.

NOTE ▶ If you already have an account named "Chris Johnson" or "chris," you will have to use a different name here and then remember to use your substitute name throughout the rest of the exercises.

5   Click Create User.

6   If a dialog appears with an "Automatic login is turned on. Do you want to turn it off?" prompt, click Turn Off Automatic Login.

7   Verify that Chris's account is selected in the account list.

8   Click the large picture beside Chris Johnson's name in the right pane, select a picture from the pop-up menu that appears, and click Done.

Note that you could configure several other account properties here, including granting Chris admin rights or using parental controls to limit the account.

Log In to the New User Account

You will now log in to Chris's user account to verify that it was created correctly.

1   Choose Log Out Local Admin from the Apple menu.

2   In the dialog asking if you are sure, leave "Reopen windows when logging back in" selected, and click Log Out.

3   At the login screen, select Chris Johnson, and enter the password.

▶   If you chose to use an iCloud password for the account, use the password of the Apple ID/iCloud account you entered earlier; then press Return.

   If you are unable to log in or do not remember the Apple ID password, you may need to log back in as Local Admin and then use https://appleid.apple.com/ to troubleshoot the Apple ID account.

▶   If you chose to use a separate password, enter the password you selected; then press Return.

4 If you chose to use a separate password, a screen will appear giving you another chance to link the account to an Apple ID. If this appears, select "Don't sign in," click Continue, click Skip in the confirmation dialog that appears, and then skip ahead to the section "Adjust Chris Johnson's Preferences" on page 150.

5 If you chose to use an iCloud password, a Welcome screen appears, giving you the option to choose a profile image for your account. Click Continue to skip this step.

6 If you used an iCloud account with two-factor authentication, you will be prompted to verify your identity via one of your devices. Follow the prompts to finish authenticating.

7 If a Terms and Conditions screen appears, read through the terms, and if they are acceptable, click Agree; then click Agree again in the confirmation dialog that appears.

8 If an iCloud Drive screen appears, this is the first time this iCloud account has been used with OS X Yosemite and has documents stored in an older format. See "Reference 18.5 iCloud Drive" on page 546 for more information about iCloud Drive.

▶ If you are performing these exercises in a classroom environment, select "Upgrade to iCloud Drive," click Continue, and then click Continue in the confirmation dialog that appears.

▶ If you are performing these exercises on your own and want to upgrade your iCloud account's document storage to iCloud Drive, select Upgrade to iCloud Drive, click Continue, and then click Continue in the confirmation dialog that appears.

▶ If you are performing these exercises on your own and do not want to upgrade your iCloud account's document storage at this time, select Not Now, click Continue, and then click Don't Upgrade in the confirmation dialog that appears.

Note that you can always upgrade later in iCloud preferences.

Adjust Chris Johnson's Preferences

Just as you did with the Local Admin account, you will adjust Chris Johnson's preferences to allow easy access to system files.

1 In the Finder, choose Finder > Preferences.

2 Select the options to show hard disks and connected servers on the desktop.

3   From the "New Finder windows show" pop-up menu, choose your system disk (typically Macintosh HD).

4   Click the Sidebar button at the top of the Finder Preferences window.

5   Select "chris" in the Favorites section of the sidebar and "Hard disks" in the Devices section. Note that "Hard disks" should be fully enabled (checkmark in the checkbox), not just partially enabled (dash in the checkbox).

6   Close the Finder Preferences window.

7   Navigate to the /Applications folder (choose Go > Applications or press Command-Shift-A).

8   Just as you did in the Local Admin account, drag the TextEdit application into the left side of Chris's Dock.

9   Navigate to /Users/Shared. Since Chris's Finder preferences are set to show the hard disks on the desktop, you can open Macintosh HD from the desktop, then open Users, and then open Shared.

10   Drag the StudentMaterials folder into the right side of Chris's Dock.

11   Open System Preferences, and click the Desktop & Screen Saver icon to open that preference pane.

12   Select a different desktop picture.

13   If you like, adjust the Mouse and Trackpad preferences to your personal taste, just like you did in the Local Admin account.

Examine Chris Johnson's Account

1   In System Preferences, open Users & Groups preferences.

Notice that you have different options than you had when logged in as Local Admin. For instance, you cannot allow yourself to administer the computer or enable parental controls for yourself. You can, however, configure a Contacts card or add login items (which will open every time you log in). Also, you cannot select any account other than your own.

2   In the lower-left corner, click the Lock button, and authenticate as Local Admin (either the full name Local Admin or the account name ladmin). This unlocks Users &

Groups preferences and allows you to make changes to other user and group accounts while remaining logged in as Chris.

3   Control-click Chris's account in the account list, and choose Advanced Options from the shortcut menu.

The Advanced Options dialog appears and displays the hidden attributes of the Chris Johnson account.

Note that your alias list will depend on whether you linked the account to iCloud and exactly how your iCloud account is configured.

4   Click Cancel (or press Command-Period) to dismiss the dialog. It is always a good
    idea to cancel a settings dialog when you have not made changes to it.

5   Leave System Preferences open for the next exercise.

Exercise 5.2
Create a Managed User Account

▶ **Prerequisites**

   ▶ You must have created the Local Admin ("Exercise 2.1 Configure a New OS X
     System for Exercises" on page 60 or "Exercise 2.2 Configure an Existing OS X
     System for Exercises" on page 63) and Chris Johnson ("Exercise 5.1 Manage
     User Accounts" on page 145) accounts.

In this exercise, you will create a managed account with parental controls applied and
observe the resulting restrictions on that account.

Create an Account with Parental Controls

1   If necessary, log in as Chris Johnson, open Users & Groups preferences, and authenti-
    cate as Local Admin (again, remember that you can use the account name ladmin
    instead of the full name Local Admin).

2   Click the New User (+) button beneath the account list, and enter the following infor-
    mation:

    New Account: Managed with Parental Controls

    Full Name: Johnson Junior

    Account Name: junior

    Password: "Use separate password"

    If you are performing this exercise in a class, enter junior in the Password and Verify
    fields. If you are performing this exercise on your own, select a more secure password
    for the Johnson Junior account. Be sure to remember the password you have chosen
    because you will need to reenter it later.

You may provide a password hint if you want.

NOTE ▶ If you already have an account named "Johnson Junior" or "junior," you will have to use a different name here and then remember to use your substitute name throughout the rest of the exercises.

3 Click Create User.

4 Verify that Junior's account is selected in the account list.

Since you created the account as managed, the "Enable parental controls" checkbox is selected.

5 Click Open Parental Controls.

This takes you to Parental Controls, another pane in System Preferences.

6 If the lock icon in the lower left is locked, click it, and enter Local Admin's account name and password.

7 Select the "Use Simple Finder" and "Limit Applications" options.

8 Click the Other Apps disclosure triangle to see what applications are allowed by default.

9 Click the Web tab to configure Junior's web restrictions.

10 Select "Allow access to only these websites," and leave the default site list.

11 Click through the People, Time Limits, and Other tabs of Parental Controls to see what other restrictions are available.

> **TIP** ▶ Your Mac computer's Parental Controls preferences can be managed remotely by another Mac running OS X. To enable this feature in Parental Controls preferences, click the Action pop-up menu (small gear icon) at the bottom of the user list, and choose Allow Remote Setup. From another Mac on the local network, open Parental Controls preferences; any Mac allowing this remote control automatically appears in the user list. You will have to authenticate using an administrator account on the selected Mac to be granted Parental Controls preferences access.

12 Quit System Preferences, and log out of the Chris Johnson account.

Test the Managed User Account

You will now log in to Johnson Junior's user account to see the effects of the parental controls you have configured.

1 At the login screen, select Johnson Junior, enter the password (junior, or whatever you chose), and press Return.

2 If you are prompted to sign in with your Apple ID, select "Don't sign in," click Continue, and then click Skip in the confirmation dialog.

Because you restricted Junior's account to the Simple Finder, the interface looks a bit different than normal.

3 Look at the options available in the Apple, Finder, File, and Help menus. Notice that most of the usual Finder capabilities are missing.

4 In the Dock, click the leftmost of the folder icons (marked with a stylized "A" for Applications).

The Simple Finder application launcher opens and shows icons for the apps Junior is allowed to open.

5   Open Safari. If Safari is not shown on the first screen of apps, click the right arrow to show more apps.

Use the Safari address bar to navigate to www.wikipedia.org.

6   Since Wikipedia is not on the list of allowed sites, an error message appears.

7   Click Add Website, and authenticate as Local Admin.

This action overrides the restriction, and the Wikipedia front page loads.

8   Quit Safari, and log out as Johnson Junior.

Lesson 6

User Home Folders

Aside from the initial account attributes, like the account name and password, every other item the user is likely to create or need is stored in that user's home folder. As mentioned earlier, the default location for a locally stored user home folder is /Users/<name>, where <name> is the user's account name.

Reference 6.1
Home Folder Contents

When a new user account is created, the system generates a home folder that contains several default folders. Users can create additional folders to store their items, but it's best practice for them to keep all personal files in their home folder using the default locations. Most applications suggest an appropriate default folder, while others don't even ask users, and simply use the assigned default folder.

GOALS

▸ Understand user home folder layout and contents

▸ Delete users and archive home folder content

▸ Migrate and restore a user's home folder

All the contents of the default folders inside a user's home folder are viewable only by that user, with the exception of the Public folder. Other users can view the contents of the Public folder, but they cannot add items or make changes, except to put files in the Drop Box folder. Others can add files there, but they cannot see its contents.

It's important to note that, by default, other users are able to view items at the root (or begging) level of any user's home folder. This is necessary in order to allow other users to navigate into the Public folder. However, this also means that if you store any items at the root of your home folder, other users will be able to see those items. Of course, you can change all these defaults by adjusting file and folder access permissions, as outlined in Lesson 11 "Permissions and Sharing".

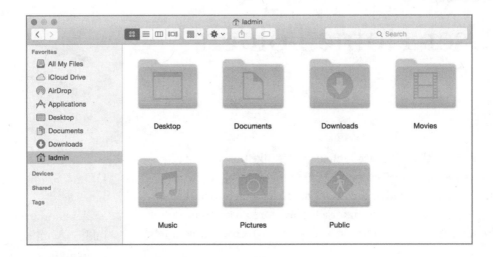

The default items in an OS X user's home folder are:

▶ Desktop—Although many Mac users store files on the desktop, it's not recommended. Along with adding to visual clutter, having an excessive number of items on the desktop may slow system login and Finder actions. More appropriate folders are provided for most user items, as covered here.

▶ Documents—This is the default storage location for any document type that does not have a dedicated folder. For example, Microsoft Office prefers this folder as the default location for all its user documents and Entourage/Outlook profiles. Putting items here is a better alternative than cluttering up the desktop—or at least a good start.

▶ Downloads—Internet applications use this folder as the default location for storing downloaded files. Sequestering all Internet downloads to this folder also makes it easier for virus and malware protection utilities to identify potentially harmful files.

▶ Library—Earlier versions of OS X showed this folder, but since OS X Lion, it has been hidden from the default Finder view. This folder is a collection point for many user resources. This includes, but isn't limited to, user-specific preference files, fonts, contacts, keychains, mailboxes, favorites, screen savers, widgets, and countless other application resources.

> **TIP** ▶ The quickest way to reveal the user's Library folder is to manually go to the folder in the Finder. While holding down the Option key, choose Go > Library to reveal the user's hidden Library folder. You can learn more about hidden items in Lesson 13 "Hidden Items, Shortcuts, and File Archives".

▶ Movies—This is the obvious default location for movie files, and therefore often preferred by applications such as iMovie and iDVD.

▶ Music—This is, naturally, the default location for music files, so it's often preferred by applications such as GarageBand, Logic, and iTunes. It is also the default location for synced iOS application resources and backups, which are managed by iTunes. Further, any movies that are part of an iTunes library end up in this folder, as opposed to the default Movies folder.

▶ Pictures—The default location for picture files, which is often preferred by applications such as iPhoto and Aperture.

▶ Public—The default location for users to share files with other users. Everyone who has access to the Mac, either directly or via remote access, can view the contents of this folder. This folder contains a Drop Box folder where others can place files that only the owner of the home folder can see.

Optional items commonly found in a Mac user's home folder are:

▶ Applications—This optional folder must be created manually, but the system recognizes it as a special folder. As the name implies, this is the preferred location for users to install their own applications.

▶ Sites—This legacy folder might appear for home folders that have been upgraded or migrated from earlier versions of OS X. It was the default location for personal websites when Web Sharing was enabled. As of Mountain Lion, OS X no longer supports enabling Web Sharing via Sharing preferences; however, other local users can still view the contents of this folder.

MORE INFO ▶ To find out more about alternatives to Web Sharing, see Apple Support article HT5230, "OS X Mountain Lion: Options for web sharing."

Reference 6.2
Deleting User Accounts

Deleting a user account in OS X is even easier than creating one. To delete a user account, simply select it from the list of users in the Users & Groups preferences, and then click the Delete (–) button at the bottom of the list. An administrator needs to make only one choice when deleting a user account: what to do with the user's home folder contents.

NOTE ▶ If a user has a particularly large home folder, the "delete user account" dialog may take several minutes to appear.

The administrator deleting the user account can choose one of three options:

▶   Save the home folder in a disk image—This option creates an archive of the user's home folder as a disk image file. The disk image file is saved in the /Users/Deleted Users folder, with the account name as the name of the disk image file. Retaining the home folder as a disk image makes it easy to transport it to other systems or to import archived items to another user's home folder.

Keep in mind you must have sufficient free disk space available on the local system disk—essentially enough to duplicate the original home folder—to create the archive disk image. This process can take quite a bit of time, depending on the size of the folder.

▶   Don't change the home folder—This option leaves the user's folder unchanged, save for its name. It simply appends "(Deleted)" to the home folder's name, letting you know that the user account no longer exists. The deleted user's home folder maintains the same access restrictions as a normal user home folder. Subsequently, however, even though this is a much quicker and more space-efficient method compared to the archival option, you have to manually adjust file ownership and permissions to access the items, as covered in Lesson 11 "Permissions and Sharing".

▶ Delete the home folder—This option deletes the home folder contents immediately. The items are not stored in a Trash folder before they are deleted, so they cannot easily be recovered if you use this method.

MORE INFO ▶ The default method used to delete a user's home folder is equivalent to a quick erase. Thus, the contents are potentially recoverable using third-party data recovery tools if you don't have FileVault enabled. If your system is not using FileVault, then you can use the "Erase home folder securely" option to make the system perform a secure erase of the user's home folder items. You can learn more about securely erasing items in Lesson 9 "File Systems and Storage".

Reference 6.3
Migrating and Restoring Home Folders

Usually, the best way to move or restore a user's account and home folder is with Apple Migration Assistant. But it's not *always* the best solution, and you may have to manually restore a user's account. In this section, you'll explore both Migration Assistant and the manual steps for restoring a home folder.

Migration Assistant

This handy application is a huge time-saver that enables you to easily transfer all the settings, user accounts, and data from another OS X or Windows system to your Mac system.

With Migration Assistant, you can migrate:

▶ From another Mac computer, Time Machine backup, or startup disk—This option scans the local network looking for other Mac computers running Migration Assistant and ready to transfer their information. If you don't have a local network, you can directly connect two running Mac computers via Ethernet, FireWire, or Thunderbolt, and the two of them will create a local network. Alternatively, this option will also scan all locally mounted disks and the local network looking for Time Machine backups. Finally, it will also scan all locally mounted disks for a previous system. This includes any external disks or other Mac computers in target disk mode connected via Fire-Wire or Thunderbolt. Using target disk mode is further detailed in Lesson 12 "File System Troubleshooting".

MORE INFO ▶ See Apple Support article HT5872, "Move your data to a new Mac."

▶ From a Windows PC—This option will scan the local network looking for Windows PCs running Migration Assistant and ready to transfer their information. OS X can migrate from Windows XP SP3 or later, assuming those systems have Windows Migration Assistant installed; it can be downloaded from the Apple Support website.

MORE INFO ▶ See Apple Support article HT4796, "About Windows Migration Assistant."

As covered in Lesson 2 "Setup and Configuration", Migration Assistant runs as part of OS X Setup Assistant on new or newly installed Mac systems. However, you can also run this application at any point by opening /Applications/Utilities/Migration Assistant.

NOTE ▶ Before using Migration Assistant, always check for Apple software updates on both the source and destination computers. This process ensures that you are using the latest copy of Migration Assistant on all computers.

NOTE ▶ Migration Assistant can only migrate a Legacy FileVault–protected user account to a Mac during the initial Setup Assistant process.

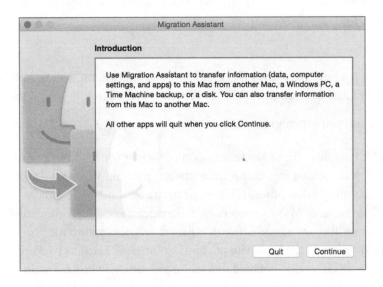

Clicking the Continue button will start the Migration Assistant process; however, you will have to first authenticate a user with administrative rights to start the process. Further, starting the Migration Assistant process will quit all running applications and log out all user accounts.

The Migration Assistant process has three modes: transfer from another Mac source, transfer from a Windows PC source, or transfer to another destination Mac. The first two options assume that you are transferring from another computer source to this Mac as the destination, while the last option assumes you are transferring from this Mac as the source to another destination Mac via network. In this case you will need to open Migration Assistant on the destination Mac as well.

How do you want to transfer your information?

◉ From a Mac, Time Machine backup, or startup disk
○ From a Windows PC
○ To another Mac

If you choose to transfer from another computer source, Migration Assistant scans all attached disks and the local network for any possible migration sources. Alternatively, you can enter a specific Time Machine server as the source by clicking the Other Server button at the bottom of the Migration Assistant screen.

Once a source is selected, Migration Assistant scans the contents and presents you with a list of items you can migrate. If multiple disks are available on a system, you can choose to migrate that data as well. However, the migration process does not create new partitions on the new system; instead, it creates folders on the new system with the contents of the migrated disks.

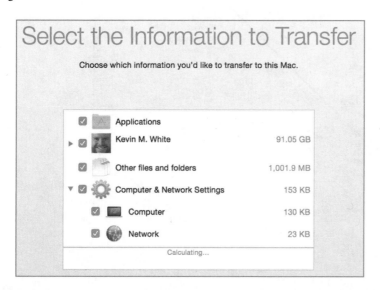

Once you make your selections, you can begin the transfer process. The more data you have selected to transfer, the longer the process will take. Mature systems with lots of data can take several hours to migrate.

Manually Restore a User's Home Folder

In certain situations, you may need to erase and install a new system to repair or update a Mac. Unfortunately, you can't always count on the user having a recent Time Machine backup of the system. Thus, erasing the system disk would also destroy any user accounts on the Mac. In this case, because you're working only with a single Mac, as opposed to moving from one Mac to another, and you don't have a Time Machine backup, Migration Assistant isn't going to work for you.

If you find yourself in a situation like this, where Migration Assistant won't fit your needs, you can manually move the user's home folder data. Although this doesn't require another Mac, it does require that you temporarily copy the user's home folder to another "backup" storage disk. Once you have additional backup storage available, log in to the user's account and, in the Finder, simply drag the home folder to the backup disk. As long as you copy the root of the user's home—the folder with the user's account name—then the Finder copies the entirety of the home folder in one move.

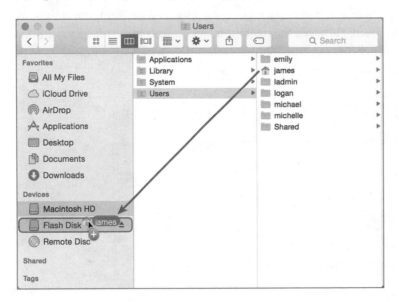

NOTE ▶ If you are creating a copy of another user's home folder contents, you are prompted to authenticate as an administrative user to continue. This is because the default file system permissions often prevent one user from accessing another user's content. Administrative users are allowed to temporarily override permissions in the Finder if they authenticate.

Once you are sure you have a complete copy of the user's home folder on the backup storage, you can erase the system disk and repair it. With the new system in place and working, first start by creating an administrator account with a different name from the user account to be restored. You must set up this other administrator account because the proper method for manually restoring a user's home folder requires that the user account not yet exist on the system.

To complete the home folder restore, in the Finder, simply copy the backup of the user's home folder into the /Users folder, making sure the home folder's name is titled appropriately.

Finally, in Users & Groups preferences, create the user's account, making sure to use the same account name. Upon creation of the new user account, if the names match, the system will automatically associate the manually restored home folder in the /Users folder with the newly created user account. This includes setting the proper home folder permissions so that the new user has access to the restored home folder content.

Exercise 6.1
Restore a Deleted User Account

In this exercise, you will create a user account and populate the home folder for the user.
Then, you will delete the account, preserving the contents of the home folder. Finally, you
will create a new account, ensuring that the new user gets the old user's home folder contents. Besides illustrating how to restore a deleted user account, this technique can be used
for changing a user's short name. It also provides an alternative to the Migration Assistant
method for moving user accounts between computers.

The scenario is that HR asked you to create an account for Marta Mishtuk. Her real name
is Mayta Mishtuk, so you'll need to fix the error.

Create Marta Mishtuk's Home Folder

1   If necessary, log in as Local Admin (password: ladminpw, or whatever you chose when
    you created the account).

2   Open System Preferences, and select the Users & Groups pane.

3   Click the Lock icon, and authenticate as Local Admin.

4   Click the Add (+) button under the user list.

5   Enter the account information for Marta Mishtuk:

    New Account: Standard

    Full Name: Marta Mishtuk

    Account Name: marta

    Password: "Use separate password"

    Password: marta

    Verify: marta

Do not provide a password hint.

6   Click Create User.

7   Control-click Marta's account, and choose Advanced Options from the shortcut menu.

Now you will take a screenshot of the System Preferences window to record Marta's account attributes for later reference.

8   Press Command-Shift-4, followed by the Space bar.

Your mouse cursor changes into a camera icon, and the region of the screen it is over is highlighted in blue. If you see a crosshair cursor instead, press the Space bar again.

9   Move the camera pointer over the System Preferences window, and then click to record its contents.

This is one of several ways of taking screenshots in OS X. Command-Shift-3 records the entire screen, Command-Shift-4 (without the Space bar) lets you select a rectangular region to record, and Command-Shift-4 with the Space bar lets you select a single window.

The image is saved to your desktop, named "Screen Shot" followed by the date and time it was taken.

10   In the Advanced Options dialog, click Cancel, or use Command-Period, which is a way to select Cancel in most OS X dialogs.

11   Log out as Local Admin.

12   Log in as Marta Mishtuk (password: marta).

13   If you are prompted to sign in with your Apple ID, select "Don't sign in," click Continue, and then click Skip in the confirmation dialog.

14 In the Dock, click the Launchpad icon.

Launchpad gives users an easy way to open applications that aren't in their Dock, without having to navigate to the Applications folder in the Finder.

15 Click the Other application group in Launchpad.

16 In the Other group, click the TextEdit icon to open TextEdit.

17 In the Untitled document, enter the text This is Mayta's project document. ("Mayta" is not a typo.)

18 From the menu bar, choose File > Save (or press Command-S) to save the file.

19 Name the file Project, and save it to Marta's desktop. You can use the shortcut Command-Shift-D to select the desktop.

20 Quit TextEdit, and log out of the Marta Mishtuk account.

Delete Marta's Account

You will delete Marta's account, preserving her home folder in a disk image file. A disk image is a file that contains a file system.

1 Log in as Local Admin.

2 Open Users & Groups preferences in System Preferences, if necessary. Unlock the preferences pane.

3 Delete Marta's account by selecting her name and then clicking the Delete (–) button.

4 In the dialog that appears, make sure "Save the home folder in a disk image" is selected.

5 Click Delete User.

While Marta's account is being archived, it is listed in the Users & Groups list as "Deleting Account."

6   Wait for the archive to complete and Marta's account to vanish from the list, and then quit System Preferences.

Restore Marta's Account for Mayta

Marta's files (actually Mayta's) have been preserved in a disk image. Now you need to copy them to Mayta's new home folder so that when the new account is created, she gets her old (the Marta account's) files.

Note that since disk images are portable and easy to store, you could use this technique to re-create the account on another computer, even long after it has been deleted.

1   Navigate to the folder /Users/Deleted Users.

You can reach this folder by opening Macintosh HD from your desktop, opening the Users folder inside of that, and then opening Deleted Users inside of that.

If you don't have permissions to open the Deleted Users folder, you may be logged in as a standard user. Log out, and log back in as Local Admin.

2   Open marta.dmg.

The disk image opens and displays the contents of the marta account's home folder. However, as "Reference 13.1 Hidden Items" on page 377 discusses, an invisible sub-folder named Library contains account settings and preferences for the marta account; to fully restore this account, you need to restore the entire home folder, not just its visible contents.

3   Close the "marta" window (but do not eject the disk image). The disk's icon is still visible on your desktop.

4   Select (single-click) the "marta" icon on your desktop.

5   From the Finder's File menu, choose Duplicate (or use the shortcut Command-D).

The Finder copies the contents of the image (including the hidden Library folder) to a folder named "marta" on your desktop.

6   Once the copy finishes, unmount the "marta" volume by clicking the Eject button next
    to its entry in the Finder sidebar. Note that you may need to scroll to view more of the
    sidebar to see the icon.

7   Select the new "marta" folder on your desktop, and press Return.

    This allows you to edit the folder's name.

8   Change the folder's name to mayta, and press Return.

9   In the remaining Finder window, navigate back to the /Users folder. You can do this by
    clicking the left arrow in the window's toolbar, by pressing Command-[(left bracket),
    or by Control-clicking the folder name in the window's title bar and choosing Users
    from the shortcut menu.

10 Drag the "mayta" folder from your desktop to the /Users folder.

The file permissions on the /Users folder do not allow you to add items to it. The Finder asks you to authenticate as an administrator in order to override this.

11 Click Authenticate; then enter Local Admin's password, and click OK.

12 Open the "mayta" folder and then the Desktop folder inside of that.

You see Mayta's Project document (Project.rtf if filename extensions are visible). Since you (Local Admin) created this copy of Mayta's home folder, you own it and have full permission to access it.

Create and Verify Mayta Mishtuk's Account

You will now create the Mayta Mishtuk user account using the restored home folder as the new account's home folder.

1 If necessary, open System Preferences, and select Users & Groups.

2 Click the Lock button, and authenticate as Local Admin.

3 Click the Add (+) button to create another account:

New Account: Standard

Full Name: **Mayta Mishtuk**

Account Name: **mayta**

Password: Use separate password

If you are performing this exercise in a class, enter **mayta** in the Password and Verify fields. If you are performing this exercise on your own, select a more secure password for the Mayta Mishtuk account. Be sure to remember the password you have chosen because you need to reenter it periodically while you use this computer.

You may provide a password hint if you want.

4   Click Create User.

5   Control-click Mayta's account, and choose Advanced Options from the shortcut menu.

6   Open the Screen Shot file on your desktop, and compare the account attributes of Mayta's new account with her original account. The User ID of the old account may have been reused for the new account, but the UUID will be different. Each account is assigned a completely new UUID when it is created.

7   Quit Preview.

8   In the Advanced Options dialog, click Cancel, and then quit System Preferences.

9   Try to reopen the Desktop folder in Mayta's home folder now. If your Finder window is still displaying the Desktop folder, click the back button, and then double-click the Desktop folder. You no longer have permission because the files are now owned by Mayta's new account.

10 Close the Finder window.

Verify Mayta Mishtuk's Home Folder

To make sure Mayta's files are all here, you will explore her restored home folder.

1   Log out as Local Admin, and log in as Mayta.

2   If you are alerted that the system could not unlock Mayta's keychain, click Update Keychain Password, and enter marta (the original password for the Marta Mishtuk account).

For more information about keychains, see Lesson 8 "Keychain Management".

3   Verify that the Project file is on the desktop.

4   In the Finder, open Mayta's home folder by choosing Go > Home (or by pressing Command-Shift-H).

5   Make sure all the usual subfolders are there: Desktop, Documents, Downloads, Movies, Music, Pictures, and Public.

6   Open the Desktop folder, and verify that you see the Project document.

7   Navigate back to the home folder, and then open the Public folder, where you see a Drop Box folder. For more information about these folders, see Lesson 11 "Permissions and Sharing".

In addition to the visible folders inside Mayta's home folder, it should contain an invisible Library folder.

8   Hold down the Option key, and choose Go > Library. Note that the Library choice is hidden except when you are holding the Option key.

Mayta's Library folder contains a large number of subfolders. For more information about this folder and its contents, see "Reference 13.1 Hidden Items" on page 377 and Lesson 14 "System Resources".

9   Close the Library folder, and log out as Mayta Mishtuk.

Lesson 7

System Security

The primary purpose of a multiple-user operating system is to provide all users with a secure work environment. OS X provides a relatively secure out-of-the-box experience for most situations. Yet some situations call for greater security than the defaults afford. This lesson focuses on the built-in advanced security features of OS X and how best to manage and troubleshoot these features.

GOALS

▶ Understand password types and their usage

▶ Use a variety of methods to reset lost user passwords

▶ Manage user and system security settings

Reference 7.1
Account Passwords

OS X relies on passwords as its primary method for verifying a user's authenticity. There are other, more elaborate systems for proving a user's identity, such as biometric sensors and two-factor random key authentication, but these require special hardware. It's a pretty safe bet that every Mac is attached to an alphanumeric input device such as a keyboard, so passwords are still the most relevant security authentication method.

Understanding Password Types

If you look closer at the security systems used by OS X, you discover that it uses a variety of passwords at different levels to secure the computer. Most users are familiar only with their account password, but the Mac can also have a firmware password, a master password, many resource passwords, and several keychain passwords.

Individual users may use several types of passwords, each with a specific purpose:

▶ Local account password—Each local user account has a variety of attributes that define the account. The local account password is the attribute used to authenticate users so they can log in to OS X. For security reasons, a user's local account password is stored as encrypted data in the account record.

▶ Apple ID and password—This is a user name and password combination that can be used to authorize many Apple and OS X services. The creation and use of an Apple ID requires an Internet connection, as Apple uses your Apple ID to keep record of a multitude of services. An Apple ID provides access to all the Apple online services, including iCloud and various stores. In the context of user security, OS X Yosemite features the ability for a user's Apple ID password to also be used as the local account password. Alternatively, even if the user's local account password is not tied to the Apple ID password, the latter can be still be used to reset a lost local account password, as covered in "Password Reset Methods" on page 182.

▶ Legacy FileVault password—Versions of OS X prior to OS X Lion supported home folder–based encryption. If an earlier system is upgraded or migrated with Legacy FileVault user accounts, the home folders remain encrypted. The password for a Legacy FileVault user account can only be reset using a known master password. Resetting and disabling Legacy FileVault user accounts is covered in the "Reset Legacy FileVault Passwords" on page 185.

▶ Keychain password—OS X protects the user's important authentication assets, other than the account password, in encrypted keychain files. Each keychain file is encrypted with a keychain password. The system attempts to keep keychain passwords synchronized with the user's local account password. However, you can maintain unique keychain passwords separate from an account password as well. Maintaining synchronization between a user's keychain password and account password is covered in "User Keychains After Reset" on page 185.

▶ Resource password—This is a generic term that describes a password used by nearly any service that requires you to authenticate. Resource passwords include email, website, file server, application, and encrypted disk image passwords. Many resource passwords are automatically saved for the user by the keychain system. Details on keychain features are covered in Lesson 8 "Keychain Management".

There are also system passwords, which are not associated with an individual user. Again, each has a specific purpose:

▶ Master password—The master password is used to reset standard, administrative, and Legacy FileVault user accounts when users forget their account password. Use of the master password is covered in "Master Password" on page 181.

▶ Firmware password—The firmware password protects the Mac during startup. By default, anyone can subvert system security settings simply by using one of the commonly known startup-interrupt keyboard shortcuts. For example, anyone can hold down the Option key during startup to select an alternate operating system, thus bypassing your secure system. Setting the firmware password prevents unauthorized users from using any startup-interrupt keyboard shortcuts. Setting a firmware password is covered in "Reference 7.5 Firmware Password" on page 200.

Password Changes

Users who already know their account password but want to change it can do so at any time from the Security & Privacy or Users & Groups preferences. In the General pane of Security & Privacy preferences, you simply click the Change Password button.

Alternatively, in Users & Groups preferences, the user first selects his or her account and then clicks Change Password. Either method reveals the same series of dialogs that allow a password change. The dialogs will vary depending on whether the user's local account is using an Apple ID password or a separate local account password.

> **NOTE ▶** It's important to recognize that a password *change* is distinctly different from a password *reset*. A known password can be "changed," but an unknown password needs to be "reset" by some other authorization mechanism. "Reference 7.2 Resetting Passwords" on page 182 discusses various tools and methods for resetting lost passwords.

Password Change: Local Account Using an Apple ID Password

When users attempt to change the password for a local account that is using an Apple ID (or iCloud) password, they are first prompted with options to switch to using separate passwords or to change their Apple ID password.

NOTE ▶ The OS X interface sometimes uses "iCloud password" instead of "Apple ID password." However, because all Apple services, including iCloud, are accessed via Apple ID authentication, this guide uses the term "Apple ID" when discussing Apple service authentication.

NOTE ▶ Changes to Apple ID passwords can only be made if the computer has Internet access. Specifically, the system must be able to communicate with Apple's authentication services.

Users who choose to change their Apple ID password here will then have to enter their Apple ID password, as well as a temporary verification code if two-step verification is enabled. After the account is verified, users will be able to change their Apple ID password. Whenever you change a password, OS X presents a dialog requiring that you enter your new password twice to avoid typos in the new password. Also, because this is an Apple ID password, there are specific password complexity requirements to ensure a strong password.

Change Password

Your password must be at least eight characters and include a number, an uppercase letter, and a lowercase letter.

Old Password: ●●●●●●●●●●●●

New Password: ●●●●●●●●●●●●

Verify: ●●●●●●●●●●●●

Cancel   Change

TIP ▶ Changes to Apple ID passwords can also be made from another Apple device that is signed into the Apple ID or via any web browser from the Apple ID website: https://appleid.apple.com. If a user changes an Apple ID password using another device or web browser, the local user account on the Mac will not take the new password until the user logs out and then back in using the new Apple ID password.

Alternatively, users who choose to switch to using a separate local password will be presented with a different dialog. In this case they must enter their Apple ID password along with a new local account password. Once they complete this dialog, their local account password will be no longer be tied to their Apple ID password. Note that because the new password is no longer tied to the user's Apple ID it doesn't have to conform to any password complexity requirements.

Password Change: Local Account *Not* Using an Apple ID Password

Users who have a separate local account password but are also signed into the iCloud service via the iCloud or Internet Accounts preferences have the option to change their local account password to their Apple ID password. Again, if the user is also signed into the iCloud service, during a local password change, the system will give the user the choice to switch to using his or her Apple ID password for the local account.

Users who choose to use their Apple ID password here will then be presented with a dialog where they enter their old local account password and then their Apple ID password. Again, the system already knows their Apple ID name because they have previously signed into the iCloud service. Assuming the correct passwords are entered, after the user completes this dialog the local user account password will be tied to the user's Apple ID password.

Alternatively, users who choose to keep a separate local password or have not signed into the iCloud service will be presented with the local account password change dialog. In this case, users must enter their old password once, followed by their new password twice, to avoid typos. Again, notice that because the user is continuing to use a local account password that is not tied to the user's Apple ID, the new password doesn't have to conform to any password complexity requirements.

Password Assistant

Regardless of how sophisticated a security system is, the protection it affords is only as strong as the password you choose. For this reason, new Apple ID passwords must meet minimum password complexity requirements. However, as you've seen in this lesson, local account passwords do not have to meet any password complexity requirements by default.

TIP ▶ Administrators can enforce local password complexity rules via a configuration profile. You can find out more about configuration profiles in "Reference 2.3 Profiles" on page 55.

To help users pick a stronger password, OS X includes a handy utility called Password Assistant that gauges the strength of your passwords or automatically creates strong passwords for you. Anytime you are creating or modifying a local password that grants access to a substantial resource, like an account or keychain password, you can use Password Assistant. It is available anytime you see the small key icon next to a password field, as you can see in the previous screenshot of the local account password change dialog.

Master Password

As mentioned previously, the master password can be used to reset regular account passwords and is required to reset Legacy FileVault user account passwords. The master password isn't tied to any local user account, so it's an effective way to provide a password reset mechanism that does not require the creation of an additional administrator account. If you are maintaining a large deployment of Mac computers that are using local accounts, setting a uniform master password is an easy method for ensuring you always have a back door in without having your own local administrator account.

New installations of OS X do not normally have the master password set. However, there are two cases in which the master password may already be set on an OS X system. The first is if you have upgraded a Mac from a previous version of OS X where the master password was set. The second is if you used Migration Assistant to transfer a Legacy FileVault user account to the OS X system, in which case the master password is transferred as well.

If you think you know the current master password, or you would like to set a new master password, you can do so in Users & Groups preferences. Once you have opened Users & Groups preferences and authenticated as an administrator, click the Action pop-up menu (the small gear icon) at the bottom of the users list. A menu with Set Master Password or Change Master Password options then appears. As you'd expect, changing the master password requires that you know the current master password.

TIP ▶ If you are logged in to a Legacy FileVault account, you can also change the master password from the Legacy FileVault pane of Security & Privacy preferences.

Reference 7.2
Resetting Passwords

Users mistyping or forgetting their password is the primary cause of most login and access issues on any platform. The second most common issue, specific to OS X, is when a user's login keychain password becomes out of sync with that user's account password. Fortunately, with a few rare exceptions, OS X provides ways to easily resolve these types of password issues.

Password Reset Methods

OS X offers several methods for resetting a local user account password:

▶ Administrator account in Users & Groups—If you have access to an administrator account on the system, you can easily reset other user account passwords from Users & Groups preferences. Simply authenticate as an administrator, select another user account, and click Reset Password. If the selected user account is configured for Legacy FileVault, you must enter the master password to reset the account password. However, in all other cases, by virtue of previously authenticating as an administrator, you can enter a new password for the user. If the selected user account is using an Apple ID password, during the reset you can change it to a separate local account password.

▶ Apple ID website—If the user account is tied to an Apple ID password, the user can try to reset the Apple ID password via any web browser from the Apple ID website: https://appleid.apple.com. If the Apple ID has two-step verification enabled, the user will need to enter the recovery key. Alternatively, for Apple IDs without this feature enabled, the user will need to successfully answer the recovery questions and respond to an email sent to the Apple ID. If the user is unable to reset the Apple ID password online, you can still reset the local user account password using the previous method as an administrator or using the Reset Password application as covered in "OS X Recovery Password Reset" on page 187.

▶ Master password at login—When the master password is set, users who enter an incorrect password three times at the login window are prompted to reset their account password. Authenticating with the current master password allows you to enter a new password for a local user account. Note that this method does not work for local user accounts with Apple ID passwords. On the other hand, this is the only method for resetting a Legacy FileVault user account at login. If you don't know the master password, it won't help you now, but eventually you can reset the master password, as covered in "Reset the Master Password" on page 186.

▶   Apple ID at login—Two conditions must be met for users to be able to reset their local account password at login using an Apple ID. First, they must not be using Legacy FileVault (most users won't be). Second, the user account must have previously signed into the iCloud service but still be using a separate local account password. As you can see in the previous screenshot, after three failed attempts at login, local users can enter their Apple ID to reset the password for a local user account. Details on setting up the iCloud service are covered in Lesson 2 "Setup and Configuration".

NOTE ▶ User accounts on Mac systems protected by FileVault 2 cannot have their local passwords reset using the Master Password or an Apple ID.

▶   FileVault 2 Recovery Key at Startup—On a Mac with FileVault 2 enabled, users who enter an incorrect password three times at startup are prompted to reset the password using a Recovery Key. "Reference 10.3 FileVault Recovery" on page 293 covers this topic in greater detail.

▶   Reset Password in OS X Recovery—Anyone with access to OS X Recovery can use the Reset Password application to reset any local account password, including the root account password, without any other authorization. While this last-resort option is useful, it's also a significant security risk, as, by default, it requires no knowledge of any other passwords. Enabling FileVault 2 or a firmware password can mitigate this risk by requiring authentication to access the system disk from OS X Recovery. Use of the Reset Password application is covered in "OS X Recovery Password Reset" on page 187, and managing firmware passwords is covered in "Reference 7.5 Firmware Password" on page 200.

User Keychains After Reset

OS X user accounts are given local encrypted keychains accessed by a password that is normally synchronized with their account password. Resetting (as opposed to changing) an account password with any of the methods just discussed does not also reset any of the user's keychain passwords. However, by default in OS X, the next time the user logs in he or she is prompted to fix the login keychain password. Lesson 8 "Keychain Management" covers this topic in greater detail.

Reset Legacy FileVault Passwords

Legacy FileVault user accounts are unique because the user's home folder is saved inside an encrypted disk image protected by that user's account password. Consequently, it is extremely important for an administrator to be able to reset a Legacy FileVault user's account password so that the user can access home folder files again.

A normal administrative user account is not enough to reset a lost Legacy FileVault user's password. After all, Legacy FileVault wouldn't be very secure if just any old administrative user could come along and break in. Therefore, if a Legacy FileVault user has forgotten the account password, the master password is required to reset the account.

As covered previously, if you know the master password, OS X provides two methods for easily resetting Legacy FileVault user passwords. The first method allows you to reset a Legacy FileVault user at the login window, and the second method involves resetting a Legacy FileVault account password in Users & Groups preferences.

If the master password as well as the user's Legacy FileVault password is lost, you are completely out of luck. You must have at least one of these two passwords to recover a Legacy FileVault user account. Otherwise, you are never, ever going to be able to recover the user's data. Not even Apple can help you. Apple designed Legacy FileVault to be as secure as possible, and thus created only one way to reset a Legacy FileVault user account: the master password. For this reason alone, you should abandon using Legacy FileVault user accounts in favor of FileVault 2 full system volume encryption.

> **MORE INFO** ▸ Turning off Legacy FileVault encryption is covered in "Security & Privacy: Legacy FileVault Settings" on page 190 . OS X full disk encryption technology is covered in Lesson 10 "FileVault".

Reset the Master Password

If Legacy FileVault user accounts are still active, it's vital that the master password be properly configured and known by an administrator. If the master password is lost, an administrative user should reset it immediately just to be able to reset normal user passwords. Resetting the master password involves simply deleting the /Library/Keychains/FileVault-Master.cer and /Library/Keychains/FilevaultMaster.keychain files.

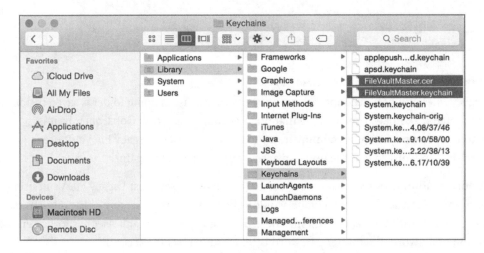

Once these files are deleted, an administrative user can return to Users & Groups preferences and set a new master password using the techniques covered previously in this lesson. However, just because you can set a new master password for your Mac doesn't mean you can recover a Legacy FileVault user account that was created with the old master password. Only the master password created when the Legacy FileVault user account was enabled can unlock an inaccessible account.

Even if a new master password is set it cannot reset existing Legacy FileVault user account passwords. This is because OS X does not support reencrypting Legacy FileVault user accounts, which is a necessary step for lost master password resets. Thus, if you lost the master password used to create a Legacy FileVault user account, there is no recovery method if users also lose their password. This is yet another reason to abandon the use of Legacy FileVault user accounts in favor of FileVault 2 full system volume encryption.

OS X Recovery Password Reset

Many Mac computers intended for personal use have only the single primary administrator user account that was created when the Mac was initially configured with Setup Assistant. Even if more than one person uses this Mac, quite often its owner is not very concerned about security. Thankfully, OS X now defaults to requiring the user to enter a password at login.

However, if the computer was upgraded to OS X, it's very common for the primary user account to automatically log in during startup and for a master password not to be set. Often this results in Mac owners forgetting their primary administrator account password and not having any way to reset it because they never enabled the master password or created another administrator account. Fortunately, Apple has prepared for these occasions by including the Reset Password application in OS X Recovery.

> **NOTE ▶** If the system disk is protected with FileVault 2 full disk encryption, you must first unlock the system disk via Disk Utility. However, if there is only one account on the Mac and its password is lost, odds are you won't know the FileVault 2 password either. In this case, the Reset Password application can't help you. Thus, your best bet to regain access to a FileVault 2 system is to use a recovery key, as outlined in "Reference 10.3 FileVault Recovery" on page 293.

The Reset Password application is available only from an OS X Recovery system, as covered in Lesson 3 "OS X Recovery". Once the Mac is running from OS X Recovery, open the Terminal application (via the Utilities menu), type resetpassword, and then press Return. Once Reset Password opens, simply select the system volume and the account you want to reset. You do not have to enter anything but the new password for the selected account.

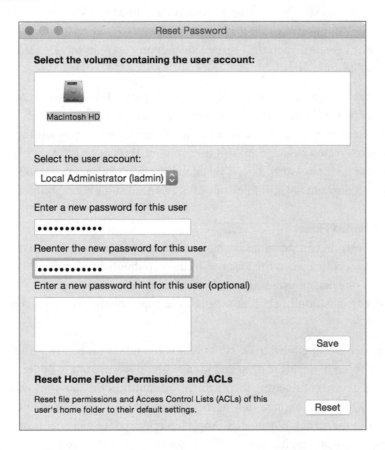

Obviously, the Reset Password utility is a dangerous application that can completely bypass any of the account security settings you've configured to protect your Mac. For this reason, the Reset Password utility does not run if copied off the original media, but this still doesn't prevent any user with access to OS X Recovery from using this utility. Once again, Apple prepared for this situation by providing another utility on OS X Recovery: the Firmware Password utility. As covered in "Reference 7.5 Firmware Password" on page 200, later in this lesson, setting a firmware password prevents any unauthorized user from circumventing normal system startup.

Reference 7.3
System Security Settings

In addition to specific user security settings, such as account passwords and keychain items, there are systemwide security preferences that affect all users on the Mac. Many of these options are disabled by default because the average Mac user would probably consider them inconveniences. However, if your environment requires greater security, these additional security features are indispensable.

Security & Privacy: General Settings

Security & Privacy preferences is a combination of both system settings and personal settings that allow you to tailor the security features of OS X. As with all other system settings, administrator authentication is required to make changes to any items that may affect the system or other users. When using Security & Privacy preferences, note that system settings are dimmed when the lock is present but personal settings are always available.

The General settings pane provides another location, besides the Users & Groups preferences, for users to change their password.

You can also choose to require a password to wake the computer from sleep or screen saver mode and to define a delay before this requirement sets in. Both standard and administrative users can set this for their account, but an administrator cannot set this for every account from Security & Privacy preferences. The exception is that systems with FileVault 2 enabled always require a password on wake. Such systems do not show the option to disable that requirement.

Administrators can also configure a custom message to show at the login window or when the screen is locked. When setting the message, you can press Option-Return to force a new line. However, the system allows for only three lines of text.

The final login option is the ability to disable automatic login for all accounts. This system setting is also always required on systems with FileVault 2 enabled. Those systems do not show the choice to disable automatic login.

Finally, at the bottom of the General pane, you'll find settings for a significant security feature of OS X, dubbed Gatekeeper. This allows administrators to restrict applications downloaded from the Internet based on the trustworthiness of the source. Lesson 17 "Application Installation" covers this topic in greater detail.

Security & Privacy: Advanced Settings

Additional security settings are available to an administrator who unlocks Security & Privacy preferences and then clicks the Advanced button in the lower-right corner.

Administrators can choose to require that users automatically log out of accounts after a certain amount of inactivity and that all system preferences with locking access require an administrator password every time. For example, the default setting allows an administrative user to change Date & Time preferences without actually authenticating. Enabling this option requires an administrator to enter his or her password to use Date & Time preferences.

Security & Privacy: FileVault Settings

This pane is where you enable and configure OS X FileVault 2 full system volume encryption. Lesson 10 "FileVault" covers this topic in greater detail.

Security & Privacy: Legacy FileVault Settings

Prior to OS X Lion, FileVault existed as a technology that secured user data by encrypting the user's home folder content. This method, though effective, has a variety of drawbacks. For one, it does not protect data outside the user's home folder. More problematic, though, is that many system management and backup utilities simply don't work properly with

FileVault home folders. With OS X now featuring FileVault 2 full disk encryption, File-Vault home folder encryption is deprecated.

The previous version of FileVault, now dubbed Legacy FileVault, is still supported by OS X for existing or migrated user accounts, but you can no longer enable it for new user accounts. If you are currently using a Legacy FileVault account on an OS X system, Security & Privacy preferences presents a window prompting you to turn off Legacy FileVault.

NOTE ▶ It is strongly suggested that you turn off Legacy FileVault and switch to the much more robust and secure FileVault 2 system volume encryption. You must completely disable all Legacy FileVault users to enable FileVault 2.

NOTE ▶ Turning off Legacy FileVault requires a logout and a potentially lengthy copy process as the system migrates the encrypted data back to "regular" data.

NOTE ▶ Turning off Legacy FileVault requires enough free space on the system disk to duplicate an entire decrypted copy of your home folder data. If there is not enough free space, you can't turn off Legacy FileVault. You may want to consider manually migrating a copy of your home folder, as covered in Lesson 6 "User Home Folders".

If you dismiss the first Legacy FileVault dialog, you can always decide later to turn off Legacy FileVault. Simply return to the Legacy FileVault pane of Security & Privacy preferences. Note that you can reset the master password from this location as well.

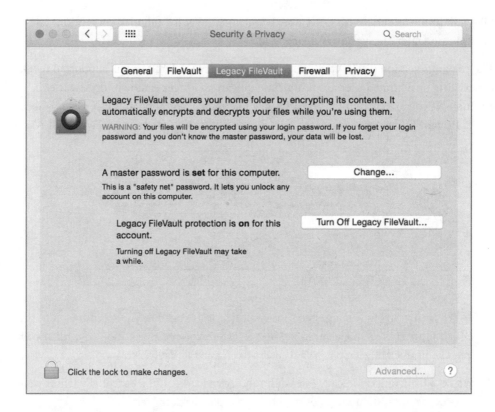

If you decide to stick with Legacy FileVault encrypted home folders, they will behave as they did in OS X v10.6. Other sections in this lesson cover techniques for managing passwords. Be sure to look for techniques pertaining to Legacy FileVault, as these accounts must be handled differently from standard user accounts.

Security & Privacy: Firewall Settings

This pane is where you enable and configure the personal network firewall settings. Lesson 24 "Host Sharing and Personal Firewall" covers this topic in greater detail.

Security & Privacy: Privacy Settings

This pane gives both administrators and standard users the ability to adjust various services' access to personal information.

When a new application requests information that is considered personal, the system automatically asks you for permission. For example, the Maps application asks you to allow Location Services so the Mac system can be located for the default map view. Any Mac with Wi-Fi capabilities can use Location Services to identify its location. Thus, Wi-Fi must be enabled to use Location Services.

TIP Anytime an application takes advantage of Location Services, the Location Services status menu appears near the upper-right corner of the screen. The menu item appears as a northeast compass arrow, similar to that seen in the Privacy pane of Security & Privacy preferences.

From the Privacy pane, a user can view all the applications that have asked for this information and choose to allow or disallow further attempts to collect information. Examples of the types of services an application may request include Location Services, Contacts, Calendars, Reminders, Twitter, LinkedIn, and Facebook information.

NOTE ▶ The list of items in the Privacy pane varies based on configured services. For example, the Twitter service appears only after the user has configured Twitter in Internet Accounts preferences.

Enabling access for assistive applications in previous versions of OS X was found in the separate Accessibility or Universal Access preferences. In OS X Yosemite, you'll find the Accessibility settings listed in the Privacy pane of the Security & Privacy settings.

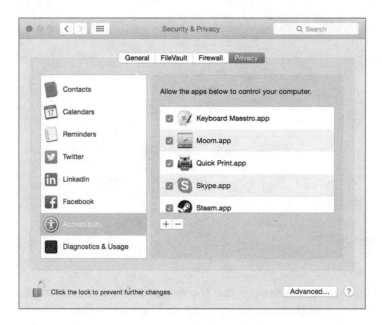

In OS X you must manually enable access for assistive applications by application. This is because, through the Accessibility mechanism, these assistive applications will be granted access to control computer input and modify the interface behavior. In other words, a malicious or poorly written assistive application has the potential to cause all kinds of trouble throughout the system. Thus, an administrative user must allow assistive applications to control the system individually.

The final privacy setting in the list, Diagnostics & Usage, allows administrators to disable the reporting of diagnostic information to Apple. The primary source of information sent with this option is application hangs or crashes. This information helps Apple resolve recurring issues faster.

Dictation Privacy

The OS X dictation feature is enabled and managed via Dictation & Speech preferences. This feature supports English (US, UK, and Australia), French, German, Japanese, Mandarin, Cantonese, Spanish, Korean, Canadian English, Canadian French, and Italian. When the system is set to one of these languages or dialects in Language & Region preferences, it helps this feature automatically enter the correct text. Further, the dictation function supports basic text-related spoken commands for formatting and punctuation.

> **MORE INFO** ▶ You can find out more about general OS X dictation features from Apple Support article HT5449, "Mac Basics: Dictation lets you speak text instead of typing."

The default behavior for the OS X dictation feature actually sends the spoken audio to Apple servers across the Internet. This may seem like an excessively complex solution, but it's the only way to create a dictation system that contains a huge library of words and doesn't require any user training or excessive local storage. Because of this round-trip between the Mac and Apple servers, the transcription response could be a few seconds.

Also, from a security perspective, this server-based dictation method isn't ideal, as you are literally sending your words directly to Apple's servers. Further, the server-based dictation in OS X also sends other user information, like your address book contacts, to provide more accurate transcription. Apple never uses this information for any purpose beyond improving the server-based dictation service, but this may still be unacceptable for those requiring greater privacy.

Alternatively, OS X Yosemite offers an "enhanced" dictation option that relies on locally stored assets to perform the transcription. Selecting the Use Enhanced Dictation checkbox downloads the dictation assets, which require roughly 760 MB. In this case, all transcription is completed by the local Mac, and nothing is ever transmitted to the Apple servers.

Obviously the Enhanced Dictation option provides a completely private method for taking advantage of the OS X dictation feature. Further, when this feature is enabled, user data and recent voice input data are removed from Apple servers. Finally, as a bonus, when the transcription is completed entirely on the local Mac, the dictation system can provide more immediate text feedback as you dictate.

Safari Privacy

With regard to privacy, another growing area of concern is the ever-expanding reach of website tracking systems. As more user services blossom across the Internet, those looking to take advantage of personal information invent more sophisticated techniques for gathering this data. While the OS X default web browser, Safari, can't prevent you from giving away your personal information, it can try to block the "hidden" methods used to gather information about your web usage.

You can find additional privacy settings in the Safari preferences window. From here you can manage existing website cookies or adjust automatic blocking of cookies. Cookies are bits of information about your web history that can be used to track your presence on the Internet. Other Safari privacy options include the ability to further limit Location Services and website tracking.

Find My Mac

From a security standpoint, one of the most significant features of iCloud is Find My Mac. This service helps you locate a lost Mac by allowing you to remotely access the computer's Location Services service. In addition to locating a lost Mac, the service also allows you to remotely lock, erase, and display a message on the Mac.

> **TIP** iCloud can also be used to locate a lost iPhone, iPod touch, or iPad. This service is collectively known as Find My iPhone, which is also the name of a free iOS app that can be used to find both OS X computers and iOS devices.

Several prerequisites must be met to use Find My Mac:

▶ The Mac system must have Wi-Fi enabled as well as an active Internet connection.

▶ The Mac system must have a local OS X Recovery partition.

▶ The Mac system must be configured for iCloud with Find My Mac enabled. As covered in Lesson 2 "Setup and Configuration", the initial system setup includes prompts to enable Find My Mac. You can also configure or disable Find My Mac at any time from iCloud preferences. Although multiple users can sign in to most iCloud services on a single Mac, only one iCloud account per device can be enabled for Find My Mac.

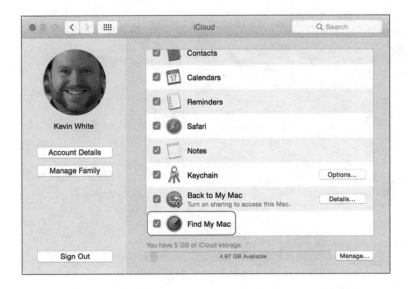

Once you configure Find My Mac, you search for a lost device from another computer by accessing the iCloud website: www.icloud.com. Simply log in with the appropriate iCloud account, and then select Find My iPhone on the iCloud homepage. As you can tell from the name, the "Find" services use the same Location Services technology for both iOS and OS X devices, but an iPhone is more vulnerable to loss than a Mac.

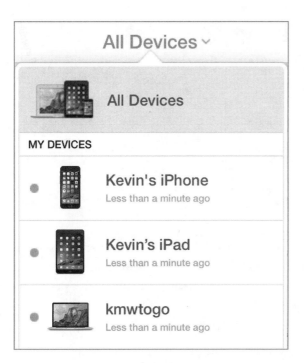

If Find My iPhone is successful, the web interface displays a map with the relative location of all the devices configured for this iCloud account. Selecting a located device on the map allows you to play a sound, send a message, or lock or wipe a device. You can even see the power status in the top-right corner of the device's view. For example, the following screenshot shows that the portable Mac is fully charged.

> **TIP** ▸ OS X Yosemite supports iCloud Family Sharing, which allows a group of iCloud accounts to access each other's devices when using Find My Mac. This allows you to easily locate a device from another user's device or iCloud account as long as they are part of your iCloud Family Sharing group. However, to prevent unintended actions, the lock and erase commands require additional authentication by the iCloud account that enabled Find My Mac on the device. You can find out more about iCloud Family Sharing at https://www.apple.com/icloud/family-sharing/.

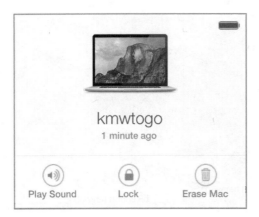

Both the remote lock and erase functions immediately restart the selected Mac system. The remote lock lets you set a new four-digit PIN for the Mac, and upon restart the Mac prompts you for the new number. If a remote erase is issued, upon restart a Mac protected by FileVault 2 erases the encryption keys necessary to decrypt the system disk, whereas other Mac computers simply delete the system partition.

Enabling Find My Mac on a system will also enable the guest account for local login. It's a trap for thieves. The intent is that a stolen Mac will be locked when found. The culprit can choose Guest as a login option upon system startup or wakeup, which allows limited access to the system. Assuming the default settings, the thief would be allowed only to select a Wi-Fi network and use Safari. This enables the stolen Mac to get back online so the owner can use Find My Mac to locate it.

NOTE ▶ Disabling the Find My Mac feature does not also disable the Guest account. Thus, if you intend to permanently disable Find My Mac, you should also disable the Guest account in the Users & Groups preferences, if you'll have no need for it.

Reference 7.5
Firmware Password

As covered previously, setting the firmware password prevents unauthorized users from using any startup-interrupt keyboard shortcuts. This protects your system from someone trying to circumvent an otherwise secure installation of OS X. A firmware password is not in any way tied to a user account. Instead, the password is saved to the Mac computer's firmware chip, so this password remains separate from the installed software.

TIP ▶ Even without setting a firmware password, enabling OS X FileVault 2 full disk encryption prevents unauthorized access to the encrypted system disk.

With a firmware password set, all startup keyboard shortcuts are disabled except for shortcuts that allow you to choose a different startup system. Further, you must provide authentication to gain access to another startup system. For example, on a Mac with a firmware password enabled, if you start up while holding down the Option key, an authentication window appears, prompting you to enter the firmware password. If you enter the correct firmware password, you can select a different startup disk from the Startup Manager. This gives the administrator the flexibility to start up from another system should the need arise, but otherwise prevents users from affecting the standard OS X startup process.

MORE INFO ▶ All the available startup keyboard shortcuts are covered in Lesson 27 "System Troubleshooting".

If you require the highest level of security for your Mac, you must set the firmware password. This is because any user with access to OS X Recovery can set the password if it hasn't already been set. You can set the firmware password using the Firmware Password utility, available when the Mac is started up from OS X Recovery, as covered in Lesson 3 "OS X Recovery".

Once the Mac is started in OS X Recovery, the Firmware Password utility is available in the Utilities menu. If the firmware password isn't currently set, simply click Turn On Firmware Password, and enter the desired password.

If a firmware password is already set for the system, you can change it or turn it off using the corresponding button. However, you must know the current firmware password to change or disable it.

If for some reason the computer's firmware password is lost, it can be reset. For many Mac models made before 2010, you can reset the firmware password by first removing some of the system memory from the Mac. This "proves" that you have access to the internals of the Mac. Then, when you restart the Mac, hold down Command-Option-P-R. Continue holding until you hear the Mac restart; then you can release the keys. At this point, the firmware password has been cleared.

However, to provide enhanced security, most Mac models from 2010 or later don't support this method of resetting the firmware password. If you are in the position where you need the firmware password cleared on a later Mac, you need to visit an Apple Authorized Service Provider.

Exercise 7.1
Reset Account Passwords in OS X Recovery

▶ **Prerequisites**

- ▶ You must have created the Local Admin ("Exercise 2.1 Configure a New OS X System for Exercises" on page 60 or "Exercise 2.2 Configure an Existing OS X System for Exercises" on page 63) and Mayta Mishtuk ("Exercise 6.1 Restore a Deleted User Account" on page 166) accounts.

- ▶ Your computer must have a local hidden Recovery HD partition. This partition is normally created by the OS X installation process.

OS X provides a number of ways to reset lost account passwords. In this exercise, you will use OS X Recovery mode to reset Mayta Mishtuk's password.

Reset a User Password in OS X Recovery

1 Restart your computer, and hold down Command-R until the gray Apple logo appears on the screen.

2 If a language selection screen appears, select your preferred language, and click the right-arrow button to continue.

3 From the menu bar, choose Utilities > Terminal.

   Terminal provides access to a command-line (text-based) interface in OS X. This guide doesn't cover the command-line interface, but using it is necessary to reach the Reset Password utility in OS X Recovery.

4 Type the command resetpassword, and press Return.

   The Reset Password utility opens.

5 In the volume list, select Macintosh HD, and then choose Mayta Mishtuk (mayta) from the user account pop-up menu.

6   Enter password1 in both password fields. Leave the hint field blank.

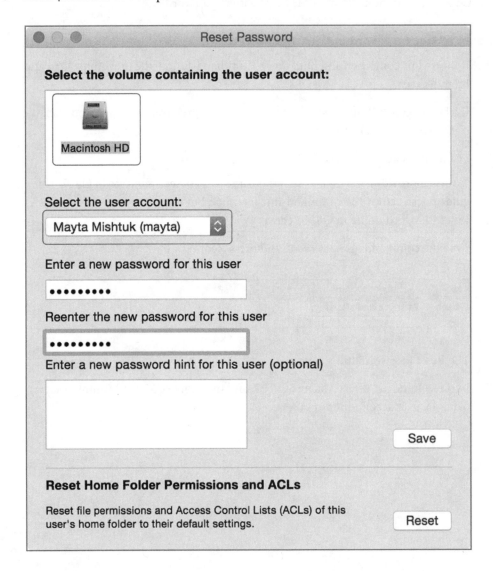

7   Click Save.

A warning appears, stating that the user's default keychain password wasn't changed (more on the implications of this in "Exercise 7.3 Synchronize Keychain Passwords" on page 211).

8   Click OK.

In addition to resetting user passwords, the Reset Password utility can repair some permissions issues with user home folders. In this case, nothing is wrong with Mayta Mishtuk's home folder permissions; resetting them anyway doesn't hurt anything.

9   Click Reset to reset Mayta's home folder permissions.

10 From the Apple menu, choose Restart.

NOTE ▶ Mayta Mishtuk's login keychain is no longer synchronized with her login password. Either you may perform "Exercise 7.2 Reset Account Passwords" on page 206 next, followed by "Exercise 7.3 Synchronize Keychain Passwords" on page 211, or you may skip directly to "Exercise 7.3 Synchronize Keychain Passwords" on page 211. In any case, resynchronize Mayta's passwords by performing "Exercise 7.3 Synchronize Keychain Passwords" on page 211 before going on to any other lesson.

Exercise 7.2
Reset Account Passwords

▶ **Prerequisites**

▶ You must have created the Local Admin ("Exercise 2.1 Configure a New OS X System for Exercises" on page 60 or "Exercise 2.2 Configure an Existing OS X System for Exercises" on page 63) and Mayta Mishtuk ("Exercise 6.1 Restore a Deleted User Account" on page 166) accounts.

OS X provides a number of ways to reset lost account passwords. In this exercise, you will reset Mayta Mishtuk's password as an administrator and then again using a master password.

Reset a User Password as an Administrator

1   If necessary, log in as Local Admin (password: ladminpw, or whatever you chose when you created the account).

2   Open System Preferences, and select Users & Groups.

3   Click the lock icon, and authenticate as Local Admin.

4   Select the Mayta Mishtuk account.

5   Click Reset Password.

6   In the dialog that appears, enter password2 in the "New password" field.

7   Click the small key icon next to the "New password" field.

Password Assistant opens to help you choose a better password. It rates the quality of this proposed password (red, to indicate it's bad), suggests a better password (in the Suggestion field), and lists tips on how to avoid such bad passwords.

8   Click the triangle next to the Suggestion field to show more suggested passwords.

9   Click one of the suggested passwords. The selected password is copied into the "New password" and Suggestion fields, and the Quality bar expands and turns green to indicate this is a much better option.

10   Type the password you chose into the Verify field, and click Change Password.

You do not need to memorize or record this password because you will not need it later.

11   Close Password Assistant.

12   If you used an iCloud password for the Chris Johnson account in Lesson 5 "User Accounts", select the Chris Johnson account, and click Reset Password.

When an account is using an iCloud password, the only ways to reset the password are by going through iCloud and by switching the account to a separate password.

13   Click Cancel to skip resetting Chris Johnson's password.

14   Click the Action (gear icon) menu under the user list, and choose Set Master Password from the pop-up menu that appears.

15   If you are performing this exercise in a class, enter masterpw in the Master Password and Verify fields. If you are performing this exercise on your own, select a more secure master password. Be sure to remember the password you have chosen since you will need to reenter it in the next section.

16 Quit System Preferences, and log out as Local Admin.

Reset a Password with the Master Password

1 At the login screen, select Mayta Mishtuk.

2 Enter the wrong password for Mayta, and press Return three times.

You'll see options for resetting Mayta's password.

3 Click the arrow next to "reset it using your Master Password."

4 Enter the master password (masterpw, or whatever you chose earlier in the exercise); then enter password2 in the "New password" and "Verify password" fields.

Do not enter a password hint.

A dialog warns that the system was unable to unlock your login keychain. Leave this dialog open for the next exercise.

NOTE ▶ Mayta Mishtuk's login keychain is no longer synchronized with her login password. You need to resynchronize her passwords by performing "Exercise 7.3 Synchronize Keychain Passwords" on page 211 before going on to any other exercise.

Exercise 7.3
Synchronize Keychain Passwords

▶ **Prerequisites**

▶ You must have created the Local Admin ("Exercise 2.1 Configure a New OS X System for Exercises" on page 60 or "Exercise 2.2 Configure an Existing OS X System for Exercises" on page 63) and Mayta Mishtuk ("Exercise 6.1 Restore a Deleted User Account" on page 166) accounts.

▶ You must perform "Exercise 7.1 Reset Account Passwords in OS X Recovery" on page 202 or "Exercise 7.2 Reset Account Passwords" on page 206 before this exercise.

Update the Login Keychain Password

After the previous exercises, Mayta Mishtuk's account password has been reset, but her login keychain is still encrypted with her old password and cannot be opened as OS X would do if both the account password and login keychain password were the same. Fortunately, the login process provides an easy way to resynchronize the login keychain's password.

1   If you aren't already logged in (or logging in) as Mayta Mishtuk, log in now (after the previous exercises, her password is either password1 or password2).

Because Mayta's account password no longer matches her keychain password, the system cannot use this password to unlock her keychain, and you receive a warning to this effect.

If you did not remember Mayta's old password, there would be no way to recover the contents of her old keychain, and you could click Create New Keychain to delete it and create a new one. In this case, however, because you do remember the old password, you can use it to recover the contents and update the keychain password.

2   Click Update Keychain Password.

3   When prompted, enter Mayta's old login password from before her account was reset (mayta, or whatever you chose when you created Mayta's new account in "Exercise 6.1 Restore a Deleted User Account" on page 166), and click OK.

Verify the Synchronization

1   In the Finder, open the Utilities folder. There are a number of ways to navigate there:

   ▶ Open the Macintosh HD icon on the desktop, then open Applications, and then open Utilities.

   ▶ From the Finder's Go menu, choose Utilities.

   ▶ Use the Finder shortcut Command-Shift-U.

2   In the Utilities folder, open Keychain Access.

Keychain Access displays the status and contents of your login keychain. Note that the keychain appears as unlocked, which means that the correct password has been supplied and its contents are available.

3 From the menu bar, choose Keychain Access > Preferences (or press Command-Comma).

Command-Comma is a shortcut for opening application preferences that works in most applications.

4 Click the First Aid tab.

5 Ensure that the "Synchronize login keychain password with account" option is selected.

6 Close the Preferences window.

7 Choose Keychain Access > Keychain First Aid.

8   In the Keychain First Aid window's Password field, enter Mayta's current account password (password1 or password2).

9   Click Start.

Keychain Access checks the login keychain for a variety of problems, including synchronization with the account password. Its report shows "No problems found." If it does find any problems, select the Repair option, and click Start again.

10   Close the Keychain First Aid window, but leave Keychain Access open.

Change Mayta's Password

Resetting Mayta's account password desynchronized it from her login password. Changing her password normally does not cause this problem. To test this, change Mayta's password the normal way.

1   Open the Users & Groups pane in System Preferences.

2   Make sure the Mayta Mishtuk account is selected.

3   Click Change Password.

Note that unlike the Reset Password options you used earlier, this has a field for the old password. It uses this old password to decrypt the login keychain and then reencrypt it with the new password.

4   Enter the following:

Old password: **password1** or **password2**

New password: **mayta** (or whatever you chose when you created her new account)

Verify: **mayta** (or whatever you chose whatever you chose when you created her new account)

You may enter a password hint if you want.

5   Click Change Password.

6   Quit System Preferences.

Reverify the Synchronization

1   If necessary, open the Keychain Access utility.

2   As you did before, choose Keychain Access > Keychain First Aid.

3   Enter Mayta's current account password (**mayta**, or whatever you chose when you created her new account) in the Password field, and click Start.

As before, it reports "No problems found," which indicates that the keychain password has stayed synchronized with the account password.

4   Quit Keychain Access.

5   Log out as Mayta Mishtuk.

Exercise 7.4
Use a Firmware Password

In this exercise, you will set a firmware password to control the startup process of your computer.

> **WARNING** ▶ If you forget the firmware password, you might have to take your computer to an Apple Authorized Service Provider to unlock it. If you do not want to risk this, please skip ahead to the next lesson.

Set a Firmware Password

1   Restart your computer, and hold down Command-R until the gray Apple logo appears on the screen.

2   If a language selection screen appears, select your preferred language, and click the right-arrow button.

3   From the menu bar, choose Utilities > Firmware Password Utility.

4   Click Turn On Firmware Password.

5   Enter the password apple in both the "New password" and "Verify" fields.

6   Click Set Password.

The utility indicates that password protection is enabled.

Test the Firmware Password

1   From the Apple menu, choose Restart.

Your computer restarts normally. The firmware password does not interfere with a normal startup.

2   At the login screen, click Restart, and then hold down Command-R until a lock icon appears onscreen.

Alternative boot modes, including OS X Recovery, are not available without entering the firmware password.

3   Enter the password (apple), and press Return.

Remove the Firmware Password

If you are performing these exercises on your own and want to leave the firmware password enabled, restart your computer normally, and skip this section.

If you are performing these exercises in a classroom or you do not want to leave the firmware password set on your own computer, follow these steps to remove the password:

1   Choose Utilities > Firmware Password Utility.

2   Click Turn Off Firmware Password.

3   When prompted, enter the firmware password (apple).

WARNING ▶ There is no simple way to remove or reset a forgotten firmware password. You might have to take your computer to an Apple Authorized Service Provider to unlock it.

The Firmware Password utility shows that password protection is disabled.

4   From the Apple menu, choose Restart.

Your computer restarts normally.

Lesson 8

Keychain Management

OS X features a sophisticated system that automatically protects all your authentication assets via the securely encrypted keychain system. Much as service workers might keep a keychain containing all the keys needed during their workday, OS X keeps all your resource passwords, certificates, keys, website forms, and even secure notes in encrypted storage. Every time you allow OS X to remember a password or any other potentially sensitive item, it saves it to the keychain system. Only your account password remains separate from all the other items saved to your keychains.

In this lesson, you first identify where the keychain system stores various keychain files. Then, the majority of this lesson shows you how to manage the keychain system, including the use of multiple keychains and advanced keychain settings. Finally, you learn how to use iCloud Keychain, a secure method for sharing your secrets among multiple Apple devices.

Reference 8.1
Keychain Architecture

Because so many important items are saved via the keychain architecture, the keychain files themselves are encrypted with a very strong algorithm: They are impenetrable unless you know the keychain's password. In fact, if you forget a keychain's password, its contents are lost forever. Not even the software engineers at Apple can help you—the keychain system is *that* secure. Yet probably the single best feature of the keychain architecture is that it's entirely automatic using the default settings. Most users never know just how secure their saved passwords are, because the system is so transparent.

Understanding Local Keychain Files

Keychain files are stored throughout the system for different users and resources. Here are a few of note:

▶ /Users/<username>/Library/Keychains/login.keychain—Every standard or administrative user is created with a single login keychain. As a default, the password for this keychain matches the user's account password, so this keychain is automatically unlocked and available when the user logs in. If the user's account password does not match the keychain's password, it does not automatically unlock during login. This keychain appears with the name "login" when using the Keychain Access application, as covered later in Lesson 8 "Keychain Management".

> **TIP** ▶ Users can create additional keychains if they want to segregate their authentication assets. For example, you can keep your default login keychain for trivial items and then create a more secure keychain that does not automatically unlock for more important items.

▶ /Users/<username>/Library/Keychains/<UUID>—This keychain folder is also created for every user account. The chosen UUID (universally unique identifier) name of the folder does not match the user's local account UUID, but this item is associated with the user due to its location in the user's home folder. This folder contains the keychain database used by the iCloud Keychain service. Even if the user hasn't enabled the iCloud Keychain service yet, this local keychain database is still created. When the iCloud Keychain service is not enabled, this keychain appears with the name Local Items in the Keychain Access application. Once the iCloud Keychain service is enabled, this keychain appears with the name iCloud in the Keychain Access application. Managing the iCloud Keychain service is covered later in "Reference 8.3 iCloud Keychain" on page 229.

▶ /Library/Keychains/System.keychain—This keychain maintains authentication assets that are not user specific. Examples of items stored here include Wi-Fi wireless network passwords, 802.1X network passwords, and local Kerberos support items. Although all users benefit from this keychain, only administrative users can make changes to it. You'll also find additional keychains in this folder for use by Legacy FileVault and the Apple Push service. This keychain appears with the name System in the Keychain Access application.

▶ /Library/Keychains/FileVaultMaster.keychain—This keychain is created when the system master password is set, so it can only be unlocked with that password. This keychain, as the name implies, is used by the Legacy FileVault and FileVault 2 systems.

Managing and troubleshooting Legacy FileVault and the master password is covered in Lesson 7 "System Security". This keychain doesn't appear in the Keychain Access application by default.

▶ /System/Library/Keychains/—In this folder are several keychain files that store root certificates used to help identify trusted network services. Once again, all users benefit from these keychains, but only administrative users can make changes to them. Most of these keychain items don't appear in the Keychain Access application by default.

NOTE ▶ Both Apple and third-party developers create keychains for securely storing a variety of data. Thus, keychain files with seemingly random names can be found throughout the system. It's best to leave these files alone unless you are specifically instructed by a trusted source to take action to resolve an issue.

Reference 8.2
Keychain Management

The primary tool you use to manage keychains is the Keychain Access application, found in the /Applications/Utilities folder. With this application you can view and modify any keychain item, including saved resource passwords, certificates, keys, website forms, and secure notes. You can also create and delete keychain files, change keychain settings and passwords, and repair corrupted keychains. Additionally, you can manage web-specific keychain items from the Safari preferences.

Manage Items in Keychain Access

To manage all keychain items, including saved passwords, start by opening /Applications/Utilities/Keychain Access. The default selection shows the contents of the user's login keychain, but you can select another keychain from the list to view its items.

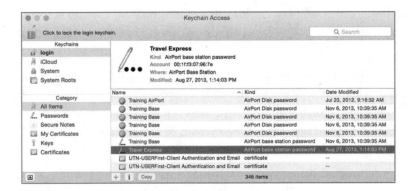

Simply double-click a keychain item to view its attributes. If the item is a password, you can reveal the saved password by selecting the "Show password" checkbox. You'll find that this, and other changes, often prompt you for the keychain's password. This is a safety measure to ensure that only the keychain's owner can make changes. Once you have authenticated, you can change any attribute in the keychain item dialog, including any saved passwords. You can also click the Access Control tab to adjust application access for the selected item.

NOTE ▶ The iCloud authentication mechanisms create many keychain items that you may not recognize. Many of these are in the form of certificates or keys, the contents of which should not be tampered with. In short, refrain from "cleaning out" keychain secrets that seem unfamiliar.

TIP ▶ To easily search through keychain items in Keychain Access, you can filter the list by selecting a keychain Category view on the left, or you can search for a specific item via the Spotlight search in the upper-right corner of the toolbar.

TIP ▶ The safest place to store secure text on your Mac is in keychains. In Keychain Access, you can create a new secure note by choosing File > New Secure Note Item.

Understanding User Keychains

At this point, you may notice differences in content between the user's login keychain and the user's Local Items/iCloud keychain. (Again, the Local Items keychain is renamed iCloud once the iCloud Keychain service is enabled.) This difference between these two user keychains is caused by technical differences in the keychain storage system.

Items in the user's login keychain are stored using an older method that is compatible only with legacy OS X applications. Items in the user's Local Items/iCloud keychain are stored using a newer method compatible only with newer OS X applications and with iOS. During initial setup of the iCloud Keychain service, a background process automatically migrates items from any legacy keychains to the iCloud keychain. Obviously, only the items in the iCloud keychain are saved to iCloud and subsequently pushed to other appropriately configured devices.

NOTE ▶ After enabling the iCloud Keychain service, if you later disable the service, you can choose to keep the items saved locally, in the renamed Local Items keychain.

The user's Local Items/iCloud keychain is accessed using the same password as the user's login keychain. In other words, the password used to unlock and manage the user's login keychain is also used to unlock and manage the Local Items/iCloud keychain. Thus, changes to the login keychain password are automatically applied to the Local Items/iCloud keychain. For this reason, the Keychain Access application does not allow you to change the Local Items/iCloud keychain password.

Manage Safari Keychain Items

The built-in OS X web browser, Safari, is a great example of where a user would interact with the keychain system on a daily basis. By default, the AutoFill system in Safari automatically prompts the user to start saving web-form information and site passwords. Further, the latest version of Safari includes new AutoFill features like the ability to suggest secure website passwords and store credit card purchasing information.

NOTE ▶ Despite the dialog's text, Safari AutoFill doesn't require the iCloud Keychain service. If the iCloud Keychain service isn't enabled, Safari will save secret information to the Local Items keychain.

When the user revisits a site or navigates to a new site with similar form information, Safari AutoFill automatically fills in information for the user, as long as the keychain file is unlocked. Safari also pulls information from the user's contact information, if allowed.

You can find the Safari AutoFill settings by choosing Safari > Preferences from the menu and then selecting the AutoFill tab. These settings give you fine-grained control over what items are automatically saved and filled. Further, Edit buttons allow you to inspect and manage individual items such as website passwords and saved credit cards.

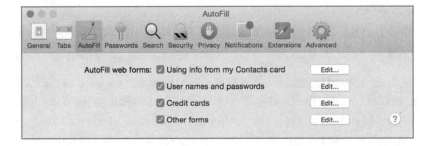

With the exception of the user's contact information, which is stored in the Contacts application, all Safari AutoFill data is securely stored in the keychain system. Thus, you can also view and manage the AutoFill items from the Keychain Access application. The easiest way to find these items in Keychain Access is to enter Safari in the Spotlight search field. Again, double-clicking any item in Keychain Access allows you to inspect that item. However, you can actually see more information about AutoFill items in the Safari preferences.

NOTE ▶ Some websites remember your authentication inside a web cookie, so you might not see an entry in a keychain file for every website that automatically remembers your account. Website cookies can be viewed and deleted from the Security tab of Safari Preferences.

Reset Keychain Passwords

The only time a user's login and Local Items/iCloud keychain passwords will be changed is if the user knows the current account password and then decides to change it. So that they remain as secure as possible, keychain passwords cannot be changed by any outside password-resetting process. Apple did not design the keychain system with a back door, as doing so would render the system less secure.

Consequently, whenever an administrative user resets a user's account or Legacy FileVault password, the user's login and Local Items/iCloud keychain passwords remain unchanged and will not automatically open when the user logs in to the account. However, by default in OS X, when a user with a recently reset password logs in, he or she will be prompted with a dialog to update or reset the keychain password.

TIP ▶ The keychain update dialog can be disabled from the First Aid tab of the Keychain Access application preferences.

The default selection, Update Keychain Password, works only if the user knows the previous keychain password, which is probably not the case if you just had to reset the password. In that case, the user should click the Create New Keychain button to create a new login keychain. The system renames the old login keychain and leaves it in the user's Keychains folder in case the user ever remembers the old password. Finally, though it's not recommended, the user can simply choose to ignore the warning by clicking Continue Log In.

NOTE ▶ Creating a new login keychain effectively erases all saved authentication secrets. This means the system will have lost saved authentication for any services, such as those configured via the Internet Accounts preferences and iCloud preferences, including access to additional secrets saved in the Local Items/iCloud keychain.

If the automatic keychain update dialog does not appear, you can still reset the user's login and Local Items/iCloud keychain passwords from the Keychain Access application, assuming the previous password is known. As you'd expect, if you do not know the user's previous keychain password, the contents of that keychain are lost forever. Using Keychain Access to manage a user's keychain is covered in the following section.

Manage Keychain Files

To manage keychain files, including resetting a keychain's password, open the Keychain Access application. You can create a new local keychain by choosing File > New Keychain and then entering a password, six characters or longer, for the keychain. The default location for new keychains is the Keychains folder inside your home folder.

NOTE ▶ The user's Local Items/iCloud keychain is automatically managed by the system for you. Thus, you cannot change the settings, change the password, or delete this keychain. Again, the Local Items/iCloud keychain password is automatically updated to match the user's login keychain password.

You can further adjust a keychain's settings by selecting it from the list and then choosing Edit > Change Settings for Keychain. A dialog appears where you can change automatic keychain locking settings for the selected keychain file.

To change a keychain's password, first select it from the list, and then choose Edit > Change Password for Keychain. You have to enter the keychain's current password first, followed by a new password and verification.

Finally, to delete a keychain, select it from the list, and choose File > Delete Keychain. When the Delete Keychain dialog appears, click Delete References to simply ignore the keychain, or click Delete References & Files to completely erase the keychain file.

It's not recommended that you delete the original keychain file manually in the Finder, as this will confuse the keychain system. Also, it's obviously not a good idea to delete the Login keychain unless another keychain is there to take its place. In other words, a user should always have access to at least one local keychain.

TIP ▸ You can move keychain items between keychains by dragging and dropping an item from one keychain to another. The exception to this is the Local Items/iCloud keychain, for which the system automatically manages the addition and removal of items.

TIP ▸ For quick access to your keychains and other security features, you can enable the Keychain menu item by choosing Keychain Access > Preferences. Then select the "Show keychain status in menu bar" checkbox to display the Keychain menu item, as indicated by a small key icon.

Repair Keychain Files

If the system is unable to open a keychain file or retrieve secrets from it, the keychain file may have become corrupted. Fortunately, the Keychain Access application can verify and repair keychain files, provided that you know the keychain's password.

To verify or repair a keychain file, start by opening /Applications/Utilities/Keychain Access. If the troublesome keychain is not already in your keychain list, choose File > Add Keychain to browse for it. When you are ready to attempt the repair, choose Keychain Access > Keychain First Aid.

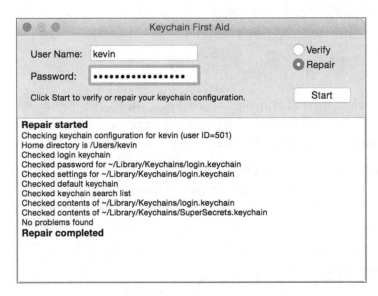

In the Keychain First Aid window, select the Repair option, and then enter a user name and password to start the repair. Note that you are allowed to repair only keychains that you can unlock with the entered password. Also note that if you enter an administrator account, Keychain First Aid attempts to repair keychains stored in /Library/Keychains. A log shows the keychain verification or repair process. More than one pass may be necessary to fully repair all keychain issues.

> **TIP** ▶ Find additional Keychain First Aid preferences by choosing Keychain Access > Preferences.

Reference 8.3
iCloud Keychain

Previous OS X versions featured Keychain synchronization through the Apple MobileMe service. Although otherwise functional, this service lacked a very important feature: iOS compatibility. Many of the same secrets are used across the two platforms, so having your secrets shared automatically between devices is hugely convenient. It's even handier given the limited screen size and absence of a physical keyboard on iOS devices, which make managing secrets even more difficult there.

Enter iCloud Keychain, supported on Mac computers with OS X Mavericks and later and iOS devices with iOS 7.0.3 and later. This service automatically shares your commonly used secrets between devices via iCloud.

> **MORE INFO** ▶ iCloud services are designed with strong personal security in mind, as detailed in Apple Support article HT202303, "iCloud security and privacy overview."

Understanding iCloud Keychain

As covered previously in this lesson, the system automatically maintains two keychains for each local user account: the legacy login keychain and the new Local Items/iCloud keychain. Note that the previous Keychain Access screenshots in this lesson show the iCloud keychain. As the name implies, contents in the iCloud keychain are also stored on the Apple iCloud servers and then automatically pushed to other configured Apple devices. Thus, this service not only provides a secure mechanism for accessing your secrets from any Apple device connected to the Internet, it also acts as a secure backup for your important secrets.

When the iCloud Keychain service is enabled, items from local keychains are automatically copied to the user's iCloud keychain. This process happens whenever you enable the iCloud Keychain service on any Apple device. On an OS X system, any compatible item from any local keychain the user has access to is copied to the user's iCloud keychain, including items from the System keychain. As covered previously in this lesson, only keychain items compatible with iOS are copied to the iCloud keychain.

As new secrets are saved or created on behalf of the user, the keychain system automatically saves compatible items to the iCloud keychain and legacy items to the user's login keychain. Importantly, items in the iCloud keychain will never migrate back to the local keychain files. This step would be unnecessary anyway, because as long as your devices can see the iCloud keychain, they can access its content without copying items to a legacy local keychain. Again, if the user chooses to disable the iCloud Keychain service, the iCloud keychain will be renamed Local Items, and the user can choose to keep the secret items intact locally.

> **NOTE ▶** Only standard or administrator user account types can take advantage of iCloud Keychain.

iCloud Keychain Security Code

Keeping the contents of your iCloud keychain safe is of paramount importance. After all, once it's enabled, your secrets are stored in a manner that makes them accessible to anyone on the Internet who knows your credentials. In short, no matter how strong your Apple ID password is, single-factor authentication is still not good enough for the iCloud Keychain service. Thus, when you first enable the iCloud Keychain service for a specific Apple ID, the system prompts you to choose an iCloud Security Code that is used to further protect your valuable secrets.

> **NOTE ▶** It's important to recognize that the iCloud Security Code is a separate security mechanism from the two-step verification for Apple ID. Although a single Apple ID simultaneously benefits from both security mechanisms, they are set up independently from each other. You can find out more about two-step verification for Apple ID in Apple Support article HT5570, "Frequently asked questions about two-step verification for Apple ID."

In addition to Apple ID authentication, enabling the iCloud Keychain service prompts you to select one of the following security code options:

▶   Code plus verification. The default iCloud Security Code mechanism is a simple code paired with SMS text message verification. This requires that you select a four-digit numeric code and provide a phone number that can receive SMS text messages for further verification.

► An advanced option to manually set a complex iCloud Security Code. You can create a code up to 32 characters long, but it's your responsibility to keep track of this code in a safe place.

► An advanced option to have a random complex iCloud Security Code generated and then paired with an SMS text message verification. The system first randomly generates a 32-character code, but again, it's your responsibility to keep track of this code in a safe place. Then you provide a phone number that can receive SMS text messages for further verification.

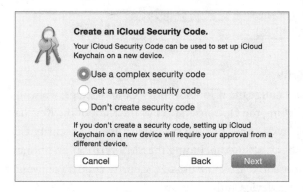

As the preceding dialog states, you do not have to use an iCloud Security Code for initial setup of the iCloud Keychain service. If you choose not to, enabling the iCloud Keychain service on any additional devices requires physical access to another device that has already been configured for the service.

After you have made your choice for the iCloud Security Code, the iCloud Keychain service is enabled for your first device. As described earlier, on OS X, the iCloud keychain appears in Keychain Access and is made available to all compatible applications and services.

iCloud Keychain Device Authorization

After initial setup of the iCloud Keychain service on the first device, you can grant access for additional devices via a simple device authorization mechanism. The idea is that any device currently configured with the iCloud Keychain service is a trusted device. Thus, any trusted device can be used to verify additional devices for the iCloud Keychain service.

For example, after setup of the iCloud Keychain service on an OS X computer, when you attempt to enable this service on a different OS X computer, you have to approve this action from the original OS X computer. Alternatively, if you set up an iCloud Security Code, you can use the code as additional verification instead of device-based authorization.

Manage iCloud Keychain Security

If at any point you want to verify or change the iCloud Security Code settings, you can do so from the iCloud preferences. Clicking the Options button to the right of the Keychain item in the iCloud preferences displays a pane showing the current iCloud Security Code settings and allows you to change these settings, including the SMS verification phone number. Note that you can also choose to disable the use of a security code if you want to allow iCloud Keychain access only via device authorization.

Resetting iCloud Keychain

Not only does the iCloud Security Code give you an additional way to add new devices, it also provides a last resort should the iCloud Keychain service become unavailable to all your devices. In other words, if you lose access to all your devices, a new device can be authorized via the iCloud Security Code. However, if you don't create an iCloud Security Code, and somehow all your devices are lost or have disabled the iCloud Keychain service, then your iCloud Keychain contents are no longer accessible and must be reset.

> **NOTE** ▶ If you lose both your iCloud Security Code and access to authorized devices, the iCloud Keychain service must be reset to regain access to the service. However, if you lose access only to the SMS text message phone number, you can contact Apple Support to help resolve this issue.

> **NOTE** ▶ Resetting the iCloud Keychain service destroys all previously saved items in the iCloud Keychain. After a reset, enabling this service will again prompt you to set up an iCloud Security Code.

Also covered previously, as the local login keychain goes, so does the iCloud keychain. If the login keychain is locked, the iCloud keychain is also locked.

Further, if the login keychain password is lost, so is the user's access to the local instance of the iCloud keychain. If a new login keychain is created, as is recommended by the keychain update dialog, the local iCloud keychain is also automatically reset. This results in a new empty Local Items keychain for the user, but the contents of the iCloud Keychain service remain "in the cloud." You can then gain access to your secrets by reenabling the iCloud Keychain service; however, doing so will treat the device as if it were a new device. Thus, you will again be prompted to authenticate with an Apple ID and to use either the iCloud Security Code or device authorization to regain access to the iCloud Keychain service.

MORE INFO ▶ You can find out more about iCloud Keychain from the Apple Support site at www.apple.com/support/icloud/keychain/.

Exercise 8.1
Manage Keychains

▶ **Prerequisite**

> ▶ You must have created the Chris Johnson account ("Exercise 5.1 Manage User Accounts" on page 145).

As you've seen, in most cases a user's keychain password and account password are the same. When you create a user account, the login keychain file is created to store the user's passwords and is secured with the account password. However, in environments where more security is desired, a user can decouple the keychain password from the account password by using the Keychain Access application to change the login keychain's password. In this case, the user must enter the login keychain's password before applications such as Mail and Safari can access stored passwords. The system provides various features to help users keep their account and keychain passwords synchronized.

In this exercise, you will explore various keychain management techniques.

Show Keychain Status in the Menu Bar
You will prepare the keychain environment for more advanced users using Keychain Access.

1   Log in as Chris Johnson (using the password for the linked iCloud account or whatever you chose when you created the account).

2   Open Keychain Access from the Utilities folder.

3   From the menu bar, choose Keychain Access > Preferences (or press Command-Comma).

4   Select "Show keychain status in menu bar."

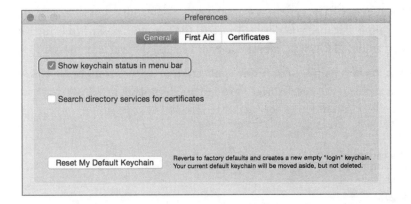

This places a lock icon in the menu bar, making it more convenient to perform various security-related functions.

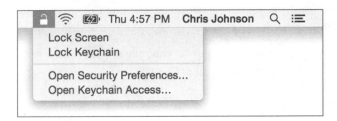

5 Close Keychain Access preferences.

6 Choose Edit > Change Password for Keychain "login."

7 Enter Chris's current password, then enter a new password (keychain), and finally verify the new password.

This desynchronizes the keychain password from Chris's account password.

NOTE ▶ Normally you would want to test the strength of your passwords by clicking the key icon to open Password Assistant. However, this exercise uses simple passwords for academic purposes only.

8 Click OK.

9 Log out and back in as Chris Johnson.

Notice that the message "The system was unable to unlock your login keychain" did not appear this time. Because you desynchronized the keychain password using Keychain Access, it assumed this was intentional and disabled the warning message.

However, since the keychain is locked, any application or system component that wants to access items in the keychain will prompt you to unlock it.

10   If you receive any requests for the keychain password, try clicking Cancel (or using the shortcut Command-Period) to dismiss a few of them.

Since Chris's account has iCloud services configured, you may receive a large number of unlock requests. You do not have to dismiss all of them.

11   Look at the Keychain menu bar icon.

Notice that the lock icon appears locked, not open, which means that although you logged in successfully to your account, your keychain did not automatically unlock. If Keychain Access reopened automatically, it also shows the keychain status as locked.

When the keychain and login passwords are the same, the login keychain unlocks when the user logs in, to allow applications to access the passwords stored on it. Because the account and login passwords don't match, Chris has to enter his login keychain password in order for applications to access stored passwords.

12   If you are still receiving requests for the keychain password, enter it (keychain), and click OK.

The lock icon in the menu bar opens, indicating that your login keychain is unlocked.

13   If you receive any more requests for the keychain password (from system components that requested access before you unlocked it), click Cancel to dismiss them.

Store a Password in a Keychain

Your keychain already has a number of automatically created entries. In this section, you will create an entry manually.

1   Open the StudentMaterials/Lesson8 folder. Remember that you created a shortcut to StudentMaterials in your Dock.

2   Open the file named "Chris's private files.dmg."

This disk image is encrypted, so the system prompts you for the password to open it.

3   Select "Remember password in my keychain."

4   Enter the password private.

5   Click OK.

If you have not already unlocked the login keychain, the system again prompts you for the keychain password. The keychain must be unlocked to store passwords in the keychain as well as to access them.

6   If you are prompted to, enter the keychain password (keychain), and click OK.

7   Select the disk image on your desktop, and press Command-E to eject it.

8   Open the disk image again.

Since the password is now stored in your keychain and the keychain is unlocked, the image opens without asking you for the password.

9   Eject the disk image again.

Retrieve a Password in a Keychain

Even though passwords are stored to make them conveniently available for applications, there may be times when a user needs to retrieve a stored password. For example, a user who wants to use webmail on a different computer may want to retrieve her email password in order to do so. In this section, you will use the keychain to retrieve a forgotten password.

1   If necessary, open Keychain Access from the Utilities folder.

2   Double-click the password entry named "Chris's private files.dmg." Use the search filter at the upper-right corner of Keychain Access if you need to.

A window opens, displaying information about this password entry.

3   Click the Access Control tab.

The Access Control pane displays information about what applications or system components are allowed access to the keychain entry. In this case, the diskimages-helper application can automatically access the password, but if any other application requests access, the system asks the user for confirmation first.

Normally, the application that created a keychain entry is the only one that is allowed automatic access to it, but you can change this policy as needed.

4   Click the Attributes tab.

5   In the Attributes pane, select Show Password.

A dialog informs you that Keychain Access wants to use your confidential information stored in "Chris's private files.dmg" in your keychain. Even though your keychain is unlocked, this item's access policy requires confirmation before anything other than diskimages-helper is allowed to read the password.

6   Enter your keychain password (keychain), and click Always Allow.

The disk image password becomes visible.

7   Click the Access Control tab.

Keychain Access has now been added to the "Always allow" list for this item. If you had clicked "Allow" instead, Keychain Access would have been allowed access to the password but would not have been added to this access control list. Since it has been added to the list, Keychain Access can now display the password without asking for confirmation.

8   Close the "Chris's private files.dmg" window.

Sync Keychain Password with Account

If you want to resynchronize the login keychain password with the login password, you can use Keychain First Aid to synchronize the two. In addition to the synchronization feature, Keychain First Aid can repair certain application issues with stored passwords, such as when an application erroneously asks for a password that has previously been stored.

1   Still logged in as Chris Johnson, open Keychain Access preferences, and then click the First Aid tab.

2   Select "Synchronize login keychain password with account."

This preference setting controls whether the system warns you at login if your keychain password is out of sync with your account password. It is normally enabled by default, but when you changed Chris's keychain password in Keychain Access (intentionally desynchronizing it), Keychain Access disabled this preference setting automatically.

3   Close the Preferences window.

4   Choose Keychain Access > Keychain First Aid.

5   Enter Chris's account password (the password for the linked iCloud account or whatever you chose when you created the account), select Repair, and click Start.

6   If asked to provide the keychain password for the login keychain, enter it (`keychain`), and click OK.

The bottom section of the Keychain First Aid window displays a log of the repair process.

7   If the log indicates that the repair failed, repeat the repair process.

8   After the repair completes successfully, quit Keychain Access.

9   Log out and back in again.

10 Check the Keychain menu item in the menu bar. Note that the keychain is automatically unlocked because the login password and the keychain password are synchronized.

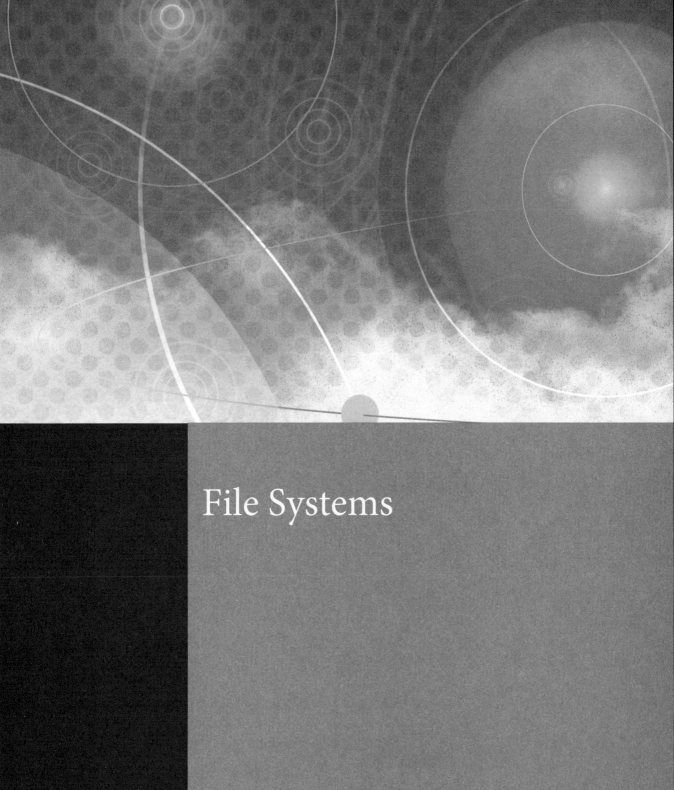

File Systems

Lesson 9
File Systems and Storage

Although personal computer processor speed has increased around a thousandfold since the first Mac was introduced in 1984, storage capacity has easily increased a million times over. Compare 1984's 400 KB floppy to today's average desktop disk at 1 TB, which is roughly equivalent to 1,000,000,000 KB, or 2.5 million 400 KB floppies. Users have responded by moving thousands of pictures and hundreds of hours of music and video, historically stored in analog form, to digital storage. Even though the Internet has recently changed our perception of what a computer is used for, it's clear that the computer's primary role continues to be a tool to organize, access, and store our stuff.

In this lesson, you examine the storage technology used by OS X. Storage hardware, such as flash disks, are covered alongside logical storage concepts like partitions and volumes. Naturally, you will learn how to properly manage and troubleshoot these storage assets as well.

GOALS

▶ Recognize the various file systems supported by OS X

▶ Manage disks, partitions, and volumes

▶ Properly unmount and eject disks and volumes

Reference 9.1
File System Components

Before you begin managing storage in OS X, it is important to understand the distinction between storage, partitions, and volumes. Traditionally, computer storage has been defined by spinning disk hardware. After all these years, spinning disk hardware still maintains the storage lead, though it has changed from removable floppy disks to enclosed hard disks. However, alternative formats have become extremely popular as they have increased in capacity and performance. These formats primarily include internal solid-state disks or flash storage, and removable storage like USB flash disks (also called key or thumb disks) and compact flash cards. All are equally viable storage destinations for OS X.

Storage Concepts

Without proper formatting, though, any storage technology is nothing more than a big empty bucket of ones and zeros, and consequently not very useful to the Mac. Formatting is the process of applying logic to storage in the form of partitions and volumes. Partitions are used to define boundaries on a storage device. You can define multiple partitions if you want the physical storage to appear as multiple separate storage destinations. Even if you want to use the entire space available on a device as a single contiguous storage location, the area must still be defined by a partition.

Once partitions have been established, the system can create usable volumes inside the partition areas. Volumes define how the files and folders are actually stored on the hardware. In fact, it's the volume that you see represented as a usable storage icon in the Finder. Obviously, a storage device with several partitions, each containing a separate volume, appears as several storage location icons in the Finder.

Partition schemes:

- GUID Partition Table (GPT)
- Apple Partition Map (APM)
- Master Boot Record (MBR)

Most common volume formats:

- Mac OS Extended (Journaled)
- Mac OS Extended (Journaled, Encrypted)
- Mac OS Extended
- MS DOS File System (FAT32, ExFAT)
- NT File System (NTFS) *

    * read only

Partition Schemes

As mentioned earlier, disks must be partitioned to define and possibly segregate the disk's usable space. Every disk requires at least one partition, but OS X can support up to 16 partitions per disk. You learned the advantages and disadvantages of using single and multiple partitions in Lesson 1 "Install OS X Yosemite".

OS X supports three types of partition schemes. This may seem excessive, but it's necessary for Mac computers to support multiple partition schemes to start up computers using modern Intel processors, support older Mac disks, and use standard PC-compatible volumes.

The three partition schemes supported by OS X are:

▶ GUID Partition Table (GPT)—This is the default partition scheme used by Intel-based Mac computers. It is also the only partition scheme supported for Intel-based Mac computers to start up using disk-based storage. PowerPC-based Mac computers running OS X v10.4.6 or later can also access this type of partitioning, but they cannot start up from it. Windows Vista or later and Windows Server 2003 SP1 or later also support disks using GPT.

▶ Apple Partition Map (APM)—This is the default partition scheme used by previous PowerPC-based Mac computers. It is also the only partition scheme that PowerPC-based Mac computers can start up from. However, all Intel-based Mac computers can also access this type of partitioning. No version of Windows includes built-in support for disks using APM.

▶ Master Boot Record (MBR)—This is the default partition scheme used by most non-Mac computers, including Windows-compatible PCs. Consequently, this is the default partition scheme you find on most new preformatted storage disks. This partition scheme is also commonly used by peripherals that store to flash memory, such as digital cameras or smartphones. Even though no Mac can start up from this type of partitioning, all Mac computers can fully use MBR partitioned disks.

Obviously, if you have any additional disks formatted with APM or MBR, you have to repartition those disks for them to act as a startup disk for an Intel-based Mac. But if you don't plan on ever using any of these additional disks as a system disk, there is no advantage to repartitioning. Also, you should keep MBR disks unmodified if you want them to be backward-compatible with generic PCs or peripherals.

TIP Intel-based Mac computers can start up from USB, FireWire, and Thunderbolt external disks.

Volume Formats

The volume format defines how the files and folders are saved to the disk. To maintain compatibility with other operating systems and provide advanced features for later Mac computers, OS X supports a variety of storage volume formats.

Volume formats supported as read/write in OS X are:

- ▶ Mac OS Standard—This is the legacy volume format used by the classic Mac OS. This format, though a precursor to Mac OS Extended, is not supported as a startup volume for OS X.

- ▶ Mac OS Extended—This is the legacy volume format designed and supported by Apple for Mac computers. This format is itself an update from the earlier Mac OS Standard format. Mac OS Extended supports all the advanced features required by OS X, including Unicode filenames, rich metadata, POSIX (Portable Operating System Interface) permissions, access control lists, UNIX-style links, and aliases.

- ▶ Mac OS Extended (Case-Sensitive)—This Mac OS Extended format adds case sensitivity to the file system. Normally, Mac OS Extended is case-preserving but case-insensitive, which means that a normally formatted Mac volume remembers what case you chose for the characters of a file's name but cannot differentiate between similar filenames where the only difference is the case. In other words, it would not recognize "MYfile" and "myfile" as different filenames. By adding support for case sensitivity, Apple resolved this issue. However, case sensitivity is generally an issue only for volumes that need to support traditional UNIX clients, like those shared from Mac computers running OS X Server. Further, many third-party applications exhibit significant issues when running from a case-sensitive file system. Thus, the case-sensitive option is not supported as a default for OS X client systems.

- ▶ Mac OS Extended (Journaled) or Mac OS Extended (Case-Sensitive, Journaled)—This feature is an option for the Mac OS Extended format that adds advanced file-system journaling to help preserve volume structure integrity. The journal records what file operations (creation, expansion, deletion, and so on) are in progress at any given moment. If the system crashes or loses power, the journal can be "replayed" to make sure operations that were previously in process are completed, rather than left in a half-completed, inconsistent state. This helps avoid the possibility of file corruption and greatly reduces the amount of time it takes to complete the check-and-repair process on the volume after a crash. Because of these enhancements, the required format for an OS X system volume is Mac OS Extended (Journaled).

  NOTE ▶ While journaling protects the file structure, it cannot protect the contents of files themselves against corruption. If a large file was half-written when the system crashed, the journal makes sure that half-file is consistently entered in the volume's file-tracking databases, but it's still only half a file.

- ▶ Mac OS Extended (Journaled, Encrypted) or Mac OS Extended (Case-Sensitive, Journaled, Encrypted)—This feature is an option to the Mac OS Extended format that adds full disk, XTS-AES 128 encryption. This is the technology behind FileVault system volume encryption. Lesson 10 "FileVault", covers this topic in greater detail.

NOTE ▶ Encrypted Mac OS Extended volumes are not compatible with versions of OS X prior to OS X Lion.

NOTE ▶ No version of Windows includes built-in support for any form of Mac OS volume formats. Thus, if you require a disk that's compatible across both of these common platforms, you should choose a volume format supported by Windows.

▶ File Allocation Table (FAT)—FAT is the legacy volume format used by Windows PCs and by many peripherals. This format has evolved over the years, with each progressive version supporting larger volumes: FAT12, FAT16, FAT32. Apple Boot Camp supports running Windows XP from a FAT32 volume, but OS X itself cannot start up from such a volume.

▶ Extended File Allocation Table (ExFAT)—Created specifically for large flash storage disks, ExFAT basically extends the legacy FAT architecture to support disks larger than 32 GB. Many flash-based digital camcorders use ExFAT to support the large storage volumes required for high-definition video. OS X v10.6.5 and later includes full support for ExFAT volumes. Updated versions of Windows XP and Windows Server 2003 and later also support ExFAT formatted volumes.

▶ UNIX File System (UFS)—UFS is the legacy native volume format supported by UNIX systems. UFS served as the default UNIX file system for decades. Beginning with OS X v10.5, though, UFS volumes are no longer supported as startup volumes. Further, Disk Utility does not support the creation of UFS volumes.

Volume formats supported as read-only in OS X are:

▶ New Technology File System (NTFS)—Windows 7, Windows Vista, Windows XP, and Windows Server all use this as their default native volume format. Once again, Boot Camp supports running Windows from an NTFS volume, but OS X itself cannot write to or start up from such a volume. Further, Disk Utility does not support the creation of NTFS volumes.

TIP▶ You can add NTFS volume write support to OS X by installing the free, open source NTFS-3G + Ntfsprogs software, available at www.tuxera.com/community/ntfs-3g-download/.

▶   ISO 9660 or Compact Disc File System (CDFS)—This is a common standard for read-only CD media. Note, however, that "Mac formatted" CD media can also contain Mac OS Standard formatted volumes.

▶   Universal Disk Format (UDF)—This is a common standard for read-only DVD media. Again, note that "Mac formatted" DVD media can also contain Mac OS Standard volumes.

> **MORE INFO** ▶ Wikipedia has a great comparison of the wide variety of file systems: http://en.wikipedia.org/wiki/Comparison_of_file_systems.

Core Storage

OS X also features an advanced file system management technology known as Core Storage. This technology is an additional management layer between the traditional partition scheme and volume formats of a disk. Although this adds complexity to the file system, it also adds significant flexibility. For example, Core Storage allows OS X to encrypt (or decrypt) a volume without interrupting use of the volume, as used by FileVault system volume encryption. Core Storage also allows for more complex arrangements of multiple disks, as used by Fusion Drive. Further, Core Storage offers increased file system crash protection and more reliable methods for storing file system metadata and catalog data.

In previous versions of OS X, Core Storage was enabled only if the system used either FileVault system volume encryption or Fusion Drive. With OS X Yosemite, Core Storage is enabled by default for late-model Mac portable computers even if they aren't using FileVault or a Fusion Drive. Specifically, during an upgrade to OS X Yosemite, the installer will automatically enable Core Storage on any Mac portable that supports accelerated disk encryption. Further, on these systems, the Setup Assistant will encourage the user to enable FileVault, as covered in Lesson 2 "Setup and Configuration".

> **MORE INFO** ▶ You can find out if your Mac computer's system disk is managed by Core Storage by inspecting the disk using either Disk Utility or System Information, as detailed in "Reference 12.1 File System Inspection" on page 341.

The following graphic represents a typical OS X Yosemite system disk. As you can see, the disk uses GPT to define two partitions. The first partition, occupying the majority of the disk, contains the system volume. This partition is managed by Core Storage and is formatted as either a Mac OS Extended (Journaled) volume or a Mac OS Extended (Journaled, Encrypted) volume if FileVault system volume encryption is enabled.

The second partition, occupying the final ~650 MB of the disk, is an "Apple_Boot" formatted volume that contains the Recovery HD system. Aside from providing OS X Recovery functionality, this second partition is intentionally not managed by Core Storage, as it provides the software necessary for a Mac computer's (relatively simple) firmware to understand Core Storage volumes. Thus, the initial startup of OS X is facilitated by the Recovery HD volume.

Partitioning:

- GUID Partition Table (GPT)
- Core Storage Logical Volume

"Macintosh HD" Volume:

- Mac OS Extended (Journaled)
- Mac OS Extended (Journaled, Encrypted)

"Recovery HD" Volume:

- Hidden Apple_Boot Volume
- ~650 MB

Fusion Drive

Mac computers featuring Fusion Drive break from the traditional disk, partition, and volume paradigm. Courtesy of Core Storage, a Mac with Fusion Drive uses two separate physical disks to form one logical storage device. This provides a hybrid storage solution that has both the speed of flash storage and the size of traditional spinning disk media.

The following graphic represents a typical OS X Yosemite system disk on a Mac with Fusion Drive. As you can see, each separate physical disk uses GPT to define two partitions. The first partitions of each disk, occupying the majority of each disk, contain the combined system volume. These two partitions, again from two separate disks, are managed by Core Storage, which has the ability to merge the two separate physical volumes into a single logical volume. The resulting combined volume is formatted as either a Mac OS Extended (Journaled) volume or a Mac OS Extended (Journaled, Encrypted) volume if FileVault system volume encryption is enabled.

The second partition on each disk is intentionally not managed by Core Storage, as it provides the software necessary for the Mac computer's (relatively simple) firmware to understand Core Storage volumes. In the case of Fusion Drive, the smaller flash storage disk contains an ~185 MB "Boot OS X" volume, while the larger spinning disk contains the ~650 MB Recovery HD system. As you can tell from the name, the Boot OS X volume is used to facilitate the initial OS X system startup.

Physical Disks:
- Smaller Flash Storage
- Larger Spinning Disk

Partitioning:
- GUID Partition Table (GPT)
- Core Storage Logical Volume

"Macintosh HD" Volume

"Boot OS X" Volume

"Recovery HD" Volume

MORE INFO ▶ Find out more about Fusion Drive from Apple Support article HT202574, "Mac mini (Late 2012 and later), iMac (Late 2012 and later): About Fusion Drive."

Reference 9.2
Managing File Systems

The internal storage originally included with your Mac is probably the only new storage device you will ever come across that is already properly formatted for full Mac compatibility. Most new storage devices are either completely blank or formatted for Windows. For the most part, you can use Windows-formatted disks on the Mac without reformatting. However, if you want to install the Mac operating system on a disk, or you have a new disk that is completely blank, you have to format the disk.

The primary storage management tool included in OS X is /Applications/Utilities/Disk Utility. You may have already used this utility from OS X Recovery to reformat the system disk before you installed the operating system. Here, you are going to explore all the aspects of this tool for managing disks.

TIP In the Finder, you can rename any volume without having to reformat or erase its content. Simply edit the volume name as you would any other item in the Finder or, from the Finder sidebar, use secondary (or Control-) click to rename it. Curiously, you cannot rename a volume from Disk Utility without reformatting or erasing.

Formatting or Reformatting a Disk

Despite all the choices OS X gives you for configuring storage, actually formatting a disk is quite easy. If you attach an unformatted device, the Mac automatically prompts you to open Disk Utility. On the other hand, if you have an already-formatted disk and you want to change the partition scheme or the volume structure, you can just as easily reformat the disk using the same steps.

Remember that reformatting (or initializing) a disk destroys any existing formatting; a reformatted disk is effectively losing its contents. The disk is not technically erased by default—all the bits are still stored on the device. Reformatting simply replaces the previously populated partition and volume structure with new partitioning and empty volume structures. Truly erasing the contents of a disk is covered in "Securely Erasing Files" on page 258.

Opening Disk Utility reveals a list of connected storage devices and volumes. Storage devices are typically identified by the size, manufacturer, and model number of the device. The exceptions to this are disks managed by Core Storage, like Mac computers with Fusion Drive and system volumes protected by FileVault.

In Disk Utility, the default label for a Fusion Drive is simply "Internal Drive," whereas disks containing an encrypted volume are often labeled with the same name as the encrypted volume. For example, the following screenshot of Disk Utility shows a Mac with File-Vault encryption enabled for the system volume named Macintosh HD. This computer also has an unformatted external USB disk attached, showing the device information.

Select the storage device you want to format, and then click the Partition tab. To reformat a disk, you must select the Partition Layout pop-up menu and define the number of desired partitions. Once you have selected the number of partitions, you can define the remaining parameters for the storage device, including partition scheme, volume formats, and names.

> **NOTE** ▶ You cannot select any disk encryption options from the Disk Utility Partition interface. You can, however, select encryption options from the Erase interface, as covered in "Erasing a Disk or Volume" on page 256.

> **NOTE** ▶ You can change the partition scheme of a disk by clicking the Options button below the Partition Layout view. If the Options button is unavailable, simply pick a new partition layout from the pop-up menu to indicate your intent to reformat the disk.

Repartitioning a Disk

Disk Utility also allows you to dynamically repartition a disk without destroying any data currently stored on the disk. This functionality was introduced in OS X v10.5, primarily to facilitate the Boot Camp setup process. OS X upgrade installations also use this functionality to create the hidden OS X Recovery HD on an existing system disk.

The only downside to dynamic repartitioning is that some disks may not support the partition changes you want to make. For instance, some disks may be too full for you to repartition. Also, Disk Utility is less flexible in its ability to modify disks containing encrypted volumes or Fusion Drive disks, and does not support dynamically repartitioning disks formatted with the Master Boot Record partition scheme. If you come across any of these issues, you will have to resort to using the previous method for repartitioning a disk, which does erase any previous formatting and data.

NOTE ▸ Always back up important data before making changes to a disk's file system.

NOTE ▸ Modifying an OS X system disk often requires relocating the hidden OS X Recovery HD. Fortunately, Disk Utility in OS X handles this automatically for you.

NOTE ▸ Using Disk Utility to add a partition to a Fusion Drive disk only adds the partition to the larger spinning disk. Thus, additional partitions are not able to take advantage of the flash storage performance increase normally seen with Fusion Drive. For more information, see Apple Support article HT202574, "Mac mini (Late 2012 and later), iMac (Late 2012 and later): About Fusion Drive."

Again, opening Disk Utility reveals a list of connected storage devices and volumes. Storage devices are identified by the size, manufacturer, and model number of the device. Select the storage device you want to format, and then click the Partition tab. Any data currently on the disk appears as a light blue area in the partition layout diagram. White areas indicate free space.

The partition layout area in Disk Utility allows you to:

▶ Resize a volume—Click and drag from the lower-right corner until you reach the desired new size. You cannot shrink a volume past the light blue area that represents data on the disk. You may choose to leave parts of the disk empty if you plan on formatting those parts later using another operating system.

▶ Add a new volume—Click the Add (+) button below the partition diagram. Remember, you can have as many as 16 partitions per disk, each containing a unique volume. Be sure to choose an appropriate name and volume format from the pop-up menu for each new volume.

▶ Delete a volume—Select it from the partition diagram, and click the Delete (–) button below the partition diagram. If you are deleting an existing partition, you're presented with a verification dialog. If you are certain you want to delete the selected partition, click Remove to finish the process. The volume is deleted immediately, leaving free space you can use to resize other volumes or create new volumes.

Erasing a Disk or Volume

You have seen earlier in this lesson how Disk Utility can be used to quickly erase an entire disk or volume by reformatting it. Yet the default reformatting process does not actually erase any files from the disk; Disk Utility simply creates new blank volumes by simply replacing the file and folder structure data of any volume. The old data files still remain on the disk and can be recovered using third-party recovery tools.

In fact, there is no such thing as erasing data from a disk—all you can do is write new data on top of the old data. Therefore, if you want to truly "erase" a disk or volume, you must somehow write new nonsensitive data on top of it. Disk Utility includes a variety of options for securely erasing old data. You can securely erase an entire disk or volume, or just a volume's remaining free space.

Again, opening Disk Utility reveals a list of connected storage devices and volumes. Storage devices are identified by the size, manufacturer, and model number of the device. Volume names vary, but they always appear indented below the storage device. Select the storage device or volume you want to erase, and then click the Erase tab.

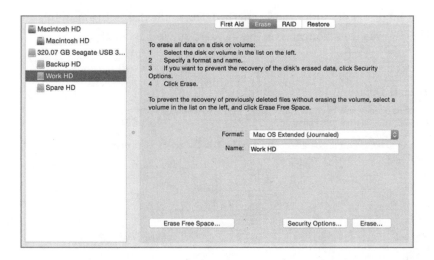

NOTE ▶ When you erase an entire disk, the Disk Utility application automatically creates a new partition scheme as well. Disk Utility chooses the most appropriate partition scheme based on the volume format you've selected. To select a different partition scheme, you must repartition the disk, as detailed earlier in this lesson.

To quickly erase the selected item, simply click the Erase button. You also have the option of selecting a different volume format or name for the erased volume. If you require a secure erase, click Security Options to display a dialog with four options along a slider:

▶ Fastest: Don't Erase Data—This is the default action that occurs when you erase or reformat a disk or volume. Obviously, this does not provide any security from disk-recovery utilities. On the other hand, this choice provides a nearly instantaneous erase option.

▶ Second Choice: Single-Pass Erase—This option writes zeros over all the data once. This is the quickest of the secure erase options, and for most users provides an adequate level of security.

▶ Third Choice: 3-Pass Erase—This is a very secure option that writes two passes of random data followed by a single pass of known data to the disk. According to Apple, this option meets U.S. Department of Energy standards for securely erasing data. The downside is that this method takes three times longer than the standard single-pass method.

▶ Most Secure: 7-Pass Erase—This is the most secure option, which according to Apple meets U.S. Department of Defense standards for securely erasing data. The Mac writes seven different passes of random and patterned data to the disk. Obviously, this method takes seven times longer than the standard single-pass method.

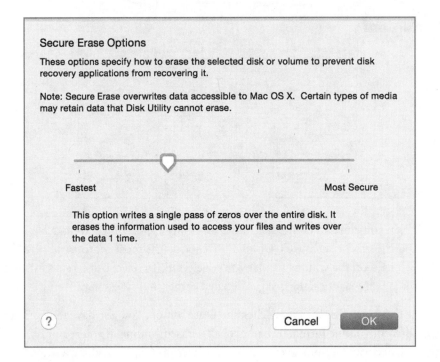

NOTE ▶ When erasing solid-state or flash disks, no more than a three-pass erase is recommended. In fact, multipass erasing of this type of media can lead to degraded disk performance over time.

NOTE ▶ Depending on the size of the selected disk or volume and the secure erase option you chose, this process can take anywhere from seconds to days.

NOTE ▶ If you have selected an encrypted volume type, a dialog appears, allowing you to set the encrypted volume's password. Note that, as the dialog states, you are not able to recover data from the encrypted volume if you lose the password. Choose the password wisely.

Securely Erasing Files

Again, the default OS X behavior simply marks deleted files as free space, leaving the files intact until written on top of by another action. Unfortunately, securely erasing an entire disk or volume can take quite a bit of time. As an alternative, you may find it's much quicker to use a more subtle secure erase method. Also, you may not want to erase the entire contents of a volume or disk—you may just want to securely erase a few specific files or only the free space on your disk. Fortunately, OS X provides targeted secure erase options from the Finder and Disk Utility.

> **NOTE ▶** Studies show that, due to the complex nature of solid-state and flash disk controllers, attempting to securely erase individual files on these types of disks is generally not sufficient. If security is truly a concern, a better solution would be to store your data on encrypted volumes.

> **NOTE ▶** The data stored on an encrypted volume is always scrambled to those who don't have authorization to access its contents. Thus, securely erasing individual files on an encrypted volume is a waste of time.

Finder Secure Erase

From the Finder, you can securely erase any item in the Trash by choosing Finder > Secure Empty Trash. The Secure Empty Trash feature in the Finder is a secure erase method that writes seven different passes of random and patterned data on top of the erased files. According to Apple, this feature even meets U.S. Department of Defense standards for securely erasing data. Depending on the number and size of the files to be erased, this process can take anywhere from seconds to days. The Finder shows you a progress indicator, but not estimated time.

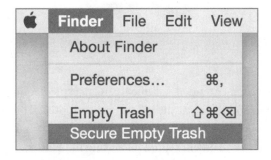

Disk Utility Secure Erase

If past users have neglected to securely erase trash items, you can ensure these items are fully erased by securely erasing a volume's free space. In Disk Utility, from the column on the left, select the volume with the free space you want to securely erase. Be sure not to select the storage device, only a volume of the disk. Next, click the Erase tab, and then click Erase Free Space.

The dialog that appears presents three available secure erase options, similar to those for erasing an entire volume or disk: Fastest is a single-pass erase, the second choice is a three-pass erase, and Most Secure is a seven-pass erase. Again, depending on the amount of free space to erase and the erase option you choose, this process can take anywhere from seconds to days.

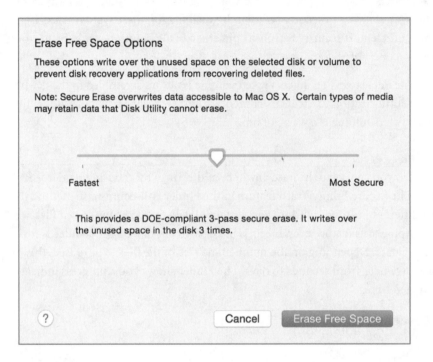

Encrypting a Disk

Disk Utility cannot convert an existing Mac OS Extended volume to an encrypted volume. Instead, as covered earlier, it can only erase and reformat the volume as encrypted. This is obviously inconvenient if you want to encrypt the contents of an existing disk. Fortunately, in OS X you can easily convert an existing disk to an encrypted disk using the Finder.

> **NOTE** ▶ Encrypted Mac OS Extended volumes are not compatible with versions of OS X prior to OS X Lion.

> **NOTE** ▶ To encrypt the system volume, you need to enable FileVault. Lesson 10 "File-Vault", covers this topic in greater detail.

NOTE ▶ Due to the complex nature of solid-state and flash disk controllers, encrypting a disk may still leave some parts of the original data in a recoverable form. To minimize the security risk, it's ideal to encrypt a disk before saving any sensitive data to it.

NOTE ▶ The Finder can convert volumes only on disks formatted with the GPT partition scheme. Attempting to encrypt a volume on a disk with another partition scheme results in either the "Encrypt disk" menu option not appearing or an error message appearing. If this is the case, you have to resort to erasing and reformatting the disk with Disk Utility.

To encrypt a disk in the Finder, use secondary (or Control-) click to select the disk you want to encrypt, and from the shortcut menu choose Encrypt <diskname>, where <diskname> is the name of the disk you've selected.

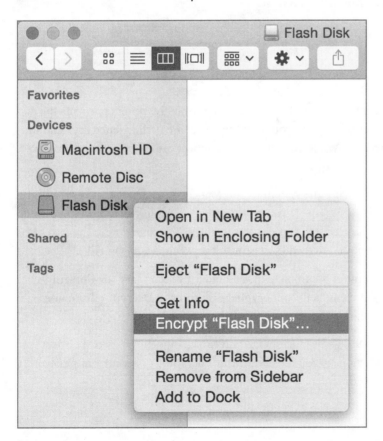

The Finder prompts you to set a password and a password hint for the encrypted disk. You must set a password hint, as it's the only thing that will help you recover a lost password.

Should you lose the password, there is no way to recover the disk's data. Once you enter these items and then click Encrypt Disk, you may notice the disk quickly disappears, and then after a few seconds it reappears in the Finder as the system begins encrypting the contents of the disk.

Amazingly, you can continue to use the disk as usual while the system encrypts the disk's contents in the background, though you might notice some performance degradation. From this point forward, anytime you attempt to connect the encrypted disk, you are prompted for the disk's password.

> **TIP** ▶ You can configure the system to automatically authenticate an encrypted disk by using the keychain system. This can be configured when you're prompted for the disk's password by selecting the option to remember the password in the user's keychain. Using keychain is covered in Lesson 8 "Keychain Management".

You can see if the encryption is complete in the Finder by secondary (or Control-) clicking the disk. In the shortcut menu, a fully encrypted disk shows a Decrypt <diskname> option, where <diskname> is the name of the disk you've selected.

> **TIP** ▶ From the Disk Utility File menu, you can change the password or decrypt an encrypted disk. Obviously, you must know the encrypted disk's current password to perform these operations.

Reference 9.3
Mounting, Unmounting, and Ejecting

Mounting a volume is the process by which the system establishes a logical connection to a storage volume. This is not something users normally concern themselves with on the Mac, because the system automatically mounts any volume connected to the Mac. Simply plug a disk in, and the disk's volumes automatically appear in the Finder and Disk Utility. The only exception to this rule is for Mac OS Extended (Journaled, Encrypted) volumes, which require that you enter a password to unlock the disk's contents.

On the other hand, ensuring that users properly unmount and eject volumes is very important to maintaining data integrity. Unmounting is the process of having the Mac cleanly disconnect from a disk's volumes, whereas ejecting is the process of having the Mac additionally disconnect electronically from the actual hardware disk or media. When you choose to eject a disk from the Finder, the computer actually unmounts the volumes first and then ejects the disk.

Ejecting Disks

There are three ways to unmount and eject a disk from the Finder:

▶ In the Finder, drag the disk icon to the Trash icon in the Dock. You'll note the Trash icon changes to an Eject icon, indicating the appropriate action.

▶ In the Finder sidebar, select the volume you want to unmount and eject, and then choose File > Eject.

▶ In the Finder sidebar, click the small Eject button next to the volume you want to unmount and eject.

NOTE ▶ Pressing and holding the Eject key (the farthest top-right key on some Mac keyboards) for a few moments unmounts and ejects only optical media, like CDs or DVDs. If you have more than one optical disc drive, press Option-Eject to eject the second optical disc.

When you use the Finder to unmount and eject a single volume that is part of a disk with several mounted volumes, you see a warning dialog giving you the choice to unmount and eject all the volumes on the disk or just the one you originally selected. You shouldn't experience any problems with a disk if some volumes are mounted while others remain unmounted. Just remember to properly unmount the remaining volumes before you physically disconnect the disk.

TIP ▶ In the Finder, you can eject all the volumes of a disk without additional confirmation by holding down the Option key while you click the Eject button.

Disk Utility Mount Management

If you're using the Finder, remounting volumes on a connected disk is a bit of a hassle. You must first unmount and eject any remaining volumes, and then physically disconnect and reconnect the disk. Alternatively, you can use Disk Utility to manually mount, unmount, and eject items without physically disconnecting and reconnecting the disk.

In the following screenshot of Disk Utility, a variety of volumes are shown. Notice that the volume names from the second disk appear in dimmed text; those volumes are physically connected to the Mac but are not mounted.

In Disk Utility, select the disk or volume you want to manage. To mount an unmounted volume on a connected disk, click the volume's dimmed name, and then click the Mount button in the toolbar. The volume immediately mounts and appears in the Finder and as normal text in Disk Utility.

If you select an unmounted Mac OS Extended (Journaled, Encrypted) volume, the Mount button is replaced by an Unlock button. Clicking the Unlock button opens a dialog where you enter a password to unlock the disk's contents. Once authenticated, the volume immediately mounts.

If you have selected a volume to unmount, simply click the Unmount button in the tool-bar. If you have selected an entire disk, to unmount all its volumes and eject it, click the Eject button in the toolbar. All the disk's volumes unmount, and then the disk disconnects from the system, disappearing from the Finder and from Disk Utility. In this case, you have to physically disconnect and reconnect the disk for its volumes to be remounted.

Ejecting In-Use Volumes

Any volume that contains files currently in use by an application or system process cannot be unmounted or ejected. The obvious reason for this is to avoid data corruption when a process attempts to write to files on that volume. If you try to eject a volume with in-use files, the Finder does not allow you to do so, but, depending on the situation, it may try to help you eject the volume. If the application or process using the volume belongs to your account, the Finder lets you know via the following dialog. In this case, the resolution is as simple as quitting the suspect application and attempting to eject the volume again.

NOTE ▶ As the screenshot shows, using Terminal can prevent you from ejecting a vol-ume. Even if no process is active, just having Terminal open, with the volume as the current working directory, prevents unmounting.

If you don't own the application or process using the volume, the Finder asks if you want to attempt to forcibly eject the volume. To do that, you have to click the Force Eject button twice; the Finder then tries to quit the offending application or process to release the vol-ume you're attempting to eject. If the volume is successfully ejected, you are notified by the dialog.

If this doesn't work or the Finder doesn't tell you which application is the problem, you can always log out the current user to quit all of his or her processes and then log in again, or fully restart the Mac to clear the issue. While this may seem excessive, it is not advisable to physically disconnect a volume without first unmounting it, as covered in the next section.

Improperly Unmounting or Ejecting

Disconnecting a volume from a Mac that you did not first unmount can lead to data corruption. If you forcibly eject a disk by physically disconnecting it before you unmount it, or if the system loses contact with the disk due to power failure, the Mac warns you with a device removal dialog. You should immediately reconnect the device so the Mac can attempt to verify or repair its contents.

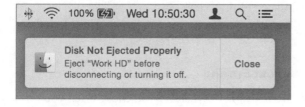

Anytime you reconnect a disk that was improperly unmounted, the Mac automatically runs a file system diagnostic on the disk before it remounts any volumes. Depending on the format and size of the disk, it may take anywhere from a few seconds to several hours for the system to verify the contents of the disk. Again, journaled volumes, like Mac OS Extended (Journaled), verify quite quickly.

If you connect a disk and notice a fair amount of disk activity, but the volumes have not mounted yet, the system is probably running a diagnostic on the disk. You can verify that the system is diagnosing a volume by opening the /Applications/Utilities/Activity Monitor application and looking for a background process with "fsck" in its name. Monitoring processes is covered in Lesson 19 "Application Management and Troubleshooting".

Exercise 9.1
Repartition a Disk Dynamically

▶ **Prerequisites**

- ▶ You must have created the Local Admin account ("Exercise 2.1 Configure a New OS X System for Exercises" on page 60 or "Exercise 2.2 Configure an Existing OS X System for Exercises" on page 63).

- ▶ Your startup volume must be less than half full.

In early versions of OS X, using Disk Utility to partition a disk meant erasing the disk first. Since Mac OS X v10.5, Disk Utility has been able to live-partition GPT-formatted disks without destroying the data.

In this exercise, you will partition your computer's internal disk. If you do not want to repartition your internal disk, you can skip this exercise; however, if you choose to skip this exercise, you will need an external disk to use as a Time Machine backup volume in Lesson 16 "Time Machine". You can also partition your disk now and then remove the additional partition after you have finished testing Time Machine.

As always, backing up your data before partitioning is a good idea.

Repartition Your Startup Disk Without Erasing

1 Log in as Local Admin (password: ladminpw, or whatever you chose when you created the account).

2 If any applications other than Disk Utility are running, quit them.

3 Open Disk Utility from the Utilities folder.

   Do not use any other applications while Disk Utility is working to repartition the disk.

4 In Disk Utility, select the upper (unindented) entry for your startup volume. Depending on whether your startup volume is being managed by Core Storage, this will either represent the Core Storage "logical volume group" that the volume is in or represent the physical disk device that the volume is on.

NOTE ▶ Depending on whether your startup disk is being managed by Core Storage, you will see slightly different options. The following screenshots show the Core Storage version, but the steps are the same in either case.

5   Click the Partition tab.

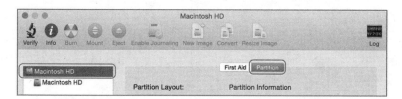

6   If necessary, select your startup volume in the graphical depiction of the partition layout.

7   Click the Add (+) button below the partition layout.

    The disk's layout appears divided into two equally sized partitions.

8   Select the second partition, and change its name to Backup.

9   Click Apply.

Disk Utility opens a dialog asking you to confirm partitioning the disk. Note that the dialog indicates that no partitions will be erased.

10 Click Partition.

Disk Utility partitions the disk, which can take a few minutes. Disk Utility has to move any data that resides in the space allocated to the second partition. It also verifies the file system before beginning its work.

11 Wait for Disk Utility to finish repartitioning before going on to the next exercise.

Exercise 9.2
Erase and Partition a Disk

▶ **Prerequisites**

- ▶ You must have created the Local Admin account ("Exercise 2.1 Configure a New OS X System for Exercises" on page 60 or "Exercise 2.2 Configure an Existing OS X System for Exercises" on page 63).

- ▶ This exercise is best performed with an erasable external disk, such as a flash drive.

In this exercise, you will use Disk Utility to erase and partition a disk using a new partition scheme. The exercise is written to use an external disk, such as a USB flash drive, but if no erasable external disk is available, it can be performed on a disk image in the StudentMaterials folder.

Use Disk Utility to Create a New Partition Scheme

Most external storage systems (USB flash drives, USB and FireWire hard disks, and so on) come preformatted, most of those for Windows. Many of them are partitioned using Master Boot Record (MBR). To start up your computer from one of these devices, you need to erase all existing partitions in order to switch to the GUID partition table (GPT) scheme.

1　If necessary, log in as Local Admin (password: ladminpw, or whatever you chose when you created the account).

2　Plug in the external disk you're using for this exercise. If you do not have an external disk that can be erased for this exercise, open the disk image StudentMaterials/ Lesson9/Partitionable_Image.dmg. Remember that you have a shortcut to the StudentMaterials folder in your Dock.

　　Note that the screenshots in this exercise were taken using an external disk; if you are using the disk image, things will look slightly different.

　　WARNING ▶ This exercise erases all information on the external disk. Do not perform this exercise with a disk that contains any files you want to keep.

3　If necessary, open Disk Utility from the Utilities folder.

4　In the source list, select the external disk device (or Partitionable_Image.dmg). Be sure to select the device, not the volume or volumes it contains.

5　Click Partition, and view the partitioning options available.

　　If the Partition tab is not shown, make sure you have the disk device selected, not the volume and volumes it contains.

　　Note that the Partition Layout field displays a diagram of the disk's current partitions, and at the bottom of the Disk Utility window, the disk's current partition map scheme is listed. Both of these depend on what this disk has been used for in the past.

6　Choose "2 Partitions" from the Partition Layout pop-up menu.

　　If all the controls in the Partition pane are disabled, you may not be logged in as Local Admin. In this case, eject the disk (or Partitionable_Image.dmg), and then log out and return to step 1.

This option gives you two equally sized partitions.

7   Click Options to choose a partition scheme.

8   If it is not already selected, select GUID Partition Table, and then click OK. This is generally the best partition scheme for disks that will be used only in OS X.

9   Select the first partition, and then choose Mac OS Extended (Journaled) from the Format pop-up menu.

10   In the Name field, change the partition's name to Partition 1.

Note that if you try to change the name first, you may not be able to use lowercase letters. This is because lowercase volume names are not supported by some volume formats.

11   Repeat for the second partition, choosing Mac OS Extended (Journaled) from the Format menu and renaming the partition Partition 2.

12 When you have finished, click Apply.

A confirmation dialog appears.

Note that the dialog may differ from the screenshot shown here.

13 Click Partition to confirm that you want to destructively repartition this disk image.

Disk Utility unmounts the disk volume (or volumes), repartitions it as two volumes using GPT, formats those volumes, and mounts those volumes.

You may now proceed to any of the other exercises in this lesson and use the same disk to explore other features of OS X (although note that you cannot perform "Exercise 9.4 Encrypt a Volume" on page 278 if you are using a disk image). If you are not going to perform any further exercises in this lesson, eject the disk (or image), and quit Disk Utility.

Exercise 9.3
Examine Disk Ejection

▶ **Prerequisites**

▶ You must have created the Local Admin account ("Exercise 2.1 Configure a New OS X System for Exercises" on page 60 or "Exercise 2.2 Configure an Existing OS X System for Exercises" on page 63).

▶ You must have just performed "Exercise 9.2 Erase and Partition a Disk" on page 270.

In this exercise, you will investigate disk ejection, including options for forcing the ejection of disks that are in use. You will use the same disk (or disk image) that you erased and partitioned in the previous exercise.

Create a Text Document

To support this exercise, you need to create a document on the disk.

1   If necessary, log in as Local Admin, and mount the disk (or disk image) you partitioned in "Exercise 9.2 Erase and Partition a Disk" on page 270.

2   Open TextEdit. Remember that you have a shortcut to TextEdit in your Dock.

    TextEdit opens a new Untitled document.

3   Type some text into the TextEdit document.

4   Choose Format > Make Plain Text.

5   Choose File > Save (Command-S).

6   Name the document Example document, and choose Partition 1 from the Where pop-up menu (or from the sidebar if you have expanded the Save dialog).

7 Click Save.

8 Quit TextEdit.

9 Open the Partition 1 volume in the Finder.

10 Control-click the Example document, and choose Open With > Console from the shortcut menu.

The Example document opens in the Console utility. Console is primarily used for viewing system logs, but it can also display the contents of plain-text documents. In this exercise, you are using it because it keeps the file continuously open to monitor it for changes (such as new log entries).

Leave the document open in Console for use in the next section.

Eject Volumes as Local Admin

1 If necessary, open Disk Utility. Since you used Disk Utility in the previous exercise, you can open it from the Apple menu's Recent Items submenu.

2   In Disk Utility, select Partition 1 in the sidebar.

Note that the Disk Utility toolbar has separate buttons for Unmount (which unmounts only this partition, not the entire disk) and Eject (which ejects the entire disk).

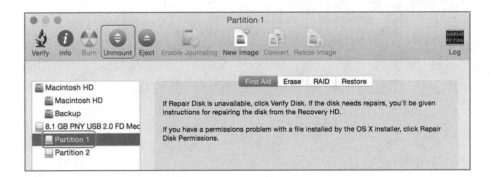

3   Click the Unmount button.

Since Console is using a file on the Partition 1 volume, the unmount operation fails.

4   Click OK.

5   Drag the Partition 1 icon from the desktop to the Trash. The Trash icon turns into an eject symbol.

6   If a dialog asks whether you want to eject one or both partitions, click Eject All.

Partition 2 is ejected successfully, but again Partition 1 cannot be ejected. The Finder identifies that Console is the app using Partition 1.

7   Click OK.

Eject Volumes as Chris Johnson

1   Use fast user switching to switch to Chris Johnson (using the password for the linked iCloud account or whatever you chose when you created the account).

2   Drag the Partition 1 icon from the desktop to the Trash.

3   If you are prompted to, authenticate as Local Admin.

Since the volume is in use by another user, the Finder does not display what app is using it. Instead, it gives you the options to try again or to force-eject the volume.

4   Click Force Eject.

5   In the confirmation dialog that appears, click Force Eject.

6   If you are prompted to authenticate again, authenticate as Local Admin.

This time, the disk ejects successfully.

7   If necessary, click OK to dismiss the success dialog.

8   If you are using an external disk (not a disk image), unplug it from your computer.

9   Log out as Chris Johnson.

10   Log back in as Local Admin.

11   Quit Console.

You may now proceed to "Exercise 9.4 Encrypt a Volume" on page 278 or "Exercise 9.5 Securely Erase Disk Data" on page 282 and use the same disk to explore other features of OS X (although note that you cannot perform "Exercise 9.4 Encrypt a Volume" on page 278 if you are using a disk image). If you are not going to perform any further exercises in this lesson, eject the disk (or image), and quit Disk Utility.

Exercise 9.4
Encrypt a Volume

▶ **Prerequisites**

▶ You must have created the Local Admin account ("Exercise 2.1 Configure a New OS X System for Exercises" on page 60 or "Exercise 2.2 Configure an Existing OS X System for Exercises" on page 63).

▶ This exercise requires that you have just performed "Exercise 9.2 Erase and Partition a Disk" on page 270 (and optionally "Exercise 9.3 Examine Disk Ejection" on page 274) using an external disk (not a disk image).

The Finder in OS X has an option to encrypt an existing volume, preserving all existing files. In this exercise, you will test this feature using the same disk you used for "Exercise 9.2 Erase and Partition a Disk" on page 270.

Note that if you performed "Exercise 9.2 Erase and Partition a Disk" on page 270 with a disk image, you will not be able to use it for this exercise; disk images can be encrypted, but they use a different encryption mechanism.

Encrypt a Volume in the Finder

1   If necessary, log in as Local Admin.

2   If necessary, plug the disk you used for "Exercise 9.2 Erase and Partition a Disk" on page 270 back into your computer.

3   Click the desktop to bring the Finder to the foreground.

4   In the Finder, Control-click the Partition 1 volume, and choose Encrypt "Partition 1" from the shortcut menu.

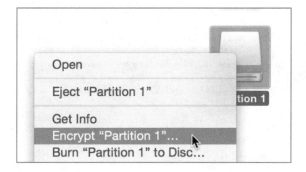

5   In the dialog that appears, enter encryptPW in the "Encryption password" and "Verify password" fields, and enter an appropriate hint.

6   Click Encrypt Disk.

After a delay, the Partition 1 icon vanishes from your desktop and then reappears.

7   Switch to Disk Utility, and note that your disk's entry in the sidebar has changed. There is now a main entry named Partition 1, with Partition 1 and Partition 2 listed as the volumes under it.

8   Select the main (upper) Partition 1 entry.

The information at the bottom of the window now lists this as a logical volume group. To support encryption, the disk has been converted to Core Storage format.

9   Select the Partition 1 volume (lower) entry.

Its format is listed as an encrypted logical partition. The volume is actually being encrypted in the background, so the data it contains is not completely secure until the encryption is complete.

10 Click the Disk Utility File menu, and look at the options available.

The menu contains options to change the volume's encryption password or turn off encryption.

11 Quit Disk Utility.

You do not need to wait for the encryption process to finish before proceeding. You can even eject the disk before it has finished encrypting, although its contents will not be fully secure yet.

> **NOTE ▶** Disk Utility cannot erase disks that contain encrypted volumes. If you want to erase or repartition the disk, you must first either erase the encrypted volume in Disk Utility or decrypt it in the Finder.

Exercise 9.5
Securely Erase Disk Data

▶ **Prerequisite**

> ▶ You must have created the Local Admin account ("Exercise 2.1 Configure a New OS X System for Exercises" on page 60 or "Exercise 2.2 Configure an Existing OS X System for Exercises" on page 63).

The Finder has an option to securely empty the Trash to make sure the data from deleted files is not left on a disk. However, if a file is deleted insecurely, it may be necessary to overwrite all free space on the volume to make sure none of the file's data remains. In this exercise, you will explore the Disk Utility options to erase either just the free space on a volume or an entire volume.

Since secure erasure on a real disk can take a long time, you will test secure erasure on a disk image instead. You could follow essentially the same steps to securely erase a real disk, but it could take quite a while and might interfere with other exercises.

Securely Erase Free Space on a Volume
The first secure erasure option you will explore removes remnants of deleted files but leaves existing files intact.

1   If necessary, log in as Local Admin.

2   Open StudentMaterials/Lesson9/Pretendco Documents.dmg. Remember that you have a shortcut to the StudentMaterials folder in your Dock.

The Pretendco SSED Plans volume mounts.

3   Open the Pretendco SSED Plans volume in the Finder.

The only item visible in the volume is a file named Note.rtf. However, it used to contain Pretendco's secret plans to develop a next-generation solid-state encabulation device (SSED), and those plans were not deleted securely.

4   If necessary, open Disk Utility.

5   In Disk Utility, select the Pretendco SSED Plans volume in the sidebar.

6   Click the Erase tab.

7   Click Erase Free Space.

A dialog appears with a slider that lets you choose the level of speed or security you would like. The Fastest option is good enough for almost all purposes.

8   Leave the slider at Fastest, and click Erase Free Space.

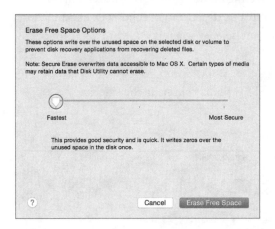

Since this is a small disk image, the erasure finishes quickly. A disk might take minutes or even hours depending on its size, its speed, and the amount of free space.

9   Open Pretendco SSED Plans in the Finder.

Notice that Note.rtf is still there.

Securely Erase an Entire Disk

If you want to make sure a disk does not contain leftover data, you may want to erase the entire disk, including existing files. Disk Utility has an option to do this as well.

1   Switch back to Disk Utility.

2   If necessary, select Pretendco Documents.dmg in the sidebar.

Selecting the disk (rather than the volume it contains) ensures that the entire contents of the disk will be securely erased, including the partition table and any hidden partitions.

3   If necessary, click the Erase tab.

Note that the Erase Free Space button is dimmed when an entire disk is selected.

4   Click Security Options.

A dialog appears with a slider that looks similar to the one in the previous section. In this case, however, the Fastest option provides no real security.

5   Drag the slider one tick to the right.

As mentioned in the following screenshot, this option writes a single pass of zeros over the entire disk. This is equivalent to the Fastest option of Erase Free Space.

6   Click OK.

7   Click Erase.

8   In the confirmation dialog that appears, click Erase.

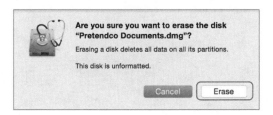

If you receive a message that the disk could not be unmounted, make sure TextEdit is not running, and try again.

As before, the operation completes quickly.

9   Open the volume (now named Untitled) in the Finder.

This time, notice that Note.rtf is not present because it was erased.

10 In Disk Utility, click the Eject button to eject the disk image.

Lesson 10

FileVault

Prior to OS X Lion, the Apple solution for protecting user data involved encrypting just the user's home folder content. This system, now dubbed Legacy FileVault, came with a list of caveats about issues that would prevent many system features and third-party software applications from behaving as expected. Further, it did not meet the security requirements of many organizations that required full-system volume encryption.

Although third-party solutions for full-system volume encryption did emerge for previous versions of OS X, they often exhibited issues whenever Apple updated hardware or software. Many third-party full-system volume encryption schemes would simply stop working, leaving users literally stranded, with no way to reach their encrypted data.

GOALS

▶ Understand how FileVault helps protect your data

▶ Enable FileVault protection

▶ Recover a FileVault system when all passwords are lost

With OS X Lion, Apple engineers decided to take this problem into their own hands and introduced a new version of FileVault (sometimes called FileVault 2). In this lesson, you will learn how FileVault protects the system volume and how to enable this protection. You will also learn how to recover a system protected with FileVault when all local users' passwords are lost.

NOTE ▶ All instances of "FileVault" in this guide refer to the newer FileVault 2 system volume encryption technology, unless otherwise specified.

Reference 10.1
FileVault Technology

In OS X Lion and later, FileVault 2 protects the entire system volume by converting it to Mac OS Extended (Journaled, Encrypted) format, which uses XTS-AES 128 encryption. This adoption of a full-system volume encryption scheme resolves all the limitations of Legacy FileVault by performing the encryption at the file system driver level of the operating system. In other words, most processes and applications don't even know the system volume is encrypted, so they simply behave as usual.

NOTE ▶ Enabling FileVault encrypts only the system volume. If you make use of more than one volume, consider encrypting the other volumes, as covered in Lesson 9 "File Systems and Storage".

This was not the case with Legacy FileVault, as the system and applications were unable to access an encrypted user's home folder contents when the user was logged out of the system. Obviously, by encrypting the entire system volume, FileVault 2 in OS X Lion and later provides better protection than Legacy FileVault did. Further, because the current version is fully supported by Apple, changes to Apple hardware and software should no longer cause compatibility issues.

NOTE ▶ You can't enable FileVault 2 if any local user is still configured to use Legacy FileVault. Details on Legacy FileVault, including how to disable it for a user account, are covered in Lesson 7 "System Security".

The current FileVault solution is more than just a new volume format; it's a system of new technologies that enables your Mac to transition from a standard system volume to a protected system volume. Full details of all the changes required to engineer FileVault are beyond the scope of this guide, but the primary new technologies instrumental in the current version include seamless volume format conversion, user account password synchronization, secure key storage on Apple servers for lost password recovery, OS X Recovery for initial system startup, and a new firmware login window.

You can see many of these new pieces at work during startup to an encrypted system volume. What was traditionally a straightforward task—starting up the system—takes on a new level of complexity when you can't read the system volume to start with. Thus, Apple had to devise a method to authenticate and access the protected system volume during startup.

When starting up from an encrypted system, the Mac actually starts from the hidden OS X Recovery HD volume first, to present users with a login window. Users enter their account password, which is then used to access the decryption key that ultimately unlocks the protected system volume. Once the Mac has access to the system volume, startup continues normally, with one exception: Users, having already authenticated to unlock encryption, are automatically logged in to their accounts.

NOTE ▶ If the system disk is missing the hidden OS X Recovery HD volume, you cannot enable FileVault. Fortunately, OS X also makes it impossible to accidentally engage it without that volume. Re-creating the Recovery HD volume is covered in Lesson 3 "OS X Recovery".

Reference 10.2
Enabling FileVault

In typical Apple style, despite the underlying complexity of transitioning an existing system to a secure encrypted system, turning on FileVault requires only a few simple steps. In fact, as covered in Lesson 2 "Setup and Configuration", late-model Mac portable computers will prompt the user to set up FileVault during the Setup Assistant process.

Even if Setup Assistant doesn't prompt you to enable FileVault, an administrative user can enable it at any time from Security & Privacy preferences. Clicking the Turn On FileVault button initiates the setup process.

Configuring FileVault Recovery

During the FileVault setup, a dialog appears that offers two methods for recovering should all FileVault-enabled user passwords be lost. This is a very important decision, because if you do not have authentication or recovery access to the FileVault-protected system volume, then all data will be lost. In this case, the security mechanisms used by FileVault are so strong that not even Apple can help you recover the data.

The first method for recovery is to use an Apple ID (or iCloud) account to unlock the FileVault volume and reset the user's lost password. This new recovery method, introduced with OS X Yosemite, generates a random FileVault recovery key and then saves it to the user's iCloud account on Apple servers. Although the user cannot see the recovery key, should the need arise, the system will be able to retrieve the key from the user's iCloud service.

NOTE ▶ The OS X interface sometimes uses "iCloud password" instead of "Apple ID password." However, because all Apple services, including iCloud, are accessed via Apple ID authentication, this guide uses the term "Apple ID" when discussing Apple service authentication.

This recovery method obviously requires that the system have Internet access and that the user be signed into the iCloud service (via the iCloud preferences). However, it does not require that the user's local account password be linked to his or her Apple ID. In other words, the user can continue to use a separate local account password even if the Apple ID account is configured for FileVault recovery.

Finally, it's important to note that only one user's Apple ID account can be configured for FileVault recovery. Other users can be given the ability to log in to the FileVault protected system, but they do not have access to the recovery key stored in iCloud. Thus, for multi-user systems, it's best that an administrative user enable FileVault and use an appropriate Apple ID account to save the key.

NOTE ▶ If you choose to use an Apple ID account for FileVault recovery, it's strongly recommended that you also take advantage of two-step verification for the Apple ID. For more information about two-step verification, see Apple Support article HT5570, "Frequently asked questions about two-step verification for Apple ID."

NOTE ▶ Previous versions of OS X allowed you to save a FileVault recovery key with Apple without using an Apple ID. This recovery method is no longer available with OS X Yosemite.

An alternative method for FileVault recovery that doesn't involve Apple ID services is the creation of a locally saved recovery key. This randomly generated key can be used later to unlock the FileVault protected volume and reset the user's lost password. As the dialog states, you will need to manually copy this key and store it somewhere safe other than the computer on which you are currently enabling FileVault. A good choice may be to take a photo with a mobile device, providing it uses strong local security as well.

MORE INFO ▶ For organizations deploying and managing systems en masse, there are more appropriate options for configuring FileVault than the default method covered here. For example, you can use an institutional recovery key for FileVault recovery, as covered in Apple Support article HT202385, "OS X: How to create and deploy a recovery key for FileVault 2."

Enabling Users for FileVault

During the FileVault setup process, if more than one local user exists on the system, a dialog appears where you can enable existing local users to unlock the protected system volume. This grants these other users the ability to start up the system. Click the Enable User button next to each user you want to be able to access the FileVault system volume. These users must then enter their account password to enable this ability. An administrator cannot override this step, as each user must each enter his or her unique password.

Any user not initially enabled to unlock FileVault can be configured for this ability later; just click the Enable User button in the FileVault pane of Security & Privacy preferences. Only local users or cached mobile network users can be FileVault enabled. New local users or cached mobile network users created after FileVault is turned on are automatically able to unlock FileVault.

Any user password changes that occur will continue to be FileVault enabled as long as those changes occur on the system protected with FileVault. In other words, if you reset the password for a cached mobile user from the network directory server, the account will not be allowed to unlock the local FileVault system volume. To resolve this issue, you can either use a FileVault recovery method or you can log in as another administrative user and then reenable the reset local account by clicking the Enable User button in the FileVault pane of Security & Privacy preferences.

Restarting and Encrypting

Most Mac computers will need to be restarted to begin the system volume encryption. Upon restart, notice that the login window appears much more quickly than usual. This is the new FileVault login window, hosted from the hidden OS X Recovery HD volume. You will also notice that only FileVault enabled users appear here. Authenticate as any FileVault enabled user, and system startup continues until the user is automatically logged in to his or her account.

From the FileVault pane of Security & Privacy preferences, you can view the progress of the system volume encryption as well as an estimated completion time. It may take several hours to completely encrypt a system volume. Obviously, the length of time varies greatly depending on the amount of data that must be encrypted.

> **NOTE** ▶ Due to the complex nature of solid-state and flash disk controllers, encrypting a volume may still leave some parts of the original data in a recoverable form. Thus, to minimize the security risk, it would be ideal to enable FileVault before saving any sensitive data to the system volume.

Amazingly, you can close Security & Privacy preferences and continue to use the Mac as usual, even though the system is slowly encrypting the volume it's running from. No notification appears once encryption is complete, but you can always return to Security & Privacy preferences to check the progress.

NOTE ▶ To conserve battery power, portable Mac computers may pause encryption when they aren't plugged in. The encryption will continue once the Mac portable is connected to a power source.

If for some reason you want to turn off FileVault encryption, you can do so from the same Security & Privacy pane. This requires another system restart and a potentially lengthy decryption process. However, similar to the encryption process to enable FileVault, the decryption process can continue in the background without interrupting the user.

Reference 10.3
FileVault Recovery

Although highly unlikely on multiuser systems, it's probably more common than you think for a single-user Mac computer's human to lose the login password. If by some means all FileVault enabled account passwords are lost on a system protected with FileVault, you may still be able to unlock the system.

The ability to unlock a FileVault protected system lies with the recovery key. As covered previously, this key can be stored in a user's iCloud service or simply saved manually by the user. Hopefully, the user either knows his or her Apple ID authentication or has dutifully copied and saved the FileVault recovery key somewhere safe.

Initiating the FileVault Recovery Process

To start the FileVault recovery process, at the FileVault login window, select a user, and then click the small "?" icon to the right of the password entry field. A popover appears suggesting you reset the user's password with a recovery key or an Apple ID. This message will also appear automatically should a user fail to authenticate three times in a row.

NOTE ▶ Only systems that were running OS X Yosemite during the FileVault enabling process have the option to use FileVault with Apple ID recovery. Also, on multiuser systems, you will need to select the specific user that enabled FileVault with Apple ID recovery.

The quickest recovery method is to enter the recovery key. Simply click the arrow next to Recovery Key to enter the key, if you have it. After you successfully enter the key, the system unlocks the system volume and continues the startup process. The traditional Mac login window eventually appears, prompting you to set a new password for the user. Enter a new password twice, then an optional password hint, and then click Reset Password to log in the user.

NOTE ▶ If FileVault was configured using a previous version of OS X, and you elected to save the recovery key with Apple, you must contact AppleCare directly to retrieve the key. You can find out how to directly contact AppleCare from Apple Support article HT201232, "Contacting Apple for support and service."

Apple ID FileVault Recovery

If you select the option to reset the password using an Apple ID, the system will start up into a special Reset Password Assistant that resides only on the hidden Recovery HD volume. This application looks similar to Setup Assistant, but it's specifically designed to provide a way to authenticate the user's Apple ID, retrieve the recovery key from Apple's iCloud servers, and reset the local user's password. Further, the Reset Password Assistant can also help users reset their Apple ID password if it's lost as well.

NOTE ▶ The Reset Password Assistant requires an Internet connection to reach the Apple iCloud servers. The Recovery HD system attempts to automatically connect to the previously used Wi-Fi network, but if this doesn't work you will have to manually configure a network connection. Either connect the Mac to a DHCP-enabled Ethernet network, or move the cursor to the top of the screen and select the Wi-Fi menu to configure a Wi-Fi network.

Once the user authenticates with the Apple ID, the Reset Password Assistant retrieves the recovery key from iCloud and then checks the FileVault protected system for a matching local user account. If the user's local password was linked to his or her Apple ID password, it will be reset to the new password. However, if the user's local password was separate from the Apple ID, the Reset Password Assistant presents a screen where you can enter a new password for the local user account. Once the reset process is complete, restart the system, and then authenticate with the new user account password to gain access to the system.

Lost FileVault Recovery Key

If, in a worst-case scenario, you have lost all FileVault enabled account passwords and you are unable to access the FileVault recovery key (either by local methods or with Apple), there is no way to recover the data on the system volume. You might as well start up to OS X Recovery (covered in Lesson 3 "OS X Recovery") and then repartition the system disk (covered in Lesson 9 "File Systems and Storage"). At that point, you could reinstall OS X (covered in Lesson 1 "Install OS X Yosemite") or restore from a Time Machine backup (covered in Lesson 16 "Time Machine").

Exercise 10.1
Turn On FileVault

▶ **Prerequisites**

▶ You must have created the Local Admin ("Exercise 2.1 Configure a New OS X System for Exercises" on page 60 or "Exercise 2.2 Configure an Existing OS X System for Exercises" on page 63) and Chris Johnson ("Exercise 5.1 Manage User Accounts" on page 145) accounts.

WARNING ▶ If you lose all the passwords and the recovery key for a FileVault–encrypted volume, you will not be able to regain access to the data stored in it. If you are performing this exercise on your own computer and have any files you do not want to risk losing, you must back up your computer before starting this exercise.

FileVault allows you to encrypt your startup volume and control which users can gain access to the volume. In this exercise, you will turn on FileVault protection for your startup volume. If you do not want to protect your computer with FileVault, you can turn it off in "Exercise 10.4 Turn Off FileVault" on page 308.

Use System Preferences to Turn On FileVault

1   If necessary, log in as Chris Johnson (using the password for the linked iCloud account or whatever you chose when you created the account).

2   Open the Security & Privacy pane in System Preferences.

If a dialog appears indicating that "You're using an old version of FileVault," it means you have old user accounts set up using Legacy FileVault encryption. You can either click Turn Off Legacy FileVault and follow the prompts to turn it off or click Keep Using Legacy FileVault and skip this lesson's exercises. You cannot use both Legacy FileVault and the current version, FileVault 2, at the same time.

3　Click the FileVault tab.

4　Unlock the preference pane and authenticate as Local Admin (password: ladminpw).

5　Click Turn On FileVault.

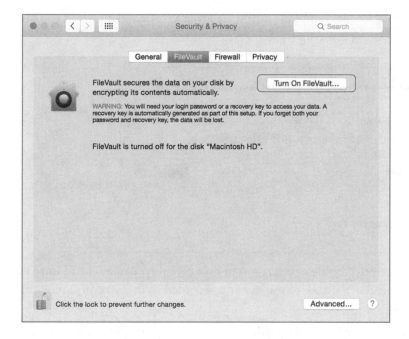

If a dialog appears saying "A recovery key has been set by your company, school, or institution," it means your computer was preloaded with an institutional recovery key (described in Apple Support article HT202385, "OS X: How to create and deploy a recovery key for FileVault 2"). In this case, click Continue and skip to step 9. You will also not be able to perform "Exercise 10.3 Use a FileVault Recovery Key" on page 304.

If an institutional key has not been set, a dialog appears giving you the choice of allowing your iCloud account to unlock the disk or creating a recovery key. Note that the dialog will be slightly different if you have not linked the Chris Johnson account to an Apple ID.

6   Select "Create a recovery key and do not use my iCloud account," and click Continue.

    If an institutional key has not been set, you are given a recovery key, which you can use to unlock the disk if you forget all users' passwords.

7   Record your recovery key.

    Recovery key: _____

    If you are performing these exercises on your own computer and intend to leave File-Vault on at the end of these exercises, store the recorded recovery key in a physically secure location.

    One convenient option for recording the key is to take a picture of it with a smart-phone (or other camera). However, you should consider the security implications of someone stealing your computer and phone together.

    You could also take a screenshot on the computer itself, but then you would need to copy it someplace else to make it available if you get locked out of your computer.

8   Click Continue.

    A dialog appears, allowing you to select which users can unlock the disk.

9   Click the Enable User button for Local Admin.

10 Enter the Local Admin password, and then click OK.

11 If the Chris Johnson account is not already enabled (green checkmark to the right of the account), enable it as well.

Do not enable any accounts other than Chris Johnson and Local Admin.

12 Click Continue.

13 Click Restart to begin the encryption process.

Your computer restarts. Encrypting the entire partition takes a while, but you can use the computer normally during the encryption process.

You can now leave your computer at the authentication screen and proceed to "Exercise 10.2 Restart a FileVault-Protected System" on page 301 or "Exercise 10.3 Use a FileVault Recovery Key" on page 304; if you do not want to leave FileVault on, wait for the encryption process to finish, and then use "Exercise 10.4 Turn Off FileVault" on page 308 to turn it off. You can also perform exercises from other lessons while you are waiting for it to finish encrypting your disk.

Exercise 10.2
Restart a FileVault-Protected System

▶ **Prerequisites**

▶ You must have created the Local Admin ("Exercise 2.1 Configure a New OS X System for Exercises" on page 60 or "Exercise 2.2 Configure an Existing OS X System for Exercises" on page 63) and Chris Johnson ("Exercise 5.1 Manage User Accounts" on page 145) accounts.

▶ You must have performed "Exercise 10.1 Turn On FileVault" on page 296.

In this exercise, you'll see how FileVault modifies the OS X startup process by requiring one of the selected user's passwords. Once the computer is fully started, all users may use the computer normally.

Your computer restarts and displays a FileVault access screen. This looks similar to the login screen, but you see only Chris Johnson and Local Admin. The operating system has not started yet because you need to unlock the disk before the system files can be read.

If Find My Mac were turned on, you would also see a Guest account listed here. Selecting Guest starts the computer in a Safari-only mode with no access to the startup volume. This exists primarily to tempt computer thieves into connecting the computer to the Internet, after which, thanks to Find My Mac, it can be located, locked, or wiped.

Log In to a FileVault-Enabled Account

1   Click Chris Johnson.

2   Enter Chris's password, and press Return.

If you lost all the selected users' passwords, you could enter an incorrect password three times to be prompted for the recovery key.

At this point, the normal OS X startup process proceeds, and you are automatically logged in as Chris Johnson. Since you already authenticated as Chris Johnson at the FileVault authentication screen, OS X facilitates an automatic login for you.

3   Open System Preferences, select Security & Privacy, and click the FileVault tab.

A progress indicator shows the encryption status. As you have just seen, FileVault provides some protection immediately, but your data is not fully secured until the encryption process finishes.

4   Quit System Preferences.

5   Select your startup volume from the desktop.

6   In the Finder, choose File > Get Info (Command-I).

7   If necessary, click the triangle to expand the General section of the Info window.

The format of the volume is now Mac OS Extended (Journaled, Encrypted).

8   Close the Info window, and log out as Chris Johnson.

Notice that even though Chris's account was used to gain access to Macintosh HD, all users can now log in normally.

9   If you plan to perform "Exercise 10.3 Use a FileVault Recovery Key" on page 304 next, click the Restart button at the bottom of the screen.

Exercise 10.3
Use a FileVault Recovery Key

▶ **Prerequisites**

▶ You must have created the Local Admin ("Exercise 2.1 Configure a New OS X System for Exercises" on page 60 or "Exercise 2.2 Configure an Existing OS X System for Exercises" on page 63) and Chris Johnson ("Exercise 5.1 Manage User Accounts" on page 145) accounts.

▶ You must have performed "Exercise 10.1 Turn On FileVault" on page 296 and recorded your recovery key.

You can use the FileVault recovery key to reset user passwords at startup. In this exercise, you will use this capability to reset Chris Johnson's password.

Reset Chris Johnson's Password

1   If your computer is not at the FileVault authentication screen, restart it.

Note that at the FileVault authentication screen, you see only the two FileVault-enabled accounts: Chris Johnson and Local Admin. If you see other accounts, you may have logged out without restarting the computer, in which case you are seeing the normal login screen, not FileVault.

2   At the FileVault authentication screen, click Chris Johnson.

3   Click the Help (?) button at the right of the Password field or fail to authenticate with the correct password three times.

You will see an option that lets you reset the password with the recovery key.

4   Click the arrow to start the reset process.

A Recovery Key field replaces the Password field.

5   Enter the recovery key you recorded earlier, and press Return.

If the Recovery Key field shakes and resets, you have not entered the recovery key correctly. If reentering it does not correct the problem, you may have recorded it incorrectly. In this case, you can't perform the password reset portion of this exercise; instead, cancel the password reset by clicking the left-arrow button, log in normally using Chris's current password (chris, or whatever you chose when you created the account), and skip ahead to "Exercise 10.4 Turn Off FileVault" on page 308.

The operating system starts up. Once the startup process finishes, a dialog appears indicating that changing your password will unlink it from your iCloud account.

6   Click Continue to unlink the account password.

7   In the Reset Password dialog, enter chrisvault in the "New password" and "Verify password" fields, and then click Reset Password.

You are now logged in to Chris's account. Since his password has been reset, you receive the warning that the system was unable to unlock his login keychain.

8   Click Continue Log In.

9   If you are prompted, enter the password for Chris's login keychain (the password for the iCloud account or whatever you chose when you created the account).

Restore Chris Johnson's Original Password

To avoid confusion for the rest of the exercises, you will now change Chris Johnson's password back to "chris."

1   Open the Users & Groups pane in System Preferences.

2   Click Change Password.

3   In the dialog that appears, click Use iCloud Password.

4   Enter chrisvault as the old password, and the password for the iCloud account you are using, then click "Use iCloud Password."

Note that this also brings Chris's account password back in sync with his keychain password.

Exercise 10.4
Turn Off FileVault

▶ **Prerequisites**

- ▶ You must have created the Local Admin ("Exercise 2.1 Configure a New OS X System for Exercises" on page 60 or "Exercise 2.2 Configure an Existing OS X System for Exercises" on page 63) and Chris Johnson ("Exercise 5.1 Manage User Accounts" on page 145) accounts.

- ▶ You must have performed "Exercise 10.1 Turn On FileVault" on page 296, and the encryption process must have finished.

FileVault encryption can be turned off as easily as it is turned on. If you are performing these exercises on your own and want to leave FileVault protection enabled on your computer, you can skip this exercise.

If you are performing these exercises in a class, you should not skip this exercise.

Turn Off Encryption on the Macintosh HD Volume

1   If necessary, log in as Chris Johnson.

2   Open Security & Privacy preferences.

3   Click the FileVault tab.

    If the encryption process has not finished, you will not be able to turn off FileVault yet. You may perform other exercises while the encryption proceeds in the background and then return to this exercise when the volume is fully encrypted.

4   Click the lock icon, and authenticate as Local Admin. Only administrators can turn FileVault on and off.

5   Click Turn Off FileVault.

    You are asked to confirm that you want to turn off FileVault.

6   Click "Restart & Turn Off Encryption."

7   If you are prompted to do so, reauthenticate as Local Admin.

Your computer restarts, and the decryption process begins. Note that since you authenticated to FileVault when you started up the computer, no special FileVault password is required at this point. As with the encryption process, you can continue to use the computer normally during the decryption process.

Lesson 11
Permissions and Sharing

The technologies collectively known as file system permissions are used to control file and folder authorization for OS X. File system permissions work alongside the user account technologies, which control user identification and authentication, to provide the secure multiuser environment of the Mac. File system permissions—just like user accounts—permeate every level of the operating system, so a thorough investigation of this system is required to fully understand OS X.

In this lesson, you will learn how file system ownership and permissions allow you to protect local files and folders. You will also explore the default permissions used by OS X to provide secure access to shared files. Finally, you will use the Finder to make ownership and permissions changes.

GOALS

► Understand file ownership and permissions

► Explore the default shared folders in OS X

► Securely manage file and folder access

Reference 11.1
File System Permissions

Every single item on the system volume has permissions rules applied to it by the operating system. These rules are used to define file and folder access for every standard, administrative, guest, and sharing user. Only users and processes with root account access can ignore file system permissions rules.

NOTE ► The OS X interface sometimes uses the word *privileges* in place of *permissions*. In general, the meaning of these two terms is similar.

Viewing File System Permissions
Any user can easily identify a file's or folder's permissions via the Info window in the Finder. First, select the file or folder whose permissions you want to identify. You can select multiple items to open multiple Info windows.

There are several ways to access the Finder Info window:

▶   Press Command-I.

▶   Choose File > Get Info.

▶   Secondary (or Control-) click the selected item, and then choose Get Info from the shortcut menu.

▶   In a Finder window toolbar, click the Action pop-up menu (the gear icon), and then choose Get Info.

Once you open an Info window, click the Sharing & Permissions disclosure triangle to reveal the item's permissions. Note that the permissions list is broken into two columns. To the left is a list of users or groups with access to this item, and to the right is the associated privilege assigned by user or group. Modifying these settings is covered in "Reference 11.3 Managing Permissions " on page 326.

TIP ▶ You can also identify ownership and permissions from the dynamic Inspector window in the Finder. This is a single floating window that automatically refreshes as you select different items in the Finder. To open the Inspector, press Command-Option-I in the Finder.

Ownership for Permissions

Every file and folder belongs to at least one owner and one group and also has an ownership setting for everyone else. This three-tiered ownership structure provides the basis for
file system permissions:

▶ Owner—By default, the owner of an item is the user who created or copied the item to
the Mac. For example, users own most of the items in their home folder. The system
or root user almost always owns system software items, including system resources
and applications. Traditionally, only the owner can change the item's ownership or
permissions. Despite this, OS X makes management easier by giving every administrative user the ability to change ownership and permissions regardless of who owns the
item.

▶ Group—By default, the group of an item is inherited from the folder it was created in.
Thus, most items belong to the staff (the primary group for local users), wheel (the
primary group for the root system account), or admin groups. Group ownership is
designated to allow users other than the owner access to an item. For instance, even
though root owns the /Applications folder, the group is set to admin so administrative
users can make changes to the contents of this folder.

▶ Everyone—The Everyone setting is used to define access for anyone who isn't the
owner and isn't part of the item's group. In other words, this means everyone *else*. This
includes local, sharing, and guest users.

The simple three-tiered ownership structure presented here has been part of traditional
UNIX operating systems for decades. However, with only three levels of permissions to
choose from, it is quite difficult to define appropriate access settings for a computer with
many user accounts and shared files, as is the case with many servers. Fortunately, as you'll
see later, access control lists were developed to allow for nearly limitless ownership and
permissions configurations.

Standard UNIX Permissions

The standard file system permissions structure of OS X is based on standard UNIX-style
permissions. This system is also sometimes referred to as POSIX-style permissions. The
system may be old, but for most Mac users it is quite adequate, because you can define
privilege rules separately at each ownership tier. In other words, the owner, the group, and
everyone else have individually specified access to each file or folder. Further, because of
the inherent hierarchy built into the file system, where folders can reside inside other fold-

ers, you can easily create a complex file structure that allows varying levels of sharing and security.

Apple has streamlined the Finder to allow for the most common permissions options. Alternatively, the full range of UNIX privilege combinations are available from Terminal, but that topic is beyond the scope of this guide.

> **MORE INFO** ▶ Wikipedia has an excellent overview of UNIX-style permissions: http://en.wikipedia.org/wiki/Filesystem_permissions.

File-level permissions options available in the Finder are:

▶   Read & Write—The user or group members can open the file and save changes.

▶   Read Only—The user or group members can open the file but cannot save any changes.

▶   No Access—The user or group members have no access to the file at all.

Folder-level permissions options available in the Finder are:

▶   Read & Write—The user or group members can browse and make changes to the contents of the folder.

▶   Read Only—The user or group members can browse the contents of the folder but cannot make changes to the contents of the folder.

▶   Write Only (Drop Box)—The user or group members cannot browse the Drop Box folder but can copy or move items into it.

▶   No Access—The user or group members have no access to the contents of the folder.

> **NOTE** ▶ Although the Finder doesn't show or allow changes to the UNIX execute permission, it automatically assigns this permission when read access is granted for folders.

Access Control Lists

Access control lists (ACLs) were developed to expand the standard UNIX permissions architecture to allow more control of file and folder access. OS X has adopted a style of ACLs similar to that available on Windows-based NTFS file systems and UNIX systems that support NFSv4. This ACL implementation is extremely flexible but increases complexity by adding more than a dozen unique privilege and inheritance attribute types.

Further, the OS X implementation of ACLs supports an essentially unlimited number of access control entries (ACEs). An ACE is a set of permissions defined for a specific user or group. In other words, ACLs provide a nearly unlimited list of permission rules or ACEs for every file or folder. Hence the *list* in *access control list*.

Finally, it's important to note that if an ACL rule applies to a user or group, this rule trumps standard UNIX permissions. However, any users or groups that don't apply to a specific ACL are still bound by the standard permissions currently in place.

Apple does not expect average users to navigate through all the options available using ACLs, so once again the Finder has been streamlined to allow only the most common ACL configurations. In fact, the Finder allows you to assign only ACL attributes that match the most common standard UNIX permissions configurations (previously listed in this lesson). The only feature of ACLs that the Finder actually implements is the ability to have an unlimited number of user or group privilege rules. In other words, the Finder uses the ACL architecture to let you configure unique privileges for an essentially unlimited number of users or groups.

Permissions in a Hierarchical Context

It is important to remember that permissions do not exist in isolation; rather, they are applied in the context of a folder hierarchy. In other words, your access to an item is based on an item's permissions in combination with the permissions of the folder in which it resides. If you're still confused, it's easiest to think of permissions as defining access to an item's content, not to the item itself. Remember the word *content* as you consider the following three simplified examples.

Example 1: You have both read and write permissions to the folder. It's obvious that you should have full access to the first file, as your permissions here are read-and-write as well. You can also view and copy the second file, but you can't make changes to the file's content because your permissions are read-only. Yet you can still move, delete, or rename the second file because you have read-and-write access to the folder's contents. Thus, the second file isn't secure in this example, because you can make a copy of the original file, change the copied file's content, delete the original file, and finally replace it with the modified copy. This is how many applications actually save document changes; thus, the file can in fact be edited.

NOTE ▶ The "*" in these examples represents that actual editing behavior varies based on the application's design. For some applications, you may need read-and-write access to both the file and the folder it's inside to save changes to the file.

Example 2: You have read-only permission to the folder. You can edit the content of the first file because you have read-and-write access to it, but you can't move, delete, or rename it because you have read-only access to the folder's contents. On the other hand, you can effectively delete the file by erasing its contents. The second file here is the only truly secure file, as you're only allowed to view or copy the file. Granted, you can make changes to the contents of a copied file, but you still can't replace the original.

Read & Write

Read & Write
Locked File

Only owner can edit the file *
Can copy, but copies locked
Only owner can move, delete
Only owner can rename

Example 3: Your permissions are identical to the first document in the first example, with one significant change. The owner of this file has enabled the locked attribute, perhaps through the new OS X version's document control feature. Even though you have read-and-write access to the example folder and file, the locked attribute prevents all users who aren't the file's owner from modifying, moving, deleting, or renaming the file. From most applications, only the owner is allowed to change the file's content or delete it, but the owner can also disable the locked attribute to return the file to normal. You can still make a copy of the locked file, but the copy will be locked as well. However, you will own the copy, so you can disable the locked attribute on the copy, but you still can't delete the original locked file unless you're the owner.

MORE INFO ▶ Managing the locked file attribute is detailed in Lesson 18 "Document Management".

Reference 11.2
Permissions for Sharing

Once you have an understanding of the available permissions options in OS X, you should explore how the local file system is set up by default to provide a secure environment that still allows users to share files.

If you don't have fast user switching enabled, as outlined in Lesson 5 "User Accounts", enable it now to make it easy to test file system permissions as different users. Further, to aid in your exploration of the file system, use the Finder Inspector window. This single floating window, which automatically refreshes as you select different items in the Finder, allows you to quickly explore the default permissions settings without having to open multiple Finder Info windows. Open the Inspector from the Finder by pressing Command-Option-I, and then click the disclosure triangle to reveal the Sharing & Permissions section.

NOTE ▶ The Inspector window sports a slightly different title bar than the Info window. Also, the Inspector always floats on top of all other windows in the Finder.

Home Folder Sharing

OS X protects the user's files by default and allows them to be shared easily when needed. This starts with the user's home folder. Notice that users are allowed read-and-write access to their home folder, while the staff group and everyone else are allowed only read access.

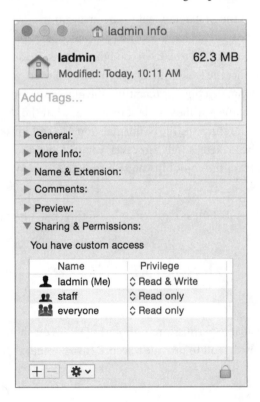

This means that every local user or guest can view the first level of every other user's home folder. (Remember, guests are allowed access to your computer without a password. This is why you can disable guest access in Users & Groups preferences.)

The default home folder permissions may seem insecure until you look at the permissions in context. Most user data is actually stored inside a subfolder in the user's home folder, and if you inspect those subfolders, you'll notice that other users are not allowed to access most of them.

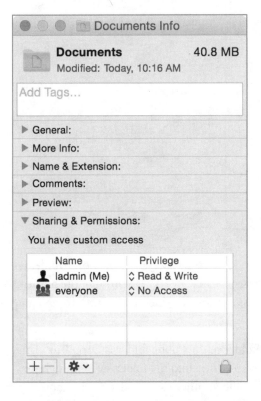

A few subfolders in a user's home folder, however, are specifically designed for sharing. The Public folder and legacy Sites folder remain readable to everyone. A user can easily share files without having to fuss with permissions by simply moving the files into those two folders. Others are able to read those files, but they still cannot make any changes to them.

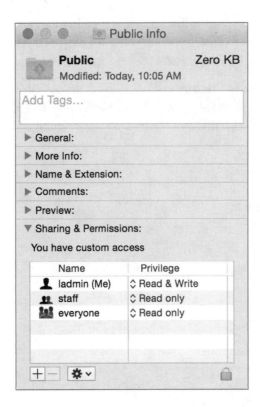

NOTE ▶ By default, user-created files and folders at the root of the home folder have permissions like the Public folder's. To secure new items at the root of the home folder, simply change the permissions, as outlined in "Reference 11.3 Managing Permissions" on page 326.

Looking deeper, you'll notice that one subfolder of the Public folder is Drop Box. This folder's permissions allow all other users to copy files into the folder, even though they cannot see the other files in that folder. This allows other users to discreetly transfer files to a specific user without others knowing.

When items are created or copied, they are owned by the user who performed the create or copy action. This would normally present a problem for a folder like Drop Box, as other users still own the items they have placed in your Drop Box folder. However, there is a custom ACE set for the Drop Box folder that ensures that users are also granted full access to the items in their Drop Box.

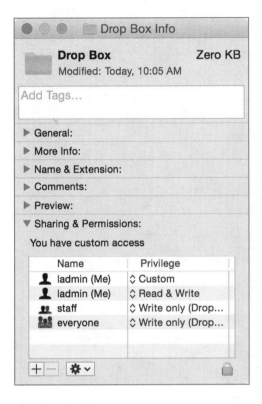

The Shared Folder

An additional folder set aside for local file sharing is the /Users/Shared folder. Notice that this is a general sharing location that allows all local users to read and write items to the folder. Normally this permissions setting would also allow any user to delete another user's item in this folder.

Yet the Inspector window is not showing you the full permissions picture here. A unique permissions setting on the Shared folder prevents other users from being able to delete items they don't own. This permissions setting, known as the "sticky bit," can be viewed and managed only from Terminal.

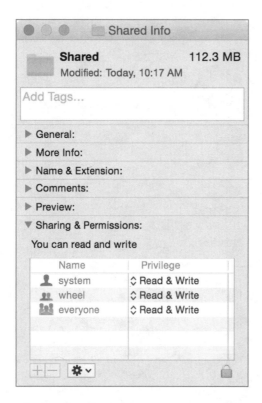

Securing New Items

Once you understand how the OS X file system security architecture works with the folder hierarchy, it's time to consider how this technology is used to secure new items. In this lesson you've already learned that OS X is preconfigured for secure file and folder sharing; however, new items are created with unrestricted read access.

For example, when users create a new file or folder at the root of their home folder, by default, all other users, including guest users, are allowed to view this item's contents. The same is true for new items created by administrators in local areas, such as the root of the system volume and the local Library and Applications folders.

New items are created this way to facilitate sharing, so that you do not have to change any permissions to share a new item. All you have to do is place the new item in a folder that other users can access, like the predefined sharing folders covered in the previous section. It's assumed that if you want to secure a new item, you will place it inside a folder that no one else has access to, like your home Desktop or Documents folder.

On the other hand, this default behavior is inconvenient if you want to safely store your items in an otherwise public area, like the root of the system volume. To store items in a public area so they are only accessible to the owner requires that you change the item's permissions using either the Finder or Terminal, as outlined later in this lesson.

Specifically, from the Sharing & Permissions section of the Info window, you must remove all other users and all group accounts from the permissions list. You cannot remove the Everyone permission, so you have to set it to No Access. Once you have made these permissions changes, only the owner has access to the item.

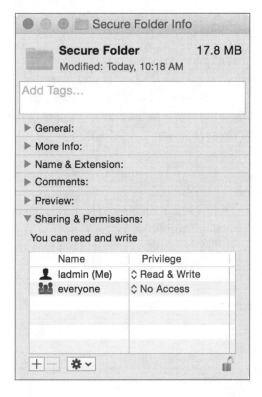

NOTE ▶ Despite appearances, in the preceding screenshot Secure Folder does indeed have a group assignment. This is because the Finder hides an item's group permission if no access is granted. Thus, clicking the Delete (–) button to "delete" an item's group permission disables access for the group, but it does not actually remove the group assignment.

Reference 11.3
Managing Permissions

You may find that although the Finder makes permissions management simple, it does so through a form of obfuscation. In other words, the Finder hides the complexity of full UNIX and ACL permissions by showing a simplified view of an item's permissions.

Thus, if you're more comfortable with standard UNIX permissions, or you simply require full access to an item's permissions, you're best served by managing permissions via Terminal. This is, however, beyond the scope of this guide. For the most common permissions settings, the simplified Finder permissions interface is still the quickest and easiest solution.

An example situation you might encounter that requires changing permissions is when you delete a user's account but retain the user's home folder. The system renames that folder to "Username (deleted)," but otherwise leaves it alone. This presents a management problem, as even administrative users won't have full access to the folder's content in the Finder. This section explores the permissions changes an admin would make to get full access to a deleted user's home folder.

Permissions Management via the Finder

As covered previously in "Viewing File System Permissions" on page 311, you can view and manage permissions in the Sharing & Permissions section of the Info window. To do so, if you aren't the owner of the item, you must click the small lock icon in the bottom-right corner of the Info window and authenticate as an administrative user.

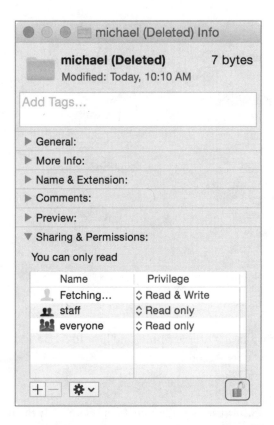

It's important to note that changes made using the Info window are applied immediately. However, as long as you keep the Info window open, the Finder also remembers the original permissions setting for the item. This is useful for testing different permissions configurations, as you can always revert to the original permissions setting. To do that, click the Action pop-up menu (gear icon) at the bottom of the Info window, and then choose "Revert changes."

Add a Permissions Entry

To add new permissions entry for a user or group, click the Add (+) button in the bottom-left corner of the Info window. A dialog appears, allowing you to search for and select a user or group. Alternatively, you can create a new Sharing user account by clicking the New Person button or selecting a contact from your Address Book. Creating a new Sharing account requires that you enter a new password for the account.

MORE INFO ▶ Details about creating Sharing user accounts and how to create additional groups are covered in Lesson 5 "User Accounts".

Change Ownership

Even though ACLs allow you to define multiple user permissions for an item, only the user closest to the bottom in the permissions list is the owner of the item. Again, an item's owner who is not an administrative user is allowed to change the privileges of an item. However, only administrative users can change both the ownership and the privileges of an item.

To assign a new owner using the Finder Info window, you must first add that user as an additional permissions entry. Once the user is added, select the user from the permissions list, and then choose "Make <username> the owner" from the Action pop-up menu, where <username> is the selected user.

Delete a Permissions Entry

To delete a user or group permissions entry, select the account from the permissions list, and click the Delete (–) button in the lower-left corner of the Info window. The Info window doesn't allow you to delete or change the original owner or delete the Everyone privilege of an item. You can use this window to seemingly delete all group privileges, but this isn't truly deleting the group privilege. Instead, it's simply removing all the privileges for the item's original group.

Modify a Permissions Entry

To assign different permissions to an entry, simply click any privilege, and then choose another access option for that user or group from the pop-up menu that appears.

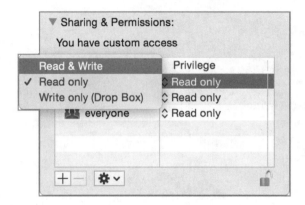

Propagate Folder Permissions

If you are changing a folder's permissions, by default, the Finder does not change the permissions of any items inside the folder. In many cases, you may want to apply the same permissions to the items inside the folder. This task is sometimes known as propagating permissions. You can accomplish this quickly by choosing "Apply to enclosed items" from the Action pop-up menu.

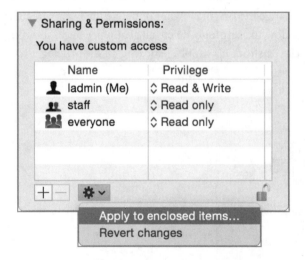

NOTE ▶ Even if you are the owner of a folder, applying permissions to the enclosed folder items may require administrator authentication.

NOTE ▶ Applying permissions to the enclosed folder items applies all permissions settings to all enclosed items, not just the changes you recently made. Further, these changes cannot be easily reverted. The exception to this is that any locked items inside the folder remain in their original state.

Permissions for Nonsystem Volumes

Portable external disks are useful tools for transferring files and folders from one computer to another. A downside to this technology, though, is that computers can't properly interpret file ownership, because they don't share the same user account database. In other words, most Mac computers don't have the exact same user accounts, so when a disk is moved from one Mac to another, the file ownership from one Mac is meaningless to another.

Unless you plan to implement a centralized network user database so all your Mac computers *do* share the same user account database, ownership on nonsystem volumes, like those found on external disks, will have to be ignored to prevent access issues. This is the default behavior in OS X for all nonsystem volumes on both internal and external disks. However, this approach introduces the security risk that all local users will have full access to the contents of any nonsystem volumes, including other partitions of a system disk. If you find this an unacceptable risk, you can disable the default behavior and force OS X to honor ownership on nonsystem volumes.

To do this in the Finder, select the nonsystem volume for which you want the system to honor the ownership, and then open the Info window. In the Sharing & Permissions section, click the small lock icon in the lower-right corner, and authenticate as an administrative user to unlock the Sharing & Permissions section. Finally, deselect the "Ignore ownership on this volume" checkbox.

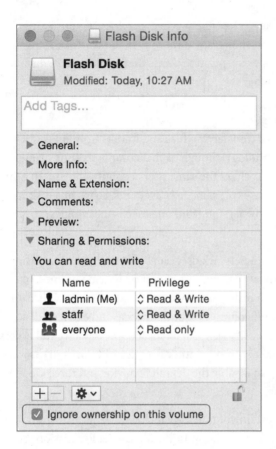

Exercise 11.1
Create Items with Default Permissions

▶ **Prerequisites**

▶ You must have created the Local Admin ("Exercise 2.1 Configure a New OS X System for Exercises" on page 60 or "Exercise 2.2 Configure an Existing OS X System for Exercises" on page 63), Chris Johnson ("Exercise 5.1 Manage User Accounts" on page 145), and Mayta Mishtuk ("Exercise 6.1 Restore a Deleted User Account" on page 166) accounts.

A thorough understanding of ownership and permissions is essential to supporting and troubleshooting OS X. Permissions control the access to files and folders by users and system services such as the printing system. This exercise gives you a brief introduction to permissions in a user's home folder.

Store Files and Folders in Chris Johnson's Home Folder

To see the effects of the OS X default permissions, you will create some items with which to experiment.

1 If necessary, log in as Chris Johnson (using the password for the linked iCloud account or whatever you chose when you created the account).

2 Navigate to your home folder in the Finder by pressing Command-Shift-H.

3 Choose File > New Folder (or press Command-Shift-N).

4 Name the new folder Payroll Reports, and be sure it is located in your home folder, along with the default user folders.

As you will see shortly, this is not a good place to store confidential documents.

5 Open TextEdit.

6 In TextEdit, choose File > Save (or press Command-S), name the new file Secret Bonus List, and save it to the desktop. (Note that in a save dialog you can use the shortcut Command-Shift-D to select the desktop.)

7 Quit TextEdit.

8 Drag the Secret Bonus List.rtf file inside the Payroll Reports folder.

Examine Permissions as Another User

Now that Chris Johnson has created a test folder and file, experiment to see what Mayta Mishtuk can do with them.

1 Use fast user switching to log in as Mayta Mishtuk (password: mayta, or whatever you chose when you created the account).

2 In the Finder, navigate to Chris Johnson's home folder.

Mayta's Finder preferences have not been customized to allow easy access outside her home folder; however, you can reach Chris's home folder by choosing Go > Computer and then opening the Macintosh HD > Users > chris folder.

3 Click the Desktop folder, and then choose File > Get Info. Expand the Sharing & Permissions section if necessary.

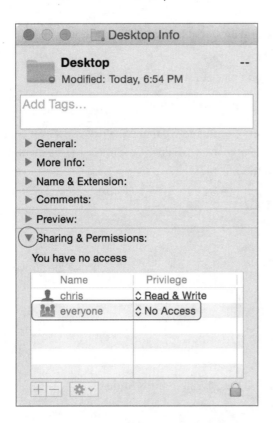

With the exception of Public, the folders that OS X creates by default in the home folder are protected from access by other users (the No Access permission).

4   Close the Info window.

5   Open the Payroll Reports folder.

The folder opens, and the Secret Bonus List file is visible.

This behavior may be contrary to what is expected by users. Be sure to guide your users to store their folders in the right place, based on the type of access they want to allow for other users. While others cannot add or remove items stored in the Payroll Reports folder, they can open and read the contents. You can see the permissions explicitly when you select the folder and choose File > Get Info.

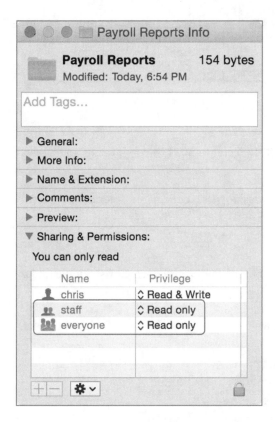

6   Open the Secret Bonus List file.

Since the file is readable by everyone but writable only by its owner, Chris Johnson, TextEdit shows that it is locked.

7 Try to enter some text into the file.

TextEdit asks if you would like to create a duplicate so that you can save your changes.

8 Click Duplicate.

A duplicate document named Untitled (Secret Bonus List copy) opens and allows you to enter text.

9 Save the duplicate document to your desktop (leave the name "Secret Bonus List copy").

10 Quit TextEdit.

11 In the Finder, navigate back to Chris's home folder, and open Chris's Public folder.

12 Try to open Chris's Drop Box folder.

The default permissions do not allow you to open another user's Drop Box folder.

13 Try to copy the Secret Bonus List copy from your desktop to Chris Johnson's Drop Box folder.

The Finder warns you that you will not be able to see the items you put into the Drop Box folder.

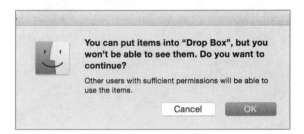

> **You can put items into "Drop Box", but you won't be able to see them. Do you want to continue?**
>
> Other users with sufficient permissions will be able to use the items.
>
> Cancel   OK

14 Click OK.

Proceed to "Exercise 11.2 Test Permissions Changes" on page 337 to see how to adjust the permissions on the Payroll Reports folder.

Exercise 11.2
Test Permissions Changes

> **Prerequisite**
>
> ▶ You must have performed "Exercise 11.1 Create Items with Default Permissions" on page 332.

Chris Johnson will now change the permissions on the Payroll Reports folder and test the results from Mayta Mishtuk's account.

Change Permissions as Chris Johnson

1 Use fast user switching to switch back to Chris Johnson's account.

2 Select the Payroll Reports folder that resides in Chris's home folder, and then choose File > Get Info.

3 If necessary, expand Sharing & Permissions.

4 Click the small lock in the Info window, and then authenticate as Local Admin.

5   Select the group (staff), and click the Delete (–) button below the permissions list.

6   Change the Privilege level for everyone to No Access.

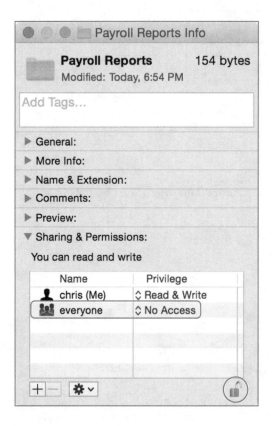

7   Close the Info window.

8   Navigate to Chris's Drop Box folder (inside the Public folder).

9   Select the Secret Bonus List copy that Mayta placed in Chris's Drop Box.

10   Choose File > Get Info. If necessary, expand the Sharing & Permissions section.

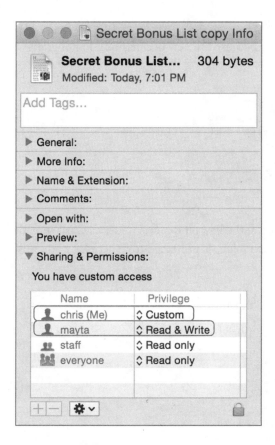

Since Mayta created this file, she is still its owner. However, when she copied it into Chris's Drop Box folder, an inheritable access control entry on the Drop Box folder granted Chris full access to it as well. This access actually goes beyond normal Read & Write access, so the Info window displays it as Custom.

11 Close the Info window.

12 Open the Secret Bonus List copy, and edit its contents.

The inherited access control granted Chris permissions to edit the file.

13 Quit TextEdit.

Test the New Permissions as Mayta Mishtuk

1 Use fast user switching to switch back to Mayta's account.

2   Try to open the Payroll Reports folder.

This time you cannot open the folder because the new permissions do not grant you read access.

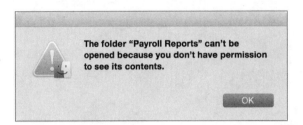

The default permissions did not protect the Payroll Reports folder as Chris intended, but after changing the permissions, the folder is protected from access by other users.

3   Log out of Mayta's account.

4   At the login window, switch to Chris Johnson.

5   Drag the Payroll Reports folder to the Trash.

Lesson 12
File System Troubleshooting

Because the operating system requires a functional file system, the software that drives the file system is very reliable. In fact, most file system failures are due to bad hardware or media. No matter how good the software is, though, if the hardware is no longer reading or writing bits, it's pretty much useless to the file system.

If, during troubleshooting, you determine that catastrophic hardware failure is the problem, there really isn't anything you can do from a software perspective to repair the device. Only a data recovery service, such as DriveSavers, might have a chance of recovering your data.

> **MORE INFO** ▸ When storage hardware suffers from catastrophic failure, DriveSavers is the most popular hard disk recovery service for Mac formatted volumes. You can find out more at www.drivesaversdatarecovery.com.

GOALS

▸ Examine file system elements

▸ Troubleshoot and repair partition and volume issues

▸ Troubleshoot and repair file system permission issues

Conversely, if you're experiencing file system issues but the storage hardware still appears to function, you may be experiencing partial hardware failure or file system corruption. In these cases, you can try some steps using the built-in utilities in OS X to repair the volumes or at least recover data. This lesson focuses on inspecting, verifying, and potentially repairing file system elements.

Reference 12.1
File System Inspection

Before attempting any fixes, you should become fully familiar with the file system configuration you're dealing with. The availability and status of storage hardware shown in the Disk Utility and System Information applications can help you determine if you are indeed experiencing hardware failure.

Examine Storage via Disk Utility

The /Applications/Utilities/Disk Utility application is your main tool for gathering file system information. When you open Disk Utility, it scans the file system for all attached devices and volumes. To gather detailed information about a specific disk or volume in Disk Utility, simply select the item from the column on the left, and then click the Info button in the toolbar.

As covered previously in Lesson 9 "File Systems and Storage", the disk storage hardware is listed first, and directly below each disk is the list of volumes. For example, the preceding screenshot shows two physical disks. The first disk contains one visible volume, and the second contains three.

For disks using standard volume management, the disk's name is a combination of the size, manufacturer, and model number. In the preceding screenshot, you can see this combination as the name for the second disk.

As covered in Lesson 9 "File Systems and Storage", many OS X systems use volumes managed by Core Storage. Disks containing volumes managed by Core Storage will often show the disk's name as similar to the volume's name, as shown by the name of the first disk in the preceding screenshot. Alternatively, for most Mac computers with Fusion Drive, the disk is labeled simply Internal Drive. If you have trouble identifying specific disks because of this odd Disk Utility behavior, consider inspecting the file system using the more accurate System Information application, as covered later in this lesson.

The information gathered from these dialogs reveals a great deal about the status of a disk or volume. A particularly helpful piece of information for identifying hardware failure is a disk's S.M.A.R.T. (self-monitoring, analysis, and reporting technology) status. S.M.A.R.T. technology can automatically determine if a disk is suffering from some sort of internal hardware failure. Unfortunately, as you can see from the following screenshot, many external disks don't support S.M.A.R.T.

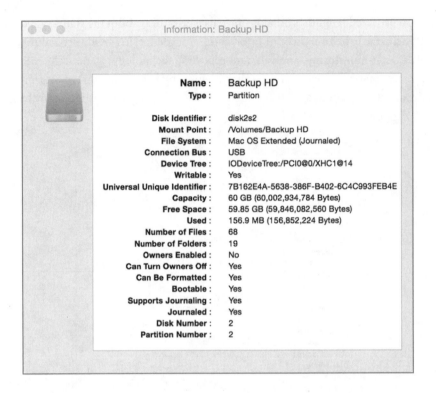

Examine Storage via System Information

There are several instances where you may want to double-check the disk's status using /Applications/Utilities/System Information . For example, it's possible that a disk has suffered such catastrophic failure that it doesn't even appear in the Disk Utility list. Another example is that the Disk Utility application doesn't properly show all aspects of volumes being managed by Core Storage, as is the case for Fusion Drive systems or disks containing encrypted volumes.

When you open System Information, your first step should be examining the contents of the Storage section. This shows you all currently mounted volumes, regardless of origin. The following screenshot of System Information was taken on the same system as the earlier screenshots of Disk Utility. Note how in System Information you can easily identify the physical storage device used for the encrypted Macintosh HD volume, APPLE SSD, and that the device's S.M.A.R.T. status is Verified.

You can further inspect the physical storage devices by selecting one of the storage inter-faces. In this example, the APPLE SSD is connected via SATA, so selecting the SATA/SATA Express section in System Information reveals more information about the hardware. Knowing how the storage device is physically connected is key to inspecting it.

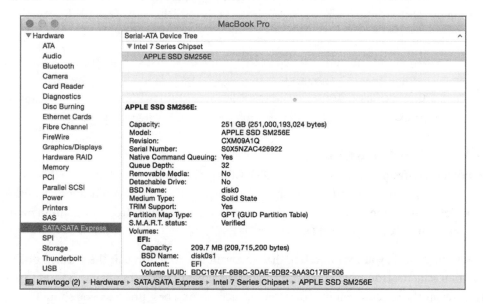

If a physical device does not appear in System Information, it is not available to the Mac in its current state. At that point, you should focus your efforts on troubleshooting the disk hardware. This includes simple fixes, such as looking for loose connections or replacing bad cables, as well as more complex fixes, such as replacing bad hardware like the disk enclosure.

Reference 12.2
Troubleshoot Partitions and Volumes

Disk Utility can be used to examine and attempt to repair a partition scheme or volume directory structure. The partition scheme is used to define the space where volumes exist. The volume directory structure is used by the file system to catalog where files and folders exist on the disk. To access data on the disk, the file system must first check with the partition scheme and volume directory structure to locate the appropriate bits on the disk that make up the requested items. Obviously, any damage to this information can lead to serious problems, including data loss.

Before any disk is mounted, the Mac automatically performs a quick consistency check to verify the disk's partition scheme and volume directory structure. The system also quickly scans the startup disk during the startup process. However, if the system is unable to mount a disk or its volumes, or you are experiencing problems accessing a disk's content, you can use Disk Utility to verify and repair the partition scheme or volume directory structures.

> **NOTE** ▶ If you're attempting to repair the system disk, first start up from OS X Recovery by holding down Command-R at startup, and then choose Disk Utility from the OS X Utilities window. If the default OS X Recovery system doesn't work, you can use any of the alternative methods detailed in Lesson 3 "OS X Recovery".

Disk Utility Verify and Repair

To use the Verify and Repair features in Disk Utility, first double-check that the disk you want to verify or repair is attached to the computer, and then open /Applications/Utilities/Disk Utility. Select the disk or volume you want to verify or repair from the column on the left, and then click the First Aid tab.

By selecting a disk, you are indicating that you want to verify or repair the selected disk's partition scheme. However, by selecting a volume, you are indicating that you want to verify or repair the selected volume's directory structure. As a best practice, you should verify or repair all components of a single disk.

First verify the selected item by clicking the Verify Disk button. The verification process may take a few minutes to complete. During this time, Disk Utility shows a progress indicator and log entries in the history area. Click the "Show details" checkbox to view more detail in the history log. You can stop the process at any time by clicking the Stop button.

If no problems are found, an entry with green text appears in the history log. If problems are uncovered, they appear in bright red text. If the disk has problems and you haven't already started the repair process, do so now. The system continues to run the repair process until no more problems are found. This may take a while, because the system may run through the repair process several times.

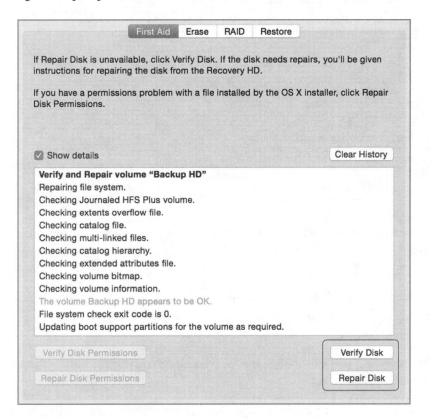

Target Disk Mode

Mac hardware has a unique ability to share its internal disks via a feature called target disk mode. Basically, when target disk mode is engaged, instead of starting up normally from the system disk, the Mac creates a connection from the internal disks to the FireWire or Thunderbolt port.

Because the target disk mode function is built into the Mac computer's hardware, you can still use this feature even if the installed operating system volume is corrupted. An administrative user can enable target disk mode on a currently running Mac by clicking the Target Disk Mode button in Startup Disk preferences. Alternatively, any user can engage target disk mode during system startup by holding down the T key while turning on the Mac.

NOTE ▶ Certain forms of hardware failure can prevent a Mac from entering target disk mode. If you suspect this is the case, try using Apple Hardware Test, as covered in Lesson 27 "System Troubleshooting".

NOTE ▶ Target disk mode is not supported on any Mac that lacks a FireWire or Thunderbolt port or that uses third-party storage interfaces like those found on PCI Express expansion cards.

NOTE ▶ Target disk mode cannot be engaged during system startup when using a Bluetooth wireless keyboard.

NOTE ▶ If the Mac you're placing in target disk mode features a Fusion Drive, you should only connect it to Mac systems using OS X v10.8.5 or later. For more information, see the Apple Support article HT202757, "OS X Mavericks: Only connect OS X Mavericks Fusion Drives to OS X Mountain Lion v10.8.5 or later."

Once target disk mode has been engaged, large FireWire and/or Thunderbolt symbols appear on the screen, and then you can simply plug the targeted Mac into another fully functioning Mac using a FireWire or Thunderbolt cable. The targeted Mac computer's internal volumes mount normally on the other Mac, as if you had plugged in a normal external disk. At this point, you can do anything to the targeted Mac computer's internal disk that you could do to any local disk, including installations, repairs, and data migration.

Recovering Data from a Nonstarting System

If you are still stuck with a Mac that refuses to fully start up from its internal system disk, you might be able to recover important data off the disk as long as it's functional. You can use the Mac computer's built-in target disk mode to easily access the internal system disk and transfer important data to another working Mac.

NOTE ▶ If your Mac doesn't support, or is unable to engage, target disk mode, your best bet is to visit an Apple Authorized Service Provider. As an alternative, you could remove the disk from the troubled computer and attach it to another fully functional Mac.

First, turn on or restart the problematic Mac while holding down the T key to engage target disk mode, and connect the computer to another fully functioning Mac using a standard FireWire or Thunderbolt cable. If the targeted Mac computer's volume appears in the Finder, first attempt to repair the volume using Disk Utility, as detailed previously in this lesson.

After repairs have been completed, you have a variety of data recovery options:

▶ Use the Finder to manually copy data from the targeted Mac to storage attached to the functioning Mac.

▶ Use Disk Utility on the functioning Mac to create a disk image archive of the targeted Mac computer's system volume. Creating disk images is covered in "Reference 13.4 File Archives" on page 388.

▶ Migrate user data to the other system either manually or using Migration Assistant. Migrating user data is detailed in Lesson 6 "User Home Folders".

▶ After you have migrated the data, use Disk Utility to reformat the targeted Mac computer's disk, and then attempt to reinstall the operating system. Lesson 1 "Install OS X Yosemite" covers this topic in greater detail.

Depending on the amount of corruption to the targeted Mac computer's system disk, you may not be able to use Disk Utility or Migration Assistant. The disk may simply be too corrupted to recover all that data. In this case, you have to resort to manually copying data.

In general, the items most important to users are stored in their home folder, so you should start there. This can be a time-consuming process, because when the Finder discovers damaged files, you have to manually restart the copy process and omit the damaged files.

> **TIP** ▶ Use the ample spare time between manual file copies to remind the Mac computer's owner (or yourself) that you wouldn't have to labor over a broken disk if there was a good backup! Lesson 16 "Time Machine" covers this topic in greater detail.

> **TIP** ▶ Several third-party disk recovery utilities are available for OS X. This guide doesn't recommend one over another; contact an Apple Authorized Service Provider for recommendations.

Reference 12.3
Troubleshoot File System Permissions

Permissions issues can be caused by a variety of situations. Many are due to user error, but others can be the result of a failure elsewhere in the system. For instance, some software installers may improperly change permissions during the installation process. You may also experience permissions issues after restarting from a power loss or system freeze.

System and application errors, such as applications that will not open or an inability to empty the Trash, may occur due to incorrect permissions. Many of these permissions issues can be resolved by utilities that are part of OS X. If you are having trouble accessing an application, try to resolve the issue using the Disk Utility Repair Disk Permissions feature. Also, if you are experiencing problems trying to access home folders, you can use the Reset Password utility in OS X Recovery to reset home folder permissions. The use of these two utilities for resolving permissions issues is covered later in this section.

Many general permissions issues are revealed in obvious ways. Users attempting to access a file or folder are immediately stopped and presented with a dialog stating that they don't have the appropriate permissions. In this case, a permissions change on the item, or the folder it's inside, is usually all that's needed to resolve the issue. If you attempt to repair the item's permissions manually, you should be familiar with the methods for managing permissions, as covered in Lesson 11 "Permissions and Sharing".

MORE INFO ▶ For further guidance on general permissions troubleshooting, you can also refer to Apple Support article HT2963, "Troubleshooting permissions issues in Mac OS X."

Disk Utility Repair Permissions

One of the most common troubleshooting techniques for OS X is to use the Disk Utility Repair Disk Permissions feature. Many novice Mac administrators use this technique every time they encounter any problem.

Actually, however, this process fixes only file permissions issues specific to certain installed Apple software. Further, this process doesn't touch any incorrect permission settings on personal or user data. In other words, this process, though a good starting point for addressing system and application issues, doesn't fix every incorrect permissions issue on a problematic Mac.

MORE INFO ▶ For more information, see Apple Support article HT201560, "About Disk Utility's Repair Disk Permissions feature."

The upside is that the repair permissions process is an easy troubleshooting step that can resolve many permissions issues. Keep in mind that many default folders are installed as part of the operating system. Thus, the repair permissions process repairs not only system items but also important folders like /Applications and /Library.

To verify or repair disk permissions, open Disk Utility on a currently running Mac or on a Mac started up from OS X Recovery. In Disk Utility, select a volume containing an OS X system you want to repair from the column on the left, and then click the First Aid tab. Click the Verify Disk Permissions button to view a log of any potential problems, or click the Repair Disk Permissions button to view and fix any permission problems.

In most cases, even though it may not be the answer to every last issue, repairing permissions issues found by Disk Utility is a good idea.

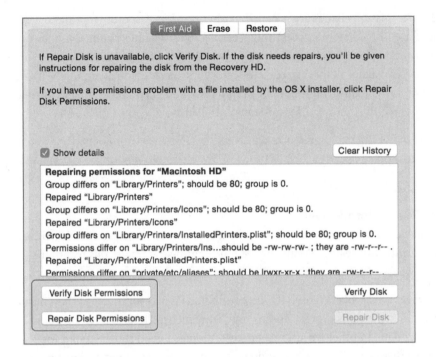

Reset Home Folder Permissions

If a user's home folder becomes inaccessible due to improper permissions, you can attempt to fix the issue by manually adjusting the permissions yourself, or you can try the Reset Password application found in OS X Recovery.

> **TIP** ▶ Obviously, you can also use the Reset Password application to change a user's lost password.

This application was primarily designed to reset user passwords; nonetheless, it also has the ability to reset a user's home folder permissions and ACLs. Keep in mind that this application resets all home folder permissions, including intentionally changed permissions that may have benefited the user.

Again, the Reset Password application is available only from an OS X Recovery system. Once running from OS X Recovery, you must open Terminal (via the Utilities menu), type resetpassword, and press Return. After Reset Password opens, simply select the system volume and the user account you want to reset, and click the Reset button in the bottom-right corner. Note that you do not have to enter a new user password to repair a user's home folder permissions.

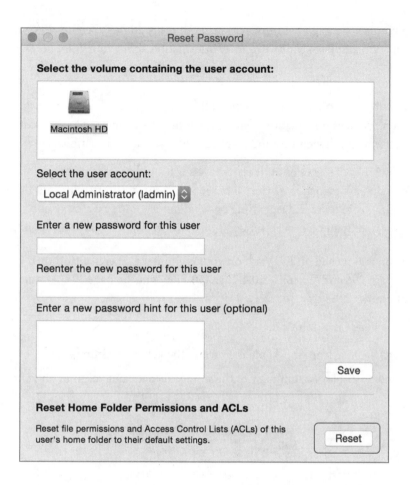

Exercise 12.1
Examine Local Storage

▶ You must have created the Chris Johnson account ("Exercise 5.1 Manage User Accounts" on page 145).

OS X provides multiple ways to gather information about disks. In this exercise, you will use System Information and Disk Utility to gather information about your computer's disk.

View Disk Information with System Information

System Information provides information about devices that are connected to your computer. In this exercise, you will view disk information with System Information.

> **NOTE ▶** At a number of places in this exercise, you will see that information displayed about volumes that are managed by Core Storage is considerably different from those that are not using Core Storage. Depending on what model of Mac you have and exactly how your computer has been set up, it might be in either mode at this point.

1 If you turned on and turned off FileVault on your computer ("Exercise 10.1 Turn On FileVault" on page 296 and "Exercise 10.4 Turn Off FileVault" on page 308), restart your computer now.

2 If necessary, log in as Chris Johnson.

3 Choose About This Mac from the Apple menu, and then click the Storage tab.

The About window displays a summary of the storage devices and volumes on your computer.

4 Click the Overview tab and then the System Report button.

System Information opens and displays a more detailed report of the hardware, network, and software configuration of your computer.

5 On the left, select the bus that's connected to your Mac computer's internal disk.

Most Mac models use Serial ATA (SATA) for internal disks, but the latest Mac Pro computers use PCI Express, and first-generation MacBook Air models use ATA.

6   If necessary, select your computer's internal disk, and make a note of the following information:

NOTE ▶ If your startup volume is being managed by Core Storage, some information will not be available here. Specifically, your startup volume will appear with a generic identifier (such as disk0s2) instead of a name, and most of its other properties will not be listed. In these cases, you will be able to find the missing information when you get to step 7.

Disk Device

▶   Partition Map Type: _____

Volume "Macintosh HD"

▶   File System (Volume Format): _____

▶   Capacity (Volume Size): _____

▶   Available (Free Space): _____

Volume "Backup"

▶   File System (Volume Format): _____

▶   Capacity (Volume Size): _____

► Available (Free Space): _____

You may also see a couple of hidden partitions: EFI (used for firmware updates) and Recovery HD (used for OS X Recovery).

The Hardware section of the source list on the left displays connection methods. The information shown in this part of System Information is bus-oriented, that is, connection-oriented. As you will see in Lesson 25 "Peripherals and Drivers", System Information is especially useful when you are troubleshooting a suspected connection issue.

7   On the left, select Storage.

The Storage section shows the volumes mounted on your computer independent of which bus and device they are on. If you were not able to find any of the volume capacity information in the bus-oriented view, you can find it here and fill in the missing information.

8   Quit System Information.

View Disk Information with Disk Utility

Disk Utility is storage device–oriented, in that it provides information on both disks connected to your computer and management tools for those disks. In this exercise, you will gather information about your computer's disk using Disk Utility.

1   Open Disk Utility.

2   Click the entry for your internal disk or Core Storage volume group (generally the top item) in the source list on the left. If you see a Core Storage volume group, skip ahead to step 5.

Without Core Storage volume management

With Core Storage volume management

3   If you see the physical disk device, click the Info button in the toolbar to view information about your hard disk.

Note that this window does not show information about space available or space used.

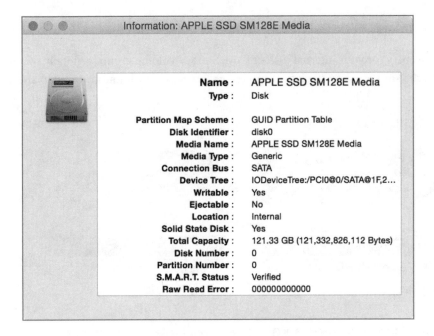

Depending on your disk, you may also see detailed S.M.A.R.T. statistics.

4   Close this information window.

5   In the source list, click the indented entry for your startup volume (generally Macintosh HD), and then click the Info button.

This window displays information for the volume, including capacity, free space, and used space.

6   Get info on the Backup volume as well, and then use these three windows in Disk
    Utility to make a note of the following information:

> **NOTE ▸** Again, if your disk is being managed by Core Storage, some information is
> not available. While System Information showed full disk-level information but left
> out information on the encrypted volume, Disk Utility shows full volume information
> but not disk-level information.

Disk Device

▶   Partition Map Scheme: _____

Volume "Macintosh HD"

▶   File System (Volume Format): _____

▶   Capacity (Volume Size): _____

▶   Available (Free Space): _____

Volume "Backup"

▶   File System (Volume Format): _____

▶   Capacity (Volume Size): _____

▶ Available (Free Space): _____

The details for your computer are likely to be different from what you see pictured. Disk Utility refers to the partition map scheme, whereas System Information refers to the partition map type. These are interchangeable terms.

7 If you are not going to perform the next exercise, quit Disk Utility.

Exercise 12.2
Repair Partitions and Volumes in Target Disk Mode

▶ **Prerequisites**

▶ You must have created the Mayta Mishtuk account ("Exercise 6.1 Restore a Deleted User Account" on page 166).

▶ You need another computer running OS X Yosemite.

▶ Both computers must have FireWire or Thunderbolt interfaces, and you need the appropriate cable to connect them.

In this exercise, you will start your computer in target disk mode and use another computer to check its file structure and system file permissions and to examine its files directly in the Finder. These are techniques that could be used to repair or recover files from a computer that could not start up normally because of file system damage.

NOTE ▶ This exercise and "Exercise 12.3 Repair Partitions and Volumes in OS X Recovery Mode" on page 368 cover many of the same operations, but they use different modes to run the disk repair tools. You do not need to perform both. Generally, if you have access to another Mac running Yosemite and both computers have FireWire or Thunderbolt (and you have the appropriate cable), this exercise is the preferred exercise. If you are participating in a classroom setting, you can perform this exercise with a partner, using one of your computers as the host and the other as the target.

Start Your "Target" Computer in Target Disk Mode

Choose one of your computers to act as a "host" (the computer that will run the disk repair tools) and one to act as a "target" (the computer that will have its disk repaired).

1 Shut down the target computer.

2 Hold down the T key on the target computer while you press the power button. Keep holding the T key until you see a FireWire or Thunderbolt logo (or both) on the screen.

3 When you see the logo on the screen, release the T key.

4 If necessary, log in to the host computer.

5 Connect the two computers with a FireWire or Thunderbolt cable.

6 If the target computer's startup disk is encrypted with FileVault, you are prompted for a password to unlock the disk; you can enter the password of any FileVault-enabled account (ladminpw, or the iCloud password for Chris Johnson, or whatever passwords you chose).

7 If a dialog appears asking whether you want to use this disk as a Time Machine device, click Don't Use.

8 On the host computer, open Disk Utility.

9 Select the target computer's internal disk device, or if it is being managed by Core Storage, select the logical volume group that appears instead. It generally appears with an orange disk icon (in contrast to the gray icons of the host computer's disk and volumes).

10 In the toolbar, click Info.

Note that the Connection Bus entry is FireWire or Thunderbolt. If the target computer is using Core Storage, the logical volume group is shown instead, which does not list the connection bus.

11 Close the Information window.

Repair the Partition Table and Volume

1 If necessary, click the First Aid tab.

2 Click Repair Disk.

Disk Utility checks (and, if necessary, repairs) the partition table as well as certain hidden disk contents such as the EFI system partition. If you are using a Fusion Drive or FileVault, checking the logical volume group checks the volumes as well, so you can skip ahead to the next section of this exercise ("Examine Files Manually in Target Disk Mode" on page 365).

Disk Utility shouldn't find any problems; if it does, use Repair Disk again to make sure that all problems were repaired successfully.

3   Select the entry for the target computer's Macintosh HD volume, and then click Repair Disk again.

This time, Disk Utility checks (and, if necessary, repairs) the file structure within the Macintosh HD volume. Since there are a large number of files in the volume, this process may take a few minutes.

As before, it should not find any problems; if it does, use Repair Disk again to make sure that all problems are repaired successfully. You can also verify or repair the Backup volume.

Note that the Verify Disk Permissions and Repair Disk Permissions buttons are dimmed; this is because the volume is external and your computer is ignoring file ownership on it. You will change this shortly.

4   Select the host computer's startup volume.

For this volume the Repair Disk button is dimmed because you cannot repair a volume that is in use. You can verify it, but even that may not work if the volume is too active.

Examine Files Manually in Target Disk Mode

1   In the host computer's Finder, open the Computer view by pressing Command-Shift-C.

Both computers' volumes appear. Generally, you can distinguish them by the target computer's orange volume icons (and FireWire symbols if appropriate).

2   Select the target computer's Macintosh HD volume, and choose File > Get Info (Command-I).

The bottom of the Sharing & Permissions section shows that "Ignore ownership on this volume" is selected. Because the host computer sees this as an external disk, it assumes that file ownership and permissions relate to user accounts from some other computer, and it shouldn't attempt to apply them to users on this computer. This was discussed in "Reference 11.3 Managing Permissions " on page 326.

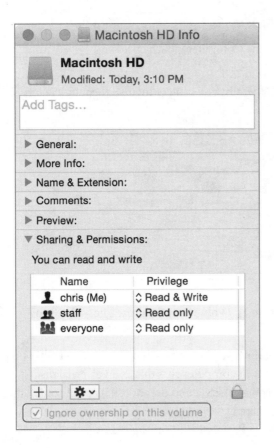

3   Open the target computer's Macintosh HD volume, and then navigate into Users/
    mayta/Desktop.

    Because ownership is being ignored, you can access Mayta's files directly. If necessary,
    you could recover files from a computer this way even if the computer could not start
    up normally.

4   In the volume's Info window, click the small lock icon, and authenticate as Local
    Admin.

5   Deselect the "Ignore ownership on this volume" checkbox.

6   Close the Info window.

Repair System File Permissions

1   Switch back to Disk Utility.

2   Select the entry for the target computer's Macintosh HD volume.

Since ownership is not being ignored, the Verify Disk Permissions and Repair Disk Permissions buttons are available.

3   Click Repair Disk Permissions.

Disk Utility checks the system files against their installation records and repairs any discrepancies. Again, since there are a large number of files to check, this process may take a few minutes.

It is normal for a few errors to be listed here; usually they do not represent a real problem. See Apple Support article HT203172, "Mac OS X: Disk Utility's Repair Disk Permissions messages that you can safely ignore," for more information.

Note that the Disk Utility permissions repair function does not fix user files. If you need to repair user home directories, you need to use the Reset Password utility in OS X Recovery mode (shown in the next exercise).

4   In the Disk Utility toolbar, click the Eject button.

Note that the Eject button ejects the entire disk (including all volumes on it), whereas the Unmount button operates only on the selected volume. The exception is that encrypted volumes are treated separately, so ejecting them does not eject the rest of the disk.

5   If any of the target computer's volumes remain undimmed in the list, select them, and click Eject again.

6   Quit Disk Utility.

7   Press and hold the power button to shut down the target computer, and then unplug the cable after the computer has been turned off.

8   If you are not going to perform the next exercise, restart the target computer normally.

Exercise 12.3
Repair Partitions and Volumes in OS X Recovery Mode

▶ **Prerequisites**

▶   You must have created the Chris Johnson account ("Exercise 5.1 Manage User Accounts" on page 145).

▶   Your computer must have a local hidden Recovery HD partition.

In this exercise, you will start your computer in OS X Recovery mode and check its file structure, system file permissions, and home folder permissions. These are techniques that you can use to repair a computer that will not start up normally because of file system damage.

NOTE ▶ This exercise and "Exercise 12.2 Repair Partitions and Volumes in Target Disk Mode" on page 360 perform many of the same operations but use different modes to run the disk repair tools. You do not need to perform both.

Repair the Partition Table and Volume

1   Restart your computer, and then hold down Command-R until the gray Apple logo appears on the screen.

2   At the Utilities screen, select Disk Utility, and click Continue.

3   If your startup volume is encrypted with FileVault, it appears dimmed in the disks and volumes list; select it, and click the Unlock button in the toolbar, and then enter the password of any FileVault-enabled account (**ladminpw**, or the iCloud password for Chris Johnson, or whatever passwords you chose).

4   Select your computer's internal disk device, or if it is being managed by Core Storage, select the logical volume group that appears instead. In either case, it is generally the top entry in the sidebar.

5   If necessary, click the First Aid tab.

6   Click Repair Disk.

   Disk Utility checks the partition table as well as certain hidden disk contents such as the EFI system partition and Recovery HD partition and attempts to repair any problems it finds. If it is being managed by Core Storage, checking the logical volume group actually checks the volumes as well, so you can skip ahead to "Repair System File Permissions" on page 367.

NOTE ▶ If you receive a message that says "Live file system repair is not supported," there is a problem with the partition table that Disk Utility was not able to repair while started up from that disk. Note that in Recovery mode, even though the normal startup volume is not in use ("live"), the partition table is. To repair this problem, you need to perform the repair via target disk mode ("Exercise 12.2 Repair Partitions and Volumes in Target Disk Mode" on page 360), create an external install disk ("Exercise 3.2 Create an OS X Install Disk" on page 99), and run the repair from that; or use Internet Recovery by restarting your computer with Command-Option-R (note that this requires recent firmware; see Reference "Reference 3.1 Startup from OS X Recovery" on page 87).

7 Select the entry for the Macintosh HD volume, and then click Repair Disk again.

This time, Disk Utility checks the file structure within the Macintosh HD volume and repairs it if necessary.

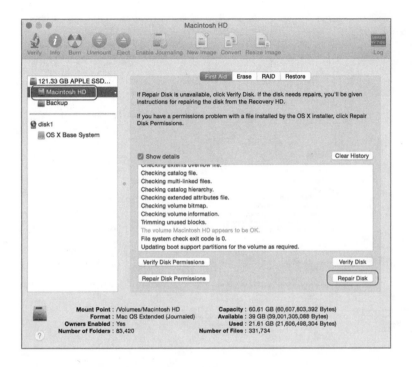

You can also verify or repair the Backup volume.

Repair System File Permissions

1   If necessary, select the entry for the Macintosh HD volume.

2   Click Repair Disk Permissions.

Disk Utility checks the system files against their installation records and repairs any discrepancies.

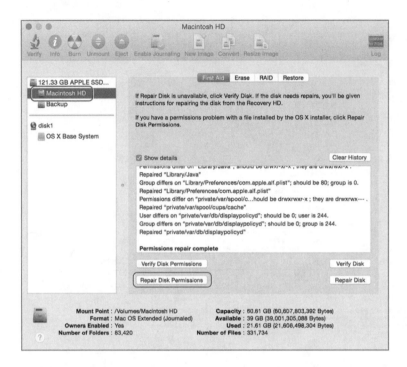

It is normal for a few errors to be listed here; usually they do not represent a real problem. See Apple Support article HT203172, "Mac OS X: Disk Utility's Repair Disk Permissions messages that you can safely ignore," for more information.

3 Select the entry for the Backup volume.

The Verify Disk Permissions and Repair Disk Permissions buttons are dimmed since this volume does not have OS X installed on it.

4 Quit Disk Utility.

Repair Home Folder Permissions

1 From the Utilities menu, choose Terminal.

The Terminal utility provides access to a command-line (text-based) interface in OS X. We do not cover the command-line interface in this guide, but it is necessary to reach the reset password utility in OS X Recovery.

2 Type the command resetpassword, and press Return.

The Reset Password utility opens.

3   Select Macintosh HD in the volume list, and then choose Chris Johnson (chris) from the user account pop-up menu.

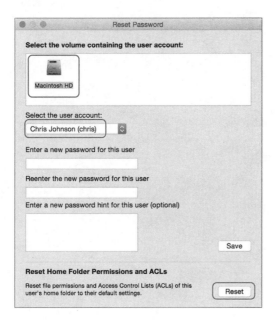

4   Click Reset.

The Reset Password utility checks (and, if necessary, repairs) the ownership for Chris Johnson's home folder and its contents.

This tool does not report whether it found any problems.

5   Choose Restart from the Apple menu to restart your computer normally.

Data Management

Hidden Items, Shortcuts, and File Archives

OS X includes several technologies for making complex file system structures appear simple. An excellent example of this is how the Finder displays the OS X file system to the user. By default, the Finder hides much of the complexity of OS X from the user and reveals only four folders at the root (beginning) level of the system volume. Applications also appear to be single icons, despite containing all the resources necessary for modern complex software. Also, many items are shown in intentionally convenient locations but are actually stored elsewhere. Further, archiving technology allows multiple items to be combined into a single compressed file.

In this lesson, you will explore the file system technologies that assist in hiding, redirecting, and archiving items. This includes an exploration of the hidden items in OS X, including bundles and packages. You will also learn how to manage file system aliases and links. Finally, you will open and create zip archives and disk images.

GOALS

▸ Navigate to hidden files and folders

▸ Examine packages and bundles

▸ Manage aliases and links

▸ Create and open zip archives and disk images

Reference 13.1
Hidden Items

OS X is a fully UNIX-compliant operating system, and as such includes a number of files that the average user never touches. The root level of the Mac system volume contains many resources that UNIX processes require and UNIX administrators expect. Apple made the wise choice of configuring the Finder to hide these items from the average user. On a daily basis, the average user—and even most administrative users—does not need to access any of these items from the graphical interface.

Realistically, the only people who even care about these normally hidden resources are going to be using the command-line interface via Terminal to do their work anyway. In other words, keeping these system items hidden in the Finder not only provides a tidier work environment but also prevents average users from poking around in places they shouldn't go.

As a hybrid of previous UNIX and Mac OS technologies, OS X uses two methods to hide files and folders. The first is a UNIX tradition: simply using a period at the beginning of the item's name hides the item both in the Finder and while using the default options to list items in Terminal. The second method is a Mac OS tradition: enabling an item's hidden file flag. This method, however, only hides the item in the Finder.

> **NOTE** ▶ To prevent user confusion, OS X does not let you hide items using the Finder or any of the default applications. Only from Terminal can a user name items beginning with a period or manage the hidden file flag. Use of Terminal is beyond the scope of this guide.

Navigating Hidden Folders in the Finder

Should you want or need to open normally hidden items in the Finder, you have a choice of several methods. The first two provide access to the most commonly accessed hidden folder, the user's Library folder. The last method involves using the Go menu in the Finder to open any folder, including hidden folders.

User's Hidden Library Folder

As detailed later in Lesson 14 "System Resources", the user's Library folder is full of important resources, but it is hidden in the Finder. Fortunately, the Go menu provides a quick shortcut to this often-visited location. Simply hold down the Option key while clicking the Go menu to reveal the Library menu item.

Go	Window	Help	
Back			⌘[
Forward			⌘]
Enclosing Folder			⌥⌘↑
	📖 All My Files		⇧⌘F
	📄 Documents		⇧⌘O
	🖥 Desktop		⇧⌘D
	⬇ Downloads		⌥⌘L
	🏠 Home		⇧⌘H
	📁 Library		
	💻 Computer		⇧⌘C
	📶 AirDrop		⇧⌘R
	🌐 Network		⇧⌘K
	☁ iCloud Drive		⇧⌘I
	Applications		⇧⌘A
	🛠 Utilities		⇧⌘U

If you frequently access the user's Library folder, you may want to make it permanently visible. OS X Yosemite (and Mavericks) provides the ability to always show the user's Library folder. Start by making sure the user's home folder appears in the Finder sidebar. You can enable that behavior in the Sidebar settings of the Finder preferences, accessed by choosing Finder > Preferences or pressing Command-Comma. After you have selected the user's home folder in the Finder sidebar, choose View > Show View Options, or press Command-J. From the View Options window, you can select the checkbox to permanently show the user's Library folder.

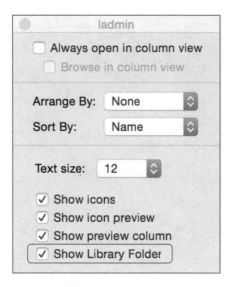

Go to Folder

To reveal any hidden folder in the Finder, choose Go > Go to Folder, or press Command-Shift-G. This opens a dialog that allows you to enter an absolute path to any folder on the Mac. A good starting place is the /private folder, as this folder contains many common UNIX system resources.

TIP An incredibly useful shortcut is to use Tab key completion when entering file system paths. Simply press Tab once you have started a pathname, and the system attempts to automatically fill in the rest of the name. For example, navigating to the /private folder requires only that you enter **/p** and then press Tab.

Click the Go button after you have entered a path. The Finder reveals the hidden folder in a window. Note the dimmed folder icon representing the normally hidden folder. To save time when you return to the Go dialog, the last path you entered appears there.

NOTE ▶ Some folders, both visible and hidden, have permissions that do not allow standard or administrative users to view the contents.

Reference 13.2
Bundles and Packages

Sometimes hiding individual items isn't the most efficient solution for hiding data, especially if you need to hide a lot of related files. Conveniently, there is a built-in method for combining files: the common folder. Apple simply modified this existing file system container by adding the ability to optionally hide a folder's content.

Bundles and packages are nothing more than common folders that happen to contain related software and resources. This allows software developers to easily organize all the resources needed for a complicated product into a single bundle or package while also discouraging normal users from interfering with the resources.

Bundles and packages use the same technique of combining resources inside special folders. The difference is that the Finder treats packages as opaque objects that users, by default, cannot navigate into. For example, where a user sees only a single icon in the Finder representing an application, in reality it is a folder filled with, potentially, thousands of resources.

The word *package* is also used to describe the archive files used by applications to install software—that is, installer packages. This is appropriate, as users cannot, by default, navigate into the contents of an installer package, because the Finder again displays it as a single opaque object. Starting with OS X v10.5, Apple allowed the creation of fully opaque installation packages, wherein the entire contents are inside a single file, further preventing users from accidentally or intentionally revealing installation content.

NOTE ▶ Because bundles and packages are really just special folders, these items simply copy over to volumes other than Mac OS Extended as regular folders. The Finder continues to recognize the items as bundles or packages even when they reside on a third-party volume.

Revealing Package Content

Although the Finder default is to hide the contents of a package, you can view the contents of a package from the Finder. To access a package's contents in the Finder, secondary (or Control-) click the item you want to explore, and then choose Show Package Contents from the shortcut menu.

Be very careful when exploring this content. Modifying the content of a bundle or package can easily leave the item unstable or unusable. If you can't resist the desire to tinker with a bundle or package, always do so from a copy, and leave the original safely intact.

MORE INFO ▶ Tools for creating and modifying bundles and packages are available to those who have Mac Dev Center access. You can find out more about the Apple developer programs at https://developer.apple.com/.

Package Resources

The anatomy of an installer package is quite simple; it usually contains only a compressed archive of the software to be installed and a few configuration files used by the installer application. Other software bundles and packages, on the other hand, are often much more complex, as they contain all the resources necessary for the application or software.

Software bundles or packages often include:

▶ Executable code for multiple platforms

▶ Document description files

▶ Media resources such as images and sounds

▶ User interface description files

▶ Text resources

▶ Resources localized for specific languages

▶ Private software libraries and frameworks

▶ Plug-ins or other software to expand capability

Reference 13.3
File System Shortcuts

Another example of OS X being a hybrid of both UNIX and the classic Mac OS is the multiple methods used for file system pointers or shortcuts. Generally speaking, file system shortcuts are files that refer to other files or folders; this allows you to have a single item appear in multiple locations or with multiple names without having to create multiple copies of the item. Both the system and users take advantage of file system shortcuts to provide access to items from more convenient locations without having to duplicate those items.

> **NOTE** ▶ Do not confuse the shortcuts found in the Dock or the Finder sidebar with true file system shortcuts. Both the Dock and Finder save their references to original items as part of their configuration files, whereas file system shortcuts appear as individual files that can be located anywhere on a volume.

File System Shortcut Comparison

OS X uses three primary file system shortcut types: aliases, symbolic links, and hard links. To help compare these shortcut types, this section uses a 7.1 GB disk image file named

BigFile.dmg. This file will be referred to using each shortcut type, and you will see the differences illustrated in the Finder Info window.

Aliases

Aliases are a holdover from the classic Mac OS but have been updated for OS X duties. Aliases can be created using the Finder but are not recognized by command-line tools in Terminal. Command-line tools think that aliases are nothing more than data files and do not know how to follow their references back to the original items.

Aliases, however, are more resilient than other shortcut types in that, if the original item is replaced or moved, the alias almost never loses the original item. An example of how aliases are used by the operating system is the Finder Burn Folder feature, which allows you to organize files before you burn them to an optical disc. To save space, the Finder populates the burn folder with aliases instead of copies of the original items.

The following screenshot shows the Finder Info window inspecting an alias pointing to BigFile.dmg. Note that the kind is reported as Alias and the file is much smaller than the 7.1 GB original, weighing in at roughly 760 KB. The extra information in the alias is what allows the system to keep track of the original item should it ever change location.

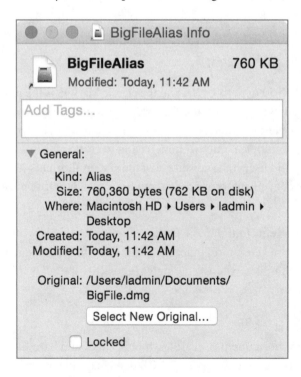

Symbolic Links

Symbolic link shortcuts are part of the traditional UNIX file system; they are simple pointers to the file system path of the original item. Thus in many cases, if you move the original item, the symbolic link is broken. However, replacing the original item works, because the path remains the same.

You can create symbolic links only in Terminal. The Finder cannot create symbolic links, but it can follow them to the original item. An example use of symbolic links in OS X is the way the system layout stores several fundamental UNIX folders in the /private folder but also makes those items available at the root of the file system using symbolic links.

The following screenshot shows the Finder Info window inspecting a symbolic link pointing to BigFile.dmg. Note that the kind is also reported as an Alias, but the file itself is tiny, at only 35 bytes. This illustrates that a symbolic link is merely saving a path to the original item. Also note the lack of a Select New Original button, indicating that the Finder cannot repair a symbolic link.

Hard Links

Hard-link shortcuts are also part of the traditional UNIX file system; they are actual additional references to the original item. Think of a normal file as two parts: the bits on the physical disk that make up the file's actual content and a name that points to those bits.

Technically, every file always uses at least one hard link. Creating an additional hard link is like creating another name that points to the same bits on the physical disk.

As a result, removing additional hard links does not delete the original item. Furthermore, deleting the "original" item does not delete the actual data or additional hard links. This is because the other hard links still point to the same bits on the disk, which won't be freed until there are no links left to them. This is unlike aliases and symbolic links, where deleting the original item leaves the shortcut pointing at nothing.

You can create hard links only in Terminal. The Finder cannot create hard links, but it can follow them. An example use of hard links in OS X is for Time Machine backups. Time Machine uses hard links to refer to items that have not changed since the previous backup, thus saving a tremendous amount of space. Finally, OS X is unique in its ability to use hard links of both files and folders; again, this is to support Time Machine backups.

The following screenshot shows the Finder Info window inspecting a hard link pointing to BigFile.dmg. Notice that the hard link is reported as a Disk Image (as opposed to an Alias) and it has the exact same file size as the original item, indicating that they share the same bits on the physical disk.

Managing Aliases

To create an alias in the Finder, simply select the item you want to create an alias for, and then choose one of the following methods:

▶ Choose File > Make Alias.

▶ Press Command-L.

▶ In a Finder window, choose Make Alias from the Action pop-up menu (small gear icon).

▶ In the Finder, secondary (or Control-) click the item, and then choose Make Alias from the shortcut menu.

▶ Click and drag the original item while holding down the Option and Command keys to drop the alias in another location. This is the only method that doesn't append *alias* to the new alias filename.

▶ Drag an application to the desktop. This gives users access to the application without the risk of them accidentally removing it from its original installed location.

After you have created the alias, you can rename it or move it anywhere you like. As long as the original item remains somewhere on the original volume—even if it's replaced or its name changes—the Finder can locate the alias. An alias file is easy to recognize by the small curved arrow that appears at the lower-left corner of the icon. From the Finder, you can locate the alias's target by secondary (or Control-) clicking the alias and then choosing Show Original from the shortcut menu, or by pressing Command-R.

In the rare case that an alias is broken—most likely because the original item was copied to another volume and then deleted off the original volume—you can repair the alias in the Finder. One method is to double-click the broken alias; the Finder automatically prompts you to select a new original.

Another option, which can also be used to redirect an existing alias, is to open the Finder Info window and then, in the General area, click the Select New Original button. Both methods open a browser dialog, allowing you to select a new original for the alias.

Reference 13.4
File Archives

At its essence, archiving is the practice of saving copies of important information to another location or format better suited for long-term storage or network transfer. Archiving and backup are both synonymous with copying data to another location for safekeeping, but in the context of this guide they are different processes serving different purposes. If you want to know more about backup in OS X, see Lesson 16 "Time Machine".

Unlike automated backup solutions, archiving is typically a manual process that involves creating compressed copies of selected data. Archive formats are efficient from a storage and data transfer perspective, but they generally require user interaction. This section focuses on the archive technologies in OS X: zip archives and disk images.

File Archive Comparison

OS X includes two archiving technologies—zip archives and disk images—both of which allow you to combine multiple files and compress the data into a more efficient file suited for long-term storage or network data transfer.

Zip archives can be created in the Finder from a selection of files or folders. This is an efficient method for archiving relatively small amounts of data quickly. The zip archive format is also widely compatible, as many operating systems include software to decompress zip archives back to their original items. However, zip archives in OS X do not offer the flexibility provided by disk images.

Disk images, created using Disk Utility, are more widely used in OS X for archiving purposes, because they offer many features not available from zip archives. Primarily, disk images allow you to archive the contents of an entire file system, including all files, folders, and their associated metadata, into a single file. The resulting disk image can be compressed, encrypted, or both. Disk images can also be created as read/write, so you can easily make changes to them over time. The only downside to disk images created using Disk Utility is that, by default, only Mac computers can access the content—other systems require third-party software to access Mac disk-image content.

Zip Archives

The Finder allows you to quickly create a compressed zip archive from any number of selected items or expand a zip archive to its original number of items. By default, creating a zip archive in the Finder doesn't delete the original items, and expanding a zip archive doesn't delete the original archive.

Creating Zip Archives

To create a zip archive in the Finder, select the items you want to archive and compress in the Finder. You can hold down the Shift key to quickly select contiguous lists of items or hold down the Command key to select noncontiguous items. Then simply choose File > Compress <Items> or secondary (or Control-) click the items and choose Compress

<Items> from the shortcut menu, where <Items> is the name of a single item or the number of items you have selected.

If the archiving process is going to take more than a few seconds, the Finder shows a progress dialog with the estimated time required to complete the compression task. You can also choose to cancel the archive by clicking the small x button on the far right. When the process finishes, you are left with a zip archive named either Archive.zip or <Item>.zip, where <Item> is the name of the single item you chose to archive and compress.

After the archiving process is complete, it's always interesting to compare the size of the original item(s) with the archive's size using the Info or Inspector window in the Finder. In many cases, you can expect at least a 50 percent decrease in file size. On the other hand, many media formats are already quite compressed in their original form, so you may not experience very good results when compressing these types of files.

Expanding Zip Archives

Expanding a zip archive in the Finder is as simple as double-clicking the archive file. The Finder, by default, decompresses the entire archive file and places the resulting files and folders in the same folder as the original zip archive. The Finder cannot list or extract individual items from a zip archive. Also by default, the Finder does not delete the original archive.

If you need more control over how zip archives are expanded, open /System/Library/CoreServices/Applications/Archive Utility.app (also searchable via Spotlight), and then choose Archive Utility > Preferences. These preferences allow you to adjust how zip archives are both expanded and compressed. Specifically, these preferences include options about how original items are handled after an archive transition.

Alternatively, the Archive Utility contains a system preference pane that can be installed if you find you are making frequent changes to these settings. To install this preference pane, secondary (or Control-) click the Archive Utility.app icon, and choose Show Package Contents from the shortcut menu. Once you're viewing the package contents in the Finder, navigate to and double-click /Contents/Resources/Archives.prefPane.

Disk Images

Disk images are files that contain entire virtual disks and volumes. OS X relies on disk images for several core technologies, including software distribution, system imaging, OS X Recovery, NetInstall, Legacy FileVault, and network Time Machine backups. Disk images are also useful as a personal archive tool. Though disk images created on a Mac work only on Mac computers by default, they offer much more flexibility than zip archives. Disk images provide advanced compression and encryption, but their greatest benefit is that they can be treated like a removable volume.

Mounting Disk Images

If in the past you have manually installed any Apple or third-party software downloaded from the Internet, you have already used a mounted disk image. By default, the Safari web browser automatically mounts any downloaded disk image, but you can also manually mount disk images at any time from the Finder. To access the contents of a disk image, simply double-click the disk image file in the Finder.

This mounts the volume inside the disk image file as if you had just connected a normal storage device. Even if the disk image file is located on a remote file server, you can still mount it as if it were a local disk. You can treat the mounted disk image volume as you would any other storage device by navigating through its hierarchy and selecting files and folders as you need them. Further, if the disk image is read/write, you can add to the contents of the disk image by simply dragging items to the volume.

Disk Image File.dmg   Disk Image Volume

NOTE ▶ When you are done with a disk image volume, be sure to properly eject it as you would any other removable volume.

Creating Empty Disk Images

Using /Applications/Utilities/Disk Utility to make disk images allows you to create blank images, or images containing copies of selected folders or even entire file systems. OS X supports disk images of nearly any size, limited only by local storage capacity.

To create an empty disk image, which you can then fill with content over time, open Disk Utility and then choose File > New > Blank Disk Image. Alternatively, with nothing selected in the Disk Utility window disks list, you can click the New Image button.

In the New Blank Image dialog you can define the parameters for the new disk image. At minimum, you need to select a name and destination for the resulting disk image file. You should also enter a name for the volume inside the disk image. The disk image file and volume names do not have to match, but they should be similar so that you can recognize their relationship.

As for disk image size, again you are limited only by the storage destination. However, a very efficient option is to select "sparse disk image" for the image format. With this option selected the resulting image file will only be as large as it needs to be to store items that are actually in the disk image volume. Any "empty" space inside the disk image volume will occupy zero real storage space. This way, you can define a very large size without having to initially fill the entire storage space.

After you have defined your disk image options, click Create to create the disk image. After the system has created the new blank disk image, it automatically mounts it. If you have elected to create a sparse disk image, you can open Info windows in the Finder for both the disk image file and the disk image volume to verify that the volume size is much larger than the image size. As you copy files to the volume, the disk image file automatically grows accordingly.

TIP You can change the format of a disk image at any time in Disk Utility by choosing Images > Convert. This opens a dialog where you can select the image you want to change and save a copy of the image with new options.

Creating Disk Image Archives

To create a disk image that contains copies of specific items, open Disk Utility, and choose File > New > Disk Image from Folder. This opens a file browser window in which you can select the folder you want to copy into a new disk image.

To create a disk image from the contents of an entire volume or disk, first select the source from the Disk Utility window disks list, and then choose File > New > Disk Image from "<Source>"—where <Source> is the name of the selected volume or disk. Alternatively, with the source selected in the Disk Utility window disks list, you can click the New Image button.

NOTE ▶ Disk Utility can only make disk images of volumes that it can temporarily unmount. Thus, you cannot make a disk image of the currently running system volume.

Once you've selected the disk image source, a Save dialog appears. At minimum, you need to select a name and destination for the resulting disk image file. The name of the volume inside the disk image is automatically set to the name of the selected source. Your options include the ability to compress the disk image contents, which is recommended to save storage space. Also, if the contents of the archive are sensitive, you have the option to enable encryption for the disk image. Selecting that option requires setting a password and hint for the resulting secure disk image.

NOTE ▶ Be sure you have enough free space on the destination volume where you plan to save your disk image file.

After you have defined your disk image options, click Save to create the disk image. Depending on the amount of data to be copied and the image format you choose, it can take anywhere from minutes to hours for the disk image copy process to complete. Disk Utility opens a small progress dialog that also allows you to cancel the copying process.

NOTE ▶ To create an image containing items for which you don't have read permissions, you must authenticate as an administrator.

Exercise 13.1
Navigate Hidden Items

OS X hides certain portions of its folder structure, both to simplify the user experience and to prevent users from accidentally damaging the workings of the operating system. As an administrator, however, it is sometimes useful to know what these hidden folders are and how to reach them. In this exercise, you will explore some of the hidden folders in OS X.

Examine Your User Library Folder

1   If necessary, log in as Chris Johnson.

2   In the Finder, open your home folder. You can do this by choosing Go > Home or by using the shortcut Command-Shift-H.

   Note that no folder named Library is visible.

3   In the Finder, open the Go menu, but don't choose anything yet.

4   Press the Option key.

   As long as you have the Option key held down, a "Library" choice appears in the menu.

5   With the Option key held down, choose Library.

   This opens the hidden Library folder in Chris's home folder.

6   If necessary, change to column view by choosing View > as Columns or by clicking the Column View button in the Finder toolbar.

Chris's user Library folder is now shown inside Chris's home folder but is dimmed to indicate that it's normally invisible.

7   Explore some of the subfolders under Chris's user Library folder. Note that you can navigate into them normally.

8   Close the Finder window showing Chris's user Library.

9   Press Command-Shift-H to open Chris's home folder in a new Finder window.

The Library folder is not shown.

10   Choose Go > Go to Folder, or press Command-Shift-G.

11   In the "Go to the folder" dialog, enter ~/Li, and press Tab.

The field automatically completes the path to ~/Library/.

This is an example of specifying a folder by the path to reach it. In this case, the tilde (~) means "start at my home folder," and "/Library" means "then go into the Library folder." This is another way to reach your user Library folder.

12   Click Go.

As before, Chris's user Library is shown in the Finder.

Note that you could also have reached this folder by entering the full path, "/Users/chris/Library," but the tilde (~) shorthand is an easier way to specify locations inside your home folder.

Examine Hidden System Folders

1 Press Command-Shift-G to reopen the Go to Folder dialog.

2 This time, enter /L, and press Tab.

The field automatically completes the path to /Library/. This path looks similar to the previous one, but because it does not start with a tilde (~), it specifies a completely different folder. When a path starts with a slash (/), it starts at the top level of the startup volume (sometimes called the "root" of the file system).

3 Click Go.

This time, the Finder opens the Library folder at the top of the startup volume. The various Library folders are discussed in the next lesson.

This Library folder is not hidden, but you can use the same technique to reach any folder you know the path to, whether it is hidden or not.

4 Use Go to Folder to reach the /private/var/log/ folder (remember, you can type part of a name and then press Tab to complete it).

The /private folder holds some of the OS X "private" system files. The /private/var/log folder holds some of the system log files (there are more in /Library/Logs and ~/Library/Logs). Normally, you do not need to access these in the Finder, so they are hidden from view unless you specifically navigate to them.

5 Use Go to Folder to reach the /var/log/ folder.

This also takes you to /private/var/log because /var is a symbolic link to /private/var.

Lesson 14

System Resources

It is not unusual for an OS X system volume to contain well over 100,000 folders and 500,000 files just to support the operating system and its applications. As you can imagine, the number of items in a user's home folder varies widely, depending on the user, but even the most frugal of users has thousands of items in the home folder. With this many files on hand, attempting to explore and fully comprehend the OS X file layout may seem like a monumental task. The contrary is true, however: The OS X system files are streamlined and organized in an easy-to-understand layout that is easy to manage and provides strong security.

This lesson focuses on the composition and organization of the files and folders that make up OS X. In this lesson, you, acting as an administrator, will use the file layout to strategically allocate resources. The exercises in this lesson specifically discuss management of font resources, as they are one of those most commonly modified by users. However, many of the same management techniques can be used for other system resources.

Reference 14.1
OS X File Structure

The OS X system layout is designed to strike a balance between ease of use and advanced functionality. For the basic user, looking at the root (beginning) of the file system from the Finder reveals only four default folders: Applications, Library, Users, and System.

The contents of these four folders represent all that most users, and many administrators, ever need to access. Yet when advanced users look at the system root from Terminal, they see many more items that the Finder would normally hide. Thus, the complexity and flexibility of a UNIX operating system remains accessible to those users who require it.

Following are descriptions of the default system root folders you see from the Finder:

▶ Applications—Often called the local Applications folder, this is the default location for applications available to all local users. Only administrative users can make changes to the contents of this folder.

▶ Library—Often called the local Library folder, this is the default location for ancillary system and application resources available to all users of the system. Once again, only administrative users can make changes to the contents of this folder.

▶ System—This folder contains resources required by the operating system for primary functionality. Users very rarely have to make changes to the contents of this folder. Even administrative users can't make changes to items in the System folder without reauthenticating. Further, it is not recommended to make any changes to the System folder, as a system update may negate any changes you have made.

▶ Users—This is the default location for local user home folders. Lesson 6 "User Home Folders", covers this topic in greater detail.

System Resource Types

All OS X–specific system resources can be found in the various Library folders throughout the system volume. A system resource can be generally categorized as any resource that is not a general-use application or user file. That's not to say that applications and user data can't be found in the Library folders. On the contrary, the Library folder is designed to keep both user and system resources organized and separated from the items you use every day. This keeps the /Applications folder and user home folders free from system resource clutter.

Opening any of the Library folders reveals several dozen categories of items. It is not necessary to explore every possible Library item, but there are several system resources you should be familiar with:

▶ Application Support—This folder can be found in both the user and local Library folders. Any ancillary data needed by an application may end up in this folder. For example, it often contains help files or templates for an application. Once again, application resources are placed here to keep the /Applications folders tidy.

▶ Extensions—Also called kernel extensions, these items are found only in the system and local Library folders. Extensions are low-level drivers that attach themselves to the kernel, or core, of the operating system. Extensions provide driver support for hardware, networking, and peripherals. Extensions load and unload automatically, so there is little need to manage them, as is common in other operating systems. Extensions are covered in greater detail in Lesson 25 "Peripherals and Drivers".

▶ Fonts—Found in every Library folder, fonts are files that describe typefaces used for both screen display and printing. Font management is covered in "Exercise 14.1 Manage Font Resources" on page 414.

▶ Frameworks—Found in every Library folder, frameworks are repositories of shared code used among different parts of the operating system or applications. Frameworks are similar to extensions in that they load and unload automatically, so again, there is little need to manage these shared code resources. You can view your Mac computer's currently loaded frameworks from the /Applications/Utilities/System Information application.

▶ Keychains—Found in every Library folder, keychains are used to securely store sensitive information, including passwords, certificates, keys, Safari AutoFill information, and notes. Keychain technology was covered previously in Lesson 8 "Keychain Management".

▶ LaunchDaemons and LaunchAgents—Both items can be found in the local and system Library folders, and LaunchAgents can also be found in users' Library folders. These launch items are used to define processes that start automatically via the launchd process. OS X uses many background processes, which are all started by launchd. Further, every single process is a child of the launchd process. LaunchAgents are for processes that need to start up only when a user is logged in, whereas Launch-Daemons are used to start processes that always run in the background, even when no users are logged in. More about launchd can be found in Lesson 27 "System Trouble-shooting".

▶ Logs—Many system processes and applications archive progress or error messages to log files. Log files can be found in every local Library folder and also the /var/log folder. Technically, an application or process can save log files to any writable location, but the previously mentioned folders are the defaults. Log files can be viewed using the /Applications/Utilities/Console application.

▶ PreferencePanes—PreferencePanes can be found in any Library folder. These items are used by the System Preferences application to provide interfaces for system config-uration. Using System Preferences is covered in Lesson 2 "Setup and Configuration".

▶ Preferences—Preferences, found in both local and user libraries, are used to store sys-tem and application configuration settings. In other words, every time you configure a setting for any application or system function, it is saved to a preference file. Because preferences play such a critical role in system functionality, they are often the cause of software problems. Troubleshooting preference files is covered in Lesson 19 "Applica-tion Management and Troubleshooting".

▶ Startup Items—Found in only the local and system Library folders, these are precur-sors to LaunchAgents and LaunchDaemons. Since OS X v10.5, Apple has been offi-cially discouraging the use of Startup Items. In fact, you will have Startup Items only if you've installed third-party software that hasn't been updated. In OS X the launchd process still supports many Startup Items, but this may not be true for future versions.

System Resource Hierarchy

Library folders, and thus system resources, are located in each of the four domain areas: user, local, network, and system. Segregating resources into four domains provides increased administrative flexibility, resource security, and system reliability. Resource domains allow for administrative flexibility, because you can choose to allocate certain resources to all users or just specific users. Using resource domains is also more secure, because standard users can add resources only to their own home folder and cannot access other users' resources. In addition, resource domains are more reliable, because in most cases you don't have to make changes to the core system functionality to provide more services.

TIP ▶ The quickest way to reveal a user's Library folder is to manually go to the folder in the Finder. While holding down the Option key, choose Go > Library to reveal the hidden folder. You can learn more about hidden items in Lesson 13 "Hidden Items, Shortcuts, and File Archives".

The four system resource domains are, in order:

▶ User—Each user has his or her own Library folder in the home folder for resources. When resources are placed here, only the user has access to them. The user's Library folder is hidden by default to prevent users from accidentally making changes that could be detrimental. However, you can still find many thousands of items in this folder, as many applications and processes continue to rely on this location for resources. Also, users can have their own Applications folder within their home folder, providing they create the folder and name it, precisely, Applications.

▶ Local—Both the root Applications and root Library folders are part of the local resource domain. This is why they are known as the *local* Applications and *local* Library folders. Any resources placed in these two folders are available to all local user accounts. By default, only administrative users can make changes to local resources.

▶ Network—OS X can access system resources in a Library folder and applications in an Applications folder residing on a network file share. Administrators must configure an automounted share to enable the Network resource domain. Configuring automounted shares is beyond the scope of this guide.

▶ System—Finally, the system domain encompasses all the items necessary to provide core system functionality. Many hidden items at the root of the system volume make up the system resource domain, but the only one you see in the Finder is the /System/Library folder. In many cases, you do not need to add or manage any resources here.

With four different domains containing resources, a strong likelihood exists for overlap in resources, meaning there may be multiple copies of similar resources available to the system and user at any given time. The system is designed to handle this by searching for resources from the most specific (those in the user domain) to the least specific (those in the system domain). The following graphic represents the order in which resource contention is resolved from the user's home folder (1) to the System folder (4).

If multiple similar resources are discovered, the system uses the resource most specific to the user. For example, if multiple versions of the font Times New Roman are found—one in the local Library and one in the user's Library—the system uses the copy of the font in the user's Library. In other words, resources in the user's home folder take first priority, thus trumping all other resource locations.

Application Sandbox Containers

A recent addition to OS X, application sandbox containers add a bit more complexity to file system organization but greatly enhance the security of running applications. Sandboxed applications are designed in such a way that they are allowed access only to the specific items they need to function. Because application sandboxing is a recent addition to OS X, many legacy applications do not take advantage of this technology. However, most applications built into OS X and all applications from the Mac App Store are created as sandboxed applications.

As the term *sandbox* implies, these applications are allowed to "play" only in their specific area. These areas are special folders that are referred to as containers. The system manages the content of these containers to ensure an application is not allowed access to any other items in the file system. In other words, sandboxed applications are more secure because they are allowed access only to the items in their own containers.

Users can also allow a sandboxed application access to other files outside the container, but they must do so by opening the item in the application. In other words, the specific action of a user opening a document outside of an application's container is the only way a sandboxed application is allowed access outside of its container.

Application containers can be found in the user's Library folder. Specifically, the ~/Library/Containers folder contains individual application containers. When a sandboxed application starts up the first time, the system automatically creates a container folder for the application, named with its bundle identifier. The bundle identifier is used for development purposes to identify an application by its creator and application title. For example, the container folder for Text Edit is ~/Library/Containers/com.apple.TextEdit.

The root content of an application container is a property list file containing application information, a Data folder, and possibly an OldData folder. The Data folder is the application's current active container. Any OldData folder you might find contains previously used application items. The content of the Data folder mostly mimics the user's home folder, but with one key distinction: It contains only the items that the application is allowed to access. Thus, in the Data folder you will find only items specific to the application's function or items the user has explicitly opened in the application.

Items created and managed by the sandboxed application are the only original items in the container Data folder. As covered previously in this lesson, common resource folders used by an application include Application Support and Preferences. If the user has enabled iCloud Drive, you may also find a CloudKit folder for maintaining items stored in iCloud.

Items that originated from other applications or a user's file-opening action are represented as symbolic links that point to the original item outside of the container. The system automatically creates these symbolic links when the user opens an item in the sandboxed application. By representing external items this way, an original item can stay where the user wants it while also being accessible to a sandboxed application that can only see its own container.

Application Group Containers

Although a user can explicitly allow sandboxed applications to access specific files beyond the application's container, the secure design of sandboxing prevents applications from doing this automatically for themselves. As you can imagine, this keeps applications from automatically taking advantage of each other's resources. Thus, in order to facilitate sharing application resources automatically, developers of sandboxed applications can request that the system create a shared application group container.

Application group containers can also be found in the user's Library folder. Specifically, the ~/Library/Group Containers folder contains shared application containers. When a sandboxed application starts up the first time and requests access to share application resources, the system automatically creates a group container folder for the application, named with its bundle identifier.

Unlike application sandbox containers that simulate an entire user's home folder, application group containers hold only items to be shared between applications. For example, in the previous screenshot you can see that the Preview application is sharing its property list file. In this specific instance, the Preview preference file is shared so that other applications can read the settings for the Markup app extension included with the Preview application.

(The Markup app extension itself is inside the Preview application bundle and accessed via a different security mechanism.) App extensions are detailed in Lesson 19 "Application Management and Troubleshooting".

System Resource Troubleshooting

System resource issues are rare, and they are generally easy to identify. You may occasionally see an error message calling out an issue with a specific item, but you may also experience a situation where the item appears to be missing. In some cases, the system resource in question may actually be missing, but many times the system simply ignores a system resource if it determines that the resource is in some way corrupted. The solution for both of these situations is to simply replace the missing or suspect item with a known working copy.

When troubleshooting system resources, you must also remember to heed the resource domain hierarchy. Using fonts as an example, you may have loaded a specific version of a font in the local Library, as required by your workflow to operate properly. In spite of this, a user may have loaded another version of the same font in his or her home folder. In this case, the system loads the user's font and ignores the font you installed. Therefore, this user may experience workflow problems even though it appears that he or she is using the correct font.

TIP If fonts are missing from within applications but appear to be properly installed, remember to check Font Book, as the font may be temporarily disabled. Font Book is covered in the next section of this lesson.

Logging in with another account on the Mac is always a quick way to determine if the problem is in the user's home folder. You can also use /Applications/Utilities/System Information to list active system resources. System Information always shows the file path of the loaded system resources, so it's easy to spot resources that are loading from the user's Library.

Reference 14.2
Font Resources and Font Book

An excellent way to experience the system resource domain hierarchy is by managing fonts. OS X has advanced font-management technology that enables an unlimited number of fonts using nearly any font type, including bitmap, TrueType, OpenType, and all Post-Script fonts. As mentioned previously, fonts are installed in the various Font folders located in the Library folders throughout the system. A user can manually install fonts simply by dragging them into a Fonts folder.

> **MORE INFO** ▶ OS X includes a wealth of high-quality fonts for many different languages. For a full list of these fonts, see Apple Support article HT201375, "OS X: Fonts included with Mavericks."

Installing Fonts via Font Book

On the other hand, OS X includes a rather nice font-management tool, /Applications/Font Book, which automatically installs fonts for you. Font Book can also be used to organize fonts into more manageable collections, enable or disable fonts to simplify font lists, and resolve duplicate fonts.

NOTE ▶ Third-party font-management tools, such as Extensis Suitcase Fusion or Universal Type Server, interrupt Font Book and take over font management for the system.

By default, when a user double-clicks a font in the Finder, Font Book opens and displays a preview of the font. When the user clicks the Install Font button, Font Book automatically copies the font into the Fonts folder in the user's Library folder.

NOTE ▶ Font Book, by default, automatically validates a font before installing and enabling it. This helps prevent font problems by making sure the font file isn't compromised. Thus, installing fonts via Font Book is favored over manual installation via the Finder.

When a new font is installed, the Font Book main window appears with the font preview at right. Manually opening Font Book also opens the main window. To preview any currently installed font, simply click it in the list of fonts. If you want to install additional fonts without leaving the Font Book application, you can do so by clicking the Plus button in the Font Book toolbar.

NOTE ▶ Some applications may need to be restarted to take advantage of recently added fonts.

With Font Book open, you can adjust the default install location for fonts by choosing Font Book > Preferences. If you are an administrative user, you can choose to install fonts to the local Library folder by choosing Computer from the pop-up menu. Close the Font Book Preferences dialog after you have made your selections.

Disabling Fonts via Font Book

If you, or the application you're using, have difficulties choosing fonts from a large list, you can temporarily disable fonts within Font Book by selecting a font and then clicking the Enable/Disable button (appears as a selected or deselected checkbox) in the toolbar. Disabled fonts appear dimmed in the font list, with "Off" shown next to their name. To enable the font, simply select it again, and click the same checkbox button at the bottom of the font list.

Fonts that have multiple copies on your system show a small dot next to their name in the font list. You can automatically disable duplicate fonts with Font Book by choosing Edit > Look for Enabled Duplicates.

If you feel the need to remove a font, simply select it from the font list and then press Delete. A summary dialog appears, reminding you that continuing will move the selected fonts to the Trash. If you are sure this is what you want to do, click Remove. Remember, however, you can always disable a font instead of deleting it entirely.

Resolving Font Issues via Font Book

If you're having font issues, you can identify problem fonts by forcing the system to revalidate all the fonts on your system. To do this, select a single font in the Font list, and then press Command-A to select all the fonts. Choose File > Validate Fonts to start the validation process.

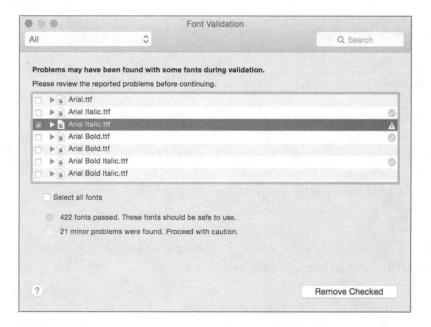

The Font Validation window opens and scans all the selected fonts. This window clearly shows any problem font with a status indicator (exclamation mark icon) next to the font's name. To view details about a font issue, click the disclosure triangle to the left of the font name. To remove a problem font, simply select the checkbox next to its name and then click the Remove Checked button.

If you're still having problems with fonts, a final option in Font Book is to restore all the system fonts to the defaults for OS X. To do this, choose File > Restore Standard Fonts. A dialog appears, verifying your choice. Click Proceed to remove third-party fonts from the system.

Exercise 14.1
Manage Font Resources

▶ **Prerequisites**

▶ You must have created the Local Admin ("Exercise 2.1 Configure a New OS X System for Exercises" on page 60 or "Exercise 2.2 Configure an Existing OS X System for Exercises" on page 63), Chris Johnson ("Exercise 5.1 Manage User Accounts" on page 145), and Mayta Mishtuk ("Exercise 6.1 Restore a Deleted User Account" on page 166) accounts.

In this exercise, you will remove a font from /Library/Fonts, where it is available to all users, and install it in a single user's Fonts folder.

Remove a Font

You can use Font Book to watch what happens when you move a font to the Trash.

1   Verify that no users have fast user switching sessions active. If any users other than Chris are logged in, log them out.

2   If necessary, log in as Chris Johnson.

3   Open the Font Book application, which is located in the /Applications folder.

4   Locate Andale Mono in the Font column.

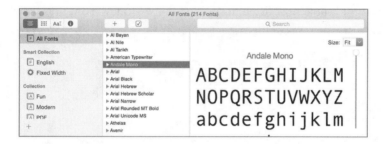

5   In the Finder, navigate to the folder /Library/Fonts. If Macintosh HD is not displayed on Chris's desktop, you can find it in the Computer view, available by choosing Go > Computer (or pressing Command-Shift-C).

6   To verify your location, choose View > Show Path Bar.

    Make sure the path bar at the bottom of the window matches the following screenshot (although the rest may not match unless you are in column view):

These fonts are available to all users on the system.

7   Locate the file Andale Mono.ttf.

8   Drag Andale Mono.ttf to the desktop. As you drag, a cursor with a green badge with a plus sign on it appears attached to the pointer. This indicates that the file will be copied rather than moved.

This will be your backup copy of the Andale Mono font.

9   Move the original Andale Mono.ttf file from /Library/Fonts to the Trash. To do so, you have to authenticate as Local Admin.

10   Click the Font Book window to make it the active application.

The Andale Mono font is no longer listed in the Font Book window. Font Book shows a real-time display of all the fonts in the system search path.

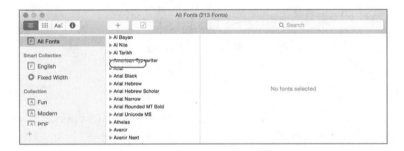

Add a Font for Only One User

You can use Font Book to install a font that only one user of the computer can use.

1   In Font Book, choose Font Book > Preferences.

2   Ensure that the Default Install Location is set to User.

3   Close Font Book Preferences.

4   Switch to the Finder, and double-click Andale Mono.ttf on the desktop.

This opens Andale Mono.ttf in Font Book, which gives you the option to install the font.

5   Click Install Font.

Andale Mono reappears in the Font column of Font Book.

6   In the Collection list, select User. Andale Mono is the only font listed there.

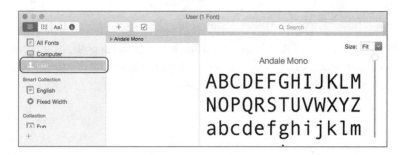

7   Quit Font Book.

The Andale Mono font is now installed in the Fonts folder located in Chris's Library folder. The user Library folder is hidden, but the Finder has a hidden menu option to open it.

8   In the Finder, hold down the Option key, and choose Go > Library. This menu selection appears only when you hold down the Option key.

9   Open the Fonts folder.

Andale Mono.ttf is the only font installed in Chris's Fonts folder.

Confirm the Font Is Unavailable to Other Users

If you log in as a different user, you don't have access to the fonts in Chris's Fonts folder.

1   Use fast user switching to switch to Mayta Mishtuk's account (password: mayta, or whatever you chose when you created the account).

2   Open Font Book, and look for the Andale Mono font.

Notice that Andale Mono is not visible in Font Book for Mayta's account. At this time, you could add Andale Mono to Mayta's user account, just as you added it to Chris's account earlier. You would have to copy the font file to a location that Mayta can access.

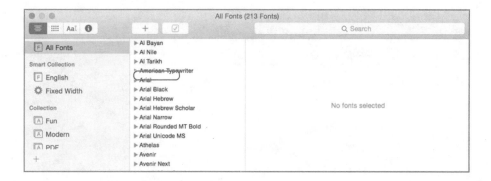

3 Quit Font Book, and log out of Mayta's account.

Validate Fonts

Since you have changed your font configuration, you will use Font Book to check your new setup.

1 Log back in to the Chris Johnson account.

2 Open the Font Book application.

3 Select the All Fonts collection, click any font in the Font column, and then press Command-A to select all the fonts.

4 Choose File > Validate Fonts.

Font Book reads and validates all the font files, checking for any corruption.

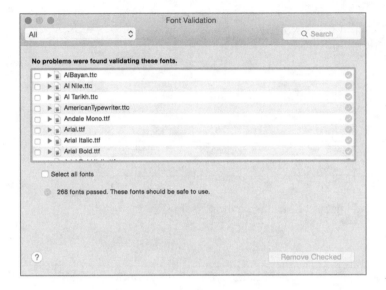

5   When the validation scan finishes, quit Font Book.

Metadata and Spotlight

Metadata is data about data. More specifically, metadata is information used to describe content. The most basic forms of file and folder metadata employed by nearly every operating system are names, paths, modification dates, and permissions. These metadata objects are not part of the item's content, yet they are necessary to describe the item in the file system. OS X has used several types of additional file system metadata for a variety of technologies that ultimately lead to a richer user experience. As of OS X Mavericks, Apple expanded upon this already rich base by offering a new metadata mechanism—tags—which can be found throughout the system.

This lesson details how OS X makes use of file metadata and how this metadata is stored on various file systems. It also demonstrates how to take advantage of all this metadata by using the file system tags feature and the OS X advanced Spotlight search technology.

GOALS

▶ Understand how OS X stores and uses file metadata

▶ Use metadata, such as tags and comments, to organize your files

▶ Leverage file metadata by using Spotlight for advanced searching

Reference 15.1
File System Metadata

Resource forks, dating back to the original Mac OS, are the legacy metadata technology in the Mac operating system. To simplify the user experience, Apple created a forked file system to make complex items, such as applications, appear as a single icon. Forked file systems, such as Mac OS Extended, allow multiple pieces of data to appear as a single item in the file system. In this case, a file appears as a single item, but is actually composed of two separate pieces: a data fork and a resource fork. This technology also enables the Mac OS to support file type identification in the data fork, whereas the extra information specific to Mac resides in the resource fork. For many years, the Mac OS has relied on forked files for storing both data and associated metadata.

OS X not only continues but also expands the use of metadata, even going so far as to allow developers to take advantage of an arbitrary number of additional metadata items. This enables Apple and other developers to implement unique file system solutions without having to modify the existing file system. For instance, OS X v10.6 introduced compressed application code, wherein the actual executable program files are all compressed to save space and then, when needed, automatically decompressed on the fly. To prevent previous versions of OS X or older applications from improperly handling these compressed executables, Apple chose to hide the compressed bits in additional metadata locations.

The downside to legacy resource forks, and other types of additional file system metadata, is that some third-party file systems, like FAT, do not know how to properly store this additional data. The solution to this issue is addressed with the AppleDouble file format, covered later in this lesson.

File Flags and Extended Attributes

OS X also uses metadata in the form of file system flags and extended attributes to implement a variety of system features. In general, file system flags are holdovers from the original Mac OS and are primarily used to control user access. Examples of file system flags include the hidden flag, covered in Lesson 13 "Hidden Items, Shortcuts, and File Archives", and the locked flag, covered in Lesson 18 "Document Management".

With OS X, Apple needed to expand the range of possible attributes associated with any file or folder, which is where so-called extended attributes come into play. Any process or application can add an arbitrary number of custom attributes to a file or folder. Again, this allows developers to create new forms of metadata without having to modify the existing file system.

For example, the OS X file system tags feature is stored as an extended attribute. The system also uses extended attributes for several general file features, including the stationery pad option, hide extension option, and comments. All of these items can be accessed from the Info window in the Finder. The following Info window screenshot shows a document featuring Red and Work file system tags and a searchable text comment.

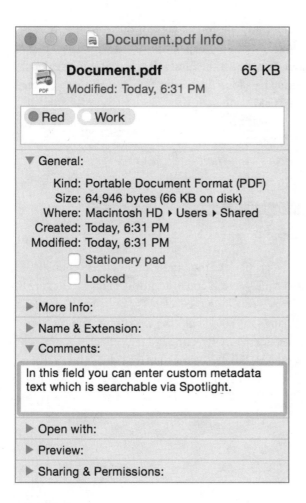

File System Tags

The OS X file system tags feature is really an upgrade to a previous OS X metadata technology, Finder labels. In versions of OS X prior to Mavericks, you can set a single color label for any item in the Finder. File system tags expand upon this by allowing you to assign multiple tags with custom user-defined tag colors and tag names. Further, in previous versions of OS X you could edit labels only in the Finder.

NOTE ▶ Similar to how developers must update their applications to support iCloud, an application must be updated to support file system tags. Thus, some applications may not recognize file system tags.

In OS X Mavericks and later, you can modify file system tags for documents within any application that presents a Save dialog. You can define tags for documents saved locally and in iCloud. The default file system tags match the Finder labels found in previous versions of OS X. However, when selecting tags for a document, you can create a new tag by simply typing a new name in the Tags field.

You can further customize tags in the Tags pane of the Finder preferences (choose Finder > Preferences). From this this pane you can create additional tags by clicking the Add (+) button, and delete existing tags by clicking the Delete (–) button. To rename a tag, simply click the tag's name, and to change the color, click the tag's color. You can also define which tags are shown in Finder sidebar by selecting the tag's checkbox, and set the tag order by dragging tag entires in the list. Finally, below the tags sidebar list, you can define favorite tags so they will appear in Finder menus.

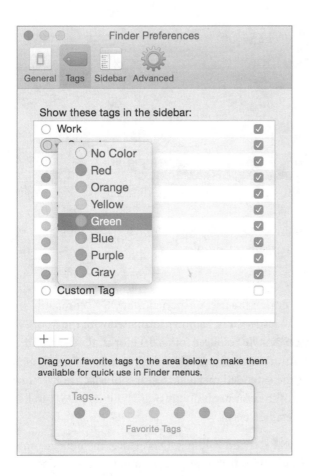

NOTE ▶ Items from previous versions of OS X with Finder labels appear as file system tags in OS X Mavericks and later. However, previous versions of OS X are not fully compatible with items using custom tags or with items that use more than one tag. Previous versions of OS X display only the last saved tag of an item, and even then will only display it as a standard Finder label color.

Most importantly, though, OS X includes interfaces that enable you to quickly search for your items or organize your items by file system tag. In the Finder, you can find tags in the Spotlight search field or the sidebar. In updated applications, you can access tags from a similar Spotlight search and sidebar as well. Using Spotlight for searching is detailed in "Reference 15.2 Spotlight Search" on page 427.

MORE INFO ▶ You can find out more about file system tags in Apple Support article HT202754, "OS X: Tags help you organize your files."

AppleDouble File Format

Although file system metadata helps enrich the user's experience in OS X, compatibility with third-party file systems can be an issue. Only volumes formatted with the Mac OS Extended file system fully support OS X style resource forks, data forks, file flags, and extended attributes. Third-party software has been developed for Windows-based operating systems to allow them to access the extended metadata features of Mac OS Extended. More often, though, users make use of the compatibility software built into OS X to help other file systems cope with these metadata items.

For most anything other than Mac OS Extended volumes, OS X stores metadata from the file system in a separate hidden data file. This technique is commonly referred to as AppleDouble. For example, if you copy a file containing metadata named My Document.docx to a FAT32 volume, OS X automatically splits the file and writes it as two discrete pieces on the FAT32 volume. The file's internal data would be written with the same name as the original, but the metadata would end up in a file named ._My Document.docx that would remain hidden from the Finder. This works out pretty well for most files, because Windows applications only care about the contents of the data fork. But some files do not take well to being split up, and all the extra dot-underscore files create a bit of a mess on other file systems.

NOTE ▶ Recent Windows systems default to automatically hiding these dot-underscore files. In fact, to acquire the Windows XP screenshot shown here, showing hidden files had to be manually enabled.

OS X includes a method for handling metadata on SMB network shares from NTFS volumes that doesn't require the AppleDouble format. The native file system for current Windows-based computers, NTFS, supports something similar to file forking known as alternative data streams. The Mac file system writes the metadata to the alternative data stream, so the file appears as a single item on both Windows and Mac systems.

NOTE ▶ OS X always reverts to using dot-underscore files when writing to FAT volumes, some Xsan volumes, and older NFS shares.

Reference 15.2
Spotlight Search

With Spotlight on OS X, you can perform nearly instantaneous searches that go wider and deeper than any other desktop computer search technology. For any query, Spotlight can go beyond simple file system searches and actually find relevant information from inside local documents, application function results, and even Internet sources.

Simple Spotlight Search

OS X Yosemite introduces a redesigned Spotlight interface that combines the search results list and search results preview into a new Spotlight window that appears in the center of the screen. However, you can still initiate a search by clicking the Spotlight (spyglass) icon at the top-right corner of the screen or by using the default keyboard shortcut, Command-Space bar.

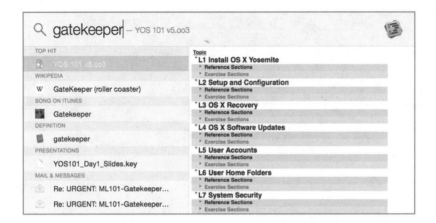

The Spotlight search is so fast that the results actually change in real time as you type in your search query. The left side of the Spotlight window is a list of the search results; the right side is a preview area. Use the arrow keys to navigate the results list, or select an item (by clicking once) to show a preview. Both the results list and preview area are scrollable to reveal more content. Finally, double-clicking an item or pressing Return will open the selected item immediately.

Spotlight Search Results

The preceding screenshot shows the results of a Spotlight search for the query "gatekeeper." As you can see, the results list contains documents, mail messages, and even results from Internet sources. The selected item being previewed is a document (used for the creation of this very guide), created by a third-party application called OmniOutliner. Note the icon of the third-party application at the top-right of the Spotlight search window.

Spotlight also has the ability to search inside application databases. As another example, the Contacts application stores user contact information in a database that appears opaque to the file system. Nevertheless, Spotlight can return search results from Contacts along with results from other sources nearly instantly. In some cases, Spotlight can even take advantage of an application's functions. For example, Spotlight can perform mathematic calculations and unit conversions (including market-based currency conversion) via integration with the Calculator application.

The file system metadata covered previously in this lesson is also searchable via Spotlight, including filenames, file flags, modification dates, and file system tags. Additionally, many files also contain internal metadata used to describe the file's content. For example, many digital camera image files contain additional camera setting information embedded as metadata inside the file. Spotlight can search through this document-specific metadata information as well.

In addition to local files, Spotlight can also search through the contents of shared files from other Mac clients, servers, AirDisk volumes (disks shared via AirPort Wi-Fi access points), Time Machine backups, and iCloud Drive.

Extending beyond local network services, Spotlight can search through a variety of Internet sources, including the results of Microsoft Bing web searches and an Apple service called Spotlight Suggestions. Spotlight Suggestions uses a combination of Spotlight usage history, location information, and user information to generate relevent search results.

Spotlight Indexing

Spotlight is able to perform wide and deep searches of local items and shared files quickly because it works in the background to maintain highly optimized databases of indexed metadata for each attached local volume. When you first set up OS X, it creates these databases by indexing all the available local volumes. The system also indexes new volumes when they are first attached.

On OS X, a background process automatically updates the index databases on the fly as changes are made throughout the file system. Because these indexes are kept current, the Spotlight process only needs to search the databases to return thorough results. Essentially, Spotlight preemptively searches everything for you in the background, so you don't have to wait for the results when you need them.

> **NOTE ▶** Spotlight does not create index databases on read-only volumes or write-once media such as optical discs.

> **NOTE ▶** Your Mac computer's Spotlight service directly indexes Time Machine and AirDisk volumes (drives shared via AirPort Extreme), but does not index shared volumes from other computers. However, Spotlight can connect to indexes on shares hosted from other OS X systems.

You can find the Spotlight general index databases at the root level of every volume in a folder named .Spotlight-V100. A few applications maintain their own databases separate from these general index databases. One example is the built-in email application Mail, which maintains its own optimized email database in each user's folder at ~/Library/Mail/V2/MailData/Envelope Index.

If you are experiencing problems with Spotlight, you can force it to rebuild the index databases by deleting them and restarting your Mac or by managing the Spotlight preferences, as covered in "Spotlight Preferences" on page 433 later in this lesson.

Spotlight Plug-ins

Spotlight is able to create indexes, and thus search, from an ever-growing variety of metadata using a plug-in technology. Each Spotlight plug-in is designed to examine specific types of files or databases. Many Spotlight plug-ins are included by default, but Apple and third-party developers can create additional plug-ins to expand the Spotlight search capabilities.

Included Spotlight plug-ins enable you to:

▶ Search via basic file metadata, including name, file size, creation date, and modification date

▶ Search via media-specific metadata from picture, music, and video files, including timecode, creator information, and hardware capture information

▶ Search through the contents of a variety of file types, including text files, iLife-related files and databases, Photoshop files, PDF files, iWork files, and Microsoft Office files

▶ Search through personal information like that found in the Contacts and Calendar applications

▶ Search for correspondence information like the contents of Mail emails and Messages chat transcripts

▶ Search for highly relevant information like your favorites or web browser bookmarks and history

▶ Perform Internet searches using Microsoft Bing or Apple Spotlight Suggestions

Spotlight plug-ins, like any other system resource, are stored inside the various Library folders. The Apple built-in Spotlight plug-ins can be found in both the /System/Library/Spotlight folder and the /Library/Spotlight folder. Third-party plug-ins should always be installed in either the /Library/Spotlight or the ~/Library/Spotlight folder, depending on who needs access to it.

TIP ▶ You can create custom metadata for Spotlight by entering Spotlight comments in the Info and Inspector windows from the Finder.

Spotlight Security

To provide security on par with the rest of the file system, Spotlight also indexes every item's permissions. Even though Spotlight indexes every item on a volume, it automatically filters search results to show only items that the current user has permissions to access. For example, you can't search the content of another user's Documents folder. Also, the Spotlight index database for a Legacy FileVault user is stored at the root level, inside the user's encrypted home folder, so it's not searchable when the user is logged out.

There is still a security concern, though, when users search through locally attached nonsystem volumes, because they can choose to ignore ownership on these volumes. In other words, all users can search through locally attached nonsystem volumes, including mounted disk images, even if another user attached the device.

Spotlight searches that take advantage of Internet sources adhere to the Apple Privacy Policy. Apple takes user privacy very seriously and always attempts to keep the user's information as safe as possible while still providing advanced services. Further, you can disable Internet searching in the Spotlight preferences, as covered in "Spotlight Preferences" on page 433 later in this lesson.

MORE INFO ▶ Apple's Privacy Policy is clearly outlined and constantly updated at www.apple.com/privacy/.

Advanced Spotlight Search

The default Spotlight search serves the needs of most users quite well, but as you've read thus far, Spotlight has a powerful range of search features. You can perform advanced file system Spotlight searches by opening a new Finder window and entering your search in the Spotlight field, by choosing File > Find, or by pressing Command-F. Selecting an item from the search results shows you the path to the selected item at the bottom of the Finder window. Selecting an item and then pressing the Space bar opens a preview of the selected item.

You can refine your Spotlight search from a Finder search window by clicking the small plus buttons below the search field; this allows you to add as many specific search attributes as you need. After you add a new search attribute, click the first word in the search attribute to choose another type from the pop-up menu.

If you don't see the search attribute you're looking for, you can add literally dozens of other attributes that aren't enabled by default. To add search attributes, select any attribute and choose Other from the pop-up menu. In the dialog that appears, you can add search attributes to the pop-up menu. Two especially useful search attributes for administrators are "File visibility" and "System files," neither of which is shown by default in any Spotlight search.

TIP Take some time to explore the additional search attributes; you may be surprised at the depth of the Spotlight search capabilities. Search attributes include specifying audio file tags, digital camera metadata, authorship information, contact information, and many other metadata types.

Clicking the Save button on the right saves these search criteria as a Smart Folder. Smart Folders are like normal folders in that they can be given a unique name and placed anywhere you like, including the Finder sidebar. Smart Folders are special because their contents always match your search criteria no matter how the file system changes. In fact, the All My Files and Tags items in the Finder sidebar are simply predefined Smart Folders.

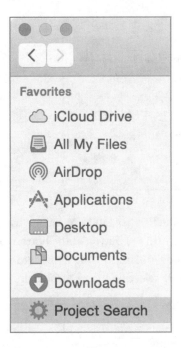

Spotlight Preferences

From Spotlight preferences, any user can choose to disable specific categories from appearing in Spotlight searches. For example, users can choose to disable Spotlight Suggestions if they don't want any information sent to the Apple servers. A user can also prevent some volumes from being indexed by specifying those volumes in the privacy list. However, by default, all new volumes are automatically indexed, so the user must manually configure Spotlight to ignore a volume.

The Spotlight privacy list is a computer-level setting that remains the same across all user accounts, but it's not protected by administrative access, which means any user can change the privacy list. In this case, the Spotlight privacy list isn't any less secure than the rest of the file system, as any user can still have full access to locally connected nonsystem volumes, because the system defaults to ignoring ownership on those volumes.

Opening Spotlight preferences defaults to the Search Results tab, where you can disable specific categories from the search results. Simply deselect the checkboxes next to the categories you want to ignore. You can also drag categories to change their order in the search results. Each user has his or her own separate Search Results settings.

To prevent Spotlight from indexing specific items, click the Privacy tab to reveal the list of items for Spotlight to ignore. To add new items, click the Add (+) button at the bottom of the privacy list and choose the items from a browser dialog, or simply drag items into the privacy list. You can delete an item from the privacy list by selecting it and then clicking the Delete (–) button at the bottom of the list.

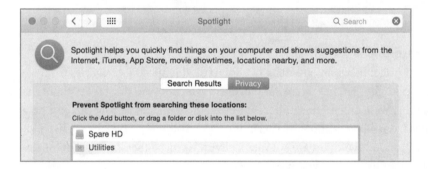

All Spotlight settings are applied immediately. If you add an entire volume to the privacy list, the system deletes the Spotlight index database from that volume. In turn, removing a volume from the privacy list rebuilds the Spotlight index database on that volume. This technique—rebuilding the Spotlight index databases by adding and then removing a volume from the privacy list—is the most common method for resolving problematic Spotlight performance.

Exercise 15.1
Examine File Metadata

▶ **Prerequisite**

▶ You must have created the Chris Johnson account ("Exercise 5.1 Manage User Accounts" on page 145).

In this exercise, you will examine some file metadata in the Info window in the Finder and add custom metadata.

Use Tag and Comment Metadata

1   If necessary, log in as Chris Johnson.

2   Open Safari, and navigate to www.apple.com.

3   Choose File > Save As (Command-S).

If File > Save As is not available, the page may not have fully loaded. Click the "X" in the right side of the URL/search field, and the Save As option should become available.

4   In the Tags field, enter Apple Info, and then click "Create new tag 'Apple Info.'"

5   If necessary, click elsewhere in the dialog to dismiss the Tags pop-up.

6 Ensure that the location (the Where option) is set to Documents and that Format is set to Web Archive, and then click Save.

7 Quit Safari.

8 In the Finder, navigate to your Documents folder (Choose Go > Documents, or press Command-Shift-O).

9 Select the web archive file, and then choose File > Get Info (or press Command-I).

10 If necessary, expand the General, More Info, and Comments sections of the Info window.

The Info window in the Finder displays a variety of information about the file, from basic metadata such as its size to information about where on the web it came from, as well as the tag you added when you saved it. It also lets you edit some types of metadata.

11 In the Comments section, type **The Apple Orchard.**

This field adds custom metadata to the file, allowing you to attach searchable comments and keywords. You will see how to use this comment later in this exercise.

12 Close the Info window.

13 If necessary, change the Finder view of the Documents folder to list view (click the List View button in the toolbar, choose View > as List, or press Command-2).

14 Choose View > Show View Options (or press Command-J).

15 In the Show Columns section, select Comments and Tags.

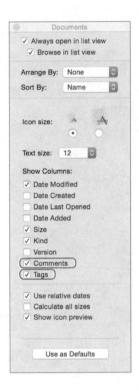

Note that this setting applies only to this specific folder. Clicking "Use as Defaults" would make it the default for all folders.

16 Close the View Options window, and, if necessary, widen the Documents window until you can see the Tags and Comments fields.

17 Close the Documents window.

Use Spotlight to Search for Documents

1   In the Finder, choose File > Find (Command-F).

2   In the search field of the window that opens, type `orchard`.

The search finds the web archive you saved earlier because the word "orchard" appears in its Spotlight comment. Note that you can also restrict the search to files with "orchard" in the name.

Spotlight can search a wide variety of file metadata as well as the contents of files. It generally displays all possible matches and then suggests ways to narrow the search (for example, only filename matches or "downloaded from" matches).

3   Change the search to `apple info`.

This time it finds the archive file by its tag and gives you options to restrict the search to name or tag matches only. Since it is searching all file attributes, it may find other matching files.

4 Change the search to www.apple.com.

Again, the web archive is found, this time because your search matches the site it was downloaded from. It also finds the Energy_Saver.mobileconfig file in the StudentMaterials/Lesson2 folder, because it contains a document type descriptor that says it conforms to a format defined at www.apple.com/DTDs/PropertyList-1.0.dtd. If you had any text files or PDFs that mentioned www.apple.com, they would be listed as well.

Time Machine

Several mature and relatively easy-to-use backup solutions are available for OS X, so you may be wondering why Apple chose to invent its own backup architecture for OS X. A little research revealed that, before the introduction of Time Machine, only a small percentage of Mac users were backing up their data on a regular basis. This was an unacceptable number, so Apple decided that the only way to convince users to back up their systems was to create a new backup process that would be as easy to use as possible. The Apple solution was Time Machine.

In this lesson, you will learn how Time Machine enables users to easily browse the backup history of their entire file system. You will become familiar with the configuration of Time Machine. Finally, you will explore multiple methods for recovering data from Time Machine backups.

GOALS

▸ Understand the technology behind Time Machine

▸ Configure Time Machine to back up important data

▸ Restore data or entire systems from a Time Machine backup

Reference 16.1
Time Machine Architecture

Aside from being built into the operating system, Time Machine has two features that make it fundamentally different from any other solution currently out there. First, configuring Time Machine is so easy it's nearly automatic. The system practically begs you to set up Time Machine if you haven't done so already, and with as little as one click, it's configured.

The second, more significant feature is that Time Machine is so tightly integrated with the operating system that users don't even have to exit the application they are currently using to recover data. Applications, both built-in and third-party, can tie directly into the Time Machine backup system.

From applications supporting Time Machine, a user can activate the Time Machine interface and travel back through time to see the application's data as it was in the past. If an application doesn't yet support Time Machine, you can use the Finder while in the Time Machine interface to browse the entire file system through time.

Time Machine Disks

Time Machine can back up to any locally connected Mac OS Extended volume that is not the startup volume. You are allowed to select a backup disk that resides as another partition on the system disk—but this is an incredibly bad idea: If the system disk dies, so does your backup. Consequently, many choose an external USB, FireWire, or Thunderbolt disk as their Time Machine backup disk.

However, external disks have the potential to be lost or stolen. Thus, OS X includes support for an encrypted local backup disk. This option automatically reformats the backup disk as Mac OS Extended (Journaled, Encrypted). Using this option requires setting a password, which is used to access the encrypted Time Machine backup disk.

> **NOTE ▶** Remember that a Time Machine backup can contain a full copy of all your important files. Thus, it's recommended that you choose the encrypted backup disk option, in case your backup disk is ever lost or stolen.

When configured, the encrypted Time Machine disk password is saved to the secure keychain system for automatic retrieval. However, if the encrypted disk is connected to another system, the user must enter the password to access the backup items. Further, if the original system is lost, you will need to manually enter the disk password to access the backup disk contents. In other words, it is very important that you store the backup disk password using a secure mechanism outside of the Mac system.

> **NOTE ▶** If you lose the password used to unlock an encrypted Time Machine backup disk, its contents are lost forever. Not even Apple can recover the data.

If you don't have a local volume suitable for backup, you can select a shared network volume as your backup disk. Time Machine supports network shares by creating a disk image on the share to store the backups. Time Machine currently supports backing up only to network shares hosted from OS X Server or Time Capsule wireless access points.

The storage on network shares used for Time Machine may not be encrypted, but access to a network share is likely to be configured to require authentication. While this prevents unauthorized access over a network, it doesn't offer any security if the device providing the share is physically located in an insecure environment. Thus, remember to consider the physical aspects of security when placing a Time Machine server or Time Capsule.

MORE INFO ▶ You can find out more about configuring OS X Server as a Time Machine backup disk from *OS X Server Essentials 10.10: Using and Supporting OS X Server on Yosemite.*

MORE INFO ▶ You can find out more about the Apple Time Capsule wireless base station at www.apple.com/airport-time-capsule/.

OS X Mountain Lion introduced support for selecting more than one Time Machine backup disk. This is especially useful for those who are away from their primary Time Machine backup disk for extended periods. For example, you can choose to back up to a Time Capsule wireless base station at home and also use a portable external disk when traveling.

Time Machine Schedule

Logistically, Time Machine uses a sophisticated background process, named backupd, to automatically create new backups of the entire file system every hour. This only works, though, if the backup disk is readily available. As more users go for portable Mac computers, it's becoming increasingly possible that users may be away from their backup disks for quite a while.

So, starting with OS X Lion, Time Machine began supporting local snapshots. As the name implies, Time Machine takes local snapshots if the backup disk is unavailable. Even when away from the backup disk, the user at least has access to restore from the local snapshots. This feature is enabled only on Mac portables with Time Machine left in the On state. Once the Mac can locate the backup disk again, the local snapshots are converted to traditional backups and saved to the disk. Time Machine attempts to keep a history of local snapshots available as well, in case you need to restore when the backup disk is offline. To save space, though, this local snapshot history is not as deep as the full backup.

While the Time Machine local snapshots are a convenient new feature, they certainly aren't true backups, as they are located on the same disk they are backing up. If the system disk fails, the local snapshots are lost as well. This is why, when a Mac is not backed up to the backup disk for ten consecutive days, the system warns the user on a regular basis to reconnect that disk. Train your users to ensure their Mac computers are connected to their Time Machine disks on a regular basis. Again, as long as the Mac can connect to the disk, Time Machine automatically handles the backup maintenance.

Another issue that may prevent Time Machine backups is system sleep. Quite simply, if the computer is asleep, it may not run the backup job. To rectify this situation, OS X Mavericks and later include the ability to back up to Time Machine while the system is in

Power Nap mode. For Mac systems that support Power Nap, even while the system is "sleeping" it still attempts to perform Time Machine backups or local snapshots every hour. Obviously, even with Power Nap enabled, the availability of the backup disk likewise affects the ability of a sleeping system to back up.

> **MORE INFO** ▶ Power Nap details are covered in Lesson 27 "System Troubleshooting".

Time Machine Backup Format

Time Machine uses several tricks to keep backups as small as possible so that you can maintain a deep history, but the backup starts out big. The initial Time Machine backup copies almost the entire contents of your file system to the specified backup volume.

To provide fast backups and convenient restores, Time Machine does not use a compressed archive format like many other backup systems. Instead, it simply copies the items as is to the backup disk. As you'll see later, this permits easy access to those items.

The space-saving comes into play with each subsequent backup. Between backups, a background process similar to the one used by the Spotlight search service automatically tracks any changes to the original file system. When the next scheduled backup occurs, only the items that have changed are copied to the backup volume. Time Machine then combines this new content with hard-link file system pointers (which occupy nearly zero disk space) to the previous backup content, and creates a simulated view of the entire file system at that point in time.

Time Machine also saves space by ignoring files that do not need to be backed up—ones that can be re-created after a restoration. Generally speaking, Time Machine ignores temporary files, Spotlight indexes, items in the Trash, and anything that can be considered a cache. Of particular note, Time Machine doesn't back up system log files, which you could need for later troubleshooting. Software developers can also instruct Time Machine to ignore specific application data that does not need to be backed up.

> **MORE INFO** ▶ Specifically, Time Machine always ignores files as defined by a configuration file that lives at /System/Library/CoreServices/backupd.bundle/Contents/Resources/StdExclusions.plist.

Eventually, so as not to waste space on your backup volume with historical data that has outlived its usefulness, Time Machine starts "aging out" backups: It keeps hourly backups for only a day, daily backups for a week, and weekly backups until your backup volume is full. After your backup volume is full, Time Machine starts deleting the oldest items first.

However, it always keeps at least one copy of every item that is still on your current file system.

> **NOTE ▶** Do not confuse Time Machine with snapshot technology common on other operating systems. While snapshots do create multiple instances of a file system through time, they do not provide you with a backup, as they don't actually copy data to another storage device. In other words, if a disk containing file system snapshots dies, those snapshots are just as lost as the current data on the dead disk.

Time Machine Limitations

Although Apple has put a lot of work into Time Machine, it is not entirely without issues. The Time Machine backup architecture does not lend itself to handling large files that change often. For example, many database files appear as large, single files to the file system. While the database application may be able to change just a few bytes of the large file as a user edits the database, Time Machine doesn't recognize this, so it creates another copy of the entire database file during the next backup. Obviously, this fills your backup volume much more quickly than if the database had been stored as many smaller files.

This leads to the next Time Machine issue: running out of backup space. Once Time Machine fills up the backup volume, it begins deleting older items to make room for newer ones. Therefore, the depth of your backup history varies based not only on the size of your backup volume but also on how often you change your files and how Time Machine recognizes those changes. Because you cannot change how Time Machine chooses to delete older items, you may discover that items you thought would still be on the backup volume have already been deleted.

> **TIP ▶** By default, Time Machine lets you know if it needs to delete older items to ~~~pace for new backups.

~~~sue is that Time Machine can only back up Legacy FileVault accounts when the ~~~d out of the system. The solution to this problem is to simply stop using Leg-~~~t in favor of OS X FileVault 2, as covered in Lesson 10 "FileVault".

~~ce 16.2
Configuring Time Machine

Despite the rather complex process going on behind the scenes to make Time Machine possible, configuration couldn't be easier. In fact, Time Machine is enabled by default and simply waiting for you to pick a backup disk. If you haven't configured a Time Machine backup disk, the system automatically scans the network for a Time Machine network share or waits for you to attach an external disk. If the system locates either, you are prompted to select it as your backup disk. If you select your backup disk with this method, after you click the Use as Backup Disk button, Time Machine is fully configured. It's just that easy.

If you make the wise choice to encrypt backups, you need to specify a password to protect the encryption, along with a password hint. The system automatically remembers the password in a local keychain to perform automated backups. However, as covered previously, if you ever need to access this encrypted disk from another computer, or even on the same Mac using a different system, you must enter the password to gain access to the disk's contents.

NOTE ▶ Again, if you lose the password used to unlock an encrypted Time Machine backup disk, its contents are lost forever. Not even Apple can recover the data.

NOTE ▶ Selecting the option to encrypt the Time Machine backup disk erases the disk's current contents.

Depending on the amount of data that has to be backed up and your choice of encryption format, it can take from minutes to hours for the initial backup to complete. The system can encrypt the disk and back up at the same time. Consequently, even if it takes only a few minutes to create the initial backup, the system may have to continue the disk encryption process, which could take several hours, depending on the size and speed of the disk. You can check the progress of any backup task from Time Machine preferences. From this interface, you can cancel the backup by clicking the small x button to the right of the progress bar.

TIP If you need to eject the Time Machine disk during a backup, you can also stop the backup and eject the disk from the Finder sidebar.

Time Machine lets you know when backup operations are complete. Subsequent backups occur automatically in the background. You can verify the last backup, or force an immediate backup, from the Time Machine menu near the clock in the menu bar. You can also open Time Machine preferences from this menu.

Time Machine Preferences

If you need to select a network backup disk, verify the backup status, or manually configure backup settings to better suit your needs, you can do so in Time Machine preferences. You can open Time Machine preferences from System Preferences, from the Time

Machine menu, or by secondary (or Control-) clicking the Time Machine icon if it's in the Dock.

TIP ▶ If you want Time Machine to back up only when you say so, simply switch it to Off in Time Machine preferences, and then initiate manual backups from the Time Machine menu. You can also postpone backups by disconnecting from the backup disk, though this works only with locally attached backup disks.

Configure Backup Disks

Again, OS X has the ability to select multiple Time Machine backup disks. Depending on the number of backup disks currently configured, the Time Machine preferences will look a bit different.

To add the first backup disk, click the Select Backup Disk button. If you want to modify the configuration of a single backup disk, click the Select Disk button. Finally, if you want to modify the configuration of multiple backup disks, select the text that reads "Add or Remove Backup Disks." Any of these methods reveals the Time Machine backup disk management dialog, which allows you to both add and remove backup disks.

If you select an additional backup disk, you are prompted to choose whether to replace the originally selected backup disk or to use both disks. You can configure multiple backup disks; however, the system completes backups for each destination separately and tries to back up at least once an hour to each destination. If you have two backup disks configured, Time Machine has to complete the backup for the first disk before it begins on the second. Backups can be completed out of order if one of the disks is missing, but the system still runs only one backup at a time. The system tries to keep a complete backup on every backup disk, but if the backup disks are of different sizes, the system starts to delete older items from the backup. Thus, one backup disk may have a deeper history than another, smaller backup disk.

As covered previously, if you selected a locally connected external disk and the encryption option, you need to specify a password and password hint. If you selected a network share or Time Capsule as the disk, you need to specify an authentication that allows you to access the share. Further, if you elect to encrypt the backup on a network share or Time Capsule, you also need to specify a password and password hint. Note that the password used to access the shared storage doesn't, and ideally shouldn't, match the password you specify for the encrypted backup.

Again, all Time Machine authentication information is saved to the keychain system, so backups can occur unattended. Once again, though, it's strongly recommended that you securely save any authentication information needed for Time Machine somewhere outside the system(s) you're backing up.

If you configure a new backup disk, Time Machine waits two minutes, allowing you to make further configuration changes before it starts the backup. Again, you can always return to the Time Machine backup disk management dialog to add or remove backup disks.

NOTE ▶ If your portable Mac supports local backup snapshots, this feature is enabled automatically. More information about using local snapshots is covered later in this lesson.

Time Machine Options

Clicking the Options button at the bottom of the Time Machine preferences reveals a dialog where you can adjust backup settings.

The most important configuration choice you can make with Time Machine is to exclude items from the backup. Obviously, excluding items reduces the amount of space needed for your backups. Note that the system automatically excludes any backup disk; this is to prevent multiple backup disks from backing up each other. It's not uncommon to leave only the /Users folder as the single item to back up—after all, that's where the important user items reside.

You can drag items into the list field, or you can click the Add (+) button at the bottom of the list to reveal a file browser, allowing you to select specific folders or volumes to exclude. Be sure to click Save to close this dialog, as backups will not be made until you have set the options here.

NOTE ▶ If you want to save space by excluding system items, simply add the /System folder to the exclude list; you will be prompted to exclude all system files or just the /System folder. When presented with this choice, it's best to exclude all system files.

NOTE ▶ If you do not perform a full backup of your system volume, you won't be able to perform a full restoration of it. Instead, you will have to install OS X first, and then you restore the remainder using Migration Assistant, as covered later in this lesson.

Reference 16.3
Restoring from Time Machine

Ultimately, a backup solution is only as good as its ability to restore the user's lost data. Time Machine delivers this ability in several different ways. First, you can easily restore individual items by entering the Time Machine interface. Second, you can restore user accounts and entire home folders with Migration Assistant. Third, you can restore an entire OS X system with OS X Recovery. Finally, advanced users can directly navigate through the Time Machine backup via the Finder and manually restore items.

NOTE ▶ Legacy FileVault users cannot access their home folder backup via the standard Time Machine interface. They can, however, use any of the other methods to restore their home folder from a Time Machine backup.

Restoring via Time Machine

The restore process for many backup solutions is geared for trained administrators, making user-initiated restoration a difficult proposition. OS X avoids this problem by providing an easy-to-use restore interface. The restore interface is considered by many to be Time Machine's best feature, because of the dynamic interface Apple has created to "look through time." This interface is available by opening the Time Machine application or using the Time Machine menu.

TIP ▸ For quick access to Time Machine, you can also drag its icon to the Dock. From the Time Machine icon you can secondary (or Control-) click to reveal a shortcut menu featuring additional Time Machine commands.

Few applications currently support the Time Machine restore interface, so in most cases you are presented with a historical view in the Finder. The Finder windows let you browse as usual, with one significant addition. You can use the navigation arrows to the right of the window, or the navigation timeline further to the right, to view Finder contents as they have changed over time.

NOTE ▸ If you use an encrypted disk or network share for your backup disk, and you are trying to restore from a different system, you will have to enter a password to access the backup data.

To aid in your search through time, the Spotlight search field remains active, and you can quickly preview any item by selecting it and then pressing the Space bar. Once you have found the item you are looking for, select it, and then simply click the Restore button. The Finder returns to "the present" with your recovered file intact where it once was.

Unlike in previous versions of OS X, the Time Machine restore interface in OS X Yosemite does not differentiate between items backed up to a local snapshot or a backup disk.

Instead, to avoid confusion, all snapshots appear similar in the timeline, regardless of backup destination.

If you are concerned about the amount of disk space occupied by local backups, you can examine disk space usage by opening the About This Mac dialog (from the Apple menu) and selecting the Storage tab. Any space on the system volume used for local snapshots appears as Backups. The system automatically adjusts the space used for local snapshots to a number in line with the disk's size.

Restoring via Migration Assistant

You can restore a complete user home folder or other nonsystem data from a Time Machine backup using Migration Assistant. You cannot, however, restore an entire system with Migration Assistant. Restoring an entire system is covered in the next section of this lesson.

When Migration Assistant opens, either during new system setup or when opened from /Applications/Utilities, simply choose to restore from a Time Machine backup. Once you have selected the backup disk and authenticated to access its content, the remainder of the Migration Assistant process is similar to the standard migration process covered in Lesson 2 "Setup and Configuration" for applications and settings, or in Lesson 6 "User Home Folders" for user-specific items.

> **NOTE** ▶ After completing the OS X Setup Assistant, only a user with administrative rights can initiate the Migration Assistant process. Starting the Migration Assistant process quits all running applications and logs out all user accounts.

> **NOTE** ▶ Legacy FileVault user accounts can be fully restored only by running Migration Assistant during the initial OS X system setup.

Restoring an Entire System

You can restore an entire system volume when the Mac is started up from an OS X Recovery system. However, this technique assumes you did not exclude any items from your system volume; that is, you left the Time Machine defaults and backed up the entire system volume.

You can start up the Mac using the normal OS X Recovery techniques, as covered in Lesson 3 "OS X Recovery", or you can actually start up from the OS X Recovery system hidden on a local Time Machine backup disk. When a local Time Machine backup disk is configured, the system automatically copies a disk image of the hidden Recovery HD volume from the system disk to the backup disk. This hidden recovery system can be a lifesaver if the original system disk suffers a catastrophic failure.

To start from this system, first make sure the backup disk is connected locally to the Mac, and then start up the Mac while holding down the Option key. This allows you to select the Time Machine disk as the startup disk.

External Backup HD

NOTE ▶ If the Mac has a firmware password enabled, you must enter the password to start up from another system volume. You can find out more about firmware passwords in Lesson 7 "System Security".

NOTE ▶ If the Time Machine backup disk is encrypted, you must enter the password to access its contents. This includes starting up from the backup disk's OS X Recovery system.

Once the system has started from OS X Recovery, select Restore From Time Machine Backup in the OS X Utilities window to open the Time Machine System Restore Assistant. The assistant first scans for local and network Time Machine backup volumes. Once you have selected the Time Machine volume, you can restore the entire system from any backup instance on that volume to your new system disk.

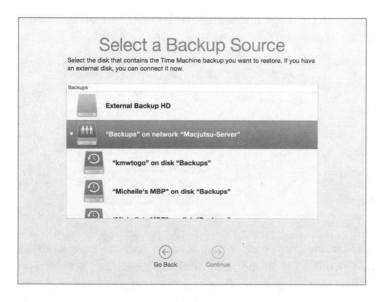

Manually Restoring via Finder

If you are experiencing problems using one of the other Time Machine restoration inter-faces, you can always browse the backup from the Finder. The Time Machine backup tech-nology uses file system features that are part of standard Mac OS Extended volumes, so no special software is needed to browse through backup contents.

> **NOTE** ▶ Do not directly modify the contents of a Time Machine backup, as doing so could damage the backup hierarchy. The default file system permissions do not give you write access to these items.

> **NOTE** ▶ Legacy FileVault home folders remain inside an encrypted disk image in the Time Machine backup. Thus, you need users' passwords to access their secure home folder contents.

> **NOTE** ▶ If your Time Machine configuration supports local snapshots, those snap-shots are cached locally to a hidden /.MobileBackups folder. Although you can navi-gate here and look around, the items in this location aren't permanent, as they are eventually copied to a backup disk and then erased on the local disk to save space.

If you're accessing a locally attached Time Machine backup disk, the backup files are loca-ted on the root of the backup disk in a folder named Backups.backupdb. Inside the backup database folder are folders with the name of each computer backed up to that disk. Inside each computer folder are folders named using the date and time of each backup. Finally, inside each dated folder are folders representing each backed-up volume.

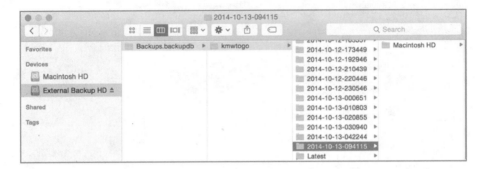

If you're accessing Time Machine over a network, you need to manually connect to the Time Machine share first. (Connecting to shares is covered in Lesson 23 "Network Services".) Once connected, you need to locate the Time Machine backup disk images. They are at the root of the Time Machine share, most commonly named Backups. Each Mac computer's backup is saved as a separate sparse disk image file named with the computer's sharing name.

Double-click to mount the Time Machine backup disk image volume, which is named "Backup of" followed by the computer's name. Remember, if the backup is encrypted, you will have to authenticate again to mount the backup disk image. Inside this volume is the same Backups.backupdb folder and contents you would find on a directly connected Time Machine backup.

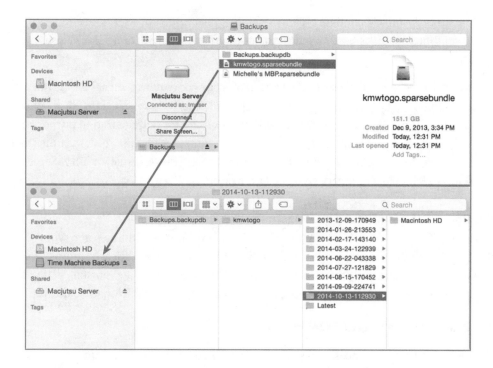

Exercise 16.1
Configure Time Machine

▶ **Prerequisites**

- ▶ You must have created the Local Admin ("Exercise 2.1 Configure a New OS X System for Exercises" on page 60 or "Exercise 2.2 Configure an Existing OS X System for Exercises" on page 63) and Chris Johnson ("Exercise 5.1 Manage User Accounts" on page 145) accounts.

- ▶ You must have partitioned your internal disk to create a Backup partition ("Exercise 9.1 Repartition a Disk Dynamically" on page 268), have an external disk in Mac OS Extended format, or have a Time Capsule appliance to use for backups.

In this exercise, you will configure Time Machine to back up your user home folders to either your internal disk's Backup partition, an external disk drive, or a Time Capsule appliance.

NOTE ▶ Backing up to a second partition on your computer's internal disk is not a recommended backup strategy because it provides no protection against disk failure or loss of the computer. It is presented in this exercise for demonstration purposes only. If you are performing these exercises on a computer you use for tasks other than exercises, configure it to back up to an external disk, Time Capsule, or OS X Server with the Time Machine service turned on instead.

Configure Exclusions for Time Machine

By default, Time Machine backs up the entire startup volume (excluding some types of files), but for this exercise you will configure it to back up only user files. In most situations, this is sufficient since the system and applications can always be reinstalled; if you want to be able to do a full system restore, do not exclude anything from the backup.

1   If necessary, log in as Chris Johnson.

2   Open System Preferences, and select the Time Machine preference pane.

3   If necessary, click the lock icon, and authenticate as Local Admin.

4   Select the "Show Time Machine in menu bar" checkbox if it is not already selected.

5   Click the Options button to reveal a dialog allowing you to exclude folders from backup.

6   Click the Add (+) button at the bottom of the dialog.

7   Navigate to your startup volume (generally Macintosh HD), and select the Applications, Library, and System folders.

Note that you can Command-click folders to add them to the selection.

8 Click Exclude.

9 When you see the message "You've chosen to exclude the System folder," click Exclude All System Files.

10 Click the Add (+) button again to add another exclusion.

11 This time, exclude the /Users/Shared/StudentMaterials/Lesson3 and Lesson4 folders, if they exist. If neither exists, click Cancel.

12 Click Exclude.

Your exclusion list now looks like this (although the Lesson3 or Lesson4 folders, or both, may not exist, and the sizes may be different):

Make sure you have just the Lesson3 and/or Lesson4 folders excluded, not the entire StudentMaterials folder.

Note that the option to back up while on battery power appears only on laptop computers.

13 Click Save.

Select a Backup Volume

1 If you want to back up this computer to an external disk, connect the disk to the computer now.

2 If a dialog appears asking if you want to use the disk to back up with Time Machine, click Decide Later so that you can configure the backup manually.

3 Turn on Time Machine by sliding the switch to On.

A dialog appears with a choice of backup targets.

4 Select the volume or Time Capsule you want to back up to. If you do not have an external disk or Time Capsule, use the Backup volume for demonstration purposes.

Storing the backup on the same disk as your original data does not protect you in the event of a hard disk failure. It will, however, be sufficient for the purposes of these exercises.

Note the checkbox that allows you to encrypt the backups. This encrypts the backup volume the same way as encrypting it in the Finder, as you did in "Exercise 9.4 Encrypt a Volume" on page 278.

If you are performing these exercises in a class, do not encrypt the volume since doing so delays the initial backup. If you are performing them on your own, you can encrypt the backup volume if you want; however, you have to wait for the conversion to encrypted format before you can start "Exercise 16.2 Restore Using Time Machine" on page 465.

5   Click Use Disk.

6   If a dialog appears asking if you are sure you want to back up to the same device, click Use Selected Volume.

Time Machine will start backing up in two minutes. You do not have to wait for it before proceeding.

7   Quit System Preferences.

Import vCards into Contacts

To demonstrate Time Machine, you will import some contacts that you can delete and then recover.

1   Open /Users/Shared/StudentMaterials/Lesson16.

2   Open the vCards.vcf file.

The Contacts app opens, and a dialog appears to confirm that you want to add the contacts.

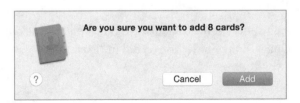

If the dialog indicates that some cards are duplicates, this may be because a previous student left them in the iCloud account you are using.

3   Click Add or Import.

This imports eight vCards into Contacts. If you have set up iCloud, they are also pushed to the iCloud servers.

4   Quit Contacts.

You should now perform "Exercise 16.2 Restore Using Time Machine" on page 465 to test the backup.

Exercise 16.2
Restore Using Time Machine

> **Prerequisite**
>
> ▶   You must have performed "Exercise 16.1 Configure Time Machine" on page 459.

In this exercise, you will learn how to use the Time Machine interface to recover lost files from the backup.

Make a New Snapshot

Before testing the backup, make sure it has finished backing up and is up to date.

1   If necessary, log in as Chris Johnson.

2   Click the Time Machine menu. If the menu indicates that it is still backing up, wait for it to finish.

3   If you are notified that the backup is complete, click Close.

4   From the Time Machine menu, choose Back Up Now.

This creates a new backup snapshot. Since little has changed since the initial backup, it should finish quickly.

5   Wait for the new backup to finish before proceeding.

Delete a Contact

Here you will delete one of the new contacts and the vCard file it was imported from.

1   Open the Contacts app.

You are going to delete some data so that you can test restoring it.

2   Select Carl Dunn.

3   Press Delete.

4   When asked if you are sure, click Delete.

5   Quit Contacts.

6   In the Finder, open /Users/Shared/StudentMaterials/Lesson16.

7   Move the vCards.vcf file to the Trash.

8   If you are prompted to, authenticate as Local Admin.

9   Choose Finder > Empty Trash. In the confirmation dialog, click Empty Trash.

    You have now removed all copies of Carl's contact information from your startup volume.

Restore a Contact Using Time Machine

Some apps integrate the Time Machine restore capability to allow you to restore their contents without needing to know how they are stored in the file system. You will test this capability with the Contacts app.

1   Imagine you are trying to call Carl Dunn. Open Contacts, and search for his phone number.

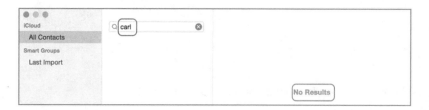

2   With Contacts the active application, choose Enter Time Machine from the Time Machine menu.

    Time Machine opens and shows snapshots of your contacts fading into the past.

3   Navigate to an earlier time by clicking the up arrow. This arrow points back in time.

    You can also navigate through time using the timeline along the right side of the screen. Carl Dunn's entry appears in the Contacts app.

4   Type **carl** in the search field.

    Time Machine finds Carl's entry in the old version of Contacts.

5   Select Carl's card, and click Restore below the Contacts window.

    Time Machine mode ends, and you are returned to Contacts. Contacts asks if you are sure you want to add one card to your contacts.

    If you are not prompted to add the contact, you may not have selected the card before clicking Restore. Return to step 2 and try again.

6   Click Add.

    Carl's entry is added back into your live contacts.

7 Quit Contacts.

Restore a File Using Time Machine

1 Switch to the Finder, and, if necessary, navigate to /Users/Shared/StudentMaterials/ Lesson16.

The Lesson16 folder is empty.

2 From the Time Machine menu, choose Enter Time Machine.

3 Navigate back in time until the vCards.vcf file appears.

4 Select vCards.vcf, and press Command-Y.

A Quick Look preview opens. Quick Look is available in Time Machine so you can verify that you have the right file before restoring it.

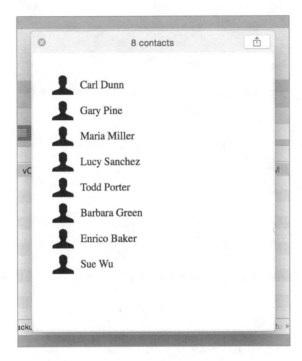

5   Press Command-Y again to close Quick Look.

6   With the file still selected, click Restore.

7   If you are prompted, authenticate as Local Admin.

You are returned to the Finder, and vCards.vcf is restored into the Lesson16 folder.

Restore Directly from Time Machine

When backing up to a local volume, Time Machine stores its backups in the file system. This means you can restore files by directly inspecting the backup and copying files out of it. If you are backing up to a Time Capsule, directly accessing backups is more complex; in that case, you should skip this section of the exercise.

1   In the Finder, open the volume you have chosen to back up to.

2   Open the Backups.backupdb folder. In this folder is a folder for your client. Open it.

This folder contains a series of folders, the names of which are date/timestamps. There is also an alias named Latest that always points to the latest backup.

3   Browse through these folders: Latest/Macintosh HD/Users/Shared/StudentMaterials/
    Lesson16.

4   Drag a copy of vCards.vcf to your desktop.

5   If prompted, authenticate as Local Admin.

Applications and Processes

Lesson 17

Application Installation

People use computers because they want to run applications, not operating systems. Most users don't care about the technologies underneath as long as the applications they want run smoothly. This is why, despite the growing popularity of Mac computers, users of other platforms are apprehensive about switching. It cannot be ignored that many applications run only on Windows-based computers.

Yet many applications that work only on Mac computers tempt other users because they represent the best solutions available. For several years now, Apple has been responsible for some of the most popular media creation applications with the iLife and Pro production suites. Third-party developers have stepped up their game in the last few years as well, as OS X provides a robust development platform with many unique features. For hundreds of examples, you need look no further than the Mac App Store.

In this lesson you will install applications using both the Mac App Store and traditional installation methods. You will also explore the various application environments and application security measures used in OS X.

Reference 17.1
The Mac App Store

With traditional installation methods, acquiring the software is often more difficult than actually installing it. Purchasing software in the traditional way means having to search through a variety of distribution channels with different delivery methods and possibly different pricing and versions.

Apple has taken a page from the iOS playbook and simplified software acquisition with the Mac App Store included in OS X. It gives users a single easy-to-use interface for locating, downloading, and installing software via the Internet. Further, applications from the Mac App Store do not require complex serial numbers or activation codes. Instead, all purchases are associated with an Apple ID and can be installed on any number of computers you own or control.

> **MORE INFO** ▶ If you support Mac computers for a large organization, Apple offers the Volume Purchase Program to acquire multiple licenses for Mac App Store items. You can find out more about this program for business customers at www.apple.com/business/vpp/, and for education customers at www.apple.com/education/it/vpp/.

Chances are you are already familiar with the Mac App Store, as it's the primary distribution method for all Apple software updates. However, if you have a new Mac with OS X Yosemite preinstalled, you may not have used the Mac App Store yet. Even if you have used it, you may not be familiar with all its features. This section provides an introduction to the Mac App Store from a support perspective.

> **MORE INFO** ▶ The Mac App Store has its own support site with more details available. You can find the site at www.apple.com/support/mac/app-store/.

Mac App Store Requirements

Introduced in OS X v10.6.6, the Mac App Store is the premier location for Mac-compatible software, and it's increasingly the only location where you can get new Apple software. The Mac App Store combines all the steps of acquiring new software into a single interface. These steps, covered in greater detail in the next section, include browsing and searching for new software, downloading and installing software, managing an account for purchasing software, updating installed software, and managing purchased software.

Aside from having OS X v10.6.6 or later, you must meet two additional requirements to install software from the Mac App Store: an Internet connection and an Apple ID. Obviously you must have an Internet connection to access content from the Mac App Store. A high-speed broadband connection is recommended, but slower connections are adequate, as long as you have the time to wait for the download.

An Apple ID with a verified email address is required to install anything from the Mac App Store, free or otherwise. If you intend to buy non-free items, you must also associate a valid credit card with your Apple ID. However, free items can be downloaded without a credit card. All Apple ID account management can be handled via the Mac App Store, as covered in "Store Account Management" on page 481.

NOTE ▶ Unlike previous versions of OS X, local administrator authentication is not required to install items when using the Mac App Store on OS X Mavericks or later. As covered later in this lesson, an administrative user can disable the Mac App Store for standard account users from the Parental Controls preferences.

Browse, Search, and Install

Even if you don't have an Apple ID, you can easily browse and search the Mac App Store. To get started, open the App Store in the Dock, or choose App Store from the Apple menu. When the Mac App Store opens, you are greeted with the Featured view.

Browsing the Mac App Store

The main area of the Featured view allows you to browse new, popular, and staff favorite items. To the right of the Featured view you'll find Quick Links, which link to specific categories and Mac App Store management features. Across the top of the Mac App Store window is a toolbar. Note the arrow buttons in the top-left corner that allow you to navigate backward and forward much like a web browser's history. If you're still browsing for new applications, you can click Top Charts to see the most popular items, or click Categories to browse for a specific type of application.

TIP ▶ The buttons in the Mac App Store toolbar correspond to keyboard shortcuts Command-1 through Command-5. For example, use the Command-2 keyboard shortcut to quickly navigate to the Top Charts page.

Searching the Mac App Store

The most direct route for finding a particular application is the search field in the top right of the window. Simply start typing part of the name, and the search immediately returns a list of matching items.

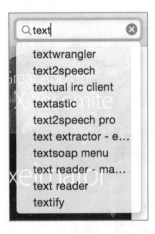

Pressing the Enter key or selecting an item from the list returns a search results page, giving you a more detailed view of the matching items. Click an application's icon or name to view the details page.

Once you're at an application's details page, you can read more about the application, view application screenshots, and at the bottom browse or write your own customer ratings and reviews. To the far right you'll also see developer and application information, including version, download size, and system requirements.

Installing from the Mac App Store

Directly under the application's icon, you'll see the application's price. Some applications on the Mac App Store are free and can be purchased without entering any payment information. Paid items require that a valid credit card or PayPal account be associated with the Apple ID that will be used to purchase items. To download and install an item, click the purchase button. The purchase button will either read as "Get" for a free application or the purchase price for a paid application. Click either to start the installation process.

TIP Clicking the small arrow to the right of the Install button reveals a pop-up menu allowing you to copy or share a link to the selected Mac App Store item.

If you have yet to sign in to the Mac App Store with an Apple ID, or you did not enter an Apple ID during system setup, you are prompted to do so now. If you don't have an Apple ID yet, you can create one in the Mac App Store. Details of the creation and management of accounts in the Mac App Store are covered in the next section. If, however, you already have an Apple ID that has been previously used to purchase items from any Apple online store, enter it to continue the installation process.

NOTE ▶ You will receive a warning if you try to install an application from the Mac App Store that replaces an earlier version of the same application that was purchased outside the Mac App Store.

Once your Apple ID is validated, the selected application downloads and installs directly to what appears to be the Launchpad. In reality, the application is being installed to the /Applications folder. Thus, if you prefer to use the Finder, you can also open the application from this folder. While the application is downloading, a progress bar is shown in both Launchpad and the Finder. Once the application has been installed, it will literally sparkle with anticipation waiting for you to open it for the first time.

Any item your Apple ID has been used to purchase is always available to update or reinstall from the Mac App Store. You can find out more about this in the "Managing Purchases" on page 486 section later in this lesson.

Store Account Management

Again, an Apple ID is required to purchase anything from the Mac App Store. If you have purchased items from Apple previously using the Apple Web Store, iTunes Store, or the iOS App Store, you can use the same Apple ID you used for those previous purchases. If you have not purchased anything from Apple via an online store, you can add purchasing information to an existing Apple ID or create a new Apple ID.

The only requirement for creating a new Apple ID is a unique email address, which is used for contact and verification. If your primary email address is from a non-Apple source, you can use that email to define an Apple ID. Alternatively, you can use a free iCloud account, which also provides a free email address, acts as an Apple ID, and can be used to make purchases from any of Apple's online stores. OS X Yosemite also includes Family Sharing, which allows one user to organize a group of up to six Apple IDs that can share downloaded Apple items. The Family Sharing organizer is even allowed to create new Apple IDs for children that give them limited access to online purchases from Apple.

You can begin the account management process by clicking the Sign In link, found on the right side of the Mac App Store in the Quick Links list, or by choosing Store > Sign In.

Quick Links

Sign In

Account

Redeem

Support

The Mac App Store authentication dialog appears. If you already have an Apple ID, enter it now. If you don't have an Apple ID, or you want to create a new one just for purchases, click Create Apple ID. What happens next depends on the state of your Apple ID: You can proceed to install items, you need to verify or update your Apple ID information, or you must enter some information to create a new Apple ID.

Your Apple ID Is Ready to Install

If your Apple ID has been used to purchase items from Apple previously, it may be ready to go for the Mac App Store. If this is the case, you won't see any other screens. When you are signed in, the first Quick Links item is Welcome followed by your first name. You can also verify the signed-in Apple ID by clicking the Store menu. Note that you can sign out from the Store menu as well.

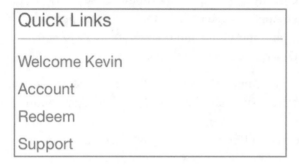

Your Apple ID Needs Updating

If your Apple ID information needs to be verified or updated, you're prompted to review your account. You first need to agree to the App Store terms and conditions, and then you need to verify your Apple ID security details. Sometimes this is all the verification that's needed. However, in some cases, your existing billing information may be incomplete or out-of-date and you will need to verify or update your billing information to continue with purchases.

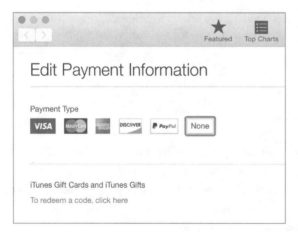

You have the choice of either entering credit card information for making purchases or choosing the None option if you plan to install only free items. Alternatively, if you have previously entered credit card information for an existing account, you can remove payment information and set the account to None by editing the account payment options as covered later in this lesson.

MORE INFO ▶ For more information about using any of Apple's online stores without a credit card, see Apple Support article HT204034, "Create an iTunes Store, App Store, or iBooks Store account without a credit card or other payment method."

You're Creating a New Apple ID

If you don't have an Apple ID, or you want to create a new one just for making purchases, you can do so almost entirely from the Mac App Store. After agreeing to the terms and conditions, you are prompted to enter details for a new Apple ID. Any time you create a new Apple ID, you must first provide account details that include a verifiable email address, three security answers, and your birthday.

After entering your details, you're prompted to provide a payment method. Finally, when creating a new Apple ID, you have to verify the email address specified. The Mac App Store system sends an email verification; click the link inside the email to open a webpage where you can authenticate and verify the account. Once you've done so, you have to sign in to the Mac App Store again to purchase or install any items.

NOTE ▶ An individual must be over the age of 13 to create an Apple ID. However, a Family Sharing organizer can create Apple IDs for children that can be granted limited online purchasing ability. Education institutions can create Apple IDs for minors by taking advantage of the Apple ID for Students program at http://deploy.apple.com.

NOTE ▶ Purchases made from different Apple IDs cannot be merged. However, a Family Sharing organizer can invite existing Apple IDs into a group so that purchases can be shared.

Verifying and Managing Your Apple ID

Anytime you want to make changes to your Apple ID, you can do so from within the Mac App Store by clicking the Account link in the Quick Links section or by choosing Store >

View My Account. From the Account Information page, you can change your Apple ID, payment information, and country or region setting.

Also, the Apple ID verification screen is the only location where you can create a nickname or change an existing one. Your Apple nickname is used to hide your personal identification in any reviews you post in any of Apple's various online stores.

Managing iCloud Family Sharing

OS X Yosemite introduces iCloud Family Sharing, allowing families of up to six people to share each other's iTunes, iBooks, and Mac App Store purchases without sharing account information. In other words, family members can sign in to the Mac App Store with their own personal Apple ID and share purchases with up to five other people in the Family Sharing group.

While the effects of iCloud Family Sharing can be seen in the Purchases view of the Mac App Store, all management of the Family Sharing group is via the iCloud preferences. An adult user who is signed into iCloud on OS X can start, or organize, a Family Sharing group by clicking the Manage Family button in the iCloud preferences.

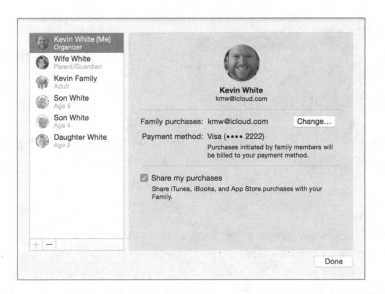

This first Apple ID is designated the "organizer" of the Family Sharing group. The organizer account must be set up with credit card payment information, as all other family members can be allowed to purchase using this payment information. The organizer can invite other adults via their Apple ID to the Family Sharing group and also create new iCloud accounts for children under 13 years of age. Child accounts are given full iCloud service access, including an email address using the @icloud.com domain.

Each member who joins the Family Sharing group is allowed to share existing Apple online purchases with the other group members. However, new purchases for any member of the Family Sharing group are all made via the organizer's payment method. The exception to this rule is that all Family Sharing members can make their own purchases using redemption codes, this includes both monetary and item-specific redemption codes.

Family Sharing users who are children can be required to ask for approval for any purchase, including free items. By default, the organizer is the only person who can approve such requests. Other adult members of the Family Sharing group can also approve purchases if the organizer specifies the adult as a parent or guardian. Adults who can approve purchases will receive a notification on their Apple devices to approve (or decline) each purchase. Adults can also authenticate directly on the device that the child is using to approve a purchase.

MORE INFO ▶ iCloud Family Sharing also includes the ability to share other services between family members. You can find out more at https://www.apple.com/icloud/family-sharing/.

Managing Purchases

A significant feature of the Mac App Store is that applications are associated with an Apple ID. According to Apple, "Apps from the Mac App Store may be used on any Macs that you own or control for your personal use." This means that if you personally use multiple Mac computers, you can install items from the Mac App Store on all of them. This is possible because Apple keeps track of the items purchased or installed by your Apple ID. Further, as covered previously, iCloud Family Sharing allows you to easily share Mac App Store purchases.

To install an application on a Mac that has already been purchased by you or another member of your Family Sharing group, open the Mac App Store, sign in with your Apple ID, and then click the Purchases icon in the toolbar. The Purchases page defaults to showing all the items owned by the signed-in Apple ID, both installed and not installed on the Mac.

If the currently signed-in Apple ID is part of a Family Sharing group, you can also view another family member's purchases by selecting the person's name from the Purchases pop-up menu just above the purchases list. Note that some Mac App Store items cannot be shared. The option to allow purchases to be shared is at the discretion of the application's developer.

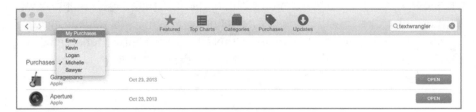

Once you have located an already purchased item, simply click the Install button to download and install the latest version of the application to the local Mac. If the button next to a purchased item reads "Open," then the item is already installed on the Mac.

> **TIP** If the Mac App Store is in the process of downloading a particularly large item, you can check the item's progress from the Purchases page.

> **TIP** New Mac computers have additional Apple software preinstalled at the factory. Thus, the first time you view purchases in the Mac App Store, you may note these items listed at the top. You can associate these items with your Apple ID by clicking the Accept button.

> **TIP** If you use more than one Mac, you may want to enable automatic downloading of purchased applications. This option can be set from the Mac App Store preferences pane in the System Preferences for every Mac that has been configured with your Apple ID.

Mac App Store Updates

Updating applications you originally installed from the Mac App Store is also extremely easy. As covered in Lesson 4 "OS X Software Updates", OS X includes an automatic software update mechanism that is built in to the Mac App Store. Automatic updates are enabled by default, and the system reminds you via notification when they are available for installation. Further, you can enable updates to install automatically without the need for user interaction.

However, you can also manually check for updates by simply opening the Mac App Store. Every time you open the Mac App Store, it scans your local Mac for any Apple-installed items and compares the results to what's current on the Apple servers.

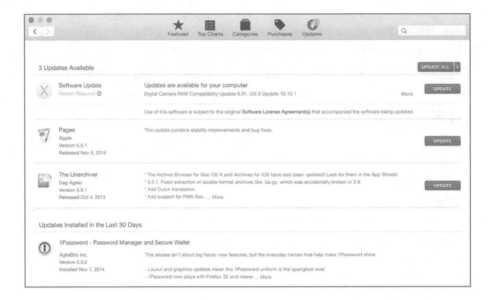

TIP ▶ If the proper updates don't seem to be appearing for your system, you can force the Mac App Store to reevaluate your installed software by holding down the Option key while opening the Mac App Store. Continue to hold the Option key while you click the Updates button as well.

If updates are available, you may notice in the toolbar that the Updates button has a small number by it. This represents applications that have updates available. Click the Updates button to reveal the list of available updates. You can choose to install individual updates by clicking specific Update buttons, or you can click the Update All button to install all updates.

Limiting Access to the Mac App Store

Some items on the Mac App Store, specifically games, may contain content not suitable for children. Because software on the Mac App Store is rated with a system similar to that for motion pictures, you can limit a user's access to specific ratings. Further, if your organization prevents users from installing their own applications, then you may want to disable access to the Mac App Store altogether. If you want to limit access or completely disable the Mac App Store for a user, you can do so via the parental controls.

NOTE ▶ The system will not allow you to delete the Mac App Store, as it is needed to perform system updates.

In Parental Controls preferences, you have several ways to limit applications from the Mac App Store. The easiest method is to simply choose an age requirement from the Allow App Store Apps pop-up menu. Selecting a minimum age here limits the user's ability to both purchase new applications and open any applications already installed from the Mac App Store.

Alternatively, you can click the disclosure triangle next to App Store and then individually deselect the applications you want to disallow. Scrolling down through the allowed applications list also reveals an option, under the Other Apps disclosure triangle, to disallow the Mac App Store itself. This obviously prevents the restricted user account from installing or updating of any item available from the Mac App Store.

MORE INFO ▶ Managing users using the parental controls is further covered in Lesson 5 "User Accounts".

Reference 17.2
Application Environments

Obviously, applications from the Mac App Store are made specifically to work on OS X. Once you venture beyond the Mac App Store though, you'll find there are thousands of other applications that also work on OS X. Aside from the Mac App Store, software can be delivered through a variety of mechanisms.

OS X supports several different application environments. Application developers create their products based on support for these environments. Several are specific to OS X, while others add support for popular UNIX-based tools. Most importantly, though, average users do not need to concern themselves about which environment their application is using—the system will provide the appropriate resources automatically. The four primary application environments in OS X are native OS X applications, UNIX commands, Java applications, and UNIX applications that use the X Window System.

> **MORE INFO** ▸ To learn more about OS X system architecture and application environments, see the Apple development resources at http://developer.apple.com/technologies/mac.

Native OS X Applications

Most native OS X applications are created using a development environment known as Cocoa. Unsurprisingly, Cocoa is the application environment most specific to OS X, as Cocoa-based applications run only on iOS and OS X. Cocoa is primarily based on the Objective-C programming language.

> **MORE INFO** ▸ To learn more about the Cocoa application environment, refer to the Apple development resources at http://developer.apple.com/technologies/mac/cocoa.html.

OS X Yosemite continues to support earlier OS X applications created using a development environment known as Carbon. The Carbon application environment is a streamlined and significantly updated version of the previous Mac OS 9 environment. Developers could update their legacy Mac applications, often with little work, to run natively in OS X. Carbon is based on the industry-standard C and C++ programming languages.

On the surface, it's hard for a user to identify any differences between Carbon and Cocoa applications. As OS X advanced, Apple further blurred the lines between Cocoa and Carbon by allowing applications to use a mix of both environments.

However, Apple drew the line in OS X v10.6 by adding full 64-bit support for Cocoa graphical applications but not for Carbon graphical applications. Apple has made it clear that going forward, new development for OS X should be exclusively in Cocoa. Often, developers must use the Cocoa environment if they want to take advantage of the latest OS X features. As an example, only Cocoa-based applications can integrate with Auto Save and iCloud services.

For this reason, nearly all Apple software and most third-party software available from the Mac App Store is developed for the Cocoa application environment. Further, while OS X Yosemite still supports Carbon applications, the technology has officially been deprecated, indicating future releases of OS X may not support Carbon-based applications.

Legacy Mac Applications

Previous versions of OS X supported applications created for Mac OS 9 and for PowerPC processors. The Classic compatibility environment, which enables users to run software created for Mac OS 9, ceased to be supported as of OS X v10.5. The Rosetta compatibility environment, which enables users to run software created for PowerPC processors, is not supported as of OS X Lion.

UNIX Applications

Since the introduction of OS X v10.5, the system has been both POSIX- and UNIX 03–compliant. Thus, OS X is compatible with most UNIX software. The OS X system foundation, named Darwin, is based on the open source Free Berkeley Software Distribution (FreeBSD) UNIX command-line interface. The command line is most often accessed via the /Applications/Utilities/Terminal application.

MORE INFO ▶ To learn more about Darwin, see the Apple open source development resources at http://developer.apple.com/opensource/.

Java Applications

Java is an application environment originally developed by Sun Microsystems but now owned and primarily maintained by Oracle Corporation. The goal of developing software in Java is to create cross-platform applications. This means a developer can write software code that can run on many environments. At the time of this writing, there are two versions of the Java runtime available for OS X: Apple still supplies the older Java SE 6, whereas Oracle supplies the latest Java 8.

NOTE ▶ JavaScript, another technology, is used almost exclusively by web browsers and is fundamentally quite different than the Java application runtime. The web browser included in OS X, Safari, provides robust support for JavaScript.

While there is Java application runtime support for OS X, it is not included with the default OS X system installation. The first time you run a standard Java applet or application, you are prompted to navigate to the download page for the latest version of Apple's Java SE 6.

As with any system software installation, administrative user access is required to install the Java runtime. Thus, if you know that your users require access to Java applications, you may want to manually download and install the Java runtime as part of your standard OS X configuration. The latest Java runtime for OS X from Apple can be found at Apple Support article DL1572, "Java for OS X."

With Java from Apple installed, the system supports both 32-bit and 64-bit Java SE 6 version 1.6.x. Going forward, Apple will only be providing updates for this older Java technology. Similar to other Apple-supplied software, updates to Java SE 6 from Apple can be automatically installed via the Mac App Store software update mechanism.

NOTE ▶ For security reasons, the Apple implementation of Java SE 6 disables automatic opening of web browser-based Java applets and applications. If you need this functionality, it's recommended that you install Oracle's implementation of Java 8.

Historically, Java for other computing platforms was delivered by Java's primary developers, originally Sun and now Oracle. With Java 8, Oracle is the official developer for OS X versions of the Java runtime. Thus, to acquire the latest versions of Java for OS X, you must download and install the Java runtime from http://java.com/. At the time of this writing, Oracle supports only Java 8 on OS X Yosemite.

The Java website provides the Java runtime in the form of a standard Apple installer package. Note that installation of this package requires administrator authentication. Again, if you know that your users require access to Java applications, you may want to manually download and install the Java 8 runtime as part of your standard OS X configuration. Also note that you can have both the Apple-supplied Java SE 6 and the Oracle-supplied Java 8 installed at the same time.

With Java from Oracle installed, the system supports 64-bit Java 8 version 1.8.x. You can verify the specific Java version supplied by Oracle and adjust other Java settings by opening the Java preference, which appears in the Other section of System Preferences. Oracle's implementation of the Java runtime features its own proprietary updater mechanism, which can also be managed from the Java preferences.

X Window System Applications

The X Window System is an extension of the UNIX environment that provides a common graphical applications platform for UNIX workstations. Previous versions of OS X included the Apple version of a popular implementation of the X Window System known as X11. Open /Applications/Utilities/X11 to access X Window System applications.

However, opening this application in OS X Yosemite redirects you to Apple Support article HT201341, "About X11 and OS X." From that article you are redirected to an open source implementation known as XQuartz, available at http://xquartz.macosforge.org. This is the Apple-supported implementation of the X Windowing System on OS X. Upon installation the /Applications/Utilities/X11 application is replaced with /Applications/Utilities/XQuartz.

Open Source Software

By now you may have noticed that quite a bit of OS X is based on something called open source software. Generally speaking, open source is a method of software creation based on the free distribution and contribution of software source code. In other words, it's software whose code is available at no cost to anyone for general use or further modification. Interested individuals are expected and usually encouraged to provide improvements to open source software by adding to the software's code. It's expected that over time this community involvement will yield software products of exceptional quality, often free of cost.

Apple is deeply involved with many open source projects, including not just building upon open source but also contributing to existing projects and creating entirely new open source projects. In fact, the core of OS X, Darwin, is an entirely open source operating system that includes more than 200 individual open source projects. Keep in mind, though, that Apple maintains proprietary closed software solutions as part of OS X as well. Apple charges for these proprietary parts of OS X, but that is what allows Apple to employ hundreds of talented developers to create exceptional software.

MORE INFO ▶ To learn more about how Apple is involved in open source development, visit http://developer.apple.com/opensource/.

The astounding growth of open source software in the last decade has not only produced some great software but also led to the rise of an entirely new operating system, Linux.

With the growing popularity of Linux, high-quality open source applications have taken off as well. Because of the open source and UNIX heritage of OS X, you can also take advantage of many of these open source applications on your Mac. Some open source applications run in the command line, others through XQuartz, and some have even been converted to full-fledged Mac applications. Take some time to explore these free open source solutions for your Mac, as they may be suitable replacements for commercially purchased software.

> **MORE INFO** ▶ The MacPorts project hosts over 15,000 open source software titles for OS X at www.macports.org.

Reference 17.3
Application Security

One of the primary benefits of acquiring applications from the Mac App Store is knowing that Apple has processes for ensuring the applications are free of malicious software, also known as malware. No system is perfect, but even if a bad application slips by the Apple procedures, the application can be pulled quickly from the store.

Despite the popularity of the Mac App Store, there are thousands of Mac applications that are available only outside of the store. There are many reasons a developer might need to distribute software outside of the Mac App Store, including both technical and licensing issues. Apple recognizes the need for software developers to distribute their wares outside of the Mac App Store. At the same time, though, there is the need to ensure that OS X users are protected from bad software. To this end, OS X includes several application security technologies that help protect users when they install third-party applications.

Process Security

OS X inherits relatively robust process security due to its UNIX foundation. At both the command line and graphical interface, applications and processes are not allowed to access resources unless they are authorized. Access restrictions in the form of file system permissions are responsible for much of the security here. Simply, a running process is owned by a user, and is therefore granted file system access similar to that of the user.

However, system privileges are allowed when needed. The most obvious example of this is the Installer application, which requires administrative authorization to install software that affects more than one user. The moral of this story is to beware of applications that require administrator authorization, as you are granting that application system-level access. Of note, the only applications on the Mac App Store that may ask for administrative authorization are those developed by Apple. For example, setup of the OS X Server application requires administrative authorization as it installs additional system services.

Application Sandboxing

Even with the OS X default process security mechanism in place, an application could still access all the files owned by a user. This gives an application the potential to read all your files and potentially gain unauthorized access to personal information.

A significant security feature in OS X is support for full application and process sandboxing. As the name implies, applications and processes in OS X can "play" inside a protected environment that has little or no access to other parts of the system. With application sandboxing, applications are granted access only to the items they need through a sophisticated arrangement of rules. This is implemented in OS X via application sandbox containers, as covered in Lesson 14 "System Resources".

It's important to note that application sandboxing is an optional feature. Despite this, Apple has already sandboxed any application or process built into OS X that could benefit from this feature. Further, as of June 2012, all applications available from the Mac App Store must use application sandboxing.

Code Signing

Code-signed applications and processes include a digital signature, which is used by the system to verify the authenticity and integrity of the software code and resources. Code is verified not only on disk but also as it is running. Therefore, even if some part of the application's or process's code is inappropriately changed while it's active, the system can automatically quit it.

In addition to identifying changes to applications, code signing provides guaranteed application identification for other parts of the system, including the keychain, the personal application firewall, Parental Controls preferences, application sandboxing, and Managed Client settings.

Finally, in OS X, code signing is used as the basis of identification for trusting newly installed items. Though code signing is optional, applications that have it are automatically trusted by the system. All Apple software and applications from the Mac App Store are always code signed, and thus trusted by OS X upon installation.

Software developers that choose not to use the Mac App Store can still take advantage of this system. A developer can code sign its installers and applications using an Apple-granted Developer ID. In this way, code-signed applications installed from any origin can be trusted by OS X.

File Quarantine

OS X includes a file quarantine service that displays a warning when you attempt to open an item downloaded from an external source like the Internet. Quarantined items include many file types, including documents, scripts, and disk images. This lesson focuses primarily on quarantine as it relates to downloaded applications.

File quarantine goes into effect only when an item is marked for quarantine by the application that downloaded it. This is true for all applications built into OS X, but it may not be true for third-party applications that can download files. Also, files copied to the Mac using any other method are not marked for quarantine. For example, using the Finder to copy an application from a USB disk does not engage the quarantine system.

When a file is marked, the system requires you to verify your intent to open the item or cancel if you have any suspicions about the safety of an item. Any administrative user can permanently clear the quarantine by clicking Open. After an administrator clears the quarantine, the system will no longer show the quarantine warning. On the other hand, when a standard user clicks Open on a quarantined item, the item opens but the quarantine remains. Thus, subsequent users who try to open the item still get the quarantine warning.

"TextWrangler.app" is an application downloaded from the Internet. Are you sure you want to open it?

Safari downloaded this file today at 12:23 AM from www.barebones.com.

[?]   [Cancel]   [Show Web Page]   [Open]

NOTE ▶ The version of TextWrangler that was used to generate the previous screenshot was downloaded from the developer's website. TextWrangler is also available from the Mac App Store; however, the Mac App Store version is not quarantined because it's from a trusted source: Apple.

Apple has further enhanced this feature by maintaining a list of known malicious software. If you attempt to open any software on this list, the system presents a warning dialog suggesting that you move the item to the Trash. The list of malicious software is automatically updated via the OS X software update mechanism and is located on your Mac in the file /System/Library/CoreServices/CoreTypes.bundle/Contents/Resources/XProtect.plist.

MORE INFO ▶ File quarantine can also be removed using the xattr command line tool. This is useful for removing quarantine on multiple files at once, or in cases where the Finder can't properly remove the quarantine. To use this tool in the Terminal application, enter **xattr –dr com.apple.quarantine**, followed by the path of the item.

MORE INFO ▶ To find out more about file quarantine, see Apple Support article HT201940, "About the 'Are you sure you want to open it?' alert (File Quarantine / Known Malware Detection) in OS X."

Gatekeeper

Gatekeeper is a system that leverages both code signing and file quarantine to further protect your Mac from malicious applications. It does this by giving you the choice to allow only trusted application sources. Although originally introduced with OS X Mountain Lion v10.8, Apple believes that Gatekeeper is important enough that it was also retroactively added to OS X Lion v10.7.5.

NOTE ▶ Because Gatekeeper relies on the file quarantine system, it restricts only applications downloaded by applications that properly set file quarantine.

From the General pane of Security & Privacy settings, you can adjust the settings for Gatekeeper. Gatekeeper allows for three modes of application restriction:

▶ Mac App Store—This is the most limited option, as it allows only applications from the Mac App Store to open. Even when a version of the application is available from the Mac App Store, if you download the application from somewhere else, it will still be blocked.

▶ Mac App Store and identified developers—This is the default option for OS X. As covered previously, developers can use an Apple-verified code-signing certificate to identify their application. If a developer has done this, the application is allowed to open, but the system still presents the file quarantine dialog for downloaded items. If an application isn't properly signed, it will be blocked.

▶ Anywhere—This option is similar to the behavior of previous versions of OS X. All applications are allowed regardless of source, but again the system presents the file quarantine dialog for downloaded items.

Gatekeeper also identifies modified or damaged applications regardless of your security settings. In this case you are seeing code signing at work, as the system has identified changes to an application from its original state. Thus, the application is either damaged due to file corruption or someone other than the original developer has modified it. In either case you will not be allowed to open the application, as it may cause harm.

MORE INFO ▶ To find out more about Gatekeeper, see Apple Support article HT202491, "OS X: About Gatekeeper."

Temporarily Bypassing Gatekeeper

Even with Gatekeeper in place, an administrative user can override the system's settings and allow untrusted applications. In the Finder, an administrative user can secondary (or Control-) click the application file and then choose Open from the shortcut menu. The Gatekeeper warning appears to verify the administrator's intent.

TIP ▶ An administrative user can also override the previous item blocked by Gatekeeper in the General tab of Security & Privacy preferences.

Clicking Open opens the application and clears the file quarantine. However, this may not be enough for all unsigned applications, because some applications may automatically open other background or child applications. Examples include applications that also provide background software to facilitate hardware functionality.

These secondary applications also trigger Gatekeeper. Unfortunately, you may not be able to override the appropriate files from the Finder. In these cases, you may have to temporarily allow Anywhere in the General tab of Security & Privacy preferences. Once you have launched the application and verified its full functionality, the quarantine is cleared, and you can then return the Gatekeeper settings to something more secure.

Reference 17.4
Traditional Installation Methods

Traditional installation methods fall into one of two categories: drag-and-drop installations or installation packages. Application developers can choose any method they want to deploy their wares. Often the distinction between the two traditional methods is the complexity of the software being deployed.

If a software developer creates a product that requires only a folder of a few items or even one single item, it's often deployed as a drag-and-drop installation. However, if a software developer creates a product that requires a set of items that must be installed in multiple specific locations throughout the system, it's often deployed as an installation package.

> **NOTE** ▸ As covered previously in this lesson, applications downloaded from any source outside of the Mac App Store are subject to file quarantine and Gatekeeper rules.

Drag-and-Drop Installations

Apple pioneered the era of drag-and-drop in computing, so it should come as no surprise that many traditional software installations in OS X are of the simple drag-and-drop variety. In general, OS X doesn't care where an application or process resides. So long as the application itself doesn't have a specific location requirement, applications can run from any location on the Mac. That said, as covered in previous lessons, some locations are more appropriate and secure than others.

Specifically, OS X makes the /Applications folder the default location for applications available to all users. Only administrative users can manually make changes to the /Applications folder. If users want to install their own drag-and-drop applications, they can create their own Applications folder in their home folder. However, users can place applications anywhere they please inside their own home folders. Again, many drag-and-drop applications work from any location on the system.

Drag-and-Drop Application Security

Also, it's important to recognize that because of the default security and permissions model in OS X, any application a standard user is allowed to install and open cannot interfere with other users on the system. Poorly written or malicious software could potentially harm items in the user's home folder, but as long as the user is not allowed to authenticate as an administrator, it is extremely difficult for the software to cause damage to the system or other users.

Keep in mind, the same is true for a user's intentional actions as well. A user could deliberately cause similar damage. In short, allowing nonadministrative users the ability to install software is no more dangerous than allowing them to use the computer in the first place.

Installing Drag-and-Drop Items

Drag-and-drop software deployed via optical disc, or any other physical medium, is often ready to copy to wherever the user wants to install it. On the other hand, software downloaded from the Internet is almost always deployed in some kind of archive format. As covered in "Reference 13.4 File Archives" on page 388, zip files and disk images are the most common archive formats for OS X.

In OS X, the Safari browser automatically unarchives zip files, by default, to the ~/Downloads folder. Users could technically leave the application in the ~/Downloads folder and continue to open it from there, but they should be trained to move the new application to a more appropriate location in their home folder.

In OS X the Safari browser does not, however, automatically mount a downloaded disk image. A user must double-click a disk image to make its contents available to the Finder. Once the disk image volume is mounted, again the user could technically leave the application inside the disk image and open it from there, but users should be trained to move the new application to another location. This is especially true of disk images, because if the user logs out or restarts the computer, the disk image unmounts.

For many novice users, this would result in their "losing" the application. Fortunately, many developers use a helpful Finder window background graphic that should encourage the user to copy the software to a more appropriate location. An example of this type of installation is found later in this lesson, "Exercise 17.3 Use a Drag-and-Drop Install" on page 517.

Installation Packages

Installation packages are the default deployment mechanism for most Apple software updates and third-party software that requires the installation of items in multiple locations. Installation packages are deployed via user interaction with the Installer application. When a user opens an installation package, the Installer application opens automatically. This application has the user walk through a few simple screens to configure and initiate the installation process.

Most significantly, installation packages often require administrative user authentication, as they are frequently used to install items that can affect other users and the operating system. Lesson 4 "OS X Software Updates" details using and troubleshooting installation packages for Apple software updates. The same techniques apply to third-party installation packages deployed via the Installer application.

That said, on occasion you will find third-party installers that do not use the Apple Installer application. These installations are easily identified because the installation assets are themselves an application using the .app filename extension. The Apple native installation assets come only in the form of installation packages using the .pkg or .mpkg filename extensions. If you have problems with a third-party installer, you must contact the developer for any issues regarding installation, as it has elected to use a proprietary installation mechanism.

Updating Installed Software

Similar to installation, there are a variety of methods for keeping installed software up to date:

▶ Apple software and Mac App Store software—Any software acquired via the Mac App Store, including both Apple and third-party software, is also updated via the Mac App Store software update mechanism, as covered previously in this lesson and in Lesson 4 "OS X Software Updates".

▶ Automatically updating third-party software—Automatic update mechanisms for third-party software vary widely. Prior to the Mac App Store, no unified method for providing third-party software updates existed. Thus, software developers often implemented their own automatic update methods. Unfortunately, this means there is no standard method to determine if an application has automatic update capability. You can start by looking in common locations, including the application menu (the menu that appears with the application's name), the application's preferences window, or the application's Help menu. If the third-party item installed a preference pane, it's highly likely any automatic update mechanism will be found within. Finally, it's important to note that nearly all automatic update mechanisms require administrative user authentication.

▶ Manually update third-party software—In some cases the only update mechanism for third-party software is to simply install a newer version. Keep in mind, only administrative users can replace or update software in the /Applications folder. Further, many package installations require administrative user authentication.

Reference 17.5
Removing Installed Software

In many cases, removing installed software is much easier than installing it in the first place. One thing that often surprises veteran Windows support specialists who are new to the Mac is that there's no default Apple software removal mechanism. This is because the vast majority of Mac software can simply be moved to the Trash. That said, it's never recommended to remove any part of the OS X system software.

Software removal methods include:

▶   Mac App Store software—Although it's true that applications installed from the Mac App Store can be dragged to the Trash, you can also remove these applications from Launchpad. To engage Launchpad, double-click its icon in the /Applications folder, or from a Multi-Touch trackpad use the "pinch with thumb and three fingers" gesture. In Launchpad, hold down the Option key, and a small x button appears next to applications installed from the Mac App Store. Click one of the buttons, and the system will remove that application.

▶   Drag to the Trash—Yes, it's true that most applications are "removed enough" if you simply move the primary application icon into the Trash. If the software item is a type of resource, like a preference pane or font, just locate the item in one of the Library folders and drag it to the Trash. This method may leave some residual support files, but by removing the primary application or resource file you have rendered the software inoperable. This method works for applications installed using a traditional method and via the Mac App Store. Just don't forget to empty the Trash before continuing with your work—a user logout wouldn't hurt either.

▶   Application uninstaller—Only in very rare occasions will third-party software require an uninstaller. The only times you will find an uninstaller are in situations where the software's developer has deemed the removal process complicated enough to warrant an uninstaller. If this is the case, the software developer must provide the uninstaller; it often comes along with the original software installer.

Exercise 17.1
Use the Mac App Store

▶ **Prerequisite**

▶ You must have created the Local Admin ("Exercise 2.1 Configure a New OS X System for Exercises" on page 60 or "Exercise 2.2 Configure an Existing OS X System for Exercises" on page 63) and Chris Johnson ("Exercise 5.1 Manage User Accounts" on page 145) accounts.

In this exercise, you will use the Mac App Store to purchase, download, and install a free application on your computer.

Select an App to Purchase

NOTE ▶ The exact process of configuring Chris Johnson's account with an Apple ID for the App Store will depend on whether you want to use the same Apple ID for iCloud and App Store purchases, and what the Apple ID has been used for in the past. The instructions in this exercise attempt to cover most of the possibilities, but if you find that your experience does not match these instructions, the App Store will be able to guide you through the process.

1   If necessary, log in as Chris Johnson.

2   Open System Preferences, and select the App Store preference pane.

The settings in this preference pane allow you to automate updating and downloading App Store purchases, as well as system software. By default, the App Store automatically checks for all updates and downloads system updates in the background. It also automatically installs new security updates. There is also an option to automatically update purchased apps, as well as an option to automatically download apps purchased on other Mac computers using the same Apple ID.

3   If "Automatically download apps purchased on other Macs" is selected, click the lock, authenticate as Local Admin, and deselect the checkbox.

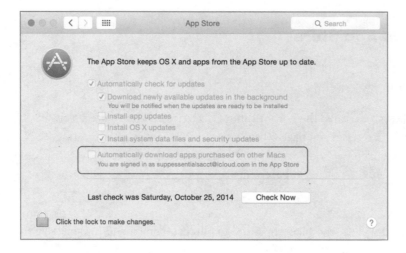

4 Close System Preferences.

5 From the Apple menu, choose App Store.

6 In the App Store, pull down the Store menu, and see if it shows you are signed in (it will list "View My Account") or not ("Create Account").

You may have been automatically signed in to the Apple ID you used for iCloud. Apple recommends using the same account for both (see Apple Support article HT204053, "Set up your Apple ID for iCloud and iTunes"), but it is also possible to use different Apple IDs for these different functions.

7 If you are signed in but want to use a different Apple ID for App Store purchases, choose Store > Sign Out. Otherwise, dismiss the menu.

8   Enter **the unarchiver** into the search field (at the top right of the App Store window), and press Return.

> **NOTE ▶** If you are performing these exercises in a class, the instructor may recommend a different app for this exercise; in that case, substitute that recommendation for The Unarchiver throughout this exercise.

The App Store may find more than one relevant app. Find a free app named The Unarchiver (or the app your instructor recommended). Note that free apps have a button labeled "Get" instead of a price (although if the app has already been purchased under this Apple ID, the button will be labeled "Install").

9   Click the free app's name.

The App Store displays more details about this app. Again, there will be a button labeled either "Get" or "Install."

10 Click the Get or Install button.

11 If the app begins downloading immediately, skip to "Test the App" on page 512.

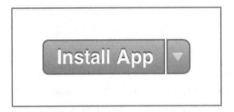

12 If it changes to an Install App button, click that to confirm the download.

If additional confirmation or configuration is required, a dialog appears asking you to sign in to download the app. Note that an Apple ID is required even though this is a free application. If you are already signed in to the iCloud account, the Apple ID field will already be filled in.

You have several choices for which account to use:

▶ If you want to use the same Apple ID for both iCloud services and App Store purchases, follow Option 1 with that account. If you are performing these exercises as part of a class, you should use this option.

▶ If you have another existing Apple ID, you can use that (follow Option 1).

▶ If you have access to an existing email account that is not already in use as an Apple ID, you can create a new Apple ID linked to it and use that for the App Store (follow Option 2).

Depending on which choice you prefer, perform the steps in the corresponding section.

Option 1: Use an Existing Apple ID (Either Yours or Provided by an Instructor)

Follow these steps if you already have an Apple ID that you want to use for the App Store or if you are performing the exercise in class and the instructor has provided an Apple ID for you to use.

Note that you may need to search for the app again (step 8 of the previous section).

1   Enter the Apple ID and password, and click Sign In.

2   If you receive a message that you need to ask permission for the purchase, you are using an iCloud child account. In this case, you can do any of the following:

▶ Click Ask, and then continue the exercise after a parent has approved the purchase.

▶ Switch to a different Apple ID by clicking Cancel, choosing Store > Sign Out, and then starting over using a different Apple ID.

▶ Click Cancel, quit the App Store, and skip this exercise.

3   If you receive a message that this Apple ID has not been used with the iTunes Store, you can do any of the following:

▶ Enable this Apple ID for use with the App Store by clicking Review and following the prompts (the process is not covered in detail here). Note that this may require you to supply a credit card or other payment source.

▶ Switch to a different Apple ID by clicking Cancel, and start over using an Apple ID that has been used with the App Store.

▶ Click Cancel, quit the App Store, and skip this exercise.

4   If you are asked to verify billing information for your Apple ID account, click Billing Info, and enter it as requested. If the requested information is not available, click Cancel, then choose Store > Sign Out, and either start over using an instructor-provided Apple ID instead of your own or use one of the other options for an Apple ID.

5   If you receive a warning that the terms and conditions have changed, click OK, and read the new terms. If you are using your own Apple ID and do not want to agree to them, click Cancel, then choose Store > Sign Out, and either use an instructor-provided Apple ID instead of your own or skip this exercise.

6   Once the app starts downloading (shown under the Launchpad icon in the Dock), skip to "Test the App" on page 512.

Option 2: Create a New Apple ID for the App Store

Follow these steps if you have access to an existing email account and want to create an Apple ID linked to that email and use it for the App Store:

1   Click the Create Apple ID button.

2   In the "Welcome to the App Store" screen, click Continue.

3   In the "Terms and Conditions" screen, review the terms.

If the terms are not acceptable to you, you cannot use the App Store. Quit the App Store, and proceed to the next exercise.

If the terms are acceptable, select "I have read and agree to these terms and conditions," and then click Agree.

4   In the Provide Apple ID Details screen, enter your existing email address, choose a (new) password and security questions, enter your date of birth, and adjust the email options to your preferences. Click Continue.

5   In the "Provide a Payment Method" screen, select None as the payment type, and enter your name and billing address. Click Create Apple ID.

Apple sends a test message to verify the email address you provided.

6   Check your email. When you receive the verification message from Apple, click the Verify Now link in the message.

This link takes you to a web form where you can verify the address.

7   In the web form that opens, enter your Apple ID (the email address you provided) and the password you chose, and then click Verify Address.

8   When the email address has been verified, quit the browser.

9   In the App Store, click OK.

10   At the Congratulations screen, click Start Shopping.

Since you have now signed in to a new account, the App Store may reset to its starting screen. You need to find the app (generally The Unarchiver) and reselect it for purchase. See the earlier section "Select an App to Purchase" on page 505 for details.

11   Once the app starts downloading (shown under the Launchpad icon in the Dock), proceed with the section "Test the App" on page 512.

Test the App

1   In the Dock, click the Launchpad icon.

If the app has not finished downloading, Launchpad displays its progress. When it finishes, you will see the app's regular icon (with sparkles around it, indicating that it is new).

2   Click The Unarchiver's icon.

The app launches.

3   If The Unarchiver asks where to extract archives, click "Extract to the same folder."

4   Quit the app.

Examine the App Store

1   In the App Store toolbar, click the Purchases icon.

2   Choose Store > Reload Page (Command-R) to make sure the purchases list is up to date.

The App Store lists all the applications purchased with this Apple ID. If you are using your own Apple ID, you see your previous purchases; if you are using an instructor-supplied Apple ID, you may see apps that previous students purchased.

Note that if you had enabled the "Automatically download apps purchased on other Macs" option in Software Update preferences, any additional apps would be automatically downloaded and installed. Since this option is disabled, you see Install buttons that allow you to download and install them manually.

NOTE ▶ The App Store terms and conditions limit the situations in which an app may be installed on several computers. See www.apple.com/legal/itunes/us/terms.html for the current terms and conditions.

If any other apps are listed, do not install them at this time.

3   In the App Store toolbar, click the Updates button. If you are prompted, authenticate as Local Admin.

This displays updates available for both system software and App Store purchases installed on this computer.

4   Quit the App Store.

Exercise 17.2
Use an Installer Package

► **Prerequisite**

► You must have created the Local Admin ("Exercise 2.1 Configure a New OS X
System for Exercises" on page 60 or "Exercise 2.2 Configure an Existing OS X
System for Exercises" on page 63) and Chris Johnson ("Exercise 5.1 Manage
User Accounts" on page 145) accounts.

Traditionally, one common way of distributing software is in the form of an installer package. Although this installation process involves more steps than the App Store method, it
also offers some additional capabilities, such as allowing the developer to install files outside of /Applications, allowing the user to choose which optional components to install,
and so on. Packages can also be distributed on physical media (CDs and DVDs), as well as
by download. For these reasons, package-based installation is likely to continue to be used
for complex applications and other software. In this exercise, you will use it to install a
simple application.

Install an App with an Installer Package

1   If necessary, log in as Chris Johnson.

2   Open the /Users/Shared/StudentMaterials/Lesson17 folder.

3   Open Hello World.dmg.

    The image mounts, with the Hello World package inside it.

4   Open Hello World.pkg.

The Installer opens and prepares to install the Hello World application.

5   Click the lock icon at the upper right of the Installer window.

The lock icon indicates that this is a signed package; clicking it displays information about the certificate it was signed with. In this case, it was signed with Gordon Davisson's Developer ID Installer certificate, which was signed by the Developer ID Certification Authority, which in turn was signed by the Apple Root CA. Essentially, this means that the Apple Root CA vouches for the authenticity of the Developer ID Certification Authority, which vouches for the authenticity of Gordon Davisson's certificate, which vouches for the authenticity of the installer package.

This is the standard format of an Apple-issued Developer ID certificate.

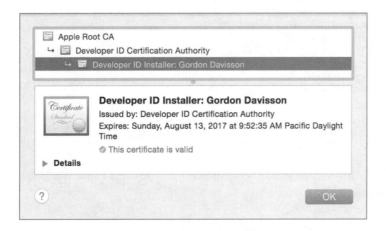

6   Click OK to dismiss the certificate dialog.

7   Choose File > Show Files.

8   In the window that appears, click the disclosure triangle next to Hello World.

This shows what files the installer package contains. In this case, it is a folder named Hello World containing Hello World.app, Uninstall.app, and some metadata files.

9   Close the "Files from Hello World" window.

10 In the main Installer window, click Continue.

Some packages include additional steps, such as readme information, license agreements, choices of components to install, and so forth. This is a simple package, so it proceeds straight to the install pane.

11 In the Standard Install pane, click Install.

12 Authenticate as Local Admin when prompted.

The installation completes quickly, and the Installer informs you that it was successful.

13 Click Close, and the Installer exits.

14 Eject the disk image.

15 In the Finder, navigate to the Applications folder (you can use the shortcut Command-Shift-A).

Note that a Hello World subfolder has been installed. Inside is the Hello World application and an Uninstall script.

16 Open Launchpad.

Even though it was installed in a subfolder, the new app is displayed along with your other applications.

17 Open Hello World.

Because this application was installed with a package (and the package was properly signed), Gatekeeper does not activate, and no warning is displayed. You will see what happens with an untrusted application in the next exercise.

18 Quit Hello World.

Note that unlike the App Store, there is no standard update process for package-installed applications. Some apps manage their own updates, while others require you to manually download and install updates.

Exercise 17.3
Use a Drag-and-Drop Install

▶ **Prerequisites**

    ▶   You must have created the Local Admin ("Exercise 2.1 Configure a New OS X System for Exercises" on page 60 or "Exercise 2.2 Configure an Existing OS X System for Exercises" on page 63) and Chris Johnson ("Exercise 5.1 Manage User Accounts" on page 145) accounts.

In this exercise, you will examine the process of installing a downloaded application via the drag-and-drop method. The way you will get this application depends on whether you have a server available to support these exercises (either one provided by the classroom, or one you set up yourself). If you have a "Mainserver" available, follow Option 1; otherwise, follow Option 2.

Option 1: Download an Application from Mainserver

Follow these steps if you have an OS X server configured to support these exercises:

1 If necessary, log in as Chris Johnson.

2 Open Safari.

3 Enter mainserver.local.

4   If you receive a warning that Safari can't verify the identity of the website, click Continue.

Note that continuing after this warning is not generally safe since the web server might be a fake or impostor; but in this particular case, it should not be a problem.

5   Near the bottom of the page, click the link to download Dead End. When the download is complete, quit Safari.

6   Open Dead-End.dmg from your Downloads folder. Note that there is a shortcut to Downloads in your Dock.

Option 2: Use an Application from StudentMaterials

Follow these steps if you do not have an OS X server configured to support these exercises:

1   If necessary, log in as Chris Johnson.

2   Open the /Users/Shared/StudentMaterials/Lesson17 folder.

3   Open Dead-End.dmg.

Note that this disk image contains an application that was previously downloaded from a website and is still in quarantine, so OS X treats it as coming from an untrusted source.

Copy the Application to /Applications

Some applications distributed for drag-and-drop installations come with instructions or hints about how to install them, while others simply assume the user will know what to do. The Dead End app comes as a disk image with instructions in the background image.

1   Drag the Dead End icon onto the Applications icon (which is a symbolic link to /Applications).

A dialog appears telling you that modifying Applications requires an administrator name and password.

2   Click the Authenticate button, authenticate as Local Admin, and click OK.

The Finder now copies Dead End into /Applications.

OS X is tolerant, and it allows you to run applications no matter where they're stored, even if they are not in /Applications. Running the copy in the disk image you downloaded would work, but it may cause confusion or slightly odd application behavior, so you should avoid doing this.

Do not launch the Dead End app yet.

3   Eject the disk image.

Test the Gatekeeper Security Settings

1   Open System Preferences, and select the Security & Privacy pane.

2   Click the General tab.

3   If necessary, authenticate and set the "Allow apps downloaded from" option to "Mac App Store and identified developers."

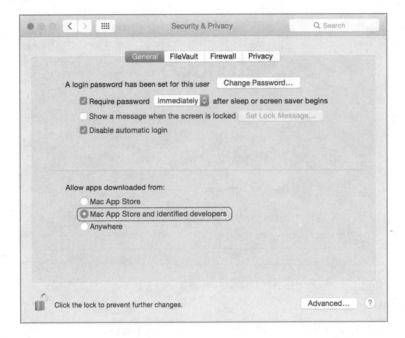

4   Quit System Preferences.

5   In the Finder, navigate to the Applications folder (you can use the shortcut Command-Shift-A).

6   Double-click Dead End.

The file is labeled with some additional metadata to indicate that it is in quarantine because it was downloaded from the Internet. The first time you open it, Gatekeeper checks it against your allowed applications policy. Since the application is not signed with a Developer ID, Gatekeeper does not allow it to open.

7   Click OK.

8   Control-click Dead End, and choose Open from the shortcut menu.

This time, Gatekeeper warns you about the app but gives you the option to bypass its normal policy and open the application.

9   Click Open.

10 When you are prompted, authenticate as Local Admin.

11 If necessary, click the Dead End icon in the Dock to bring it to the foreground.

Do not click "Download the Internet" at this time. If you do, see "Exercise 19.1 Force Applications to Quit" on page 603 for information on forcing applications to quit. While this app is not particularly malicious, it doesn't do anything useful either.

12 Quit Dead End.

13 Double-click Dead End to reopen it.

This time it opens without the warning. Since you opened it once, your Gatekeeper policy has been modified to allow it to run normally.

14 Quit Dead End again.

Note that unlike the App Store, there is no standard update process for applications installed via the drag-and-drop method. Some apps manage their own updates, while others require you to manually download and install updates.

Exercise 17.4
Remove Applications

▶ **Prerequisites**

▶ You must have performed "Exercise 17.1 Use the Mac App Store" on page 505 and "Exercise 17.2 Use an Installer Package" on page 514.

Since OS X applications are usually just packages (or even single files), all that's necessary to remove them is to drag them to the Trash. A few more complex programs consist of more than just an application, and these will generally include their own uninstaller.

View Installed Applications

1 Open System Information by holding the Option key and choosing Apple menu > System Information.

System Information opens and displays the system report.

2 From the Software section of the sidebar, select Installations.

This part of the report shows software that has been installed on the computer both by the App Store and by package, so it shows both The Unarchiver (or whatever app you installed in "Exercise 17.1 Use the Mac App Store" on page 505) and Hello World. It does not show software installed by other methods, so even if you installed Dead End (by the drag-and-drop method), it does not appear here.

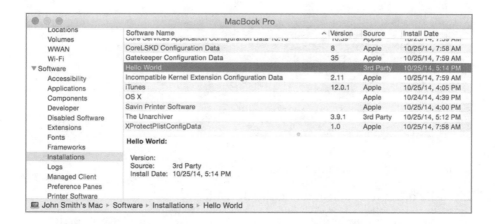

3   Quit System Information.

Remove an Application in Launchpad

1   Open Launchpad.

2   Click The Unarchiver (or whichever app you installed from the App Store), and hold down the mouse until an "X" appears at its top left and the other icons begin to wobble.

In this mode, Launchpad lets you drag app icons around to rearrange them and also use the "X" button to delete apps purchased from the App Store. Since The Unarchiver is the only one you purchased from the App Store, it is the only one that has an "X" by its icon.

3   Click The Unarchiver's "X" button.

4   In the confirmation dialog that appears, click Delete.

5   If you are prompted, authenticate as Local Admin.

The Unarchiver is now uninstalled from your computer. Note that your preference file or files and user data still exist, so if you ever decide to reinstall the program, all of your settings are kept.

Reinstall an Application in the App Store

1   Open the App Store.

2   In the toolbar, click the Purchases icon.

Since you purchased The Unarchiver, it is listed here and available to reinstall. Depending on the history of the Apple ID you are using, other apps may be listed as well.

If you are using Family Sharing, a pop-up menu will allow you to switch from My Purchases to other family members' purchases. If you have not set up Family Sharing, this menu does not appear.

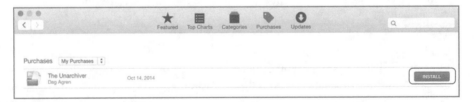

3   Click the Install button for The Unarchiver.

4   If you are prompted, enter your Apple ID's password to authenticate to the App Store. The app is downloaded and reinstalled.

5   Wait for the download to finish, and then quit the App Store.

Remove an Application in the Finder

1   In the Finder, navigate to the Applications folder.

2   Select The Unarchiver, and drag it to the Trash icon in your Dock.

3   When you are prompted, authenticate as Local Admin.

4   Choose Finder > Empty Trash, and then click Empty Trash in the confirmation dialog.

    The Unarchiver is now uninstalled from your computer.

Remove an Application with an Uninstaller

Since most applications can be uninstalled with the Finder, they don't provide any special uninstaller. Applications that do will vary as to how they provide the uninstaller and exactly how it works. This exercise presents a simple example.

1   In the Finder, navigate to the Applications folder.

2   Open the Hello World folder.

3   Open the Uninstall script in the Hello World folder.

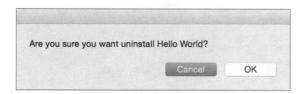

4   At the confirmation dialog, click OK.

5   When you are prompted, authenticate as Local Admin.

6   Reopen the Applications folder.

    The entire Hello World folder has been removed from your computer.

Lesson 18

Document Management

For most users, document management is one primary day-to-day computing task. For many years, the act of opening and saving documents on a Mac system has remained the same. Yet, with the introduction and ultimate success of iOS, Apple has been seriously rethinking how Mac users interact with documents. OS X Lion included significant changes to how documents are saved with Auto Save and Versions. OS X Mountain Lion featured integration that allowed you to save documents from applications to iCloud. OS X Yosemite introduces iCloud Drive, which finally puts iCloud on par with local storage. Items saved in iCloud Drive appear just like any other local storage and are fully manageable via the Finder.

This lesson first introduces OS X Launch Services, which is the system that determines an action when the user double-clicks a document. You will also learn to use Quick Look for previewing most common document types. Then a significant portion of this lesson is dedicated to document management via Auto Save, Versions, and documents in iCloud Drive. Finally, you will see how OS X attempts to automatically resume documents and applications on the user's behalf.

GOALS

▶ Manage Launch Services settings

▶ Use Quick Look to preview documents

▶ Work with applications that support Auto Save and Versions

▶ Save and open documents in iCloud Drive

Reference 18.1
Launch Services

Aside from a file's name, the most fundamentally important piece of information about a file is its type. A file's type identification allows OS X to almost always choose the correct application to open when you double-click a file. Launch Services is the technology responsible for helping OS X make the connection between a file's type and the appropriate application. When you double-click a file from the Finder, it asks Launch Services to open the file with the appropriate application. Launch

527

Services identifies the file based on its type and then references an application registration database to determine which application should open the file.

File Type Identification

Apple pioneered file type identification when it first introduced the Mac OS. Apple designed the file identification system to use four-character file type and creator signature file attributes, which were normally hidden from the user. This was a brilliant design that separated the file's type and default application binding from the file's name.

Unfortunately, the popularity of other operating systems forced the awkward practice of adding a file type identifier to the end of a filename. This complicated the practice of naming files by requiring the user to identify and maintain the appropriate filename extension, such as .mp3 for compressed audio files, .jpg for compressed picture files, or .doc for Microsoft Word files.

Using filename extensions has become standard practice, so current operating systems have been designed to work around this poor design choice by simply hiding the filename extension from the user. For the sake of compatibility, Apple adopted this later method of file type identification as the default for all versions of OS X.

> **NOTE** ▶ OS X still supports the legacy file type attribute but no longer supports the creator code attribute. Thus, some files may not default to opening in the application that created them. However, you can change the default behavior, as covered later in this section.

Since the Finder hides many filename extensions by default, you can toggle file type extension visibility from the Finder preferences by choosing Finder > Preferences. Then click the Advanced button and select or deselect the checkbox next to "Show all filename extensions."

NOTE ▶ Choosing to show all file extensions in the Finder overrides the individual file attribute for hiding the extension, as configured from the Info and Inspector windows in the Finder.

Application Registration

When a user attempts to open a file of a certain type, Launch Services reads from a database of applications and the types of files each can open to determine a match. Successful file and application match information is cached, so future attempts to open an application are resolved as quickly as possible. However, after every startup or login, a background process automatically scans for new applications and updates this database. Further, both the Finder and Installer keep track of new applications as they arrive on your system and add their supported file types to the database.

The application registration system is pretty good at finding matches, so odds are if the system gives you an error message, then you probably don't have the correct application for the file. In OS X, Launch Services maps many common file types to the built-in Preview and TextEdit applications if the primary application is missing. For example, Numbers or Excel documents open in Preview and Pages, and Word documents open in TextEdit.

TIP ▶ The OS X Quick Look feature can also preview many common file types even without the applications installed. This includes both iWork and Microsoft Office documents. Quick Look details are covered later in "Reference 18.2 Quick Look" on page 532.

If Preview, or any other application, cannot properly open a specific file type, you can change the Launch Services settings to force those files to open in a more appropriate application, as outlined in the following section. Other times, though, Launch Services may not have any idea which application to use for the file type. If you attempt to open a file type that is not stored in the Launch Services database, the computer prompts you to find an application that supports the file. Alternatively, you can use a new feature in OS X that searches the Mac App Store for a compatible application.

Launch Services Settings

From the Info or Inspector windows in the Finder, you can override the Launch Services default application settings for any specific file type.

> **MORE INFO** ▶ Using the Info window to inspect files and folders is detailed in Lesson 11 "Permissions and Sharing".

Once you have selected the files you want to change Launch Services settings for and have opened an Info window, click the "Open with" disclosure triangle to reveal the default application selected by Launch Services. To change just the selected files' default application, simply select another application from the pop-up menu. This information is saved to the files' metadata and defines Launch Services settings only for the selected items.

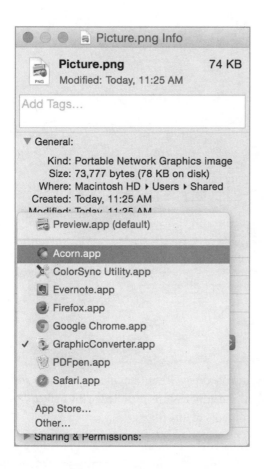

To change the default application for all files of this type, select the application you want to define as the default, and then click the Change All button. This setting is saved per user, so one user's application preferences do not override another's. A user's custom Launch Services settings are saved to the com.apple.LaunchServices.plist preference file in each user's ~/Library/Preferences folder.

You can also modify Launch Services settings in the Finder by secondary (or Control-) clicking the selected files and then choosing Open With from the shortcut menu. Additionally, holding down the Option key changes the menu command to Always Open With.

Reference 18.2
Quick Look

Quick Look enables you to preview nearly any file type without having to open any additional applications, or without even having those applications installed. This makes Quick Look the most convenient way to view the contents of any file.

Quick Look previews can be accessed, or dismissed, by pressing the Space bar from any Finder view, the Time Machine restore interface, most Open and Save browser dialogs, the Mail application, or any other application that supports Quick Look. Later versions of OS X keep the Quick Look preview window open in the Finder until it's closed. Selecting another item in the Finder changes the Quick Look preview to the newly selected item.

The Quick Look close button is in the top-left corner, just as in a traditional window. You can also quickly dismiss the Quick Look preview by pressing the Space bar again. With the Quick Look preview window open, you can resize the window by clicking and dragging any edge of the window, or you can go to full-screen view by clicking the twin arrow button at the top-right of the preview window.

Quick Look technology is also used to provide the Finder with previews for files in icon view, previews in column view, and the preview section of the Info and Inspector windows. Finally, Quick Look also provides previews for the Cover Flow view. This view allows you to browse folder content in a similar way to browsing on Apple iOS mobile devices or in iTunes. Cover Flow view can be accessed from any Finder window by clicking its icon in the toolbar, which you can find two icons to the left of the action (gear icon) menu, also in the toolbar.

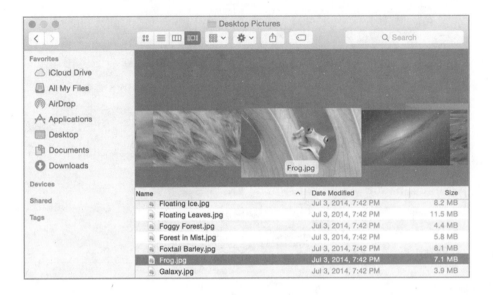

The Quick Look Window

In the titlebar of the Quick Look window, you'll find other useful options for previewing the selected item. For example, you can open the selected item in an application by clicking the "Open with <Application>" button, where <Application> is the name of the default application for the selected file. Also note the Share button (box with upward arrow) that allows you to quickly share the document.

MORE INFO ▶ The list of options in the Share menu varies depending on the file type of the item being previewed, installed App Extensions, and services configured in Internet Accounts preferences. You can find out more about managing App Extensions in "Reference 19.2 App Extensions " on page 582, and about configuring Internet services in "Internet Accounts Preferences" on page 732.

Use the arrow keys to navigate and preview the items adjacent to the original previewed item in the Finder. If the previewed file has multiple pages, you'll be able to scroll through the document. In some cases—Keynote presentations, for example—Quick Look shows a thumbnail preview of each slide, allowing you to scroll through the thumbnails as well. Finally, if you select multiple items to preview, the Quick Look window allows some basic slideshow features via buttons at the top left of the window.

Quick Look Plug-ins

Quick Look is able to preview an ever-growing variety of file types using a plug-in technology. Each Quick Look plug-in is designed to preview specific types of files. Many Quick Look plug-ins are included by default, but Apple and third-party developers can create additional plug-ins to expand the Quick Look preview capabilities.

Included Quick Look plug-ins enable you to:

▶ Preview any audio or video file that can be decoded by QuickTime

▶ Preview a variety of graphics files, including many digital camera files, PDF files, EPS files, and any standard graphics file

▶ Preview a variety of productivity files, including standard text files, script files, and files created by the iWork and Microsoft Office suites

▶ Preview a variety of Internet-centric files, including mailboxes, iChat transcripts, and web archives

Quick Look plug-ins, like any other system resource, are stored inside the various Library folders. The built-in Apple Quick Look plug-ins are always found in the /System/Library/QuickLook folder and sometimes appear in the /Library/QuickLook folder. Third-party plug-ins should always be installed in either /Library/QuickLook or the ~/Library/QuickLook folder, depending on who needs access to them.

Reference 18.3
Auto Save and Versions

For over 30 years, most applications have relied on users to remember to save their work. It's true that for many years some applications have featured optional auto save features. In fact, many Apple applications have always provided an environment where users don't have to remember to save. Examples include Aperture, iPhoto, and iTunes.

With OS X Lion, Apple introduced a sophisticated automatic document management model that can be used by any application. Not only does the system automatically save for the user, it also automatically maintains a history of versions for the user's documents as well.

In this section, you will learn how the OS X Auto Save and Versions features work together. These two features also work hand in hand with another OS X feature, document locking and resume, to maintain a current state of users' work environment even if they log out or restart the computer.

Auto Save and Versions Architecture

A primary goal of later versions of OS X is to incorporate many of the iOS features and workflows. One of the main tenets of iOS application design is that users never have to remember to save their work. However, Mac users are accustomed to having more control over their documents. Further, Mac computers in general have more storage and computing resources than iOS devices. Thus, with OS X Lion Apple took the auto save concept and extended it with support for document versions.

For applications that support Auto Save, once the user saves the first time, no further dialogs appear asking if the application should save changes. In addition, if the user wants to use the document in another application or share it with another user, he or she doesn't have to remember to save the latest version of the document. From the user's point of view, the document seen in the Finder is always the same as the document seen in the application—the location where the document was first saved will always be the latest version.

In addition, applications that support Auto Save also support document Versions. This provides an environment where the system automatically maintains a history of changes for any document. The user can easily return a document to a previous state with just a few clicks, or can navigate to an earlier version of a document and quickly copy specific elements to the latest version of the document.

The user can access a document's version history using an interface very similar to the Time Machine Restore interface. However, from a technical perspective, the document version histories are saved in a hidden folder named .DocumentRevisions-V100 at the root of the disk containing the original document. Again, the most recent version of a document is always automatically saved to its original location and can be copied or shared with other applications or users immediately after a change is made.

Applications that support OS X Auto Save and Versions are easily identified by the content of the File menu in the application. Applications that support Auto Save can be most easily identified by their File > Duplicate menu option (instead of the traditional Save As menu option). Applications compatible with Auto Save also include File > Rename and File > Move To menu options. Updated applications still feature File > Save for saving a document the first time, but upon subsequent usage, the behavior of this menu option changes to saving a version of the document. Most Apple-designed applications already support Auto Save and Versions, including TextEdit, Preview, Pages, Numbers, and Keynote.

File	Edit	Format	View	
New				⌘N
Open...				⌘O
Open Recent				▶
Close				⌘W
Save				⌘S
Duplicate				⇧⌘S
Rename...				
Move To...				
Revert To				▶
Export as PDF...				

Auto Save

Saving the first time in an application that supports Auto Save is much like using a traditional application. Users may not be prepared for what comes next, though. The irony is that many users may find it difficult to move to this new method even though it requires less work. Simply, most users have grown accustomed to the traditional save methods and will have to "unlearn" them. Thus, training may be required to enable users to get the most out of OS X Auto Save and Versions.

TIP ▶ The Auto Save behavior can be disabled from General preferences, as covered in "Disabling Auto Save" on page 554 later in this lesson.

When you open an application that supports Auto Save for the first time, one of two things happens. If you are not signed in to iCloud, or the application does not support saving to iCloud, the application automatically opens a new document. If you are signed in to iCloud and the application supports saving documents to iCloud, you are prompted with an Open dialog. Saving documents to iCloud is covered in the next section of this lesson.

When you start a new document in an application that supports Auto Save, it's actually already saved even though you've not yet set a location for it. In other words, changes you make to the new document are automatically saved, even if you have yet to explicitly save the document. This is because the document is actually saved to the Versions history database on the system volume.

By default, if you choose to close the document window or application, the system prompts you to save the document. Obviously you can also manually choose File > Save or press the Command-S keyboard shortcut. The resulting Save dialog is similar to that in earlier versions of OS X, allowing you to choose a name and location for the document.

TIP ▶ You can expand a minimized Save dialog to show a full file system browser by clicking the small arrow to the right of the filename.

Alternatively, you can save a document simply by clicking its name in the title bar. This reveals a popover dialog similar to the traditional Save dialog. One significant exception is the lack of Cancel or Save buttons. Again taking cues from iOS, entering a change here

immediately saves once you click somewhere outside of the dialog. As you'll see throughout the remainder of this lesson, you can return to this popover dialog to save changes to
the document as well. For example, renaming the document is as simple as entering a new
name and then clicking elsewhere to dismiss the popover dialog.

TIP ▶ Holding the Command key and clicking the document's name in the menu
bar reveals its path in the file system.

After you have picked a location for the document, you'll never have to save it again. There
are many instances that will trigger an auto save, including making a significant change to
the document, closing the document window, closing the application, selecting the Finder,
or attempting to access the document from another application. Applications also save
during pauses in your work and, if you work continuously, they will at the very least, save
your work every five minutes.

As you make changes to the document, you may see "Edited" in the document title bar.
This is also a visual cue to let the user know the system is automatically saving changes.
You can test this by making some changes to the document and then immediately using
Quick Look to preview the document by selecting it in the Finder and pressing the Space
bar. The Quick Look preview is identical to the open document in the application.

Duplicate and Save As

If you need to save another copy of a document, you do so by using the Duplicate option.
With the document open, simply choose File > Duplicate or press the Shift-Command-S
keyboard combination. A new window appears with a copy of the document. Note that the
filename in the title bar is highlighted, indicating you can change the name of the duplicate document.

TIP ▶ The Move To command in the Document menu moves the original document to a new location without creating a new copy. Even though the document has been moved, in most cases the version history will be preserved.

The document itself is saved in the same folder as the original document. Again, because Auto Save is at work, you never have to manually save this document again. The system always saves the changes for you.

If you or your users are more comfortable with the traditional Save As process, this is available as well. If you hold down the Option key, the File > Duplicate menu option changes to File > Save As. Alternatively, you can press the Option-Shift-Command-S keyboard shortcut.

Selecting Save As will reveal a slightly modified Save dialog that gives you the option to also save the changes to the original document. This option is enabled by default, meaning that any changes made up to this point will also be saved to the original document. Disabling this option will cause Save As behavior similar to that in a legacy application that does not support Auto Save. In other words, disabling this feature will revert the original document to its previous state, before the user made any recent changes, and then save a new document with the latest changes.

Selecting the Save As command is effectively the same process as Duplicate, only it also presents the full Save dialog again, allowing you to choose a different filename and location, and then closes the original document. However, this close action is quite subtle, as the new document replaces the original document in the active window without any obvious animation.

Save As:	Important Stuff.rtf
Tags:	● Red ○ Work
Where:	📁 Desktop
File Format:	Rich Text Document
	Cancel Save

Document Versions

With Versions in OS X, applications always maintain a history of your changes. Anytime an application is saved, automatically or manually, a new document version is also saved. If users, perhaps out of habit, attempt to manually save by choosing File > Save or by pressing Command-S, they are essentially telling the system to save another version of the document in the version history.

If you're editing a document and have yet to trigger a manual or automatic save, you can easily revert to the previously saved state by choosing File > Revert To > Last Saved or File > Revert To > Last Opened. If a deeper version history is available, OS X allows you to browse the entire history of a document. To open the version history browser, choose File > Revert To > Browse All Versions.

It's important to remember that a document's version history is not saved within the document itself. Instead, document history is stored only on the volume where the original document is saved, specifically in the .DocumentRevisions-V100 folder at the root of the volume. Thus, if you share the document by creating or sending a copy of the document, other users will not have access to the document's version history.

> **NOTE** ▶ Version history is not always maintained on files being edited from a shared network volume. If you want to ensure that a version history is maintained, you must copy the shared file to a local disk.

If you've ever used Time Machine, the Versions browser interface will look pretty familiar. To the left you'll see the current version of the document, and to the right you can see previous versions. Navigate by either clicking a previous version's title bar or using the timeline to the right.

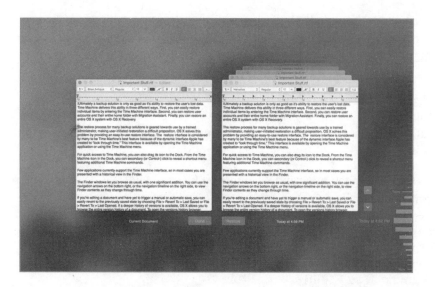

If you want to restore a previous version in its entirety, click Restore. However, if you just want a specific section of a previous version copied to the latest version, simply make a selection inside the previous document, and then copy and paste to the current document. When you are done making targeted edits, click Done to return to the standard application interface.

> **TIP** In the Versions browser, you can copy and paste using the Command-C and Command-V keyboard shortcuts, or by using the secondary (or Control-) click to reveal a shortcut menu.

> **TIP** To delete a previous document version, in the Versions browser, select the document name in the title bar to reveal a pop-up menu allowing you to choose Delete This Version.

> **TIP** If you have Time Machine enabled, as covered in Lesson 16 "Time Machine", an application's version history can go much deeper by showing you versions also saved in the Time Machine backup.

Reference 18.4
Document Locking

OS X includes a special file and folder attribute that trumps all write privileges and even administrative user access. Users can choose to lock a file or folder that they own from any application that supports Auto Save or the Finder Info window.

Locking an item renders it completely unchangeable by any user except the item's owner. Even administrative users are prevented from making changes to another user's locked file in the graphical interface.

Managing Locking from the Finder

The Finder and the Info or Inspector windows can be used to view and change a file's lock state. Once an item is locked, no other users can modify, move, delete, or rename it in the Finder.

MORE INFO ▶ Using the Info window to inspect files and folders is detailed in Lesson 11 "Permissions and Sharing".

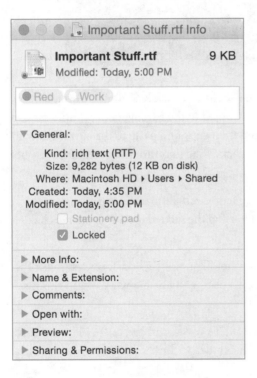

Once the file is locked, the Finder also prevents the owner from moving, renaming, or changing ownership and permissions for the locked item. In fact, if you as the owner try to move a locked item, the Finder defaults to making a copy. However, unlike other users, the owner can return the file to the normal state by disabling the locked attribute from the Info or Inspector windows.

NOTE ▶ Duplicating a locked document in the Finder simply results in another locked copy of the document. In OS X, only applications that support Auto Save can create an unlocked duplicate of a locked file.

Managing Locking from an Application

Applications that support Auto Save also provide easy access to document locking. Document locking may seem like an inconvenience, but in a system where changes are automatically saved, document locking provides a useful service. Specifically, locking a document prevents users, or more appropriately their applications, from accidentally auto-saving changes. Users can choose to manually lock or unlock documents within applications that support Auto Save.

NOTE ▶ OS X Lion automatically locked documents if they had not been edited after a certain amount of time. This feature confused a lot of users, and as a result it is no longer available in later versions of OS X.

As long as you are the owner of a document, which is often the case if you created the document or are editing a copy of the document, you can manually lock it to prevent further changes. To manually lock a document in an application that supports Auto Save, select the document's filename in the title bar to reveal a popover dialog allowing you to select the Locked checkbox.

You'll note that locked documents are clearly marked in the title bar with "Locked" and a small lock icon. As long as you are the owner of a document, you can deselect the Locked checkbox to enable changes. Alternatively, you can simply start modifying a locked document that you own. A dialog appears, allowing you to verify your intent to unlock and edit the document. Note the Duplicate button, a choice that encourages the user to make a copy for editing.

If you aren't the owner of a locked document, you aren't allowed to unlock it; thus you aren't allowed to edit it. Also, as covered in Lesson 11 "Permissions and Sharing", if you don't have write file permissions, you are not allowed to edit a document. In both cases the document's title bar displays "Locked."

However, you can treat a locked document as a template by duplicating the document and then editing the copy. Attempting to edit a locked, or otherwise unwritable, document reveals a prompt that allows the user only to duplicate the document.

As covered previously, you can also manually duplicate a locked document by choosing File > Duplicate or File > Revert To > Browse All Versions. Again, once the application has duplicated a copy, you can then save the copy as you would a new document.

Reference 18.5
iCloud Drive

The introduction of Auto Save and Versions in OS X Lion was ultimately a precursor to what was to come in future versions of OS X: saving documents to iCloud. By allowing OS X applications to automatically open and save documents to iCloud, Apple has added the last fundamental bit of feature parity between iOS and OS X. Quite simply, saving your documents to iCloud is the easiest way to manage documents between multiple Apple devices. OS X Yosemite introduces support for the new iCloud Drive service, which gives you even greater flexibility when saving documents to iCloud.

> **MORE INFO** ▶ Although iCloud Drive is covered here in some detail, you can find out more about iCloud Drive from Apple Support Article HT201104, "iCloud Drive FAQ."

Configuring iCloud Drive

To store files in iCloud on OS X Yosemite, a user must be signed in to iCloud and have the iCloud Drive service enabled. Users who have created a new iCloud account with iOS 8 or OS X Yosemite will automatically have iCloud Drive enabled when they sign in to iCloud. However, existing iCloud accounts need to be upgraded to support iCloud Drive. When an existing iCloud account signs into an iOS 8 or OS X Yosemite device, the user is asked to upgrade to iCloud Drive. This most often happens during the Setup Assistant process.

In many ways, iCloud Drive is a better service than the previous iCloud document storage mechanism, so most users will want to upgrade their service. However, a user may want to delay this upgrade, because iCloud Drive is only compatible with iOS 8 and OS X Yosemite or later, and the upgrade process to iCloud Drive is one way. Unfortunately, iCloud document storage features will not be available to users on OS X Yosemite until they choose to upgrade their iCloud account to include the iCloud Drive service.

TIP ▶ A solution for users stuck using both old and new Apple systems is to go ahead and upgrade to iCloud Drive. When working on older Apple systems (or systems from other vendors) they can access iCloud Drive documents via most web browsers by logging into www.icloud.com.

Users who have delayed the upgrade to iCloud Drive can initiate the upgrade in the iCloud preferences simply by selecting the iCloud Drive checkbox. This will prompt the user to verify the upgrade process.

You can verify that iCloud Drive is has been enabled from the iCloud preferences. Also, iCloud Drive can be disabled by deselecting the iCloud Drive option.

Finally, clicking the iCloud Drive Options button reveals an interface allowing you to hide specific iCloud Drive items. By default, all applications designed for iCloud Drive can store documents and will allow other iCloud Drive users to look up your account for sharing documents.

In the Documents tab of the iCloud Drive options, you can deselect a checkbox next to an application to hide documents and data from that application. Hiding doesn't delete any existing data in iCloud, it simply prevents the application from accessing iCloud Drive and hides the associated folder from the Finder. In the Look Me Up By Email tab you can also prevent iCloud Drive applications from allowing other users to find your information for document sharing.

Using iCloud Drive

Previous incarnations of iCloud document storage only allowed the user to access items stored in iCloud via specific compatible applications. While this type of document management is ideal for the app-specific nature of iOS, it was often confusing and limiting on OS X. Not only does OS X have a long history of flexible document management via the Finder interface, it's also an operating system designed for multitasking.

iCloud Drive brings iCloud document management in line with traditional OS X behavior. The "Drive" in iCloud Drive is not a misnomer, as iCloud storage now appears as if it was a normally connected disk. All Finder document management features work as expected on iCloud Drive content: move, copy, rename, folder creation, and so forth.

TIP ▶ By default, iCloud Drive appears in the Finder's sidebar, but it can also be accessed from the Finder's Go menu or by using the Command-Shift-I keyboard shortcut.

iCloud Drive also appears in Open and Save dialogs for any application. In other words, with iCloud Drive, applications do not have to be specifically designed to support iCloud document storage.

Again, just like a normal disk, with iCloud Drive on OS X Yosemite you can create custom folder hierarchies and save documents inside any folder you choose. You may notice that iCloud Drive is automatically populated with application-specific folders. These folders are created by the applications to facilitate iOS-style document management.

> **TIP** In the previous screenshot you'll notice "TextEdit" in the sidebar just below "iCloud" and also a TextEdit folder in iCloud Drive. These two locations are the same; the sidebar location is simply a shortcut to the TextEdit-specific folder in iCloud Drive.

It's important to remember that even though you are allowed to create custom folders for documents, iOS 8 apps will recognize only documents located in their specific folders. In other words, custom folders at the root of the iCloud Drive cannot be seen by iOS 8 apps. However, you can create custom folders inside each application-specific folder to organize your documents. These folders will appear in iOS 8, although they will only be visible to the app associated with the folder.

> **TIP** Custom folders and documents saved to iCloud Drive can be accessed via the iCloud website, www.icloud.com. Further, items in iCloud Drive can be easily shared with others, which allows for collaborative document editing.

iCloud Drive Architecture

Documents saved in iCloud Drive are maintained locally in each user's ~/Library/Mobile Documents/ folder. While you can see this folder in the Finder, double-clicking this folder will automatically redirect you to the root iCloud Drive view in the Finder.

However, if you were to navigate to the Mobile Documents folder via Terminal, you would indeed be able to view and manipulate the folder's content. Be forewarned, you should avoid modifying any content with unclear names in the Mobile Documents folder. On the other hand, application-specific folders, custom user folders, and all documents are clearly visible via Terminal navigation. Also keep in mind that any changes to the contents of the Mobile Documents folder are automatically saved to iCloud Drive the moment you make them.

Speaking of making changes to iCloud Drive, the actual transfer process is highly sophisticated and efficient. In the worst case, a user should only notice a few moments' delay before the changes are reflected to all devices configured for iCloud Drive. This is because, if multiple devices on the same network share an iCloud account, they transfer the data locally to improve performance. Also, if you make changes to iCloud Drive while offline, the system caches the changes and then silently pushes them the very next moment an Internet connection to the iCloud servers becomes available.

Reference 18.6
Automatic Resume

An OS X feature ancillary to Auto Save is automatic application resumption. This feature allows supported applications to maintain their current state even if the user logs out or the application is quit. When an application quits, not only are any open documents automatically saved, the state of the application is saved as well.

Upon application restart, everything returns to how it was when the user quit the application. This includes automatically saving and restoring documents and windows open in the application, the view and scrolling position of each window, and even the user's last selection.

NOTE ▶ Applications that support resume can also be automatically quit by the system when it's determined that the system resources, specifically memory, are running low. The system quits only applications that are idle (not in active use).

Resuming After Log Out

Automatic resumption of applications and windows after logout is, by default, enabled in OS X. A user can, however, permanently prevent this behavior by deselecting the option when prompted to verify logout. This selection remains persistent through multiple user sessions, and will only change when the user clicks the checkbox.

TIP If the resume after logout feature is turned off, you can temporarily enable it by holding down the Option key when you log out.

Resuming After Quit

In the General preferences you'll find other options for automatic resumption. The default behavior for OS X is to close open documents and windows when quitting an application. An alternate option allows for the iOS-like behavior of automatically resuming documents and windows when opening an application. Deselect the "Close windows when quitting an app" checkbox to effectively enable automatic resume of an application's state when you quit it.

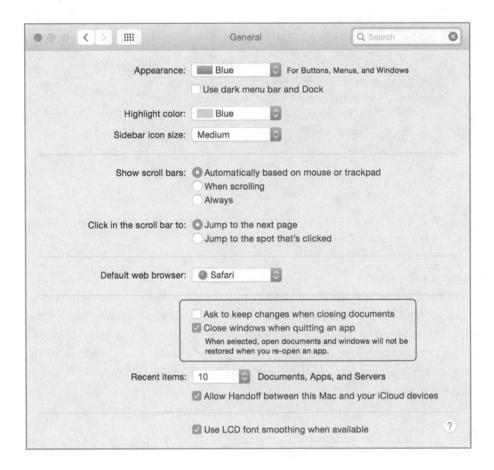

Disabling Auto Save

Another option in General preferences allows you to bring back the legacy OS X behavior of asking the user to save changes upon closing a document. For users who are more comfortable with how the legacy OS X save system behaved, selecting the "Ask to keep changes when closing documents" checkbox will disable the Auto Save feature for any application that supports it.

Many would argue that selecting this option defeats one of the primary advantages of Auto Save: less bother for the user. Further, this may also cause an inconvenient delay or cancellation of the logout process as the system will have to wait for applications to quit.

NOTE ▶ Even if you disable the Auto Save feature, applications that support Auto Save will still retain the rest of their current document management behavior. For example, these applications will still offer a Duplicate menu option and will automatically maintain a version history whenever documents are manually saved.

Exercise 18.1
Use Alternate Applications

▶ **Prerequisite**

    ▶ You must have created the Chris Johnson account ("Exercise 5.1 Manage User Accounts" on page 145).

In this exercise you will learn different ways to set which applications open files, both when making a one-time choice of a different application and when permanently changing the default application for a particular file type. You will also use the OS X Quick Look feature, which lets you see the contents of common file types without opening an application.

View a File with Quick Look

1   If necessary, log in as Chris Johnson.

2   In the Finder, open the StudentMaterials/Lesson18 folder.

3   Copy the file Pet Sitter Notes to your desktop.

    The file has no visible extension, although the icon may indicate its file type.

4   Select (single-click) the Pet Sitter Notes document on your desktop.

5   Choose File > Quick Look "Pet Sitter Notes" (or press Command-Y).

    Quick Look displays a preview of the document. Note that it has a button near the top right that allows you to open the document in TextEdit (currently the default application for this type of document).

TIP You can also use Quick Look to view a document by selecting it in the Finder and pressing Space bar. However, if you have the filename selected rather than the file itself, pressing Space bar will begin to edit the filename. If you do this by mistake, you can delete the filename and press Return; since the filename cannot be blank, the Finder displays an error and restores the original filename. Alternatively, you can use the Finder's undo capability to restore the file's name.

TIP Yet another way to use Quick Look is to Control-click the document and choose Quick Look "filename" from the shortcut menu.

6   Press Command-Y to close the Quick Look preview.

Choose an Application to Open a File Once

1   Double-click Pet Sitter Notes on your desktop.

The file opens in TextEdit. Note that TextEdit does not display the document's headings or background image.

2   On your desktop, Control-click the file.

3   In the shortcut menu, mouse over the Open With choice.

A submenu opens showing the applications available that can open this type of document.

4   In the Open With submenu, choose Preview.

The file opens in Preview.

Note that editing the same file in two different applications at the same time can lead to unpredictable results. In this case you are only viewing the file, so it is not a problem.

5   Compare how the file is displayed in TextEdit and in Preview.

Preview gives a richer view of the file, showing a background image and headings that TextEdit does not show. On the other hand, TextEdit lets you edit its content, while Preview does not. Depending on what you want to do with the document, you might prefer either one.

6   Close the document in both applications.

7   Double-click the document again.

It opens in TextEdit because the Open With choice you made earlier was not a permanent setting.

8   Close the document.

Permanently Change the Default Application for a File Type

1   In the Finder, select the Pet Sitter Notes document.

2   Choose File > Get Info (Command-I).

3   If necessary, expand the General and Name & Extension sections of the Info window.

This is a Word 97 document, and it has a file extension of .doc, which is hidden.

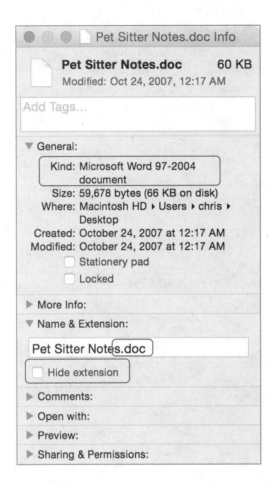

4 Deselect "Hide extension." The extension will now be visible in the view of your desktop in the Finder.

5 Expand the "Open with" section of the Info window, and then choose Preview from its pop-up menu.

Note that this menu shows the same possible applications as the Open With submenu in the Finder. Choosing an application here makes a permanent setting, but only for this specific file.

6 Click Change All.

7 In the confirmation dialog, click Continue.

You have now changed the default application for opening documents with the extension .doc in Chris Johnson's account. This setting is permanent (until you change it to something else).

8   Close the Info window.

9   Double-click the document on your desktop.

It opens in Preview.

10   Quit Preview.

11   Move Pet Sitter Notes.doc from your desktop to the Trash.

12   In the Finder, reopen the StudentMaterials/Lesson18 folder, and examine the original Pet Sitter Notes document there.

Note that its filename extension is not shown. When you used Get Info to show the extension of the copy on your desktop, it affected only that specific file.

13   Double-click the original Pet Sitter Notes.

It opens in Preview because you used Change All in the Info window to apply the setting to all Word 97-2004 documents.

14   Quit Preview.

Exercise 18.2
Use Auto Save and Versions

▶ **Prerequisite**

▶   You must have created the Chris Johnson account ("Exercise 5.1 Manage User Accounts" on page 145).

Many support issues derive from users losing work either because they did not save changes to a document or because they did save after making unfortunate changes. In applications that support it, OS X provides the capability to periodically save changes automatically and to keep multiple previous versions of a document. This means users don't have to worry about whether they should—or shouldn't—save the documents they're working on.

In this exercise, you will edit a file in TextEdit, save several versions, and roll back to an earlier version.

Experiment with Auto Save

1   If necessary, log in as Chris Johnson.

2   Open System Preferences, and select the General pane.

3   Ensure that "Ask to keep changes when closing documents" is not selected and that "Close windows when quitting an app" is selected.

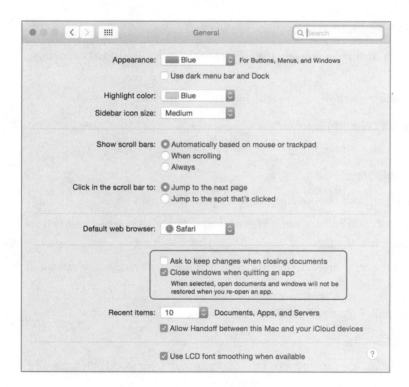

4   Quit System Preferences.

5   If necessary, navigate to /Users/Shared/StudentMaterials/Lesson18.

6   Copy Pretendco Report.rtfd to your desktop, and open the copy.

7   Add some text to the file.

Notice that the window's title bar now indicates its status as Edited.

8   Switch to the Finder, and select your copy of the Pretendco Report file, and choose File > Get Info (Command-I).

Notice that it has been modified within the last minute or so (your edits were saved automatically).

9   Close the Info window.

10   Switch to TextEdit, and add some more text to the file.

11   Select the file in the Finder, and choose File > Quick Look "Pretendco Report.rtfd" (Command-Y).

The Quick Look view shows all the text you added to the file.

12   Close the Quick Look window.

Work with Multiple Versions

1   Switch to TextEdit, and choose File > Save (or press Command-S).

Note that this looks like a "normal" save command, but what it actually does is save a restorable version of the file.

While TextEdit saves changes to the live document frequently, it saves a restorable version only when explicitly told to.

2   Delete the graphic from the document.

3   Quit TextEdit.

Notice that you are not prompted to save changes; they were saved automatically.

4   Reopen the Pretendco Report.rtfd file.

5   Choose File > Revert To > Previous Save.

The graphic is restored.

6   Add more text to the document, and choose File > Save (Command-S) again.

7   Add still more text, and examine the File > Revert To submenu.

It now lists options to restore to the last-saved version, to restore to the last-opened version, or to browse all versions.

8   Choose File > Revert To > Browse All Versions.

TextEdit displays a full-screen version browser, showing the current document state on the left and saved versions on the right. This view is similar to the Time Machine restore interface and actually shows versions from the Time Machine backups as well as restorable versions created by the application.

9   Experiment with the two windows. Note that you can switch between saved versions either by clicking their title bars in the stack or by using the timeline on the right side of the screen. You can also use editing controls, including copying and pasting content between versions.

10   Scroll back to the oldest version, and click Restore.

The document reverts to its original state.

11   Choose File > Revert To > Browse All Versions again.

TextEdit again switches to the full-screen version browser. Note that "newer" versions are still available, even though you reverted to the original state.

12   Click Done to exit the history browser.

13   Quit TextEdit.

Exercise 18.3
Manage Document Locking

▶ **Prerequisites**

▶ You must have created the Local Admin ("Exercise 2.1 Configure a New OS X System for Exercises" on page 60 or "Exercise 2.2 Configure an Existing OS X System for Exercises" on page 63) and Chris Johnson ("Exercise 5.1 Manage User Accounts" on page 145) accounts.

In this exercise you will explore options for locking documents to prevent accidental changes.

Lock and Unlock a Document

1 If necessary, log in as Chris Johnson.

2 If you have not performed "Exercise 18.2 Use Auto Save and Versions" on page 560, copy /Users/Shared/StudentMaterials/Lesson18/Pretendco Report.rtfd to your desktop.

3 Select your copy of the Pretendco Report.rtfd document and choose File > Get Info (Command-I).

4 In the General section of the Info window, select the Locked checkbox.

Notice that the document's icon now has a small padlock in its corner.

5 Close the Info window.

6   Open the document.

Notice that the window's title bar now indicates its status as Locked.

7   Attempt to add some text to the document.

A dialog appears telling you the file is locked and gives options for how to deal with the locked file.

8   Click Unlock.

The padlock vanishes from the document's icon on your desktop.

9   Add some text to the document.

10   Click the document name in the title bar, then select the Locked checkbox.

The padlock reappears on the document's icon on your desktop.

Since you are the owner of the document, you can lock and unlock it freely, in either the Finder or an editor that supports Auto Save.

11   Quit TextEdit.

Exercise 18.4
Store Documents in iCloud

> **Prerequisites**
>
> ▶ You must have created the Chris Johnson ("Exercise 5.1 Manage User Accounts" on page 145) and Mayta Mishtuk ("Exercise 6.1 Restore a Deleted User Account" on page 166) accounts.

OS X Yosemite allows applications to save documents to the Internet by way of iCloud Drive and then access them from any computer tied to the same iCloud account.

Enable iCloud Features

1   If necessary, log in as Chris Johnson.

2   Open System Preferences, and select the iCloud pane.

If you are already signed into iCloud, skip to the next section, "Configure iCloud Drive " on page 567.

3   If you are not already signed in to use iCloud, enter your iCloud Apple ID and password, and then click Sign In.

Note that if you do not already have an Apple ID, you can create one here; however, the ID creation process is not covered in this exercise.

4   If you are prompted to accept the iCloud terms and conditions, read through the new terms. If they are acceptable to you, agree to the terms, and click Continue; otherwise, click Cancel, and skip this exercise.

5 If the Apple ID is protected by two-step verification, follow the prompts to complete the authentication process.

6 When you are prompted for which features to set up, leave "Use iCloud for mail, contacts, calendars, reminders, notes, and Safari" selected, deselect Use Find My Mac, and then click Next.

7 If a dialog appears recommending requiring a password to unlock your screen, click Not Now.

8 If a dialog appears asking for your Apple ID password to set up iCloud Keychain, click Cancel.

9 If a dialog appears asking if you want to upgrade to iCloud Drive, this indicates that your iCloud account is being used to store documents in an older format and must be upgraded to use iCloud Drive. Skip to the warning in the next section.

Configure iCloud Drive

1 If iCloud preferences requires you to enter your password, click Enter Password, and authenticate to iCloud.

2   In iCloud preferences, verify that iCloud Drive is selected. If it is, skip to step 5.

If iCloud Drive is not selected, this normally indicates you are using an iCloud account that was set up by an older version of OS X or iOS and does not yet support iCloud Drive.

3   If you want to upgrade to iCloud Drive, select the checkbox iCloud Drive.

WARNING ▶ If you still use this iCloud account from a Mac running OS X v10.9 or earlier or an iPhone or iPad running iOS 7 or earlier, upgrading to iCloud Drive will make the documents currently stored in iCloud inaccessible to those devices until they are upgraded to OS X v10.10/iOS 8. See "Reference 18.5 iCloud Drive" on page 546 for details.

If you do not want to upgrade at this time, click Cancel, quit System Preferences, and skip the rest of this exercise.

4   If you are sure you want to upgrade the iCloud account to iCloud Drive, click Continue in the confirmation dialog.

5   Click the Options button to the right of iCloud Drive.

The iCloud Drive Options dialog lets you control which applications have access to your iCloud documents and your email address.

6   In the Documents tab, make sure TextEdit is selected.

7   Click Done.

8   Quit System Preferences.

Save a Document to iCloud

1   If you have not performed "Exercise 18.2 Use Auto Save and Versions" on page 560, copy /Users/Shared/StudentMaterials/Lesson18/Pretendco Report.rtfd to your desktop.

2   Open the Pretendco Report.rtfd document.

3   Click the document's name in the title bar.

4   If necessary, deselect Locked.

5   From the Where pop-up menu, choose iCloud Drive.

6   If a dialog appears indicating that an item with the same name (Pretendco Report.rtf) already exists in the same folder, a previous student may have left this item in the iCloud account. Click Replace to replace the old copy with yours.

The document's icon vanishes from your desktop.

7   Quit TextEdit.

8   Open the Contacts application.

If you performed "Exercise 16.1 Configure Time Machine" on page 459, the contacts you imported in that lesson are listed.

9   If the contacts from "Exercise 16.1 Configure Time Machine" on page 459 (Enrico Baker, Carl Dunn, Barbara Green, and so on) are not listed, open the file /Users/Shared/StudentMaterials/Lesson16/vCards.vcf to import them into Contacts.

10   Quit Contacts and log out as Chris Johnson.

Open a Document from iCloud

Now that your document and contacts are stored in iCloud, they are available from any computer account tied to the same iCloud account. For simplicity, you will demonstrate this using the Mayta Mishtuk account on your computer; but iCloud could push the documents and contacts to an account on a different computer just as well.

1   Log in to the Mayta Mishtuk account (password: **mayta**, or whatever you chose when you created the account).

2   Open System Preferences, and select the iCloud preference pane.

3   If iCloud is not set up in Mayta's account, enter the iCloud Apple ID and password you used with the Chris Johnson account, and click Sign In.

4   If the Apple ID is protected by two-step verification, follow the prompts to complete the authentication process.

5   When you are prompted for which features to set up, leave Use iCloud for mail, contacts, calendars, reminders, notes, and Safari" selected, deselect Use Find My Mac, and then click Next.

6   If a dialog appears recommending requiring a password to unlock your screen, click Not Now.

7   If a dialog appears asking for your Apple ID password to set up iCloud Keychain, click Cancel.

8   Make sure that iCloud Drive is selected.

9   Quit System Preferences.

10   In the Finder, choose Go > iCloud Drive (Command-Shift-I).

11   Open Pretendco Report.rtfd.

The document opens in TextEdit.

12   Add some text to the document.

Your edits are automatically saved to the iCloud servers and are available to any other computers using this iCloud account.

13   Quit TextEdit.

14   In the Finder, choose Go > All My Files (Command-Shift-F).

Pretendco Report.rtfd is listed; the All My Files view shows both local documents and those in iCloud Drive.

15   In the search field, enter pretendco.

Pretendco Report.rtfd is shown in the results, even though it is stored in iCloud Drive.

Use Contacts from iCloud

1   Open the Contacts application.

The contacts from the Chris Johnson account appear.

2   Quit Contacts, and log out as Mayta Mishtuk.

Exercise 18.5
Manage Automatic Behaviors

▶ **Prerequisites**

- ▶ You must have created the Chris Johnson account ("Exercise 5.1 Manage User Accounts" on page 145).

- ▶ You must have performed "Exercise 18.4 Store Documents in iCloud" on page 566.

By default, OS X Yosemite remembers what apps are open when you log out, but the apps themselves do not reopen the documents they had open before. In this exercise, you will experiment with changing these defaults.

Examine the Default Behavior

1   Log in as Chris Johnson.

2   Open System Preferences and select the General preference pane.

3   If necessary, select the checkbox "Close windows when quitting an app."

This is the default setting in OS X Yosemite.

4   Leave System Preferences open, and open TextEdit.

5   In the TextEdit Open dialog, open the file Pretendco Report.rtfd you saved in iCloud in the previous exercise.

Note that you may have to wait a few moments for the edit you made (as Mayta) to appear.

6   Create a new TextEdit document by choosing File > New (Command-N).

7 Type some text into the new document.

8 From the Apple menu, choose Log Out Chris Johnson (Command-Shift-Q).

9 In the confirmation dialog, make sure that "Reopen windows when logging back in" is selected, and click Log Out.

Note that you are not prompted to save the new (unsaved) document.

10 At the login screen, log back in as Chris Johnson.

System Preferences and TextEdit both automatically reopen, and TextEdit opens both of the documents it had open before.

11 Quit TextEdit.

Since the option to close windows when quitting is selected, you are prompted for whether you want to keep the new document.

12 Click Delete.

13 Reopen TextEdit.

This time it does not automatically open any documents but instead shows the dialog to let you select a document to open.

14 Reopen Pretendco Report.rtfd.

Experiment with Other Options

1 Switch to System Preferences.

2 Deselect "Close windows when quitting an app."

3 Bring TextEdit to the foreground (you can do this by clicking in its window or by clicking its icon in the Dock).

4 Quit TextEdit.

5 Reopen TextEdit.

This time it automatically reopens Pretendco Report.rtfd.

6 Switch to System Preferences, and select "Close windows when quitting an app."

7 Quit System Preferences.

8 From the Apple menu, choose Log Out Chris Johnson (Command-Shift-Q).

9 This time, deselect "Reopen windows when logging back in," and click Log Out.

10 At the login screen, log back in as Chris Johnson.

This time, neither System Preferences nor TextEdit reopen.

11 From the Apple menu, choose Log Out Chris Johnson.

Note that the "Reopen windows when logging back in" option is deselected. This setting is remembered, although you can always change it when logging out.

12 Click Cancel to remain logged in.

Turn Off Auto Save

1 Open System Preferences, and select the General preference pane.

2 Select "Ask to keep changes when closing documents."

3 Open TextEdit, and reopen Pretendco Report.rtfd.

4 Add some more text to the Pretendco Report document.

Like before, the title bar shows its status as Edited, but now there is also a dot in the close button, which indicates unsaved changes in the document.

5 Click the close button for the document (Command-W).

You are asked whether you want to save changes to the document.

6 Click Save.

7 Quit TextEdit.

8 In the General preference pane, deselect "Ask to keep changes when closing documents."

This restores the normal Auto Save behavior.

9 Close System Preferences.

Lesson 19

Application Management and Troubleshooting

For many OS X support professionals, their most common day-to-day task is troubleshooting application issues. The successful resolution of an application issue most often depends on previous experience with the specific application. Specific application issues, however, are beyond the scope of this guide.

On the other hand, support professionals dealing with new applications or new issues must rely on their ability to effectively gather relevant information and their knowledge of general system technologies. This lesson primarily addresses these two application troubleshooting aspects. So that you have a better understanding of the pieces in play, this lesson first defines key elements of the OS X process architecture. You will then learn to gather information about applications and processes. The remainder of this lesson covers a variety of general troubleshooting techniques that can be used for any type of application.

GOALS

▸ Understand and support the various application types

▸ Manage app extensions and widgets in Notification Center

▸ Monitor and control processes and applications

▸ Explore various application troubleshooting techniques

Reference 19.1
Applications and Processes

A *process* is any instance of executable code that is currently activated and addressed in system memory. In other words, a process is anything that is currently "running" or "open." OS X handles processes very efficiently, so even when a process is idle, and probably consuming no processor resources, it's still considered active, because it has dedicated address space in system memory. The four general process types are applications, commands, daemons, and agents.

OS X Process Types

Applications are a specific category of process that is generally identified as something the user opened in the graphical interface. *Commands* are also normally opened by the user but are only available at the command-line interface. The key similarity between most applications and commands is that they are running in the user's space. In other words, most applications and commands are started, stopped, and limited to accessing resources available only to the user.

Processes that run on behalf of the system fall into another category, *daemons*, also referred to as background processes because they rarely have any user interface. Daemons usually launch during system startup and remain active the entire time the Mac is up and running; consequently, most daemons run with root or systemwide access to all resources. These background daemons are responsible for most of the automatic system features like detecting network changes and maintaining the Spotlight search metadata index.

Agents are technically also daemons, or background processes. The primary difference is that agents run only when a user is logged in to the system. Agents are always started automatically for the user by the system. While applications and commands can also be opened automatically, they are not controlled by the system the way agents are. Most important, all three of these process types are considered part of the user's space because they are executed with the same access privileges the user has.

OS X Process Features

OS X is a desirable platform for running applications and other processes because it combines a rock-solid UNIX foundation with an advanced graphical user interface. Users will most likely recognize the interface elements right away, but it's the underlying foundation that keeps things running so smoothly. Specifically, a few fundamental features of OS X are responsible for providing a high level of performance and reliability.

OS X Process Performance Features

▶ Preemptive multitasking—This gives OS X the ability to balance computing resources without letting any single process take over. It allows the system to run dozens of processes without significantly slowing down user applications.

▶ Symmetric multiprocessing—Whenever possible, the system uses all available computing resources to provide the best performance. This is a key feature, because every currently shipping Mac includes at least two processor cores. OS X v10.6 introduced two new unique multiprocessing features, Grand Central Dispatch and OpenCL, which provide for even greater performance than previous versions of OS X. Grand

Central Dispatch makes it much easier for application developers to take full advantage of not just multiprocessor systems but also multicore processors. OpenCL takes this even further by allowing applications to use your Mac computer's powerful graphics processor to accelerate general computing tasks.

► Simultaneous 32-bit and 64-bit support—OS X supports both 32-bit and 64-bit modes simultaneously. A process running in 64-bit mode has the ability to individually access more than 4 GB of system memory, can perform higher-precision computational functions much faster, and can take advantage of Intel's updated x86-64 architecture for improved performance and security. All Mac computers compatible with OS X Yosemite feature 64-bit-capable processors and can take advantage of 64-bit system features. With OS X v10.6, Apple updated nearly all included software to take advantage of 64-bit resources, including the core of OS X, the system kernel.

► Optimized power management—OS X includes several advanced power management technologies that are designed to specifically increase battery life for portable Mac computers. Much of this technology works behind the scenes, so the average user shouldn't even notice. Two users might notice are App Nap and Safari Power Saver. App Nap essentially puts applications in a temporary sleep mode when their windows are hidden by other applications. This shouldn't affect the user's experience, but it can be turned off on a per-application basis from the Finder's Info window if it causes problems. On the other hand, users will see the effects of Safari Power Saver. In Safari, plug-ins like Flash all start out as inactive and are not activated until the user clicks the website item requesting the plug-in. This feature can be turned off as well, in the Advanced tab of Safari preferences.

OS X Memory Management Features

► Protected memory—Similar to how the file system prevents users from meddling with items they shouldn't, processes are also kept separate and secure in system memory. The system manages all memory allocation so that processes are not allowed to interfere with each other's system memory space. In other words, an ill-behaved or crashed application does not normally affect any other process on the system.

► Dynamic memory allocation—The operating system automatically manages system memory for processes at their request. Though real system memory is clearly limited by hardware, the system dynamically allocates both real and virtual memory when needed. Thus, the only memory limitations in OS X are the size of installed RAM and the amount of free space you have available on your system volume.

▶ Secure memory allocation—OS X includes two additional memory management features that further protect the system from malicious processes. The first feature is known as execute disable memory, which creates a strong barrier between memory used for data and memory used for executable instructions within an individual process. This helps prevent malicious process code from improperly accessing user data. Another feature, known as address space layout randomization, changes the location in memory where a process stores key items, thus making it much less vulnerable to an attack that attempts to inject malicious actions into a normally benign process.

▶ Compressed memory—OS X includes a memory management feature that both increases performance and reduces energy usage. Instead of the wasteful practice of swapping memory out to disk when too many processes are active, the system first compresses the content used by less active processes to free up space for more active processes. This greatly reduces traffic between active memory and the virtual memory swap files on the system disk.

64-Bit Versus 32-Bit Mode

In OS X Yosemite, nearly the entire operating system and almost all included applications run in 64-bit mode. In fact, only one of the main built-in applications is still limited to 32-bit mode: DVD Player.

While moving most of the applications to support 64-bit mode generally improves performance, this advancement is not without drawbacks. Namely, applications that run in 64-bit mode can't take advantage of any 32-bit code. This means any application that uses plug-in technology may suffer from compatibility issues with third-party plug-ins that have not been updated to support 64-bit mode.

Examples of plug-in software affected by this issue include:

▶ Printer drivers that add interfaces for the printer dialog

▶ Screen savers

▶ Audio device drivers known as audio units

▶ Spotlight metadata import plug-ins

▶ Quick Look preview plug-ins

▶ Dashboard widgets that require plug-in code (though most widgets don't use extra code, so they should work without issues)

► Safari plug-ins

In short, applications running in 64-bit mode do not load 32-bit plug-ins. If you need to use a third-party 32-bit plug-in with a 64-bit-capable application, you have to force the application to run in 32-bit mode on most Mac systems. This can be accomplished from the Finder Info or Inspector window by simply selecting the "Open in 32-bit mode" checkbox. Obviously, forcing 32-bit mode may make the application run more slowly, but this is required to use nonupdated plug-ins.

NOTE ► The Open in Low Resolution checkbox appears only on new Mac computers featuring Retina displays. This option prevents the use of high-resolution application assets, which also may not be compatible with older application plug-ins.

One system application automatically switches modes for you: System Preferences. When a user tries to open a third-party 32-bit System Preferences plug-in, often called a System Preferences pane, a prompt to restart System Preferences appears. If the user clicks OK (the default), System Preferences restarts in 32-bit mode and loads the selected pane.

NOTE ▶ With the exception of Dashboard and System Preferences, third-party plug-ins that tie into a system resource or background process must support 64-bit mode to work with OS X.

Reference 19.2
App Extensions

OS X Yosemite introduces app extensions, which allow applications to take advantage of functionality and content from another applications. In this section you will explore how app extensions blur the line between separate applications in OS X.

NOTE ▶ Don't confuse app extensions with kernel extensions. App extensions add functionality to applications, while kernel extensions primarily add hardware compatability to the system. You can find out more about kernel extensions in "Peripheral Device Drivers" on page 850.

App Extensions Architecture

OS X has long included cross-application integration through methods like copy and paste, the Services menu, and AppleScript. While these older methods are still viable, app extensions provide a standard framework that allows applications from completely different developers to directly interact with each other—so much so that with app extensions one application's features can appear as if they are built-in to another application.

Examples of app extensions possible for OS X include:

▶   Finder—App extensions can add file system functionality exposed in the Finder. As an example, the popular third-party cloud storage solution Dropbox includes an app extension that adds a pop-up menu to the Finder toolbar where you can manage Dropbox settings for specific files.

▶   Sharing menu—App extensions can add more options to the Share menu, allowing users to directly share content from one application with other applications or Internet services.

► Action menu—App extensions can add more options to the Action menu. The Action menu is an interface that allows a user to manipulate a document. With app extensions, the features from one application can be used in another application to manipulate the document.

► Today view—App extensions can add functionality to the Today view of Notification Center. In OS X Yosemite, this ability largely replaces the need for Dashboard widgets.

As an example of app extensions in OS X Yosemite, the Preview application includes markup features that allow you to manipulate pictures or PDF documents. This includes the ability to add custom shapes, text, or even your digital signature to existing documents. You can access these features in Preview by clicking the Markup button (toolbox icon) in the toolbar.

The markup features of Preview are also available as an app extension that can be used by any other application. In OS X Yosemite, the Mail application can take advantage of markup features within an email that contains a picture or PDF document. When replying to a message in Mail, click the Include Attachments button in the toolbar and then the Action button (downward arrow icon) at the top-right of the document to reveal the markup features. Again, other app extensions can add their custom actions here as well.

Managing App Extensions

Several app extensions are included with OS X Yosemite, and additional app extensions are "installed" automatically with the application providing the additional functionality. In other words, applications that integrate via app extensions include the app extension resources inside the application bundle. Thus, the user will never have to see or install specific app extensions.

A user can inspect the installed app extensions and enable or disable their functionality from the Extensions preferences. The following screenshot shows the markup action included with OS X via the Preview application. For example, deselecting the checkbox next to the Markup item would prevent that app extension from appearing in other applications. Also note the Dropbox app extension listed under Finder. This app extension is installed automatically with the Dropbox application.

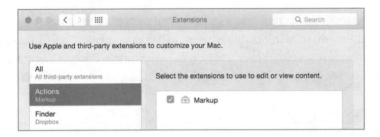

Items in the Share menu can also be enabled or disabled from the Extensions preferences. However, keep in mind that the user will need to be signed in to any Internet-based sharing service to activate the associated app extension. Users can sign into most Internet services via the Internet Accounts preference, as covered in "Internet Accounts Preferences" on page 732.

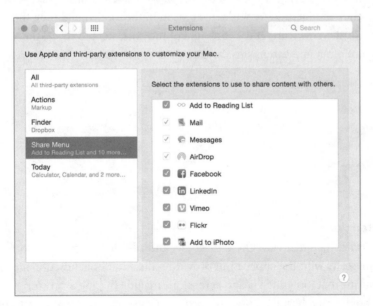

Notification Center Today View

OS X Yosemite introduces the new Today view in the Notification Center. This view offers a range of information and functionality that can be customized to the user's preference. Notification Center is accessed by clicking the farthest right button in the menu bar, and the default view is Today.

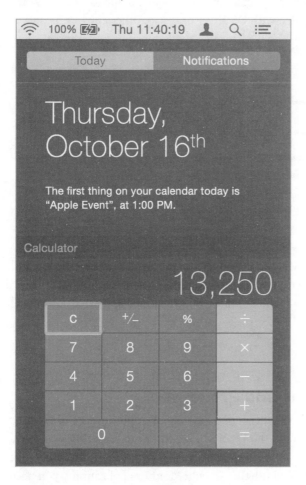

The Today view largely replaces functionality found in an older OS X technology, Dashboard widgets. In fact, app extensions that can be used in the Today view are referred to as widgets. However, from a technology standpoint, legacy Dashboard widgets are not the same. Widgets in the Today view of Notification Center are implemented through app extensions, whereas older Dashboard widgets were installed in their own Widgets folder within a Library folder.

TIP OS X Yosemite still includes the ability to use legacy Dashboard widgets, although it's hidden by default. Access to the Dashboard can be managed via the Mission Control preferences.

Like other app extensions, widgets in the Today view are included with the application providing the functionality or service. For example the Calculator app extension is built in to the Calculator application included with OS X. Also, as with other app extensions, you can disable or enable widgets in the Today view from the Extensions preferences.

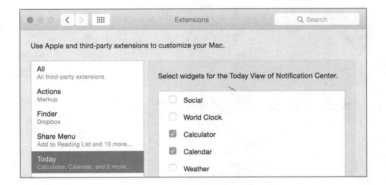

TIP Widgets in the Today view can also be managed by clicking the button at the bottom-center of Notification Center. This button most often says Edit, but it can also display as <#> New, where <#> is the number of newly added app extensions that can present widgets in the Today view.

Reference 19.3
Monitoring Applications and Processes

OS X provides several methods for identifying and managing applications and processes. As covered previously, you can still use the Finder Info window to inspect basic application information, but you can find out a lot more about an application from System Information. On the other hand, you would use the Activity Monitor application if you need to inspect an application or process as it's running on the Mac.

Applications via System Information

If you want to quickly gather information about all the applications on your Mac, use the /Applications/Utilities/System Information application. When you select the Applications category in System Information, the content of all available Application folders is scanned. This includes /Applications, /Applications/Utilities, ~/Applications, /System/

Library/CoreServices, and any other Applications folders at the root of any mounted volumes.

From the applications list, select an entry to reveal its name, version number, application source modification date, and application type. The application's source, in the "Obtained from" column, is based on the code-signing certificate used to create the application. Unidentified applications do not contain this code signature. Also note that applications installed as part of OS X do not show as being purchased from the Mac App Store, but instead show just "Apple."

	Application Name	^ Version	Obtained from	Last Modified	64-Bit (Intel)
▼ Network	Boom	1.9.1	Identified Developer	5/20/14, 8:45 AM	No
Firewall	Boot Camp Assistant	5.1.2	Apple	9/30/14, 2:37 PM	Yes
Locations	Bridge Constructor FREE	2.5.1	Mac App Store	1/11/14, 12:19 AM	No
Volumes	BrokenAge	1.2.2	Unknown	2/26/14, 12:54 PM	No
WWAN	Brother MFC-8860DN	10.0	Apple	9/30/14, 2:37 PM	Yes
Wi-Fi	Brother Scanner	2.3.1	Apple	1/28/13, 10:39 AM	Yes
▼ Software	Brother Status Monitor	3.9.1	Apple	1/28/13, 10:39 AM	Yes
Accessibility	Build Web Page	10.0	Apple	9/30/14, 2:37 PM	Yes
Applications	Calculator	10.8	Apple	9/30/14, 2:37 PM	Yes
Components	Calendar	8.0	Apple	9/30/14, 2:37 PM	Yes

Calculator:

Version: 10.8
Obtained from: Apple
Last Modified: 9/30/14, 2:37 PM
Kind: Intel
64-Bit (Intel): Yes
Signed by: Software Signing, Apple Code Signing Certification Authority, Apple Root CA
Location: /Applications/Calculator.app
Get Info String: 10.8, Copyright © 2001-2013, Apple Inc.

kmwtogo ▸ Software ▸ Applications ▸ Calculator

Monitoring Processes via Activity Monitor

The primary application in OS X for monitoring processes as they are running is /Applications/Utilities/Activity Monitor. This extremely useful tool shows you the vital signs of any currently running process and of the system as a whole. If an application has stopped responding or has become noticeably slow, check Activity Monitor. Also check here if the overall system is running noticeably slower. Activity Monitor helps you identify an application or background process that is using a significant percentage of system resources.

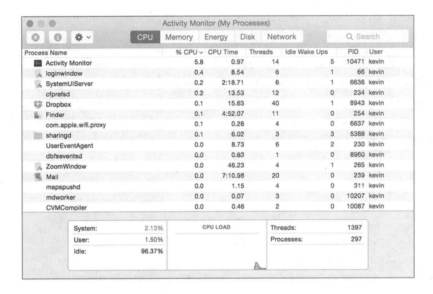

The main window of Activity Monitor presents a list of running processes and applications that belong to the current user. Below the process list you'll see overall system statistics. The default columns in Activity Monitor allow you to examine various process statistics:

▶ Process Name—This is the name of the running process chosen by the developer who created it.

▶ % CPU—This number is the percentage of total CPU usage the process is consuming. Note that the maximum percentage possible is 100 percent times the number of processor cores. For example, a Mac featuring an Intel Core i7 presents a total of eight processor cores to the system.

▶ CPU Time—This is the amount of time a process has been active on the system since the last startup.

▶ Threads—Each process is further broken down into the number of thread operations. Multithreading helps increase a process's responsiveness by enabling it to perform multiple simultaneous tasks. Multithreading also increases performance, as each thread of a single process can run on a separate processor core.

▶ Idle Wake Ups—This is the number of times a process has been woken up from a paused "sleep" state since the process was last started.

▶ Process Identification (PID)—Each process has a unique identifier number. The numbers are assigned in sequence as processes are opened after system startup. Note that the PIDs are "recycled" after 65,535 has been reached.

▶ User—Per the UNIX application security model, each process is opened on behalf of a particular user. Thus, each application has file system access corresponding to the assigned user account.

By default, Activity Monitor only shows processes running for the currently logged-in user. To increase your view of all active processes, choose View > All Processes. You can also adjust the number of statistics shown in the columns and the update frequency from the View menu.

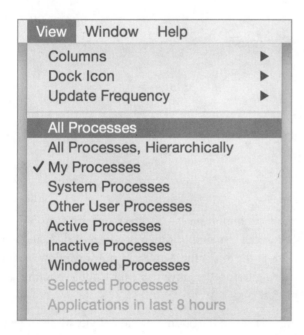

TIP ▶ To narrow down your view, use the Spotlight search filter in the upper-right corner of the Activity Monitor window.

To sort the process list by column, simply click any column title. Click the column title again to toggle between ascending and descending sorts. By viewing all processes and then re-sorting the list by % CPU, you can determine whether any process is using excessive resources.

To further inspect an individual process, double-click its name in the Activity Monitor list. This reveals a window showing detailed process information.

While CPU utilization generally is the most important statistic for monitoring process activity, the Activity Monitor application can also monitor memory, energy, disk, and network utilization. Click through the tabs at the top of the Activity Monitor window to view the different categories. These monitoring features are invaluable for troubleshooting, as they show you real-time system statistics.

TIP Hold the pointer over any statistic at the bottom of the Activity Monitor window to view a description of the statistic.

Of particular note are the Swap Used and Compressed statistics under the Memory tab. These numbers are a historical account, since last system startup, of how much active process data has been swapped out to local storage or compressed to save space. Compression is preferred to swapping, as it's a higher-performance approach to making more room in memory.

Physical Memory:	16.00 GB	MEMORY PRESSURE	App Memory:	9.08 GB
Memory Used:	14.10 GB		File Cache:	3.22 GB
Virtual Memory:	16.00 GB		Wired Memory:	1.79 GB
Swap Used:	0 bytes		Compressed:	0 bytes

A low number of swap usage is acceptable, but a high number of swap usage indicates the system does not have enough real memory to meet the user's application demands. In other words, the system only "swaps out" when it does not have enough real memory, thus slowing system performance.

TIP ▶ Take time to explore all the features available from the Activity Monitor menu options. For an even more detailed process inspector, check out the Instruments application installed as part of the optional Xcode Developer Tools found on the Mac App Store.

Reference 19.4
Application Troubleshooting

Application issues are as diverse as the applications themselves. Just as each application is designed to provide unique features, problems often manifest in unique ways as well. Fortunately, there are a variety of general troubleshooting steps you can take when diagnosing and resolving an application issue.

MORE INFO ▶ Apple maintains a list of software known to be incompatible. You can find out more about how OS X handles incompatible software in Apple Support article HT201861, "OS X: About the incompatible software folder."

General Application Troubleshooting

The actions in the following list are in order from the least to the most invasive and time-consuming. Actions are also generally presented according to the likelihood of their success in resolving the issue, from most to least likely. Generally, when troubleshooting applications, start with one of these actions:

▶ Restart the application—Often, restarting an application resolves the issue, or at least resolves application responsiveness. In some cases, the application may become unresponsive and you may have to forcibly quit it to restart it, as detailed later in "Forcibly Quitting Applications" on page 593.

▶ Try another known working document—This is an excellent method to determine if a document has become corrupted and that is the cause of the problem. If you discover that the problem's source is a corrupted document file, usually the best solution is to restore the document from an earlier backup. As covered in Lesson 16 "Time Machine", OS X includes a sophisticated and easy-to-use backup system.

▶ Try another application—Many common document types can be opened by multiple Mac applications. Try opening the troublesome document in another application. If this works, save a new "clean" version of the document from the other application.

▶ Try another user account—Use this method to determine if a user-specific resource file is the cause of the problem. If the application problem doesn't occur when using another account, search for corrupted application caches, preferences, and resource files in the suspect user's Library folder. Creating a temporary account to test—and then deleting it—is quite easy, as covered in Lesson 5 "User Accounts".

▶ Check diagnostic reports and log files—This is the last information-gathering step to take before you start replacing items. Few applications keep detailed log files; however, every time an application crashes, the OS X diagnostic reporting feature saves a diagnostic report of the crash information. Using the Console application to view diagnostic reports is detailed later in "Viewing Diagnostics via Console" on page 595.

▶ Delete cache files—To increase performance, many applications create cache folders in the /Library/Caches, ~/Library/Caches, and ~/Library/Saved Application State folders. A specific application's cache folder almost always matches the application's name. Although not the most likely application resource to cause problems, cache folders can be easily deleted without affecting the user's information. Once you delete an application's cache folder, the application creates a new one the next time you open it. One cache type that can't be removed easily from the Finder are the various font caches. However, the system font caches are cleared during a safe boot, as covered in Lesson 27 "System Troubleshooting".

TIP The ~/Library folder is hidden by default in OS X. The easiest way to reveal this folder in the Finder is to hold down the Option key and choose Go > Library.

▶ Replace preference files—Corrupted preference files are one of the most likely of all application resources to cause problems, as they change often and are required for the application to function properly. Application preference troubleshooting is detailed later in "Preference Troubleshooting" on page 597.

▶ Replace application resources—Although corrupted application resources can certainly cause problems, they are the least likely source of problems, since application resources are rarely changed. Application resource troubleshooting is also detailed later in "Application Resource Troubleshooting" on page 602.

Forcibly Quitting Applications

It's pretty easy to tell when an application becomes unresponsive—it stops reacting to your mouse clicks, and the pointer often changes to a wait cursor (spinning pinwheel) and stays that way for more than a minute. Hence, the terms *spinning-wheel* and *beach-balling* have become slang for a frozen Mac application.

Because the forward-most application controls the menu bar, it may seem as if the application has locked you out of the Mac entirely. But moving the cursor from the frozen application window to another application window or the desktop usually returns the pointer to normal—and you can then click another application or the desktop to regain control of your Mac.

OS X provides no less than three methods for forcibly quitting applications from the graphical interface:

▶ From the Force Quit Applications dialog—Choose Apple menu > Force Quit, or press Command-Option-Escape to open the Force Quit Applications dialog. A frozen application appears with "(not responding)" next to its name. To forcibly quit, select any application and click Force Quit. Note that you can only restart the Finder from this dialog.

▶ From the Dock—Use secondary (or Control-) click, or hold down the application's icon in the Dock, to display the application shortcut menu. If the Dock has recognized that the application is frozen, simply choose Force Quit from this menu. Otherwise, hold down the Option key to change the Quit menu command to Force Quit.

▶ From Activity Monitor—Open /Applications/Utilities/Activity Monitor, and then select the application you want to quit from the process list. Next, click the "X in an octagon" button on the far-left edge of the Activity Monitor toolbar, and then click the Force Quit button. Activity Monitor is the only built-in graphical application that also allows administrative users to quit or forcibly quit any other user process or background system process.

NOTE ▶ In Activity Monitor, individual web pages in Safari are shown as separate processes. This gives you the ability to force quit individual pages that may have crashed in Safari.

Diagnostic Reports

To help diagnose persistent issues, the OS X diagnostic reporting feature springs into action any time an application quits unexpectedly (commonly known as a *crash*) or stops functioning and you have to forcibly quit it (commonly known as a *hang*). This process displays a warning dialog that lets the user know a problem has occurred.

More importantly, this process records log files that detail the circumstances surrounding the application's crash or hang. If you click the Report button when the warning dialog appears, you can see the diagnostic report and, optionally, add comments to send to Apple.

TIP You can turn off the automatic sending of diagnostic reports to Apple from Security & Privacy preferences.

Viewing Diagnostics via Console

Even if you don't send the report to Apple, you can revisit diagnostic reports later, as they are always saved to the system volume. If the problem report was generated by something running for the user, the log is saved to the user's ~/Library/Logs/DiagnosticReports folder. However, if the problem report was generated by something running as the system, the log is saved in the local /Library/Logs/DiagnosticReports folder.

The easiest way to view these reports is to open the /Applications/Utilities/Console application and then click the Show Log List button in the toolbar. The diagnostic reports are chronologically listed in the Diagnostic and Usage Information section. Each problem report entry is named by the application followed by the date and time in 24-hour notation.

These diagnostic report logs include highly technical information that many won't understand, but they also include key pieces of information that may help the average troubleshooter diagnose the issue. For example, diagnostic reports often indicate which files were being used by the application at the time. One of the reported files could be the source of the problem due to corruption.

Another method in the Console application for reviewing hangs and crashes is to choose File > New System Log Query, which allows you to construct a custom search to precisely target key items across the most common logs.

Much like constructing a custom Spotlight search in the Finder (as covered in Lesson 15 "Metadata and Spotlight"), you can click the Add (+) button to add multiple search criteria. Each new search criteria is an "and" by default, but you can define an "or" by holding down the Option key when you click the Add (+) button. For example, the preceding screenshot shows a search that looks for any log sender that contains "crash" or "spin" or any log sender that includes "hang" and does not contain "change" in the message. In this example, because the word *hang* is contained in the word *change,* the final condition is necessary to avoid finding log entries with just the word *change.*

Preference Troubleshooting

Applications primarily access two types of often-changing files when they are in use: the documents for which the application handles viewing or editing, and the preference files that contain all the application's settings. From an administration perspective, preference files are often more important, as they may contain settings that are required for an application to work properly. For instance, an application's serial number or registration information is often stored in a preference file.

Preference files can be found in any Library folder, but most application preferences end up in the user's Library. Application preferences are kept in user home folders because the local Library should only be used for system preferences. More important, this enables each user to have his or her own application settings that do not interfere with other users' settings. By this logic, it's clear that if you're troubleshooting a system process, then you should look for its preferences in the /Library folder.

> **TIP** The ~/Library folder is hidden by default in OS X. The easiest way to reveal this folder in the Finder is to hold the Option key and choose Go > Library.

Most application and system preference files are saved as property list files. The naming scheme for a property list file usually has the unique bundle identifier for the application first, followed by the file type .plist. For example, the Finder preference file is named com.apple.finder.plist. This naming scheme may seem strange at first, but it helps avoid confusion by identifying the software's developer along with the application itself.

Many applications are still not sandboxed, so they use the default preference folder for standard applications: the ~/Library/Preferences folder. The full path to the Finder preference file is /Users/<username>/Library/Preferences/com.apple.finder.plist, where <username>;is the account name of the user.

NOTE ▶ Any lock files associated with a preference file can be largely ignored, as they don't contain any data and are simply the result of a legacy OS X Lion behavior.

For sandboxed applications, the preference will be located in either the Containers or Group Containers folder. Specifically these folders are ~/Library/Containers/<BundleID>/Data/Library/Preferences and ~/Library/Group Containers/<BundleID>/Library/Preferences, where <BundleID> is the unique bundle identifier for the application.

For example, the identifier for the Mail application is com.apple.mail. Therefore, for a user with the account name "ladmin," the full path to the Mail application's preference file is /Users/ladmin/Library/Containers/com.apple.mail/Data/Library/Preferences/com.apple.mail.plist.

Application preference files are a common application resource known historically to cause problems. Because these files can contain both internal application configuration information and user-configured preferences, even if you haven't changed any preferences, odds are the application is constantly storing new information in this file. It is the only file required by most applications that is regularly being rewritten, so it has the potential to become corrupted.

Apple has worked to make its own applications and the user preference system wary of corrupt preference files. Many applications that use the Apple preference model, including third-party applications, simply recognize the corrupt preference file, ignore it, and create a new one. On the other hand, many other third-party applications use their own proprietary preference models that are not as resilient. In these cases, corrupted preferences typically result in an application that crashes frequently or during startup.

Resolving Corrupted Preferences

The most convenient method of isolating a corrupted preference in the latter case is to rename the suspect preference file. If any part of the preference filename is different than expected, the application ignores it and creates a new preference file. So, in the Finder, add an identifier to the end of the suspect preference filename—something like ".bad." Alternatively, to make the preference file easier to find later, you could simply put a tilde (~) at the beginning of the file's name, which causes the Finder to put it at the beginning of the file listing when sorted alphabetically.

The preference architecture in OS X is maintained by a background server process known as cfprefsd. To improve performance, this process uses memory caching to store preference information. After you remove a potentially corrupt preference you should restart this process to clear its cache. As covered previously, you can force any process to quit from Activity Monitor. Because cfprefsd should always be running, the system automatically restarts it when you force it to quit. Also, make sure to force only the cfprefsd process owned by the appropriate user to quit.

After you have removed the preference file and restarted the cfprefsd process, opening the application or process creates a new preference file based on the code's defaults. If this resolves the issue and doesn't remove any irreplaceable settings, go ahead and trash the old preference file; if not, move on to resource troubleshooting.

If you eventually resolve the problem elsewhere, you can then restore the previous settings by deleting the newer preference file and then removing the filename identifier you added to the original preference file. Again, don't forget to restart the `cfprefsd` process. The benefit of replacing the previous preference file is that you don't lose any of the settings or custom configuration saved in the file.

Viewing and Editing Preferences

One of the primary advantages of using the property list file format is that it can generally be understood by humans. During your troubleshooting, you may find it advantageous to verify settings by directly viewing the contents of the configuration property list file. Many applications and processes keep additional settings items in these files and may not have a graphical interface for configuration.

> **NOTE** ▸ Some third-party applications do not store their preference files as property lists. Thus, they will likely use a different naming convention, and you will probably not be able to view or edit the file's contents.

The content of a property list file is formatted as either plain-text Extensible Markup Language (XML) or binary. The XML format is relatively human-readable with normal text interspersed with special text tags that define the data structure for the information. Thus, you can view and attempt to decipher the XML code of plain-text-formatted property list files using any text-reading application.

Binary-encoded files are, on the other hand, only readable using special tools designed to convert the binary code into human-readable format. Fortunately, OS X includes a Quick Look plug-in that allows you to easily view the contents of either type of property list file by simply pressing the Space bar while you have the file selected in the Finder.

If you need to edit a property list file, avoid using TextEdit, as it will improperly format any property list file that is saved as a binary. The most complete graphical application from Apple for editing property list files is Xcode. The Xcode application can decode binary property list files, and it enables you to view and edit any property list in an easy-to-read hierarchical format. Again, Xcode is an optional install that can be found on the Mac App Store.

NOTE ▶ Avoid editing property list files that are currently in use by a running application or process. However, if you need to edit a property list that may be in use, make sure to restart the `cfprefsd` process, as covered earlier in "Forcibly Quitting Applications" on page 593.

Application Resource Troubleshooting

Although it's rare, corrupted application software and associated nonpreference resources can be a source of application problems. These types of files rarely, if ever, change after the initial application installation, so the likelihood that such a resource is the cause of a problem is low.

However, keep in mind that many applications use *other* resources from the local and user Library folders, such as fonts, plug-ins, and keychains, as well as items in the Application Support folder. The hard part is locating the suspect resource; once you have, the fix is to simply remove or replace the corrupted resource and restart the application.

> **NOTE ▶** Applications running in 64-bit mode do not load plug-in resources that only support 32-bit mode. This compatibility issue is covered in the section "64-Bit Versus 32-Bit Mode" on page 580.

Remember that corrupted resources in the user's home folder Library affect only that user, whereas corrupted resources in the local Library affect all users. Use this fact to narrow your search when looking for a corrupted resource. Further, application and diagnostic report logs, covered earlier in "Viewing Diagnostics via Console" on page 595, may tell you which resources the application was attempting to access when it crashed. Obviously, those resources should be your primary suspects.

If the application exhibits problems with only one user, attempt to locate the specific resource at the root of the problem in the user's Library folder. Start with the usual suspects; if you find a resource that you think could be causing the problem, move that resource out of the user's Library folder and restart the application.

> **NOTE ▶** Some applications have a habit of storing their resources in the user's Documents folder, so you may want to check there as well.

If you've determined that the application issue is persistent across all user accounts, start by reinstalling or upgrading to the latest version of the application. You will probably find that a newer version of the application is available—one that likely includes bug fixes. At the very least, by reinstalling you replace any potentially corrupted files that are part of the standard application. If you continue to experience problems after reinstalling the application, search through the local Library resources to find and remove or replace the corrupted resource.

> **NOTE ▶** If you are discovering a large number of corrupted files, this probably indicates a much more serious file system or storage hardware issue. Troubleshooting these items is covered in Lesson 12 "File System Troubleshooting".

Exercise 19.1
Force Applications to Quit

In this exercise, you will learn how to determine when an application has become unresponsive. You will learn different ways to force unresponsive applications to quit: from the
Dock, using the Force Quit window, and using Activity Monitor. Even background processes without a user interface can have issues and stop running, so you'll learn how to
manage these processes as well. You will also see how to open an application in 32-bit
mode.

Force an Application to Quit via the Dock

1 If necessary, log in as Chris Johnson.

2 Open the Dead End application you installed in "Exercise 17.3 Use a Drag-and-Drop
    Install" on page 517.

   The sole purpose of Dead End is to become unresponsive, giving you an opportunity
   to practice different ways to force an application to quit.

   Dead End opens a window with a "Download the Internet" button.

3 Click "Download the Internet."

   Dead End becomes unresponsive. After a few seconds you may see the wait cursor (a
   colored pinwheel). Note that the wait cursor appears only when you mouse over the
   Dead End window or (if Dead End is in the foreground) the menu bar.

4 Control-click the Dead End icon in the Dock, and then choose Force Quit from the
    shortcut menu. Alternatively, you could click and hold the Dead End icon in the
    Dock, and then choose Force Quit from the pop-up menu.

If Force Quit does not appear in the menu, repeat step 3 or hold down the Option key. When you hold down the Option key, Quit changes to Force Quit, and you then choose it to force Dead End to quit.

Use the Force Quit Window

1 Open the Dead End application again so you can try another method of forcibly quitting.

One way to open applications you've used recently is by going to the Apple menu and choosing Recent Items. By default, the system remembers the last ten applications you've opened.

2 Click "Download the Internet."

3 Press Command-Option-Escape to open the Force Quit Applications window.

Note that it will take about 15 seconds before Dead End is shown as "not responding."

4 Select Dead End, and click Force Quit.

5 In the confirmation dialog, click Force Quit.

6 If you are given the opportunity to send a report to Apple, click Ignore.

7 Close the Force Quit Applications window.

Use Activity Monitor

There may be times when you need another method to force an application to quit. Activity Monitor not only forces applications to quit but also allows you to review all processes running on the computer, gather information, and quit them when necessary.

1 Open Dead End.

2 Click "Download the Internet."

3 Open Activity Monitor (from the Utilities folder).

Even though the wait cursor appears in Dead End, you can still click the desktop to make the Finder active or click in the Dock to use Launchpad. A single unresponsive application should not affect the rest of the system.

Activity Monitor displays a list of all running processes. When you open this window, it shows processes that you will recognize as applications. It also shows other processes running in the background that do not have a graphical user interface.

4   If necessary, click the CPU tab above the process list.

5   If the "% CPU" in the table header is not already selected, click it twice to get a top-down (most to least) list of processes in terms of their CPU usage. The arrowhead that appears next to % CPU should point downward.

Process Name	% CPU ⌄	CPU Time	Threads	Idle Wake Ups	PID	User
Dead End (Not Responding)	199.5	2:38.48	4	0	1472	chris
Activity Monitor	0.8	2.02	6	0	1483	chris
cfprefsd	0.0	1.42	7	0	553	chris
loginwindow	0.0	0.51	2	1	1373	chris
identityservicesd	0.0	0.66	5	1	1418	chris

6   Look for the Dead End process by name. It should be at the top.

The name of an unresponsive application appears in red with a note declaring the application is "Not Responding." As you look at the Dead End process, notice how the CPU usage is close to 200 percent. You can see how an application can hijack your CPU, even though the application is not responding and appears to be doing nothing.

Note that the % CPU statistic can be misleading since it refers to the percentage of a CPU core being used. Current Mac computers have multiple cores and hyperthreading, so even "200%" CPU utilization is not fully using the computer's CPU power.

7   Choose Window > CPU Usage. This opens a window that displays how many cores your computer has and how busy each one is.

This example screenshot was taken on a computer with two physical cores, but hyper-threading allows each of those to do two things at once, giving it four virtual cores. As you can see, 200 percent is only half what it is capable of.

8 Select Dead End in the process list, and then click the quit process button (its icon is an "X" in an octagon) on the toolbar.

9 When asked to confirm, click Force Quit.

Note that Quit is the default option in the dialog that appears. However, since Dead End is not responding, it will not respond to a normal Quit command either. Therefore, you need to use Force Quit in order to stop this process from running.

Dead End disappears from the process list in the Activity Monitor window and from the Dock. After a few seconds, the CPU Usage window updates to show that utilization has decreased.

Unlike the Dock and Force Quit Applications window, Activity Monitor is capable of forcing background processes to quit. Background processes are generally programs that are launched automatically to provide some part of the system's functionality. Normally, you will not have to manage them explicitly, but in a few cases forcing them to quit is useful.

10 Select SystemUIServer in the process list. It may help to click Process Name in the table header. Remember its process ID (PID) number, shown in a column to the right.

SystemUIServer manages the menu items on the right side of the menu bar. Each menu item runs as a plug-in inside of the SystemUIServer, and if one of them locks up, it might be necessary to force SystemUIServer to quit.

11 With SystemUIServer selected, click the quit process button, and then watch the right side of the menu bar as you click Force Quit.

The right side of the menu bar goes blank, and then the menu items reappear. Examine your process list, and notice that SystemUIServer is running but with a different process ID than it had before.

What has happened is that the launchd process (another background process) has detected that SystemUIServer exited and has automatically relaunched it. launchd is responsible for starting and monitoring many of the system's background processes and restarts them if necessary.

Not all processes can be safely forced to quit this way. For example, forcing launchd to quit would leave the computer running in a degraded state. Lesson 27 discusses launchd in more detail.

12 Leave Activity Monitor open for the next section.

Open an App in 32-Bit Mode

Most applications that come with OS X Yosemite can run only in 64-bit mode. Some can run in either 32- or 64-bit mode but normally run in 64-bit mode. If you need to, you can run them in 32-bit mode (for example, in case they need to load a plug-in that runs only in 32-bit mode).

1 In Activity Monitor, choose View > Columns > Kind.

This adds a Kind column to the display, showing what mode each process is running in. Normally, all the processes run in 64-bit mode.

2 Open Dead End.

3 In Activity Monitor, find the Dead End process, and note that its Kind is also listed as 64 bit.

4 Quit Dead End.

5 In the Finder, select the Dead End app and choose File > Get Info (Command-I).

6 In the General section of the Info window, select "Open in 32-bit mode."

You will also see several other options; exactly which are available depends on the app, as well as whether you are using a Retina display.

7   Close the Info window, and reopen the Dead End app.

8   In Activity Monitor, find the new Dead End process.

Its Kind is now listed as 32 bit.

9   Quit Dead End.

View System Processes and Usage

1   In Activity Monitor, choose View > All Processes.

You see many more processes appear in the process list. In addition to the background processes within your user session (sometimes called "agents"), OS X has many background processes (sometimes called "daemons") running outside of your login session.

2   At the top of the Activity Monitor window, switch through the CPU, Memory, Energy, Disk, and Network tabs, and examine the information they display for each process, as well as the overall statistics at the bottom of the window.

3   If you are continuing to Exercise 19.2, leave Activity Monitor running because you will use it again.

Exercise 19.2
Troubleshoot Preferences

▶ **Prerequisite**

▶   You must have created the Chris Johnson account ("Exercise 5.1 Manage User Accounts" on page 145).

Most application preferences are created and stored for individual users in their personal Library folder. This compartmental approach can help when troubleshooting application issues. You'll learn how to set and restore a preference and see the effect of moving a preference file out of the ~/Library folder.

Create and Locate Preview Preferences

1   If necessary, log in as Chris Johnson.

2   Open Preview from the Applications folder.

3   Open Preview preferences by choosing Preview > Preferences (Command-Comma).

Note that the default setting for "When opening files" is "Open groups of files in the same window."

4   Select "Open all files in one window."

5   Close the Preferences window, and quit Preview.

6   In the Finder, open ~/Library.

Remember that since the user Library folder is invisible, the easiest way to navigate to this folder is to hold down the Option key and choose Go > Library.

Preview is a sandboxed app, so its real preference file is not in the ~/Library/Preferences folder but in a sandbox container. See "Reference 14.1 OS X File Structure" on page 401 for more details about sandbox containers.

If Preview stored its preferences in its private sandbox container, they would be in ~/Library/Preferences/Containers/com.apple.Preview/Data/Library/Preferences. But since Preview provides the Markup extension and needs to share its preferences with that extension, it stores its preferences in an application group container instead.

7   In the ~/Library folder, open the Group Containers folder.

There is a com.apple.Preview folder inside Group Containers. In this case, the application group has the same identifier as the application. If it didn't, you might have to use Spotlight to find the relevant group container.

8   Navigate down to Group Containers/com.apple.Preview/Library/Preferences, and select the com.apple.Preview.plist file.

9   Use Quick Look to view the preference file's contents (Command-Y).

The preferences setting you made is listed here, although in somewhat cryptic form.

```
com.apple.Preview.plist                    Open with TextEdit

<?xml version="1.0" encoding="UTF-8"?>
<!DOCTYPE plist PUBLIC "-//Apple//DTD PLIST 1.0//EN" "http://www.apple.com/DTDs/PropertyList-1.0.dtd">
<plist version="1.0">
<dict>
        <key>NSToolbar Configuration com.apple.NSColorPanel</key>
        <dict>
                <key>TB Is Shown</key>
                <integer>1</integer>
        </dict>
        <key>NSWindow Frame NSNavPanelAutosaveName</key>
        <string>284 262 712 448 0 0 1280 777 </string>
        <key>NSWindow Frame PVPreferences</key>
        <string>390 389 454 172 0 0 1280 777 </string>
        <key>PVGeneralSelectedPane</key>
        <integer>0</integer>
        <key>PVImageOpeningMode</key>
        <integer>0</integer>
</dict>
</plist>
```

10   Close the Quick Look window.

Disable and Restore Preferences

Moving an application's preferences file is not always enough to reset its preferences since the preferences agent (named cfprefsd) may remember its old settings. To make sure the preferences reset, quit the program and then the preferences agent, and then move the file.

1   If the Activity Monitor utility is not running, open it.

2   In Activity Monitor, choose View > My Processes.

3   Make sure Preview is not running (it may help to sort the process list by Process Name). If it is running, quit it.

4   Select cfprefsd in the process list, and then click the quit process button (the "X" in an octagon icon) in the toolbar.

5   In the confirmation dialog, click Quit.

A new `cfprefds` process will start automatically when it is needed. This sometimes happens so quickly that you may not see it vanish from the Activity Monitor list.

6   Switch to the Finder, and drag the com.apple.Preview.plist file to your desktop. Leave the Preferences folder open for later.

7   Open Preview again, and open its preferences (choose Preview > Preferences, or press Command-Comma).

The setting for "When opening files" has reset to its default of "Open groups of files in the same window."

8   Quit Preview.

9   Switch back to Activity Monitor, and quit `cfprefsd` again.

10 In the Finder, move the com.apple.Preview.plist file from your desktop back into the Preferences folder.

11 If you are notified that a newer item named com.apple.Preview.plist already exists, click Replace.

12 Open Preview again, and open its preferences.

This time your custom preference setting ("Open all files in one window") has been restored.

13 Quit Preview.

Manage Corrupted Preferences

OS X has some built-in features for dealing with corrupted preference files. You will explore what happens when a preference file becomes corrupt.

1 Use Activity Monitor to quit `cfprefsd` again.

2 In the Finder, Control-click the com.apple.Preview.plist file, and choose Open With > TextEdit from the shortcut menu.

Some .plist files are stored in an XML/text format, which TextEdit can edit like any other text document. This .plist file, however, is stored in a binary format TextEdit cannot fully display or edit. As a result, you see only part of the file's contents.

3 Add some new text anywhere in the document.

4 Quit TextEdit. Note that the changes are saved automatically.

5 Try to view the file using Quick Look (select it and press Command-Y).

By editing the file as if it were plain text, you have damaged its binary structure. As a result, Quick Look cannot display its contents and shows a generic view.

6 Close the Quick Look window.

7 Reopen Preview, and open its preferences.

Since the preferences file was damaged, the system has reset it, and the setting for "When opening files" has reset to its default of "Open groups of files in the same window."

8   Quit Preview.

9   Use Quick Look to view com.apple.Preview.plist again.

Preview has rewritten its preference file, removing the corruption you introduced.

Exercise 19.3
Examine Application Diagnostics

▶ **Prerequisites**

▶   You must have created the Local Admin ("Exercise 2.1 Configure a New OS X System for Exercises" on page 60 or "Exercise 2.2 Configure an Existing OS X System for Exercises" on page 63) and Chris Johnson ("Exercise 5.1 Manage User Accounts" on page 145) accounts.

▶   You must have performed "Exercise 19.1 Force Applications to Quit" on page 603.

The Console utility is the primary tool in OS X for viewing system logs. In this exercise, you will use it to view application diagnostic logs and to search the system log for application events.

View a Diagnostic Report

1   If necessary, log out as Chris Johnson.

2   Log in as Local Admin.

Some of the log files you'll examine in this exercise are readable only by administrators.

3   Open the Console utility.

Console is the primary tool in OS X for viewing log files. Its Log List sidebar lets you view specific log files or the catchall All Messages.

4   In the Log List sidebar, examine the entries under User Diagnostic Reports and System Diagnostic Reports. If necessary, click the disclosure triangles next to each one to show the individual reports.

User Diagnostics Reports may be turned off if there are no report logs under the Local Admin account.

A separate log file is created each time a program crashes or is forced to quit while hung, so you should have a number of entries from forcing Dead End to quit in "Exercise 19.1 Force Applications to Quit" on page 603. Note that these are listed under System Diagnostic Reports, even though it was Chris Johnson who forced them to quit.

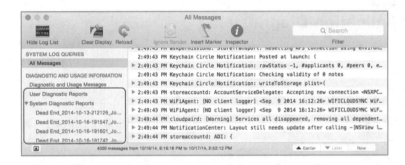

5   Select one of the diagnostic reports. It includes detailed information about what the program was doing when it crashed or hung.

Create a Custom Search Query

You can also use Console to search for particular types of events in the computer's logs.

1   Choose File > New System Log Query (Command-Option-N).

2   Change the search name to **Crashes**.

3   Click the "Message" and "contains" pop-up menus, and look at the options for filtering messages.

4   Leave the pop-up menus set to "Message" and "contains," and enter **crash** in the field to the right.

5   Click OK.

A new window opens showing entries in the system log that contain "crash." Depending on your computer's history, there might not be any messages to show.

Your custom query is also added to the Log List sidebar, in the System Log Queries section.

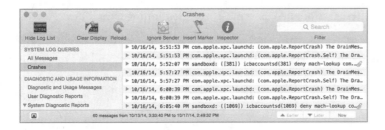

6   Control-click the Crashes entry in the sidebar, and choose Edit Log Database Query from the shortcut menu.

7   Change the search name to **Crashes & Hangs**.

8   Option-click the Add (+) button to the right of the "Message contains crash" line.

Holding Option makes it create an "or" clause; that is, it makes it display entries that match one search criterion *or* the other.

9 Change the new search clause to "Message contains `hang`."

This search now includes all messages containing the text "hang." Unfortunately, this also matches other words, such as "change," "changed," and so on.

10 Without holding down the Option key, click the Add (+) button to the right of the "Message contains hang" line.

11 Set the new search clause to "Message does not contain `change`."

12 Click OK.

The new search criteria are applied, and messages mentioning either "crash" or "hang" are displayed.

This custom search query is stored in Local Admin's preferences and is available in the Console sidebar any time you want to check for recent crash and hang events.

13 Quit Console.

14 Log out as Local Admin.

Network
Configuration

Lesson 20

Network Essentials

The capability to share information between computers across a network has always been important. During the early years of personal computer development, vendors designed their own proprietary local network systems. Apple was no exception with its implementation of AppleTalk and LocalTalk network standards for file sharing and network printing. Yet although these vendor-specific technologies were suitable for private networks, they didn't allow for direct communication between dissimilar networks. Special hardware or software had to be put in place to translate from one vendor's network to another.

Around the same time, researchers were working at the behest of various U.S. organizations to create a wide area network (WAN) standard for military and governmental use. From this research was born the Internet protocol suite known as TCP/IP. The marriage of the Transmission Control Protocol (TCP) and the Internet Protocol (IP) became the universal language that allows computers to communicate on the Internet. This standard became so pervasive that nearly every network today, from small local networks all the way up to the largest long-distance network on Earth, the Internet, is based on the TCP/IP suite.

It should come as no surprise, then, that OS X includes a robust TCP/IP implementation. In fact, the first computer systems to popularize the use of TCP/IP were UNIX systems. Thus, much of the TCP/IP software built into every version of OS X is based on open source UNIX software that was established long before OS X ever existed as a product from Apple.

In this lesson, you will configure basic settings for both Ethernet and Wi-Fi networks. Before that, though, you must have a fundamental understanding of core network concepts, which the first part of this lesson is devoted to.

GOALS

▶ Understand fundamental TCP/IP network concepts

▶ Configure and monitor basic network settings

▶ Connect to a Wi-Fi network

Reference 20.1
Network Concepts

Properly configuring and troubleshooting networking on any operating system requires a basic understanding of fundamental network concepts. Due to the widespread adoption of standardized network technology, the following network overview applies to nearly any operating system, OS X included. Basic network terminology is covered first, followed by an overview of the processes involved in actual data delivery across a network.

Network Terminology

It's best to explore networking from a layered perspective. In fact, there is an established seven-layer model used to describe network technologies: the Open Systems Interconnection reference model (known as the OSI model). Exploring networking using the OSI model goes well beyond the scope of this guide.

> **MORE INFO** ▶ For more details on the OSI model for describing computer networks, refer to the Wikipedia entry http://en.wikipedia.org/wiki/OSI_model.

Consequently, networking concepts will be presented in a more simplistic abstraction of three basic elements:

▶ Network interface—The *network interface* is the medium through which network data flows. Network interfaces can be physical or virtual. The most common physical network interfaces for computers are Ethernet and 802.11 wireless networking, which is most commonly known as Wi-Fi. Virtual network interfaces are also available that can be used to increase the functionality of the physical interface: for example, a virtual private network (VPN) that uses the existing physical network interface to provide a secure connection without the need for a dedicated physical interface.

▶ Network protocol—A *protocol* defines a set of standard rules used for data representation, signaling, authentication, or error detection across network interfaces. Primarily, protocols are designed to ensure that all data is communicated properly and completely. Specific protocols have a narrow focus, so often multiple protocols are combined or layered to provide a complete network solution. For example, the combined TCP/IP protocol suite provides only for the addressing and end-to-end transport of data across the Internet; dozens of other protocols are required for something as simple as checking your email or browsing a website.

▶ Network service—In the context of network preferences, the term *network service* describes a configuration assigned to a network interface. For example, in the OS X Network preferences, you will see the Wi-Fi service listed; this represents the connection settings for the Wi-Fi network interface. A fundamental feature of OS X is the ability to support multiple network services, or connections, for each individual network interface, be it physical or virtual.

NOTE ▶ A different definition of *network service* is sometimes used in Lesson 23 "Network Services" and Lesson 24 "Host Sharing and Personal Firewall". There, a network service is information provided on the network by a server for use by clients. Common examples in these lessons include file-sharing services, messaging services, and collaboration services. Often a specific set of protocols is used to define how the particular service works.

Simplifying computer network technology to only three distinct elements does not provide a detailed abstraction, but it still shows clearly how each is related to the others. When a network interface, service, or protocol is created, it is often put through a review process before it's deemed a network standard. Standards committees are formed with members from multiple network organizations and vendors to ensure that new network standards remain interoperable with existing network standards. Most networking technologies in use today have been ratified by some standards body, so you may often come across an interface, protocol, or service labeled as a "standard."

MAC Address

The Media Access Control (MAC) address is used to uniquely identify a physical network interface on a local network. Each physical network interface has at least one MAC address associated with it.

Because the most common network interface is Ethernet, people often refer to MAC addresses as Ethernet addresses. Still, nearly every other network interface type also uses some type of MAC address for unique identification. This includes, but isn't limited to, Wi-Fi, Bluetooth, and FireWire.

A MAC address is usually a 48-bit number represented by six groups of two-digit hexadecimal numbers separated by colons. For example, a typical MAC address would look something like this: 00:1C:B3:D7:2F:99. The first three number groups make up the organizationally unique identifier (OUI), and the last three number groups identify the network device itself. In other words, you can use the first three number groups of a MAC address to identify who made the network device.

MORE INFO ▶ The Institute of Electrical and Electronics Engineers (IEEE) maintains a searchable database of publicly listed OUIs on its website: http://standards.ieee.org/develop/regauth/oui/public.html.

IP Address

Communicating with computers on both local and remote networks requires an IP address. IP addresses, unlike MAC addresses, are not permanently tied to a network interface. Instead, they are assigned to the network interface based on the local network it's connected to. This means if you have a portable computer, every new network you connect to will probably require a new IP address. If necessary, you can assign multiple IP addresses to each network interface, but this approach is often only used for computers that are providing network services.

There are currently two standards for IP addresses: IPv4 and IPv6. IPv4 was the first widely used IP addressing scheme and is the most common today. An IPv4 address is a 32-bit number represented by four groups of three-digit numbers, also known as octets, separated by periods. Each octet has a value between 0 and 255. For example, a typical IPv4 address would look something like this: 10.1.45.186.

With IPv4, a little over 4 billon unique addresses exist. This may seem like a lot, but considering how many new network-ready devices come out, and the number of people who want to own multiple network-ready gadgets, this number isn't really big enough. For the time being, the available IPv4 addresses are extended by using network routers that can share a single routable, or "real world," IPv4 address across a range of reusable private network addresses. This is how most home networks are configured, but it is only a temporary solution for what's to come next.

The successor to IPv4 is IPv6, but because IPv4 is so much a part of the backbone of the Internet, the transition to IPv6 has been slow. The main advantage to IPv6 is a much larger address space—so large, in fact, that every person on Earth could have roughly 1.2×10^{19} copies of the entire IPv4 address range. This may appear to be a ridiculous number of IP addresses, but the design goal of IPv6 was to eliminate the need for private addressing and allow for easier address reassignment and changing to a new network.

An IPv6 address is a 128-bit number that is presented in eight groups of four-digit hexadecimal numbers separated by colons. Hexadecimal numbers use a base-16 digit system, so after the number 9 you use the letters A through F. For example, a typical IPv6 address would look something like this: 2C01:0EF9:0000:0000:0000:0000:142D:57AB. Long strings of zeros in an IPv6 address can be abbreviated using a double colon, resulting in an address more like this: 2C01:0EF9::142D:57AB.

Subnet Mask

The computer uses the subnet mask to determine the IPv4 address range of the local network. Networks based on the IPv6 protocol do not require subnet masks. A subnet mask is similar to an IPv4 address in that it's a 32-bit number arranged in four groups of octets. The computer applies the subnet mask to its own IP address to determine the local network's address range. The nonzero bits in a subnet mask (typically 255) correspond to the portion of the IP address that determines which network the address is on. The zero bits correspond to the portion of the IP address that differs between hosts on the same network.

For example, assuming your computer has an IP address of 10.1.5.3 and a commonly used subnet mask of 255.255.255.0, the local network is defined as hosts that have IP addresses ranging from 10.1.5.1 to 10.1.5.254.

> **MORE INFO ▶** Another way of writing the subnet mask is known as Classless Inter-Domain Routing CIDR notation. This is written as the IP address, a slash, and then the number of 1 bits in the subnet mask. The previous subnet example would be 10.1.5.3/24. You can find out more about CIDR notation from Wikipedia: http://en.wikipedia.org/wiki/Classless_Inter-Domain_Routing.

Whenever the computer attempts to communicate with another network device, it applies the subnet mask to the destination IP address of the other device to determine if it's on the local network as well. If so, the computer attempts to directly access the other network device. If not, the other device is clearly on another network, and the computer sends all communications bound for that other device to the router address.

Router Address

Routers are network devices that manage connections between separate networks; as their name implies, they route network traffic between the networks they bridge. Routing tables are maintained by routers to determine where network traffic goes. Even if a router is presented with traffic destined for a network that the router is unaware of, it still routes the traffic to another router that it thinks is closer to the final destination. Thus, routers literally are the brains of the Internet.

To reach computers beyond the local network your computer needs to be configured with the IP address of the router that connects the local network with another network or, more commonly in residential situations, an Internet service provider. Typically the router's address is at the beginning of the local address range, and it's always in the same subnet. Using the previous example, assuming your computer has an IP address of 10.1.5.3 and a commonly used subnet mask of 255.255.255.0, the local network IP address range would be 10.1.5.0 to 10.1.5.255, and the router address would most likely be 10.1.5.1.

TCP

TCP is the primary protocol used to facilitate end-to-end data connectivity between two IP devices. TCP is the preferred transport mechanism for many Internet services because it guarantees reliable and in-order delivery of data. In other words, IP provides network addressing and data routing, and TCP ensures that the data arrives at its destination complete. The combination of these two protocols encompasses the TCP/IP suite, commonly known as the Internet protocol suite.

The TCP/IP protocol suite chops continuous data streams into many individual packets of information before they are sent across the network. This is because IP networks use packet-switching technology to route and transmit data. Almost all digital networking technologies are packet-based, because this provides efficient transport for network connections that aren't always reliable. Remember, the TCP/IP protocol was originally designed with the military in mind, so packet-based network technology is ideal because it's designed to work around communications link failure. This is why sophisticated routing hardware was originally developed for TCP/IP networks: so that data could be literally rerouted and re-sent should a network link go down.

A lesser used protocol known as User Datagram Protocol (UDP) is also attached to the TCP/IP suite. UDP is a simpler protocol that does not guarantee the reliability or ordering of data sent across networks. This may seem like a poor choice for networking, but in some cases UDP is preferred because it provides better performance than TCP. Examples of network services that use UDP include Domain Name System (DNS), media streaming, voice over IP (VoIP), and online gaming. These services have been designed to tolerate lost or out-of-order data so they can benefit from UDP's increased performance.

> **MORE INFO** ▶ For more information on the Internet protocol suite, refer to this Wikipedia entry: http://en.wikipedia.org/wiki/internet_protocol_suite.

Reference 20.2
Networks in Action

Manually assigning an IP address, a subnet mask, and a router address is technically all that is needed to configure a computer to use TCP/IP-based networking on both local area networks (LANs) and wide area networks (WANs). Yet two other network services are almost always involved in basic network functionality: Dynamic Host Configuration Protocol (DHCP) and DNS. These two services, combined with TCP/IP, characterize core network functionality that provides the foundation for nearly any network service.

LAN Traffic

Most LANs use some form of wired or wireless connection. Once the network interface has been established, TCP/IP networking must be configured, either manually or via DHCP. Once both these steps are complete, network communication can begin.

TCP/IP packets are encased inside Ethernet frames to travel across the local network. The TCP/IP packet includes the originating IP and destination IP addresses along with the data to be sent. The network device applies the subnet mask setting to determine if the destination IP address is on the local network. If so, it consults its Address Resolution Protocol (ARP) table to see if it knows the MAC address corresponding to the destination IP address. Each network host maintains and continuously updates an ARP table of known MAC addresses that correspond to IP addresses on the local network. If the MAC address is not listed yet, it broadcasts an ARP request to the local network asking the destination device to reply with its MAC address, and adds the reply to its ARP table for next time. Once the MAC address is determined, an outgoing Ethernet frame, encasing the TCP/IP packet, is sent using the destination MAC address.

The other network device likely returns some information as well, using the same technique of transferring TCP/IP packets inside MAC-addressed Ethernet frames. This goes on and on for thousands of packets every second to complete a data stream. For standard Ethernet the maximum frame size is only 1500 bytes (that's roughly 1.5 kilobytes, or 0.0015 megabytes), so you can imagine how many Ethernet frames are necessary to transmit even a small file.

WAN Traffic

Sending data over a WAN differs only in that data is sent through one or more network routers to reach its intended destination. WANs exist in all shapes and sizes, from a small WAN perhaps used to connect separate LANs in a large building all the way up to the biggest and most popular WAN, the Internet.

Initially, transferring data across a WAN is similar to transferring data on a LAN. After all, the first stop for the data destined for the WAN is at the network router on the local network. The network device prepares the packets as before by encasing the TCP/IP packets inside Ethernet frames. Once again, the subnet mask is applied to the destination IP address to determine if the address is on the local network. In this case, the network device determines that the destination is not on the local network, so it sends the data to the router. Because the router is on the local network, the transmission between the local network client and the router is identical to standard LAN traffic.

Once the router receives the Ethernet-encased TCP/IP packets, it examines the destination IP address and uses a routing table to determine the next closest destination for this packet. This almost always involves sending the packet to another router closer to the destination. In fact, only the last router in the path sends the data to the destination network device.

Network routers also often perform some sort of hardware interface conversion, as WAN network links are rarely standard copper Ethernet connections. The router strips the Ethernet container away from the original TCP/IP packet and then rewraps it in another container that is appropriate for the WAN connection. Obviously, the final router has to prepare the TCP/IP packet for the last leg of the journey on the destination device's local network by rewrapping it in an Ethernet frame addressed to the destination's MAC address.

In most cases, network data is transferred back and forth several times to establish a complete connection. Remember, these packet sizes are very small. The default packet size for Internet traffic is also 1500 bytes with a maximum packet size of 65,535 bytes for most TCP/IP connections.

Network routers are highly optimized devices that can easily handle thousands of data packets every second, so for small amounts of data many WAN connections "feel" as fast as LAN connections. Conversely, a lot of latency is introduced from all the different routers and network connections involved in transferring data across a WAN, so often sending large amounts of data across a WAN is much slower than across a LAN. Thus, many users' favorite time-wasting computer practice was born: waiting for an Internet download or upload.

DNS

Most people are bad at remembering strings of seemingly arbitrary numbers used to define addresses, so additional technology is often implemented to help users find addresses. Even the simplest mobile phones feature a contact list so users don't have to remember phone numbers. For TCP/IP networks, DNS makes network addressing much more approachable to normal humans.

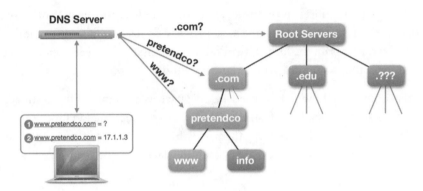

In essence, DNS is a worldwide network of domain servers with the task of maintaining human-friendly host names used to easily locate specific network IP addresses. If you've spent any time at all on the Internet, you're already familiar with the DNS naming convention: For example, the Apple website is located at www.apple.com. Any network device can have a host name, but only those network devices providing a service that needs to be easily located need to have host name entries on a DNS server. Devices providing shared services, such as printers and server computers, are the most common devices to have DNS entries.

The hierarchical DNS naming convention relates directly to the hierarchical structure of the DNS domain architecture. As you know, DNS names are broken into labels separated by periods. Each label represents a different level, or domain, of the DNS hierarchy.

The top of the DNS hierarchy is the root or "." domain. The names that are part of the root domain are the familiar abbreviations at the end of nearly every Internet resource. Common examples are .com, .edu, .gov, and others, including various country codes. These top-level domains (TLDs) are hosted by a consortium of commercial and governmental organizations.

Below the TLDs, individual organizations or users host or rent their own DNS domains. For example, Apple hosts several DNS servers that are known by the TLD servers to maintain the apple.com domain. Apple can host an unlimited number of host names inside the apple.com domain. Apple can also create unlimited names in the domain by preceding "apple.com" with any text. Examples include www.apple.com, training.apple.com and developer.apple.com.

When a local network device needs to resolve a DNS name into the corresponding IP address, it sends the name query to the IP address of a DNS server. The IP address for a DNS server is usually configured along with the other TCP/IP address information for the network device. The DNS server searches its local and cached name records first. If the requested name isn't found locally, the server queries other domain servers in the DNS hierarchy.

This process may take a while, so DNS servers temporarily cache any names they have recently resolved to provide a quicker response for future requests. Querying a DNS server to resolve an IP address given a known host name is called a forward lookup, whereas querying a DNS server to resolve a host name from a known IP address is called a reverse lookup. When initially configured, network clients query the DNS server with a reverse lookup of its own IP address to determine if the network client has its own DNS name.

> **MORE INFO** ▸ For more information on DNS, refer to this Wikipedia entry: http://en.wikipedia.org/wiki/Domain_Name_System.

> **MORE INFO** ▸ Bonjour is a name discovery service that uses a name space similar to DNS. Bonjour is covered in Lesson 23 "Network Services".

DHCP

Although not required to provide network functionality, DHCP is used by nearly all network clients to automatically acquire preliminary TCP/IP configuration. In some situations, an administrative user may still choose to manually enter TCP/IP networking configuration information. This is often the case with network devices that are providing network services. However, manually configuring multitudes of network clients is tedious work that is subject to human error. Thus, even on rigorously managed networks, DHCP is still widely used to configure network clients.

> **NOTE** ▸ DHCP is specifically designed to assign IPv4 addressing; IPv6 addressing is handled automatically via other mechanisms.

> **NOTE** ▸ A precursor to DHCP is Bootstrap Protocol (BOOTP). DHCP is backward compatible with BOOTP but provides greater functionality and reliability.

DHCP Server

Server responds if
address available

Server responds if
address available

Client requests
IP address

Client requests
IP address

IP address:
10.0.0.210

IP address:
10.0.0.211

A DHCP server is required to provide the service. On many networks, the network routers provide the DHCP service, but in some cases a dedicated server or network appliance can be used for this purpose. When a network device becomes active on the network, it first negotiates a link with the hardware interface, and then sends out a broadcast to the local network requesting DHCP information. Because the new network client doesn't yet have an IP address, it uses the network interface's MAC address for identification.

If a DHCP server that is listening has available addresses, it sends back a reply to the client with TCP/IP configuration information. At a minimum, this information includes IP address, subnet mask, router, and a DHCP lease time that defines how long the client can retain the address before it's given away. Ancillary DHCP information often also includes DNS configuration.

MORE INFO ▶ For more information on DHCP, refer to this Wikipedia entry: http://en.wikipedia.org/wiki/Dhcp.

Reference 20.3
Basic Network Configuration

Initial networking configuration is handled by Setup Assistant, which runs the first time you start up a new Mac or a fresh OS X system installation. Setup Assistant makes it easy for even a novice user to configure network settings. Yet even if you choose not to set up networking during the initial system setup process, the Mac automatically enables any active network interface, including connecting to unrestricted wireless networks, and attempts to configure TCP/IP via DHCP. Consequently, for many users OS X does not require any initial network configuration at all.

MORE INFO ▶ Advanced network configuration techniques are covered in Lesson 21 "Advanced Network Configuration".

Network Preferences

If network changes are required after initial setup, you can still use Network Setup Assistant to help guide you through the network configuration process. You can access Network Setup Assistant by clicking the "Assist me" button at the bottom of Network preferences.

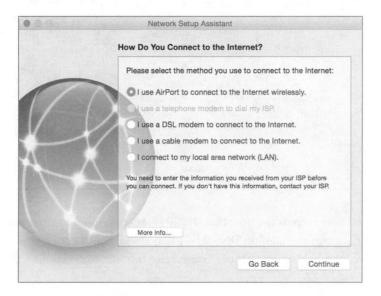

Although this tool is helpful for novice users, get familiar with all network configuration options so you're prepared for any potential network situation or troubleshooting issue. All network preferences and configuration windows are consolidated into a unified interface. Thus, all network settings can be found in Network preferences. Note that Network preferences are available only to administrative users. A standard user attempting to open Network preferences will notice a lock in the bottom-right corner. However, because DHCP is enabled by default for Ethernet and Wi-Fi interfaces, for most situations network configuration is automatic.

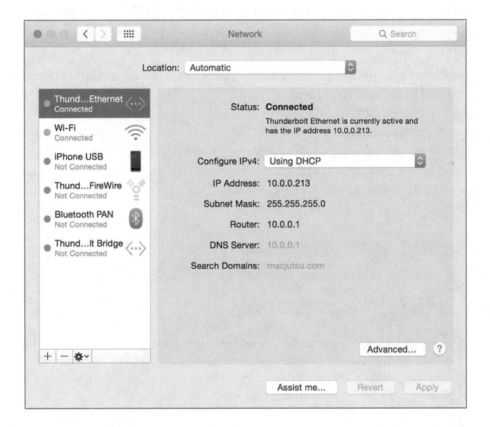

NOTE ▶ In the preceding screenshot, note that DHCP is also providing configuration for the DNS server. Recognize that if no DNS server IP address is configured, your Mac cannot resolve DNS host names. Thus, in most cases Internet connections will fail.

Basic Wi-Fi Configuration
Wireless networking, also known by the technical specification 802.11 or the more common "Wi-Fi," has become the dominant local network connectivity standard. Ethernet is

certainly still popular, but Wi-Fi has cut the cord by allowing easy network access for an ever-increasing number of portable devices. Apple made basic Wi-Fi network management a breeze with automatic Wi-Fi network discovery and the Wi-Fi status menu. These Wi-Fi setup mechanisms give nonadministrative users access to the most commonly needed Wi-Fi network settings.

OS X always remembers Wi-Fi networks that were previously connected, by default. Thus, if you start up or wake a portable Mac, it will attempt to locate and reconnect to any previously connected Wi-Fi networks. If an appropriate Wi-Fi network isn't found, you will need to manually select a new one from the Wi-Fi status menu near the top-right corner of the display. When you select this menu, the Wi-Fi background process automatically scans for any advertised networks that are within range so you can choose among them.

A service set identifier, or SSID, identifies a Wi-Fi network's name and associated configuration information. An administrator of the devices providing Wi-Fi services sets the network's name and configuration settings. OS X uses the information in the SSID configuration to automatically establish Wi-Fi network communications.

Aside from Wi-Fi network names, the most important indicator this menu shows is the relative strength of any Wi-Fi network, as indicated by the number of black bars compared to gray bars. The more black bars displayed, the greater the strength of the Wi-Fi signal.

Wi-Fi Authentication

If you select an open wireless network, the Mac immediately connects, but if you select a secure wireless network, as indicated by the small lock icon, you have to enter the network password. When you select a secure network, in most cases the system automatically negotiates the authentication type, and for many networks you need only enter a common shared Wi-Fi password.

OS X supports the most common Wi-Fi authentication standards, including Wired Equivalent Privacy (WEP), Wi-Fi Protected Access (WPA), and Wi-Fi Protected Access II (WPA2). This includes support for WPA/WPA2 in both their personal and enterprise forms. Essentially WPA/WPA2 Personal uses a common shared password for all users of the Wi-Fi network, whereas WPA/WPA2 Enterprise includes 802.1X authentication, which allows for per-user password access to the Wi-Fi network. WPA/WPA2 Enterprise authentication is covered in the next section of this lesson.

> **NOTE ▶** It is well known that WEP is an easily compromised security protocol and should be avoided. Thus, WPA/WPA2 are preferred protocols.

If you join a WEP or WPA/WPA2 Personal Wi-Fi network, the system automatically saves the passwords to the System keychain. This is what allows the Mac to automatically reconnect to the Wi-Fi network immediately after startup or waking up. Also, because the password is saved to the System keychain, all users can access the wireless network without needing to reenter the password.

> **MORE INFO ▶** Details of the Keychain system are covered in Lesson 7 "System Security".

Automatic WPA Enterprise Configuration

If you join and authenticate to a wireless network that uses WPA or WPA2 Enterprise, it's implied that the authentication is handled via 802.1X. Thus, joining this type of network automatically creates an 802.1X service configuration.

As you can see in this screenshot, when 802.1X is used, you must enter both a username and password to authenticate the connection. You may also be prompted with a server certificate verification dialog. You must accept this certificate to continue, but completing the configuration requires administrative authentication.

A user with administrative rights is required because this will add the wireless authentication server certificate to the System keychain. Assuming the server configuration doesn't change, you will only have to accept this certificate once per system. Future connections to this wireless network will require only that users enter their normal authentication credentials.

Wi-Fi Status Menu Options

In some cases, to increase security, wireless networks may not advertise their availability. You can connect to these hidden wireless networks (also called closed networks) as long as you know their network name (or SSID) by choosing Join Other Network from the Wi-Fi status menu. In the dialog you can enter all the appropriate information to join the hidden wireless network.

If you are unable to connect to a standard wireless network, you can create an ad hoc wireless network using your Mac computer's Wi-Fi connection to share files wirelessly with other computers. Choose Create Network from the Wi-Fi status menu and then enter the wireless network information that will be used to connect to your ad hoc network.

NOTE ▶ Leaving an ad hoc network enabled on your Mac is a security risk. To prevent your Mac from connecting to the ad hoc network, turn off the Wi-Fi hardware or choose another wireless network from the Wi-Fi status menu.

NOTE ▶ Do not confuse the creation of an ad hoc Wi-Fi network with the new OS X AirDrop Wi-Fi sharing feature. Creating a Wi-Fi network has permanence, and it can be used by other non-OS X systems. AirDrop allows for only temporary connections between OS X systems. You can find out more about AirDrop in Lesson 24 "Host Sharing and Personal Firewall".

Exercise 20.1
Connect to a Wi-Fi Network

▶ **Prerequisites**

- ▶ You must have created the Local Admin ("Exercise 2.1 Configure a New OS X System for Exercises" on page 60 or "Exercise 2.2 Configure an Existing OS X System for Exercises" on page 63) and Chris Johnson ("Exercise 5.1 Manage User Accounts" on page 145) accounts.

- ▶ Your computer must have a Wi-Fi interface, and you must have access to an available Wi-Fi network that you are not already connected to.

OS X makes joining a wireless network simple. In this exercise, you will examine the process of finding and joining a wireless network.

Verify Your Network Settings

1 If necessary, log in as Chris Johnson.

2 Open System Preferences, and select the Network pane.

3 If necessary, click the padlock, and authenticate as Local Admin.

4 Select the Wi-Fi service from the sidebar. If you do not have Wi-Fi service, you cannot perform this exercise.

5 If necessary, click the Turn Wi-Fi On button.

6 If necessary, select "Show Wi-Fi status in menu bar."

7 Click Advanced.

8 Examine the options available on the Wi-Fi tab.

The Preferred Networks list allows you to control which networks this computer joins automatically and includes an option to add networks to this list as your computer joins them. You can also control whether administrative authorization is required for certain operations.

9 Click OK.

10 If you made any changes, click Apply.

11 Click the Wi-Fi status menu.

A list of visible networks in your area is shown. Note that it may take a few seconds for your computer to discover all the local networks.

Note that this list is also available in Network preferences, in the Network Name pop-up menu.

If you are performing these exercises in a class, the instructor provides you with the name of the network to join (and, if necessary, security information for it).

If the network you want to join is shown in the list, follow the steps in the section "Option 1: Join a Visible Network" on page 641. If it is not shown, the network may be configured as invisible (or "SSID broadcast disabled"), in which case you need to follow the steps in the section "Option 2: Join an Invisible Network" on page 641.

Option 1: Join a Visible Network

1   Choose the network you want to join from the Wi-Fi status menu.

If the wireless network is encrypted, you are prompted for the network password. Selecting the "Remember this network" option allows your computer to automatically reconnect to this network whenever it is available.

2   If you are prompted, enter the network password, and click Join.

Skip ahead to the "Verify Your Connection" on page 642 section.

Option 2: Join an Invisible Network

1   Choose Join Other Network from the Wi-Fi status menu.

2   Enter the network's name (SSID)

3   If the network is encrypted, you need to know its encryption type as well as the password. Choose the encryption type from the Security pop-up menu, and then enter the network password. Selecting the "Remember this network" option allows your computer to automatically reconnect to this network whenever it is available.

4 Enter the security information, and click Join.

Verify Your Connection

If OS X detects that the wireless network you have joined is connected to a captive portal, it opens a window showing the portal's sign-in page.

1 If a captive portal window appears, follow its instructions to get full network access. A captive portal might require you to agree to its terms of service, authenticate, watch an advertisement, or meet other requirements before it allows you full network access.

2 In Network preferences, look at the status indicator next to the Wi-Fi service.

The status indicator will be green if the computer is connected to a network and has address information configured. If the indicator is not green, you did not successfully join the network and may have to troubleshoot the connection.

3 Click the Wi-Fi status menu.

It shows a number of arcs to indicate the signal strength of the wireless network. If all the arcs are light gray, you are not joined to a wireless network or are receiving only a weak signal.

4 Option-click the Wi-Fi status menu.

The menu opens and displays additional information about your connection, including the current wireless speed ("Transmit rate") and signal strength (RSSI; note that –50 is a very strong signal, and –100 is a very weak one).

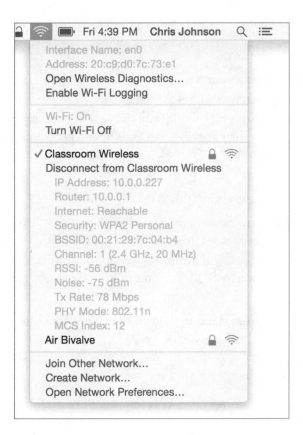

Exercise 20.2
Monitor Network Connectivity

> **Prerequisite**
>
> ▶ You must have created the Chris Johnson account ("Exercise 5.1 Manage User Accounts" on page 145).

In this exercise you will break your primary network connection and observe how that change is reflected in the Network pane of System Preferences. The Network pane dynamically updates as network connectivity changes, so it is a valuable tool for troubleshooting connectivity issues.

Monitor Connectivity via Network Preferences

The Network Status view of Network preferences shows the status of all active configured network interfaces. User-initiated connections such as PPP and VPN are also listed. Users can view the Network Status pane to verify their active connections in order of priority.

1 If necessary, log in as Chris Johnson.

2 If necessary, open System Preferences, and select the Network pane.

Notice the status of your network connections on the left side of the window. The green status indicators show which network services are active, and their order shows their priority. Whichever service is at the top of the list is your current "primary" service, and it is used for all Internet connectivity. Make a note of which service is currently the primary service.

If you do not have any services with green status indicators, you do not have a network connection and cannot perform this exercise.

3 Select the current primary service.

4 Watch the status indicators and service order as you disable the connection for your primary network service. How to do this depends on what type of service it is:

▶ If it is an Ethernet service, unplug the Ethernet cable from your computer.

▶ If it is a Wi-Fi service, click the Turn Wi-Fi Off button.

▶ If it is a dial-in or mobile broadband service, click the Disconnect button.

When the service is disabled, its status indicator turns red or yellow, and it drops down in the service order. If you have another active service, it becomes the new primary service.

The detailed view on the right also changes to indicate why the service is disabled.

5   Again, watch the status indicators and service order as you reenable the connection. How to do this depends on what type of service it is:

▶   If it is an Ethernet service, plug the Ethernet cable back into your computer.

▶   If it is a Wi-Fi service, click the Turn Wi-Fi On button, and if necessary choose the network from the Network Name pop-up menu.

▶   If it is a dial-in or mobile broadband service, click the Connect button.

It may take a few seconds for the network connection to appear and the service to reconfigure itself. When the service becomes fully active, its status indicator turns green, and it rises to the top of the service list.

Lesson 21
Advanced Network Configuration

A strong understanding of network fundamentals is required to properly configure advanced network settings without error. Consequently, this lesson builds on the network essentials topics covered in the previous lesson. This lesson focuses squarely on the unique and powerful OS X user interface for managing network configuration, Network preferences. First, this lesson presents an overview of the OS X network configuration architecture and supported network interfaces and protocols. You will then dive deeper into the more advanced network configuration options.

Reference 21.1
Network Locations

Similar to how applications are designed to save information to any number of individual documents, OS X enables you to save network settings to any number of individual network configurations, known as network locations. A network location contains all network interface, service, and protocol settings, allowing you to configure as many unique network locations as you need for different situations. For example, you could create one network location for home and a different one for work. Each location would contain all the appropriate settings for that location's network state.

A network location can contain any number of active network service interfaces. This allows you to define a single location with multiple network connections. The system automatically prioritizes multiple service interfaces based on a service order that you set. Details about using multiple network service interfaces are covered in the "Multiple Simultaneous Interfaces" on page 656 section later in this lesson.

It is not necessary to add new network locations to change network settings, but it is more convenient, as you can easily switch back to the previous network location should you make a mistake. Thus, creating additional network locations is an essential network troubleshooting technique. Also, because OS X always requires one active network location, if you ever want to temporarily turn off networking, you have to create a new location with all the network service interfaces disabled.

Configuring Network Locations

The default network location on OS X is called Automatic. Despite this, this first location is no more automatic than any other network location you create. The initial location is simply called Automatic to indicate that it attempts to automatically initialize any network service interface to establish a TCP/IP connection via DHCP; but all network locations, regardless of their name, attempt this as well.

To configure network locations, open Network preferences by choosing Apple menu > System Preferences, and then clicking the Network icon. You may have to click the lock icon in the bottom-left corner and authenticate as an administrative user to unlock Network preferences. Choose Edit Locations from the Location pop-up menu to reveal the interface for editing network locations.

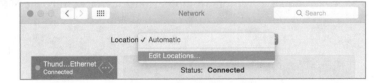

To add a new location with default settings, click the Add (+) button, and then enter a new name for the location. Or you can duplicate an existing location by selecting its name from the Locations list and clicking the Action button (gear icon) and then choosing Duplicate Location from the pop-up menu. Finally, double-clicking a location name allows you to rename it.

When you are finished making location changes, click Done to return to Network preferences. Network preferences automatically loads the newly created location but won't apply the location settings to the system. If you want to work with another location, simply choose it from the Location pop-up menu, and Network preferences loads it but won't apply it to the system.

You may have noticed that the network settings are different from all the other system preferences in that you must click Apply to activate the new settings. This allows you to easily prepare new network locations and services without disrupting the current network configuration.

TIP ▶ If you make a mistake at any time using Network preferences, click Revert to return to the current active network configuration.

Changing Network Locations

Though you can certainly choose and apply a different network location from Network preferences, only administrative users have this ability, as normal users do not have access to Network preferences. Conversely, all users (including standard users) can quickly and easily change the network location by choosing Apple menu > Location > location name.

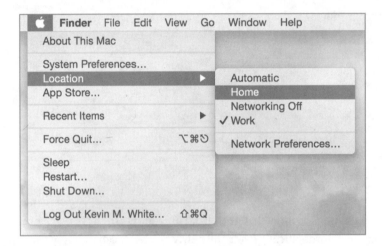

This applies the selected network location. Keep in mind that changing locations may interrupt network connections. Once a network location is selected, it remains active until another location is selected. Even if other users log in to the Mac or the Mac is restarted the selected network location remains active.

> **NOTE** ▶ The Location menu option does not appear in the Apple menu if only one network location exists. Thus, from an administrative perspective, if you want to configure the system so standard users cannot change network locations, do not configure additional network locations.

Reference 21.2
Network Interfaces and Protocols

Mac hardware has a long history of providing built-in network connectivity. Apple started including Ethernet on Mac computers as early as 1991, and it was the first manufacturer to have wireless as a built-in option when it introduced the iBook in 1999. Mac models have varied over the years as network technologies have grown increasingly faster and more affordable.

Network Hardware Interfaces

You can identify the hardware network service interfaces available to your Mac from the /Applications/Utilities/System Information or /Applications/Utilities/Network Utility applications. Many of these interfaces automatically appear as a network service in Network preferences.

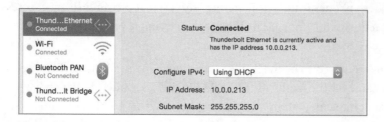

NOTE ▶ The newest hardware interface on Mac systems is Thunderbolt, a very high-speed connection technology. Thunderbolt is also extremely flexible, allowing for a wide variety of adapters. For example, Apple offers a Thunderbolt to gigabit Ethernet adapter and a Thunderbolt to FireWire adapter. In the previous screenshot, note the awkward name truncation for the attached Thunderbolt adapters.

OS X includes built-in support for the following hardware network interfaces:

▶ Bluetooth—This relatively low-speed wireless interface has become popular as a short-range connectivity standard. Every recent Mac that includes Wi-Fi support also includes Bluetooth. OS X supports Bluetooth as a network bridge to some mobile phones and hotspots, like iPhones, that can provide Internet connectivity via a cellular network.

▶ Ethernet—Ethernet is the family of IEEE 802.3 standards that define most modern wired LANs. Every Mac desktop since 1997 has included standard built-in Ethernet connectivity, with some models even featuring multiple Ethernet interfaces. Until recently most Mac portables also included standard built-in Ethernet connectivity. However, with the prevalence of Wi-Fi networks and the popularity of smaller portable devices, recent Mac portables are dropping standard Ethernet connectivity. For these systems Apple offers optional USB Ethernet (100baseT) and Thunderbolt to Gigabit Ethernet adapters.

▶ FireWire—FireWire is the Apple marketing name for the IEEE 1394 connection standard. Though not a common network standard, OS X includes software that allows you to create small ad hoc networks using daisy-chained FireWire cables. FireWire is standard on many older Mac models.

▶ Thunderbolt Bridge—As with FireWire, you can create small ad hoc networks using daisy-chained Thunderbolt cables. Thunderbolt is standard on most newer Mac systems, and offers higher performance than FireWire.

▶ USB—Although USB is not technically a network connectivity standard, OS X supports a variety of USB adapters that provide Internet access via cellular networks. Also, many modern phones feature a "tethering" service that provides Internet access via a USB connection to the phone. The iPhone is an example of a device that offers tethering connectivity.

▶ Wi-Fi—Previously referred to by the Apple marketing name AirPort, Wi-Fi is the more common name for the family of IEEE 802.11 wireless standards, which have become the default implementation for most wireless LANs. The AirPort name is still used in reference to the Apple family of Wi-Fi network base stations: AirPort Express and AirPort Extreme. Every desktop and portable Mac since 2006 has included standard built-in Wi-Fi connectivity. Wi-Fi was an option for older Mac Pro computers, but starting with the new smaller Mac Pro design in 2013, Wi-Fi is standard.

Cellular Internet Connections

Internet access via cellular networks is nothing new, but in the last few years this type of connectivity has seen a huge growth in popularity. With most major carriers offering ever-faster near-broadband speeds and expanded geographical coverage, many people are relying on cellular networks as their primary Internet access. As a result, a variety of devices and methods are available for providing cellular Internet access for your Mac.

NOTE ▶ The capabilities and configuration of cellular devices vary greatly. Check with your cellular device vendor about how to enable Internet access for your specific device.

OS X supports use of cellular Internet connections via:

▶ Bluetooth personal area network (PAN)—Many current cellular devices allow for Internet connectivity by acting as a small router providing a PAN available via Bluetooth wireless. For example, an iPhone can provide Internet access via Bluetooth PAN. As with any Bluetooth device, you must first pair your Mac with the mobile device, as covered in Lesson 25 "Peripherals and Drivers". Once the two are paired, configuration should be automatic, as the Mac should configure TCP/IP using DHCP hosted from the cellular device. You have to initiate the connection by clicking the Connect button in Network preferences or by choosing the device and Connect to Network in the Bluetooth status menu.

▶ USB cellular network adapters—Again, USB is not technically a network connectivity standard, but OS X supports a variety of USB adapters and tethered phones that provide cellular Internet access. The iPhone is an example of such a device, and in typical Apple fashion all configuration on the Mac is automatic. If tethering is available on your mobile phone data plan, simply plug an iPhone in via the USB adapter cable, and then on the iPhone turn on the Personal Hotspot feature. Conversely, third-party cellular Internet devices vary, and many require the installation and configuration of third-party drivers.

▶ Wi-Fi PAN—As with Bluetooth, many cellular devices can act as a small Wi-Fi access point. Thus, any device that supports Wi-Fi can connect to the cellular device without any special software. On any iOS device that supports cellular connections, you can enable Personal Hotspot for Wi-Fi. Simply select the Wi-Fi network the iOS device is hosting and provide authentication, if necessary. If the iOS device is running iOS 8 or later and you have the Handoff feature enabled, OS X Yosemite will automatically authenticate to the device's personal hotspot. Once you're connected, inspecting the Wi-Fi connection in Network preferences reveals that the iOS device appears identical to a traditional Wi-Fi router.

Virtual Network Services

A virtual network service is a logical network within a hardware network interface. Think of a virtual network service as providing another unique network interface by carving out a section of an established network connection.

Some virtual network services are used to increase security by encrypting data before it travels across an IP network, and others are used to segregate or aggregate network traffic across LAN connections. OS X includes client software that enables you to connect to many common virtual network services and establish a virtual network service interface.

If necessary, you can define multiple separate virtual network service interfaces for each network location. Virtual network service interfaces are not always tied to a specific physical network interface, as the system attempts to seek out the most appropriate route when there are multiple active connections. Likewise, any virtual network service interface that is not destined for a LAN connection is always routed to the primary active network service interface.

NOTE ▶ Third-party virtualization tools, like Parallels Desktop and VMware Fusion, also use virtual network interfaces to provide networking for multiple simultaneous operating systems.

OS X includes built-in support for the following virtual network services:

▶ Point-to-Point Protocol over Ethernet (PPPoE)—This protocol is used by some service providers to directly connect your Mac to a modem providing a high-speed digital subscriber line (DSL) Internet connection.

▶ Virtual private network (VPN)—By far the most commonly used virtual network service, VPNs are primarily used to create secure virtual connections to private LANs over the Internet.

▶ Virtual local area network (VLAN)—The OS X VLAN implementation allows you to define separate independent LAN services on a single physical network interface.

▶ Link aggregate—This service allows you to define a single virtual LAN service using multiple physical network interfaces. OS X uses the standard Link Aggregation Control Protocol (LACP), also known as IEEE 802.3ad.

▶ 6to4—This service creates a VPN, of sorts, to transfer IPv6 packets across an IPv4 network. There is no enhanced security when using a 6to4 connection, but your Mac will appear to be directly connected to a remote IPv6 LAN. The differences between IPv4 and IPv6 were covered in the previous lesson.

Network Protocols

Each network service interface provides connectivity for a number of standard networking protocols. Network preferences show primary protocol settings whenever you select a service from the services list, but many protocol configuration options are available only by clicking the Advanced button.

NOTE ▶ AppleTalk works only with OS X v10.5 or earlier.

OS X includes built-in support for the following network protocols:

▶ TCP/IP configured via DHCP—As explained in Lesson 20 "Network Essentials", TCP/IP is the primary network protocol for LANs and WANs, and DHCP is a popular network service that automatically configures TCP/IP clients.

▶ TCP/IP configured manually—If you do not have DHCP service on your local network, or if you want to ensure that the TCP/IP settings never change, you can manually configure TCP/IP settings.

▶ DNS—As covered in the previous lesson, DNS provides host names for IP network devices. DNS settings are often configured alongside TCP/IP settings either by DHCP or manual configuration. OS X supports multiple DNS servers and search domains.

▶ Wireless Ethernet (Wi-Fi) protocol options—The wireless nature of Wi-Fi often requires additional configuration to facilitate network selection and authentication.

▶ Authenticated Ethernet via 802.1X—The 802.1X protocol is used to secure Ethernet networks (both wired and Wi-Fi) by allowing only properly authenticated network clients to join the LAN.

▶ Network Basic Input/Output System (NetBIOS) and Windows Internet Naming Service (WINS)—NetBIOS and WINS are protocols most often used by older Windows-based computers to provide network identification and service discovery.

▶ IP proxies—Proxy servers act as intermediaries between a network client and a requested service and are used to enhance performance or provide an additional layer of security and content filtering.

▶ Ethernet hardware options—OS X supports both automatic and manual Ethernet hardware configuration, as covered later in "Manual Ethernet Configuration" on page 675.

▶ External (analog) modem with PPP—For many years this was the only method for accomplishing any sort of digital computer-based communication. OS X still supports this method, but since it is so rarely used in this age of broadband Internet, analog modem configuration is not covered in this guide.

▶ Point-to-Point Protocol (PPP)—PPP is an older protocol originally intended for use with analog modems. Again, OS X still supports PPP for analog modems, but it also supports PPP for Bluetooth dial-up networking and PPPoE connectivity. Again, the rarity of this protocol's use today means that PPP configuration is not covered in this guide.

Reference 21.3
Network Services

Typically, having multiple active network service interfaces means you also have multiple active IP addresses. To handle multiple IP addresses, OS X also features IP network multi-homing. In fact, OS X supports multiple IP addresses for each physical network interface. Thus, the network service list can contain multiple instances of the same physical network interface. Again, a network service in this context is a single configuration of a physical network interface.

Multiple Simultaneous Interfaces

OS X supports a multilink networking architecture, which means that OS X supports multiple simultaneous network service interfaces. For example, you can have both an active wired Ethernet connection and an active Wi-Fi, or wireless Ethernet, connection at the same time. In other words, you can configure as many separate network service interfaces with as many unique IP addresses as you need. This may seem like overkill for most Mac clients, but remember that OS X acts as the foundation for OS X Server as well.

For some servers, multilink multihoming networking is a requirement, but Mac clients can also benefit from this technology. You may have a work environment where you have one insecure network for general Internet traffic and another network for secure internal transactions. With OS X, you can be on both of these networks at the same time. However, the first fully configured active service in the list is the primary network service interface.

In most cases the primary network service interface is used for all WAN connectivity, Internet connectivity, and DNS host name resolution. The exception to this is if the primary network interface is lacking a router configuration. In this case, the system treats the next fully configured active service as the primary network service interface.

When multiple IP addresses are available, the system can communicate via any of those network service interfaces, but it will attempt to pick the most appropriate route for every network connection. As described in the previous lesson, a network client uses the subnet mask to determine if an outgoing transmission is on the LAN. OS X takes this a step further by examining all active LANs when determining a destination for outgoing transmission. Because a LAN connection is always faster than a WAN connection, OS X always routes outgoing transmissions to the most appropriate LAN.

Any network connections that are not destined for a LAN that your Mac is connected to are sent to the router address of the primary active network service interface, which should be the topmost service listed in Network preferences. Again, in most cases this means the primary active network service interface is responsible for all WAN connections, Internet connections, and DNS host name resolution. Any active network service interface with a valid TCP/IP setting is considered, but the primary active network service interface is automatically selected based on the network service order. You can manually configure the network service order, as outlined later in "Manage Network Services" on page 658.

Using the previous example, in which you have a Mac active on both wired Ethernet and Wi-Fi, the default network service order prioritizes wired Ethernet over Wi-Fi because wired is almost always faster. Thus, in this example, even though you have two active valid network service interfaces, the primary active network service interface is the wired Ethernet connection.

NOTE ▸ OS X features automatic source routing. This means incoming connections to your Mac over a specific network service interface are always responded to on the same interface, regardless of the service order.

Network Services List

Every time you open Network preferences, the system identifies all available network service interfaces. Even if a physical network interface is not connected or properly configured, it creates a configuration for that interface, which shows up in the network services list. In Network preferences, each network interface is tied to one or more network services.

A quick glance at the network services list clearly shows the status of all network interfaces and their configured services. Network services with a red indicator are not connected, a yellow indicator shows services that are connected but not properly configured, and a green indicator shows connected and configured network services.

The active service at the top of this list is the primary network service interface, as defined by the network service order. This list updates dynamically as new services become active or as active services become disconnected, so it's always the first place to check when attempting to troubleshoot a network issue.

Manage Network Services

To manage network interfaces and their configured services, open and (if necessary) unlock Network preferences. First, make sure the network location you want to edit is selected in the Location pop-up menu, or configure a new network location, as detailed previously in "Configuring Network Locations" on page 648.

To configure a specific network service, simply select it from the network services list. Remember, each network service has its own settings separate from the other services. The configuration area to the right of the list changes to reflect primary options available to the selected service. Clicking Advanced reveals all the advanced network protocol options available to the selected network service. Advanced network configuration is covered later in Lesson 21 "Advanced Network Configuration".

To create another configurable instance of a network interface, click the Add (+) button at the bottom of the network services list. This reveals a dialog that allows you to choose a new interface instance from the pop-up menu and then assign it a unique service name to identify it in the services list. Creating additional instances of a network service enables you to assign multiple IP addresses to a single network interface.

Select the interface and enter a name for the new service.

Interface: Thunderbolt Bridge

Service Name: Thunderbolt Bridge 2

Cancel   Create

To make a service inactive, select it from the services list, click the Action button (gear icon), and then choose Make Service Inactive from the pop-up menu. An inactive service never activates, even if connected and properly configured. You can also delete an existing network service by selecting its name from the services list and then clicking the Delete (–) button at the bottom of the list. Deactivating or deleting a network service from this list is the only way to disable a hardware network interface in OS X.

NOTE ▶ You are not allowed to delete network service interfaces configured as part of a configuration profile. To delete these network services, you must delete their associated configuration profile from the Profiles system preference.

Clicking the Action button (gear icon) at the bottom of the network services list reveals a pop-up menu with several management options. For example, you can duplicate an existing network service by selecting its name from the services list and then choosing Duplicate Service from the pop-up menu. Using this menu, you can also rename an existing network service. Finally, you can modify the active network service interface order by choosing Set Service Order from the pop-up menu.

The Service Order dialog allows you to drag network services into your preferred order for selection as the primary network interface. Click OK when you have finished reordering, and the system automatically reevaluates the active network service interfaces based on the new order. Also, don't forget that you must also click Apply in Network preferences to activate and save all the changes to the currently selected network location.

TIP ▶ If you make a mistake at any time using Network preferences, click Revert to return to the currently active network configuration.

Reference 21.4
VPN Configuration

A VPN is an encrypted tunnel from your client to the network routing device providing the VPN service. Once it is established, your Mac will appear to have a direct connection to the LAN that the VPN device is sharing. So even if you're on a wireless Internet connection thousands of miles away from your LAN, a VPN connection provides a virtual network interface as if your computer were directly attached to that LAN. OS X supports three common VPN protocols: the Layer 2 Tunneling Protocol over Internet Protocol Security (L2TP over IPSec), Point-to-Point Tunneling Protocol (PPTP), and Cisco's IPSec.

NOTE ▶ Some VPN services require a third-party VPN client. Third-party VPN clients usually include a custom interface for managing the connection. Although you may see the virtual network interface provided by the third-party VPN client in Network preferences, it's usually not configurable from there.

VPN Configuration Profile

By far the easiest method for managing VPN configuration is to do so via a configuration profile. As detailed in Lesson 2 "Setup and Configuration", a configuration profile is a file that contains instructions for specific settings. The administrator of a VPN system can provide a VPN profile whose relevant settings can easily be configured by simply opening the profile on a Mac.

Installed configuration profiles can be verified from Profiles preferences. Once a configuration profile is installed, all the appropriate VPN settings should be configured for you. To establish the VPN tunnel, a user needs only to initiate the VPN connection, as covered in the "Establishing VPN Connections" on page 664 section later in this lesson.

Manual VPN Configuration

Even with a VPN configuration profile, you may find it necessary to verify or further manage VPN connections from Network preferences. Or if the administrator of the VPN service is unable to provide a configuration profile, you need to manually configure VPN services. To add a VPN interface, click the Add (+) button at the bottom of the network services list in Network preferences. This reveals a dialog where you can add a new network service interface.

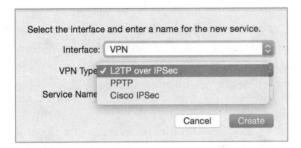

From the new network service interface dialog you must choose the appropriate VPN protocol from the VPN Type pop-up menu. Again, OS X supports the L2TP over IPSec, PPTP, and Cisco IPSec VPN protocols. All three have similar configuration options, but for the purposes of this lesson L2TP is used because it has a few more authentication and advanced options. If you're going to have more than one type of VPN protocol, you may want to enter a descriptive name for the service.

Once you create the new VPN interface, select it from the network services list, and basic VPN configuration settings appear to the right. To configure VPN settings, first enter the VPN server address and, if you use user-based authentication, an account name.

TIP ▶ If you do want to set multiple VPN configurations, choose Add Configuration from the Configuration pop-up menu. In the dialog, you can name and create a new VPN configuration. You can also delete and rename your configuration from this pop-up menu.

You must also define authentication methods by clicking the Authentication Settings button and then specifying user and computer authentication settings. The VPN administrator can provide you with the appropriate authentication settings. Supplying a password here adds it to the system keychain. If the field is left blank, the user is prompted for the password when connecting.

User Authentication:

○ Password: [_____]

● RSA SecurID

○ Certificate [Select...]

○ Kerberos

○ CryptoCard

Machine Authentication:

● Shared Secret: [•••••••••••••••]

○ Certificate   [Select...]

Group Name: [_____]

(Optional)

[Cancel]   [OK]

To configure advanced VPN settings, click the Advanced button in Network preferences. In the Advanced Settings dialog, click the Options tab to view general VPN options. The most important optional setting is to send all traffic over the VPN connection. By default, active VPN connections do not move to the top of the network service list. Thus, the system only routes traffic to the VPN service if the destination IP address is part of the LAN that the VPN service is providing or if the VPN server supplies special routing information.

NOTE ▶ OS X supports automatic VPN connections via certificate-based authentication and the VPN on Demand service. However, this can only be configured through the use of configuration profiles.

NOTE ► The built-in Cisco IPSec client does not feature any advanced options or VPN on Demand settings.

Establishing VPN Connections

VPN connections are not typically always-on connections. OS X supports automatic VPN connections with the VPN on Demand feature, but many users may still manually enable VPN connections when necessary. You can make accessing VPN connectivity options much easier by selecting the "Show VPN status in menu bar" checkbox in Network preferences. The VPN menu bar item allows you to easily select VPN configurations and connect, disconnect, and monitor VPN connections. You can also manually connect and disconnect the VPN link from Network preferences.

VPNs are usually implemented in situations where user authentication is required, so for many, initiating a VPN connection prompts an authentication dialog. Note that the VPN connection dialog does not offer to save the user's authentication information to the keychain. This is an intentional design decision, as some VPN protocols require manual authentication every time a connection is established.

Once the connection is authenticated and established, the VPN process automatically configures TCP/IP and DNS settings using the PPP protocol. VPN interfaces are, by default, set at the bottom of the network service order, so they do not automatically become the primary network interface when activated. This behavior is overridden when the optional "Send all traffic over VPN connection" checkbox is selected in Network preferences. You can also manually reorder the network service order, as explained earlier in this lesson.

TIP ► When troubleshooting VPN connections, it's useful to view the connection log info in /var/log/system.log. From the /Application/Utilities/Console application, you can view the system log.

Reference 21.5
Advanced Network Configuration

The advanced network configuration techniques covered in this section are largely optional for many configurations. However, for those who are tasked with supporting OS X systems, it's important to have a full understanding of all the configuration choices available in Network preferences.

Manual TCP/IP Configuration

Many network situations do not require any manual intervention to configure TCP/IP and DNS, as the DHCP or PPP services automatically acquire these settings. The default configuration for all Ethernet and Wi-Fi services is to automatically engage the DHCP process as soon as the interface becomes active. To verify TCP/IP and DNS settings for hardware or virtual Ethernet services when using the DHCP service, simply select the service from Network preferences.

NOTE ▸ IPv6 addressing information is automatically detected as well, if available. However, automatic IPv6 configuration is not provided by standard DHCP or PPP services.

NOTE ▸ Automatically configured DNS settings show as gray text, which indicates that you can override these settings by manually entering DNS information, as covered later in this section.

Network service interfaces that may require a manual connection process, like Wi-Fi, VPN, and PPPoE interfaces, automatically engage the DHCP or PPP process to acquire TCP/IP and DNS settings. To verify TCP/IP and DNS settings when using these interfaces, select the service from the services list, and then click Advanced in Network preferences. In the Advanced Settings dialog, you can click the TCP/IP or DNS tabs to view their respective settings. You can also verify network settings of any other interface this way.

Despite the convenience of automatic TCP/IP and DNS configuration, there may be times where manual configuration is required. For example, the network server providing the DHCP service requires a manual configuration. In fact, most network devices that provide services, like servers or printers, use manually entered network configuration information so they don't run the risk of changing to a different TCP/IP address should DHCP reset.

NOTE ▸ In some DHCP configurations, a DHCP client ID must be set. You can access this setting by clicking Advanced and then selecting the TCP/IP tab.

If you want to keep using DHCP but manually assign just the IP address, choose "Using DHCP with manual address" from the Configure IPv4 pop-up menu. You only have to manually enter an IPv4 address for the Mac, as the rest of the TCP/IP settings remain as populated by DHCP.

However, if you want to manually enter all TCP/IP settings, choose Manually from the Configure IPv4 pop-up menu. At a minimum you have to manually enter the IP address, the subnet mask (for this you can also use CIDR notation), and the router address. The user interface caches the TCP/IP settings from the DHCP service, so you may only have to enter a new IPv4 address.

If you have to manually set up IPv6 settings as well, choose Manually from the Configure IPv6 pop-up menu. At a minimum you have to manually enter the IPv6 address, router address, and prefix length. The user interface caches any automatic IPv6 settings, so you may only have to enter a new IPv6 address.

Anytime you choose to manually configure IPv4, you should also verify DNS server settings. To configure DNS, click the DNS tab to view the DNS settings. Again, the user interface caches the DNS settings from the DHCP service, so you may not have to enter any DNS settings at all.

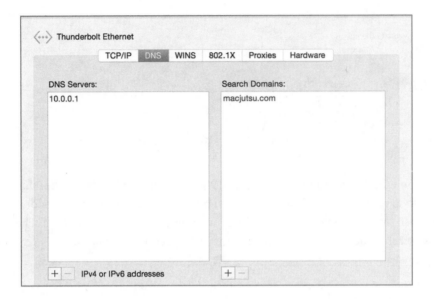

NOTE ▶ If the IP address of a DNS server is not specified, the Mac will not be able to resolve DNS host names.

If you are configuring manually, configure at least one DNS server. Click the Add (+) button at the bottom of the DNS server list to add a new server, and then enter the server's IP address. Entering a search domain is optional. Click the Add button (+) at the bottom of the Search Domains list, and then enter the domain name.

If you configure multiple DNS servers or search domains, the system attempts to access those resources in the order in which they appear in the list. To edit an address, double-click its entry in the list, or you can delete an entry by selecting it and clicking the Delete (–) button at the bottom of the list.

When you have entered all the appropriate IP and DNS settings, click OK to dismiss the Advanced Settings dialog, and then click Apply in Network preferences to save and activate the changes.

Whenever you manually configure TCP/IP or DNS settings, always test network connectivity to verify that you properly entered all information. Using standard applications to access network and Internet resources is one basic test, but you could also test more thoroughly using the included network diagnostic utilities, as covered in Lesson 22 "Network Troubleshooting".

Advanced Wi-Fi Configuration

Some administrators may find a need to restrict some of the wireless features. You may want to require that the Mac connect only to specific secure wireless networks, for example, or that the Mac always connect to one particular network. In these situations, you can use the advanced Wi-Fi configuration options in Network preferences.

To manage advanced Wi-Fi options and connections, open and (if necessary) unlock Network preferences, and then select the Wi-Fi service from the services list. At this point you can configure basic Wi-Fi settings in much the same way that you would do it from the Wi-Fi status menu, including the ability to join or create another wireless network, from the Network Name pop-up menu.

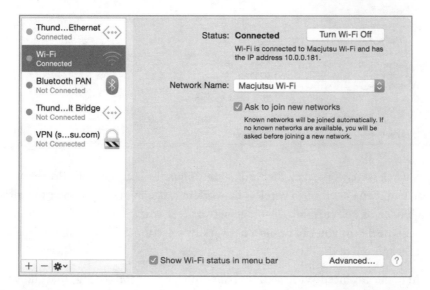

At this point you can also manage the ability for nonadministrative users to select Wi-Fi networks:

▶ When optionally enabled, the "Ask to join new networks" checkbox will have the system prompt the user to select another Wi-Fi network in the area when the Mac can't find a preconfigured wireless network.

▶ Enabled as a default, the "Show Wi-Fi status in menu bar" checkbox will allow any user to select a wireless network from the Wi-Fi status menu. However, disabling this doesn't prevent a user from choosing a wireless network if the Mac presents a wireless discovery dialog.

Clicking the Advanced button reveals the Advanced Settings dialog. If the Wi-Fi tab at the top is not selected, click it to view the advanced Wi-Fi settings.

From the top half of the advanced Wi-Fi settings pane, you can manage a list of preferred wireless networks. By default, wireless networks that were added previously appear here as well. If you disable user access to Wi-Fi settings as just described, the system connects only to the preferred wireless networks in this list.

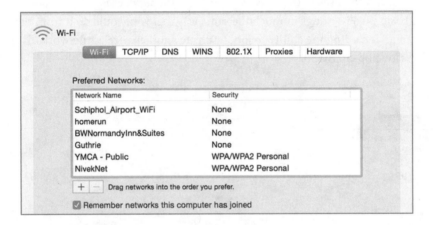

To add a new wireless network, click the Add (+) button at the bottom of the Preferred Networks list, and then either join a wireless network in range or manually enter the information for a hidden or not-currently-in-range network. To edit a network, simply double-click its entry in the list; or you can delete a network by selecting it and clicking the Delete (–) button at the bottom of the list.

At the bottom of the advanced Wi-Fi settings pane, you have several settings that allow for more specific Wi-Fi administration options. Thus, if you choose to leave the Wi-Fi status menu available to regular users, you can restrict certain settings to only administrative users. Remember to close the Advanced dialog and then click Apply in Network preferences to save and activate the changes.

802.1X Configuration

The 802.1X protocol is used to secure both wired and wireless (Wi-Fi) Ethernet networks by allowing only properly authenticated network clients to join the LAN. Networks using 802.1X do not allow any traffic until the network client properly authenticates to the network.

To facilitate 802.1X authentication, OS X provides two methods for automatic configuration:

▶ User-selected Wi-Fi network with WPA or WPA2 Enterprise authentication—As covered in the previous lesson, if a Wi-Fi network is selected that uses WPA or WPA2 Enterprise authentication, the system automatically configures 802.1X. You can verify the 802.1X configuration by selecting Wi-Fi in Network preferences, though you cannot modify the connection details in any way.

▶ Administrator-provided 802.1X configuration profile—The 802.1X architecture often relies on shared secrets or certificates to validate client connections; thus a network administrator must securely deploy these items to client computers. In OS X, the only way to set up non-Wi-Fi or managed 802.1X configurations is via a configuration profile. This profile can be deployed by simply double-clicking a local copy of a configuration profile or by having the Mac managed by a mobile device management (MDM) solution. From the local Mac, however, you can verify the 802.1X configuration by selecting the 802.1X tab from among the Advanced Configuration panes of Network preferences.

MORE INFO ▶ OS X Server can provide MDM services through Profile Manager, as covered in *OS X Server Essentials 10.10: Using and Supporting OS X Server on Yosemite.*

NetBIOS and WINS

NetBIOS and WINS run on top of TCP/IP to provide network identification and service discovery. NetBIOS and WINS are used primarily by legacy Windows-based systems to provide identification and service discovery on LANs, while WINS is used to identify and locate NetBIOS network devices on WANs. You can think of WINS as a form of DNS for NetBIOS network clients.

Current Windows networks now use Dynamic DNS as a solution for network client discovery, but OS X still supports NetBIOS and WINS to support legacy network configurations. Further, these discovery protocols are mainly used to provide naming for the Server Message Block (SMB) protocol commonly used to share files and printers. In other words, the NetBIOS name is there to provide support for SMB sharing services hosted from your Mac, as covered in Lesson 24 "Host Sharing and Personal Firewall".

NOTE ▶ OS X supports NetBIOS and WINS on any active network interface except for VPN connections.

OS X automatically configures your computer's NetBIOS name based on your Mac computer's sharing name, and for many networks this should be sufficient. If your Mac is on a larger legacy Windows network and you want to share resources from your Mac with other network clients, you may want to manually select the NetBIOS workgroup. NetBIOS workgroups are used to make navigation easier on large networks by grouping devices into smaller collections. You may have to manually configure the WINS service to provide faster NetBIOS resolution.

NOTE ▶ It's not required that you configure NetBIOS and WINS to connect to Windows resources. For certain legacy Windows clients, however, it may help.

To manually configure NetBIOS and WINS settings, open and (if necessary) unlock Network preferences, select the network service you want to configure from the network services list, and then click Advanced. In the Advanced Settings dialog, click the WINS tab to view the NetBIOS and WINS settings.

To manually configure NetBIOS, start by entering a unique name, and then choose a workgroup from the pop-up menu. It may take a while for the NetBIOS workgroup list to refresh, thus preventing you from selecting it from the pop-up menu. If you already know the name of the workgroup you want the Mac to be in, you can manually enter the workgroup name.

NOTE ▶ NetBIOS names and workgroup names are in all capital letters and cannot contain any special characters or spaces.

To enable WINS, enter at least one WINS server IP address. Click the Add (+) button at the bottom of the WINS server list to add a new server, and then enter the server's IP address. If you configure multiple WINS servers, the system attempts to access those resources in the order in which they appear in the list. To edit a server address, double-click its entry in the list, or you can delete a server by selecting it and clicking the Delete (–) button at the bottom of the list.

When you have entered all the appropriate NetBIOS and WINS settings, remember to close the Advanced dialog and then click Apply in Network preferences to save and activate the changes.

Network Proxies

Proxy servers act as intermediaries between a network client and a requested service. Proxy servers are often used to enhance the performance of slow WAN or Internet connections by caching recently requested data so future connections appear faster to local network clients. Primarily, though, proxy servers are implemented so that network administrators can limit network connections to unauthorized servers or resources. Administrators can manage lists of approved resources, having the proxy servers allow access to those resources only.

OS X supports proxy services for File Transfer Protocol (FTP), web protocols (HTTP and HTTPS), streaming (RTSP), SOCKS, and Gopher. For proxy configuration, OS X supports manual configurations, automatic proxy configuration using local or network-hosted proxy autoconfiguration (PAC) files, and fully automatic proxy discovery via the Web Proxy Autodiscovery Protocol (WPAD).

NOTE ▶ It's highly likely that you will have to acquire specific proxy configuration instructions from a network administrator.

To enable and configure proxy settings, open and (if necessary) unlock Network preferences, select the network service you want to configure from the network services list, and then click Advanced. Click the Proxies tab at the top to view the proxy settings.

At this point you will perform one of three routines, depending on your network's proxy implementation:

▶ If your proxy service supports WPAD, simply enable the Auto Proxy Discovery check-box.

▶ If you have access to a PAC file, select the Automatic Proxy Configuration checkbox at the bottom of the proxy protocols list. You must then specify a network-hosted .pac file by entering the full network path to the file in the URL field.

▶ To manually configure proxy settings, select the checkboxes next to each protocol you want to send through the proxy servers. Select each protocol individually to enter the proxy connection information provided by the network administrator. At the bottom you can also elect to bypass the proxy for specific additional hosts and domains.

When you have entered all the appropriate proxy information, remember to close the Advanced dialog and then click Apply in Network preferences to save and activate the changes.

Manual Ethernet Configuration

Ethernet connections are designed to establish connection settings automatically. Yet OS X allows you to manually configure Ethernet options from Network preferences should the automatic selections prove problematic.

The most common case for this is when you have an environment with gigabit Ethernet switches and old or substandard wired infrastructure. In this case it's common for the Mac to attempt to automatically establish a gigabit connection but ultimately fail because the wired infrastructure doesn't support the high speeds. The most common symptom is that even with the Ethernet switch showing that the Mac has an active connection, Network preferences on the Mac shows Ethernet as disconnected.

To manually configure Ethernet settings, open and (if necessary) unlock Network preferences, select the Ethernet service you want to configure from the network services list, and then click Advanced. Click the Hardware tab at the top to view the current automatically configured Ethernet hardware settings.

To manually configure Ethernet options, choose Manually from the Configure pop-up menu. The system caches the current automatically configured Ethernet settings so you do not have to change all the settings. The system also populates the Speed, Duplex, and MTU options based on your Mac computer's network hardware. Make your custom selections from these pop-up menus.

When you have selected all the appropriate Ethernet hardware settings, remember to close the Advanced dialog and then click Apply in Network preferences to save and activate the changes.

Exercise 21.1
Configure Network Locations

Prerequisites

► You must have created the Local Admin ("Exercise 2.1 Configure a New OS X System for Exercises" on page 60 or "Exercise 2.2 Configure an Existing OS X System for Exercises" on page 63) and Chris Johnson ("Exercise 5.1 Manage User Accounts" on page 145) accounts.

► This exercise requires a specific network configuration; it can be performed only in a classroom with the proper network setup or if you have configured your network according to the Optional Network Setup Instructions (available after you register your copy of this guide at www.peachpit.com/redeem).

Some network configurations do not have a Dynamic Host Configuration Protocol (DHCP) server, or there may be times when the DHCP server fails. In these instances, to establish and maintain network access, an OS X computer configured to obtain an IP address via DHCP self-assigns an IP address.

Turn Off the DHCP Service

If you are performing these exercises in a class, the instructor will turn off the classroom DHCP service.

If you are performing these exercises on your own, follow the instructions in the "Turn Off DHCP for Exercise 21.1" section of the Optional Network Setup Instructions.

Examine Your DHCP-Supplied Configuration

1   If necessary, open System Preferences, and select the Network preference pane.

2   If necessary, click the padlock, and authenticate as Local Admin.

3   Select the primary network service.

Even though the DHCP service has been turned off, the service still indicates that it is configured using DHCP and has valid network settings. This is because the DHCP service gave it the configuration information before it shut down, and the information is still valid.

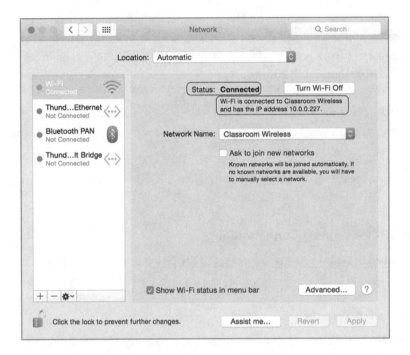

Note that your display probably appears different from this screenshot, especially if you have different network services connected.

Create a DHCP-Based Network Location

1   From the Location pop-up menu, choose Edit Locations.

2   Click the Add (+) button under the Locations list to create a new location.

3   Enter Dynamic as the name of the new location.

4 Click Done.

5 If necessary, choose the new Dynamic location from the Location pop-up menu.

6 Click Apply.

Network preferences is one of a few places in OS X where you must click Apply before your settings take effect.

7 If necessary, select the network service that is set up for these exercises (that is, the one that DHCP was just turned off for). If it is a wireless network, rejoin it.

The network service enters a Not Connected state with no IP address while it tries to acquire new DHCP configuration information. After a few seconds, it gives up and selects a "self-assigned" IP address beginning with 169.254.

The status indicator for the service will be yellow, indicating that it is connected but not properly configured.

Note that with this "self-assigned" configuration, there is no router or DNS server for that service. Therefore, this network service cannot be used to reach the Internet.

8 Open Safari, and try to browse the web.

If you have another active network service with a valid Internet connection, you can still reach the Internet. OS X Yosemite uses the router and DNS from lower-priority network services if the primary service does not have a router configured.

If you do not have another active network service, you cannot reach the Internet. Internet connectivity is available on the network you are connected to, but you cannot use it without proper IP settings.

9 If you have a server set up to support these exercises (either in a classroom or because you set one up according to the Mainserver Setup Instructions), try to browse to mainserver.local.

As long as you are on the same network as Mainserver, this works. Even though you have a self-assigned IP address, you can still communicate with other computers on your network. Bonjour allows you to look up .local names using multicast DNS (mDNS), giving you an easy way of connecting to local resources.

10 Quit Safari.

11 In Network preferences, check for any other active network services (other than the network set up for these exercises). If there are any, select them one by one and choose Make Service Inactive from the Action (gear icon) pop-up menu to inactivate them.

12 If necessary, click Apply.

Create a Static Network Location

You will configure a new location called Static with a static IP address. The IP address you will use for your computer will be in the form 10.0.0.n2.

If you are performing these exercises in a class, your instructor will provide you with a student number you should use as n. For example, student #3 would use 10.0.0.32, and student #17 would use 10.0.0.172.

If you are performing these exercises on your own, use the address 10.0.0.12.

1 From the Location pop-up menu, choose Edit Locations.

2 From the Action (gear icon) pop-up menu, choose Duplicate Location.

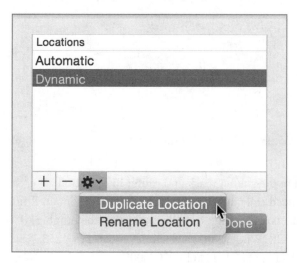

3 Name the new location Static, and click Done.

4 Use the Location pop-up menu to switch to the new Static location, if it is not already selected.

5 Click Apply.

6 Select the network service that is set up for these exercises from the service list on the left. It will most likely be either Ethernet or Wi-Fi.

7 Click Advanced.

8 If necessary, click the TCP/IP tab.

9 From the Configure IPv4 pop-up menu, choose Manually.

10 In the IPv4 Address field, enter 10.0.0.*n*2/24 (where *n* is either your student number if you are in class or 1 if you are on your own).

In other words, if you are on your own, you enter 10.0.0.12/24; if you are student #17 in a class, you enter 10.0.0.172/24.

11 Press Tab.

This fills in the subnet mask (255.255.255.0) and router (10.0.0.1) when you tab out of the field.

You are using a shortcut to fill in the subnet mask and router information. 10.0.0.$n2$/24 is CIDR (pronounced *cider* and short for Classless Interdomain Routing) notation. It specifies an IP address and subnet mask by indicating the number of "on" bits (1s) in the subnet mask. In CIDR notation, a /24 subnet equates to a 255.255.255.0 subnet mask (binary 11111111 11111111 11111111 00000000).

It also assumes that the default gateway (router) is the first usable address on the subnet. Although common practice, this is not a given. Some network administrators place the default router at the last usable address on the subnet. The gateway can be at any address on the subnet, so you may need to edit the router information to reflect the configuration of your network. Addressing doesn't tell the computer anything about the DNS environment, so you still have to enter that information manually.

12 Click DNS.

13 Click the Add (+) button under the DNS Servers list, and enter the appropriate address:

▶ If you are performing these exercises in a classroom or have an OS X server configured to support the exercises, enter 10.0.0.2.

▶ If you are performing these exercises without an OS X server, enter 10.0.0.1.

14 Click the Add (+) button under the Search Domains list, and enter pretendco.com.

15 Click OK to dismiss the advanced settings dialog.

16 Click Apply.

17 Quit System Preferences.

Test Web Access

At this point you have correctly configured your computer to work on the network. Now, use Safari to verify that you can access the Apple website.

1 Open Safari.

You will use Safari to test network access throughout this exercise. But to make sure you are testing actual network connections rather than just loading pages from Safari's caches, you will need to empty its caches first.

2 Choose Safari > Preferences (Command-Comma).

3 Click the Advanced tab in the preferences toolbar.

4 Select "Show Develop menu in menu bar," and then close the preferences window.

5 Choose Develop > Empty Caches (Command-Option-E).

6 In the address bar, type **www.apple.com**, and press Return.

If Safari is already trying to load a page from the Internet, you don't need to wait for it to finish or time out. If everything is working, the Apple website appears.

7   Quit Safari.

Exercise 21.2
Configure Network Service Order

▶ **Prerequisites**

▶ You must have created the Local Admin ("Exercise 2.1 Configure a New OS X System for Exercises" on page 60 or "Exercise 2.2 Configure an Existing OS X System for Exercises" on page 63) and Chris Johnson ("Exercise 5.1 Manage User Accounts" on page 145) accounts.

▶ You must have performed "Exercise 21.1 Configure Network Locations" on page 676.

The network service order determines which service is used to reach the Internet. Because of this, it is important to understand how network service order is determined and what its effects are.

Create a Multihomed Location

1   If necessary, open the Network pane in System Preferences, and authenticate as Local Admin.

2   From the Location pop-up menu, choose Edit Locations.

3   Select the Static location, and then choose Duplicate Location from the Action (gear icon) pop-menu below the locations list.

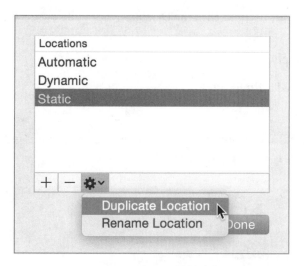

4   Name the new location **Multihomed**, and click Done.

5   Switch to the Multihomed location, if necessary.

6   Click Apply.

7   Select the primary network service (the one at the top of the list on the left).

8   From the Action (gear icon) pop-up menu, choose Rename Service.

9   Enter **With DNS** in the New Name field, and click Rename.

10 Click Apply.

11 From the Action (gear icon) pop-up menu, choose Duplicate Service.

12 Enter **Without DNS** in the Name field, and click Duplicate.

You now have two network services using the same interface. Essentially, this means you have two sets of network configurations (IP address, subnet mask, and so on) running through the same connector (or wireless network).

13 Select the Without DNS service, and click Advanced.

14 Click TCP/IP.

15 Increase the last number of the IPv4 address by 1 (for example, if it was 10.0.0.172, change it to **10.0.0.173**).

16 Click DNS.

17 Select the entry in the DNS Servers list, and click the Delete (–) button below the list to remove it.

The DNS Servers list is now empty.

18 Click OK to dismiss the advanced settings.

19 Click Apply.

At this point, both the With DNS and Without DNS services have a green status indicator, and the With DNS service is at the top of the list.

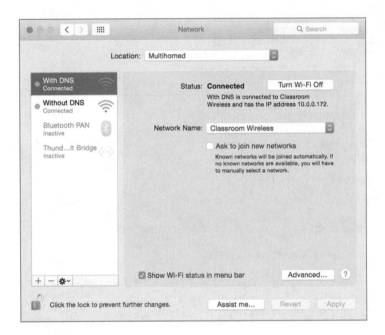

20 Open Safari, and attempt to browse the web.

You can now browse the web normally. If it does not work, check the setup you have done.

Change the Service Order

1 Switch to Network preferences.

2 From the Action (gear icon) pop-up menu, choose Set Service Order.

This list controls the normal order of the services. The system always reprioritizes the services based on their status (active services always bubble up to the top), but among the active services, this controls which is the primary.

3   Drag the Without DNS service to the top of the list, and then click OK.

The Without DNS service now moves to the top of the service list, but it is not actually used as the primary service until you apply the change.

4   Click Apply.

5   Quit and reopen Safari.

6   Choose Develop > Empty Caches (Command-Option-E).

7   Again, try to browse the web.

You are presented with a page that tells you that "You Are Not Connected to the Internet." Specifically, what this means is that it cannot find a name server to resolve the name.

The Without DNS service now has priority over the With DNS service (it is higher on the list). Because Without DNS is not configured with any name servers, it cannot look up any websites by name and so fails with this message.

8   From the Apple menu, choose Location > Static.

This submenu allows you to switch locations without having to open Network preferences.

9 Reload the page in Safari (note that it may reload automatically after a short delay). This time it works because the Static location has DNS settings associated with its highest-priority (and only) service.

10 If you are not going on to the next exercise, quit Safari.

Exercise 21.3
Configure VPN Settings

▶ **Prerequisites**

▶ You must have created the Local Admin ("Exercise 2.1 Configure a New OS X System for Exercises" on page 60 or "Exercise 2.2 Configure an Existing OS X System for Exercises" on page 63) and Chris Johnson ("Exercise 5.1 Manage User Accounts" on page 145) accounts.

▶ You must be performing these exercises in a class or have set up your own server configured as in the Mainserver Setup Instructions.

Virtual private networks (VPNs) are commonly used to securely access a remote network. With a VPN connection you establish an encrypted tunnel over the public Internet to the remote network. The encryption protects your data while it is transmitted. OS X supports three types of VPNs: Point-to-Point Tunneling Protocol (PPTP), Layer 2 Tunneling Protocol over IPSec (L2TP), and Cisco IPSec. You can configure a VPN service manually in OS X, but the preferred way to set one up is with a configuration profile.

In this exercise, you will use a configuration profile to set up a VPN connection from your computer to Mainserver's private network.

Try to Connect to a Private Service

1 If necessary, log in as Chris Johnson.

2 If necessary, open Safari.

3 Use the address bar to access internal.pretendco.com.

Safari may try to reach the site for a while, but it will eventually fail to connect. The site internal.pretendco.com is accessible only from the private network, and you have not yet joined that.

4   Leave Safari open in the background.

Configure a VPN Service

1   Open the file StudentMaterials/Lesson21/VPN.mobileconfig.

The profile opens in the Profiles pane of System Preferences.

2   Click Show Profile.

The profile contains the settings to connect to mainserver.local using the L2TP proto-col.

3   Click Continue, and then click Continue again to install the profile.

The profile does not specify a username to authenticate to the VPN server, so you need to enter one.

4   Enter the username student, and click Install.

5   When you are prompted, authenticate as Local Admin.

   Profile preferences now lists the VPN profile as installed on this computer.

6   Switch to the Network preferences pane.

7   Select the VPN service that has been added to your current location.

   All the settings in the profile have been applied, along with the username you entered.

8   Select "Show VPN status in menu bar."

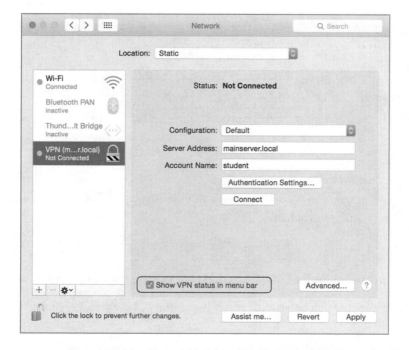

The Connect button in Network preferences may be dimmed, but you can still use the menu item to connect.

9   From the VPN menu item, choose "Connect VPN (mainserver.local)."

10   When you are prompted to authenticate to the VPN server, enter the password **student** (the username is already filled in), and click OK.

It may take a few seconds to connect. When it does, the VPN service's status changes.

Check Your VPN Connectivity

Now that you are connected to the classroom network via VPN, you will access a network resource that was previously unreachable.

1 Switch to Safari.

2 If the internal website didn't load, use the address bar to access **internal.pretendco.com**.

3 If you receive a warning that Safari can't verify the identity of the website, click Continue.

The page loads successfully this time. Since you are now connected to the private network, you have access to internal services and resources.

4 From the VPN menu item, choose "Disconnect VPN (mainserver.local)."

5 In Safari, press Command-R to reload the internal website.

Safari may continue to display the page while it attempts to reload it, but the progress bar under the address bar shows that it does not get far.

After a delay, you are informed that Safari can't open the page.

6 Quit Safari.

Exercise 21.4
Advanced Wi-Fi Configuration

In this exercise, you will learn to use the Preferred Networks list to control how your computer joins Wi-Fi networks.

Create a Wi-Fi-Only Location

1 If necessary, log in as Chris Johnson, open Network preferences, and authenticate as Local Admin.

2 Make a mental note of the currently selected location so that you can return to it at the end of the exercise.

3 From the Location pop-up menu, choose Edit Locations.

4 Click the Add (+) button under the Locations list to create a new location.

5 Enter Wi-Fi Only as the name of the new location.

6   Click Done.

7   If necessary, choose the new Wi-Fi location from the Location pop-up menu.

8   Click Apply.

9   In the network service list, make the services other than Wi-Fi inactive. Do this one by one by selecting a service and then, from the Action (gear icon) pop-up menu, choosing Make Service Inactive.

When you are done, all services except Wi-Fi are listed as Inactive.

10   Click Apply.

11   Select the Wi-Fi service.

12   If necessary, click Turn Wi-Fi On.

13   If necessary, deselect "Ask to join new networks."

This prevents your computer from suggesting networks to you when it can't find any of your preferred networks.

14 If necessary, select "Show Wi-Fi status in menu bar."

15 If your computer has not already joined a wireless network, join one by following the instructions in "Exercise 20.1 Connect to a Wi-Fi Network" on page 639.

Clear the Preferred Networks List

1 Click Advanced.

2 Examine the Preferred Networks list.

This is the list of wireless networks that your computer will join automatically any time it is in range of them. If there is more than one in range, it joins the one that is highest on the list.

3 Clear the list by selecting each entry and then clicking the Delete (–) button at the bottom of the list to remove it.

4 Make sure "Remember networks this computer has joined" is selected.

5 When the list is empty, click OK, and then click Apply. If prompted, authenticate as Local Admin.

Note that your computer is still joined to the same wireless network. The Preferred Networks list controls which networks your computer joins automatically; but once it is joined to a network, it stays joined until it loses the connection or you tell it to disconnect.

6 Click Turn Wi-Fi Off.

7 Wait ten seconds, and then click Turn Wi-Fi On.

The wireless interface turns on but does not connect to any network.

Add a Network to the Preferred List Manually

1 Click Advanced.

2 Click the Add (+) button under the Preferred Networks list.

3 Enter the network name and security information for another network you have access to.

Note that you have to enter the network's security mode and password even if they are already recorded in your keychain.

4 Click OK to add the entry.

Note that the new entry is added to the bottom of the list.

5 Click OK to dismiss the advanced settings, and then click Apply. If prompted, authenticate as Local Admin.

Your computer should automatically join the wireless network. If it does not, there may be a problem with the manual entry, such as a typo in the name or password or an incorrect security mode. In this case, you could remove it from the list and then try adding it back in.

Add a Network to the Preferred List by Joining It

1   From the Network Name pop-up menu, choose one of the wireless networks you have access to.

2   If necessary, enter the network password to join it.

3   Click Advanced.

    The network you joined has been added to the preferred list. This is because the "Remember networks this computer has joined" option is selected.

4   Click OK to dismiss the advanced settings dialog.

Test the Preferred Network Order

The network you added by joining is now at the top of the list.

1   Click Turn Wi-Fi Off. Wait ten seconds, and then click Turn Wi-Fi On.

    After a short delay, your computer rejoins the first network you joined it to.

2   Click Advanced.

3   Change the Preferred Networks order by dragging the current wireless network to the bottom of the list.

4   Click OK, and then click Apply.

5   Click Turn Wi-Fi Off. Wait ten seconds, and then click Turn Wi-Fi On.

    This time, your computer joins the network you added by joining because it is first in the Preferred Networks list.

6   Switch back to the network location you were in at the beginning of the exercise (generally the Static location, if you have one), and click Apply.

7   Quit System Preferences.

Lesson 22

Network Troubleshooting

This lesson builds on the network topics covered in Lesson 20 "Network Essentials" and Lesson 21 "Advanced Network Configuration". A solid understanding of general network technologies and the OS X network configuration architecture is necessary to effectively troubleshoot network issues from a Mac system. This lesson first covers general network troubleshooting and common network issues. Then, digging deeper, you will learn how to use the built-in OS X network troubleshooting tools, including the Network Diagnostics and Network Utility applications.

GOALS

▶ Identify and resolve network configuration issues

▶ Verify network configuration via Network preferences

▶ Understand how to use Network Utility to aid in troubleshooting

Reference 22.1
General Network Troubleshooting

The most important thing to remember about troubleshooting network issues is that it is often not the computer's fault. There are many other points of failure to consider when dealing with LAN and Internet connection issues. So the second most important thing to remember about troubleshooting network issues is that you need to isolate the cause of the problem before attempting generic resolutions.

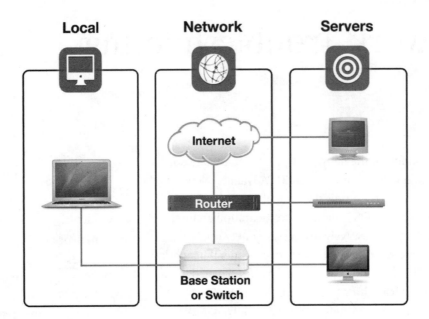

To help isolate network issues, you can categorize them into three general areas:

▶ Local issues—These are usually related to either improperly configured network settings or disconnected network connections.

▶ Network issues—These are by far the hardest to pinpoint, as there could be literally hundreds of points of failure involved. It always helps to be familiar with the physical topology of your network. Start by checking the devices that provide network access closest to your Mac. Something as simple as a bad Ethernet port on a network switch can cause problems. As you move on to investigating devices further away from your Mac, you will find that it's often easiest to start your investigation using the network diagnostic utilities included with OS X.

▶ Service issues—These issues are related to the actual network device or service you are trying to access. For example, the devices providing DHCP or DNS services could be temporarily down or improperly configured. It's often easy to determine if the problem is with the service alone by testing other network services. If the other network services work, you're probably not dealing with network or local issues. Again, OS X provides some useful diagnostic tools for testing service availability. Troubleshooting network services is also covered in Lesson 23 "Network Services".

You will be using three main tools for diagnosing network issues in OS X: Network preferences, Network Diagnostics, and Network Utility.

MORE INFO ▶ Many of the issues beyond the general scope of this guide are covered by the Apple networking support website at www.apple.com/support/networking/.

Network Preference Status

One of the diagnostic tools you should always check first is Network preferences. Network preferences features a dynamically updating list that shows you the current status of any network interface. If a network connection is not working, you will find out about it here first.

Network status indicators are:

▶ Green—The connection is active and configured with TCP/IP settings. This, however, does not guarantee that the service is using the proper TCP/IP settings.

▶ Yellow—The connection is active but the TCP/IP settings are not properly configured. If you are still experiencing problems with this service, double-check the network settings. If the settings appear sound, move on to the other diagnostic utilities.

▶ Red—This status usually indicates either improperly configured network settings or disconnected network interfaces. If this is an always-on interface, check for proper physical connectivity. If this is a virtual or Point-to-Point Protocol connection, double-check the settings and attempt to reconnect.

Common Network Issues

A good starting point for resolving network issues is to quickly verify some of the most common causes. You can think of this list as items you should check every time you're having an issue. To put it another way, verify common issues before hunting down exotic ones. This includes verifying Ethernet connectivity, Wi-Fi connectivity, DHCP services, and DNS services.

Ethernet Connectivity Issues

For well over a century, those supporting any electronic device have heeded these words: "Check the cable first!" If you're using an Ethernet connection, always verify the physical connection to the system, and if possible verify the entire Ethernet run back to the switch. If that's not possible, try swapping your local Ethernet cable or use a different Ethernet port.

You should also verify the Ethernet status from Network preferences, as detailed in the next section. Also, keep an eye out for substandard Ethernet cabling or problematic switching hardware. A symptom of these issues would be a large amount of packet errors, which you can verify with Network Utility, as covered later in "Reference 22.2 Network Utility" on page 707.

You may also find that while the Ethernet switch registers a link, Network preferences still shows the link as down. This issue may be resolved by manually setting a slower speed in the advanced hardware settings of Network preferences, as covered in Lesson 21 "Advanced Network Configuration".

Wi-Fi Connectivity Issues

A modern version of "Check the cable first!" would certainly be "Check the Wi-Fi first!" After all, when using Wi-Fi networking, the wireless signal represents the "physical" network connection. Start by verifying you are connected to the correct SSID from the Wi-Fi status menu or Network preferences. Note that the Wi-Fi status menu in the following screenshot sports an exclamation point (!), indicating there is a problem with the wireless network.

The Wi-Fi status menu can also serve as a diagnostic tool if you hold down the Option key when choosing this menu item. This view shows connection statistics for the currently selected Wi-Fi network. Of particular note is the Transmit Rate, which shows (in megabits per second) the current data rate for the selected Wi-Fi network. The Wi-Fi status menu is capable of other diagnostic tricks, including helping you quickly identify network issues and opening the Wireless Diagnostics application.

MORE INFO ▶ You can find out more about specific Wi-Fi status icons from Apple Support article HT201974, "OS X: Using the Wi-Fi status menu."

The Wireless Diagnostics application requires administrative authentication, but it can collect a huge amount of information about the Mac system's wireless and network configuration. Opening the Wireless Diagnostics application reveals an assistant interface. The primary goal of this assistant is to create a compressed archive of all the relevant files that would help experienced technical support staff diagnose a tricky connection issue. Of course, you can certainly expand the archive generated by the Wireless Diagnostics application and explore the contents on your own. However, the details of the collected items are beyond the scope of this guide.

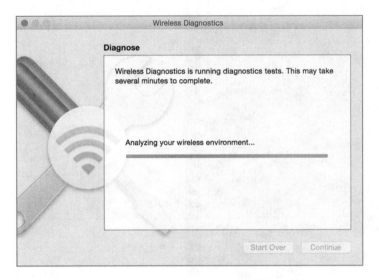

You'll also find a variety of advanced wireless network utilities in the Wireless Diagnostics application. Anytime you have the application open, you can reveal these additional utilities from the Window menu.

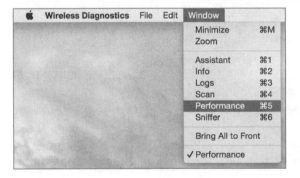

Again, use of these advanced wireless tools is beyond the scope of this guide. However, when working with wireless vendors or support specialists in trying to resolve tricky wireless issues, these wireless utilities are extremely valuable. For example, the Performance window provides a real-time view of the radio signal quality. With the wireless performance utility open, you can physically move a Mac portable device around an area to identify wireless "dead zones."

MORE INFO ▶ You can find out more about Apple Wireless Diagnostics from Apple Support article HT202663, "About Wireless Diagnostics."

DHCP Service Issues

Most client network connections are configured automatically via DHCP. If the DHCP server has run out of available network addresses, or there is no DHCP service available, as is the case with small ad hoc networks, the client automatically generates a self-assigned address. Sometimes this automatic assignment of addressing is referred to as "link-local addressing," but Network preferences shows it as Self-Assigned.

Self-assigned addresses are always in the IP address range of 169.254.xxx.xxx with a subnet mask of 255.255.0.0. The network client automatically generates a random self-assigned address and then checks the local network to make sure no other network device is using that address.

Once a unique self-assigned address is established, the network client can establish connections only with other network devices on the local network. Consequently, a client configured with a self-assigned address may be able to communicate with other devices on the LAN, but it doesn't have access to WAN or Internet resources.

DNS Service Issues

Aside from TCP/IP settings, DNS is a requirement for most network services. As always, you should start by verifying the DNS server configuration in Network preferences. Remember, in most cases the topmost network service interface is the primary one, and as such is used for all DNS resolution. The exception is if the primary network service is lacking a router configuration, in which case DNS resolution falls to the next fully config-ured network service interface.

Though it's rare, the OS X DNS resolution services can sometimes cache out-of-date DNS information and return inaccurate results. If you suspect your DNS issues are due to old information, you can either restart the system or flush the DNS service caches. You can find out more about this process from Apple Support article HT202516, "OS X: How to reset the DNS cache."

Network Diagnostics

OS X includes Network Diagnostics Assistant to help you troubleshoot common network issues. Some networking applications automatically open this assistant when they encounter a network issue. You can also open it manually by clicking the Assist Me button at the bottom of Network preferences, and then clicking the Diagnostics button.

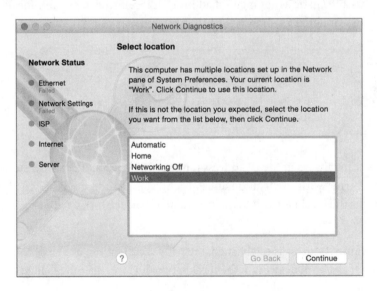

Network Diagnostics Assistant asks you a few simple questions about your network setup, and then, based on your answers, it runs a battery of tests to determine where the problem might be occurring. Test results are displayed using colored indicators on the left side of the window. If there are problems, the assistant makes suggestions for resolution.

Reference 22.2
Network Utility

Network preferences and Network Diagnostics Assistant are good places to start troubleshooting network issues, but the most powerful application in OS X for diagnosing network issues is Network Utility. In OS X, this application is buried in the /System/Library/CoreServices/Applications folder. The quickest way to find it, or really anything on the Mac, is to use Spotlight.

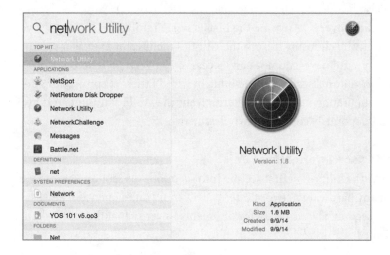

TIP ▶ You can also use Spotlight to search for and open the Wireless Diagnostics application, or any other useful application found in /System/Library/CoreServices/Applications.

Network Utility provides a selection of popular network identification and diagnostic tools. In fact, most of the tools in Network Utility are based on UNIX command-line network utilities that have been used by network administrators for years.

Network Utility is broken up into the following sections:

▶   Info—Allows you to inspect details regarding hardware network interfaces

▶ Netstat—Shows routing information and network statistics

▶ Ping—A fundamental network troubleshooting tool that lets you test network connectivity and latency

▶ Lookup—Lets you test DNS resolution

▶ Traceroute—Helps you analyze how your network connections are routed to their destination

▶ Whois—Lets you query whois database servers and find the owner of a DNS domain name or IP address of registered hosts

▶ Finger—Enables you to gather information based on a user account name from a network service

▶ Port Scan—A handy tool for determining if a network device has services available

Network Utility can also be opened when your Mac is started from OS X Recovery, as covered in Lesson 3 "OS X Recovery". Anytime the Mac is started from OS X Recovery, you can open Network Utility by choosing it from the Utilities menu. However, when running from an OS X Recovery system, you do not have access to Network preferences. This means the Mac does not automatically activate built-in wired Ethernet connections and attempt to acquire configuration via DHCP. Alternatively, the Wi-Fi status menu is available, allowing you to temporarily connect to wireless networks.

Network Utility: Interface Information

When you open Network Utility, you first see the Info section. This section lets you view the detailed status of any hardware network interface. Even if you've opened Network Utility to use another section, always take a few moments to verify that the network interface is properly activated.

Start by selecting the specific interface you're having issues with from the pop-up menu. You'll notice the selections here do not necessarily match the service names given in Network preferences. Instead, this menu shows the interfaces using their interface type and UNIX-given names.

Once you have selected an interface, you can view general interface information to the left and transfer statistics to the right. The primary pieces of information you're looking for here are link status, link speed, and IP address(es). Only active hardware network interfaces show as such, and the link speed indicates if the interface is establishing a proper connection. Obviously, a proper IP address is required to establish a TCP/IP connection. You can also identify the selected interface's MAC address, which is used to identify this particular interface on the LAN.

As a final validation of the selected network interface, you can view recent transfer statistics. If you open other network applications to stir up some network traffic, you can verify that packets are being sent and received from this interface. If you are seeing activity here but still experiencing problems, the issue is most likely due to a network or service problem and not the actual network interface. Or, if this interface is experiencing transfer errors, a local network hardware connectivity issue may be the root of your problem.

To resolve hardware network interface issues, always start by checking the physical connection. With wired networks, try different network ports or cabling to rule out physical connection issues. With wireless networks, double-check the Wi-Fi settings and the configuration of any wireless base stations. On rare occasions, you may find that the Mac computer's network hardware is somehow no longer working properly, in which case you should take your Mac to an Apple Authorized Service Provider.

Network Utility: Ping

If you have determined that your network settings are properly configured and the hardware network interface appears to be working correctly, but you are still experiencing network issues, your next step is to test network connectivity using the ping tool. The ping tool is the most fundamental network test to determine if your Mac can successfully send and receive data to another network device. Your Mac sends a ping data packet to the destination IP address, and the other device returns the ping packet to indicate connectivity.

To use ping, open Network Utility and then click the Ping tab. Start by entering an IP address to a device on the LAN that should always be accessible, like the network router. Remember, using a domain name assumes that your Mac is properly communicating with a DNS server, which might not be the case if you're troubleshooting connectivity issues.

Click the Ping button to initiate the ping process. If the ping is successful, it returns the amount of time it took for the ping to travel to the network device and back. This is typically within milliseconds; experiencing ping times any longer than a full second is unusual.

> **NOTE ▶** Some network administrators view excessive pinging as a threat, so many configure their firewalls to block pings or set up their network devices not to respond to any network pings.

Once you have established successful pings to local devices, you can branch out to WAN or Internet addresses. Using the ping tool, you may find that everything works except for the one service you were looking for that prompted you to start troubleshooting the network.

Network Utility: Lookup

If you are able to successfully ping other network devices by their IP address but attempting to connect to another device by its host name doesn't work, you are experiencing issues related to DNS. The network lookup process allows you to test name resolution against your DNS server.

To verify DNS lookup, open Network Utility and then click the Lookup tab. Start by entering the host name of a device or service in your local domain. If you can resolve local host names but not Internet host names, this indicates that your local DNS server is resolving local names but is not properly connecting to the worldwide DNS network. If you don't have a local domain, you can use any Internet host name.

> **NOTE ▸** The DNS results in the Lookup feature of Network Utility are considerably briefer than in previous versions of OS X. This simplified output shows only those IP addresses the system will attempt to connect with given the host name specified.

Click the Lookup button to initiate the network lookup process. A successful forward lookup returns the IP address of the host name you entered. A successful reverse lookup returns the host name of the IP address you entered. If you are unable to successfully return any lookups, your Mac is not connecting to the DNS server. You can verify this by pinging the DNS server IP address to test for basic connectivity.

Network Utility: Traceroute

If you are able to connect to some network resources but not others, use the network traceroute utility to determine where the connection is breaking down. Remember that WAN and Internet connections require the data to travel through many network routers to find their destination. The traceroute tool examines every network hop between routers using the ping tool to determine where connections fail or slow down.

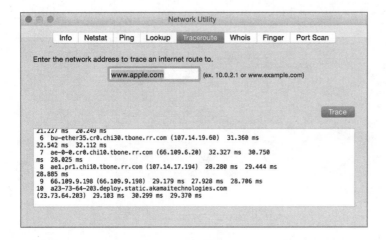

To verify a network TCP/IP route, open Network Utility, and then click the Traceroute tab. Start by entering an IP address to a device on the LAN that should always be accessible, like the network router. Remember, using a domain name assumes that your Mac is properly communicating with a DNS server, which might not be the case if you're troubleshooting connectivity issues.

Click the Trace button to initiate the traceroute process. If traceroute is successful, it returns with the list of routers required to complete the connection and the amount of time it took for the ping to travel to each network router. Note that it sends three probes at each distance, so three times are listed for each hop. Again, the delay is typically measured in milliseconds; experiencing delay times of any longer than a full second is unusual.

> **NOTE** ▶ If traceroute doesn't get a reply from any router along the way, it shows an asterisk instead of listing the router address.

> **NOTE** ▶ Again, some network administrators view excessive pinging as a threat, so many configure their firewalls to block pings or set up network devices not to respond to any network pings.

Once you have established successful routes to local devices, you can branch out to WAN or Internet addresses. Using the traceroute tool, you may find that a specific network router is the cause of the problem.

Exercise 22.1
Network Troubleshooting

▶ **Prerequisite**

▶ You must have created the Local Admin ("Exercise 2.1 Configure a New OS X System for Exercises" on page 60 or "Exercise 2.2 Configure an Existing OS X System for Exercises" on page 63) and Chris Johnson ("Exercise 5.1 Manage User Accounts" on page 145) accounts.

Network connectivity issues can be complex, but familiarity with the arsenal of tools included in OS X will help you develop a solid plan of attack for their resolution. In this exercise you will misconfigure your network settings and then use the built-in troubleshooting tools in OS X to see how they show the symptoms of the problem and allow you to isolate the problem.

Break Your Network Settings

1   If necessary, log in as Chris Johnson.

2   If necessary, open the Network pane in System Preferences, and authenticate as Local Admin.

3   Note the currently selected location so that you can return to it at the end of the exercise.

4   From the Location pop-up menu, choose Edit Locations.

5   Select the current location, and then choose Duplicate Location from the Action (gear icon) pop-up menu below the location list.

6   Name the new location Broken DNS, and then click Done.

7   Switch to the Broken DNS location, if necessary.

8   Click Apply.

9   Select the primary network service (the one at the top of the list on the left), and click Advanced.

10 Click DNS.

11 Click the Add (+) button under the DNS Servers list, and add the server address
127.0.0.55.

No DNS server is available at this address. The 127.0.0 prefix is reserved for computers to talk to themselves (known as "local loopback" addresses), but OS X uses only
127.0.0.1 for this. As a result, this is effectively an invalid address.

12 If there are any other entries in the DNS Servers list, make a note of them so you can
add them back later, and then use the Delete (–) button to remove them.

13 Click OK, and then click Apply.

Observe the Problem

1 Open Safari.

2 Enter **www.apple.com** in the address bar, and press Return.

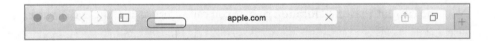

Safari attempts to load the webpage, but its progress bar does not get far because it is
not able to reach anything. If you leave it long enough, it will eventually give up and
display an error, but you do not need to wait for this.

3 Quit Safari.

Check the Network Status in Network Preferences

When you are experiencing a network problem, one of the first things to check is the network service status in the Network preference pane. This allows you to spot simple problems without having to go into more detailed diagnostics.

1 If necessary, open System Preferences, and select the Network pane.

2 Examine the status indicators next to the network services, as well as the order they appear in the list.

> If the network service you expected to be active were not showing a green status indicator, it would immediately tell you that something was wrong with the connection (loose cable, not joined to wireless network, and so on) or that critical settings were missing (no IP address, and so on).

> If the wrong service were at the top of the list, it would indicate either that the service order was set incorrectly, or that unexpected services were active.

> In this case, the expected service is green and at the top of the list, so more detailed troubleshooting is necessary.

Use Ping to Test Connectivity

This section walks you through the steps required to determine whether a computer is reachable using ping. Ping is one of the tools included in Network Utility. Network Utility is in /System/Library/CoreServices/Applications, but you can launch it easily with Spotlight.

1 Press Command–Space bar to activate Spotlight.

2 Enter **network**, and then click Network Utility in the search results.

3   In Network Utility, click the Ping tab.

4   In the "Enter the network address to ping" field, type the domain name of the server you are trying to reach: www.apple.com.

5   Enter 5 in the "Send only" field, and make sure it is selected.

6   Click the Ping button.

After about 30 seconds, you receive a message telling you that it could not resolve www.apple.com. This message indicates that the ping tool was not able to use DNS to look up, or "resolve," the name www.apple.com and match it to an IP address to send the ping to. In this case, you know that the name www.apple.com is valid because you have used it before, so this indicates that something is wrong with DNS.

Although this gives you some information about the problem, it does not tell you where the problem is. It can be hard to tell the difference between a DNS problem and a complete network failure. If DNS resolution is the only thing failing, it can mimic a complete failure because almost all network access starts with (and depends on) a DNS lookup. On the other hand, if the network is completely disconnected, most attempts to use the network fail at the DNS step, so the only visible symptoms will be DNS errors.

NOTE ▶ At this point you could use the Network Utility Lookup feature to test DNS lookups more directly, but you would not learn anything you don't already know from the ping error.

One good way to distinguish between a DNS-only problem and a complete network failure is to try to reach a server by its numeric IP address. This bypasses the usual DNS lookup and hence works even if DNS is broken.

7   In the "Enter the network address to ping" field, enter the numeric IP address 8.8.8.8. This is an easy-to-remember address of a public server maintained by Google.

8   Click Ping.

This time, ping reaches the remote computer successfully and shows statistics for its five test pings.

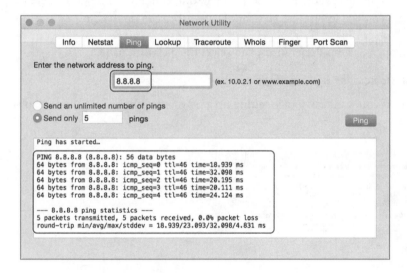

This tells you that your basic network connectivity is OK; it is likely just DNS that is not working.

NOTE ▶ If ping is unable to reach the server at 8.8.8.8, it may indicate that your computer is behind a tightly locked-down firewall. Ping probes are sometimes used in network attacks, and as a result some firewalls are configured to block them. Firewalls increase network security, but they can also complicate troubleshooting considerably.

TIP If ping was unable to reach the remote server, you could use the traceroute tool to test connectivity in more detail. Traceroute attempts to find out what network routers your packets go through on their way to the remote computer. If your packets are not making it all the way to the remote computer, traceroute can often tell you how far they are getting, which tells you more about where the problem is.

Use Network Diagnostics

Network Diagnostics helps users diagnose and fix basic network problems. Now that you've determined that there's something seriously wrong and have some idea where the problem is (DNS), you will learn what Network Diagnostics can do to help.

1   If necessary, open System Preferences, and select the Network pane.

2   Click Assist Me near the bottom of the window.

A dialog asks if you want assistance setting up a new network configuration or solving a problem.

3   Click Diagnostics.

Network Diagnostics opens and automatically runs some basic tests. Several status indicators show the results.

In the following example, the Ethernet, Network Settings, and ISP tests passed (that is, there is a live Ethernet connection, it has network settings associated with it, and it can reach as far as your Internet provider), but the Internet and Server tests failed. Your results may differ depending on what type of connection you have.

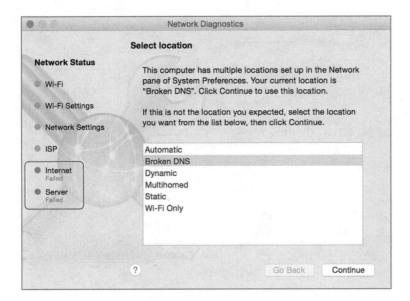

NOTE ▶ The exact results that Network Diagnostics gets depend on what type of network service and configuration you are using. While the following steps include most of the possibilities, you may run into a test result or prompt that is not covered. If this happens, use your best judgment on how to proceed.

Network Diagnostics can troubleshoot this problem further, but you need to tell it what to test and how it's supposed to work. First, you need to tell it which network location to test.

4   Ensure that the Broken DNS location is selected, and then click Continue.

5   If you are prompted, authenticate as Local Admin.

Network Diagnostics asks which network service you use to connect to the Internet.

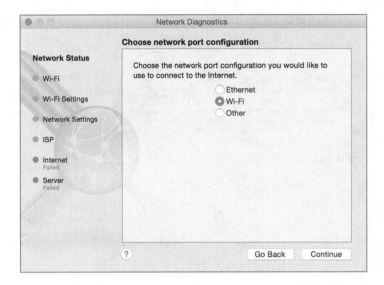

6   Ensure that your primary network service is selected, and then click Continue.

7   If you are using a Wi-Fi service, it asks which wireless network you want to join. Select the appropriate network, and click Continue. If necessary, authenticate to the wireless network or allow Network Diagnostics access to the key stored in your keychain.

8   If it reports that a network change was detected, click OK to continue.

9   If it asks whether you are sure you want to use manual settings, select Yes, and click Continue.

10 If your primary network service is configured manually, it asks you to verify the current settings. In this situation you need to know how computers on this network should be configured in order to work properly.

The current settings include the invalid DNS server 127.0.0.55, which you configured at the beginning of the exercise:

▶   Change the DNS Servers list back to what it should be. If you are using the Static location you created in "Exercise 21.1 Configure Network Locations" on page 676, it should be 10.0.0.1 or 10.0.0.2; refer to Exercise 21.1 for details. If you do not remember what the old DNS server list was, enter 8.8.8.8 as a temporary fix (you will switch back to the old location with the proper settings later).

▶   When you have corrected the manual settings, click Continue.

11 If your primary service is configured using DHCP, it reports that the DNS server is unavailable and gives you the option to use DNS servers provided by DHCP.

Select "Use DNS servers provided by DHCP," and click Continue.

If the bad DNS server setting was coming from the DHCP service, this would not help; in this case, however, the problem was the incorrect setting you entered manually, so this solves the problem.

12 If Network Diagnostics requires you to authenticate to make the change, authenticate as Local Admin.

13 If it reports that a network change was detected, click OK to continue.

14 If it asks whether you use a DSL or cable modem, select No, and click Continue.

If you select Yes here, it simply suggests restarting the device. This is generally a good troubleshooting step but irrelevant to the current problem, so you can skip it.

At this point, Network Diagnostics reports that your Internet connection appears to be working correctly.

Since the problem in this case was a misconfiguration on your computer, changing your computer's settings was sufficient to fix the problem. If your computer was properly configured but the DNS server was offline or unreachable, you would have seen essentially the same symptoms. Often, telling the difference between a network or server problem and misconfiguration on the client requires knowing the correct settings for a particular network.

15 Click Quit to close Network Diagnostics.

Use Lookup to Test DNS

At this point, you have fixed the problem with the DNS settings on your computer. Now, use the Network Utility Lookup pane to verify that it is working properly.

1 In Network Utility, click the Lookup tab.

2 In the "Enter an Internet address to lookup" field, enter the address www.apple.com.

3 Click Lookup.

The lookup tool queries your configured DNS server for the IP address corresponding to the domain name www.apple.com.

Note that the address you see may be different from the one shown since the Apple website is served by a number of servers scattered around the Internet and uses DNS to direct you to a server near your network location for faster access.

If you knew what specific address the name should resolve to, you could verify that, but the fact that it resolved to an IP address at all is a good indication that DNS is working.

Use Safari to Test Web Access

Different applications rely on different network components to work properly. In the previous section, you corrected your network settings. In this section, you will use Safari to test browsing with your current network settings.

1   Open Safari, and try browsing a website.

     This time, Safari is able to successfully load webpages from the Internet.

Monitor Network Traffic

You can use the Network Utility Info pane to view low-level network interface settings and to monitor network throughput on a per-interface basis.

1   Switch to Network Utility, and click the Info tab.

2   Select your computer's primary network interface from the pop-up menu.

The left side of the pane shows information about the active network connection, and the right side shows statistics about the network packets sent and received through this interface.

3   Arrange the Safari and Network Utility windows so that Safari is in front but not blocking the Transfer Statistics section of the Network Utility window.

4   In Safari, press Command-R to reload the current page.

The Sent Packets and Recv Packets entries increase while Safari reloads the current page.

5   In Network Utility, select another network interface from the pop-up menu.

6   Switch to Safari, and reload the current page.

The packet counts for this interface might increase slightly because of miscellaneous network chatter but should not respond specifically to refreshing in Safari.

You can use this feature of Network Utility to see which network interface your connections are actually running through.

Reset Your Network to Normal

1   Use the Apple menu's Location submenu to switch from the Broken DNS location to the one you were using at the beginning of this exercise.

2   Reload in Safari to make sure this location is working as well.

3   Quit Safari, Network Utility, and System Preferences.

Network Services

Lesson 23

Network Services

Current operating systems provide a wide range of network and Internet service options, but all of them share the basic network architecture of client software, which accesses network services, and server software, which provides network services. OS X includes support for many popular network protocols, allowing you to connect and access a wide variety of shared network services.

This lesson first discusses the architecture of network services, in a general sense. Then you will be introduced to the key network service applications built into OS X. You will then learn how OS X can access popular file-sharing services. Finally, this lesson covers techniques for troubleshooting network services when problems arise.

GOALS

▶ Understand how OS X accesses shared network services

▶ Configure built-in OS X network applications

▶ Browse and access network file services using the Finder

▶ Troubleshoot network shared service issues

Reference 23.1
Network Services Architecture

From an architectural standpoint, shared network services are defined by client software (designed to access the service) and server software (designed to provide the service). The network service communication between the client and server software is facilitated by commonly known network protocols and standards.

By adhering to such standards, software developers can create unique yet compatible network client and server software. This allows you to choose the software tool that best fits your needs. For instance, you can use the built-in OS X Mail client created by Apple to access mail services provided by Apple, Google, Yahoo, or Microsoft.

Network Services Software

Some client software takes the form of dedicated applications, as is the case with many Internet services like email and web browsing. Other client software is integrated into the operating system

—file and print services, for example. In either case, when you establish a network service connection, settings for that service are saved on the local computer to preference files. These client preferences often include resource locations and authentication information.

On the other side of this relationship is the server software, which is responsible for providing access to the shared resource. Properly setting up server software is usually a much more complicated affair. Server administrators may spend weeks designing, configuring, and administering the software that provides network services. Server-side settings include configuration options, protocol settings, and account information.

Network Services Communication

Network clients and servers, sometimes of different makes, communicate using commonly known network protocols or network standards. A protocol becomes a standard once it is widely adopted and ratified by a standards committee. Part of what defines a specific network protocol is which TCP or UDP (User Datagram Protocol) ports are used for communications.

A primary feature of both the TCP and UDP transport mechanisms is the ability to handle multiple simultaneous connections and service protocols. This is accomplished by assigning each communication service to a specific port number or port range. Both TCP and UDP connection ports are defined between 0 and 65,535.

For instance, the standard TCP port for web traffic is port 80. When troubleshooting a network service, you must know the port numbers or ranges for that service. Apple maintains a list of commonly used network services and their associated TCP or UDP ports at Apple Support article HT202944, "Well known TCP and UDP ports used by Apple software products."

> **NOTE ▶** This guide assumes the default port numbers and port ranges for each network service. Network administrators may choose to use a different port number than the default for testing, to "hide" a service, or to bypass router restrictions.

Network Service Identification

At a minimum, accessing a network service requires knowledge of service's local network or Internet location. Some network services feature dynamic service discovery, which allows you to easily locate a network service by simply browsing a list of available services, as covered in "Dynamic Service Discovery" on page 729. In other cases, you must manually identify the service's location with a specific network host address or name, as covered in "Network Host Addressing " on page 731. Finally, there are some network services so popular that OS X includes built-in mechanisms for automatically locating the appropriate network service resources. Services in this last category are mainly configured via the Internet Accounts preferences, as covered in "Reference 23.2 Network Service Applications" on page 732.

Once you have located and connected to a network service you often need to prove your identity to that service provider. This process is called authentication. Successful authentication to a network service is usually the last step in establishing a connection to that service. Once a connection is established, security technologies are normally in place to ensure that you're allowed to access only certain resources. This process is called authorization. Both of these fundamental network service concepts, authentication and authorization, will be covered throughout this lesson and the next, Lesson 24 "Host Sharing and Personal Firewall".

Dynamic Service Discovery

Requiring users to manually enter network addresses to access a network service isn't very user friendly. What if you join a new network without knowing the exact names of all its available resources? Or what if the shared resource you need is hosted from another client computer that doesn't have a DNS host name or the same IP address every time? To address these issues, OS X supports dynamic network service discovery protocols.

Dynamic network service discovery protocols allow you to browse local area and wide area network resources without knowing specific service addresses. In a nutshell, network devices providing services advertise the availability of their services on the network. As available network resources change, or as you move your client to different networks, the service discovery protocols dynamically update the list of available services.

OS X makes ample use of dynamic network service discovery throughout. For example, dynamic network service discovery allows you to browse for available network file shares with the Finder, or locate new network printers from Print & Scan preferences. Other network applications built into OS X use service discovery to locate a variety of shared resources, including Messages, Image Capture, iPhoto, iTunes, Safari, and the OS X Server application. Third-party network applications also take advantage of dynamic network service discovery.

It is important to remember the discovery protocol is used only to help you and the system locate available services. Once the discovery protocol provides your computer with a list of available services, its job is done. When you connect to a discovered service, the Mac establishes a connection to the service using the service's protocol. For example, the

Bonjour service discovery protocol can provide the Mac with a list of available screen-sharing systems, but when you select a Mac server from this list, the Mac establishes a screen-sharing connection to the server using the Virtual Network Computing (VNC) protocol.

> **NOTE ▶** OS X v10.6 and later are no longer compatible with the AppleTalk network browsing or service connections.

Bonjour

Bonjour is the Apple implementation of Zero Configuration Networking, or Zeroconf, a collection of standards drafts that provide automatic local network configuration, naming, and service discovery. Bonjour uses a broadcast discovery protocol known as multicast DNS (mDNS) on UDP port 5353.

> **MORE INFO ▶** You can find out more about Zeroconf at www.zeroconf.org.

Bonjour is the primary set of dynamic network service discovery protocols used by OS X native services and applications. Bonjour is preferred because it is based on TCP/IP standards, so it integrates well with other TCP/IP-based network services. OS X v10.5 added support for Wide-Area Bonjour, allowing you to browse WAN resources as well as LAN resources.

While local Bonjour requires no configuration, Wide-Area Bonjour requires that your Mac be configured to use a DNS server and search domain that supports the protocol. Configuring DNS is covered in Lesson 20 "Network Essentials" and Lesson 21 "Advanced Network Configuration".

> **MORE INFO ▶** OS X also supports network identification via the Back to My Mac feature in iCloud. However, a Back to My Mac system can only be located by the iCloud user who set it up. In other words, it doesn't help other users locate your system. You can find out more about Back to My Mac from www.apple.com/support/icloud/back-to-my-mac/.

Server Message Block

Originally designed by Microsoft, Server Message Block (SMB) has become the most common network service for sharing files and printers. SMB also includes a network discovery service that runs on UDP ports 137 and 138. Most current operating systems that provide support for SMB sharing also support dynamic discovery via SMB.

Despite the preferred status of SMB as the default file-sharing protocol in OS X Yosemite, the network discovery portion of SMB is still not preferred over Bonjour. However, OS X does support browsing through the legacy NetBIOS and WINS protocols. Details on configuration of NetBIOS and WINS are covered in Lesson 21 "Advanced Network Configuration".

Network Host Addressing

At a minimum, all network hosts can be reached by their IP address. For most people though, IP addresses are hard to remember, so other technologies have been created to give network hosts human-friendly network names.

Network host identification methods include:

▶ IP address(es)—The primary network identifier for your Mac, an IP address, can always be used to establish a network connection.

▶ DNS host name—All Mac computers have a host name configured via one of two methods. Traditionally, these names are hosted on a DNS server configured by administration at the DNS server. The Mac attempts to resolve its host name by performing a DNS reverse lookup on its primary IP address. However, many network clients don't have properly configured DNS host names because of the administrative overhead required to create and update client DNS entries. So if the Mac can't resolve a host name from the DNS server it uses the Bonjour name instead.

▶ Computer name—This name is used by other Apple systems to identify your Mac. The computer name is part of the Apple Bonjour implementation and is set in Sharing preferences. The computer name is also used by AirDrop peer-to-peer file sharing.

▶ Bonjour name—As covered previously, Bonjour is the OS X primary dynamic network discovery protocol; in addition, Bonjour provides a convenient naming system for use on a local network. The Bonjour name is usually similar to the computer name, but it differs in that it conforms to DNS naming standards and ends with .local. This allows the Bonjour name to be supported by more network devices than the standard computer name, which is generally recognized only by Apple systems. This name is also set in Sharing preferences.

▶ NetBIOS/WINS name—This name is used for the legacy Windows dynamic network discovery protocols as part of the SMB service. This name is set in either Sharing or Network preferences.

Identifier	Example	Set in	Used by
IP address	10.1.17.2	Network preferences	Any network host

Identifier	Example	Set in	Used by
DNS host name	client17.pretendco.com	Defined by DNS server	Any network host
Computer name	Client 17	Sharing preferences	Mac systems (Bonjour or AirDrop)
Bonjour name	Client-17.local	Sharing preferences	Any Bonjour host
NetBIOS name	CLIENT17	Network preferences	Any SMB host

Reference 23.2
Network Service Applications

Because of the widespread adoption of TCP/IP for nearly all LAN, WAN, and Internet communications, there really isn't any difference between how you access a "standard network service" and an "Internet service." With few exceptions, nearly all network services work the same way across a LAN as they do across the Internet. The primary difference between the two is the scope of service. Services like email and instant messaging can certainly work on a local level, but these services are also designed to communicate across separate networks and between servers. OS X includes a range of client applications designed to access different network services.

> **TIP** Although this guide focuses on the network client software built into OS X, many excellent third-party network clients are available for the Mac. In fact, when troubleshooting a network access problem, using an alternative network client is an excellent way to determine if the issue is specific to your primary client software.

Internet Accounts Preferences

A feature clearly influenced by iOS, Internet Accounts preferences provides a single unified interface for configuring network service accounts. Formerly known as Mail, Contacts & Calendars preferences, Internet Accounts preferences is used to configure a variety of OS X applications and services. In other words, entering a single network service account in Internet Accounts preferences configures all appropriate network service applications built into OS X.

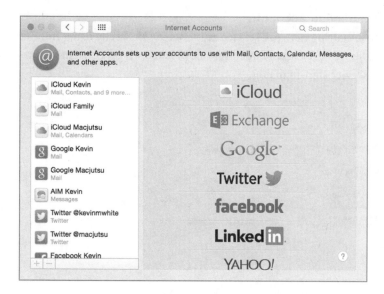

Through Internet Accounts preferences, OS X can be configured to use network service accounts for Apple iCloud, Microsoft Exchange, Google, Twitter, Facebook, LinkedIn, Yahoo, AOL, Vimeo, Flickr, and other common network service protocols, including those hosted from a system running OS X Server.

> **NOTE ▶** OS X requires Microsoft Exchange Server 2007 Service Pack 1 Update Rollup 4 or later, with Exchange Web Services enabled. The Mail application also supports the various Microsoft-hosted Exchange services.

> **NOTE ▶** Internet Accounts preferences also includes support for services popular in non-English-speaking countries. These services appear automatically when the appropriate region is selected in Language & Region preferences.

Each different service type includes varying levels of support for built-in OS X applications and services. For example, signing in with a Twitter account configures the system so you can tweet from the Notification Center or any supported application. Whereas signing in to a service that provides multiple features, like Google or Yahoo, in turn configures multiple applications including Mail, Notes, Calendar, Reminders, Contacts, and Messages. Apple iCloud includes support for even more features, including iCloud Drive, Photos, Safari, iCloud Keychain, Back to My Mac, and Find My Mac.

Configuring Network Service Accounts

The best method for configuring network service accounts in OS X is by using Internet Accounts preferences. Simply click an included service provider to get the sign-up process started. This reveals a service sign-in dialog.

TIP If you don't see the Internet Accounts list of services, simply click the small plus button at the bottom-right corner of the preference pane.

If you are signing in to a service with multiple features, after you successfully authenticate, you will be allowed to enable any available options for the service. You can also return to Internet Accounts preferences at any point to enable or disable a service feature. Additionally, from there you can verify or reenter account information by clicking the Details button.

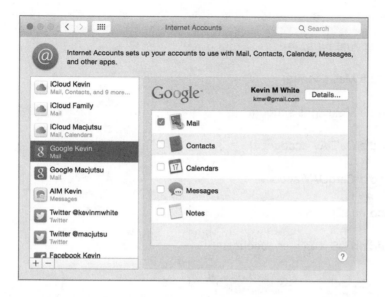

If you need to configure an Internet service that's not listed in Internet Accounts preferences, or you need to configure a local service provided by your organization, click Add Other Account at the bottom of the services list. This reveals a dialog allowing you to manually configure services for Mail, Notes, Calendar, Reminders, Contacts, and Messages. In many cases, if you add a service this way you will likely have to define additional configuration information. This information should be provided to you by an administrator of the service.

If you choose "Add an OS X Server account," the following dialog searches the local network for an OS X Server v10.7 or newer system that provides compatible services. You can select your server from the list or enter the host name of a server that's not on your local network. Because OS X can automatically detect OS X Server services, you'll only need to enter network account authentication to complete the setup.

OS X can also accept a configuration profile for automatic configuration of network service accounts settings. A network administrator would provide a configuration profile containing all the necessary settings to properly configure the OS X network applications for a specific network service account. These settings can be deployed by simply double-clicking a local copy of a configuration profile or by having the Mac managed by a Mobile Device Management (MDM) solution.

> **MORE INFO ▶** OS X Server can provide MDM services through Profile Manager, as covered in *OS X Server Essentials 10.10: Using and Supporting OS X Server on Yosemite.*

Safari Web Browser

OS X Yosemite includes the updated Safari 8 web browser. Safari is an efficient and robust browser that supports most websites. Apple continues to add new features to Safari with every new version of OS X. For example, Safari in OS X Yosemite features a new Smart Search field (replacing the standard URL field) that automatically searches for relevant content or web address. This latest version of Safari also supports Handoff, which provides continuity between OS X and iOS devices. As long as you are signed in to iCloud on your Apple devices, sites open in Safari on one device are instantly available on any of the other devices.

By far the most popular and ubiquitous network service, the Hypertext Transfer Protocol (HTTP) handles web communication using TCP port 80. Secure web communication, known by the acronym HTTPS, encrypts HTTP over a Secure Sockets Layer (SSL) connection and by default uses TCP port 443. Generally, little additional network configuration is required to use web services, as you only need to provide the web browser with the Uniform Resource Locator (URL) or web address of the resource you want to connect to. The only exception is if you have to configure web proxies, as described in Lesson 21 "Advanced Network Configuration".

> **MORE INFO ▶** You can find out more about Safari from the Apple website at www.apple.com/safari.

Mail and Notes

OS X includes the Mail application for handling email communications. Mail supports all standard email protocols and their encrypted counterparts, along with a variety of authentication standards. Mail also includes support for Exchange-based services.

With this many service options, properly configuring mail service settings can be quite daunting. Ideally, Mail is configured automatically via Internet Accounts preferences or via a configuration profile. In fact, in the Mail application, selecting the menu option Mail > Accounts will redirect you to the Internet Accounts preferences.

Mail also includes its own account setup assistant that will walk you through the process of configuring mail account settings. This assistant starts automatically if no account has been set when Mail is opened, but you can start it anytime by selecting Mail > Add Account. The assistant first presents an interface similar to that found in Internet Accounts preferences.

When you select one of these default mail account types, the assistant attempts to automatically determine the appropriate mail protocol, security, and authentication settings. This includes support for the Autodiscovery feature of Microsoft Exchange Server. Further, when you set up a mail account here, the system will automatically attempt to configure Notes, Calendar, Reminders, and Contacts as well.

If you need to configure Mail for an account type not listed in the defaults, select the Add Other Mail Account option. After entering basic mail account information, the assistant attempts to automatically determine the appropriate mail settings. If your mail service uses a nonstandard configuration or is unreachable, you may have to manually enter the mail service settings here. This means you may need to work with the service administrator to obtain the appropriate configuration settings.

Add a Mail Account

To get started, provide the following information:

Full Name: Michelle White

Email Address: mkw@pretendco.com

Password: ●●●●●●●●●●●●●●●

Cancel   Create

NOTE ▶ If you need to further tweak mail service settings, you'll find advanced options in Mail Accounts preferences, accessed by selecting Mail > Preferences. When the Mail preference window opens, select the Accounts button in the toolbar to view and manage all Mail accounts.

Closely related to Mail is the Notes application , which allows you to maintain a library of personal text notes. Notes allows for saving text notes on the local system, but you can also have text notes available on multiple devices when the Notes application is configured for access to mail services. This is because Notes utilizes EWS (Exchange Web Services) or IMAP (Internet Message Access Protocol) mail services as the mechanism for saving the notes. The Notes application creates a special Notes mailbox on your mail service and automatically manages this mailbox; thus the Mail application ignores this mailbox. However, you may notice this mailbox when using older versions of Mail or third-party mail clients.

Ideally, Notes will have been configured automatically along with other services via the Internet Accounts preferences or a configuration profile. In fact, in the Notes application, selecting the menu option Notes > Accounts will redirect you to the Internet Accounts preferences. As an option, the Internet Accounts preferences allows you to configure Notes without also configuring Mail. However, Notes still requires use of an EWS or IMAP mail service from a network service provider.

Also like the Mail application, Notes includes its own account setup assistant, which will walk you through the process of configuring mail account settings. This assistant doesn't start automatically when the Notes application is opened, but you can start it anytime by selecting Notes > Add Account. The assistant presents an interface nearly identical to the Mail Setup Assistant because again, Notes connects to mail services.

> **TIP** ▶ Notes can also be shared through other network services by clicking the Share button (right-pointing arrow inside a box) at the bottom of the Notes window.

In summary, OS X Mail and Notes support the following email services:

▶ Standard mailbox access protocols—The standard protocol used between mail clients and mail servers for receiving mail is either Post Office Protocol (POP) on TCP port 110 or IMAP on TCP port 143. However, Notes can only utilize servers that host IMAP mailboxes. Both protocols can also be encrypted with an SSL connection. By default, encrypted POP uses TCP port 995 and encrypted IMAP uses TCP port 993. Finally, iCloud defaults to secure IMAP.

▶ Standard mail sending protocols—The standard protocol used for sending mail from clients to servers and from server to server is Simple Mail Transfer Protocol (SMTP) on TCP port 25. Again, SMTP can be encrypted with an SSL connection on port 25, 465, or 587. The port used for secure SMTP vary by mail server function and administrator preference. Finally, iCloud defaults to secure SMTP.

▶ Exchange-based mail service—Although popular, these services do not use mail standards for client communication. Instead, Mail communicates using the EWS protocol. EWS uses the standard ports for web traffic: TCP port 80 for standard transport and TCP port 443 for secure transport.

Calendar and Reminders

OS X includes a scheduling application, Calendar, previously known as iCal. While Calendar can certainly work on its own for managing your calendar information on your local Mac, it also integrates with a variety of network calendar services based on the EWS or CalDAV protocols. CalDAV, or Calendaring Extensions to WebDAV, as its name states, extends WebDAV (Web Distributed Authoring and Versioning), which is itself an extension of HTTP.

Ideally, Calendar will already have been configured automatically along with Mail via the Internet Accounts preferences or a configuration profile. In fact, in the Calendar application, selecting the menu option Calendar > Accounts redirects you to the Internet Accounts preferences.

Calendar also includes its own account setup assistant, which will walk you through the process of configuring mail account settings. This assistant doesn't start automatically when the Calendar application is opened, but you can start it anytime by selecting Calendar > Add Account.

When you select one of these default calendar account types, the assistant attempts to automatically determine the appropriate calendar service security and authentication settings. This includes support for the Autodiscovery feature of Microsoft Exchange Server. Further, when you set up a calendar account here, the system will automatically attempt to configure Mail, Notes, Reminders, and Contacts as well.

If you need to configure Calendar for an account type not listed in the defaults, select the option to Add CalDAV Account. After entering the user mail address and account password, the assistant attempts to automatically determine the appropriate CalDAV settings. If your mail service uses a nonstandard configuration or is unreachable, you may have to manually enter the CalDAV service settings here. This means you may need to work with the service administrator to obtain the appropriate configuration settings.

NOTE ▶ If you need to further tweak calendar service settings, you'll find advanced options in the Calendar Accounts preferences, accessed by selecting Calendar > Preferences. When the Calendar preferences window opens, select the Accounts button in the toolbar to view and manage all calendar service accounts.

Closely related to Calendar is the Reminders application, which allows you to maintain a personal to-do list. Reminders enables to-do lists to be saved on the local system, but you can also have to-do lists available on multiple devices when the Reminders application is configured for access to calendar services. This is because Reminders utilizes EWS or CalDAV network calendar services as the mechanism for saving the notes. Reminders creates to-do calendar events and automatically manages these events. Thus, the Calendar application ignores to-do events. However, many third-party calendar applications support to-do events within their interface; this includes previous versions of OS X iCal.

Ideally, Reminders will have been configured automatically along with other services via the Internet Accounts preferences or via a configuration profile. In fact, in the Reminders application, selecting the menu option Reminders > Accounts redirects you to the Internet Accounts preferences. As an option, the Internet Accounts preferences allows you to configure Reminders without also configuring Calendar. However, the Reminders application still requires use of an EWS or CalDAV calendar service from a network service provider.

Also like the Calendar application, Reminders includes its own account setup assistant, which will walk you through the process of configuring mail account settings. This assistant doesn't start automatically when the Reminders application is opened, but you can start it anytime by selecting Reminders > Add Account. The assistant presents an interface similar to the Calendars Setup Assistant because again, Reminders only connects to EWS or CalDAV services. At the time of this writing, Reminders doesn't support Facebook or Google calendar services.

In summary, Calendar and Reminders support the following network calendar services:

▶ CalDAV collaborative calendaring—Calendars supports a network calendar standard known as CalDAV. This standard uses WebDAV as a transport mechanism on TCP port 8008 or 8443 for encrypted communication, but CalDAV adds the administrative processes required to facilitate calendar and scheduling collaboration. The OS X Server Calendar service is based on CalDAV. Furthermore, CalDAV is being developed as an open standard, so any vendor can create software that provides or connects to CalDAV services.

▶ Internet-based calendar services—Calendars and Reminders can use a variety of Internet-based calendar services, including iCloud, Yahoo, and Google calendar services. All three of these services are based on CalDAV and use the encrypted HTTPS protocol over TCP port 443.

▶ Exchange-based calendaring service—Calendars includes support for this popular calendar service. Again, the OS X Exchange integration relies on EWS, which uses TCP port 80 for standard transport and TCP port 443 for secure transport.

▶ Calendar web publishing and subscription—Calendars allows you to share your calendar information by publishing iCalendar files to WebDAV-enabled web servers. Because, as mentioned, WebDAV is an extension to the HTTP protocol, it runs over TCP port 80, or TCP port 443 if encrypted. You can also subscribe to iCalendar files, identified by the filename extension .ics, hosted on WebDAV servers. Configuration is fairly easy, as accessing a shared calendar is identical to accessing a webpage. Simply provide the Calendar application with the URL of the iCalendar file. Although calendar publishing enables you to easily share calendars one way over the web, it doesn't provide a true collaborative calendaring environment.

MORE INFO ▶ Apple hosts dozens of compatible calendars at www.apple.com/downloads/macosx/calendars.

▶ Calendar email invitation—Calendars, again using iCalendar files, is integrated with Mail to automatically send and receive calendar invitations as email attachments. In this case the transport mechanism is whatever your primary mail account is configured to use. While this method isn't a calendaring standard, most popular mail and calendar clients can use this method.

Contacts

OS X includes a contact management application, Contacts, previously known as Address Book. Similar to other OS X network applications, while Contacts can certainly work on its own for managing nonshared contact information on your Mac, it also integrates with a variety of network contact services based on EWS, CardDAV (Card Distributed Authoring and Versioning), or LDAP (Lightweight Directory Access Protocol).

Again, ideally Contacts is configured automatically via Internet Accounts preferences or a configuration profile. However, Contacts also features an easy-to-use setup assistant for configuring specific contact or directory network service accounts. You can start it any-time by selecting Contacts > Add Account. The assistant first presents an interface similar to that found in Internet Accounts preferences.

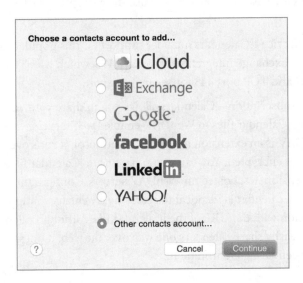

When you select one of these default contacts account types, the assistant attempts to auto-matically determine the appropriate account settings. This includes support for the Auto-discovery feature of Microsoft Exchange Server. Further, when you set up a contacts account here, the system will automatically attempt to configure Mail, Notes, Calendar, and Reminders as well.

If you need to configure Contacts for an account type not listed in the defaults, select the last option, to add another contacts account. The only two other account types supported by the Contacts application are CardDAV and LDAP. Select the account type from the pop-up menu, and then provide the server and authentication information. You may need to work with the service administrator to obtain the appropriate configuration settings.

NOTE ▶ If you need to further tweak contact service settings, you'll find advanced options in the Contacts Accounts preferences, accessed by selecting Contacts > Preferences. When the Contacts preferences window opens, select the Accounts button in the toolbar to view and manage all contact service accounts.

In summary, Contacts supports the following network contact services:

▶ CardDAV contacts service—Contacts supports a network contacts service standard known as CardDAV. Here again, as the name implies, this standard uses WebDAV as a transport mechanism on TCP port 8800 or 8843 for encrypted communication. The OS X Server Contacts service is based on CardDAV. Furthermore, CardDAV is being developed as an open standard, so any vendor can create software that provides or connects to CardDAV services.

NOTE ▶ The Apple selection of TCP ports 8800 and 8843 for CardDAV is not based on any assigned standard. Some implementations of CardDAV may use the standard ports for HTTP(S) and TCP ports 80 and 443 for encrypted communication.

▶ Internet-based contact services—Contacts can use a variety of Internet-based contact services, including iCloud, Google, Facebook, LinkedIn, and Yahoo contact services. All of these services are based on CardDAV and use the encrypted HTTPS protocol over TCP port 443.

▶ Exchange-based contact service—Contacts includes support for this popular contact sharing service. Again, the OS X Exchange integration relies on EWS, which uses TCP port 80 for standard transport and TCP port 443 for secure transport.

▶ Directory service contacts—Contacts can search contact databases via LDAP, the standard for network directory services, which uses TCP port 389 for standard transport and TCP port 636 for secure transport. Contacts can be configured for LDAP services either directly from its account setup assistant or via integration with the OS X systemwide directory service, as configured in User & Groups preferences.

Messages

Instant messaging has grown well beyond text chatting with Messages, the application formerly known as iChat, included with OS X. Messages supports ten-way audio conferencing, four-way video conferencing, peer-to-peer file sharing, remote screen sharing, and high-resolution Messages Theater for sharing video from supported applications. Finally, Messages also includes support for the iCloud push-based messaging service iMessage, which allows you to communicate with iOS devices as well.

Again, ideally Messages will have been configured automatically via Internet Accounts preferences or a configuration profile. However, Messages also includes its own account setup assistant that will walk you through the process of configuring messaging account settings. This assistant starts automatically if no account has been set when Messages is opened, but you can start it anytime by selecting Messages > Add Account.

If you haven't signed in to iCloud, you are first prompted to configure iMessage. You can enter any valid Apple ID to configure iMessage. After authentication, you may be prompted to choose additional iMessage identifiers that can be used to reach you, like other email accounts or mobile numbers.

If you choose to skip configuration of iMessage, the Messages Setup Assistant then presents an interface similar to that found in Internet Accounts preferences. You can also start this assistant any time by selecting the menu option Messages > Add Account.

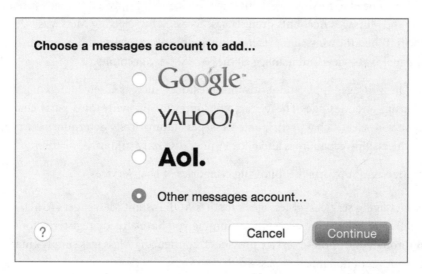

When you select one of these default messaging account types, the assistant attempts to automatically determine the appropriate account settings. If you need to configure

Messages for an account type not listed in the defaults, select the last option, to add another messages account. The only other account type supported by Messages is a manually configured Jabber service. Curiously, you can also choose to configure the three account types seen from the default list.

Select the account type from the pop-up menu and then provide the server and authentication information. You may need to work with the service administrator to obtain the appropriate configuration settings.

NOTE ▶ If you need to further tweak message service settings, you'll find advanced options in the Messages Accounts preferences, accessed by selecting Messages > Preferences. When the Messages preferences window opens, select the Accounts button in the toolbar to view and manage all message service accounts.

NOTE ▶ The Messages application's advanced features, such as video conferencing, screen sharing, and Messages Theater, are not supported by many third-party chat clients. When you select a chat participant, Messages automatically determines the client software's messaging capabilities and allows you to use only supported features.

In summary, Messages supports the following categories of chat services:

▶ Internet messaging services—Messages supports AOL Instant Messenger (AIM), Google Talk, and Yahoo chat accounts. Assuming you have already registered for an account through one of these service providers, configuring Messages simply entails entering your account name and password.

▶ iMessage—Based on the Apple push technology, the iMessage service is unique among chat services. The Apple push technology is highly efficient for devices that rely on battery power and may occasionally lose network connectivity. This makes the iMessage service ideal for messaging with iOS devices. Again, you can only configure iMessage via Internet Accounts preferences or iCloud preferences.

NOTE ▶ The iCloud iMessage service is not compatible with advanced features such as video conferencing, screen sharing, and Messages Theater. These services are only available when using traditional chat services like AIM or Jabber.

▶ Privately hosted messaging services—Messages works with open source Jabber servers, including the OS X Server Messages service. Jabber servers are based on the Extensible Messaging and Presence Protocol (XMPP), which uses TCP port 5222 or 5223 for encrypted communication.

▶ Ad hoc messaging—Messages can use the Bonjour network discovery protocol to automatically find other Messages or iChat users. No configuration is necessary to access Bonjour messaging. Bonjour details are covered in Lesson 24 "Host Sharing and Personal Firewall".

Messages is compatible with a wide variety of messaging features and instant messaging protocols—which means it uses far too many TCP and UDP ports to list here. As covered previously, you can find a full list of ports used by Apple products in Apple Support article HT202944, "Well known TCP and UDP ports used by Apple software products."

Reference 23.3
File-Sharing Protocols

Many protocols exist for transferring files across networks and the Internet, but the most efficient are those designed specifically to share file systems. Network file servers can make entire file systems available to your client computer across the network.

Client software built into the OS X Finder can mount a network file service much as it would mount a locally connected storage volume. Once a network file service is mounted to the Mac, you can read, write, and manipulate files and folders as if you were accessing a local file system.

Additionally, access privileges to network file services are defined by the same ownership and permissions architecture used by local file systems. Details on file systems, ownership, and permissions are covered in Lesson 11 "Permissions and Sharing".

OS X provides built-in support for these network file service protocols:

▶ Server Message Block version 3 (SMB 3) on TCP ports 139 and 445—This is the default (and preferred) file-sharing protocol for OS X Yosemite. Historically, the SMB protocol was mainly used by Windows systems, but many other platforms have adopted support for some version of this protocol. The SMB 3 implementation in OS X works with advanced SMB features such as end-to-end encryption (if enabled on the server), per-packet signatures and validation, Distributed File Service (DFS) architecture, resource compounding, large maximum transmission unit (MTU) support, and aggressive performance caching. Finally, OS X maintains backward compatibility with older SMB standards.

▶ Apple Filing Protocol (AFP) version 3 on TCP port 548 or encrypted over Secure Shell (SSH) on TCP port 22—This is the traditional Apple native network file service. The current version of AFP is compatible with all the features of the Apple native file system, Mac OS Extended. Further, AFP is still the default for backup systems that are based on Time Machine.

▶ Network File System (NFS) version 4, which may use a variety of TCP or UDP ports—Used primarily by UNIX systems, NFS supports many advanced file system features used by OS X.

▶ WebDAV on TCP port 80 (HTTP) or encrypted on TCP port 443 (HTTPS)—As mentioned earlier, this protocol is an extension to the common HTTP service and provides basic read/write file services.

▶ File Transfer Protocol (FTP) on TCP ports 20 and 21 or encrypted on TCP port 989 and 990 (FTPS)—This protocol is in many ways the lowest common denominator of file systems. FTP is supported by nearly every computing platform, but it provides only the most basic file system functionality. Further, the Finder supports only read capability for FTP or FTPS shares.

NOTE ▶ Don't confuse FTPS (FTP-SSL) with another similar protocol, SFTP (SSH File Transfer Protocol). The distinction is that FTPS uses SSL encryption on TCP port 990, and SFTP uses SSH encryption on TCP port 22. The Finder does not support FTPS. However, both are supported in Terminal.

Reference 23.4
Connecting to File Shares

The Finder provides two methods for connecting to a network file system: automatically discovering shared resources by browsing them in the Finder Network folder or manually connecting by entering the address of the server providing the file service.

Browsing to File Shares

You can browse for dynamically discovered file services from two locations in the Finder. The first location is the Shared list located in the Finder sidebar. If it's enabled in Finder preferences, the Shared list is ideal for quickly discovering computers providing file services on a small network. The Shared list shows only the first eight discovered computers providing services. If additional servers are discovered, the last item in the Shared list, All, is a link to the Finder Network folder.

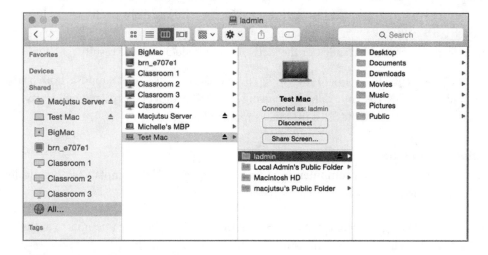

TIP The sidebar also appears in any application's Open dialog with exactly the same items as are available from the Finder.

TIP The Finder Shared list shows servers that you are currently connected to, even if they didn't originally appear in the Shared list.

TIP The Finder also lets you browse to screen-sharing (Virtual Network Computing, or VNC) hosts via Bonjour, as covered in Lesson 24 "Host Sharing and Personal Firewall".

The Finder Network folder is a special place in OS X. The Network folder is not a standard folder at all; it's an amalgamation of all dynamically discovered network file services and all currently mounted file systems, including manually mounted ones. Obviously, the Network folder is constantly changing based on information gathered from the two dynamic network service discovery protocols compatible with OS X—Bonjour and SMB/NetBIOS/WINS—so you can only browse SMB or AFP file services from the Network folder.

Smaller networks may have only one level of network services. Conversely, if you have a larger network that features multiple service discovery domains, they appear as subfolders inside the Network folder. Each subfolder is named by the domain it represents. Items inside the domain subfolders represent shared resources configured for that specific network area.

To browse and connect to an SMB or AFP file service from the Finder sidebar, select the computer you want to connect to from the Shared list, or select a computer from the Finder Network folder. In the Finder, the quickest route to the Network folder is either to choose Go > Network from the menu bar or to press Shift-Command-K. Selecting a computer from either the Shared list or the Network folder yields similar results.

> **NOTE** ▶ When browsing in the Finder, if you select a server that supports both SMB and AFP, OS X Yosemite defaults to using the SMB protocol. Further, it will always use the latest version of the SMB protocol supported by the sharing service.

Automatic File Service Authentication

The moment you select a computer providing services, the Mac attempts to automatically authenticate using one of three methods:

▶ If you are using Kerberos single sign-on authentication, the Mac attempts to authenticate to the selected computer using your Kerberos credentials.

▶ If you are using non-Kerberos authentication but you have connected to the selected computer before and chose to save the authentication information to your keychain, the Mac attempts to use the saved information.

▶ The Mac attempts to authenticate as a guest user. Keep in mind that guest access is an option on file servers that many administrators disable.

If the Mac succeeds in authenticating to the selected computer, the Finder shows you the account name it connected with and also lists the shared volumes available to this account. Selecting a shared volume connects and mounts its file system.

Manual File Service Authentication

If the Mac was unable to automatically connect to the selected computer, or if you need to authenticate with a different account, click the Connect As button to open an authentication dialog.

You can authenticate to a sharing service using one of three methods:

▶ Selecting the Guest radio button, if available, indicates that you wish to connect anonymously to the file service.

► Selecting the Registered User radio button enables you to authenticate using a local or network account known by the computer providing the shared items. Optionally, you can select the checkbox that saves this authentication information to your login keychain.

► Selecting the Using an Apple ID radio button enables you to authenticate to an SMB or AFP share using an Apple ID. For this option to appear, both the local Mac and the computer hosting the share must be running OS X. Further, the local accounts on both systems must be tied to an Apple ID, as covered in Lesson 5 "User Accounts".

Click the Connect button, and the Mac authenticates and shows you a new list of shared volumes available to the account. Each available share appears as a folder. Click once on a shared item to connect and mount its file system.

Manually Connecting File Services

To manually connect to a file service, you must specify a network identifier (URL) for the file server providing the service. You may also have to enter authentication information and choose or enter the name of a specific shared resource path. When connecting to an SMB or AFP service, you can authenticate first and then choose a shared item, or optionally provide a path. Conversely, when connecting to an NFS, WebDAV (HTTP), or FTP service, you may have to specify the shared items or full path as part of the server address and then authenticate if required.

Manually Connecting to SMB or AFP

To manually connect to an SMB or AFP file service from the Finder, choose Go > Connect to Server, or press Command-K to open the Finder Connect to Server dialog. In the Server Address field, enter smb:// or afp:// followed by the server's IP address, DNS host name, computer name, or Bonjour name.

> **TIP** ▶ If you don't specify a protocol prefix, the Connect to Server dialog will attempt to pick the appropriate file sharing protocol. Again, the preferred default file sharing protocol for OS X Yosemite is SMB 3.

> **TIP** ▶ Optionally, after the server address, you can enter another slash and then the name of a specific shared item. This bypasses the dialog for selecting a specific file share.

> **TIP** ▶ Clicking Browse in the Connect to Server dialog brings you to the Finder Network folder, allowing you to browse for a server, as covered previously in "Browsing to File Shares" on page 751.

If automatic file service authentication is available, as covered earlier in the "Automatic File Service Authentication" on page 752 section of this lesson, you do not have to enter authentication information. If it isn't, a dialog appears requiring you to enter authentication information. This authentication dialog is identical to the one covered earlier in the "Manual File Service Authentication" on page 753 section of this lesson.

Once you have authenticated to the file service, you are presented with the list of shared volumes that your account is allowed to access. Select the shared item you want to mount. Optionally, you can hold down the Command key to select multiple shared items from the list.

Manually Connecting to NFS, WebDAV, or FTP

To manually connect to an NFS, WebDAV, or FTP file service from the Finder, choose Go > Connect to Server, or press Command-K to open the Finder Connect to Server dialog.

In the Server Address field, enter one of the following:

▶ **nfs://** followed by the server address, another slash, and then the absolute file path of the shared items.

▶ **http://** for WebDAV (or **https://** for WebDAV encrypted via SSL), followed by the server address. Each WebDAV site has only one mountable share, but you can optionally enter another slash and then specify a folder inside the WebDAV share.

▶ **ftp://** (or **ftps://** for FTP encrypted via SSL), followed by the server address. FTP servers also have only one mountable root share, but you can optionally enter another slash and then specify a folder inside the FTP share.

Depending on the protocol settings, you may be presented with an authentication dialog. Specifically, NFS connections never display an authentication dialog. The NFS protocol uses the local user that you're already logged in as for authorization purposes or Kerberos single sign-on authentication.

If you are presented with an authentication dialog, enter the appropriate authentication information there. Optionally, you can select the checkbox that saves this authentication information to your login keychain. When connecting to NFS, WebDAV, or FTP file services, the share mounts immediately after authentication.

Mounted Shares

Once the Mac has mounted the network file share, that share can appear in several locations from the Finder or any application's Open dialog, including the Computer location, the desktop, and the sidebar's Shared list, depending on configuration. However, mounted network volumes *always* appear at the Computer location in the Finder, accessible by choosing Go > Computer or by pressing Shift-Command-C. By default, connected network volumes do not show up on the desktop. You can change this behavior from the General tab of the Finder Preferences dialog.

TIP ▶ Remember, the sidebar also appears in any application's Open dialog with exactly the same items that are available from the Finder.

Manually entering server information every time you connect to a server is a hassle. Two features in the Connect to Server dialog make this process efficient for your users. The dialog maintains a history of your past server connections. You can access this history by clicking the small clock icon to the right of the Server Address field. Also, you can create a list of favorite servers by clicking the plus button to the right of the Server Address field.

Disconnecting Mounted Shares

It is important to recognize that the Mac treats mounted network volumes similarly to locally attached volumes, so you must remember to always properly unmount and eject network volumes when you're done with them. Mounted network volumes are unmounted and ejected from the Finder using the same techniques you would use on a locally connected volume. Unmounting and ejecting volumes is covered in Lesson 9 "File Systems and Storage". One difference in working with mounted volumes is that the Eject button appears multiple times in the Finder, wherever the server name or the shared items appear.

In practice, though, it's difficult for users to remember they have network shares mounted, as there is no locally attached hardware device to remind them. Further, laptop users often roam out of wireless network range without even thinking about what network shares they may have mounted.

If a network change or problem disconnects the Mac from a mounted network share, the Mac spends several minutes attempting to reconnect to the server hosting the shared items. If after several minutes the Mac cannot reconnect to the server, the system will fully disconnect from the share.

Automatically Connecting File Shares

On a positive note, because the Finder treats mounted network shares as similar to other file system items, you can save time and make life easier for you and your users by creating automatic connections to network shared items. One method is to have a network share mount automatically when a user logs in by adding the network share to the user's login items. Managing login items is covered in Lesson 5 "User Accounts".

Alternatively, you can create easy-to-use shortcuts to often-used network shares. One method involves creating Dock shortcuts by dragging network shares or their enclosed items to the right side of the Dock. You can also create aliases on the user's desktop that link to often-used network shares or even specific items inside a network share. (Creating aliases is covered in Lesson 13 "Hidden Items, Shortcuts, and File Archives".) Either method you use automatically connects to the network share when the item is selected.

TIP ▶ You cannot drag items from the Finder sidebar or the Network browser to the login items on the Dock. Instead, select the network share from the desktop or the Computer location in the Finder. You can access the Computer location in the Finder by choosing Go > Computer.

TIP ▶ Remember that by using Kerberos single sign-on authentication or by saving authentication information to the keychain, you can bypass authentication dialogs as well.

Reference 23.5
Network Service Troubleshooting

To effectively troubleshoot a network issue, you must isolate the issue into one of three categories: local, network, or service. Most issues involving failure to access network services probably fall under the service category. This means that you should probably focus most of your efforts on troubleshooting the specific service you're having issues with.

However, before digging too deep into troubleshooting the specific network service, quickly check for general network issues. First, check to see if other network services are working. Opening a web browser and navigating to a few different local and Internet websites is always a good general network connectivity test.

To be thorough, also test other network services, or test from other computers on the same network. If you're experiencing problems connecting to a file server but you can connect to web servers, chances are your TCP/IP configuration is fine, and you should concentrate on the specifics of the file server. If you're only experiencing problems with one particular service, you probably don't have local or network issues, and you should focus your efforts on troubleshooting just that service.

Conversely, if other network clients or services aren't working either, your issue is likely related to local or network issues. Double-check local network settings to ensure proper configuration from both the Network preferences and Network Utility. If you find that other computers aren't working, you might have a widespread network issue that goes beyond troubleshooting the client computers. For more information on general network troubleshooting, see Lesson 22 "Network Troubleshooting".

TIP ▶ If you're experiencing problems with a service provided by Apple, you can check real-time Apple service status at this website: www.apple.com/support/systemstatus/.

Network Utility: Port Scan

Once you decide to focus on troubleshooting a problematic network service, one of your most important diagnostic tools is the network Port Scan utility. Part of the Network Utility application, Port Scan scans for any open network service ports on the specified network address.

TIP ▶ The quickest way to open Network Utility is via the Spotlight search menu. Usually searching simply for "net" will list Network Utility in the search results.

As covered earlier in this lesson, network service protocols are tied to specific TCP and UDP network ports. Network devices providing a service must leave the appropriate network ports open to accept incoming connections from other network clients. Port Scan reveals whether the required ports are indeed open. If the ports aren't open, that device either is not providing the expected service or is configured to provide the service in a nonstandard method. Either way, this indicates that the issue lies with the device providing the service, not your Mac.

To verify network service availability, start by opening Network Utility and clicking the Ping tab at the top. Before scanning the ports, check for basic network connectivity by attempting to ping the device that is supposed to be providing the service. Enter the device's network address or host name and click the Ping button. If the ping is successful, it returns with the amount of time it took for the ping to travel to the network device and then return. Assuming you have network connectivity to the other device, continue the scan.

To scan for a network service, click the Port Scan tab. Again, enter the network address or host name of the device that is supposed to be providing the service. If you're only trouble-shooting a specific service, limit the scan to just that service's default ports by selecting the appropriate checkbox and entering a beginning and ending port range. Click the Scan button to initiate the scan process.

NOTE ▶ There are 65,535 available TCP and UDP network ports, so scanning all of them is unnecessary and overly time intensive. Even if you don't know the specific port, most common ports are between 0 and 1024.

NOTE ▶ Network administrators view repeated network pings and broad port scans as a threat. Thus, some network devices are configured not to respond even when working properly. In general, you should avoid excessive network pinging and scanning an unnecessarily broad range of ports when testing others' servers.

Depending on the scan range you choose, it may take several minutes to complete the scan. Any open ports discovered are listed along with the associated network protocol, if known.

NOTE ▶ There are some inaccuracies with the protocol reporting of the Port Scan feature. For example, port 106 (listed as 3com-tsmux) is actually the OS X Server password service, and port 625 (listed as dec_dlm) is actually the directory service proxy. This is because these ports are registered by the Internet Assigned Numbers Authority (www.iana.org) for the reported protocols. However, Apple is using these numbers for its own purposes.

Troubleshooting Network Applications

Aside from general network service troubleshooting, you can try a few application-specific troubleshooting techniques. First, double-check any application-specific configuration and preference settings. It takes only a few moments, and you may find that users have inadvertently caused the problem by changing a setting they shouldn't have.

Be aware of these specifics when troubleshooting network applications:

▶ Safari—Safari is a good web browser, but it's not perfect. You may find that some websites do not render properly or work correctly with Safari. If you are unable to access certain websites with Safari, try a third-party web browser. Several are available for the Mac, including Google Chrome, Firefox, OmniWeb, and Opera.

▶ Mail—Improper mail account configuration settings are the most common cause of Mail application issues. Fortunately, the Mail application includes a built-in account diagnostic tool called Mail Connection Doctor that attempts to establish a connection with all configured incoming and outgoing mail servers. To open Mail Connection Doctor, choose Window > Connection Doctor within the Mail application. If a problem is found, a suggested resolution is offered, but for a more detailed diagnostic view, click the Show Detail button to reveal the progress log, and then click the Check Again button to rerun the tests.

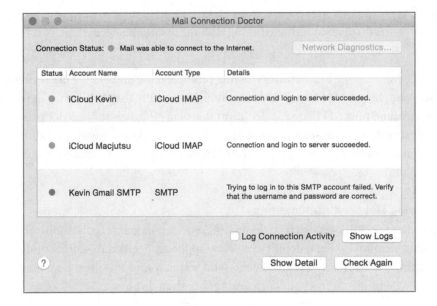

TIP Apple also provides an online Mail Setup Assistant database that may help you identify mail client configuration issues: https://www.apple.com/support/mail-settings-lookup/.

► Messages—Messages also suffers from occasional improper account configuration, but it's a less frequent occurrence than with Mail. More often, Messages experiences connectivity issues when attempting advanced messaging features like voice and video conferencing. Consequently, Messages also features a Connection Doctor that lets you view conference statistics, chat capabilities, and the Messages error log. In Messages, choose Video > Connection Doctor. If you have experienced recent errors, the Connection Doctor opens to the error log, but you can view other information from the Show pop-up menu.

File-Sharing Service Troubleshooting

There are a few known OS X file-service issues you should be aware of. They aren't software bugs in the sense that something is broken and requires a fix. Rather, these issues represent compatibility and design choices that are intentional but may still cause you problems.

AppleDouble Issues

As covered in Lesson 15 "Metadata and Spotlight", OS X uses separate metadata stores. The NFS and WebDAV file-sharing protocols do not support metadata of this type. Thus, when files are written to a mounted NFS or WebDAV volume, OS X automatically splits these files into two separate files.

With this practice, commonly known as AppleDouble, the data retains the original name, but the metadata is saved with a period and underscore before the original name. The Finder recognizes these split files and shows only a single file to the user. However, users on other operating systems see two separate files and may have trouble accessing the appropriate one.

Microsoft's Services for Macintosh Issues

You may encounter another issue when trying to access an AFP network volume from a Windows file server. Windows servers prior to 2008 include Services for Macintosh (SFM), which provides only the legacy AFP 2 file service. OS X is still compatible with AFP 2 but is optimized for AFP 3.1.

There are many known performance issues with AFP 2, so you should avoid it at all costs. Ideally, you should use a system running OS X Server to provide AFP services for your network. However, if you must keep the Windows file server, you can add AFP 3.1 support by installing the Group Logic ExtremeZ-IP (www.grouplogic.com). Also remember that OS X clients include a robust SMB client that natively connects to your Windows server with a high degree of reliability and performance.

> **MORE INFO** ▶ OS X works with legacy AFP only if you follow the steps in Apple Support article HT200160, "Connecting to legacy AFP services."

Exercise 23.1
Configure a Network Service Account

▶ **Prerequisites**

- ▶ You must have created the Chris Johnson account ("Exercise 5.1 Manage User Accounts" on page 145).

- ▶ You must be performing these exercises in a class or have set up your own server configured as in the Mainserver Setup Instructions.

The client applications built into OS X can use a wide variety of network services, and the Internet Accounts pane in System Preferences makes setting up suites of services easy. You have already set up iCloud-based services on your computer. In this exercise, you will also configure your computer to use services provided by an OS X Yosemite server.

View Your Existing Network Accounts

1   If necessary, log in as Chris Johnson.

2   Open the Contacts application.

3   Open the Contacts preferences by choosing Contacts > Preferences (Command-Comma).

4   Click the Accounts button to see the accounts your Contacts application is configured to use.

If you have configured iCloud services for the Chris Johnson account, you will see the iCloud account listed here.

This pane of the Contacts preferences can be used to view and add network accounts for Contacts, but often you have accounts that are used for groups of related services.

5   Close the Preferences window, and quit Contacts.

6   Open System Preferences, and select the iCloud pane.

Your iCloud account information appears, along with options for controlling which apps and capabilities are turned on for iCloud. Note that these settings are also available in the Internet Accounts pane.

7   If you are signed in to iCloud, deselect the Mail service for your iCloud account.

Not having iCloud mail mixed with the new account will simplify testing later in the exercise.

Set Up a New Network Account

1 In System Preferences, switch to the Internet Accounts pane.

   If you are signed in to iCloud, that account will be listed here. No other accounts are listed.

2 If a list of account types is not shown on the right, click the Add (+) button under the account list.

3   Scroll to the bottom of the list, and click Add Other Account.

    This option lists additional account types you can set up.

4   Select "Add an OS X Server account," and click Create.

Mainserver is available in the nearby server list.

5 Select Mainserver, and click Continue.

You are prompted for the server account you want to use. If you are performing these exercises in a class, your account name will include your student number or seat number. If you are performing these exercises on your own, use 1 as your student number.

6 Enter the following for your account information:

Name: Student *n* (where *n* is your student number)

Account: student*n* (where *n* is your student number)

Password: student

7   Click Set Up. If you receive an error message, check the settings, and try again.

8   In the "Select the apps..." dialog, deselect VPN, and click Done.

Setting up the VPN service would make changes to the computer's network configuration, which would require administrative authentication. Also, you may have already configured the VPN service using a configuration profile in "Exercise 21.3 Configure VPN Settings" on page 688.

9   If you receive a message that a secure connection couldn't be established, click Continue.

It may take a few moments to set up all of the accounts.

10   When the account setup finishes, quit System Preferences.

Test Your New Account

1   Open the Mail application.

A dialog may appear indicating that Mail can't verify the identity of the server; if it does not, you have already configured your computer to trust the server, and you can skip to step 5.

This appears because Mail is attempting to make a secure connection using SSL but the SSL certificate the server presents has not been signed by a trusted authority. Thus, Mail cannot tell whether the server is the one you intend to connect to or an impostor.

This problem can occur because the server is not properly configured but also might indicate that you have reached a malicious fake. Unfortunately, there is often no reliable way to tell whether there is a real problem or not. In this case, it is occurring because Mainserver is not run by the legitimate owner of pretendco.com; it is a fake, but it is a harmless fake.

2   Click Show Certificate.

The dialog expands and displays more details about the server's SSL certificate.

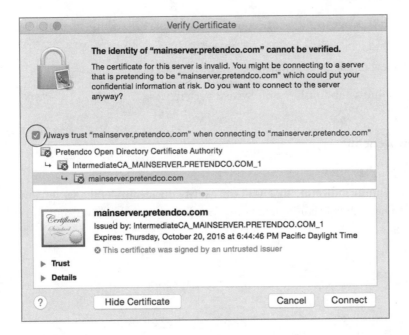

3   Select "Always trust," and then click Connect.

This adds the certificate to your keychain and creates a trust policy so that this server certificate will automatically be trusted in the future. Note that if you had been connected to a "real" server (especially one that handles sensitive information, such as your bank's web server), it would have been safer to cancel the connection.

4   Authenticate as Chris Johnson to confirm the new trust policy.

Mail checks for new messages in your OS X Server account. You should have a welcome message from the server team.

5   Quit Mail.

If you also had iCloud messages, you may have missed the step to turn off iCloud mail; return to the iCloud preferences pane, and turn off its mail service.

6   Open the Contacts application.

You see an OS X Server account listed in the left side of the window. You do not receive the certificate warning because when you selected "Always trust," you created a policy that applies to all applications, not just Mail.

7   Open Contacts preferences by choosing Contacts > Preferences (Command-Comma).

Your OS X Server account is now listed here as well as the iCloud account.

8   Close the Preferences window, and quit Contacts.

Scan the Server

To prepare for "Exercise 23.3 Troubleshoot Network Services" on page 784, you will record a baseline of what services Mainserver provides when everything is working normally.

1   Open Network Utility (remember that you can press Command–Space bar and use Spotlight to find it).

2 Click the Port Scan tab.

The Port Scan pane scans a server or other IP address to see what network ports are accepting connections. This is explored in more detail in Exercise 23.3.

3 Enter the server address mainserver.local in the IP address field.

4 Select the "Only test ports between" option, and set the range to 1 through 1024.

5 Click Scan.

6 Wait for it to finish scanning, and then expand the Network Utility window until all the results are visible.

Your results may not exactly match those shown here. To record your results, you will take a screenshot of the Network Utility window. For more about taking screenshots in OS X, see "Exercise 6.1 Restore a Deleted User Account" on page 166.

7 Press Command-Shift-4; then release those keys, and press Space bar.

The cursor changes to a camera icon, and the region of the screen it is over is highlighted in blue.

8   Move the pointer over the Network Utility window, and then click to record its contents.

The image is saved to your desktop with the name "Screen Shot" followed by the date and time it was taken.

9   Quit Network Utility.

Exercise 23.2
Use File-Sharing Services

Prerequisites

► You must have created the Chris Johnson account ("Exercise 5.1 Manage User Accounts" on page 145).

► You must be performing these exercises in a class or have set up your own server configured as in the Mainserver Setup Instructions.

Many protocols can be used to transfer files across networks and over the Internet, but some of the most efficient are designed specifically to share file systems, such as AFP and SMB. In this exercise, you will use a Finder window and the Connect to Server command from the Finder Go menu to connect to shared AFP and SMB volumes on another computer, copy a file from the server to your desktop, and copy the file back to the server.

Browse to an SMB Share

These steps will lead you through the process of using the sidebar to mount an SMB volume on the desktop.

1   If necessary, log in as Chris Johnson.

2   In a Finder window, select Mainserver in the Shared section of the sidebar.

If Mainserver is not shown, click All in the sidebar, and then double-click Mainserver in the network view.

Your computer contacts Mainserver and logs in automatically as a guest.

3   Click the Connect As button.

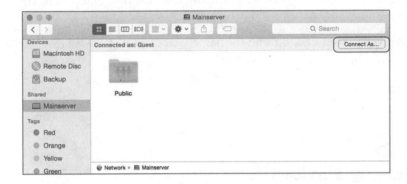

4   When prompted to authenticate, select Registered User, enter the name **student** and the password **student**, select "Remember this password in my keychain," and click Connect.

You are now connected to Mainserver with the "student" account. The Finder window shows that you now have access to more shared folders than you did as a guest. The SMB Shared folder is available only over the SMB protocol, so its appearance here indicates that this is the protocol being used to connect to Mainserver.

Now you will take a look at what you can see in the Public folder on the server.

5 Open Finder preferences using Finder > Preferences (or Command-comma), click General, and select "Connected servers," if it is not already selected.

This shows mounted server volumes on the desktop. Since you have not mounted any shared folders yet, nothing new appears on the desktop at this point.

6 Close the Finder Preferences window.

7 Open the shared folder named Public.

The folder displays in the Finder, and a new network volume icon appears on the desktop. Also, an Eject button appears next to Mainserver in the Finder sidebar.

In the Public folder you see a file (copy.rtf) along with the StudentMaterials folder.

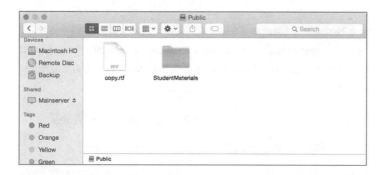

Copy Files to a Network Share

You will use the Finder to copy files to a shared folder mounted over SMB.

1   Drag copy.rtf to your desktop. Since you are dragging from one volume to another, this copies the file rather than moving it.

2   Rename your copy of copy.rtf to Student *n*.rtf (where *n* is your student number if you are in a class or 1 if you are performing these exercises on your own).

You can rename a file by selecting it and pressing Return or by clicking the filename and waiting a moment.

3   Select Mainserver in the Finder sidebar. This returns you to the view of available shared folders.

4   Open the SMB Shared folder. Its icon will appear on your desktop.

5   Drag the renamed file from your desktop onto the SMB Shared folder.

Automatically Mount a Network Share

OS X provides several ways to memorize a share point to allow easy access to it. In this section, you will configure your user preferences to automatically mount a share point whenever you log in.

1   Open System Preferences, and select the Users & Groups preferences pane.

2   With Chris Johnson selected in the user list, click the Login Items tab.

Note that you do not need to authenticate as an administrator to access your login items; they are a personal preference, so standard users can manage their own login items.

3   Drag the SMB Shared icon from your desktop to the login items list.

Anything in your login items list will be automatically opened every time you log in. It can include applications, documents, folders, and so on. By adding a shared folder, you have configured it to mount every time you log in. Since you also memorized the server account name and password when you connected, the connection should be fully automatic.

4   Quit System Preferences.

5   Disconnect from Mainserver by clicking the Eject button next to Mainserver in the Finder sidebar.

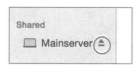

Disconnecting from the server automatically unmounts both the Public and SMB Shared folders. You can also unmount them individually if you prefer.

6   Log out and back in as Chris Johnson.

The SMB Shared folder is automatically remounted and opened in the Finder. Note that if you are connecting via Wi-Fi, it may take a minute or so to reconnect.

7   Reopen Users & Groups preferences.

8   Click Login Items.

9   Remove SMB Shared from the login items list by selecting it and then clicking the Delete (–) button under the list.

10 Quit System Preferences.

11 Disconnect from Mainserver again.

Manually Connect to an AFP Share

These steps will lead you through the process of using "Connect to Server" (in the Finder) to mount an AFP volume on the desktop.

1   In the Finder, choose Go > Connect to Server (or press Command-K).

2   In the Server Address field, enter afp://mainserver.local to connect using the AFP proto-col.

3   Before you click Connect, click the Add (+) button to the right of the Server Address field.

This adds the server URL to your Favorite Servers list. This is another way to allow easy access to a shared folder.

4   Click Connect.

5   Use the same credentials you used when connecting over SMB, and select "Remember this password in my keychain." Click Connect.

Note that although you have already memorized the SMB password for the server, this is a different file service, and you must also memorize its password.

Since you entered a connection URL that did not specify a shared folder to mount, you will be asked which folders you want to mount. Note that this time you do not see the SMB Shared folder, but you do see the AFP Shared folder.

6   Select the Public and AFP Shared folders, and click OK.

The volumes mount, and you see the same files in Public that you saw when connecting using SMB. You have connected to the same folder on the server, so this is not surprising.

7   Drag the Student *n*.rtf file from your desktop to the AFP Shared folder.

8   Disconnect from the server, either by dragging the volume icons to the Trash or by clicking the Eject button in the Finder sidebar.

Exercise 23.3
Troubleshoot Network Services

> ### Prerequisites
>
> ► You must have created the Chris Johnson account ("Exercise 5.1 Manage User Accounts" on page 145).
>
> ► You must be performing these exercises in a class or have set up your own server configured as in the Mainserver Setup Instructions.
>
> ► You must have performed "Exercise 23.1 Configure a Network Service Account" on page 768.

In this exercise, the mail service will fail, and you will use several network service troubleshooting tools to investigate the problem.

Turn Off the Mail Service or Wait for the Instructor to Do So

If you are performing these exercises in class, notify the instructor that you are ready for the mail service to be turned off, and wait for the instructor to tell you to proceed; then skip to the "Troubleshoot with the Mail.app Connection Doctor" on page 785.

If you are performing these exercises on your own, follow these steps on your server computer to turn off the mail service:

1   On your server computer, log in as Local Admin.

2   Open the Server application.

3   Select Mail from the sidebar.

4   Turn the service off.

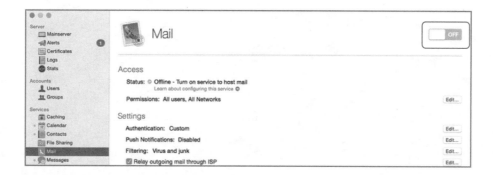

5   Quit the Server application, and return to your regular exercise computer.

Troubleshoot with the Mail.app Connection Doctor

1   If necessary, log in as Chris Johnson.

2   Open the Mail application.

3   Choose File > New Message (Command-N).

4   Address the message to david@pretendco.com, and add a Subject.

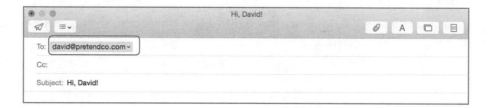

5   Click the Send button (the paper airplane icon near the top left).

You are notified that the message cannot be sent because the server refused to allow a connection.

Note that depending on your network setup, the error you see may refer to "main-server.local" instead of "mainserver.pretendco.com."

The Mail application has a built-in Connection Doctor that can do basic service diagnostics.

6   Click Connection Doctor in the error dialog.

The Connection Doctor opens and runs a series of tests to see which parts of your mail service are working. In this case, it detects that your Internet connection is working (the green Connection Status indicator at the top) but that neither the mail sending service (SMTP) nor the receiving service (IMAP) is working because it cannot connect to either service.

Note that an iCloud IMAP service may be listed. The Connection Doctor tests it even though the service is turned off.

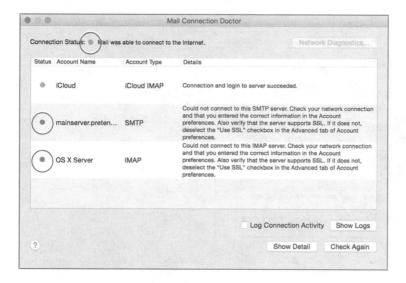

If this were a minor glitch, the Mail Connection Doctor might be able to point you to a solution. Since the server appears to be completely unreachable, you will now turn to Network Utility for further troubleshooting.

7   Close the Mail Connection Doctor window.

8   In the outgoing message error dialog, click Try Later.

9   Quit Mail.

Troubleshoot with the Network Utility

1   Open Network Utility. Remember that you can use Spotlight to find it.

Since Mail is unable to reach the server, you should first test to make sure the network connections between your computer and the server are working.

2   Click the Ping tab.

3   In the "Enter the network address to ping" field, enter mainserver.local.

4   Click Ping.

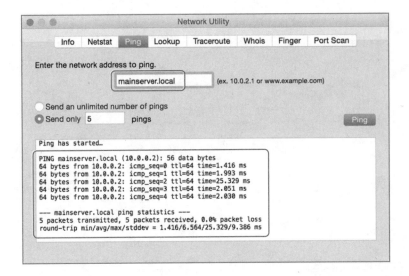

The ping probes are able to reach the server. This tells you that the network connection between your computer and the server is working, so you need to move on to the services you are trying to use.

5   Click the Port Scan tab.

The Port Scan can scan a server to see what TCP port numbers it has services running on; usually, you can tell what services are available based on the port numbers.

NOTE ▶ Many malicious network attacks start with or employ port scans, so this type of troubleshooting might be interpreted as an attack. Before you scan ports on a target computer, request permission from its owner or a network or server administrator, if possible. As a general rule, only scan ports on computers you have responsibility for. Many environments employ automatic countermeasures. Simply scanning a server may get your computer or IP address blacklisted, preventing you from knowing if you have resolved the problem you are troubleshooting.

6   If necessary, enter the server address mainserver.local in the IP address field.

7   If necessary, select the "Only test ports between" option, and set the range to 1 through 1024.

8   Click Scan.

9   Watch the scan as it identifies the open ports.

Port Scan lists the open ports it finds, along with the names of the services usually associated with them. For example, port 80 is the standard (or "well-known") port for web services (the HTTP protocol), and port 548 is the standard port for the Apple Filing Protocol ("afpovertcp"). These well-known ports are commonly used in the industry and facilitate interoperability across different vendors' implementations of the same protocols. To test whether a computer has an HTTP (web) server, you would run a port scan on it and test whether TCP port 80 is open. HTTPS (an SSL-secured web service) normally uses TCP port 443, so if HTTPS requests are not working, port 443 might be blocked or inactive.

For a listing of many ports used by Apple products, see Apple Support article HT202944, "Well known TCP and UDP ports used by Apple software products."

10 Open the screenshot you took in "Exercise 23.1 Configure a Network Service Account" on page 768 showing which ports were open when the services were working, and compare it with the current scan.

In this case, you are trying to troubleshoot the mail service, which normally involves TCP ports 25 (SMTP), 110 (POP3), 143 (IMAP), 587 (message submission), 933 (IMAPS), and 995 (POP3S). Note that mail servers that use proprietary protocols such as Exchange provide access to those protocols over other port numbers.

All of those ports are listed in the earlier scan but not in the current scan. This indicates either that the server does not offer mail service (which is true here since the service is switched off) or that a firewall is blocking access to the service.

This is as far as you can resolve this problem from the client side; further troubleshooting would mean looking in detail at the server and network firewalls, which is beyond the scope of this exercise.

11 Quit Network Utility.

Lesson 24

Host Sharing and Personal Firewall

Although OS X Server requires a separate purchase on the Mac App Store, OS X already includes many of the core technologies that make OS X Server possible. Of course, OS X Server supports additional advanced network services and administration tools, but the two systems share the same software for providing several network services.

In this lesson, you will focus on using OS X as both a network client and a shared resource for a variety of network and Internet services. After an introduction to the general concepts of providing shared services, you will delve into remotely controlling OS X systems via screen sharing. Then you will see how to use AirDrop—the easiest way to share files between Apple devices. You will also learn how to secure access to shared resources from an OS X system using the built-in firewall. Finally, this lesson covers some general troubleshooting methods to resolve issues that may arise when you attempt to share services from your Mac.

GOALS

▸ Examine the host-sharing services built into OS X

▸ Use screen-sharing tools to access other network hosts

▸ Use AirDrop to quickly and easily share files

▸ Secure shared services by configuring the firewall

▸ Troubleshoot shared service issues

Reference 24.1
Host-Sharing Services

OS X includes an assortment of shared network services, and you'll now see how to manage them. These shared services vary in implementation and purpose, but they all allow users to remotely access resources on the Mac providing the service. They are also all easily enabled and managed from Sharing preferences.

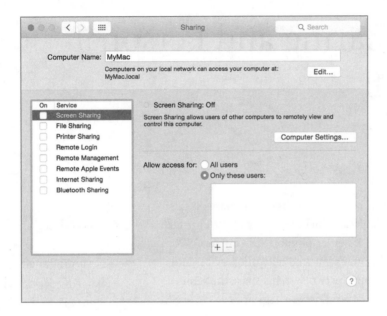

NOTE ▶ Users cannot access services on a Mac in sleep mode. You can turn off your Mac computer's automatic sleep activation or enable automatic waking for network access from Energy Saver preferences. Automatic wake on both wired and wireless networks works on OS X if your network hardware supports it. You can find out more from Apple Support article HT201960, "About Wake on Demand and Bonjour Sleep Proxy."

It's important to recognize the security risk involved in providing a service that allows other users to control processes on your Mac. Obviously, if you're providing a service that allows remote control and execution of software, it's certainly possible for an attacker to cause trouble. Thus, it's paramount that when you enable these types of services you choose strong security settings. Using strong passwords is a good start, but you can also configure limited access to these services from Sharing preferences.

Configuring Network Identification

You may be unable to control your Mac computer's IP address or DNS host name, because the network administrator usually controls these. But as long as the Mac has properly configured TCP/IP settings, as outlined in Lesson 20 "Network Essentials", your configuration is complete for these two identifiers. If your Mac has multiple IP addresses or DNS host names properly configured, it also accepts connections from those.

For dynamic network discovery protocols, though, your Mac uses network identification that can be set locally by an administrator. By default, your Mac automatically chooses a name based either on its DNS name or on the name of the user created with the Setup Assistant. However, at any time an administrative user can change the Mac computer's network identifier from Sharing preferences. Simply enter a name in the Computer Name field, and the system sets the name for each available discovery protocol.

For example, if you enter the computer name My Mac, the Bonjour name is set to My-Mac.local and the NetBIOS/WINS name is set to MY_MAC. If the name you choose is already taken by another local device, the Mac automatically appends a number to the end of the name. NetBIOS/WINS may require additional configuration if your network uses multiple domains or workgroups, as covered in Lesson 21 "Advanced Network Configuration".

The local Bonjour service needs no additional configuration, but if you want to set a custom Bonjour name, click the Edit button below the Computer Name field to reveal the Local Hostname field. From this interface you can also register your Mac computer's identification for Wide-Area Bonjour. To do so, select the "Use dynamic global hostname" checkbox to reveal the Wide-Area Bonjour settings.

Use this name to reach this computer from machines on your local subnet.

Local Hostname: `MyMac`.local

☑ Use dynamic global hostname

Hostname:

User:

Password:

☐ Advertise services in this domain using Bonjour

(?)   Cancel   OK

Shared Services

The OS X sharing services include:

▶ DVD or CD Sharing (Remote Disc)—Allows you to share your Mac computer's optical disc, if available, via the network. It's primarily designed to let you install software for Mac systems that lack a built-in optical disc. Do not confuse Remote Disc with standard file-sharing services covered later in this lesson. This service differs in several key respects: it shares only what is on the optical disc, you cannot configure user-specific access, and it can only be accessed via Bonjour. By enabling this service, the launchd control process starts the ODSAgent background process, which listens for Remote Disc requests on a very high randomly selected TCP port. This service can be accessed only by other Mac computers from the Finder sidebar or the Migration Assistant application.

MORE INFO ▶ For more information about Remote Disc, see Apple Support article HT5287, "DVD or CD sharing: Using Remote Disc."

MORE INFO ▶ Details on the launchd control process are covered in Lesson 27 "System Troubleshooting".

▶ Screen sharing—Allows remote control of your Mac. Using this service is covered later in "Reference 24.2 Screen Sharing" on page 796.

▶ File sharing—Allows remote access to your Mac computer's file system via the Server Message Blocks (SMB) and Apple Filing Protocol (AFP) network file-sharing services.

When you enable the File Sharing service, the `launchd` control process listens for SMB service requests on TCP port 445 and automatically starts the `smbd` process as necessary to handle any requests. Further, the `launchd` control process listens for AFP service requests on TCP port 548 and automatically starts the `AppleFileServer` process as necessary to handle any requests. By default on OS X, only standard and administrative users have access to File Sharing services, but you can modify access for other users as outlined in Lesson 11 "Permissions and Sharing".

MORE INFO ▶ Connecting OS X systems to file-sharing services is covered in Lesson 23 "Network Services".

▶ Printer sharing—Allows network access to printers that are directly attached to your Mac. Using this service is covered in Lesson 26 "Print and Scan".

▶ Scanner sharing—Allows network access to document scanners that are configured for your Mac. This service works only with other Mac computers on a local network (Bonjour) via the Image Capture application. This service also operates only on a per-user basis, and is available only when the user is logged in. When this service is enabled, the `launchd` control process listens for scanner-sharing requests on a very high randomly selected TCP port and starts the `Image Capture Extension` background process as needed, to handle any requests. The only additional configuration is that you can, from Sharing preferences, enable specific scanners if you have more than one attached.

▶ Remote login—Allows remote control of your Mac computer's command line via Secure Shell (SSH). Further, SSH remote login allows you to securely transfer files using Secure File Transfer Protocol (SFTP) or the secure copy command `scp`. With Remote Login enabled, the `launchd` control process listens for remote login service requests on TCP 22 and starts the `sshd` background process as needed to handle any requests. By default, all standard and administrative user accounts are allowed to access the service. Command-line usage is beyond the scope of this guide, thus using SSH is beyond the scope of this guide.

▶ Remote management—Augments the screen-sharing service to allow remote administration of your Mac via the Apple Remote Desktop (ARD) application. Using this service is covered later in "Enabling ARD Remote Management" on page 806.

▶ Remote Apple events—Allows applications and AppleScripts on another Mac to communicate with applications and services on your Mac. This service is most often used to facilitate automated AppleScript workflows between applications running on separate Mac computers. When this service is enabled, the launchd control process listens for remote Apple Events requests on TCP and UDP port 3130 and starts the AEServer background process as needed, to handle any requests. By default, all nonguest user accounts are allowed to access the service, but you can limit this to specific users from Sharing preferences.

▶ Internet sharing—Allows your Mac to "reshare" a single network or Internet connection with any other network interface. For example, if your Mac had Internet access via a cellular network USB adapter, you could enable Internet Sharing for the Mac computer's Wi-Fi and turn it into a wireless access point for the other computers. When you enable the Internet Sharing service, the launchd process starts several background processes. The natd process performs the Network Address Translation (NAT) service that allows multiple network clients to share a single network or Internet connection. The bootpd process provides the DHCP automatic network configuration service for the network devices connected via your Mac. When a network device connects to your Mac computer's shared network connection, it automatically obtains an IP address, usually in the 10.0.2.X range. Finally, the named process provides DNS resolution for network devices connected to the Internet via your Mac.

▶ Bluetooth sharing—Allows access to your Mac via Bluetooth short-range wireless. Using this service is covered in Lesson 25 "Peripherals and Drivers".

NOTE ▶ OS X Mavericks and later are not compatible with Xgrid sharing or services.

NOTE ▶ OS X no longer includes a graphical interface for enabling web sharing services. To find out more about alternatives to web sharing, see Apple Support article HT5230, "OS X Mountain Lion: Options for web sharing."

Reference 24.2
Screen Sharing

Providing remote phone support can be arduous. Inexperienced users don't know how to properly communicate the issues they are experiencing and may not be able to describe what they are seeing on the screen. Further, attempting to describe the steps involved in performing troubleshooting or administrative tasks to an inexperienced user over the phone is, at best, time-consuming for both parties.

When it comes to troubleshooting or administration, nothing beats actually seeing the computer's screen and controlling its mouse and keyboard. OS X includes built-in software that allows you to view and control the graphical interface via three methods: system screen sharing, Messages screen sharing, and Apple Remote Desktop (ARD) remote management.

Screen-Sharing Architecture

Both system screen sharing and Messages screen sharing are included with the standard system software, and their use is covered in the following sections of this lesson. However, the standard installation of OS X includes only the client-side software for ARD; the administrative side of ARD used to control other Mac systems is a separate purchase.

Yet screen sharing is a subset of ARD, so when you enable ARD remote management, you are also enabling screen sharing. This may seem a bit confusing if you look at the Sharing preferences interface, which deselects the Screen Sharing checkbox when remote management is enabled. Rest assured, though, enabling remote management also enables screen sharing. Thus, you can save yourself a step by initially configuring remote management, which allows for both ARD and screen-sharing access. Configuring ARD remote management is also covered later in this lesson, as it can still be used to provide system screen sharing.

All Apple screen sharing is based on a modified version of the Virtual Network Computing (VNC) protocol. The primary modification is the use of optional encryption for both viewing and controlling traffic. Another change is the ability to copy files and clipboard content between Mac computers using screen sharing.

Further, OS X allows you to access a virtual desktop on another Mac via screen sharing. In other words, on OS X systems, screen sharing allows you to have your own virtual login on another Mac, completely separate from the login currently being used by the local user. This feature is similar to fast user switching (covered in Lesson 5 "User Accounts") except the second user is entirely remote via screen sharing and potentially using the computer at the same time as the local user.

> **NOTE** ▶ OS X screen sharing is backward compatible with OS X v10.5 or later screen sharing. Further, OS X can control previous OS X systems that have ARD remote management or other VNC software enabled.

> **NOTE** ▶ Using screen sharing to copy files and clipboard content is only supported when using ARD or when using OS X Lion or later. Using screen sharing to a virtual desktop works with OS X Lion or later.

NOTE ▶ VNC is a cross-platform standard for remote control; so, if configured properly, the OS X screen-sharing technology integrates well with other third-party VNC-based systems. Thus, your Mac can control (or be controlled by) any other VNC-based software regardless of operating system or platform.

Enabling System Screen Sharing

Obviously, before you can access a Mac remotely via screen sharing the remote Mac must first have screen sharing enabled. To enable screen sharing, open Sharing preferences, click the lock icon in the bottom-left corner, and authenticate as an administrative user to unlock Sharing preferences.

NOTE ▶ The screen-sharing service is part of the ARD remote management service. Thus, if Remote Management is enabled, the Screen Sharing checkbox is unavailable.

Select the Screen Sharing checkbox in the Service list to enable screen sharing. The launchd control process starts the AppleVNCServer background process, which listens for screen-sharing service requests on TCP and UDP port 5900. By default, only administrative user accounts are allowed to access the service.

Optionally, you can adjust screen-sharing access by selecting the "All users" radio button, or using the Add (+) and Delete (–) buttons at the bottom of the users list. When adding accounts, a dialog appears allowing you to select the specific users or groups you want to grant screen-sharing access. You can select existing users or groups, or create a new Sharing user account by clicking the New Person button or selecting a contact from your Contacts.

Also optionally, you can allow a wider range of operating systems to access your Mac computer's screen-sharing service by clicking the Computer Settings button. This reveals a dialog where you can enable guest and standard VNC screen-sharing access.

```
☐ Anyone may request permission to control screen
☑ VNC viewers may control screen with password: [••••••••]

                          Cancel    OK
```

When attempting to access your Mac computer's screen sharing, the currently logged-in user must authorize the session. By default, only local authorized users and groups are allowed to use screen sharing. Select the "Anyone may request permission to control screen" checkbox to allow anyone (from another Mac) to ask permission to share the screen. Keep in mind, for this feature to work you must remove any access restrictions for screen sharing by allowing access to all users.

Standard third-party VNC viewers cannot authenticate using the secure methods employed by the OS X screen-sharing service. Thus, if you select the "VNC viewers may control screen with password" checkbox, you must also set a specific password for VNC access. Remember that all standard VNC traffic is unencrypted. Further, standard VNC viewers cannot use screen sharing's clipboard copy, file copy, or virtual desktop features.

Connecting via Screen Sharing

The process to connect to and control another computer for screen sharing is similar to how you connect to a shared file system. From the Finder, you can connect to another computer that has screen sharing, ARD 3 remote management, or VNC enabled. You can initiate the connection using one of two methods. The first method works only for screen sharing or ARD hosts on the local network. In the Finder, browse to and select the computer from the Finder sidebar Shared list or the Finder Network folder, and then click the Share Screen button.

The second method allows you to connect to and control any host providing screen sharing, ARD, or standard VNC services. In the Finder, choose Go > Connect to Server. In the Connect to Server dialog, enter vnc:// followed by the computer's IP address, DNS host name, or Bonjour name, and then click Connect.

Regardless of the connection method, the system automatically opens the /System/Library/CoreServices/Applications/Screen Sharing application and initiates a connection to the specified host. You are presented with a dialog that requires you to make an authentication choice.

NOTE ▶ If you are using Kerberos single sign-on or have previously saved your authentication information to a keychain, the computer automatically authenticates for you and doesn't present the authentication dialog.

The first authentication choice, which appears only if you are connecting to an OS X system with this option enabled, is to ask the current user for permission. The second authentication choice, the default for any system, is to authenticate with a user account. As a final option, you can select the checkbox that saves this information to your login keychain. Once you have made your authentication selection, click Connect to continue.

Depending on the remote computer's system, one of three situations occurs when the screen sharing establishes the connection:

▶ If the remote computer is not a Mac running OS X, you will instantly connect to the current screen of the remote computer.

▶ If the remote computer is a Mac running OS X and no one is logged in, or if you authenticated as the currently logged-in user, or if the currently logged-in user is not an administrator, you will instantly connect to the current screen of the remote Mac.

▶ If the remote computer is a Mac running OS X and you authenticated as a different user from the administrator that is currently logged in to the Mac, you are presented with a dialog allowing you to choose between asking permission or logging in as yourself to a virtual desktop.

When presented with this Screen Sharing dialog, if you choose the option to ask for permission, the remote administrative user is prompted with a dialog to either allow or deny you access. The remote user's choice dictates whether you can connect. If, however, you choose to log in as yourself, you are instantly connected to a new virtual screen that logs in to your account. In this case, the other user does not directly know that you are remotely using the computer, but they could verify by examining the Fast User Switching menu or the Users & Groups preferences.

> **TIP** ▶ If you need the ability to control another user's session without asking permission, you should enable the Remote Management service instead of the Screen Sharing service. With Remote Management enabled, when you connect via Screen Sharing, the remote user is not asked for permission. The Remote Management service is also designed for use with the Apple Remote Desktop management application, as covered later in this lesson.

Controlling Another Mac via Screen Sharing

Once you are connected to the remote computer, a new window opens, titled with the controlled computer's name, showing a live view of the controlled computer's screen(s). Anytime this window is active, all keyboard entries and mouse movements are sent to the controlled computer. For example, pressing Command-Q quits the active application on the computer being controlled. Thus, to quit the Screen Sharing application, you have to click the close (X) button in the top-left corner of the window. More options are available in the Screen Sharing toolbar when you select View > Show Toolbar.

Note the buttons in the toolbar reveal additional screen-sharing features, including the option of sharing clipboard content between your Mac and the remote Mac. Optionally, if the remote computer is running OS X, you can drag files from your Finder to the Mac computer's remote desktop. Doing so opens a File Transfers dialog allowing you to verify the transfer progress or cancel the file transfer.

While using the Screen Sharing application, be sure to check out the preference options by choosing Screen Sharing > Preferences. Use these preferences to adjust screen size and quality settings. If you are experiencing slow performance, adjust these settings for faster performance. Keep in mind that some network connections, such as crowded wireless or dial-up connections, are so slow that these preferences don't matter much; you simply have to wait for the screen to redraw.

Screen Sharing via Messages

The included Messages application, formerly known as iChat, can be used to initiate screen sharing and, as an added bonus, simultaneously provides voice chat services between the administrator Mac and the controlled Mac. Messages screen sharing also makes it much easier to locate other Mac computers to control, as Messages automatically resolves the location of remote computers based on your active chats or available buddies. Further, Messages also supports reverse screen sharing—the administrator Mac can push its screen to display on another Mac for demonstration purposes.

NOTE ▶ Messages does not require either Mac to have screen sharing enabled in Sharing preferences. This is because Messages includes a quick and easy authorization process for initiating a screen sharing session.

NOTE ▶ Messages screen sharing works only with other Mac systems running OS X v10.5 or later. When you select chat participants, Messages automatically determines if their computer is using a compatible version of iChat or Messages.

To initiate a Messages screen-sharing session, select an available chat user from a buddy list and then click the Screen Sharing button at the bottom of the buddy list. This opens a pop-up menu where you can choose Share My Screen with <Chatuser> or Ask to Share <Chatuser>'s Screen, where <Chatuser> is the name of the user whose computer you are asking to control.

The user on the other computer sees an authorization dialog offering the choice to accept or decline your request to share screens. If the other user clicks the Accept button, the screen-sharing session begins.

> **NOTE ▶** Even as an administrative user, you cannot force other users to share screens using Messages; they have the sole power to allow or deny your request.

The following screen capture is from the screen-sharing "controller's" point of view. The full screen shows the remote Mac and the small My Computer window is the local Mac. The other user does not see the small My Computer window. Clicking that window allows you to switch back and forth between your local Mac and the remote Mac.

Further, if both computers support voice chat, Messages automatically starts a voice chat session between the two computers. You may need to configure Audio/Video settings in Messages preferences for this feature to work properly.

Both users have simultaneous control of the Mac being shared, including the ability to end the screen-sharing session at any time from the Screen Sharing menu item on the right side of the menu bar.

Enabling ARD Remote Management

Remote Management is client-side software that allows the Apple Remote Desktop (ARD) administration tool to access your Mac. ARD, at version 3.7.2, supports both OS X Mavericks and OS X Yosemite and is the ultimate remote management tool for OS X computers. In addition to screen sharing, ARD allows administrators to remotely gather system information and usage statistics, change settings, add or remove files and software, install software packages, send UNIX commands, and perform nearly any other management task you can think of.

The real power of ARD is that you can execute all these tasks simultaneously on dozens of Mac systems with just a few clicks. Again, if you plan to use ARD in the future, but you want to enable screen sharing for now, you can enable remote management in one step and take advantage of both remote control features. At the time of this writing, ARD is available on the Mac App Store for $79.99.

To enable ARD remote management, open Sharing preferences and authenticate as an administrative user to unlock the preferences. Select the Remote Management checkbox to enable both screen sharing and the ARD client-side services. The launchd control process then starts the ARDAgent background process, which listens for incoming administration requests on UDP port 3283 and also starts AppleVNCServer, which listens for screen-sharing requests on TCP port 5900.

NOTE ▶ The screen-sharing service is part of the ARD remote management service. Thus, if Remote Management is selected, the Screen Sharing checkbox is inaccessible.

If this is the first time you have enabled remote management, you'll see a dialog that allows you to select the ARD options you want to allow for all nonguest local users. You can select options individually, or you can hold down the Option key and then select any checkbox to enable all options.

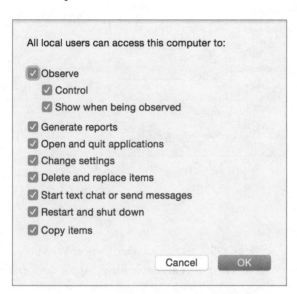

Optionally, to further limit ARD access, select "Only these users" and click the Add (+) button. Then select a standard or administrative local user you want to grant ARD access to. When you're done, another dialog appears where you select the ARD options this particular user can access. You can further edit a user's ARD options at any time by double-clicking that user's name in the user access list.

Additional ARD computer options are available by clicking the Computer Settings button. This opens a dialog where you can enable guest and VNC screen-sharing access (covered earlier in this lesson) and turn on the Remote Management menu bar item that allows users to request help from administrators. You can also add any additional information here to help identify this particular Mac.

☑ Show Remote Management status in menu bar

☐ Anyone may request permission to control screen

☐ VNC viewers may control screen with password: [   ]

Computer Information
These fields are displayed in the System Overview Report.

Info 1: [TAG# 123456   ]   Info 3: [   ]

Info 2: [   ]   Info 4: [   ]

[Cancel]   [OK]

Reference 24.3
AirDrop

In addition to traditional file-sharing services, OS X features a peer-to-peer Wi-Fi file sharing service called AirDrop. Although AirDrop isn't available for all Apple devices, it's the easiest way to share files between Apple devices, both OS X and iOS, that are in close proximity.

AirDrop Architecture

AirDrop uses Wi-Fi networking, but the radio frequencies it uses are outside the Mac computer's normal network connection; thus it does not travel across your established network. In fact, you don't need a network at all to use AirDrop, as it creates a closed network between local devices.

The most significant feature of AirDrop is that it requires no setup or configuration. Users who want to share items need only navigate to the AirDrop sharing interface, and the system presents a browser where they can select other users to easily share files with. AirDrop handles all the details of peer-to-peer file sharing, including discovery, easy authentication, and secure file transfer using Transport Layer Security, or TLS, encryption.

AirDrop does have a few significant caveats. First, it works only between devices within local Wi-Fi and Bluetooth range. This range varies based on many factors, but it's generally limited to 30 feet. Also, AirDrop was specifically designed to provide direct file sharing for selected items, as opposed to traditional file sharing, which allows the user to browse another computer's file system. Finally, AirDrop is supported only on devices with the appropriate system software and wireless hardware.

There are currently two implementations for AirDrop. The most recent method for AirDrop utilizes Bluetooth 4.0 wireless for discovery (due to its low power requirements) and then faster Wi-Fi for the data transfer. This later AirDrop method allows for sharing between both iOS and OS X devices and is available on iOS 7 and later and OS X Yosemite. The previous AirDrop method uses only Wi-Fi, and is limited to sharing only between OS X computers; it is available on OS X v10.7 and later. AirDrop hardware compatibility varies depending on the Wi-Fi and Bluetooth capabilities built into the Apple devices.

MORE INFO ▶ AirDrop hardware requirements for iOS devices can be found in Apple Support article HT5887, "Use AirDrop to wirelessly share content," and for Mac models, in HT203106, "Mac Basics: AirDrop lets you send files from your Mac to nearby Macs and iOS devices."

You can also verify whether a Mac supports AirDrop in the Finder by clicking the Go menu. If an AirDrop menu option appears, the Mac supports AirDrop.

Go	Window	Help
Back		⌘[
Forward		⌘]
Enclosing Folder		⌘↑
📄 All My Files		⇧⌘F
📄 Documents		⇧⌘O
🖥 Desktop		⇧⌘D
⬇ Downloads		⌥⌘L
🏠 Home		⇧⌘H
💻 Computer		⇧⌘C
📡 AirDrop		⇧⌘R
🌐 Network		⇧⌘K
☁ iCloud Drive		⇧⌘I
🅰 Applications		⇧⌘A
🔧 Utilities		⇧⌘U

Using AirDrop

To quickly share files between Apple devices that support AirDrop, you start by finding other devices in the AirDrop discovery interface. On OS X computers, you can open this interface by selecting the AirDrop icon in the Finder sidebar, choosing Go > AirDrop, or pressing Shift-Command-R. Any of these methods opens the AirDrop discovery interface in a Finder window, ultimately allowing you to share any item you can drag to this Finder window.

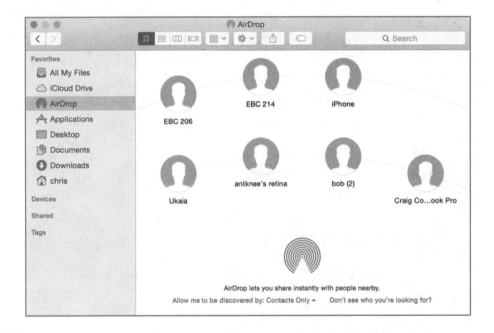

NOTE ▶ If the Mac computer's Wi-Fi or Bluetooth interfaces are turned off, click the Turn On button to enable AirDrop.

Alternatively, you can engage AirDrop to share a specific open document by clicking the Share button (box with an up-pointing arrow) at the top of the document window. This will also open the AirDrop discovery interface, but it will ultimately also share the currently selected document. On an iOS device, tapping the Share button is the only way to share an item with another AirDrop device.

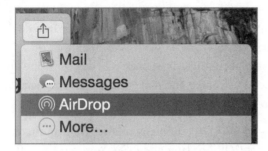

Anytime you open the AirDrop discovery interface, the system automatically scans for other AirDrop devices within local wireless range. Other AirDrop devices will appear automatically as long as AirDrop is enabled and using a compatible discovery method. The reasons you might not be able to find a specific AirDrop device are covered in the next section of this lesson.

Once AirDrop has found the other device you want to transfer an item to, sending the item is quite simple. If you are in the Finder, drag a file or folder on top of the icon representing the other device. If you are in a Share window, simply click the icon representing the other device. In either case, AirDrop will notify the other device that you would like to share something.

On the other device, a notification appears where the user can accept (or decline) the incoming item. On a Mac, the user is given three choices: If the Save button is clicked, the item is transferred to the user's Downloads folder. Clicking Save and Open saves to the same location and then automatically opens the item. Clicking Decline cancels the transfer and notifies the other user in the AirDrop interface.

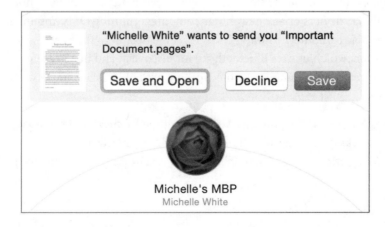

AirDrop Discovery Issues

There are several reasons your Mac might not be able to discover another AirDrop device. First, start with the basics: Is AirDrop enabled on the other devices? On another Mac, open the AirDrop window in the Finder to enable AirDrop. On an iOS device, swipe up from the bottom of the screen to open Control Center, and make sure AirDrop is enabled. If this doesn't solve your AirDrop discovery issues, things get a bit complicated.

As covered previously, there are currently two AirDrop implementations: The more recent method works only on newer Apple devices (iOS 7 or later and OS X Yosemite), and the earlier method works on older Mac computers or previous versions of OS X. The two AirDrop methods are not compatible. Thus, it's possible you won't be able to find the other device you're trying to share with in the AirDrop discovery interface.

If you are using an older Mac running OS X Yosemite, it's possible that your computer doesn't have Bluetooth 4.0 and therefore defaults to the previous AirDrop discovery method. You can confirm this on your Mac from the AirDrop discovery interface; the text below the AirDrop icon will read, "To share with someone using a Mac..."

AirDrop lets you share instantly with people nearby.
To share with someone using a Mac, ask them to go to AirDrop in the Finder.

In this case, even though your older Mac computer is running OS X Yosemite, the wireless hardware is compatible only with the previous AirDrop discovery method. You will not be able to share files with iOS devices or any newer Mac computers running OS X Yosemite. This is because newer Mac computers running OS X Yosemite default to the latest AirDrop implementation, which utilizes Bluetooth 4.0 for discovery, and that prevents AirDrop discovery on newer Mac computers from working with older Mac models or previous versions of OS X.

You can force a newer Mac to use the previous AirDrop method by clicking the words "Don't see who you're looking for?" at the bottom of the AirDrop interface. Clicking the Search for an Older Mac button will switch to the previous AirDrop discovery method.

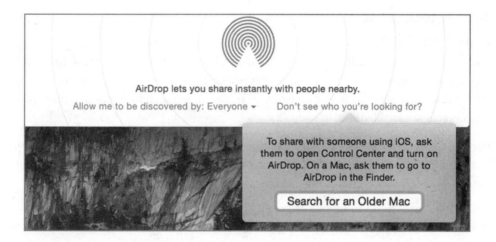

Again, this will allow your newer Mac with OS X Yosemite to discover older Mac computers and previous versions of OS X, but you will temporarily lose iOS devices and other newer Mac computers with OS X Yosemite. Keep in mind that every time you open the AirDrop interface on a newer Mac computer, it resets to the new AirDrop discovery method.

For devices using the newer AirDrop method, AirDrop defaults to a safer mode that limits discovery to only users with matching information in your Contacts. This may also limit your ability to discover other devices in the AirDrop discovery interface. To resolve this issue, on the other device you can set AirDrop discovery to allow everyone. To change AirDrop discoverability on OS X, click the words "Allow me to be discovered by:" at the bottom of the AirDrop interface. To change AirDrop discoverability on iOS, in Control Center tap the AirDrop button.

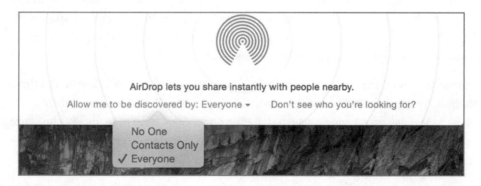

Reference 24.4
Personal Firewall

From a network services standpoint, your Mac is already very secure, because, by default, only a few essential services are running that respond to external requests. Even once you start providing individual shared services, your Mac is designed to respond to only those services that are enabled.

Further, services that could cause trouble if compromised, like file or screen sharing, can be configured to have limited access authorization. Still, users can open third-party applications or background services that could leave a Mac vulnerable to a network attack.

> **TIP** To maintain a high level of network security, you should leave sharing services off unless absolutely necessary. If you do enable sharing services, be sure to limit authorization access as much as possible.

Personal Application Firewall

The most common method for securing network services is to configure a firewall, which blocks unauthorized network service access. Most networks use a firewall to limit inbound traffic from an Internet connection.

In fact, most home routers, like AirPort base stations, are by design also network firewalls. While network-level firewalls block unauthorized Internet traffic into your network, they don't block traffic that originated from inside your network to your Mac. Also, if your Mac is mobile and is often joining new networks, odds are that every new network you join will have different firewall rules.

Thus, to prevent unauthorized network services from allowing incoming connections to your specific Mac, you can enable the built-in personal application firewall. A personal firewall blocks unauthorized connections to your Mac no matter where they originated. The OS X firewall also features a single-click configuration that provides a high level of network service security, which works for most users.

A standard firewall uses rules based on service port numbers. As you've learned in this lesson, each service defaults to a standard port or set of ports. However, some network services, like Messages, use a wide range of dynamic ports. If we were to manually configure a traditional firewall, we would have to make dozens of rules for every potential port the user may need.

To resolve this issue, the OS X firewall uses an adaptive technology that allows connections based on applications and service needs, without you having to know the specific ports they use. For example, you can authorize Messages to accept any incoming connection without configuring all of the individual TCP and UDP ports used by the Messages application.

The personal application firewall also leverages another built-in feature, code signing, to ensure that allowed applications and services aren't changed without your knowledge. Further, code signing allows Apple and third-party developers to provide a guarantee that their software hasn't been tampered with. This level of verifiable trust allows you to configure the firewall in default mode with a single click, automatically allowing signed applications and services to receive incoming connections.

Finally, because the personal application firewall is fully dynamic, it opens only the necessary ports when the application or service is running. Again, using Messages as an example, the personal application firewall allows only incoming connections to the required ports if Messages is running. If the application quits because the user logs out, the firewall closes the associated ports. Having the required ports open only when an application or service needs them provides an extra layer of security not found with traditional firewalls.

Configuring the Personal Firewall

To enable and configure the OS X personal application firewall, open Security & Privacy preferences, click the lock icon in the bottom-left corner, and authenticate as an administrative user to unlock Security & Privacy preferences. Select the Firewall tab, and then click the Turn On Firewall button to enable the default firewall rules. Once enabled, this button changes to a Turn Off Firewall button, allowing you to turn off the firewall.

The default firewall configuration is to allow incoming traffic for established connections (connections that were initiated from your Mac and are expecting a return) and for any signed software or enabled service. This level of security is adequate for most users.

TIP Firewall logging is always on and can be viewed from the Console application. The firewall log is located at /private/var/log/appfirewall.log.

Advanced Firewall Configuration

If you want to customize the firewall, you can reveal any additional firewall configuration by clicking the Firewall Options button. From the firewall options window, a list of services currently allowed appears. Without any additional configuration, sharing services enabled from Sharing preferences automatically appear in the list of allowed services. Conversely, deselecting a shared service from Sharing preferences removes the service from the list of allowed services.

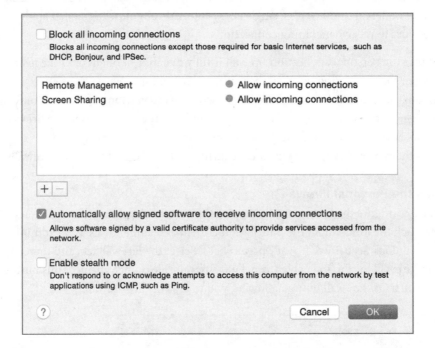

Optionally, for a bit more control, you can manually set which applications and services the firewall allows by deselecting the checkbox to automatically allow signed software. With this firewall choice, as you open new network applications for the first time or update existing network applications, you see a dialog where you can allow or deny the new network application. This dialog appears outside Security & Privacy preferences anytime a new network application requests incoming access.

If you are manually setting network application and service firewall access, you can always return to the Advanced Firewall dialog to review the list of items, and either delete items from the list or specifically disallow certain items.

For a bit more security, you can select the "Enable stealth mode" checkbox to prevent response or acknowledgment of a failed attempt to the requesting host. With this enabled, your Mac does not respond to any unauthorized network connections, including network diagnostic protocols like ping, traceroute, or port scan.

In other words, your computer simply ignores the request instead of returning a response of failure to the requesting host. However, your Mac still responds to other allowed services. This includes, by default, Bonjour, which dutifully announces your Mac computer's presence, thus preventing your Mac from being truly hidden on the network.

When the utmost security is needed, you can select the "Block all incoming connections" checkbox. Notice that selecting this option automatically selects stealth mode as well.

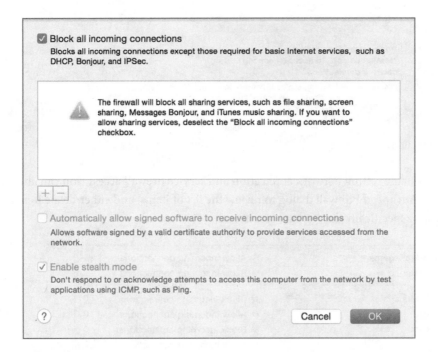

When blocking all incoming connections, your Mac does not respond to any incoming network connections except for those required for basic network services or established connections, such as those needed to browse the web or check email. Obviously, this prevents any shared service or application hosted on your Mac from working remotely.

Viewing Firewall History

Like all system services, the personal application firewall maintains an activity log. Firewall logs are always especially interesting because they reveal how inundated a typical Internet-connected computer is by external sources. The current personal application firewall log is located at /var/log/appfirewall.log. As covered previously, the best way to view log files is with the /Application/Utilities/Console application.

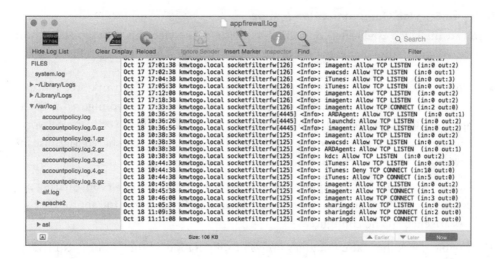

Reference 24.5
Shared Service Troubleshooting

If you're providing a shared service from your Mac, and others are having trouble reaching it, you must first consider how established the service is to determine where to focus your efforts. For example, if your Mac has been reliably providing a shared service for a while but now a single client computer has trouble accessing the service, troubleshoot the client computer before troubleshooting your shared Mac.

Otherwise, if multiple clients cannot access your shared Mac, you may indeed have an issue with the sharing service. After ruling out other potential local client and network issues, you can safely assume that the problem lies with the Mac providing shared services. If so, shared network service issues fall into two general categories: service communication and service access.

Service communication issues are manifested by an inability to establish a connection to the shared service. Keep in mind that if you are presented with an authentication dialog, the client and server are establishing a proper connection, and you should troubleshoot the issue as a service access issue. However, if authentication fails, or you can authenticate but you're not authorized to access the service, then you are experiencing a service access issue.

Network Service Communication Issues

If you are unable to establish a connection to the shared service, this may signal a network service communication issue. Use these methods to troubleshoot that type of issue:

▶ Double-check the shared Mac network configuration—From Network preferences, make sure the Mac computer's network interfaces are active and configured with the appropriate TCP/IP settings. You can also use Network Utility to verify the network configuration. If a DNS server is providing a host name for your shared Mac, use the Lookup tool in Network Utility to verify the host name.

▶ Double-check the Mac computer's sharing service configuration—From Sharing preferences, verify the Mac computer's sharing name and ensure that the appropriate services are enabled and configured.

▶ Double-check the Mac computer's firewall configuration—From Security & Privacy preferences, first temporarily stop the firewall to see if turning it off makes a difference. If you are able to establish a connection, adjust the list of allowed services and applications before you restart the firewall.

▶ Check for basic network connectivity to the shared Mac—First, turn off the firewall's stealth mode, and then, from another Mac, use the Network Utility ping tool to check for basic connectivity to the shared Mac. If you can't ping the shared Mac, you're probably having a network-level issue that goes beyond service troubleshooting.

▶ Check for network service port connectivity to the shared Mac—First, turn off the firewall's stealth mode, and then, from another Mac, use the Network Utility port scan tool to verify that the expected network service ports are accessible. If the shared Mac is configured properly, the appropriate network service ports should register as open. If there are network routers between the network clients and the shared Mac, consider the possibility that a network administrator has decided to block access to those ports.

Network Service Access Issues

Failure to authenticate or be granted authorization to a shared service is considered a network service access issue. Use the following to troubleshoot these access issues:

▶ Verify the local user account settings—When using local user accounts, make sure the correct authentication information is being used. You may find that the user is not using the right information, and you may have to reset the account password. (Troubleshooting user account issues was covered in Lesson 5 "User Accounts".) Also, keep in mind that some services do not allow the use of guest and sharing-only user accounts. Further, the standard VNC service uses password information that is not directly linked to a user account.

▶ Double-check directory service settings—If you use a network directory service in your environment, verify that the Mac is properly communicating with the directory service by checking its status in the Directory Utility application. Even if you're only trying to use local accounts, any directory service issues can cause authentication problems. Also, keep in mind that some services, like ARD remote management, do not by default allow you to authenticate with accounts hosted from network directories.

▶ Double-check shared service access settings—Several authenticated sharing services allow you to configure access lists. Use Sharing preferences to verify that the appropriate user accounts are allowed to access the shared service.

Exercise 24.1
Use Host-Sharing Services

▶ **Prerequisites**

    ▶ You must have created the Local Admin ("Exercise 2.1 Configure a New OS X System for Exercises" on page 60 or "Exercise 2.2 Configure an Existing OS X System for Exercises" on page 63) and Chris Johnson ("Exercise 5.1 Manage User Accounts" on page 145) accounts.

    ▶ You need another computer running OS X Yosemite on the same network as your primary computer. If you are performing these exercises in a class, you will work with a partner.

In this exercise, you will use the OS X screen-sharing capability to control another computer remotely. You will use both the option to share the current user's session and the option to use a virtual display to log in as a different user.

Enable Screen Sharing

1   If the Local Admin account is logged in (even as a background session), log it out.

2   If necessary, log in as Chris Johnson.

3   Open System Preferences, and select the Sharing pane.

4   Click the lock icon, and authenticate as Local Admin.

5   Select the checkbox next to Remote Management, if it is not already selected.

Note that although you will be using screen sharing, you are configuring it via the Remote Management service. Remote Management includes screen sharing as an optional capability. If you look at the checkbox for the Screen Sharing service, you'll see that it is dimmed; this does not mean the service is unavailable but rather that it is being controlled by Remote Management.

6   Ensure that "All users" is selected for "Allow access for."

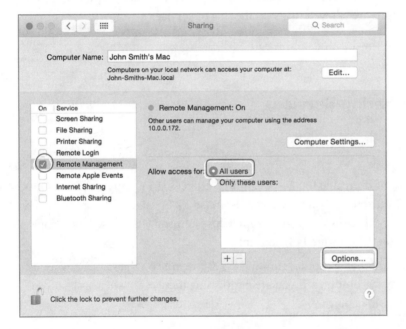

7   Click Options.

8   Ensure that all options are selected. An easy way to do this is to Option-click a check-box until all of the checkboxes are selected.

9   Click OK, and then quit System Preferences.

Remotely Control Another Computer's Screen

In this section you will use screen sharing to control another computer. Which computer you will control depends on whether you are performing these exercises in a class or on your own:

▶ If you are in a class, you will work with a partner and take turns controlling each other's computers.

▶ If you are performing these exercises on your own, you will perform this section from another computer and use it to control your primary exercise computer.

1 If you are working with a partner, wait for her to finish enabling and configuring Remote Management, and then decide who will go first. If your partner goes first, wait for her to finish this section before starting.

2 If you are on your own, log in to the other computer.

3 In the Finder, choose Go > Network (or press Command-Shift-K).

The computer you are going to control appears in the display of shared computers on the local network. Note that this shows computers offering file sharing, screen sharing, or both.

The Finder sidebar also displays local computers offering sharing services, but it shows only a limited number. The network view shows all of them.

4 Double-click the computer you will control in the Network window.

Since the other computer does not offer file-sharing service, your computer only has the option to share its screen.

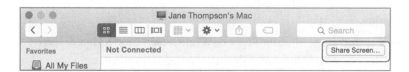

5 Click Share Screen.

6 Authenticate as Chris Johnson. Note that you can use the account's short name (chris) and that if you are working with a partner who used a different password for the Chris Johnson account, you must use her password.

7   Click Connect.

Screen sharing begins, and you see a window with a live, interactive picture of the other computer's desktop.

8   Open System Preferences on the other computer, and select the "Desktop & Screen Saver" pane.

9   Select a different picture for the other computer's desktop.

10   Press Command-Q.

This quits System Preferences on the other computer. You cannot use standard short-cuts to control the Screen Sharing application itself.

11   Click the green Full Screen button in the title bar of the Screen Sharing window.

Like many OS X apps, Screen Sharing supports a full-screen mode. In full-screen mode, your display is a virtual mirror of the other computer's display.

12   Move your mouse to the very top of the screen.

The Screen Sharing menu and toolbar appear at the top of the screen. This allows you to exit full-screen mode or access the Screen Sharing controls.

13   Choose Screen Sharing > Quit Screen Sharing.

14 If you are working with a partner, switch roles, and have your partner repeat these steps.

Connect to a Virtual Display

By connecting to another computer as a different user, you can work with a virtual display instead of sharing the local user's display. As in the previous section, you will either work with a partner (although this time you can both work at once, rather than taking turns) or connect to your primary exercise computer from another computer.

1 If necessary, wait for your partner to finish the previous section.

2 If necessary, reopen the Network view (press Command-Shift-K), and select the computer you will control.

3 Click Share Screen.

4 This time authenticate as Local Admin (you can use the short name ladmin), and click Connect.

Since you authenticated as a different user than is logged into the other computer, you are now presented with the choice of sharing the current user's display or logging in as a different user with a virtual display.

5 Select "Log in as yourself," and click Share Screen.

A screen-sharing window opens and displays a login screen for your partner's computer.

6   Log in to your partner's computer as Local Admin.

This virtual screen capability makes it easy to remotely manage users' computers without disturbing them. Note that if you are in a class, your partner is connecting to your computer at the same time, but you do not see any indication of this.

7   On the other computer, open System Preferences, and select the Users & Groups pane.

If you use the Apple menu or the Dock, be sure to use the one contained in the window, not the one at the edge of your screen.

Do not make any changes in Users & Groups preferences at this time.

8   Quit System Preferences on your partner's computer.

9   Click the fast user switching menu on the other computer.

You see that both Chris Johnson (either your partner or the session you left logged in there) and Local Admin (you) are logged in to the other computer. Your virtual display is treated as a fast user switching session.

10 From the remote menu bar, choose Apple menu > Log Out Local Admin, and then click the Log Out button.

If you disconnect screen sharing without logging out first, you leave behind an orphaned fast user switching session.

11 From the menu bar at the top of the screen, choose Screen Sharing > Quit Screen Sharing.

12 If you are working with a partner, wait for him to finish before starting the next exercise.

13 If you are working on your own, move back to your primary exercise computer for the first part of the next exercise.

Exercise 24.2
Configure the Personal Firewall

▶ **Prerequisites**

▶ You must have created the Local Admin ("Exercise 2.1 Configure a New OS X System for Exercises" on page 60 or "Exercise 2.2 Configure an Existing OS X System for Exercises" on page 63) and Chris Johnson ("Exercise 5.1 Manage User Accounts" on page 145) accounts.

▶ You need another computer running OS X Yosemite on the same network as your primary computer. If you are performing these exercises in a class, you will work with a partner.

A firewall blocks network traffic based on port numbers and protocols. The OS X firewall allows only ports based on application and service requests. The OS X built-in firewall is simple to configure from the user interface. In this exercise you will turn on the firewall and start a network-aware application. Then, you will view the firewall log. You will also configure the advanced stealth option and see that it blocks responses to network pings.

Enable the Firewall

1   If necessary, log in as Chris Johnson.

2   Open the Security & Privacy pane in System Preferences.

3   Click the Firewall tab.

4   Click the lock icon, and authenticate as Local Admin.

5   Click Turn On Firewall.

6   Click Firewall Options.

Notice that Remote Management and Screen Sharing are already on the list as "Allow incoming connections." The system assumes that if you enable a service in the Sharing pane, you must want users to be able to connect to it, so it automatically allows those services through the firewall.

7   Deselect "Automatically allow signed software to receive incoming connections."

8 Click OK.

9 Quit System Preferences.

> **NOTE ▸** With the firewall in this mode, you may receive alerts about various system components attempting to accept incoming connections. A common example is "ubd" (the ubiquity daemon, part of iCloud). It is generally safe to allow these through the firewall.

Test Firewall Settings

1 Open iTunes, which is in the Applications folder.

2 If you see the iTunes software license agreement, click Agree.

3 If you see a message telling you a new version of iTunes is available, click Don't Download.

4 If an iTunes Tutorials window opens, close it.

5 Choose iTunes > Preferences (Command-Comma).

6 Click the Sharing icon.

7 Select the checkbox "Share my library on my local network."

8 Click OK.

9 In the copyright reminder dialog, click OK (you may need to drag an iTunes dialog out of the way to get to it).

10 If a dialog appears asking if you want the application iTunes.app to accept incoming connections, click Deny. Note that clicking Allow would prompt for an administrator password to allow the exception to the firewall rules.

iTunes displays a dialog indicating that the firewall settings prevent you from using some iTunes features.

If you click Ignore here, iTunes music sharing would turn on, but other computers would not be able connect to it and listen to your songs.

11 Click Open Firewall Preferences.

12 In the Firewall pane of the Security & Privacy pane of System Preferences, authenticate if necessary, and then click Firewall Options.

Notice that iTunes has been added to the list and is set to "Block incoming connections."

13 Click "Block incoming connections," and choose "Allow incoming connections" from the pop-up menu that appears.

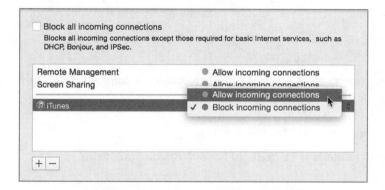

Since you have authenticated as an administrator, you can change the firewall policy for any specific application.

14 Click OK to dismiss the Firewall Options dialog.

15 Quit iTunes, but leave System Preferences open.

View the Firewall Log

1 Open Console from the Utilities folder.

2 If the source list sidebar is not shown, click the Show Log List button in the toolbar to make it appear.

3 In the files section of the source list on the left, select /var/log. This is one of the standard log locations on the system.

4 Click the disclosure triangle next to /var/log, and select appfirewall.log. This is the log file that the firewall service logs to and that records which applications have attempted to listen for network connections.

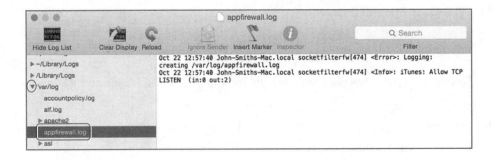

5   Quit the Console utility.

Test Stealth Mode

As in the previous exercise, you will either work with a partner or connect to your primary exercise computer from another computer.

1   In System Preferences, switch to the Sharing pane.

Note your computer's Bonjour name, listed beneath its computer name.

2   If you are working on your own, switch to your other computer.

3   Open Network Utility. Remember that you can find it with Spotlight.

4   Click the Ping tab.

5   If you are working with a partner, ask him for his computer's Bonjour name, and enter it as the network address to ping. If you are working on your own, enter the Bonjour name of your primary exercise computer.

6   If necessary, set it to send only 5 pings and click Ping.

   You should see successful pings.

7   If you are working with a partner, wait for him to finish pinging your computer. If you are working on your own, switch to your primary exercise computer.

8   Switch to System Preferences, switch to the Security & Privacy pane, and open Firewall Options.

9   Select "Enable stealth mode," and click OK.

10   If you are working with a partner, wait for him to finish turning on stealth mode. If you are working on your own, switch to your other computer.

11   Switch to Network Utility, and click Ping to rerun the connectivity test.

   After about 15 seconds, "Request timeout" messages appear in Network Utility.

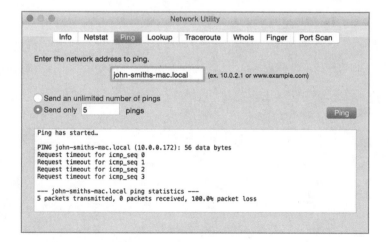

NOTE ▶ While stealth mode is an excellent security feature, it interferes with network troubleshooting. If a computer does not respond to a ping, in addition to checking cables, you should check firewall settings.

12 On your computer, turn off the firewall.

13 Quit all running programs.

System Management

Lesson 25

Peripherals and Drivers

Apple pioneered the concept of automatic peripheral support with the original Mac. This feature, commonly known as plug-and-play, is now supported with varying success in all current operating systems. Peripheral hardware has also improved, as now the most common connectivity standards support hot-pluggable or even wireless connections. OS X is compatible with all popular peripheral standards, demonstrating continued commitment by Apple to making peripheral use as easy as possible.

At the start of this lesson, you'll learn how OS X supports different peripheral technologies. Then you'll learn how to manage and troubleshoot both wired and wireless (Bluetooth) peripherals connected to OS X systems.

GOALS

▶ Understand and manage OS X peripheral connectivity

▶ Pair Bluetooth devices to your Mac

▶ Troubleshoot peripheral and driver issues

Reference 25.1
Peripheral Technologies

For the purposes of this lesson, a peripheral is any non-networked device your computer system can be directly connected to. A peripheral is also controlled by the computer, whereas network devices are shared.

Given the wide range of devices included in this definition, this lesson shows you how to categorize devices by their connectivity type and device class. Understanding the available connection methods and device types is necessary to manage and troubleshoot peripherals, which is the goal of this lesson.

> **NOTE** ▶ This lesson covers only connection technologies included with Mac systems that support OS X Yosemite.

Peripheral Connectivity

Most peripherals communicate with the Mac system via a connection mechanism commonly known as a bus. Bus connections are the most common peripheral connection types because they allow for a variety of different peripheral devices. Bus connections also allow multiple peripherals to connect to your Mac simultaneously.

There have been dozens of peripheral connectivity standards developed over the years, but in the last decade three have dominated the personal computing market: Universal Serial Bus (USB), FireWire, and Bluetooth. A fourth peripheral bus, Thunderbolt, represents the fastest and most capable personal computing peripheral bus to date. However, this connection type is common only on recent Mac computers.

The status of each of these four peripheral buses (and the items they are attached to) can be examined in OS X via the System Information application. You can access System Information by holding down the Option key and choosing Apple menu > System Information. Once System Information is open, select a hardware interface from the Contents list to view its information.

MORE INFO ▶ Using System Information for further troubleshooting peripherals is covered in "Reference 25.3 Peripheral Troubleshooting" on page 848, later in this lesson.

USB 1.1/2.0/3.0

Standard on every Mac that supports OS X, USB is by far the most popular peripheral connection. In fact, every single type of peripheral can be found in USB versions. You're probably already aware of the external USB ports on your Mac, but you may not know that Intel-based Mac computers also use USB for internal connectivity. For example, the MacBook keyboard, trackpad, infrared receiver, iSight camera, and Bluetooth controller are all connected via internal USB connections.

USB was originally designed by Intel and is a hot-pluggable interface that allows the user to connect and disconnect devices while they are on, or hot. USB is also a highly expandable connection platform that allows for daisy-chained connections. So you can connect one USB device to your Mac, then connect another USB device to the first, and so on. The USB specification allows for up to 127 simultaneous devices per host controller. Most Mac computers have at least two externally accessible USB host controllers.

A USB port can supply up to 2.5 watts of power (500 mA of current at 5 volts) to the connected devices, which is all that some types of devices need to operate. Unpowered hubs, including those built into many USB keyboards, split the available power among their ports, usually supplying only 0.5 watts (100 mA) to each, enough for only very low-power devices. When the system detects that there is not enough power for a connected device, it displays a low-power notification and disables the device.

If you see this notification, you can verify the power issue by opening /Applications/Utilities/System Information and selecting USB from the report list. Selecting any USB device displays the electric current available to, and desired by, the device. You can try resolving USB power issues by connecting the peripheral directly to the Mac or through a powered hub, which uses an external power connection to supply full power to the attached device. Peripherals that require even more power to operate, such as printers or large disk drives, generally also include a separate power source.

Three USB versions are currently supported by Apple hardware: USB 1.1, USB 2.0, and USB 3.0. Despite significant upgrades in performance, all USB ports on Mac systems are backward compatible with USB 1.1 cabling and devices. The various USB versions offer the following performance characteristics:

▶ USB 1.1 supports low-speed connections at 1.5 megabits per second (Mbit/s) and full-speed connections at up to 12 Mbit/s. All Mac systems that support OS X Yosemite also support USB 1.1.

▶ USB 2.0 supports high-speed connections up to a theoretical maximum of 480 Mbit/s. In practice, though, high-speed USB 2.0 connections fall short of the theoretical maximum due to the compression algorithms in use. All Mac systems that support OS X Yosemite also support USB 2.0.

▶ USB 3.0 supports superspeed connections up to a theoretical maximum of 5 Gbit/s (5 gigabits per second, or about 5000 Mbit/s). Peripherals and devices that support USB 3.0 are often identified by the use of bright-blue plastic for the interior of the physical connection, although no Apple device uses blue for identification. Mac systems introduced in mid-2012 and later support USB 3.0. You can also verify USB 3.0 support from the USB section of System Information.

MORE INFO ▶ You can find out more about USB at the official USB Implementers Forum website: www.usb.org.

FireWire 400/800

Also standard on most Mac systems that support OS X, FireWire is a high-speed, general-purpose peripheral connection originally developed by Apple. FireWire has been ratified by the Institute of Electrical and Electronics Engineers (IEEE) as standard IEEE-1394 and has been adopted as a standard interface for many digital video devices.

Like USB, FireWire supports hot-pluggable and daisy-chained connections. Using hubs, each FireWire host controller can support up to 63 devices simultaneously. FireWire host controllers also allow your Mac to be used in target disk mode without the need for a functional operating system, as covered in Lesson 12 "File System Troubleshooting".

All Mac systems with FireWire ports support FireWire 400 with a maximum transfer rate of up to 400 Mbit/s, and most newer Mac computers support FireWire 800 with a maximum transfer rate of up to 800 Mbit/s. These two FireWire standards use different port connections, but Mac computers with FireWire 800 ports can connect to FireWire 400 devices with an appropriate adapter. Newer Mac systems that feature Thunderbolt ports also support FireWire via the Apple Thunderbolt to FireWire Adapter.

Finally, FireWire ports on Mac systems generally supply about 7 watts per port, compared with the 2.5 watts of a USB. This increased power capacity makes FireWire ideal for use with external portable hard drives, as no additional power source is required to run the disk.

Alas, the FireWire standard's days are numbered, as the additional cost and complexity of FireWire host controllers makes the technology impractical for many simple peripherals, such as mice, keyboards, and flash drives, which are well served by USB. And at the high end, the tremendous speed and flexibility of the newer Thunderbolt standard makes FireWire obsolete.

MORE INFO ▶ You can find out more about FireWire at the official 1394 Trade Association website: www.1394ta.org.

Thunderbolt

Originally designed by Intel, then later in collaboration with Apple, Thunderbolt represents the latest in peripheral connectivity. This new standard folds PCI Express and DisplayPort data into a single connection and cable. One Thunderbolt host computer connection supports a hub or daisy chain of up to six devices, with up to two of these devices being high-resolution displays. Further, Mac systems with Thunderbolt can be used in target disk mode without the need for a functional operating system, as covered in Lesson 12 "File System Troubleshooting".

Thunderbolt provides for unmatched peripheral flexibility due to its mix of PCI Express and DisplayPort connectivity. With the appropriate adapters, a single Thunderbolt connection can provide access to any other networking, storage, peripheral, video, or audio connection. For example, the Apple Thunderbolt display provides not only a high-definition digital display but also a built-in camera, a microphone, audio speakers, a three-port USB hub, a FireWire port, a Gigabit Ethernet port, and an additional Thunderbolt port for another display—all through a single Thunderbolt cable from the Mac to the display.

All this connectivity through one cable means that Thunderbolt provides significant data rates. In fact, Thunderbolt is the fastest external peripheral bus to date, providing two bidirectional 10 Gbit/s (10,000 Mbit/s) channels. This means a total of 20 Gbit/s outbound and 20 Gbit/s inbound. With the first version of Thunderbolt, these channels can't be combined to provide full bandwidth to a single peripheral. Thus, a single Thunderbolt peripheral has a maximum bandwidth of 10 Gbit/s, but the full bandwidth can be used when multiple peripherals are part of a single Thunderbolt chain.

Thunderbolt 2, new in most Mac systems introduced in late 2013 and later, supports channel aggregation, wherein a single peripheral can take advantage of the full 20 Gbit/s throughput. Future versions of Thunderbolt are planned to provide up to 100 Gbit/s channels. While this technology isn't available yet, the plan bodes well for Thunderbolt's prospects for future expansion.

Copper Thunderbolt cabling also supplies up to 10 watts of power to connected devices, again providing more power than any previous external peripheral bus. Unfortunately, copper Thunderbolt cabling is limited to a maximum 3-meter length. However, optical Thunderbolt cabling is soon to be available in lengths of up to 100 meters.

Apple's contribution to the Thunderbolt standard brought the inclusion of the DisplayPort standard and use of the Mini DisplayPort connection. Thunderbolt connections are physically identical to Mini DisplayPort connections, but they provide both PCI Express and DisplayPort data via this single connection. As a result, Thunderbolt devices and cables provide full support for DisplayPort data.

However, older Mini DisplayPort devices and cables don't support the additional PCI Express data. Thus, items that only support Mini DisplayPort should be the last connection in a Thunderbolt daisy chain. You can identify items compatible with Thunderbolt by an icon that looks like a lightning bolt, while items compatible with only Mini DisplayPort feature an icon that looks like a flat-panel display.

MORE INFO ▶ You can find out more about Thunderbolt at Intel's official website: https://thunderbolttechnology.net.

Bluetooth

Bluetooth is a short-range wireless peripheral connection standard originally developed by Ericsson for mobile phone headsets. Most Bluetooth devices have a range of only 1 to 10 meters, ideal for peripherals but inadequate for wireless networking. Further, Bluetooth is designed for connections not nearly as fast as wireless Ethernet. However, Bluetooth has the advantage of working with low-power devices.

As Bluetooth increased in popularity, computer manufacturers adopted it for wireless peripherals as well. In addition to providing a wireless connection between your Mac and mobile phone, Bluetooth allows your Mac to use wireless headsets, mice, keyboards, and printers. Most Mac computers that support OS X include Bluetooth wireless, and for those that don't, you can easily add it with a USB-to-Bluetooth adapter. Configuring Bluetooth is covered later in "Reference 25.2 Manage Bluetooth Devices" on page 844.

All Mac systems compatible with OS X Yosemite (except Xserve) include built-in support for Bluetooth. Depending on the age of the Mac, one of two Bluetooth variations is included:

▶ Any Mac capable of running OS X Yosemite (except Xserve) supports Bluetooth 1.2 with a maximum transfer rate of 721 kilobits per second (kbit/s) and Bluetooth 2.1 + Extended Data Rate (EDR) with a maximum transfer speed of up to 3 Mbit/s.

▶ Mac systems dating from 2011 or later support all previous versions of Bluetooth in addition to Bluetooth 3.0 + High Speed (HS) with a maximum transfer speed of up to 24 Mbit/s, and Bluetooth 4.0 with low-energy support. Bluetooth low energy (BLE) mode isn't very fast, at a maximum of 200 kbit/s, but it uses much less energy, is quicker to pair with devices, and sports a larger maximum range. The iOS continuity features in OS X Yosemite (Handoff, Instant Hotspot, Phone Calling, SMS, and Air-Drop) are made possible due to the efficiencies of Bluetooth 4.0 wireless.

MORE INFO ▶ You can find out more about Bluetooth at the official Bluetooth Technology Information website: www.bluetooth.com.

Reference 25.2
Manage Bluetooth Devices

Because Bluetooth is a wireless technology, some configuration is required to connect your Mac to a Bluetooth device. The process of connecting Bluetooth devices is known as pairing. Once two devices are paired, they act as if they were directly connected to each other. The OS X Bluetooth preferences make the process of configuring Bluetooth devices easy.

NOTE ▶ Desktop Mac computers can be purchased with Bluetooth wireless input devices only. In this case, the Mac and its associated peripherals are factory-paired and require no further pairing.

The quickest way to manage Bluetooth devices is to click the Bluetooth status menu. First, make sure your Mac computer's Bluetooth is turned on.

Pairing a Bluetooth Device

Before you begin the pairing process, you will need to enable Discoverable mode on the Bluetooth device you're going to pair with your Mac. Each device is different, so you may need to consult the device's user guide to enable Discoverable mode.

> **MORE INFO** ▶ The iOS continuity features in OS X Yosemite (Handoff, Instant Hotspot, Phone Calling, SMS, and AirDrop) utilize Bluetooth, but traditional Bluetooth pairing isn't required. Instead, the continuity features automatically connect as long as all devices are signed in to the same iCloud account. Find out more about Handoff from Apple Support article PH18754, "OS X Yosemite: Pick up where you left off with Handoff."

From the Bluetooth status menu, select Open Bluetooth Preferences. You can also open Bluetooth preferences using any other technique you prefer to access the System Preference application. Once open, Bluetooth preferences scans for any Bluetooth devices in range that are in discoverable mode. In the following screenshot of the Bluetooth preferences you can see three states for a device: a connected device, a previously paired but currently not connected device, and a device waiting to be paired.

Alternatively, with Bluetooth preferences open, the Mac itself is put in Bluetooth discoverable mode. Discoverable mode advertises your Mac as a Bluetooth resource to any device within range, which could invite unwanted attention to your Mac. So the only time you should be in discoverable mode is when you're attempting to pair your Mac with a Bluetooth device. In other words, you shouldn't leave Bluetooth preferences open for too long.

It may take several moments for the device's name to appear. Once it does, select it and click the Pair button. For all Bluetooth devices, a passcode must be used to authorize pairing. Depending on the device, you will perform one of the following:

▶ Complete the pairing with little interaction by using an automatically generated passcode. This is often what will happen with a device that has no method to verify the passcode, such as a Bluetooth mouse.

▶ Enter a predefined passcode on your Mac, as specified in the device's user guide, and click Continue to authorize the pairing.

▶ Allow the Bluetooth Setup Assistant to create a random passcode, which you then enter or verify on the Bluetooth device to authorize the pairing. In this example of pairing to an iPhone, the passcode is generated automatically.

The Bluetooth Setup Assistant automatically detects the capabilities of your Bluetooth device and may present you with additional configuration screens. Continue through these screens until you complete the setup process. When the pairing is complete, you can verify the pairing at any time by reopening Bluetooth preferences. Again, a device doesn't have to be currently connected to maintain pairing status with the Mac.

Remember, however, that opening Bluetooth preferences puts your Mac in Bluetooth discoverable mode, so a safer (and probably quicker) method for verifying Bluetooth devices is via the Bluetooth status menu. Notice this menu indicates a connected device using bold letters.

Managing Bluetooth Settings

You can adjust settings such as the peripheral's name from Bluetooth preferences. To access all the Bluetooth management settings, open Bluetooth preferences from either the Apple menu > System Preferences or the Bluetooth status menu > Open Bluetooth Preferences.

To manage a Bluetooth peripheral, select it from the list, and then use secondary (or Control-) click to reveal a pop-up menu. From this menu you can connect or disconnect a device, and possibly rename a device; some devices, such as iPhones, are named on the device and cannot be changed from Bluetooth preferences. You can also delete a device pairing from this pop-up menu by clicking the small x button to the right.

Clicking the Advanced button at the bottom of Bluetooth preferences reveals a dialog where you can adjust additional Bluetooth settings. The settings here are extremely important for desktop systems that use only wireless keyboards and mice.

Finally, you'll find Bluetooth sharing settings in Shared preferences. Like all other sharing services, Bluetooth sharing is off by default. Enabling Bluetooth sharing should only be considered as a last resort when traditional file-sharing methods aren't possible. Lesson 24 "Host Sharing and Personal Firewall" discusses a variety of alternative file-sharing methods, including AirDrop wireless file sharing.

Reference 25.3
Peripheral Troubleshooting

Troubleshooting peripheral issues can be difficult because of the wide variety of devices out there. However, peripheral issues can usually be categorized as either software related or hardware related. The first part of this section looks at how the system software interacts with peripherals and how to identify peripheral issues related to software. As for peripheral hardware issues, replacing or repairing the peripheral or its connections usually resolves the issue. Yet a few general troubleshooting techniques can help you identify and possibly resolve the problem.

Peripheral Device Classes

Peripherals are divided into device classes based on their primary function. OS X includes built-in software drivers that allow your Mac to interact with peripherals from all device classes. Although these built-in drivers may provide basic support, many third-party devices require device-specific drivers for full functionality. Detailed information about software drivers is covered in the next section.

Device classes as defined in OS X include:

▶ Human input devices (HID)—Peripherals that allow you to directly enter information or control the Mac interface. Examples are keyboards, mice, trackpads, game controllers, tablets, and even Braille interfaces.

▶ Storage devices—Internal disks, flash disks, optical discs, and iPods. Storage peripherals are covered in Lesson 9 "File Systems and Storage".

- Printers—Printers of all types, plotters, and fax machines. Printing is covered in Lesson 26 "Print and Scan".

- Scanners—Flatbed, negative, slide, and drum scanners. OS X supports scanners via the Image Capture framework, which allows you to control scanners from /Applications/Image Capture or any other compatible third-party capture application, such as Photoshop. This topic is also covered in Lesson 26 "Print and Scan".

  TIP ▶ The Image Capture application supports both locally attached scanners and scanners being shared via the network. Further, Sharing preferences also allow you to share a locally attached scanner to the network. Network scanner discovery is accomplished using Bonjour, so usually no additional setup is required to locate shared scanning resources.

- Digital cameras—These peripherals include both directly connected cameras and camera storage cards mounted to the Mac computer's file system. Recall that many digital cameras, when connected to a computer, simply extend their internal storage to the computer. In this case, OS X accesses the camera's internal storage, or any directly attached camera storage cards, as it does any other storage device. Applications like iPhoto or Aperture then take over to copy the picture files from the camera storage to the Mac computer's storage. Some cameras support a tethered capture mode in which they are directly controlled by the Mac and send the captured picture data directly to the Mac. OS X supports this type of camera connection via the Image Capture framework, which also allows you to use /Applications/Image Capture or another compatible third-party capture application.

- Video devices—These peripherals include video cameras and video converters connected via USB, FireWire, or an expansion bus. OS X supports these video devices via the QuickTime framework, which allows you to use /Applications/QuickTime Player or any other compatible video application, such as iMovie or Final Cut Pro.

- Audio devices—These peripherals include external audio interfaces connected via USB, FireWire, or an expansion bus. OS X supports these audio devices via the Core Audio framework, so you can use any compatible audio application, such as GarageBand or Logic Pro.

Peripheral Device Drivers

One of the primary responsibilities of the system software is to act as an intermediary between peripherals and applications. If an application supports a general device class, the operating system handles all the technical details of communicating with each model of peripheral in that class.

Here's an example: For an application to receive user input, it needs to receive information from the keyboard, mouse, trackpad, and the like, but it doesn't need to know any details about how to interpret the electrical signals from that device because that's handled by the operating system. This separation of peripherals and applications by the operating system allows you to use nearly any combination of the two with few incompatibilities.

OS X supports peripherals using device drivers, specialized pieces of software that allow peripherals to interoperate with the system. Some peripherals are supported via a generic driver, but many require a device driver created specifically for the peripheral. Although OS X includes a decent selection of common device drivers, you may have to install third-party device drivers to support your peripherals. Nearly all device drivers are installed using an installer utility that places the driver software in the correct resource folder on your Mac. Device drivers are implemented in one of three ways: kernel extensions, framework plugins, or applications.

NOTE ▶ OS X uses a driver only if it's already installed. In other words, if you're adding support for a new third-party peripheral that requires custom drivers, install those drivers first before you connect the peripheral to the Mac.

NOTE ▶ It's always best to check the peripheral manufacturer's website to obtain the latest version of the driver software.

Device driver implementations in OS X include:

▶ Kernel extensions (KEXTs)—This is a special type of software created to add peripheral support at the lowest level of OS X: the system kernel. KEXTs load and unload from the system automatically, so there's no need to manage them aside from making sure they are installed in the correct locations. Although some KEXTs are hidden inside application bundles, most are located in the /System/Library/Extensions or /Library/Extensions folders. Remember, in general, nearly all the items in the /System folder are part of the standard OS X install. Examples of peripherals that use KEXTs are human input devices, storage devices, audio and video devices, and other expansion cards.

▶ Framework plugins—This type of device driver adds support for a specific peripheral to an existing system framework. For example, support for additional scanners and digital cameras is facilitated via plugins to the Image Capture framework.

▶   Applications—In some cases a peripheral is best supported by an application written just for that peripheral. Examples are the iPod, iPhone, and iPad, which are managed by the iTunes application.

Inspecting Kernel Extensions

Even though the OS X kernel is designed to manage KEXTs without user interaction, you may still need to verify that a specific KEXT is loaded. You can view the currently installed and loaded KEXTs from the System Information application (while holding down the Option key, choose Apple menu > System Information). Once System Information is open, select the Extensions item in the Contents list; it may take a few moments for the system to scan all currently installed KEXTs. Once the list appears, you can further inspect individual KEXTs by selecting them from this list. Sorting this list by the Loaded column clearly indicates which KEXTs are in use by the system.

A key feature of OS X is support for a 64-bit kernel, thus necessitating 64-bit KEXTs. Starting with OS X Mountain Lion, OS X requires that the kernel start up in 64-bit mode. From System Information, you can easily verify that all loaded kernel extensions support this mode. However, third-party KEXTs that have not made the transition won't work, as OS X simply ignores any KEXTs that don't support 64-bit mode.

General Peripheral Troubleshooting

Use the following techniques for general peripheral troubleshooting:

▶ Always check System Information first. If you remember only one peripheral trouble-shooting technique, it should be this. Connected peripherals appear in System Information regardless of whether their software driver is functioning. In other words, if a connected peripheral does not show up in System Information, then you are almost certainly experiencing a hardware failure. If a connected peripheral appears as normal in System Information, you are probably experiencing a software driver issue. In that case, use System Information to validate whether the expected kernel extensions are loaded.

▶ Unplug and then reconnect the peripheral. Doing this reinitializes the peripheral connection and forces OS X to reload any peripheral-specific drivers.

▶ Plug the peripheral into a different port or use a different cable. This helps you rule out any bad hardware, including host ports, cables, and inoperable hubs.

▶ Unplug other devices on the same bus. Another device on the shared bus may be causing an issue.

▶ Resolve potential USB power issues. As covered previously in "USB 1.1/2.0/3.0" on page 839, the USB interface can prove problematic if devices are trying to draw too much power. Try plugging the USB device directly into the Mac instead of a USB hub.

▶ Shut down the Mac, fully power down all peripherals, and then restart everything. This tried-and-true troubleshooting technique reinitializes all the peripheral connections and reloads all the software drivers.

▶ Try the peripheral with another Mac. This helps you determine whether the issue is with your Mac or the peripheral. If the device doesn't work with other computers, your Mac is not the source of the issue.

▶ Check for system software and driver software updates. Software bugs are constantly being fixed, so it's always a good time to check for software updates. You can use the OS X built-in software update system, but you should also check the peripheral manufacturer's website for the latest driver updates.

▶ Check for computer and peripheral software updates. Like software updates, firmware updates may also be necessary to resolve your peripheral issue. This possibility is especially likely for more sophisticated devices like the iPod, iPhone, and iPad, which have their own internal software as well.

Exercise 25.1
Examine Peripherals via System Information

In an earlier exercise you used System Information to view information about your hard disk. Because it is bus-oriented, System Information is extremely useful when trouble-shooting peripheral issues. In this exercise, you will use System Information to identify devices on a particular bus. Most Mac computers have several USB ports and use USB internally for several devices. In a class, your instructor may choose to do this exercise as a demonstration if the equipment in the room doesn't provide USB devices.

Examine Internal Devices

1   If necessary, log in as Chris Johnson.

2   Click the Apple menu.

3   Hold down the Option key. The first item in the Apple menu changes from "About This Mac" to "System Information."

4   With the Option key held down, choose System Information from the Apple menu.

A System Information report opens with the Hardware Overview displayed. The Contents list on the left displays all the report topics that System Information can generate, listed in three main sections: Hardware, Network, and Software.

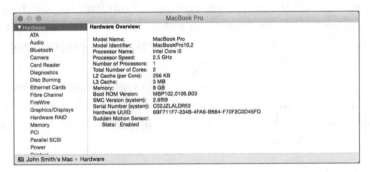

There are several ways of opening System Information. In an earlier exercise, you opened it by choosing Apple menu > About This Mac and then clicking System Report.

5   In the Hardware list on the left, click Graphics/Displays.

This shows information about your Mac computer's graphics adapters and displays.

6   In the Hardware list, click USB to view devices connected to the USB bus.

USB is a common peripheral bus. It is often used for keyboards, mice, trackpads, printers, scanners, storage devices, and digital cameras.

In this example, System Information indicates that there are four USB buses, two of which have devices connected to them. Several of the buses are internal to the computer; in this example, the FaceTime HD Camera, Apple Internal Keyboard / Trackpad, and Bluetooth USB Host Controller entries are all internal devices connected to internal USB buses.

If a device is connected to a hub, it is listed beneath the hub and indented. This example shows a Keyboard Hub entry with a Macally DotMouse and an Apple Keyboard connected. Although the hub and keyboard are separate devices at the USB level, they are both parts of a single physical device, an Apple USB keyboard. Most USB keyboards contain a built-in hub so you can attach other USB devices to them.

7   Examine the USB report for your computer and determine which devices are internal and which are external.

Examine External USB Devices (Optional)

For this section, you will need at least one external USB device connected to your computer. If you are performing these exercises in class, your instructor may be able to provide a device. If there is no suitable USB device available, quit System Information, and skip the rest of this exercise.

1   If it isn't already connected, plug in the external USB device, and refresh the System Information report by choosing File > Refresh Information (Command-R).

2   Select an external USB device in the USB report for your computer.

Details about the device appear in the lower pane.

3   Examine the Speed listed for the device.

The speed at which a USB device can run depends not only on its own capability but also on the speeds of the port and any intermediate hubs through which it is connected.

4   Examine the Current Available and Current Required figures.

Your computer can supply only a certain amount of electrical power through each of its USB ports, and if there are too many devices chained off a port, there might not be enough for all the devices. To prevent this problem, OS X keeps track of how much electrical power is available at each point in the USB bus and disables devices if it calculates that there is not enough power available for them.

5   While viewing the USB information, unplug the device from your computer (if it is a storage device, eject it first), plug it into a different USB port, and then choose File > Refresh Information (Command-R).

System Information does not update its display unless you tell it to.

6   Locate the external device in the report to see whether it has changed places or whether any of its statistics have changed.

7   If you have an external hub available, try plugging the device in via that, and then refresh the display in System Information.

Note whether there is enough power available from the hub to run the device, and whether its speed decreased because of being connected through a hub.

8   Quit System Information.

Lesson 26

Print and Scan

Apple and Adobe began the desktop publishing revolution by introducing the first high-quality printing solution for personal computers. Although Adobe created the PostScript printing system, Apple was the first to include it in both the Macintosh operating system and the first PostScript printer, the Apple LaserWriter. Apple has continued to pioneer advancements in printing software with OS X by adopting a printing workflow based on the Adobe Portable Document Format (PDF) and the Common UNIX Printing System (CUPS).

In this lesson you'll learn how OS X works with different print and scan technologies and how to manage and troubleshoot printers and multifunction devices connected to your Mac.

GOALS

▶ Understand the technologies that enable OS X to print

▶ Configure OS X for printers and multifunction devices

▶ Manage and troubleshoot print jobs

Reference 26.1
Print System Architecture

Robust printing has always been an important part of the Mac operating system because of its popularity with graphic design users. OS X continues this tradition with an updated printing system featuring redesigned and simplified printing interfaces.

CUPS

OS X uses the open source Common UNIX Printing System 1.6, or CUPS, to manage local printing. Originally an independent product, CUPS was purchased by Apple and remains an open source project. Architecturally, CUPS uses the Internet Printing Protocol (IPP) standard as the basis for managing printing tasks and uses PostScript Printer Description (PPD) files as the basis for printer drivers. Though still used by CUPS, the PPD name is a bit of a misnomer, as non-PostScript printers can also be described by these files.

A print job starts when a user prints from either an application in the graphical user interface or the print commands in the Terminal. When you print from an application, the OS X Quartz graphics system generates a Portable Document Format (PDF) file. When you print from the command line, a PostScript (PS) file is generated. In either case, the file created is called a spool file and is placed inside the /var/spool/cups folder.

The CUPS background process, cupsd, takes this spool file and passes it through a series of filter processes known as the print chain. These processes convert the spool file to a format that is understood by the destination printer, and then ultimately communicate this information to the printer.

> **MORE INFO** ▶ CUPS provides capabilities beyond the scope of this text. To find out more, visit the official CUPS website at www.cups.org.

CUPS Drivers

Before you can print, you must configure printer settings, which includes associating an appropriate printer driver with the printing device. This association happens automatically as you configure a new printing device; however, the system must have the printer driver installed before it can use the printer. Apple supplies printer drivers for most popular models, including Brother, Canon, Epson, Fuji-Xerox, HP, Lexmark, Ricoh, and Samsung.

> **MORE INFO** ▶ For A complete list of printer and scanner drivers available from Apple for OS X, refer to Apple Support article HT2201465, "OS X: Printer and scanner software available for download."

The OS X installer is designed to save space on the system volume and to avoid installation of unnecessary print drivers. New installations of OS X include only Apple and generic print drivers. OS X upgrade installations install only drivers for printers in use by the Mac. It's expected that additional print drivers will be acquired via the Internet.

If you attempt to add a printer the Mac does not have the driver for, and you are connected to the Internet, the system prompts you to automatically download and install the driver using the Apple software update service. You can also manually download and install printer drivers from the Apple support website.

> **NOTE** ▶ You should always attempt to use the Apple collection of printer drivers. These drivers provide the most native experience and automatically update via the software update system.

> **NOTE** ▶ You must log in or authenticate as an administrative user to install printer drivers either manually or via software update.

> **NOTE** ▶ The automatic printer driver installer from software update often installs multiple printer drivers from the same manufacturer simultaneously.

Obviously, if you aren't connected to the Internet, you have to acquire the printer driver manually, though some standard PostScript and Printer Command Language (PCL) printers can use the built-in generic printer drivers. Also, if Apple doesn't provide the printer driver via its software update system, you have to manually acquire the appropriate driver, often directly from the printer's manufacturer.

A few of the built-in Apple printer drivers are installed in /System/Library/Printers, but all the third-party printer drivers are installed to the /Library/Printers folder. The primary folder for drivers is the PPD folder, but you may notice other vendor folders that contain ancillary printer driver resources.

Once you've added a printer configuration, a copy of the PPD with the name of the device is placed in the /etc/cups/ppd folder and two configuration files are modified: /etc/cups/

printers.conf and /Library/Preferences/org.cups.printers.plist. Finally, the first time a user prints or accesses a printer queue, the system creates a printer queue application, again with the name of the device, in the ~/Library/Printers folder in the user's home folder.

Reference 26.2
Print and Scan Configuration

How you physically connect to a printer determines how you configure OS X to print to the printer. In many cases, printer configuration is extremely easy and mostly automatic. For example, directly attached and local network printers are automatically configured with little user interaction. However, older printers or nonlocal network printers require a bit more manual configuration.

> **TIP** ▶ When adding supported multifunction printers, scanning and faxing services are configured along with general printing services.

> **TIP** ▶ The entirety of the OS X printing configuration is stored inside the /etc/cups folder. Copying this folder to other OS X systems duplicates the entire print system configuration. Just be sure to verify the file system permissions on the copied /etc/cups folder match the original copy.

Configuring a Directly Attached Printer

If your Mac already has the correct printer driver for a directly attached USB or FireWire printer, the system automatically detects the appropriate settings and configures the new printer for you as soon as you plug it in. If the printer provides faxing and scan support, the system should automatically configure this as well.

You can verify the printer has been added by simply opening the Print dialog from any application (File > Print) or Printers & Scanners preferences. In Printers & Scanners preferences, you can tell printers are locally connected if their location has the same name as the local Mac computer's sharing name.

It's important to note, however, that this automatic configuration only occurs if the appropriate printer driver is installed. If the driver isn't installed but is available from Apple, you are prompted with the automatic software update installer when you plug the printer in.

Again, only if an administrative user is logged in is the system allowed to install the printer driver and then automatically configure the printer. Thus, if a nonadministrative user attaches a new printer for the first time, there is a good chance the system will not configure the printer because the driver is missing. Also, if a printer driver for a directly attached printer is unavailable from Apple, then nothing happens automatically when you plug it in. An administrative user has to manually acquire and install the printer driver to get it working.

Configuring a Local Network Printer

Network printer configurations must be manually added, but Apple makes this process incredibly easy for any printer that supports compatible local network discovery protocols. OS X can automatically discover standalone printers that support Bonjour (or mDNS), standalone printers that support AirPrint, and any printer shared via another Mac or AirPort wireless base station.

> **MORE INFO** ► For more information about the AirPrint protocol, including a list of printers that support this new protocol, refer to Apple Support article HT201311, "About AirPrint."

If the printer you want to add is being advertised via a supported service discovery protocol on the local network, then all you need to do is select it from the Print dialog (File > Print) from any application. Once in the Print dialog, select the Printer pop-up menu, and the system scans the local network for available printers to select.

As covered previously, the Mac either configures the printer with a preinstalled driver or prompts you to download the driver from the Apple software update service. Again, the system should also automatically configure fax and scan support for multifunction devices. If a printer driver must be added, once again only an administrative user can do that.

NOTE ▶ If a network printer requires authentication, you may have to enter the name and password of an authorized user before you can print to the shared printer.

NOTE ▶ Your Mac automatically acquires the appropriate printer drivers from any Mac that is sharing a printer via the network. In other words, the Mac hosting a shared printer automatically sends your Mac the drivers if they aren't preinstalled.

Manually Configuring a Printer

If the network printer doesn't support automatic network discovery via Bonjour, then you must configure it manually via the Add Printer window. Also, if a directly attached printer does not automatically configure, then you can manually add it. You can open the Add Printer window at any time to manually add new printers or multifunction devices. Again, nonadministrative users have to provide administrator authentication to access the Add Printer window.

NOTE ▶ OS X v10.6 and later are not compatible with the AppleTalk network protocol, so printing via AppleTalk network printers is unavailable in these versions.

NOTE ▶ Bluetooth printers are configured via the Bluetooth Setup Assistant, as covered in Lesson 25 "Peripherals and Drivers".

To manually add a new printer or multifunction device, you can open the Add Printer window via one of the following methods:

▶ From any application, open a Print dialog by choosing File > Print. Next, from the Printer pop-up menu, choose Add Printer.

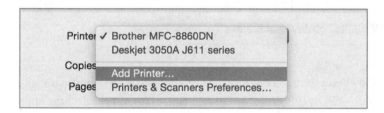

▶ Open Printers & Scanners preferences by choosing Apple menu > System Preferences and then clicking the Printers & Scanners icon. If necessary, click the lock icon in the bottom-left corner and authenticate as an administrative user to unlock Printers & Scanners preferences. Finally, click the Add (+) button at the bottom of the Printers list. If there are nearby network printers, a pop-up menu appears allowing you to easily select those printers. If the printer you need to configure doesn't appear in the menu, then select the Add Printer or Scanner option to manually configure a new printer via the Add Printer window.

▶ From the Finder, open the /System/Library/CoreServices/AddPrinter application. This application's icon can also be placed in the Dock.

The Add Printer window features several panes for selecting a printer or multifunction device. These panes are accessed by clicking the following buttons in the toolbar:

▶ Default—This browser lets you select directly attached USB and FireWire printers and network printers discovered using Bonjour (or mDNS), AirPrint, or network directory services.

▶ IP—This dialog allows you to manually enter the IP address or DNS host name of a Line Printer Daemon (LPD), IPP, or HP JetDirect printer. You must select the appropriate protocol from the pop-up menu and enter the printer's address. Entering a printer queue is usually optional.

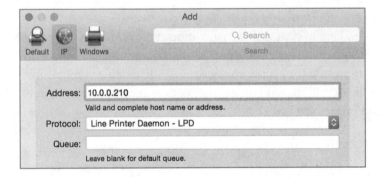

▶ Windows—This browser lets you select printers shared via the Server Message Block (SMB) printer sharing protocol. Double-click an SMB server and authenticate to access the server's shared printers.

▶ Advanced—This advanced configuration choice lets you manually enter the printer location. This is only necessary in very rare circumstances when the system cannot properly autolocate a printer. The Advanced button is hidden by default. To reveal this button, secondary (or Control-) click in the Add Printer toolbar to reveal a pop-up menu. From this menu choose Customize Toolbar and then drag the Advanced button into the toolbar.

Once you have selected a printer or multifunction device from the top half of the new printer configuration dialog, the system completes the bottom half for you using information it has discovered. This includes automatically selecting the appropriate printer driver if possible. Often this information isn't ideal, and you can easily change it. The Name and Location fields are only there to help you identify the device, so you can set those to anything you like.

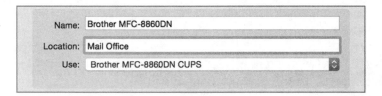

If you're configuring an LPD printer connection, you also have to manually specify the appropriate printer driver. This step can also occur with HP JetDirect and SMB printer connections.

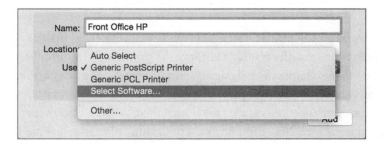

To select a specific printer driver, choose Select Software from the Use pop-up menu. You can manually scroll through the list of installed printer drivers, but using the Spotlight field to narrow the search is much quicker.

Finally, if you are configuring an IP printer, you may be presented with an additional dialog to select any special options that the printer has. Once the printer configuration is complete, you can verify the printer has been added by simply opening the Print dialog from any application or Printers & Scanners preferences. In Printers & Scanners preferences, you can tell which printers are connected via network if their location is shown as something different than your local Mac computer's sharing name. Also note that multifunction devices show a Scan tab, indicating the system has also configured the scanning driver software.

Modifying an Existing Printer Configuration

You may find it necessary to edit a printer configuration after you set it up. From Printers & Scanners preferences, you can:

▶ Delete a printer configuration—Select the item you want to delete from the printer list, and then click the Delete (–) button at the bottom of the list.

▶ Set printing defaults—From the two pop-up menus at the bottom of Printers & Scanners preferences, choose the default printer and paper size. Use caution when setting the default printer for Last Printer Used; you will effectively have no permanent default printer, as the default destination for print jobs may constantly change.

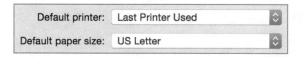

NOTE ▶ Depending on the printer model, you may not be allowed to modify the print driver settings from Printers & Scanners preferences. To change a printer's selected driver, you must delete the printer and then add it again.

▶ Open a print queue—Select a printer from the list and then click the Open Print Queue button. Details on print queues are covered later in "Managing Printer Queues" on page 876.

▶ Edit an existing configuration and check supply levels—Select a printer from the list and then click the Options & Supplies button. In the resulting dialog, you can easily edit the printer's configuration—including changing the printer's name—and, if available, check the printer supply levels and open the printer's hardware configuration utility.

▶ Manage scanning—Select a multifunction device from the list and then select the Scan tab. From this interface, you can open the scanner image capture interface or enable local network scanner sharing.

Sharing Printers

It's very easy to share printer configurations with OS X. Your Mac computer's shared print service is made available via the IPP printer sharing protocols. Although OS X and Windows are both compatible with IPP, different versions of Windows may require additional drivers for IPP. Also, the IPP protocol supports automatic printer driver configuration and installation for OS X systems, so when another Mac user connects to your Mac computer's shared print service, that user's system automatically selects, and downloads if necessary, the appropriate printer drivers.

The CUPS-shared print service also allows other network clients to easily locate your shared printer configurations with Bonjour. Again, OS X and Windows work with both discovery protocols, but whereas OS X is compatible with Bonjour, different versions of Windows may require additional drivers for Bonjour. Alternatively, network clients can manually enter your Mac computer's IP address or DNS host name to access your computer's shared print service. Configuring your Mac computer's identification for providing network services is covered in Lesson 24 "Host Sharing and Personal Firewall".

NOTE ▶ Users cannot access shared print services on a Mac in sleep mode. You can disable your Mac computer's automatic sleep activation or enable "Wake for Wi-Fi network access" from Energy Saver preferences.

To share printers from your Mac, open and unlock Sharing preferences. Select the Printer Sharing checkbox to enable printer sharing. Selecting this checkbox tells the cupsd process (which is always running in the background) to listen for IPP print service requests on TCP port 631.

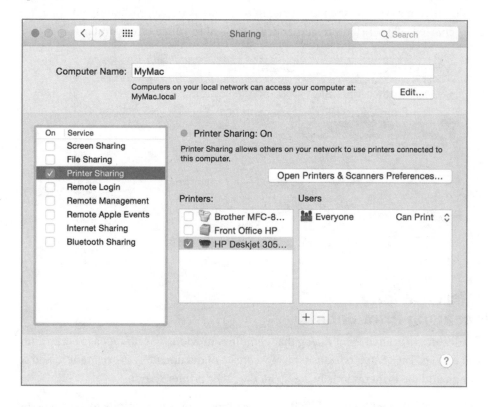

If your Mac is configured to use a document scanner, you can enable scanner sharing from Sharing preferences as well. This allows you to share the scanner with other Mac systems on the local network.

By default, no printers are shared. To enable sharing for printer configurations, simply select the checkboxes next to the printers you wish to share. Optionally, you can limit who is allowed to print to your shared printers. By default, all users are allowed access to your shared printing devices. To limit access, select a shared device from the Printers list and then click the Add (+) button at the bottom of the Users list.

NOTE ▶ To avoid confusion, you shouldn't reshare network printers using your Mac computer's shared print services if network printers are already available on your network.

A dialog appears where you can select user or group accounts you want to grant access to the printing device. When adding accounts, you can also choose to deny access to guest users by selecting No Access to Everyone in the Users list. Also, with limited printing access enabled, all users have to authenticate to print to your shared printer.

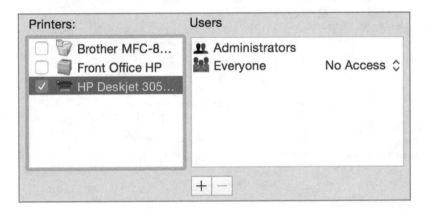

Reference 26.3
Managing Print Jobs

OS X features a unified Print dialog that combines previously separate Page Setup and Print dialogs. Page Setup options typically consist of document size, orientation, and scale settings, and the Print options make up all the other printer settings.

For backward compatibility, OS X allows older applications to continue to use separate Page Setup and Print dialogs, but older apps can also use the new, unified printing interface when you open a Print dialog. In other words, some older applications have document settings in both the Page Setup and Print dialogs.

This unified Print dialog also features two modes: The basic mode allows you to quickly preview and start a print job using default settings, and the details mode allows you to specify any page or print option and manage print setting presets.

NOTE ▶ Some applications, especially graphic design and desktop publishing applications, use custom dialogs for printing that may look different from the standard Print dialog covered in this lesson.

Basic Printing

To start a print job using default print settings, from an application, choose File > Print or press Command-P.

> **NOTE ▶** Some applications bypass the Print dialog and simply send the print job to your default printer when you use Command-P.

When the Print dialog appears, in some cases it slides out of the application's window title bar; in other cases it appears as its own separate dialog. Most applications show a print preview, but some may just show the basic print options. The default printer and print preset are selected, but you can choose the number of pages, copies, and duplex (two-sided) options, if available. Customizing printer presets is covered in the next section of this lesson.

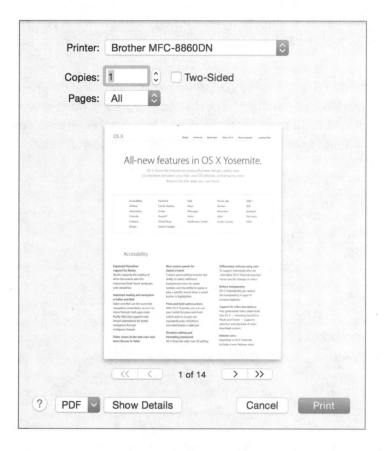

When the print job is started, the system automatically opens the print queue application associated with the destination printer. Although no window opens if the print job is successful, you can click the print queue in the Dock.

Detailed Print Settings and Presets

To start a print job that uses custom print settings, from an application, again open the Print dialog. Whenever you open the Print dialog, the default printer and print presets are selected, but you can choose any other configured printer or set of presets from the associated pop-up menu.

Clicking the Show Details button expands the Print dialog to its full details mode. In the full details mode, you can click the Hide Details button to return to the basic Print dialog mode. The Print dialog also remembers which mode you last used for each application. In other words, every application starts with a basic Print dialog the first time you print, but for subsequent print jobs, the Print dialog defaults to whatever you did last time in that application.

On the left side of the details Print dialog, you can page through a preview of the print job, much like the preview in the basic Print dialog. Any changes you make to the page layout settings are instantly reflected in the preview. On the right side of the dialog, you can configure all possible print settings for most applications. The top half features more detailed page setup and print settings.

Settings on the bottom half vary depending on the application you're printing from and your selected printer's driver. You can select a category of print settings to modify by choosing it from the pop-up menu that separates the print settings from top to bottom. The settings list and configuration options within will vary for different applications, printers, and printer drivers.

TIP ▶ If the selected printer is a multifunction device that provides fax support, one of the items in the Print Settings pop-up menu is Send Fax. From here, you can define fax settings to be used on the multifunction device to send a fax instead of printing a document.

To save the current print settings as a preset, choose Save Current Settings as Preset from the Presets pop-up menu. Select whether you want this preset to apply to all printers or just the currently selected printer. By saving a preset, you make it accessible from the Presets pop-up menu in the details view of any Print dialog. The print presets are saved to the ~/Library/Preferences/com.apple.print.custompresets.plist file, so each user has her own custom print presets.

NOTE ▶ Print presets do not save application-specific settings.

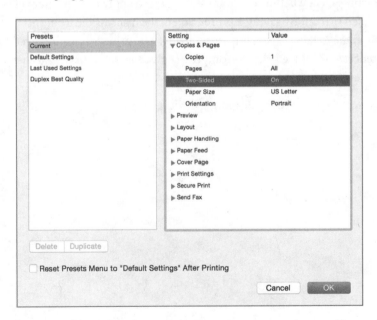

To manage existing print presets, open the print Presets dialog by choosing Show Presets from the Presets pop-up menu. In the print Presets dialog select a preset to see its settings and values, and optionally use the Delete and Duplicate buttons at the bottom of the presets list. Double-clicking a print preset allows you to rename the preset. When you are done managing print presets, click OK to save the changes and return to the Print dialog.

Using PDF Tools

OS X includes a built-in PDF architecture and editing tools. The full Adobe Acrobat suite has more advanced PDF features, but OS X includes all the tools to create PDF documents or perform basic editing. Any application that can print can also use the OS X Quartz imaging system to generate high-quality PDF documents. In any Print dialog, click the PDF button. A pop-up menu which you can use to save a PDF to any location.

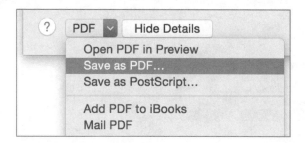

From the PDF pop-up menu, you can also specify a PDF services designed to accept and automatically process PDF files. Some preset services are built in, but you can add your own PDF services by choosing Edit Menu from the PDF pop-up menu. Or, you can manually add PDF services to the /Library/PDF Services or the ~/Library/PDF Services folders, depending on who needs access to the PDF services. To create custom PDF services, you can use either the /Applications/Utilities/AppleScript Editor application or the /Applications/Automator application.

The OS X /Applications/Preview application also offers comprehensive PDF editing functionality—you can edit and adjust individual elements, reorder pages, crop the document, add annotations, fill out form data, and apply digital signatures using an attached video camera. From Preview, you can also convert PDF files to other formats or resave the PDF file using more appropriate settings.

Managing Printer Queues

As stated previously, when a print job is started, the spool file is placed inside the /var/spool/cups folder, and then CUPS takes over to process the file and send it to the printer. When you print from the graphical interface, OS X opens a print queue application to manage the print job. If a job completes quickly, the file is only in the print queue for a few moments, and the print queue application quits when done.

However, printers always seem to be the most problematic of peripherals, so occasionally your Mac will not be able to complete the print job. The printer queue application remains open until the print job finishes or you resolve the print issue. If the system detects an error with the printer, it stops all print jobs to that device. You can still issue print jobs, but they simply fill up in the device's queue.

To manage print job queues, you can access the printer queue application using one of the following methods:

▶ If a printer queue is already open, simply click its icon in the Dock. In the following example screenshot, the printer queue's Dock icon shows a 2 in the red badge, indicating that there are currently two jobs in the queue.

- ► You can manually open a printer queue from Printers & Scanners preferences by selecting the device from the printer list and then clicking the Open Print Queue button.

- ► You can also manually open a printer queue from the Finder by navigating to the ~/Library/Printers folder.

When the printer queue opens, you immediately see the current status of the printer and any currently queued print jobs. A typical example of something you see when a printer queue is not responding is multiple versions of the same job in queue because the user has incorrectly assumed sending the print job again would fix the issue. The system automatically detects when the printer becomes available again, assuming the queue isn't paused.

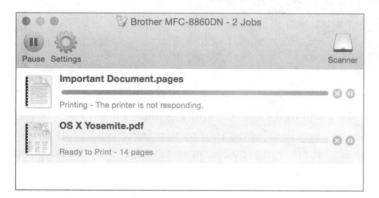

To pause or resume the printer queue, click the Pause Printer or Resume Printer button (the button toggles between the two modes) in the queue application toolbar. To hold or resume a specific print job, select it from the job list and then click the small Pause or Resume button to the right of the print job progress bar (again, the button toggles between the two). You can also delete a job by selecting it from the job list and then clicking the small x button to the right of the print job progress bar.

> **TIP** ▶ Selecting a job in the printer queue list and pressing the Space bar opens a Quick Look preview window for the print job.

> **TIP** ▶ You can reorder print jobs in the printer queue by dragging the job you want to reorder in the list. You can also drag jobs from one printer's queue window to another's.

Once you are done managing a printer queue, it's acceptable to leave the application running. You may find it useful to leave often-used printer queues in the Dock for direct access. Simply secondary (or Control-) click the queue application's Dock icon and, from the shortcut menu, choose Options > Keep in Dock.

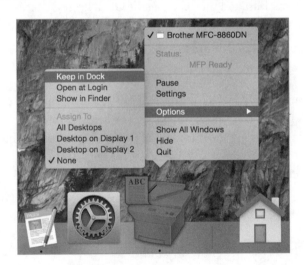

You can also provide quick access to all your printer queues by dragging the ~/Library/Printers folder from the Finder to your Dock. Clicking this folder in your Dock reveals all configured devices. An added benefit to having your printers in the Dock is that you can drag a document on top of a printer icon to quickly print a single copy of the document.

Some other features are also available in the printer queue application's toolbar. For instance, you can reconfigure the printer's settings by clicking the Settings button in the toolbar. Also, if the queue is for a supported multifunction printer, you can click the Scanner button in the toolbar to open the Scanner interface. Scanning to multifunction devices both locally and via the network is possible in OS X.

Reference 26.4
Print System Troubleshooting

You will probably experience more printing issues caused by hardware than by software. However, this being a reference about OS X, the following is a series of mostly software-based general print system troubleshooting techniques.

▶   Always check the printer queue application first. The printer queue application always shows the first symptoms of an issue, and odds are you were made aware of the issue by the queue. The printer queue lets you know if there is a printer connection issue, but you should also check to be sure that the queue is not paused and that none of the jobs is on hold. Sometimes deleting old print jobs from the queue helps clear the problem.

▶ Double-check page and print settings. If the job is printing but doesn't print correctly, double-check page and print settings using the Print dialog details mode.

▶ Review the PDF output of the application. Remember that the CUPS workflow is application > PDF > CUPS > printer. Thus, verifying whether the PDF looks correct lets you know if the source of the problem is with the application or the printing system.

▶ Print from another application. If you suspect the application is at the root of the problem, try printing from another application. You can also print a test page while in the printer queue application by choosing Printer > Print Test Page.

▶ Check the printer hardware. Many recent printers have diagnostic screens or printed reports that can help you identify a hardware issue. Many also have a software utility or a built-in webpage that reports errors. Clicking the Printer Setup button in the printer queue application toolbar accesses these management interfaces. Also, don't forget to double-check cables and connections. Finally, you may be well served by contacting the printer manufacturer to diagnose printer hardware issues.

▶ For faxing issues, check phone line and phone settings. When sending faxes via a multifunction device, you may encounter issues that are outside your control because you are relying on the phone system and another user's fax hardware. As with any faxing issue, you also need to check for fax modem problems.

▶ For directly connected printers, use peripheral troubleshooting techniques. For printers connected via USB or FireWire, use the peripheral troubleshooting techniques outlined in Lesson 25 "Peripherals and Drivers".

▶ For network printers, use network troubleshooting techniques. For printers connected via a network connection, use the network troubleshooting techniques described in Lesson 22 "Network Troubleshooting" and Lesson 23 "Network Services".

▶ Delete and then reconfigure printers. From Printers & Scanners preferences, delete and then reconfigure a troublesome printer using the techniques outlined earlier in this lesson. This resets the device's drivers and queue.

▶ Reset the entire print system. Sometimes it's necessary to reset the entire printing system. From Printers & Scanners preferences, secondary (or Control-) click in the printers list, and choose "Reset printing system" from the shortcut menu. Click OK in the verification dialog. Next you'll have to authenticate as an administrative user. This clears all configured devices, shared settings, custom presets, and queued print jobs. While this may seem drastic, it's likely to clear up any software-related printing issues.

▶ Review CUPS log files. Like other system services, CUPS writes all important activity to log files. You can access these logs while in any printer queue application by choosing Printer > Log & History. This opens the Console utility to the CUPS error_log file. While in the Console, you can also check the CUPS access_log and page_log files located in /private/var/log/cups.

NOTE ▶ The CUPS error_log file may not exist if the CUPS service hasn't yet logged any serious print errors.

▶ Reinstall or update printer drivers. Again, software bugs are always being fixed, so it's good to check for printer driver updates. You can use the OS X built-in software update system to check for system updates and many printer updates. However, be sure to also check the printer manufacturer's website for the latest printer driver updates.

▶ Repair installed software disk permissions. Third-party installers tend to mess up system software permissions. Use the Disk Utility Repair Permissions feature to resolve permissions issues with printer drivers and other print system files, as covered in Lesson 11 "Permissions and Sharing".

MORE INFO ▶ For advanced print system management and troubleshooting, you can access the Mac CUPS web interface by opening a web browser and entering the following URL: **http://localhost:631** and then following the web interface setup instructions.

Exercise 26.1
Configure Printing

> ▶ **Prerequisites**

> ▶ You must have created the Local Admin ("Exercise 2.1 Configure a New OS X System for Exercises" on page 60 or "Exercise 2.2 Configure an Existing OS X System for Exercises" on page 63) and Chris Johnson ("Exercise 5.1 Manage User Accounts" on page 145) accounts.

> ▶ You must have a network printer that supports Bonjour or a classroom server with the proper server setup or have configured your own server using the Mainserver Setup Instructions.

Configure a Bonjour Printer

In this exercise, you will discover and configure a network printer via the Bonjour service discovery protocol. If you are performing these exercises in class, you will use a print queue shared from Mainserver.

1   If necessary, log in as Chris Johnson.

2   Open System Preferences, and select the Printers & Scanners pane.

3   If necessary, click the lock icon, and authenticate as Local Admin.

4   Click the Add (+) button under the printer list.

     A pop-up menu appears giving you the option to add a nearby shared printer.

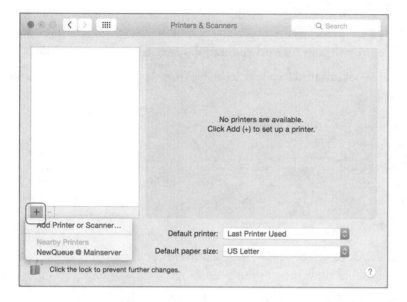

NOTE ▶ What you see on your computer will vary considerably depending on the precise model of printer you are using; the screenshot here and those that follow are intended to illustrate the range of possibilities and will not match what you actually see. If the Add window opens instead of a pop-up menu appearing, your computer did not find any Bonjour printers nearby; see "Reference 26.2 Print and Scan Configuration" on page 860 for more options.

5 Choose the printer you want to use from the pop-up menu. If you are using the print queue shared from Mainserver, it appears as "NewQueue @ Mainserver."

Depending on the type of printer, one of several things may happen:

▶ If a driver for the printer is installed on your computer or available from the computer sharing the printer, it is set up automatically.

▶ If the driver is not available locally but is available from the Apple software update servers, you are prompted to download and install the update.

In this case, click "Download & Install," then authenticate as Local Admin if prompted. The appropriate driver package downloads and installs. Depending on the package size and your Internet connection speed, this may take a while.

▶ If the driver is not installed locally or available from Apple, a generic driver may be sufficient.

In this case, click Use Generic. The generic driver may not support all the printer's features but should allow basic printing capability.

▶ If the driver is not installed locally or available from Apple, you are notified to contact the printer's manufacturer.

In this case, you need to either find a driver (probably from the printer's manufacturer) or use a generic driver (OS X comes with generic PostScript and PCL drivers) to proceed. Click Cancel, and try again after finding and installing the appropriate driver.

6 Your computer may fetch information about optional features from the printer itself (or the computer sharing it) and complete the setup process automatically. Your computer is now fully configured to print to this printer.

7 When the new print queue is set up, select it, and click the Open Print Queue button.

This lets you view and manage print jobs waiting to go to the printer, as well as view and change settings for the print queue. Depending on the printer's capabilities, you may see additional options such as a Scanner button.

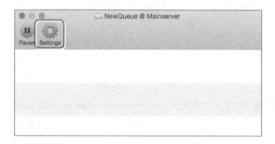

8   Click the Settings button.

A dialog opens that allows you to view and change information about the print queue's configuration. These settings are also accessible directly from Printers & Scanners preferences by clicking the Options & Supplies button.

The General pane allows you to configure the name and location displayed for the printer. It is often useful to name printers that would otherwise have only their model name listed.

You can set more descriptive names for printers by using the Printer Setup button in a queue's window. For supported printers, you also have access to supply-level information from the queue window.

9   Change the name and location to something more descriptive. If you are using "New-Queue @ Mainserver," use the following:

Name: Pretendco Network Printer

Location: Main server

If you are using an actual printer, enter a real description.

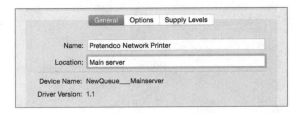

The other tabs in the Settings vary considerably between different printer models; you are unlikely to see all the options shown in the following screenshots.

10 If there is an Options tab, click it.

If this printer is shared from a Mac, that Mac controls what options are configured for the printer. If you are connecting to the printer directly, you can change the options if necessary.

11 If there is a Supply Levels tab, click it.

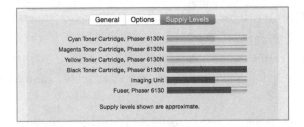

If you are connecting to the printer directly and the printer supports it, you can view the printer's supply levels here.

12 If there is a Utility tab, click it.

This tab of the printer setup gives you access to any utilities supplied by this printer's driver. The functions available here vary depending on the printer model you are using. Some drivers include a separate utility program, which can be opened from this tab.

13 Click OK to dismiss the Settings dialog.

14 Quit the printer queue. Note that although it is not really an application, it acts like one, including by offering a Quit option under its "application" menu.

Exercise 26.2
Manage Printing

▶ **Prerequisites**

- ▶ You must have created the Chris Johnson account ("Exercise 5.1 Manage User Accounts" on page 145).

- ▶ You must have at least one print queue set up on your computer. You can use "Exercise 26.1 Configure Printing" on page 882 to set up a Bonjour-based network printer or set up a different type of printer as described in "Reference 26.2 Print and Scan Configuration" on page 860.

This exercise explores both basic and advanced features of the OS X Print dialog, including saving a set of print options as a preset, printing to PDF format, and managing PDF workflows.

Print to a Printer

In this section, you will print to one of the printers you just set up. If you are printing to NewQueue on Mainserver, it does not connect to a physical printer, so no printed output appears.

1   If necessary, log in as Chris Johnson.

2   Open the Student *n*.rtf file from your desktop. If this file does not exist, open TextEdit, type some text into the blank document that opens, and save it to your desktop as Student *n* (where *n* is your student number or 1 if you are working on your own).

3   Choose File > Print (Command-P).

4   In the Print dialog, choose a printer from the Printer pop-up menu.

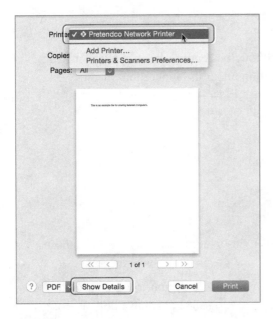

5   Click Show Details.

The Print dialog expands to show additional print settings.

6   Choose Layout from the configuration pop-up menu (initially set to TextEdit).

7   From the "Pages per Sheet" pop-up menu, choose 6.

8   From the Border pop-up menu, choose Single Thin Line.

As you change the settings, the preview on the left shows the effects of your changes.

9   From the Presets pop-up menu, choose "Save Current Settings as Preset."

10   Name the preset 6-up with border, make it available for all printers, and click OK.

These print settings are now available from the Presets menu anytime you print.

11 Use the Presets pop-up menu to switch between Default Settings and 6-up with border, and watch the effect on the print settings.

12 Click Print.

The print queue icon appears in your Dock, showing the number of jobs in the queue (1).

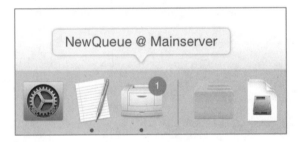

Manage a Print Queue

1 If you can, click the printer queue in your Dock before it vanishes.

In the queue window, you can watch the job get sent to the printer (or Mainserver) and be removed from the queue.

2   If the printer queue icon vanishes from your Dock before you have a chance to click it, open Printers & Scanners preferences, select the print queue on the left, and click Open Print Queue.

3   In the print queue window, click Pause.

4   Switch to TextEdit, and print the document again.

5   When you are warned that the printer has been paused, click "Add to Printer."

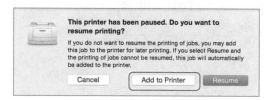

6   Switch to the print queue window. If your document is not shown, quit the print queue, and then reopen it from Printers & Scanners preferences.

Your document is shown as "Ready to Print."

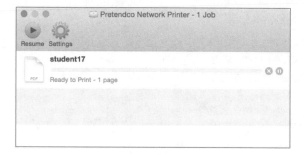

7   Double-click the document in the print queue.

A Quick Look window opens, allowing you to preview the print job.

8   Close the Quick Look window, and click the Jobs menu.

This menu has options to hold, resume, or delete individual print jobs. Most of them are also available within the print queue window.

9   Click the delete ("X") button to the right of the print job.

The job vanishes from the print queue.

10 Quit the print queue.

Print to PDF

The OS X print architecture can do a good deal more than print. In this section, you will use it to produce PDF files.

1   Switch to TextEdit, and press Command-P.

2   Click the PDF button near the bottom left of the Print dialog.

3   Choose Open PDF in Preview.

CUPS produces a PDF version of your document, and it opens in Preview. This feature provides an easy way to do a full-scale preview of documents before printing them. Note that there are Cancel and Print buttons near the bottom right of the window.

4   Click Cancel. This both closes the document and quits the Preview application.

5   In TextEdit, press Command-P again.

6   From the PDF pop-up menu, choose Save as PDF.

7   Save the PDF to your desktop.

Install a PDF Service

You can add choices to the PDF menu by placing items in a /Library/PDF Services folder. Supported item types include additional applications to open PDFs, folders in which to save PDFs, scripts and workflows to process PDFs, and aliases to any of these.

1   Open the Lesson26 folder in StudentMaterials.

2   Open "Save Encrypted PDF.workflow."

This file is a print plugin created with Automator, one of the easy-to-use Apple automation tools for OS X. Since it is a print plugin, Automator offers to install it for you.

3   Click Install.

4   When you are informed that the installation is complete, click Done.

5   Switch to the Finder; then hold the Option key, and choose Go > Library.

6   Inside the user Library, open the PDF Services folder.

When you clicked Install, the Save Encrypted PDF workflow was placed here. You can also place items in /Library/PDF Services to make them available to all users on this computer.

7   Close the PDF Services folder.

8   Switch to TextEdit, and press Command-P.

9   From the PDF pop-up menu, choose Save Encrypted PDF.

Save Encrypted PDF is an Automator workflow that takes a PDF (produced by CUPS), encrypts it, and saves it to the desktop.

10 When you are prompted to, enter and verify the encryption password of your choice.

It may take a few seconds for the workflow to do its work. When it is ready, the encrypted PDF appears on your desktop.

Student 17
(Encrypted).pdf

11 Double-click the encrypted file.

The file opens in Preview, which requests the password.

12 Reenter the encryption password you used.

Preview decrypts the document and displays it normally.

13 Quit all running applications.

Exercise 28.3
Troubleshoot the Printing System

▶ **Prerequisites**

▶ You must have created the Local Admin ("Exercise 2.1 Configure a New OS X System for Exercises" on page 60 or "Exercise 2.2 Configure an Existing OS X System for Exercises" on page 63) and Chris Johnson ("Exercise 5.1 Manage User Accounts" on page 145) accounts.

▶ You must have at least one print queue set up on your computer.

Troubleshooting printing involves understanding what goes on during the print process. In this exercise, you will examine the logs that are available from the print system as well as how to completely reset the printing configuration if needed.

Examine the CUPS Logs

OS X tracks many different events, including printing, through logs. You can view logs of both system and user events in the Console application. In this exercise, you will use Console to view the available CUPS logs.

1   If necessary, log in as Chris Johnson.

2   Open Console from the Utilities folder. If necessary, click Show Log List in the toolbar to see the list of log locations.

3   Click the disclosure triangle next to /var/log to display the list of logs, and then click the disclosure triangle next to cups.

Because the CUPS logs are located in the hidden folder /var/log in the OS X file system, they are displayed under /var/log in the Console window.

4   Click access_log in the list.

If you have printed, as you did previously, entries appear in the access log. There are also entries in the page log for each job. The access log shows interactions with the CUPS service, whereas the page log shows actual print jobs. Commands sent to CUPS appear here as well, though not exactly as you entered them at the command line.

5   Click page_log and examine its contents.

6   If there is an error_log file, view it as well.

7   Quit Console.

Reset the Printing System

If you can't print to your printer and you've tried other solutions, you can restore the printing system to "factory defaults" by resetting it. This process deletes all printers from your printer list, all information about all completed print jobs, and all printer presets. Because this completely resets information, it's likely to be your last option, rather than your first.

1   Open System Preferences, and click Printers & Scanners.

2   If necessary, click the lock icon, and authenticate as Local Admin.

3   Hold the Control key, and click in the printer list.

4   Choose "Reset printing system" from the menu that appears.

5 Click Reset when asked to confirm.

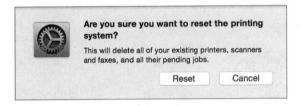

6 If you are prompted to, authenticate as Local Admin.

You can re-add your printers when the process is complete, if you like. It is not necessary for the remaining exercises.

7 Quit System Preferences.

Lesson 27

System Troubleshooting

System startup certainly isn't the most glamorous part of OS X, but it's clearly important and technically quite impressive. Apple has improved startup and runtime processes with every revision of OS X. When things work correctly, the startup process often takes under 30 seconds. Obviously, users appreciate a quick startup, but most aren't aware of what goes on during system startup, because their Mac computers usually work properly.

However, when things do go wrong during system startup, users often fear the worst. Novice users may assume that if their Mac won't start up they will lose important documents. But the system startup process can fail due to many issues that probably won't result in any user data loss. It's important to properly diagnose startup issues so you can get the Mac up and running, or at least try to recover data.

GOALS

▶ Understand the OS X startup process

▶ Examine essential files and processes required to successfully start up

▶ Learn about the various startup modes used by OS X

▶ Troubleshoot the processes used at startup and login

This lesson focuses on the process that your Mac goes through from the moment you press the power button until you ultimately reach the Finder. You will identify the essential files and processes required to successfully start up OS X. You will also explore the various OS X sleep modes, log out, and system shut down. You will then learn about the various startup shortcuts and diagnostic modes that work with Mac systems and OS X. Finally, the end of this lesson focuses on methods that will enable you to effectively troubleshoot system initialization and user session issues.

Reference 27.1
System Initialization

This section examines the main stages of the OS X system startup procedure. The stages of system startup can be categorized into either system initiation, the processes required to start the operating system, or user session, the processes required to prepare the user environment. At each stage, the Mac presents an audible or visual cue to help you validate startup progress. The startup cues discussed here are what you'll experience during a typical startup. Any deviation will be covered as you learn more about the startup process.

The four main OS X system initialization stages are, in order:

► Firmware—At this stage the Mac computer's hardware is tested and initialized, and then the booter is located and started. Successful completion of this stage results in an audible startup chime and a bright flash from the power-on light, if the Mac has one. The primary display should power on as well. On OS X Yosemite, older Mac models will start with a light gray background, but newer Mac models will start with a black background, so it might be difficult to tell if the display is active.

► Booter—The main job of the booter is to load the system kernel and essential hardware drivers, known as kernel extensions (KEXTs), into main memory and then allow the kernel to take over the system. The booter stage is indicated by the appearance of the Apple logo on the main display.

▶ Kernel—The kernel provides the system's foundation and loads additional drivers and the core BSD UNIX system. In OS X Yosemite, loading of the kernel is indicated by the appearance of a progress bar under the Apple logo on the main display.

▶ launchd—Once the core operating system is loaded, it starts the first nonkernel process, launchd, which is responsible for loading the remainder of the system. This stage is indicated by the progress bar under the Apple logo on the main display. Successful completion of this stage results in either the login screen or the Finder, if FileVault is enabled or the user is set to automatically log in.

System Initialization: Firmware

Your Mac computer's firmware, also called BootROM, resides on flash memory chips built into the main computer board. When you power on your Mac, even before it starts a "real" operating system, the firmware acts as a mini-operating system with just enough software to get things going. Specifically, the firmware tests and initializes the hardware, and then locates and starts the system software booter.

Intel-based Mac systems feature firmware based on the Intel Extensible Firmware Interface (EFI) technology. Aside from supporting the Intel processor hardware, EFI is what enables your Mac to start up from OS X, Windows, or any other Intel-compatible operating system.

> **MORE INFO** ▶ EFI is an extremely flexible boot architecture and is now managed by the Unified EFI Forum. In fact, EFI will soon be known as Unified Extensible Firmware Interface (UEFI). You can find out more at www.uefi.org.

Power-On Self-Test

The first thing your Mac firmware does when it powers on is the Power-On Self-Test (POST). The POST tests built-in hardware components such as processors, system memory, network interfaces, and peripheral interfaces. When your Mac passes the POST, you hear the startup chime, and the displays should power on. After a successful POST, the firmware goes on to locate the booter file.

> **NOTE** ▶ Mac computers perform the POST only during a startup, not during a restart.

If your Mac fails the POST, the display remains blank or off, and you may get hardware error codes. Depending on the age and model of your Mac, these error codes may manifest as audible tones, a series of flashes from the external power-on light, or internal diagnostic lights illuminating. You may even see a combination of these things. Regardless of which error code you experience, it indicates that a hardware problem exists that OS X cannot control. You can visit the Apple support website at www.apple.com/support to identify your specific Mac error code, or you can take your Mac to an Apple Authorized Service Provider.

Booter Selection

By default, the firmware picks the system booter file that was last specified from Startup Disk preferences in OS X or the Boot Camp control panel in Windows. The booter file's location is saved in your Mac computer's nonvolatile RAM (NVRAM) so that it persists across system restarts. If the booter file is found, EFI starts the booter process and OS X begins to start up. This is indicated by the appearance of the Apple logo in the center of the main display.

If the firmware cannot locate a booter file, a flashing folder icon with a question mark appears. Troubleshooting this issue is covered later in "Troubleshooting the Booter" on page 920.

NOTE ▶ During system startup, most Mac computers feature a white background with dark gray icons. However, some late-model Mac computers, after being upgraded to OS X Yosemite, will feature a black background with white icons during startup.

FileVault Unlock

If the system disk is protected with FileVault system volume encryption, the OS X booter cannot be accessed until the system disk is unlocked by a user. With FileVault, the system begins initial startup from the OS X Recovery HD, where a special EFI booter resides that presents the user with an authentication screen much like the login window. The FileVault authentication unlock screen appears just a few seconds after POST and looks very similar to the standard OS X login window.

Once the user successfully authenticates and unlocks the encrypted system disk, the EFI firmware is granted access to the system volume containing the OS X booter. Startup then continues as usual, with one exception. Because the user has already authenticated to unlock the disk, the system will automatically log in without the user having to authenticate again at the login window. This automatic login happens only once per startup and only for the user who unlocked the encrypted system disk.

Startup Shortcuts

Your Mac firmware also supports many keyboard shortcuts, which, when pressed and held down during initial power-on, allow you to modify the startup process. Some of these shortcuts alter the booter selection, while others modify how OS X starts up. Startup shortcuts are detailed later in "Reference 27.4 Startup Shortcuts" on page 916.

Firmware Updates

Boot read-only memory, or boot ROM, refers to older versions of firmware technology that are not upgradable. Your Mac firmware, however, *is* upgradable, and on Intel-based Mac systems it's even replaceable if it becomes damaged.

The OS X software update service may automatically update some Mac firmware, but you can also check the Apple Support website for the latest list of Mac firmware updates. Article HT201518, "EFI and SMC firmware updates for Intel-based Macs," maintains a list of Mac firmware updates. You can replace your Intel-based Mac computer's firmware using a firmware restoration CD, as outlined in article HT201692, "About the Firmware Restoration CD (Intel-based Macs)."

MORE INFO ▶ You can extend your Intel-based Mac computer's EFI capabilities using the rEFInd boot manager available at www.rodsbooks.com/refind.

System Initialization: Booter

The booter process is launched by your Mac firmware and is responsible for loading the OS X kernel and enough essential KEXTs that the kernel can take over the system and continue the startup process. Your Mac firmware also passes on any special startup mode instructions for the booter to handle, such as entering safe mode when the user is holding down the Shift key. The booter process itself resides at /System/Library/CoreServices/boot.efi.

To expedite the startup process, the booter loads cached files whenever possible. These files contain an optimized kernel and cached KEXTs that load much more quickly than if the system had to load them from scratch. These caches are located in the /System/Library/Caches/com.apple.kernel.caches folder. If the system detects a problem or you start OS X in safe mode, these caches are discarded and the kernel-loading process takes longer.

As covered previously, the booter process is indicated at startup by the Apple icon in the center of the main display. If the booter successfully loads the kernel, this is indicated by a small progress bar below the Apple icon. However, some modern Mac systems start up so fast you may not even see the progress bar before the next stage is indicated.

If your Mac is set to use a network disk and the firmware successfully locates the booter from a NetInstall service, you again see the Apple icon. However, in this case the booter and the cached kernel information must be downloaded from the NetInstall service. This process is indicated by a small, spinning globe icon below the Apple icon. The globe icon is replaced by the standard progress bar once the kernel has been successfully loaded from the NetInstall service.

Finally, if the booter is unable to load the kernel, a prohibitory icon takes the place of the Apple icon. Again, troubleshooting this issue is covered later in this lesson.

System Initialization: Kernel

Once the booter has successfully loaded the kernel and essential KEXTs, the kernel itself takes over the startup process. The kernel has now loaded enough KEXTs to read the entire file system, allowing it to load any additional KEXTs and start the core BSD UNIX system. Again, a progress bar below the Apple icon indicates the kernel startup progress.

Finally, the kernel starts the first normal (nonkernel) process, launchd, which is ultimately the parent process for every other process. During system startup, the progress bar below the Apple logo is an indication that the kernel has fully loaded and the launchd process is starting other items.

Again, in most cases the kernel is loaded by the booter from cached files. However, the kernel is also located on the system volume at /mach_kernel. This file is normally hidden from users in the graphical user interface, because they don't need access to it. Many other hidden files and folders at the root of the system volume are necessary for the BSD UNIX system, and again, the average user doesn't need access to these items. As covered in Lesson 25 "Peripherals and Drivers", KEXTs reside in the /System/Library/Extensions and /Library/Extensions folders.

System Initialization: launchd

Once the kernel is up and running, the Mac is ready to start running processes at the behest of the system and, eventually, human users. Again, the first normal (nonkernel) process started is launchd, located at /sbin/launchd, which runs as root and is given the process identification number of 1. In UNIX terms, launchd is the first parent process that spawns other child processes, and those processes go on to spawn other child processes.

The first task for the launchd process is to complete the system initialization by starting all other system processes. Beginning with OS X v10.5, the launchd process was highly optimized, so the system initialization process takes only a few moments and is difficult to visually discern. The best indication that you have reached this point is that the Apple logo is replaced by the login window or the user's desktop background.

If you have a Mac system with multiple displays you may also notice a brief flash coming from the secondary displays as they power on. This is a result of launchd starting the WindowServer process, which is responsible for drawing the OS X user interface, but it's still a good indication that things are progressing through the system startup process.

The launchd process is designed to expedite system initialization by starting multiple system processes simultaneously, whenever possible, and starting only essential system processes at startup. After startup, the launchd process automatically starts and stops additional system processes as needed. By dynamically managing system processes, launchd keeps your Mac responsive and running as efficiently as possible.

> **MORE INFO** ▶ launchd is an extremely powerful open source system for managing services. Learn more about launchd by reading its manual page in the Terminal.

launchd Items

As covered in Lesson 14 "System Resources", launchd manages system processes as described by launchd preference files in the /System/Library/LaunchDaemons folder. Third-party processes can also be managed when described by launchd preference files in the /Library/LaunchDaemons folder.

Apple strongly encourages all developers to adopt the launchd system for all automatically started processes, but the launchd process also supports legacy startup routines. This includes support for running the traditional UNIX /etc/rc.local script during system initialization, if present, though this script is not included on OS X by default.

> **NOTE** ▶ OS X Yosemite no longer supports legacy startup items. Thus, items from previous systems in /System/Library/StartupItems or /Library/StartupItems are ignored.

Viewing the launchd Hierarchy

You may find it beneficial to open /Applications/Utilities/Activity Monitor and examine the process listing as you learn about how OS X starts up the user environment. The Activity Monitor application lists all processes along with their identification numbers and parent-child relationships. In the Activity Monitor, you see this relationship best if you choose View > All Processes, Hierarchically. You can also view a process's parent process by double-clicking its name in the list. Detailed information about using Activity Monitor is covered in Lesson 19 "Application Management and Troubleshooting".

Process Name	% CPU	CPU Time	Threads	Idle Wake Ups	PID ∧	User
▼ kernel_task	1.3	1:24.82	112	107	0	root
▼ launchd	0.2	9.17	6	0	1	root
UserEventAgent	0.0	1.36	5	0	16	root
syslogd	0.0	2.21	7	1	17	root

Activity Monitor (All Processes, Hierarchically) — CPU Memory Energy Disk Network Q Search

Reference 27.2
User Session

Eventually, after enough system processes have started, the system begins the processes responsible for managing the user session.

The three main OS X user session stages are, in order:

▶ loginwindow—This is the process responsible for presenting the login screen and eventually logging the user in to the system. Successful completion of this stage results in initialization of the user environment, thus allowing user applications to run.

▶ launchd—the launchd process works in conjunction with the loginwindow process to initialize the user environment and start any user processes or applications.

▶ User environment—This is the "space" in which users' processes and applications exist when they are logged in to the system. Obviously, the user environment is maintained by the loginwindow and the launchd processes.

User Session: Login Window

A soon as the system has started enough processes to present the login window, the launchd process starts /System/Library/CoreServices/loginwindow.app. The loginwindow process has the ability to run as both a background process and a graphical interface application. It coordinates the login screen and, along with the opendirectoryd process, authenticates the user. After authentication, loginwindow, in conjunction with the `launchd` process, also initializes the graphical interface user environment and continues to run as a background process to maintain the user session.

By default in OS X, the user must authenticate using the login screen, or the `loginwindow` can be set to automatically authenticate a user at startup. As covered previously, the system also automatically logs in a user who provides authentication to unlock FileVault during startup. The `loginwindow` settings are stored in the /Library/Preferences/com.apple.login-window.plist preference file. As covered in Lesson 5 "User Accounts", you can configure `loginwindow` settings from Users & Groups preferences.

If no users are logged in to the Mac, the `loginwindow` process is owned by the root user. Once a user successfully authenticates, the `loginwindow` process switches ownership to this user and then proceeds to set up the graphical interface user environment with help from the `launchd` process.

User Session: launchd

The moment a user is authenticated, the `loginwindow` and `launchd` processes work together to initialize the user's environment. If fast user switching is enabled, the `launchd` process starts additional processes to initialize and maintain each user's environment.

The `loginwindow` and `launchd` processes set up the graphical interface user environment by:

▶ Retrieving the user account information from `opendirectoryd` and applying any account settings

▶ Configuring the mouse, keyboard, and system sound using the user's preferences

▶ Loading the user's computing environment: preferences, environment variables, devices and file permissions, and keychain access

▶ Opening the Dock (also responsible for Mission Control and Dashboard), Finder, and SystemUIServer (responsible for user interface elements like menu extras on the right side of the menu bar)

▶ Automatically opening the user's login items

▶ Automatically resuming any application that was open before the last logout, by default, in OS X

It's important to understand the differences among the various autostarting mechanisms in OS X: launch daemons, startup items, launch agents, and login items. Launch daemons and startup items are started during system initialization by the `launchd` process on behalf of the root user. Conversely, launch agents and login items are started only on behalf of a specific user. In other words, launch daemons and startup items affect the system as a whole, whereas launch agents and login items affect individual users.

Specifically, launch agents are started by the `launchd` process on behalf of the user. Launch agents can be started at any time, as long as the user's account is logged in to the system. Most launch agents are started during the initialization of the user environment, but they could also be started afterward or on a regular repeating basis, depending on need. Launch agents provided by the system can be found in /System/Library/LaunchAgents, whereas third-party launch agents should be located in either /Library/LaunchAgents or ~/ Library/LaunchAgents.

Finally, login items are started only at the very end of the initialization of the user environment. The `loginwindow` process, again with help from `launchd`, is responsible for starting a user's login items. The user's login item list is stored in the ~/Library/Preferences/login-window.plist preference file. As covered previously in Lesson 5 "User Accounts", you can configure a user's login item list from Users & Groups preferences.

Again, from Activity Monitor you can examine the resulting user processes. It's especially helpful if the process list is shows all processes, and you click the word User to sort the list of processes by user name.

The User Environment

The loginwindow processes continue to run as long as the user is logged in to the session. The launchd process starts all user processes and applications, while the user's loginwindow process monitors and maintains the user session.

The user's loginwindow process monitors the user session by:

▶ Managing logout, restart, and shutdown procedures

▶ Managing the Force Quit Applications window, which includes monitoring the currently active applications and responding to user requests to forcibly quit applications

▶ Writing any standard-error output to the user's console.log file

While the user is logged in to the session, the launchd process automatically restarts any user application that should remain open, such as the Finder or the Dock. If the user's loginwindow process is ended, whether intentionally or unexpectedly, all the user's applications and processes immediately quit without saving changes. If this happens, the launchd process then automatically restarts the loginwindow process as if the Mac had just started up. In other words, the loginwindow, depending on configuration, either displays the login screen or automatically logs in the specified user.

Reference 27.3
Sleep Modes, Logout, and Shutdown

At the other end of the spectrum, but still related, are the processes required to pause or end the user session. The main distinction is that your Mac computer's sleep function does not quit any open processes, whereas the user logout and system shutdown functions quit open processes. In most cases, the user manually issues a sleep, logout, or shutdown command from the Apple menu or by pressing the Mac computer's power button.

> **NOTE ▶** OS X Mavericks introduced a new behavior when you use the computer's power button to engage sleep. Quickly pressing the power button immediately puts the computer to sleep, while holding the power button down for 1.5 seconds displays an options dialog similar to earlier OS X systems. For more information, see Apple Support article HT5869, "OS X Mavericks: Using the power button."

NOTE ▶ OS X features an automatic Resume feature, enabled by default for all users. Upon login, the user's items reopen to their previous state. This feature works in conjunction with the Auto Save application, as covered in Lesson 18 "Document Management".

However, other processes and applications can also initiate sleep, logout, or shutdown commands. For instance, the Installer and Mac App Store applications can request a restart when the installation of new or updated software requires it.

Further, you can configure the Mac to automatically perform certain commands. You can put the system to sleep after a period of inactivity with settings in Energy Saver preferences; set a schedule to sleep, shut down, or start up the Mac with settings in the Schedule dialog of Energy Saver preferences; automatically log out users after a period of inactivity with settings in Security & Privacy preferences; and automatically log out managed users with settings in Parental Controls preferences. Many of these settings can be managed remotely from Apple Remote Desktop or from a management server.

The Mac sleep function is convenient because it does not quit any active processes or applications. Instead, the system kernel pauses all processes and then essentially shuts down all the hardware. This greatly reduces the amount of power used. As an example, newer portable Mac devices can remain in sleep mode for up to a month on a single battery charge. Waking your Mac from sleep mode restarts all hardware, and the kernel resumes all processes and applications from the point at which you left them.

Safe Sleep and Standby Modes

All portable Mac computers that are compatible with OS X Yosemite support safe sleep, and newer Mac computers with flash storage also support an automatic standby mode. When these Mac systems go to sleep, they also copy the entire contents of system memory to an image file on the system volume. This way, if a portable Mac computer stays in sleep mode long enough to completely drain the battery, no data is lost when the system has to fully shut down. Hence the term *safe sleep*.

A Mac in safe sleep mode must be restarted just like a Mac that was shut down. In other words, you can only restart a Mac in safe sleep mode by pressing the power button. When you restart a Mac from safe sleep mode, the booter process reloads the saved memory image from the system volume instead of proceeding with the normal startup process.

The booter process indicates that the Mac is restarting from safe sleep mode by showing a light gray version of your Mac screen as it appeared when sleep was initiated and a small progress bar at the bottom of the main display. It should take only a few moments to reload system memory, and the kernel resumes all processes and applications. If FileVault system volume encryption is enabled, the safe sleep-wake process is preceded by the FileVault authentication unlock screen.

Newer Mac computers with flash storage will enter a power-saving standby mode automatically when they are completely idle for more than three hours while connected to AC power. However, "completely idle" means that the systems detect zero network or peripheral activity for more than four hours. Unlike safe sleep, Mac computers in standby mode do not need to be restarted and can be woken by interacting with the keyboard, trackpad, or mouse. During wake you may notice a small white progress bar at the bottom of the screen, similar to that of safe sleep mode. Though in most cases, when a newer Mac wakes from standby it's so fast you may not even notice.

> **MORE INFO** ▶ You can find out more about safe sleep and standby modes, including which Mac models support these modes, from Apple Support articles HT201635, "Mac computers: Progress bar appears after waking from sleep," and HT202124, "Mac computers: About standby".

Power Nap

Mac systems introduced after mid-2011 that feature all flash storage, like MacBook Air models, gained new sleep functionality in OS X Mountain Lion with Power Nap. This feature allows your Mac to occasionally wake from sleep in a low-power mode, known as "dark wake" because the display does not power up, and perform essential background tasks. Many built-in OS X applications and services can work in Power Nap, including Mail, Contacts, Calendar, Reminders, Notes, documents in iCloud, Photo Stream, Mac App Store updates, Time Machine backup, Find My Mac updates, VPN on demand, and MDM configuration profile updates.

> **NOTE** ▶ Power Nap updates only applications that are running when sleep is initiated. Further, if the user logs out of the system before it goes to sleep, the user's items do not update.

For Mac systems that support Power Nap, it is enabled by default and will function whenever your Mac is connected to a power adapter. You can verify or adjust this setting from the Energy Saver settings. You can also optionally enable Power Nap for when your Mac is running from battery power, although this obviously means the charge won't last as long as it would during normal system sleep.

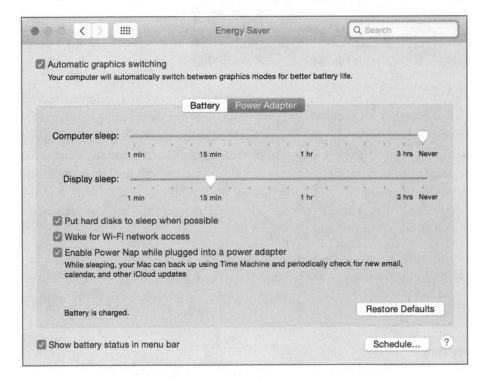

When a Mac is put to sleep with Power Nap enabled, it first waits 30 minutes before dark-waking to check for updates. After that, it dark-wakes every hour to check for updates. You can verify that Power Nap is in effect by checking its log file via Console. The Power Nap log file is located at /var/log/zzz.log.

> **MORE INFO** ▶ Some Mac systems require firmware updates to support Power Nap. You can find out more about Power Nap and any required updates from Apple Support article HT5394, "OS X: About Power Nap."

Logout

Users can log out anytime they want to end their user session, but they also have to log out to shut down or restart the Mac. When the currently logged-in user chooses to log out, the user's `loginwindow` process manages all logout functions with help from the `launchd` process.

Once the user authorizes the logout, the `loginwindow` process issues a Quit Application Apple event to all applications. Applications that support the new OS X Auto Save and Resume features can immediately save changes to any open documents and quit. Applications that do not support these features still respond to the Quit event, but they are programmed to ask the user if changes should be saved. Further, even applications that support Auto Save and Resume may still be waiting for the user if certain dialogs are left open. A great example is the Print dialog, which when left open prevents the application from quitting. If the application fails to reply or quit itself, the logout process is stopped and `loginwindow` displays an error message.

If all the user's applications successfully quit, the user's `loginwindow` process then forcibly quits any background user processes. Finally, the user's `loginwindow` process closes the user's graphical interface session, runs any logout scripts, and records the logout to the main system.log file. If the user chooses only to log out, as opposed to shutting down or restarting, the user's `loginwindow` quits, the `launchd` process restarts a new `loginwindow` process owned by the root user, and the login screen appears.

Shutdown and Restart

When a logged-in user chooses to shut down or restart the Mac, again the user's `loginwindow` process manages all logout functions with help from the `launchd` process. First, the user's `loginwindow` process logs out the current user. If other users are logged in via fast user switching, the `loginwindow` process asks for administrative user authentication and, if it's granted, forcibly quits all other users' processes and applications, possibly losing user data.

After all user sessions are logged out, the user's loginwindow process tells the kernel to issue the quit command to all remaining system processes. Processes like loginwindow should quit promptly, but the kernel must wait for processes that remain responsive while they are going through the motions of quitting. If system processes don't respond after a few seconds, the kernel forcibly quits those processes. Once all processes are quit, the kernel stops the launchd process and then shuts down the system. If the user chose to restart the Mac, the computer's firmware begins the system startup process once again.

Reference 27.4
Startup Shortcuts

Your Mac firmware supports many keyboard shortcuts, which, when pressed and held down during initial power-on, allow you to modify the startup process. Some of these shortcuts modify the booter selection, whereas others modify how OS X starts up. These alternative startup and diagnostic modes are often used for troubleshooting system issues.

> **NOTE ▶** If the Mac has firmware password protection enabled, all startup shortcuts are disabled until the user enters the computer's firmware password. Even after the user authenticates, the only two startup shortcuts that work are access to the Startup Manager and OS X Recovery. Using a firmware password is covered in Lesson 7 "System Security".

> **NOTE ▶** When using startup shortcuts, systems with FileVault system volume encryption enabled must still be authenticated and unlocked to proceed with system startup.

NOTE ▶ Some hardware does not support startup shortcuts, including some third-party keyboards and keyboards connected via certain USB hubs or a keyboard-video-mouse (KVM) switch. Also, Bluetooth wireless keyboards often do not work either. Consequently, a Mac administrator should always have a wired USB keyboard and mouse handy for troubleshooting Mac desktop systems.

NOTE ▶ Startup volumes selected with a shortcut are not saved in NVRAM, so this setting does not persist between system restarts.

Selecting an Alternate System

Mac startup shortcuts that allow you to select another system include:

▶ Option—Starts up into the Startup Manager, which allows you to select any volume containing a valid system to start up from. This includes internal volumes, optical disc volumes, some external volumes, and, on later Mac models, Wi-Fi networks and Net-Boot images.

▶ Command-Option-D—Starts up from the Apple Hardware Test via an Internet connection to the Apple servers. This option is only available to Mac models released after July 19, 2011.

▶ N—Starts up from the last-used NetBoot server, or the default NetBoot server if none was previously used. The Mac shows a flashing or spinning globe icon in the center of the main display until it locates the NetBoot server, at which point it shows the Apple logo.

▶ Option-N—This shortcut is similar to holding down the N key, but it always starts up from the current default NetBoot server instead of the last-used NetBoot server.

▶ Command-R—Starts up from the local OS X Recovery, if available. If no local OS X Recovery is found, Mac systems that support OS X Internet Recovery automatically attempt to start up from the Apple recovery servers. Lesson 3 "OS X Recovery" covers this topic in greater detail.

▶ Command-Option-R—This shortcut forces startup to OS X Internet Recovery on supported Mac systems.

Modifying OS X Startup

Mac startup shortcuts that modify the OS X default startup:

► Shift—Starts up OS X using Safe Boot, which leaves OS X running in safe mode. During Safe Boot, the system clears specific caches, carefully tests startup procedures, and limits automatically launched processes during each stage. While running in safe mode, many nonessential system and third-party items are ignored. (Details on Safe Boot and safe mode are covered throughout the troubleshooting sections later in this lesson.) You can recognize a system that has performed a Safe Boot and is now in safe mode if the words Safe Boot appear in bright red text in the top-right corner of the login screen. You can also verify Safe Boot after login by opening the System Information application and then selecting the Software item.

► Command-V—Starts up OS X in verbose mode. In verbose mode, the system does not hide the startup progress from you. Instead, you see a black background with white text showing all details of the startup process.

► Command-S—Starts up OS X in single-user mode. When starting up in single-user mode, the system only starts core kernel and BSD UNIX functionality. You must be familiar with the command-line interface to use single-user mode.

Other Startup Utilities

Other useful Mac startup shortcuts:

► T—For Mac systems with built-in Thunderbolt or FireWire ports, holding down this key powers on the Mac in target disk mode, allowing other computers to access your Mac computer's internal drives. Target disk mode details are covered in Lesson 12 "File System Troubleshooting".

► Command-Option-P-R—This shortcut resets NVRAM settings and restarts the Mac.

► Eject key, F12 key, mouse, or trackpad button—These shortcuts eject any removable media, including optical discs.

Reference 27.5
System Initialization Troubleshooting

Once you can identify the various stages—and know which processes and files are responsible for each, you are well on your way to diagnosing any startup issue. As an aid, the troubleshooting sections outlined here are organized by each stage of the system initialization process.

Also, throughout the remainder of this section, you will learn how each of the three primary OS X diagnostic startup modes—verbose mode, safe mode, and single-user mode—help resolve or identify issues. These three modes are initiated at the firmware stage but affect the remaining system initialization process at each stage. The ramifications of each diagnostic startup mode are covered with each stage throughout this section.

Troubleshooting the Firmware

Issues at the firmware stage are indicated by the inability of your Mac to reach the point where the Apple log appears. The key to troubleshooting at this point is to determine whether this issue is related to the Mac computer's hardware or system volume.

Serious Hardware Issues

If you don't hear the startup chime or see a power-on light flash, the Mac hardware did not pass the POST. You may also hear a series of diagnostic tones or see a series of power-on flashes. If this is the case, your Mac has a fundamental hardware issue.

You can always check for simple things first. Is the Mac plugged into an electrical outlet? Are the keyboard and mouse working properly? Ultimately, a failure to pass the POST is usually indicative of a serious hardware issue. If this is the case, you'll be best served by taking your Mac to an Apple Store or Apple Authorized Service Provider.

System Volume Issues

If your Mac passes the POST, but you are left with a flashing question mark folder icon, it means the firmware cannot locate a valid system volume or booter file. The Mac computer's main processor and components are probably working correctly, and you may just have a software issue. Hold down the Option key during startup and use the Startup Manager to locate system volumes.

To troubleshoot system volume issues:

▶ If the original system volume appears, select it to start up from it. If your Mac starts up from the system on the volume, open Startup Disk preferences to reset the volume as the startup disk. You can also attempt to define the startup disk when booted from another system volume, like an external OS X Recovery disk, as covered in Lesson 3 "OS X Recovery".

▶ If the original system volume appears, but your Mac still cannot find a valid system or booter, you may need to reinstall OS X on that volume. As always, back up any important data from that volume before you make significant changes.

▶ If your original system volume does not appear, the issue lies with that storage device. Start up from another system, like an external OS X Recovery disk, and use the storage troubleshooting techniques outlined in Lesson 12 "File System Troubleshooting".

Troubleshooting the Booter

Issues at the booter stage are indicated by a flashing prohibitory icon—evidence of a failure to load the kernel.

To troubleshoot the booter:

▶ If you're starting up the Mac from a volume containing a system this Mac has never booted from, the prohibitory icon usually indicates that the version of OS X on the volume is not compatible with your Mac computer's hardware. This is an extremely rare case that occurs mainly when a new Mac is restored using an older system image. The solution as this point is to reinstall OS X, using OS X Recovery, to a version of OS X that is known to work with this specific hardware.

▶ Start up the Mac while holding down the Shift key to initiate a Safe Boot. The booter first attempts to verify and repair the startup volume. If repairs are necessary, the Mac automatically restarts before continuing. If this happens, continue to hold down the Shift key. The booter verifies the startup volume again, and if the volume appears to be working properly, the booter attempts to load the kernel and essential KEXTs again. The booter uses the most judicial, and slowest, process to load these items and clears both the KEXT and font caches. If successful, the booter passes off the system to the kernel, which continues to safe-boot.

▶ If the booter cannot find or load a valid kernel, you may need to reinstall OS X on that volume.

Troubleshooting the Kernel

Issues at the kernel stage are indicated by an inability to reach the login window or automatic login process, as evidence of a failure to load KEXTs, the core UNIX system, and ultimately the launchd process. If this is the case, your Mac is stuck at the Apple logo startup screen, and the Apple icon or progress bar may stay visible indefinitely, again signaling a failure to complete the startup process.

To troubleshoot the kernel:

▶   Start up the Mac while holding down the Shift key to initiate a Safe Boot. In addition to the Safe Boot procedures covered in the "Troubleshooting the Booter" on page 920 section, this forces the kernel to ignore all third-party KEXTs. If this strategy is successful, the kernel starts the launchd process, which continues to Safe Boot. Completing the kernel startup stage via a Safe Boot indicates the issue may be a third-party KEXT, so you should start up in verbose mode to try to identify the problematic KEXT.

▶   Start up the Mac while holding down Command-V to initiate verbose mode. The Mac shows you the startup process details as a continuous string of text. If the text stops, the startup process has probably also stopped, and you should examine the end of the text for troubleshooting clues. When you find a suspicious item, move it to a quarantine folder and then restart the Mac without Safe Boot, to see if the problem was resolved. This may be easier said than done, as accessing the Mac computer's disk to locate and remove the item may not be possible if the Mac is crashing during startup. This is an example of where target disk mode really shines. As covered in Lesson 12 "File System Troubleshooting", you can easily modify the contents of a problematic Mac system volume using target disk mode and a second Mac.

> **NOTE ▶** If your troublesome Mac successfully starts up in Safe Boot and you're trying to find the issue, do not use Safe Boot and verbose mode at the same time. If the startup process succeeds, verbose mode will eventually be replaced by the standard startup interface, and you will not have time to identify problematic items.

▶   If the kernel cannot completely load during a Safe Boot, or you are unable to locate and repair the problematic items, you may need to reinstall OS X on that volume.

Troubleshooting launchd

Issues at this stage are indicated by an inability to reach the login screen or log in a user (evidence of a failure by the launchd process). If the launchd process is not able to complete the system initialization, the loginwindow process does not start.

To troubleshoot launchd issues:

▶ Start up the Mac while holding down the Shift key to initiate a Safe Boot. In addition to the Safe Boot procedures covered earlier in the "Troubleshooting the Booter" on page 920 and "Troubleshooting the Kernel" on page 921 sections of this lesson, this forces the launchd process to ignore all third-party fonts, launch daemons, and startup items. If the Safe Boot is successful, the launchd process starts the loginwindow. At this point the Mac system has fully started up and is now running in safe mode. Completing the system initialization process via Safe Boot indicates the issue may be a third-party system initialization item, and you should start up in verbose mode to try to identify the problematic item.

▶ Start up the Mac while holding down Command-V to initiate verbose mode. Again, if the text stops scrolling down the screen, examine the end of the text for troubleshooting clues; if you find a suspicious item, move it to another folder and then restart the Mac normally.

▶ At this point you may be able to successfully Safe Boot into the Finder. If so, use the Finder interface to quarantine suspicious items.

▶ While working in safe mode, you may also consider removing or renaming system cache and preference files, as they can be corrupted and cause startup issues. Begin by removing /Library/Caches, because those files contain easily replaced information. As far as system preferences go, you can remove any setting stored in the /Library/ Preferences or /Library/Preferences/SystemConfiguration folders you're comfortable with having to reconfigure. A much safer solution is to simply rename individual system preference files in these folders. Once you have moved or replaced these items, restart the Mac, and the system automatically replaces these items with clean versions.

▶ If Safe Boot continues to fail or you have located a suspicious system item you need to remove, start up the Mac while holding down Command-S to initiate single-user mode. You'll see a minimal command-line interface that enables you to move suspicious files to a quarantine folder. If you want to modify files and folders in single-user mode, you have to prepare the system volume. Start by entering /sbin/fsck -fy to verify and repair the startup volume. Repeat this command until you see a message stating that the disk appears to be OK. Only then should you enter /sbin/mount -uw / to mount the startup volume as a read-and-write file system. Once you have made your changes, you can exit single-user mode and continue to start up the system by entering the exit command, or you can shut down the Mac by entering the shutdown -h now command.

▶ If the system initialization process cannot complete during the Safe Boot or you are unable to locate and repair the problematic items, you may need to reinstall OS X on that volume.

Reference 27.6
User Session Troubleshooting

If the loginwindow process is not able to initialize the user environment, the user will never be given control of the graphical interface. You may see the user's desktop background picture, but no applications load, including the Dock and the Finder. Or it may appear that the user session starts, but then the login screen reappears.

Safe Mode Login

At this point you should first attempt a safe mode login, which is initiated by holding down the Shift key while you click the Log In button at the login screen. You can actually perform a safe mode login any time you want to troubleshoot user issues, even if you did not first Safe Boot the system.

With safe mode enabled, the loginwindow process does not automatically open any user-defined login items or applications that are set to resume. Further, the launchd process does not start any user-specific LaunchAgents. Obviously, if a safe mode login resolves your user session issue, you need to adjust the user's Login Items list from Users & Groups preferences or any items in the /Library/LaunchAgents or ~/Library/LaunchAgents folder.

If a safe mode login doesn't resolve your user session issue, there are other troubleshooting sections in this guide to which you should refer. Primarily, you should follow the troubleshooting steps outlined in Lesson 5 "User Accounts".

Troubleshoot Logout and Shutdown

An inability to log out or shut down is almost always the result of an application or process that refuses to quit. If you're unable to log out, as long as you maintain control of the graphical interface, you can attempt to forcibly quit stubborn processes using the techniques outlined in Lesson 19 "Application Management and Troubleshooting".

You may find that the `loginwindow` process has closed your user session but the Mac refuses to shut down. This is indicated by blank screen after all your applications have quit. You should let the system attempt to shut down naturally, but if it takes longer than a few minutes, it means a system process is refusing to quit. You can force your Mac to shut down by holding down the power-on button until the Mac powers off.

> **NOTE** ▶ When you restart the Mac, the firmware does not perform a full POST during the subsequent startup process. Thus, if you're troubleshooting hardware issues, you should always shut down and then start up, never restart.

Exercise 27.1
Examine System Startup

▶ **Prerequisite**

> ▶ You must have created the Chris Johnson account ("Exercise 5.1 Manage User Accounts" on page 145).

As OS X starts up, it gives auditory or visual cues as to which step of the startup process is currently being performed. If the startup process fails to complete, identifying the step where it halted can help illuminate the cause of the issue. In this exercise, you will identify steps in the startup sequence using audible and visible cues. You will then examine the processes that activate automatically when you start up your computer. After completing this exercise, you will be able to identify the sequence of startup events that occur during OS X startup.

Identify Steps in the Startup Process

In this exercise, you will watch the startup process in a standard startup. You will find that the startup process moves through some steps rapidly, while other steps only flash on the screen, such as an icon that blinks to indicate a component loading. Some steps display onscreen for a significant amount of time only if the underlying process does not start properly.

1   If your computer is on, shut it down. You can use the Apple menu or (if you are not logged in) the buttons on the login screen to shut it down.

2 Start up your computer.

3 As the computer is starting up, use the following table to note the major steps occurring during the startup process (from turning the computer on through the user environment appearing). Keep in mind that certain steps may not apply since you are not testing hardware issues or situations in which the startup device cannot be found.

Record the startup process associated with each visible or audible stage of the startup process. Refer to "Reference 27.1 System Initialization " on page 899. When you reach the login window, log in as Chris Johnson.

NOTE ▶ If your computer is encrypted with FileVault, there will be an additional startup step for the FileVault unlock screen; note where it occurs in the startup sequence.

Visual or auditory cue	Startup step or process executing at startup step
Startup chime	
Apple logo	
Apple logo and progress indicator	
Arrow pointer appears	
Login screen	
Desktop and Dock appear	

Exercise 27.2
Use Single-User Mode

▶ **Prerequisite**

▶ If your computer has a Retina display, you may need a magnifying glass to read the text in single-user mode.

When troubleshooting OS X startup issues that seem to be software-related, you might need to troubleshoot with the operating system started up in verbose or single-user mode. Verbose mode displays additional information about the startup and shutdown processes but does not change the normal operations of the computer. Single-user mode is a very primitive state of the operating system. The operating system has loaded only enough services to allow you to interact with it from the command line. It hasn't even mounted the startup disk read/write yet. Single-user mode is a low-level maintenance mode that allows you to bring the system up, look at log files, edit or replace configuration files, and so on. In this exercise, you will start up your computer in verbose mode and then single-user mode and then proceed to the user interface and identify various files used during startup.

If your computer has a Retina display, you may find that the text is too small to read easily in both verbose and single-user modes. In this case, using a magnifying glass is recommended.

Start Up in Verbose Mode

1   Before restarting in verbose mode, review the sequence you observed in "Exercise 27.1 Examine System Startup" on page 924. In verbose mode, the basic startup sequence is the same, but what you will see on the screen is different.

2   Restart your computer, and immediately hold down Command-V. Continue holding Command-V until you see text appear on the screen. When you reach the login window (or FileVault login screen), log in as Chris Johnson.

3   Fill in the following table with the sequence of cues you observe during a verbose startup, and contrast it with what you saw during a normal startup.

Normal startup	Verbose startup
Startup chime	
Apple logo	
Apple logo and progress indicator	
Arrow pointer appears	
Login screen	

Normal startup	Verbose startup
Desktop and Dock appear	

During the verbose segment of the startup process, you will see messages from the kernel and launch daemons describing what they are doing and any problems they encounter. The messages can be somewhat cryptic if you are not familiar with the details of the kernel and launch daemons' operations. Try to discern what is happening "behind the scenes" as your computer starts up.

4   Shut down your computer.

As your computer shuts down, you will see that it reenters verbose mode for a few moments. This occurs after WindowServer shuts down but before the kernel shuts down.

Use Single-User Mode

1   Restart your computer, and immediately hold down Command-S. Continue holding Command-S until the computer restarts and you see text appear on the screen. If your computer is protected by FileVault, log in as Chris Johnson to allow the computer to start up.

Single-user mode starts off a lot like verbose mode, displaying information about the startup process. But unlike verbose mode, the startup process halts just after launchd starts. The graphical user interface does not start; instead, it gives you a full-screen command-line interface.

When your computer finishes starting up into single-user mode, OS X displays instructions on how to remount the startup disk with read/write access and how to continue the startup process to multiuser mode, the usual run mode of OS X or any other UNIX system.

```
*** Single-user boot ***
Root device is mounted read-only
Enabling and disabling services is not supported in single-user
mode, and disabled services will not be respected when loading
services while in single-user mode
To mount the root device as read-write:
        $ /sbin/fsck -fy
        $ /sbin/mount -uw /
To boot the system:
```

```
        $ exit
   bash-3.2#
```

The last line is a prompt for you to enter a command. Note that the prompt ends with a # instead of the more usual $. This tells you that you are logged in as the super user (root, or System Administrator). You have unrestricted access to the startup volume and the rest of the system.

2   To force a check of the file system's integrity, enter the command "/sbin/fsck -fy", and press Return.

   NOTE ▶ Single-user mode always uses the US-English keyboard layout, no matter what your actual keyboard layout is.

   The computer runs a file system consistency check, correcting any errors that it finds and is able to repair. This is essentially the same as using Repair Disk in Disk Utility. On today's large disks, this can take a while, especially if there are many files and folders in the file system. This is one of the advantages of file system journaling. Most of the time, a complete fsck does not need to occur, so startup is much faster.

   If fsck displays something like The volume Macintosh HD appears to be OK., you may proceed to the next step. If its final message is The filesystem was modified, it found and fixed at least one issue, and you should rerun it to make sure there are no additional issues.

3   To remount the startup disk with write access enabled, type "/sbin/mount –uw /" and press Return.

   You are given a new prompt a few seconds later. This command enables you to make changes to the disk.

   This command should not generate any output if all runs correctly. If it generates an alert, double-check your typing. The most common errors with this command are leaving off the trailing / and not having spaces where they are needed.

4   Get a process listing with the command "ps -ax".

   You see a much shorter list than you will ever see in Activity Monitor. At process ID 1, you see the system launchd. Process ID 2 is bash -sh, which is the command shell with which you are interacting. The last process is your ps command. The OS is in a minimal state.

5   Examine the system log file with the command "less +G /var/log/system.log". Note that the command line is generally case sensitive, so it is important to capitalize the +G.

The +G option to less tells it to start at the end of the file (that is, show the most recent log events). Usually, when you need to examine logs in single-user mode, it is because you want to find out what happened just before the system crashed, so starting at the end is more convenient than starting at the beginning. You can scan through the log by pressing "b" to move backward in the file, and pressing the Space bar to move forward.

Unfortunately, it does not know how large the screen is, so the display can get confused as you move backward and forward. The best way to fix this is to force it to redisplay the part you are interested in by backing up past it with the "b" key, then pressing the Space bar to display forward to the part you want to read.

6   When you are through examining the log, press "q" to exit.

Create a New Administrator Account

If you lose the password to your administrator account, you now know several ways to reset its password, but if the account becomes completely unusable, this will not allow you to regain control of the computer. In this section, you will see how to use single-user mode to create a new administrator account.

1   Move to the /var/db folder with the command "cd /var/db".

2   Verify that this worked with the command "pwd".

This should print /var/db, indicating your new location in the file system. If it does not match this, the command did not work right, and you must try again before proceeding. This section of the exercise involves deleting files, and since you are running as the root user, you are capable of deleting anything (or everything). It is important to be careful when you are running commands as the root user.

3   Start typing the command "rm .AppleSe" (be sure to capitalize the A and S), but do not press Return yet.

4   Press Tab.

If you typed the command correctly, it autocompletes to rm   .AppleSetupDone. If pressing Tab does not make it autocomplete, you have not typed the command correctly and must correct it and try again. Note that you cannot use the mouse to select text to change, although you can use the Left and Right Arrow keys to move backward and forward on the command line.

If you cannot get the command to autocomplete, something is still wrong, and you should not proceed with the exercise. You can always press Control-C and then use the command "exit" to exit single-user mode.

The /var/db/.AppleSetupDone file is a placeholder file, which indicates that Setup Assistant has run on this computer; deleting it makes the computer rerun Setup Assistant the next time it starts up.

5   If the command autocompleted correctly, press Return to run it.

6   If you see a message starting with override, enter "y", and press Return.

7   If you see the message rm: .AppleSetupDone: Read-only file system, the mount command in step 3 of the previous section did not work; reenter that command, and then try again from step 2 of this section.

8   If the rm command does not display an error, exit single-user mode with the command "exit".

The computer exits single-user mode and continues starting up the operating system. With the .AppleSetupDone file gone, it runs Setup Assistant again just as though this were a new computer.

9   Step through the Setup Assistant screens (see "Exercise 2.1 Configure a New OS X System for Exercises" on page 60 for detailed instructions). When you reach the Create Your Computer Account screen, enter the following information:

Full Name: New Admin

Account Name: newadmin

If you are performing this exercise in a class, enter newadminpw in the Password and Verify fields. If you are performing this exercise on your own, you should select a more secure password for the New Admin account.

After you finish Setup Assistant, you are automatically logged in to the New Admin account.

10   Open System Preferences, and select the Users & Groups pane.

All of your old accounts are still there; New Admin has simply been added to them.

11   Quit System Preferences.

Index

Differentiate yourself. Get Apple certified.

Stand out from the crowd. Get recognized for your expertise by earning Apple Certified Pro status.

Why become an Apple Certified Pro?

Raise your earning potential. Studies show that certified professionals can earn more than their non-certified peers.

Distinguish yourself from others in your industry. Proven mastery of an application helps you stand out in a crowd.

Display your Apple Certification logo. With each certification you get a logo to display on business cards, resumés, and websites.

Publicize your certifications. Publish your certifications on the Apple Certified Professionals Registry (training.apple.com/certification/records) to connect with clients, schools, and employers.

Learning that matches your style.

Learn on your own with Apple Pro Training Series books from Peachpit Press.

Learn in a classroom at an Apple Authorized Training Center (AATC) from Apple Certified Trainers providing guidance.

Visit **training.apple.com** to find Apple training and certifications for:

OS X	Pages
OS X Server	Numbers
Final Cut Pro X	Keynote
Logic Pro X	

"The Apple Certification is a cornerstone of my consulting business. It guarantees to our clients the highest level of dedication and professionalism. And above all, the trusting smile of a client when you mention the Apple Certification can't be replaced."

– Andres Le Roux, Technology Consulting, alrx.net, inc.

Server ntials 10.10

porting OS X Server on Yosem

nd Ben Greisler

lable for download

Pro X

Music Production

Available for download

Apple Pro Training Series

OS X Support Essentials 10.10

Supporting and Troubleshooting OS X Yosemite

Kevin M. White and Gordon Davisson

Lesson and media files available for download

Apple Pro Training Series

Pages, Numbers, and Keynote

Mark Wood

Lesson and media files available for download

Apple Pro Training Series

Final Cut Pro X 10.1

Professional Post-Production

Brendan Boykin

Lesson and media files available for download

The Apple Pro Training Series

Apple offers comprehensive certification programs for creative and IT professionals. The Apple Pro Training Series is both a self-paced learning tool and the official curriculum of the Apple Training and Certification program, used by Apple Authorized Training Centers around the world.

To see a complete range of Apple Pro Training Series books, videos and apps visit: **www.peachpit.com/appleprotraining**

Apple
Certified